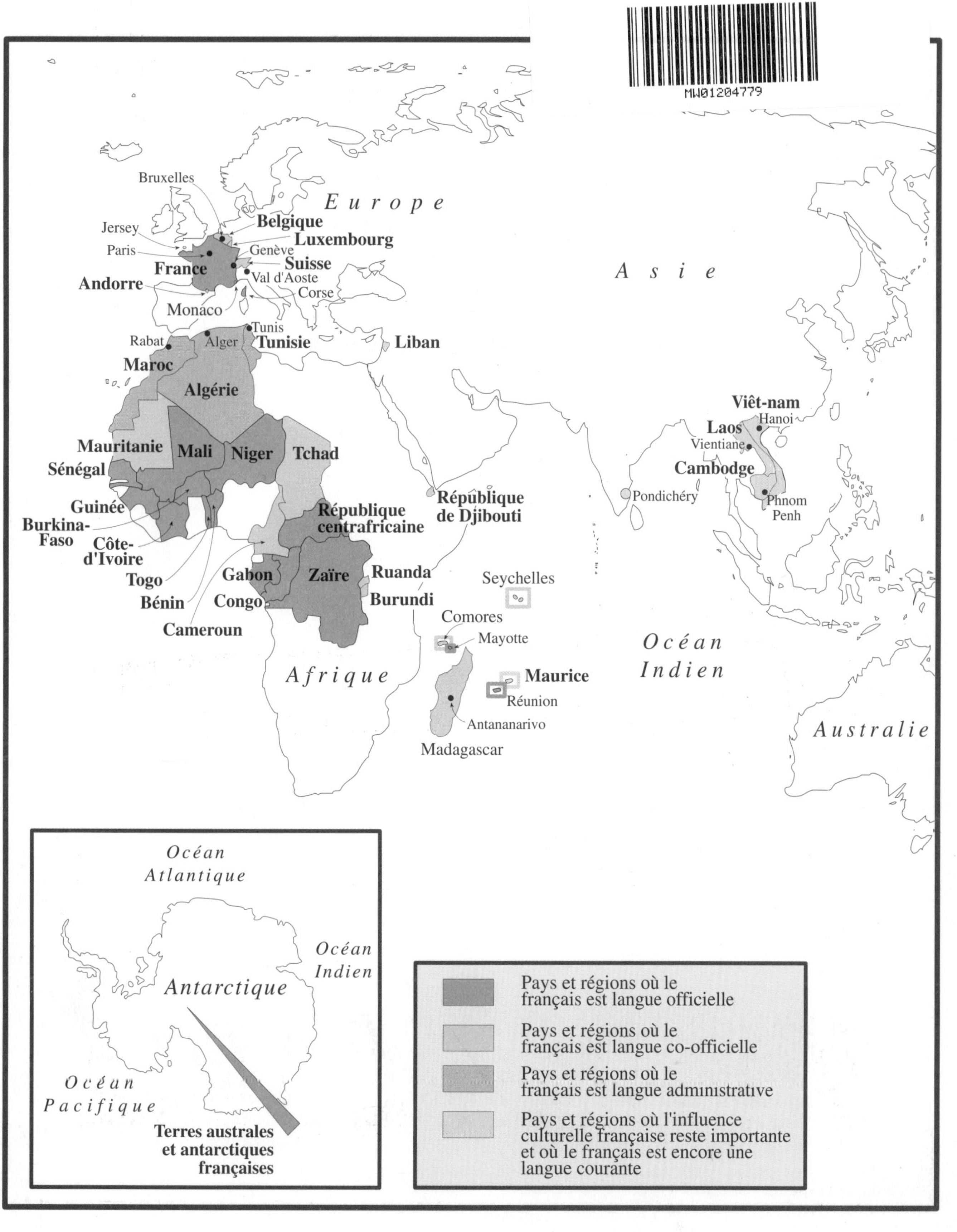
MW01204779
Europe
Asie
Bruxelles
Belgique
Jersey
Luxembourg
Paris
Genève
Suisse
France
Val d'Aoste
Andorre
Corse
Monaco
Tunis
Rabat
Alger
Tunisie
Liban
Maroc
Algérie
Viêt-nam
Hanoi
Laos
Vientiane
Mauritanie
Mali
Niger
Tchad
Cambodge
Sénégal
République de Djibouti
Pondichéry
Phnom Penh
Guinée
République centrafricaine
Burkina-Faso
Côte-d'Ivoire
Togo
Gabon
Zaïre
Ruanda
Seychelles
Bénin
Congo
Burundi
Cameroun
Comores
Mayotte
Océan Indien
Afrique
Maurice
Réunion
Antananarivo
Australie
Madagascar
Océan Atlantique
Océan Indien
Antarctique
Océan Pacifique
Terres australes et antarctiques françaises
Pays et régions où le français est langue officielle
Pays et régions où le français est langue co-officielle
Pays et régions où le français est langue administrative
Pays et régions où l'influence culturelle française reste importante et où le français est encore une langue courante

Joan H. Manley, UNIVERSITY OF TEXAS–EL PASO
Stuart N. Smith, AUSTIN COMMUNITY COLLEGE
John T. McMinn, AUSTIN COMMUNITY COLLEGE
Marc Prévost, AUSTIN COMMUNITY COLLEGE

Qu'est-ce qu'on dit?

Heinle & Heinle Publishers
Boston, Massachusetts 02116 U.S.A.

Heinle & Heinle is a division of Wadsworth, Inc.

The publication of *Qu'est-ce qu'on dit?* was directed by the members of the Heinle & Heinle College French Publishing Team:

VICE PRESIDENT & TEAM LEADER: Erek Smith
EDITORIAL DIRECTOR: Patricia L. Ménard
MANAGING DEVELOPMENTAL EDITOR: Beth Kramer
MARKETING DEVELOPMENT DIRECTOR: Marisa Garman
PRODUCTION SUPERVISOR: Barbara Browne

Also participating in the publication of this program were:

PUBLISHER: Stanley J. Galek
EDITORIAL PRODUCTION MANAGER: Elizabeth Holthaus
PROJECT MANAGER: Julianna Nielsen/Sloane Publications
MANUFACTURING COORDINATOR: Jerry Christopher
INTERIOR BOOK DESIGN: Bruce Kennett
COVER DESIGN: Jean Hammond
ILLUSTRATIONS: David Murray and Stephanie Osser
END PAPER MAPS: Magellan Geographix

Library of Congress Cataloging-in-Publication Data

Qu'est-ce qu'on dit? / Joan H. Manley . . . [et al.]. —Instructor's annotated ed.
p. cm.
Includes index.
ISBN 0-8384-4487-3
1. French language—Textbooks for foreign speakers—English.
I. Manley, Joan H.
PC2129.E5048 1994
448.3'421—dc20 93-43695
CIP

Manufactured in the United States of America

ISBN 0-8384-4487-3 Student Edition
ISBN 0-8384-4488-1 Instructor's Annotated Edition

Heinle & Heinle Publishers is a division of Wadsworth, Inc.

10 9 8 7 6 5 4 3 2 1

To our parents, our first and our best teachers.

À nos parents,
dont la sagesse et le dévouement
nous ont servi d'exemple.

Table des matières

With the exception of the *Chapitre préliminaire* and the *Chapitre de révision*, chapters have the following sections.

Pour commencer	An introduction of new vocabulary related to the chapter theme
Comment s'y prendre?	Reading or listening strategies
Qu'est-ce qui se passe?	A reading or listening passage developing the continuing story for each unit
Remarquez que...	Cultural information
Sujet de conversation 1	An introduction of a functional use of French
Sujet de conversation 2	An introduction of a functional use of French
Sujet de conversation 3	An introduction of a functional use of French
C'est à lire!	An authentic French reading
Ça y est! C'est à vous!	Global activities integrating material from throughout the chapter
Pour vérifier	A self-test correlated to the facing vocabulary list
Vocabulaire	A list of vocabulary

The following subsections are found in each of the three *Sujets de conversation.*

Qu'est-ce qu'on dit?	Vocabulary and expressions useful for a particular communicative function, followed by a dialog and recognition activities using the new vocabulary and structures
Voilà pourquoi!	Explanations of structures
Et ça se prononce comment?	Explanations of pronunciation (This section appears only when appropriate to a particular structure.)
Savez-vous le faire?	Practice of pronunciation and new structures
Remarquez que...	Cultural information (This section appears only when appropriate to a particular function or theme.)

Since no structures are introduced in the *Chapitre préliminaire*, it has a unique format. Note that page numbers appear in parentheses next to each major section head throughout the *Table des matières.*

	THEMES AND FUNCTIONS (*Qu'est-ce qu'on dit?*)	STRUCTURES (*Voilà pourquoi!*)

Unité 1 Sur la Côte d'Azur

Chapitre 1 (28) *À l'université*

Chapitre 2 (62) *Après les cours*

	THEMES AND FUNCTIONS *(Qu'est-ce qu'on dit?)*	STRUCTURES *(Voilà pourquoi!)*

Unité 2 Au Québec

Chapitre 3 (96) Un nouvel appartement

Chapitre 4 (130) Chez les parents

	THEMES AND FUNCTIONS *(Qu'est-ce qu'on dit?)*	STRUCTURES *(Voilà pourquoi!)*
Unité 3	**À Paris**	
Chapitre 5 (166)	***Des projets***	
Pour commencer (168)		
Comment s'y prendre? (171)		
Qu'est-ce qui se passe? (172)		
Remarquez que... (174)		
Sujet de conversation 1 (175)	*Suggesting activities*	Le pronom **on** et les suggestions; Le verbe **faire**; La négation et **ne... rien** Les expressions avec **avoir**
Sujet de conversation 2 (183)	*Telling what you did and when*	Le passé composé avec **avoir**
Sujet de conversation 3 (188)	*Saying where you went*	Le passé composé avec **être** Le pronom **y**
C'est à lire! (193)		
Ça y est! C'est à vous! (196)		
Pour vérifier (198)		
Vocabulaire (199)		
Chapitre 6 (200)	***Les invitations***	
Pour commencer (202)		
Comment s'y prendre? (206)		
Qu'est-ce qui se passe? (207)		
Remarquez que... (208)		
Sujet de conversation 1 (209)	*Issuing and accepting invitations*	Les verbes **devoir**, **pouvoir** et **vouloir**
Sujet de conversation 2 (215)	*Planning activities*	La date Le verbe **connaître**; Les pronoms **le**, **la**, **l'**, **les** Les verbes **savoir** et **connaître**
Sujet de conversation 3 (225)	*Offering something to eat and drink*	Le partitif; Le verbe **servir**
C'est à lire! (229)		
Ça y est! C'est à vous! (231)		
Pour vérifier (232)		
Vocabulaire (233)		

	THEMES AND FUNCTIONS *(Qu'est-ce qu'on dit?)*	STRUCTURES *(Voilà pourquoi!)*

Unité 4 Aux Antilles

Student Preface

Do you have a gift for languages?

Have you ever heard people say that they know someone who has a gift for languages? What does that mean? Are some people born with a special ability to learn languages? How do you know if you have a gift for languages? If you understood the sentence you just read, then you have a gift for languages. After all, you have already learned to speak and understand at least one language well, English. Everybody is born with a natural ability to learn languages, but some individuals seem to learn languages more quickly than others. This is because, over time, we develop different learning styles.

The process individuals use to learn languages depends a great deal on their personality. As with any other process, such as learning a new computer program or writing a composition for English class, individuals can attain similar results, although they approach the task differently. Some language learners like to plan each step before beginning. Others prefer to jump in as soon as they know enough to get started, and continue from there using a hit-or-miss method. Some language learners like to understand in detail why a language works the way it does before they try to use it, while others are ready to try speaking as soon as they know only the most basic rules, making educated guesses about how to express themselves.

Both methods have advantages and disadvantages. Some people become so bogged down in details that they lose sight of their main purpose, communication. Others pay so little attention to details that what they say is unintelligible. No matter what sort of learner you are, the most important part of the language-learning process is to constantly try to use the language to express yourself. Always alternate study of vocabulary and structures with attempts to communicate.

Since you now know that you have a gift for languages, you might think of the following pages as a user's manual that suggests how to use your language-learning capacity to learn French efficiently. Some of the learning techniques will work for you, others may not fit your learning style. You should read through the following three sections before beginning your French studies, and refer to them later to develop the language-learning process that works best for you.

- **Goals and Expectations** — How much French should you expect to learn in your first year of study and how much time and effort will be required of you?
- **Motivation** — How do you motivate yourself to study and practice the language?
- **Learning techniques** — What are some study tips that will facilitate learning French?

Goals and Expectations

Who can learn a language?

Many people believe that, as an adult, you cannot learn a language as well as you might have when you were a child. It is true that children are good language learners, but there is no reason why adults cannot learn to speak a language with near-native fluency. Children learn languages well because they can adapt very easily and they do it willingly. Being able to adapt is very important in language learning. Children are not afraid to try something new, and they are not easily embarrassed if things do not turn out as they expected. Adults, on the other hand, often are afraid of doing something wrong or looking ridiculous. Don't be afraid to experiment, using what you already know to guess at how to express yourself in French. It does no harm if you try to say something and you do not get the expected response. Just try again.

By the time people become adults, they generally learn by analyzing, rather than by doing. They have also grown so accustomed to their own way of doing things, that they are reluctant to change. Similarly, adult language learners often feel that the way English works is the natural way. They try to force the language they are learning into the same mold. In fact, languages work in variety of ways, all equally natural. Learn to accept that the French way of doing things is just as natural and valid as the English way.

Another difference in the way that children and adults learn languages is that children spend a lot more time focused on what they are doing. When children learn languages, they spend almost every hour they are awake for several years doing nothing but learning the language. Learning to communicate is their principal objective in life. Most adults, on the other hand, spend just a few hours a week studying a new language, and during this time, they are often distracted by many other aspects of their lives. In a classroom setting, where small children have contact with a foreign language for just a few hours per week, children do not learn better than adults. In fact, adults have several advantages over children, such as their ability to organize and their longer attention spans. Your ability to develop fluency in French will depend mainly on three things: the amount of time you spend with the language, how focused you are, and how willing you are to try to communicate using it.

How well will you speak after a year?

Those of you who are new to foreign language study probably have a variety of ideas about what you will be doing in this course. People who become frustrated in foreign language study generally do so because they start off with the wrong expectations. Some people begin a foreign language course with a negative attitude, thinking that it is impossible to really learn a language without going to a country where it is spoken. Although it is indeed usually easier to learn French in a French-speaking region, you can learn to speak French very fluently here as well. Once again, it is a question of spending time with the language, while focusing on how to communicate with it.

There are also some students who begin foreign language classes with expectations that are too high, thinking that they will begin speaking French with complete fluency nearly overnight. Learning a language takes time. Even after two years of concentrated study, it is reasonable to expect to have achieved only basic fluency. If you set a goal for yourself to have everyday conversation skills after your second year of study, and if you work hard toward this goal, you will be able to function in most everyday conversation settings; however, you will still frequently have to look for words, you will probably still speak in short simple sentences, and you will often have to use circumlocution to get your meaning across. In *Qu'est-ce qu'on dit?* you will learn how to function in the most common situations in which you are likely to find yourself in a francophone region. To illustrate how much you will learn during the first few weeks of study, take out a sheet of paper, and list, in English, the first eight questions you would probably ask in the following situation: Before the first day of a class, you sit down next to a student you have never seen before and you begin to chat.

In this situation, students generally ask questions like the following:

- How are you doing?
- What's your name?
- What are you studying?
- Where are you from?

- Where do you live? / Do you live on campus?
- Do you like it there?
- Do you work? Where?
- When are you graduating?

This is the extent of the conversation that you have with many people you will meet, and you will be able to do this in French after only a few weeks. To get a better idea of what you will be learning to talk about in French during the first year, look at the communication goals on the first page of each chapter, where it says **By the end of this chapter, you should be able to do the following in French** (pages 1, 28, 62, 96, 130, 166, 200, 234, 270, 312, 352, 390, 430). As you can see, in *Qu'est-ce qu'on dit?*, you will learn how to communicate the most useful information in the most common situations.

How much time and effort must you invest to be a successful language learner?

There are three P's involved in learning a language: patience, practice, and persistence. We have already said that success in learning a foreign language depends on how much time you spend studying and practicing it. You might wonder how time consuming French class will be. The amount of time required depends on your study skills and attention span. However, nobody can be successful without devoting many hours to studying and using the language. Generally, to make steady progress at the rate that material is presented in most college or university classes, you should expect to spend two to three hours on the language outside of class, for every hour that you are in class.

What is involved in learning to express yourself in another language?

Students studying a foreign language for the first time may have false expectations about what is involved in learning to speak another language. Many people think that you just substitute a French word for the equivalent word in English. Most of the time, you cannot translate word for word from one language to another. For example, if a French speaker substituted the equivalent English word for each French word in the following sentence, it would create a very unusual sentence.

> **Nous ne l'avons pas encore fait.**
> **We not it have not still done.*

You might be able to figure out that the sentence above means *We haven't done it yet*, but sometimes translating word for word can give a completely wrong meaning. For example, if you translate the following sentence word for word, you would think it has the first meaning that follows it, while it really has the second. This is because the indirect object pronoun **vous** (*to*) *you* precedes the verb in French.

> **Je voudrais vous parler demain s'il vous plaît.**
> **I would like you to speak tomorrow, if it you pleases.*
> *I would like to speak to you tomorrow, please.*

You probably noticed in this last example that one word in English may be translated by several words in French and vice versa (**voudrais** = *would like*, **vous** = *to you*, **parler** = *to speak*, **s'il vous plaît** = *please*).

Differences in languages are not due simply to a lack of one-to-one correspondence between words and structures. Cultural differences also strongly affect how we communicate. Culture and language are so interrelated that it is impossible to learn a language fluently without becoming familiar with the culture(s) where it is spoken. For example, in French, a cultural difference that affects the spoken language is that French society is not as informal as ours. Adults generally do not call each other by their first name, and the words for *sir* and *madame* are used much more frequently than in English. For example, it is normal to say **Bonjour, monsieur** (*Hello, sir*) while English speakers say *Hello.*

Cultural differences affect the spoken language and also nonverbal communication. For instance, when the French speak to each other, they generally stand closer than we do. When we are talking to a French-speaker, we may feel that our space is invaded and back away. The French interpret this as standoffishness. As you can see, learning to communicate in French entails a lot more than substituting French words for English words in a sentence.

Does practice make perfect?

Your goal in learning French should not be to say everything perfectly. If you set this goal for yourself, you will probably be afraid to open your mouth, fearing mistakes. Your goal should be to communicate clearly, but you should expect to make mistakes when speaking. If you make a mistake that impedes communication, those you are speaking to will ask for clarification or repeat what you have said to be sure of what you mean. Listen carefully to how they express themselves, and make adjustments the next time you need to convey a similar message.

Although perfection is not the goal of language learners, practice is vital to success. (Remember the three P's of language learning: patience, practice, and persistence.) You can learn every vocabulary word and rule in the book, but unless you practice regularly, attempting to listen to French and to speak it, you will not learn the language. Practicing a language is just as necessary for success as practicing a sport or a musical instrument. Imagine that you are a football player or a pianist. You might know every play in the book, or you might understand music theory completely, but unless you practice, you will never be able to perform. It is important to learn the rules of French, but you must also practice it regularly.

What do you do if foreign languages make you panic?

Most individuals feel nervous when they have to speak to strangers. This is true when you speak your own language, and it is even truer when speaking a foreign language. There is no reason to be nervous, yet fear of looking ridiculous is often difficult to control. It is normal to experience some anxiety in class. If you suffer extreme anxiety in language class, to such a degree that it impedes your ability to concentrate, it is best to recognize that you fear having to perform in class. Go see your instructor and discuss your anxiety. In order to conquer it, you must acknowledge it.

Motivation

How can learning a foreign language help you?

Learning a foreign language should be fun. After all, you will spend a lot of class time chatting with classmates, which most of us find enjoyable. However, learning French will take time and effort. No matter how much you enjoy it, there will be times when you need to motivate yourself to study or practice. You can use motivation techniques for practicing a language similar to those musicians or athletes use to practice an instrument or a sport.

Many musicians and athletes have a personal goal. They imagine themselves playing a great concert at Carnegie Hall or winning a big game, receiving applause and praise. Similarly, each time you start to practice French, imagine yourself speaking French fluently with a beautiful accent. In this mental image, you might be a diplomat, or you might be talking to the waiter at a French restaurant, impressing your friends.

Some people who practice an instrument or a sport do so for personal growth. Many people feel that learning a new language helps them discover a new side of their personality. By learning to appreciate another culture, you will learn to understand your own better. You will come to know yourself better and you will broaden your horizons.

Of course, a lot of people are motivated to practice an instrument or a sport because they make their living from it. This is good motivation for learning a language too. In today's international economy, the best jobs are going more and more to those who speak more than one language, and who have an understanding of other cultures. Many jobs in the travel industry, in communications, in government, and in companies dealing in international trade and business require proficiency in another language.

How can you learn to enjoy studying?

As with any accomplishment, learning a foreign language requires a lot of work. You will enjoy it more if you think of it as a hobby or a pastime and an opportunity to develop a skill. Here are some training techniques that can help you learn a new language.

- Get on a routine. Devote a particular time of day to studying French. It is best to find a time when you are fresh and free of distractions, so you can concentrate on what you are doing. If you study at the same time every day, getting started will become habitual, and you will have won half the battle. Once you are settled working and learning, it becomes fun.
- Make sure that the place where you study is inviting and that you enjoy being there.
- Study frequently for short periods of time, rather than having marathon sessions. After about two hours of study, the ability of the brain to retain information is greatly reduced. You tend to remember what you learn at the beginning of each study session and at the end. What you study in the middle tends to become blurred. To illustrate this, read the following words one time, then turn the page and see how many you remember.

  dog, house, sofa, cat, rooster, room, telephone, mouse, book, pencil, television

  Most people can remember the first word and the last. The longer the list, the harder it is to remember the words in the middle. The same is true with studying. Study smaller "chunks" of material more frequently. Set reasonable goals for yourself. Don't try to learn it all at once.
- Study with a classmate or a friend. It is much easier to practice talking with someone else, and it is easier to spend more time working with the language if you are interacting with another person. Also, by studying with classmates, you will come to feel more comfortable speaking in front of them, which eliminates some of the embarrassment some adults feel when trying to pronounce foreign words in front of the whole class.

- Play games with the language. It is fun to learn how to say things in a new language. For instance, ask yourself how you would say things you hear on the radio or television in French. If you do know how to say something you hear in French, your knowledge will become more certain. If you don't know how to say something in French, that's normal if you are a beginner. When you finally learn the word or expression you were wondering about, you will remember it more easily, because you have already thought about it.
- Surround yourself by French. Rent French videos, listen to French music, and read French comic books and magazines. Magazines with a lot of pictures are the best, because the pictures give you clues to the meaning of unfamiliar words. You probably will not understand very much at first in movies and songs, but they will motivate you to learn more. They will teach you about cultural differences, and they will help give you a sense of good pronunciation.
- Don't let yourself get frustrated. If you are frustrated each time you sit down to study, ask yourself why. First of all, make sure that you are not studying when you are too tired or hungry. Also, make sure that you clearly understand your assignment and its purpose. Learn to distinguish a language-learning problem from a problem understanding instructions. If you are confused about what you are to do or why, see your instructor during office hours or contact another student. (This is another reason to study with a classmate!)

Learning Techniques

How can you spend your study time most efficiently?

Individuals organize material differently as they learn it. Some people learn better by seeing something, while others learn better by hearing it. Below are some study tips for how to go about learning French. You may find that some of these methods work for you and others do not. Be creative in practicing your French, using a variety of study techniques.

General study tips

- Learn not to translate word for word. Learn to read and listen to whole sentences at a time.
- Keep a log of your study time in a small spiral notebook. This will help you learn to study more efficiently. Each time you sit down to study new material, write down the time you begin. When you finish, write down the time you stop, and two or three sentences summarizing what you studied. Students often feel frustrated that they spend a lot of time studying, but they do not retain much. By keeping a log, you will know exactly how much time you spend on French. Writing one or two sentences summarizing what you studied helps you check your retention.
- Alternate speaking, listening, reading, and writing activities. By changing tasks frequently, you will be able to study longer without losing your concentration.

Vocabulary-learning techniques

- Use your senses. Pronounce words aloud as you study them. Close your eyes as you pronounce the word and picture the thing or activity represented by nouns or verbs.
- Use flashcards, working from English to French. When possible, draw a simple picture instead of the English word. Also, write a sentence using the word on the card, trying to remember it each time you look at the card. Use different colored inks to help you visualize the meaning of words. For example, when studying colors, write them on the

flashcard in that color. When learning food items, write the words for red foods, such as strawberries and tomatoes, in red, the words for green foods in green, etc. Write words that can be associated with shapes, such as tall, short, big, small, round, or square with letters having similar shapes.

- Learn useful common phrases such as *What time is it?* or *How are you?* as a whole when using flashcards.
- Label household items in French on masking tape.
- Tape lists of vocabulary in places where you spend time doing routine tasks.
- Study vocabulary in manageable "chunks." Each morning, write out a list of 20 new words and carry it in your pocket. A few times during the day, spend two minutes trying to remember the words on the list. Take out the list and review the words you forgot for two minutes. By the end of the day, you will have spent just a few minutes and you will have learned the 20 words.
- Learn 10 useful phrases every day.
- If you know a French speaker, ask him/her to record the vocabulary words you want to learn on a cassette so you can play them at home, while you jog, or in your car.
- Make tests for yourself. At the end of a study session, write the English words or phrases on a sheet of paper. Put the sheet of paper away for a few hours. Later, take it out and see how many of the French equivalents of these words or phrases you remember.
- Group words in logical categories. For example, learn words for fruits together, words for animals together, sports-related vocabulary together, etc.
- Make flashcards with antonyms on each side such as hot/cold, near/far, to go to sleep/to wake up, etc.
- Use related English words to help you remember the French. For example, the French word for *to begin* is **commencer**. Associate it with *to commence*. Be creative in finding associations. For example, the word for *open* is **ouvert**. You can associate it with *overture*, which is the opening part of a musical piece, or an *overt* action, which is one that is done in the open. Write related English words on flashcards.

Grammar-learning techniques

- Play teacher. Try to guess what your instructor would ask you to do if he/she were giving a quiz the next day.
- Do the self-checks in the margins next to explanations of structures and check your answers in ***Appendix B***.
- Use color coding to help you remember grammatical information. For example, all nouns in French are categorized either as masculine or feminine, and you must memorize in which category each noun belongs. When you make flashcards, write feminine nouns on pink cards or with pink ink and use blue for masculine nouns. Use an eye-catching color to indicate on flashcards points you want to remember, such as irregular plurals or verbs that take **être** in the **passé composé**.
- If you like to use lists to study, organize them so that they help you remember information about words. For example, to remember noun gender, write masculine words in a column on the left and feminine words in a column on the right. If you can visualize where the word is on the list, you can remember its gender.
- Learn to accept ambiguity. Sometimes, as soon as you learn a new rule, you find out that it doesn't always work the way you expect it to.

Pronunciation-learning techniques

- Repeat everything you hear in French under your breath or in your head, even if you have no idea what it means. This will not only help your pronunciation, it will help your listening comprehension and your ability to learn vocabulary. For instance, if you keep repeating an unfamiliar word you hear in your head, when you finally find out what it means, you will remember it very easily.

- Read French words aloud as you study.
- Listen to the tapes that go with the book and the *Cahier d'activités orales* (*Lab Manual*) several times. It is impossible to concentrate both on meaning and pronunciation the first time you listen to them. Listen to them at least once focusing on pronunciation only.
- Make tapes of yourself and compare them to those of native speakers.
- Exaggerate as you practice at home. Any pronunciation that is not English will seem like exaggeration. Psychologically, it is very difficult to listen to oneself speaking another language. Pretend you are a French actor playing a role as you practice pronunciation.

Using the *Textbook Tapes* and the *Lab Manual Tapes*

There are two distinct sets of tapes that go with each chapter of the *Qu'est-ce qu'on dit?* program: the *Textbook Tapes* and the *Lab Manual Tapes.* The activities on the *Textbook Tapes* correspond to the listening sections marked by a cassette symbol in the textbook. These tapes are provided so that you can review material covered in class on your own, or prepare for the next day's class. The activities corresponding to the *Lab Manual Tapes* are found in the *Cahier d'activités orales.* These activities give you extra practice listening to and pronouncing French. When you are preparing to do a listening activity in the textbook or the *Cahier d'activités orales,* it is important to make sure that you have the right tape.

In order to get maximum benefit from the tapes, approach listening activities with the right attitude. It takes time, patience, and practice to understand French spoken at a normal conversational speed. Do not be surprised if you find it difficult at first. Relax and listen to passages more than once. You will understand a little more each time. Remember that you will not understand everything and that, for some exercises, you are only expected to understand enough to answer specific questions. Read through exercises prior to starting the tape, so that you know what to listen for.

If you find you do not have enough time to process and respond to a question before the next one, take advantage of the pause or stop button on your tape player to give yourself more time. Most importantly, be patient and remember that you can always rewind the tape and listen again.

Be willing to listen to the tapes several times. It is important to listen to them at least one separate time focusing solely on pronunciation. Practice, patience, and persistence pay!

We hope that the preceding suggestions on how to go about learning French will serve you well, helping you to become a successful language learner. We are always anxious to hear from students what works for them. If you have any study tips or ideas that you would like to share with us, please write to us in care of Heinle & Heinle Publishers, 20 Park Plaza, Boston, Massachusetts 02116-4507. Good luck with your French studies, and most of all, enjoy yourself!

Acknowledgments

We are grateful to a great many people for helping us transform our collective classroom experience into this text.

Principal among these are:

— Charles Heinle and Stan Galek, for giving us the opportunity to work with Heinle & Heinle.

— Managing Developmental Editor Beth Kramer for her unfailing support and patience through the project.

— Production Supervisor Barbara Browne, Assistant Editor Mary McKeon, and Project Manager Julianna Nielsen for their hard work down the home stretch.

— Jeff Hixson, from New College, Sarasota, Florida, for his cooperation on the workbook.

— Danielle and Philippe DeWailly for their linguistic advice.

— All of the reviewers: Diane Fagin Adler, North Carolina State University; James J. Baran, Marquette University; Lynne Breakstone, Washington University; Liette Brisebois-Kinsella, University of Illinois at Chicago; Kim Campbell, New York University; Rosalie M. Cheatham, University of Arkansas at Little Rock; James N. Davis, University of Arkansas; Victor S. Drescher, Indiana University of Pennsylvania; Mary Jane Ellis, Cornell University; Frank Friedman, Charles Stewart Mott Community College; James Gaasch, Humboldt State University; Rosalee LoGalbo Gentile, University of Illinois at Chicago; Thomas M. Hines, Samford University; Jeff Hixson, New College; Ray Horn, University of South Florida; Hannelore Jarausch, University of North Carolina at Chapel Hill; Kathryn Kinczewski, Hood College; Celeste Kinginger, University of Maryland; Rebecca R. Kline, Pennsylvania State University; Katherine Kulick, College of William and Mary; Leona B. LeBlanc, Florida State University; Stevin J. Loughrin-Sacco, Boise State University; Margaret M. Marshall, Southeastern Louisiana University; Josy McGinn, Syracuse University; Joseph Morello, The University of Rhode Island; Patricia Kyle Mosele, University of Texas at Austin; M. J. Muratore, University of Missouri—Columbia; Kathy Marshall Pederson, Wheaton College; Barbara Lomas Rusterholz, University of Wisconsin—La Crosse; Norman R. Savoie, Utah State University; Janet L. Solberg, Kalamazoo College; Kathryn Stewart, Oakland Community College; Fred L. Toner, Texas Christian University; Mary Williams, Tarrant County Junior College. Special thanks go to the following: Nicole Dicop-Hineline for her authenticity checks, Alex Silverman, from the School for International Training, Brattleboro, Vermont, for his cultural expertise, and Marie Léticée-Camboulin for the invaluable information on Guadeloupe and Martinique.

— David Murray and Stephanie Osser for their engaging drawings.

— Bruce Kennett, Julia Price, Florence Boisse-Kilgo, Esther Marshall, David Baker, Mary Taucher, Nicole Fronteau, and Carl Spector for their assistance.

— Our family and friends, for their support over the long haul, especially Jim, Bill, Daniel, and Laura.

Last but obviously not least, each other for the tolerance, mutual encouragement, and strengthened bonds of friendship such an endeavor requires.

Merci mille fois!

Chapitre préliminaire
On commence!

By the end of this chapter, you should be able to do the following in French:

- Greet others, introduce yourself, and say good-bye
- Spell your name and other words
- Count and tell addresses
- Understand what your professor tells you to do, and ask for clarification
- Make a few statements about yourself
- Tell the time and day

Nature morte
Raoul Dufy (1877–1953)
1934
Evergreen House Foundation/The Johns Hopkins University

Soyez les bienvenus!

As you begin to learn French, stop and think about how we use language and why it is so important to us. Language is how we express our thoughts and how we obtain the information we need in daily life. Usually, we are not aware of how we use language. Think back to when you first spoke to someone this morning. What did you say? To whom were you talking? Why did you say what you did? Did the person you were talking to respond or react the way you expected? Of course, you do not ask yourself these questions each time you speak to someone, but subconsciously you are always aware of all these aspects of communication. As you study French, you will need to pay attention to how and why people say what they do, and how they react to what is said.

Students in Canada

In *Qu'est ce qu'on dit?*, you will join several people as they travel in France and other francophone (French-speaking) regions of the world. Some of the situations in which they find themselves will seem quite normal to you; others may be surprising. Your job as a language learner is to observe what they say and do, and how people react to them. This will help you learn to express your own thoughts in French and to ask questions when you need information.

Students in France

SUJET DE CONVERSATION 1
Meeting and greeting people you don't know well

Qu'est-ce qu'on dit?

Use these expressions to greet adult strangers and those to whom you show respect.

— Bonjour, madame.
— Bonjour, monsieur.

— Bonsoir, monsieur.
— Bonsoir, mademoiselle.

— Je m'appelle Henri Prévost. Et vous madame, comment vous appelez-vous?
— Je m'appelle Hélène Cauvin.
— Enchanté, madame.
— Enchantée, monsieur.

Use these expressions to ask how other people are and to tell how you are doing.

Comment allez-vous? *How are you?*

Très bien, merci.
Et vous?

Assez bien.
or Pas mal.

Pas très bien.

SELF-CHECK

Self-check questions will be found throughout the book next to explanations of structures. Skim through these questions to preview what you will learn. You should always read the whole explanation before trying to answer the questions. Check your answers in *Appendix B.*

1. How do you greet someone during the day? during the evening?
2. How do you address a single woman? a married woman? a single or married man?
3. How do you ask someone's name? How do you say your name? How do you ask how someone is doing?
4. When does **enchanté(e)** have an extra **-e**? Does this extra **-e** change the pronunciation?

CULTURE NOTE

Generally, two men do not say **enchanté** to each other. Instead, they simply use **bonjour**.

NOTE

Items accompanied by a tape symbol are recorded on the textbook tape.

Savez-vous le faire?

A. Que dit-on? Look at the following people greeting each other and choose the appropriate missing statement or question.

1. a. Bonjour, monsieur.
   b. Bonjour, madame.
   c. Bonsoir, monsieur.

2. a. Bonjour, madame.
   b. Et vous, comment vous appelez-vous?
   c. Je m'appelle Hélène Cauvin. Et vous?

3. a. Enchanté, monsieur.
   b. Enchantée, monsieur.
   c. Enchanté, madame.

4. a. Bonjour, mademoiselle.
   b. Comment vous appelez-vous?
   c. Comment allez-vous?

5. a. Pas mal.
   b. Bonjour, monsieur.
   c. Comment allez-vous?

B. Conversations. You overhear the first part of several conversations. Indicate the most logical response (**a**, **b**, **c**, **d**, or **e**) to each item you hear.

a. Bonsoir, mademoiselle.
b. Bonjour, madame.
c. Je m'appelle Claude Verne. Et vous?
d. Enchanté, mademoiselle.
e. Très bien, merci. Et vous?

C. Comment vont-ils? Astérix and his friends, popular comic book heroes, are warriors fighting the Roman conquest of Gaul (ancient France) in 50 B.C. You may not understand what the characters in these scenes are saying, but use their expressions and gestures to decide how they would answer the question **Comment allez-vous?**

1. 

2. 

3. 

4. 

5. 

D. Réponses. How would you answer if someone said the following?

1. Bonjour, mademoiselle (monsieur, madame).
2. Comment vous appelez-vous?
3. Bonsoir, monsieur (madame, mademoiselle).
4. Enchanté, mademoiselle (monsieur, madame).
5. Comment allez-vous?

E. Qu'est-ce qu'on dit? What would you say in these situations?

1. You see your professor on the way to a class in the morning.
2. You want to know how he/she is.
3. You can't remember your professor's name.
4. Your professor keeps calling you by the wrong name.
5. A classmate introduces you to his grandmother.
6. You see your professor at the movies one evening.

F. Comment allez-vous? Act out the following scenes with a classmate. Greet each other, exchange names, and find out how your partner is doing.

1. 
2. 
3. 

Remarquez que...

French people who are not close friends or family members shake hands upon meeting and parting. Generally, greetings like **Bonjour** are followed by the person's name or by **monsieur**, **madame**, or **mademoiselle**. Family members and women who are good friends usually exchange **bises** (kisses on both cheeks) each time they meet or say good-bye. Men friends shake hands.

Dites ce qu'ils font. Would the following people be more likely to shake hands or exchange **bises** when meeting?

1. two women working together
2. two women friends
3. a boy and his aunt
4. a man and his boss
5. a male and a female cousin
6. two male classmates

La bise

— Bonjour, monsieur.

Qu'est-ce qu'on dit?

Use these expressions to greet classmates, friends, family members, and children; to ask how they are; and to exchange names.

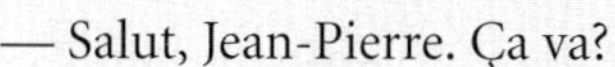

— Salut, Jean-Pierre. Ça va?
— Salut, Micheline. Ça va bien.
Et toi, comment ça va?
— Ça va.

— Bonjour, je m'appelle Henri.
Et toi, comment t'appelles-tu?
— Je m'appelle Marie-Laure.

You can use one of these expressions to say good-bye to anyone.

Au revoir.	*Good-bye.*
À bientôt.	*See you soon.*
À tout à l'heure.	*See you in a little while.*
À demain.	*See you tomorrow.*

SELF-CHECK

1. How do you greet classmates? ask their names? ask how they are?
2. What's the familiar equivalent of **Et vous**?
3. How do you say *good-bye* if you do not know when you will see someone again? if you will see someone later that day?

SUPPLEMENTAL[1] VOCABULARY

Comment vas-tu?
How are you? (informal)
Ciao! *Bye!*
Salut! *Bye!*

Bon week-end!
Have a good weekend!
Bonne journée!
Have a good day!

[1]Supplemental vocabulary enables you to personalize the material. It is not tested in the testing program.

Et ça se prononce comment?

Les consonnes muettes et la liaison

To read and write French correctly, you will learn a new system of associating written letters with spoken sounds. Many letters in French are silent.

> **NOTE**
> The textbook tape symbol indicates sections that are recorded on the textbook tape.

As you hear these greetings, tell which consonants are not pronounced.

— Bonjour. Je m'appelle Bernard. Et toi, comment t'appelles-tu?
— Je m'appelle Henri.
— Comment ça va?
— Pas mal. Et toi?

In French, consonants at the end of words are generally silent. Only the consonants **c**, **r**, **f**, and **l** (CaReFuL) are normally pronounced at the end of a word. There are a few exceptions, such as **monsieur**, where the final **r** is not pronounced. The letter **h** is always silent, in any position. Read the preceding conversation again, then pronounce the following words.

bonjour **Marc** **pas mal** **actif**

What do you notice about the pronunciation of the words **comment** and **vous** in these two examples?

Comment vous appelez-vous? **Comment allez-vous?**

Consonants at the end of French words are usually silent unless the following word begins with a vowel sound (**a**, **e**, **i**, **o**, **u**, **y**) or mute **h**. When the next word begins with a vowel sound, the final consonant sound sometimes links to the beginning of the next word. This linking is called **liaison**.

Comment vous‿appelez-vous? **Comment‿allez-vous?**

Savez-vous le faire?

A. Prononcez bien. Copy these boxes on a sheet of paper. Listen to the phrases in the two boxes, underlining the final consonants that should be pronounced, crossing out the mute h's and final consonants, and marking where **liaison** should occur with a ‿. Then go back and reorder the sentences within each box to create logical conversations to act out with a classmate.

EXEMPLE **Comment‿allez-vous, monsieur Hervé?**

A	B
1. À bientôt! 2. Pas mal. Et toi? 3. Salut, Marc! Comment ça va? 4. Eh bien, au revoir! 5. Moi, ça va assez bien.	1. Enchantée, monsieur. 2. Bonjour, monsieur. Comment allez-vous? 3. Je m'appelle Chantal Hubert. Et vous? 4. Je m'appelle Henri Châteauneuf. 5. Très bien, madame. Comment vous appelez-vous?

B. Dictée. Letter your paper from **a** to **j**. As you hear each passage, write the missing words. Be sure to spell them correctly, even if some of the letters are silent.

1. — a , Marc. b ça va?
   — Ça va bien. c toi?
   — d mal.

2. — Bonsoir, e . Comment f - g ?
   — h bien, merci. i vous?
   — j bien.

C. Formel ou familier? In which of the situations pictured, **A** or **B**, would you be most likely to hear these phrases?

1. Bonjour, madame.
2. Salut, Thomas.
3. Je m'appelle Annick.
4. Ça va?
5. Très bien, merci. Et vous?
6. Enchanté, madame.
7. Comment allez-vous?
8. Comment t'appelles-tu?
9. Ça va. Et toi?
10. Comment vous appelez-vous?

A.

B.

Now, go back and indicate how one should respond to the phrases above.

D. Et vous? With a classmate, act out the situation for each of the photos in the preceding activity. Greet your partner and ask how he/she is. Be sure to shake hands or exchange **bises**.

CULTURE NOTE
When doing ***D. Et vous?***, exchanging **bises** may feel a little awkward. It is common to feel strange doing something that is not common in your own culture. Being culturally aware will help ease the discomfort.

E. Au revoir. How would you say good-bye in the following situations?

1. You are saying good-bye to a classmate at the end of class today.
2. You will see your instructor again tomorrow.
3. You are saying good-bye to a classmate with whom you are going to study tonight.
4. You are talking on the phone to your grandparents, whom you are going to visit in a couple of weeks.
5. You are saying good-bye to a woman who just interviewed you for a job.
6. You are saying good-bye to your roommate.

F. Comment t'appelles-tu? Astérix is meeting and greeting a long-lost foreign cousin. Act out this scene with a classmate using your own names and expressions that you know.

— Salut. Je m'appelle Astérix. Et toi, comment t'appelles-tu?
— Je m'appelle Jolitorax.
— Ça va, Jolitorax?
— Ça va bien. Et toi?
— Pas mal.

Remarquez que...

French first names often have religious, historical, or legendary origins. Hyphenated names are also popular.

C'est surprenant! For which of these names can you think of an English equivalent? Does the gender of any surprise you?

PRÉNOMS MASCULINS		PRÉNOMS FÉMININS	
Adrien	Guillaume	Adrienne	Jeanne
André	Guy	Andrée	Julie
Benjamin	Jean	Béatrice	Laure
Christian	Jean-Marc	Christiane	Louise
Christophe	Jean-Paul	Claire	Marcelle
Claude	Laurent	Claude	Marie-France
Daniel	Louis	Danielle	Marie-Paule
Denis	Luc	Denise	Martine
Didier	Marc	Dominique	Michelle
Dominique	Marcel	Émilie	Monique
Émile	Martin	Fabienne	Pascale
Étienne	Michel	Françoise	Sarah
Fabien	Pascal	Gabrielle	Simone
François	René	Hélène	Véronique
Gabriel	Yves	Janine	Viviane

Qu'est-ce qu'on dit?

Here is how to count from 0 to 30 in French.

Combien? *How many? / How much?*
Comptez de zéro à trente, s'il vous plaît! *Count from zero to thirty, please!*

0	zéro				
1	un	11	onze	21	vingt et un
2	deux	12	douze	22	vingt-deux
3	trois	13	treize	23	vingt-trois
4	quatre	14	quatorze	24	vingt-quatre
5	cinq	15	quinze	25	vingt-cinq
6	six	16	seize	26	vingt-six
7	sept	17	dix-sept	27	vingt-sept
8	huit	18	dix-huit	28	vingt-huit
9	neuf	19	dix-neuf	29	vingt-neuf
10	dix	20	vingt	30	trente

Here is how to find out or tell how something is spelled.

Ça s'écrit comment? *How do you write that?*

a	a	i	i	q	ku	y	i grec		
b	bé	j	ji	r	erre	z	zède		
c	cé	k	ka	s	esse				
d	dé	l	elle	t	té	é = e accent aigu			
e	e	m	emme	u	u	è = e accent grave			
f	effe	n	enne	v	vé	â = a accent circonflexe			
g	gé	o	o	w	double vé	ï = i tréma			
h	hache	p	pé	x	iks	ç = c cédille			

Et ça se prononce comment?

Les voyelles nasales

In French, when a vowel is followed by the letter **m** or **n** in the same syllable, the **m** or **n** is silent and the vowel is pronounced nasally. Many numbers contain nasal vowels. Use the words below as models of how to pronounce each of the three nasal sounds. The letter combinations that are grouped together are all pronounced alike.

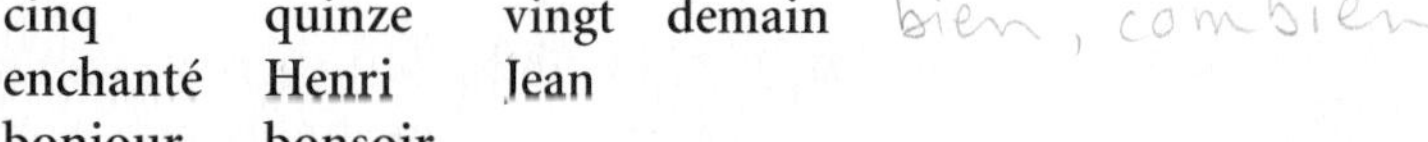

un / um / in / im / ain / aim	**un**	**cinq**	**quinze**	**vingt**	**demain**
en / em / an / am	**trente**	**enchanté**	**Henri**	**Jean**	
on / om	**onze**	**bonjour**	**bonsoir**		

Savez-vous le faire?

TEXTBOOK TAPE

A. Chiffres. Make these columns on a sheet of paper. Write out the words for the following numbers under the column indicating its nasal sound.

	A un / um / in / im / ain / aim	B en / em / an / am	C on / om
EXEMPLE 5	**cinq**		
1. 20			
2. 1			
3. 11			
4. 15			
5. 30			

Now listen to the numbers that should be in each column and check them off on your paper. Afterwards, pronounce each number.

B. C'est logique! Figure out the logical sequence of these strings of numbers. Then read the completed string.

1. 1, 3, 5, ?, 9, 11, ?, 15, 17, ?, 21, ?
2. 2, 4, ?, 8, 10, ?, 14, ?, 18, 20, ?
3. 0, 5, 10, ?, 20, ?, 30
4. 3, 6, 9, ?, 15, 18, ?
5. 20, 19, 18, ?, 16, 15, ?
6. 10, 11, 12, ?, 14, 15, ?
7. 11, 13, 15, ?, 19, 21, 23, 25, ?, 29
8. 0, 10, 20, ?

C. Sigles. The French use a lot of abbreviations. Tell what the French would call the following things by saying only the underlined initial letter of each word. Then look at the list in the right column and guess what each one refers to.

1. le train à grande vitesse = le ___
2. bon chic bon genre = ___
3. un président-directeur général = un ___
4. la taxe sur la valeur ajoutée = ___
5. la Société protectrice des animaux = la ___
6. Gaz de France = ___
7. le Mouvement de libération des femmes = le ___
8. la Communauté économique européenne = la ___

a. the Humane Society
b. a CEO
c. preppy
d. the European Community
e. the gas company
f. the high-speed train
g. the women's movement
h. sales tax

D. Présentations. With a partner, act out an introduction to a French student visiting your campus. The student asks you to spell out your name.

EXEMPLE **— Bonjour, je m'appelle Jan Wyndel.**
— Wyndel? Ça s'écrit comment?
— W-Y-N-D-E-L.

E. Messages secrets. You will hear a series of numbers. Write the letter corresponding to each number and you will discover a secret message. When you hear **zéro,** you should start another word (**un autre mot**).

EXEMPLE VOUS ENTENDEZ (*YOU HEAR*): 8, 30, 29, 9, 30, 6, 10, 0, 12, 18, 0, 15, 18
VOUS ÉCRIVEZ (*YOU WRITE*): **Bonjour, ça va?**

0	UN AUTRE MOT	8	b	16	ô	24	m
1	é	9	j	17	t	25	e
2	q	10	r	18	a	26	p
3	c	11	f	19	s	27	y
4	i	12	ç	20	h	28	è
5	d	13	g	21	l	29	n
6	u	14	x	22	w	30	o
7	z	15	v	23	à		

F. À la télévision. On which Montreal TV station(s) could you find each of these shows?

EXEMPLE Venture → CBC6 et CBS4

1. *Formule 1*
2. *Jamais sans mon livre*
3. *Life goes on*
4. *Miami*
5. *Funniest home videos*
6. *Musique vidéo*
7. *Les Amis de la forêt*
8. *La Trappe*
9. *Baseball*

Dimanche 1er août Télé-Soir TV HEBDO©

Postes	19:00	19:30	20:00	20:30	21:00	21:30	22:00	22:30
2 (RC)	SURPRISE SUR PRISE		***RENEE MARTEL—40 ANS DE SHOWBIZ***		***BEETHOVENISSIMO***			NOUVELLES
3 (CBS)	60 MINUTES		MURDER, SHE WROTE		MOVIE / IN SICKNESS AND IN HEALTH			
4 (CBS)	THE ROAD TO AVONLEA		MOVIE / MALAREK, A STREET KID WHO MADE IT				NEWS	VENTURE
5 (NBC)	MOVIE / PROBLEM CHILD				***LUCY AND DESI: A HOME MOVIE***			
6 (CBC)	THE ROAD TO AVONLEA		MOVIE / MALAREK, A STREET KID WHO MADE IT				NEWS	VENTURE
7 (TVA)	FORMULE 1		***CINEMA / VENT DE PANIQUE***				MIAMI	
8 (TVA)	FORMULE 1		***CINEMA / VENT DE PANIQUE***				MIAMI	
8 (CTV)	W5		FUNNIEST HOME VIDEOS	FUNNIEST PEOPLE	MOVIE / THE DEAD POOL			
9 (RC)	SURPRISE SUR PRISE		***RENEE MARTEL—40 ANS DE SHOWBIZ***		***BEETHOVENISSIMO***			NOUVELLES
10 (TVA)	FORMULE 1		***CINEMA / VENT DE PANIQUE***				MIAMI	
12 (CTV)	W5		FUNNIEST HOME VIDEOS	FUNNIEST PEOPLE	MOVIE / DEAD POOL			
17 (RQ)	CINEMA / LES AMIS DE LA FORET (18h30)		ONDINE		CINEMA / LA TRAPPE			LE MONDE EN MOUVEMENT(22h45)
22 (ABC)	LIFE GOES ON		FUNNIEST HOME VIDEOS	FUNNIEST PEOPLE	MOVIE / THE DEAD POOL			
33 (PBS)	WILD AMERICA	NATURESCENE	NATURE		MASTERPIECE THEATRE / THE GINGER TREE		MASTERPIECE THEATRE / THE GINGER TREE	
35 (TQS)	***THEATRE / LA NOCE*** (18h)		CINEMA / DEUX DOLLARS SUR UN TOCARD				NOUVELLES	SPORTS PLUS
57 (PBS)	THE DARLING BUDS OF MAY		EVENING AT POPS		HOLLYWOOD LEGENDS III	MOVIE / TO PLEASE A LADY (21h50)		
TV5	JOURNAL TELE-VISE DE TF1	***CHAMP LIBRE*** (19h35)	TELL QUEL	LE CHEMIN DES ECOLIERS	FROU-FROU		JAMAIS SANS MON LIVRE	
YTV	CATWALK		BLACK STALLION	MANIAC MANSION	ALL TOGETHER NOW	HOME TO ROOST	POSITIVE PARENTING	
Canaux spécialisés								
MM	SPOTLIGHT / ROXY MUSIC	ELVIS THE EARLY YEARS	VIDEOFLOW					
MP	MUSIQUE VIDEO (10h)						QUEBECPLUS	
RDS	***QUILLES***		***BASEBALL / TEXAS VS OAKLAND***					
SE	COMMANDO SUPREME (17h35) BISBILLE ET BOULES DE NEIGE (19h10)				***LES REQUINS DE LA FINANCE***			***H*** (22h50)
TMN	HEARTS OF DARKNESS: A FILMMAKER'S APOCALYPSE (17h30) MAN TROUBLE (19h15)				COOL WORLD			FINAL ANALYSIS (22h45)
TSN	***1993 BASEBALL HALL OF FAME INDUCTION CEREMONIES***		***BASEBALL / TEXAS VS OAKLAND***					

EN CARACTERES GRAS: LES SPECIAUX, PREMIERES ET EMISSIONS A SIGNALER

G. Adresses. Compare the hotel addresses you hear with those in these ads and write the letter corresponding to each one.

EXEMPLE VOUS ENTENDEZ: 4, rue Médéric
VOUS ÉCRIVEZ: c

a.

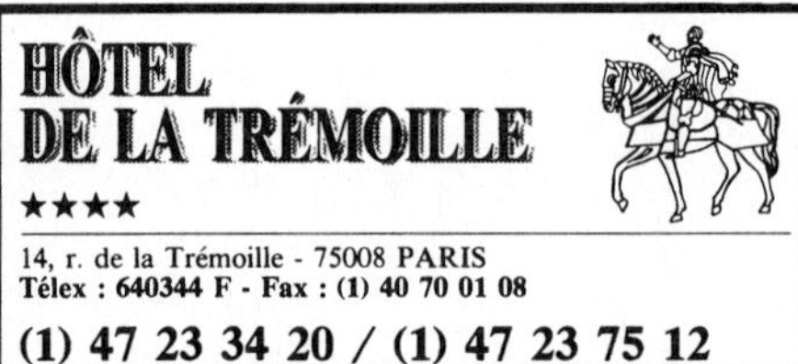

b.

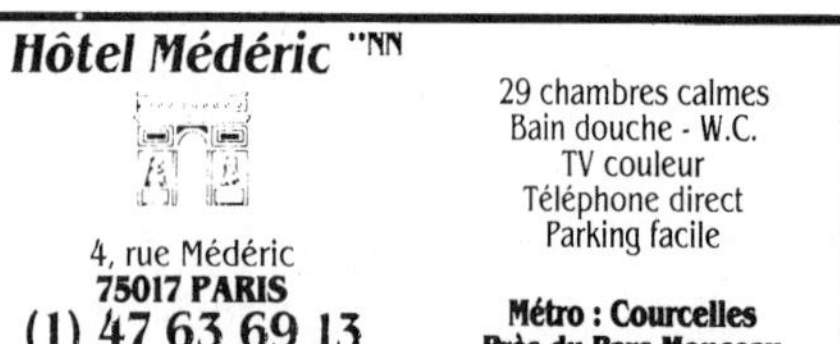

c.

d.

e.

f.

H. Mon hôtel. Choose one of the hotels above to stay in. Your friend asks you to spell out the name of the hotel and the street.

EXEMPLE
— Hôtel le Warwick, 5, rue de Berri.
— Ça s'écrit comment, Warwick?
— W-A-R-W-I-C-K.
— Et la rue de Berri?
— B-E-R-R-I.

Qu'est-ce qu'on dit?

En classe. *In class.*
Le professeur dit aux étudiants: *The professor says to the students:*

1. Levez-vous.

2. Allez au tableau.

3. Écoutez la question.

4. Répondez à la question.

5. Écrivez la phrase.

6. Retournez à votre place et asseyez-vous.

Understanding class instructions

7. Ouvrez votre livre à la page 23.

8. Prenez une feuille de papier et un stylo ou un crayon.

9. Écrivez la réponse au numéro 1 de l'exercice C.

10. Donnez-moi votre feuille de papier.

11. Fermez votre livre.

À la maison. *At home.*

12. Lisez la page 17.

13. Étudiez les mots de vocabulaire à la page 27 pour le prochain cours.

14. Faites les devoirs dans le cahier et écoutez les cassettes.

You may also need to understand or use these expressions.

Comment? Répétez, s'il vous plaît.	*What? Please repeat.*
— Est-ce que vous comprenez? — Oui, je comprends. — Non, je ne comprends pas.	*— Do you understand?* *— Yes, I understand.* *— No, I don't understand.*
Je ne sais pas.	*I don't know.*
— Comment dit-on *pen* en français? — On dit **un stylo**.	*— How do you say* **pen** *in French?* *— You say* **un stylo**.
— Qu'est-ce que ça veut dire en anglais **ouvrez**? — Ça veut dire *open*.	*— What does* **ouvrez** *mean in English?* *— It means* **open**.

Savez-vous le faire?

A. En classe ou à la maison? Would your professor normally have you do these things **en classe** or **à la maison**?

1. Fermez votre livre.
2. Étudiez les mots de vocabulaire.
3. Écoutez et répétez, s'il vous plaît.
4. Allez au tableau.
5. Prenez une feuille de papier.
6. Lisez les pages 12, 13 et 14.
7. Faites les devoirs dans le cahier.
8. Étudiez ça pour demain.
9. Retournez à votre place.
10. Asseyez-vous.

B. Dans l'ordre logique. Put each group of expressions in the logical order.

1. Levez-vous.
   Retournez à votre place et asseyez-vous.
   Écrivez votre réponse au tableau.
2. — Ça veut dire *read*.
   — Non, qu'est-ce que ça veut dire?
   — Est-ce que vous comprenez le mot **lisez**?
3. — Je ne sais pas.
   — Comment dit-on *hi* en français?
   — On dit **salut**.
4. Donnez-moi votre feuille de papier.
   Prenez une feuille de papier.
   Écrivez les réponses.
5. Lisez la page 11.
   Fermez votre livre.
   Ouvrez votre livre.

Paris, le Quartier latin

C. Pas logique. One of the commands within the parentheses does not make sense in the blank. Read only the completed commands that are possible.

1. ______ la question.
   (Lisez, Répétez, Prenez, Écoutez)
2. ______ votre livre.
   (Prenez, Allez, Ouvrez, Lisez)
3. ______ les devoirs.
   (Étudiez, Faites, Écrivez, Allez)
4. ______ la réponse.
   (Ouvrez, Répétez, Lisez, Écrivez)
5. ______ ça.
   (Lisez, Écrivez, Prenez, Allez)
6. ______ les mots de vocabulaire.
   (Lisez, Étudiez, Écrivez, Fermez)

D. En classe. Working in groups, make up commands your instructor might give you by matching items from the two columns. See which group can come up with the most.

Ouvrez...
Allez...
Lisez...
Étudiez...
Comptez...
Écoutez...
Prenez...
Écrivez...
Faites...

...la question.
...les devoirs.
...les mots de vocabulaire.
...ça.
...à la page 12.
...de 0 à 30.
...au tableau.
...une feuille de papier.
...la phrase.
...votre livre.

E. Que dit-on? What would you say in the following situations?

1. You want to ask how to say *good-bye* in French.
2. You want to ask what **enchanté** means.
3. You don't understand the question your professor is asking.
4. You want your professor to repeat a question.
5. You don't know the answer to a question.
6. You want to see how something is spelled.
7. You didn't hear what was said.

F. *Le Petit Prince.* Here is an illustration by Antoine de Saint-Exupéry, from his book *Le Petit Prince.* Make a list of what the professor might be saying to the students. What might they respond to him?

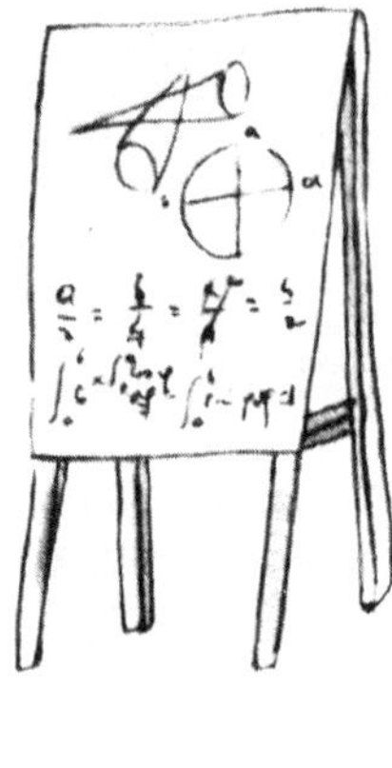

SUJET DE CONVERSATION 5
Talking about yourself

Qu'est-ce qu'on dit?

Use these expressions to talk about yourself.

J'habite...[1]	**avec** ma famille.	**Je travaille...**	**beaucoup.**
Je n'habite pas...	avec **un ami / une amie.**	Je ne travaille pas...	**pour** l'université.
	avec deux ami(e)s.		pour IBM.
	seul(e).		
	à Toronto.		

Je parle...	anglais.	**Je pense que** le français est...	(très, assez) **facile.**
Je ne parle pas...	français.		(très, assez) difficile.
	espagnol.		intéressant.
	beaucoup en classe.		

If you are female, use the following expressions on the left to describe yourself. If you are male, use those on the right.

Je suis...	étudiante.	Je suis...	étudiant.
Je ne suis pas...	professeur.	Je ne suis pas...	professeur.
	américaine.		américain.
	canadienne.		canadien.
	de Chicago.		de Chicago.
	d'ici.		d'ici.

In the following conversation, two adults meet at a Canadian-American cultural event in Montreal. Imagine what you would say in this situation.

— **Vous êtes** canadien?
— Oui, je suis d'ici. Et vous, vous êtes canadienne **aussi?**
— Non, je suis de Wichita.
— **Mais** vous parlez français **sans** accent. Vous habitez ici **maintenant**?
— Oui, **parce que** je travaille à l'université. Et vous? Vous travaillez ici aussi?
— Non, je suis étudiant.

SELF-CHECK

1. What are the two forms of the word for *I*?
2. What two words do you put around a verb to negate it?
3. What difference do you see between many of the words describing males and females?

STRUCTURE NOTES

The word **de** (*from, of*) changes to **d'** before vowel sounds or mute **h**. Similarly, **parce que** (*because*) changes to **parce qu'**. The word **seul(e)** has a final **e** when describing females but not when describing males.

---

[1] In the *Qu'est-ce qu'on dit?* section, boldfaced words are glossed at the end. Always try to guess what these words mean from the context before looking at the glosses.

j'habite *I live* **je n'habite pas** *I don't live* **avec** *with* **un ami** *a friend (male)* **une amie** *a friend (female)* **seul(e)** *alone* **je travaille** *I work* **beaucoup** *a lot* **pour** *for* **je parle** *I speak* **je pense que** *I think that* **facile** *easy* **je suis** *I am* **de (d')** *from* **ici** *here* **vous êtes** *you are (formal)* **aussi** *also, too* **mais** *but* **sans** *without* **maintenant** *now* **parce que** *because*

Savez-vous le faire?

A. Qui suis-je? Read the sentences and tell which person from the list is speaking: Gérard Depardieu, K. D. Lang, Branford Marsalis, Peter Jennings, Gloria Estefan.

1. Je suis canadien de Toronto. Je parle anglais. Maintenant, j'habite à New York. Je travaille pour ABC.
2. Je suis américaine. Je parle anglais et espagnol. Je suis de Miami.
3. Je suis canadienne. Je suis d'Alberta.
4. Je suis français. Je travaille à Paris et à Hollywood. Je parle français et anglais.
5. Je suis américain. Je suis de La Nouvelle-Orléans. J'habite à Hollywood. Je travaille à NBC avec Jay Leno.

B. Moi, je... Choose the words in parentheses so that each sentence describes you correctly.

1. (Je suis / Je ne suis pas) étudiant(e).
2. (Je suis / Je ne suis pas) en classe maintenant.
3. (Je suis / Je ne suis pas) de Los Angeles.
4. (Je suis / Je ne suis pas) canadien(ne).
5. (J'habite / Je n'habite pas) à Little Rock.
6. (J'habite / Je n'habite pas) avec ma famille maintenant.
7. (Je travaille / Je ne travaille pas) pour l'université.
8. (Je parle / Je ne parle pas) français sans accent.
9. Je pense que le français est (intéressant / facile / difficile).

C. Je suis... Finish these statements about yourself.

1. Je m'appelle...
2. Je ne suis pas français(e), je suis...
3. Je suis de (d')...
4. Maintenant, j'habite à...
5. Je parle... sans accent.
6. Je pense que le français est...

D. Et vous? Answer these questions about yourself.

1. Comment vous appelez-vous?
2. Comment allez-vous?
3. Vous êtes étudiant(e)?
4. Vous travaillez aussi?
5. Vous êtes américain(e)?
6. Vous parlez espagnol?
7. Vous êtes d'ici?
8. Vous habitez à Denver maintenant?

E. Présentations. You are at a reception given by the Canadian Embassy, where you meet several people. Complete the conversation with a classmate so that it describes you.

— Vous êtes canadien(ne)?
— Je suis de... Et vous?
— J'habite à...
— Vous êtes étudiant(e)?
— Oui, je... étudiant(e) à...

Qu'est-ce qu'on dit?

Use these expressions to ask and tell the time.

Quelle heure est-il?

Il est une heure **de l'après-midi.**

Il est deux heures.

Il est deux heures cinq.

SELF-CHECK

1. When do you use the words **et** and **le** in telling time?
2. How do you distinguish eight o'clock in the morning from eight in the evening? How do you clarify whether it is five in the morning or five in the afternoon?

Il est deux heures et quart.

Il est deux heures vingt.

Il est deux heures et demie.

STRUCTURE NOTE

Demie is spelled with an **-e** after the word **heure** but without a final **-e** in **midi et demi** and **minuit et demi.**

Il est trois heures moins vingt-cinq.

Il est trois heures moins le quart.

Il est trois heures.

Il est midi.

Il est minuit.

Use **à** *to ask or tell at what time something takes place.*

— À quelle heure ouvre **la bibliothèque?**
— À huit heures **du matin.**

— À quelle heure ferme la bibliothèque?
— À dix heures **du soir.**

de l'après-midi *in the afternoon* **la bibliothèque** *the library* **du matin** *in the morning* **du soir** *in the evening*

Use these expressions to ask and tell what day it is.

— Quel jour est-ce **aujourd'hui**?
— C'est lundi.

LUNDI	Lisez les pages 21, 22 et 23.
MARDI	Faites les devoirs dans le cahier.
MERCREDI	Faites l'exercice E à la page 23.
JEUDI	Écoutez les cassettes.
VENDREDI	Étudiez le vocabulaire.
SAMEDI	
DIMANCHE	

To say that you do something every Monday (or another day), use **le** *with the day. Do not translate the word* **on** *to say that you do something* **on** *a certain day.*

Je suis en classe **le** lundi, le mercredi et **le** vendredi.

To say that you do something ***from*** *a certain day or time* **to** *another day or time, use* **de... à**.

Je travaille **de** lundi à vendredi. Je ne travaille pas le samedi et le dimanche.
Je travaille **de** huit heures à cinq heures.

aujourd'hui *today*

Savez-vous le faire?

A. Quels sont les devoirs? Look at the calendar in the ***Qu'est-ce qu'on dit?*** box above. As you hear students ask what the homework is for a particular day, indicate what the instructor would answer.

EXEMPLE VOUS ENTENDEZ: Quels sont les devoirs pour jeudi?
VOUS RÉPONDEZ: **Écoutez les cassettes.**

B. Quel jour? Complete the following sentences with a day of the week. Remember to use **le** to say that you generally do something the same day every week.

1. Aujourd'hui, c'est...
2. Demain, c'est...
3. Je suis en classe...
4. Je ne suis pas en classe...
5. Je travaille... (*or:* Je ne travaille pas.)
6. Le cours de français est...

C. À cette heure-là. Tell whether you are usually at home at these times. Imagine that these are all afternoon and evening times.

...je suis à la maison ...je ne suis pas à la maison

EXEMPLE Le lundi à une heure...

Le lundi à une heure, je ne suis pas à la maison.

1. Le lundi à midi...
2. Le mardi à deux heures dix...
3. Le mercredi à trois heures vingt...
4. Le jeudi à cinq heures et demie...
5. Le vendredi à six heures moins le quart...
6. Le samedi à neuf heures moins dix...
7. Le dimanche à onze heures et quart...
8. Le lundi à minuit...

D. Quelle heure est-il? A classmate will ask you the time. Answer according to the clocks.

EXEMPLE **— Quelle heure est-il?**

— Il est une heure de l'après-midi.

1.

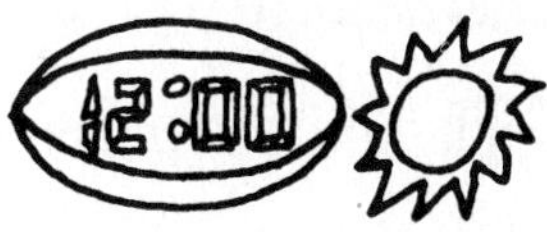

2.

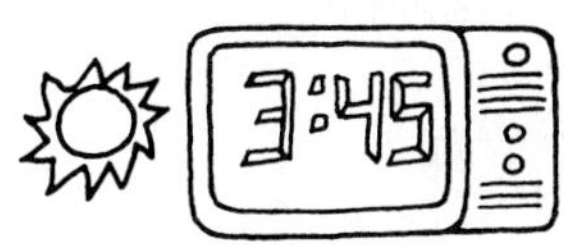

3.

4.

5.

6.

7.

E. C'est quelle heure? Complete the following sentences with the appropriate time.

1. Maintenant, il est...
2. Le lundi, je suis en classe de... à...
3. Le cours de français est de... à...
4. La bibliothèque ouvre à...
5. La bibliothèque ferme à...
6. Je travaille de... à... (*or:* Je ne travaille pas.)

F. Je préfère... Tell the station, the day, and the time of your favorite television program and see if your classmates can guess it.

EXEMPLE — **CBS, le dimanche à 7h du soir.**
— **C'est *60 minutes.***
— **Oui.**

G. Excursions. Indicate what day and time one can leave for each of these trips.

1.

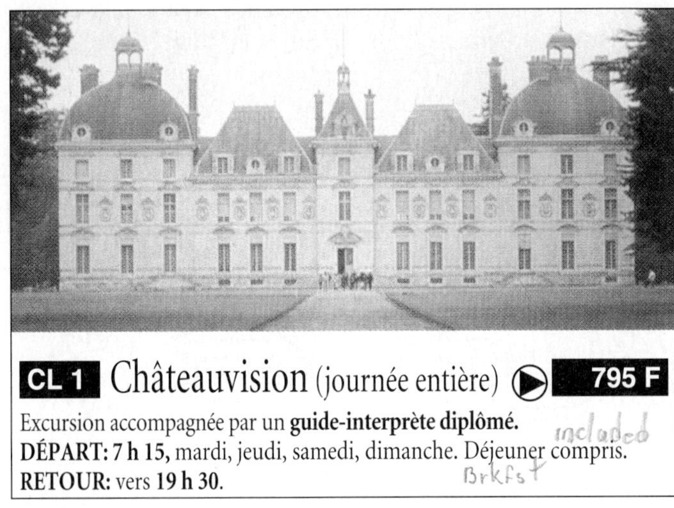

2.

3. **RC** Reims & Épernay (journée entière) **525 F**
la Route du champagne
Excursion accompagnée par un **guide-interprète diplômé.**
DÉPART: 7 h 45, mardi et vendredi. Déjeuner et boisson inclus.
RETOUR: vers **18 h 00.**

4. **RN** Giverny & Rouen (journée entière) **430 F**
Excursion accompagnée par un **guide-interprète diplômé.**
DÉPART: 8 h, le dimanche. Déjeuner non compris.
RETOUR: vers **19 h.**

5. **M** Malmaison **215 F**
Excursion accompagnée par un **guide-interprète diplômé.**
❺ **DÉPART: 9 h 30,** mercredi et vendredi.
DURÉE: 3 h environ.

Le monde francophone

You made an excellent decision when you decided to study French. It is one of the official languages of the United Nations and is spoken virtually all over the world, from Europe, to Asia, Africa, the Americas, and the South Pacific. France has long been a recognized leader in cuisine, fashion, wine, art, literature, and film, but did you know that it is also a world leader in international relations, business, and technology? You probably recognize, for example, the names of such French companies as Bic, Michelin, Lancôme, Perrier, and Renault.

Le Québec

In pursuit of the not-so-trivial

Test your knowledge of the francophone world. Before you look at the map inside the front cover, see how many of these questions you can answer.

1. French is spoken in about ___ (3, 17, 40, 200) countries of the world.
2. There are several places in the Americas where French is spoken. Name two.
3. On which three of these Caribbean islands is French an important language: the Dominican Republic, Haiti, Guadeloupe, the Virgin Islands, the Bahamas, Martinique, the Cayman Islands?
4. True or false? French is not spoken in any areas of the South Pacific.
5. True or false? Some people in Laos, Cambodia, and Vietnam speak French.
6. True or false? The existence of French-speaking people in the Americas, Africa, Asia, and the Pacific is largely due to the history of French colonialism.
7. French is spoken in several other countries of Europe, besides France. Name two.
8. French is spoken in many countries in Africa. Are most of them found in the north, west, east, or south?
9. French developed from a Latin base, whereas English developed from a Germanic base. However, English was greatly influenced by French largely due to what historical event?
10. In what country in South America is French spoken?

La Guadeloupe

Pour vérifier

Study the vocabulary on the facing page. Do the following exercises as a self-test, then check your answers in *Appendix C.*

Meeting and greeting people and saying good-bye

A. Bonjour! Complete these short conversations, using appropriate vocabulary.

1. — Comment vous appelez-vous?
   — ____________________
2. — Salut! Comment ça va?
   — ____________________. Et toi?
   — Pas mal.
3. — Au revoir. À demain.
   — ____________________
4. — À tout à l'heure!
   — ____________________

Talking about yourself

B. Autoportraits. Guess how these people would describe themselves if they were writing a self-portrait. Use these expressions in each description: **Je m'appelle..., Je suis de..., J'habite..., Je travaille...**

1. your professor 2. your best friend 3. the president / prime minister
4. a celebrity of your choice

Communicating in class and telling the time and day

C. Réponses. How would you respond if your instructor asked you the following?

1. J'ai besoin de vous voir demain. Est-ce que vous comprenez?
2. Quel jour est-ce aujourd'hui?
3. Quelle heure est-il?
4. Qu'est-ce que ça veut dire **fermez**?
5. Qu'est-ce que ça veut dire **mois**?
6. Vous êtes en classe de quelle heure à quelle heure le lundi? le mardi?

D. Chiffres. Fill in the logical numbers. If the number is larger than 30, write **beaucoup de (d')** in the blank. Spell out the numbers.

1. ______ pages dans le *Chapitre préliminaire*
2. ______ chapitres dans le livre *Qu'est-ce qu'on dit?*
3. ______ étudiants dans le cours de français
4. ______ professeur(s) dans le cours de français
5. ______ questions dans l'exercice *D. Chiffres.*

E. En classe. What has the instructor told these students to do?

1.

2.

3.

Vocabulaire

Meeting and greeting people and saying good-bye

À bientôt.
À demain.
À tout à l'heure.
Au revoir.
Bonjour, monsieur (madame, mademoiselle).
Bonsoir, monsieur (madame, mademoiselle).
Comment allez-vous? → Assez bien. / Pas mal. / Pas très bien. / Très bien, merci. Et vous?
Comment ça va? → Ça va (assez bien, très bien).
Comment t'appelles-tu? → Je m'appelle...
Comment vous appelez-vous? → Je m'appelle...
Enchanté(e).
Et toi? / Et vous?
Salut!

Talking about yourself

j'habite / je n'habite pas...
- à (+ *city*)
- avec ma famille
- avec un(e) ami(e) [deux ami(e)s]
- seul(e)

je parle / je ne parle pas...
- anglais
- beaucoup en classe
- espagnol
- français
- sans accent

je pense que...
- le français est...
  - difficile
  - facile
  - intéressant

je suis / je ne suis pas...
- à la maison
- américain(e)
- canadien(ne)
- de (d')... (+ *city*)
- d'ici
- étudiant(e)
- professeur

je travaille / je ne travaille pas...
- pour l'université

aussi
maintenant
mais
non
oui
parce que

Communicating in class and telling the time and day

Allez au tableau.
À quelle heure?
Asseyez-vous.
Ça s'écrit comment?
Combien?
Comment dit-on... en français? → On dit...
Comment? Répétez la phrase, s'il vous plaît.
Comptez de zéro à trente.
Donnez-moi votre feuille de papier.
Écoutez les cassettes.
Écrivez la réponse au numéro 1 de l'exercice E.
Est-ce que vous comprenez? → Oui, je comprends. / Non, je ne comprends pas.
Étudiez les mots de vocabulaire pour le prochain cours.
Faites les devoirs dans le cahier.
Fermez votre livre.
Je ne sais pas.
La bibliothèque ouvre / ferme...
Levez-vous.
Lisez les devoirs.
Ouvrez votre livre à la page 10.
Prenez un stylo ou un crayon.
Quel jour est-ce aujourd'hui?
Quelle heure est-il?
Qu'est-ce que ça veut dire? → Ça veut dire...
Répondez à la question.
Retournez à votre place.

Pour l'alphabet et les chiffres 0–30, voir la page 11.
Pour l'heure et les jours, voir les pages 21–22.

Unité 1 Sur la Côte d'Azur

Regional Overview
La France
(La République Française)
AREA: 211,207 square miles (549,000 sq. km.)
POPULATION: 56,500,000
CAPITAL: **Paris**
MAJOR INDUSTRIES: aeronautics, agriculture, manufacturing, mining, technology

Chapitre 1 À l'université

By the end of this chapter, you should be able to do the following in French:

- Identify and describe people
- Describe your university
- Get to know others
- Compare your classes

Baie de Cannes
Pablo Picasso (1881–1973)
1958
Paris, Musée Picasso
Giraudon/Art Resource, New York

This is a view of Cannes, a resort town on the **Côte d'Azur**, as seen from a window of Picasso's 19th-century villa, **La Californie.** The same view is the subject of many of Picasso's paintings from this period.

452

NOTE
Items accompanied by a tape symbol are recorded on the textbook tape.

Pour commencer

In the first unit, we will meet Annette and Yvette Clark, and Annette's friend David in Nice, in southern France. Use these expressions to identify people. Use **une** *to say* a *for females and* **un** *for males.* **Des** *means* some.

C'est une fille.

C'est un garçon.

C'est une jeune femme.

C'est un jeune homme.

C'est une femme (une dame).

C'est un homme (un monsieur).

Ce sont des enfants.

Ce sont des jeunes.

Ce sont des gens.

Jon

Here is the conversation between David and Annette when they first meet each other on campus and start talking.

— Salut. **Nous sommes** dans le **même** cours de français, **n'est-ce pas?** Je m'appelle David Cauvin.
— Je m'appelle Annette Clark.
— Bonjour.
— Bonjour.
— Tu es d'ici?
— Non, je suis de Paris mais maintenant j'habite ici. Et toi, tu es française?
— Non, je suis américaine.
— Ta famille habite ici?
— Non, ma famille habite à Los Angeles. Je suis ici **pour étudier. Ma sœur est** ici aussi maintenant pour **voir un peu** la France.

Later, David introduces Annette to his friend Jean-Luc.

DAVID:	Jean-Luc, c'est **mon amie** Annette Clark. Annette, c'est **mon ami** Jean-Luc. Il est aussi étudiant à l'Université de Nice.
ANNETTE:	Bonjour, Jean-Luc.
JEAN-LUC:	Bonjour, Annette.
DAVID:	Annette est américaine, de Los Angeles, mais elle parle français sans accent.
ANNETTE:	Mais maintenant j'habite à Nice parce que j'étudie à l'université.
DAVID:	Et nous sommes dans le même cours de français.

nous sommes *we are* **même** *same* **n'est-ce pas?** *right?* **pour étudier** *in order to study* **ma sœur** *my sister* **est** *is* **voir** *to see* **un peu** *a little* **mon amie** *my friend (female)* **mon ami** *my friend (male)*

Savez-vous le faire?

A. Masculin ou féminin? Indicate whether each of these words indicates a masculine or feminine person, or a group, by saying **masculin**, **féminin**, or **un groupe**.

1. un homme
2. une fille
3. des gens
4. un ami
5. une amie
6. un étudiant
7. une sœur
8. un garçon
9. des enfants
10. des jeunes
11. un jeune homme
12. une femme
13. une étudiante
14. il
15. elle

B. C'est... Below the names of the characters, list as many words as you can to identify or describe them. Use a separate piece of paper.

	DAVID	ANNETTE	DAVID ET ANNETTE
EXEMPLES	**un jeune homme**	**une étudiante**	**des jeunes**

C. Identification. Finish these statements in a logical manner.

1. David est...
2. Il est de...
3. Annette est...
4. Elle habite à... maintenant.
5. Elle parle...
6. David et Annette sont dans le même...

D. À la fac. Annette has met another foreign student at **l'Université de Nice**. Look at her new friend's passport and imagine how he answers Annette's questions.

1. Comment ça va?
2. Comment t'appelles-tu?
3. Ça s'écrit comment?
4. Tu es de Nice?
5. Tu es américain?
6. Tu habites à Nice maintenant?

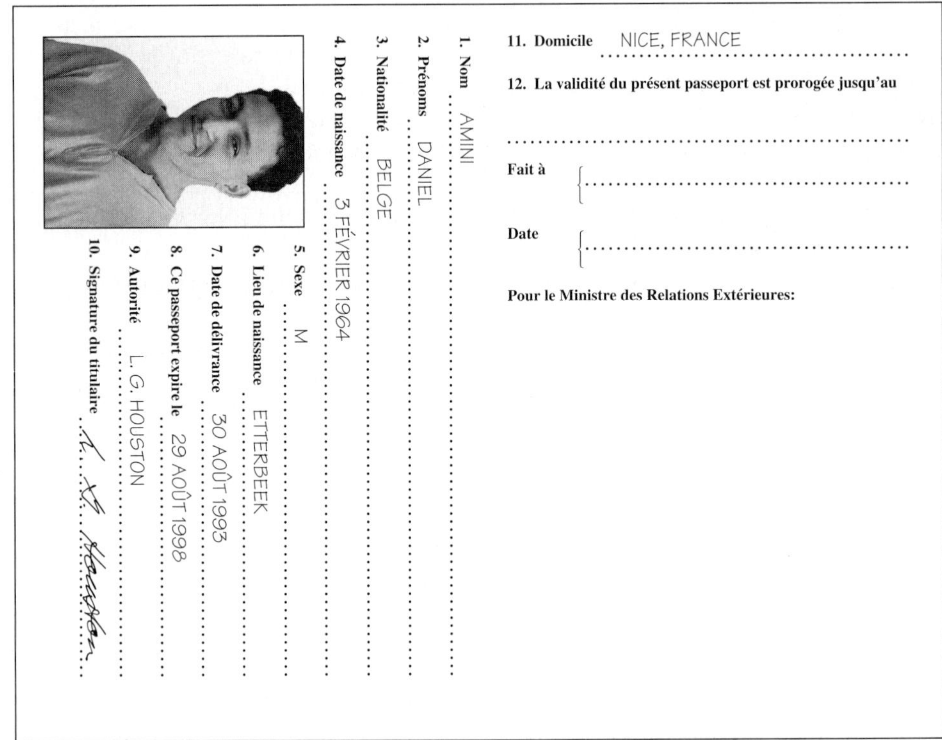

1. Nom AMINI
2. Prénoms DANIEL
3. Nationalité BELGE
4. Date de naissance 3 FÉVRIER 1964
5. Sexe M
6. Lieu de naissance ETTERBEEK
7. Date de délivrance 30 AOÛT 1993
8. Ce passeport expire le 29 AOÛT 1998
9. Autorité L. G. HOUSTON
10. Signature du titulaire L. G. Houston

11. Domicile NICE, FRANCE
12. La validité du présent passeport est prorogée jusqu'au

Fait à

Date

Pour le Ministre des Relations Extérieures:

E. Nouveaux amis. You run into one of your classmates outside of class. Introduce yourself and try to find out a few things about your new acquaintance. Use David and Annette's conversation on page 31 as an example.

F. Présentations. Introduce two classmates to each other, telling something about each. Use David's introductions on page 31 as an example.

Comment s'y prendre?

In each unit of *Qu'est-ce qu'on dit?*, you will read about someone visiting a francophone region. Before each story begins, you will be given reading tips in the ***Comment s'y prendre?*** section which will help you read French more easily.

Using cognates

Cognates are words that look the same or similar in two languages and mean the same thing. Take advantage of cognates to help you read French more easily. There are some patterns in cognates. What three patterns do you see here? What do the last two words in each column mean?

soudainement	*suddenly*	**obligé**	*obliged*	**hôpital**	*hospital*
décidément	*decidedly*	**décidé**	*decided*	**île**	*isle, island*
complètement	*???*	**vexé**	*???*	**honnête**	*???*
généralement	*???*	**sauvé**	*???*	**hôte**	*???*

Reading for the gist

You will run across a lot of unknown words as you read French, but this should not prevent you from understanding. You do not need to understand every word to get the gist. Be flexible. Change forms of words or word order if necessary and skip over little words that may not be needed to get the message. You do not know all of the words in the following sentences but you probably can figure out what they mean.

Je suis à la caméra invisible?
C'est juste à ce moment qu'Annette arrive. La pauvre Yvette est sauvée.

Recognizing words you have already learned in different forms will also help you read. Use the phrases you already know on the left to guess the meaning of those on the right.

Qu'est-ce que ça veut dire?	«Oui... euh... non... euh... je veux dire... oui.»
Comment dit-on *pen* en français?	Qu'est-ce que tu dis?

Savez-vous le faire?

A. Quelle expression? Tell in which classroom expression from the ***Chapitre préliminaire*** you saw the boldfaced words in the following sentences (or a form of them). Then guess what each of these sentences means.

1. Yvette ne **sait** pas quoi répondre.
2. **Qu'est-ce que** tu dis, Annette?
3. Ce jeune homme **ne comprend rien**.
4. Annette **dit**: «Permets-moi de te présenter ma sœur.»

B. Devinez. State the general idea of each sentence in English.

1. Yvette hésite un moment avant de répondre.
2. Yvette pense: «*He thinks I'm Annette. How do I tell him...?*»
3. C'est juste à ce moment qu'Annette arrive.
4. Annette sauve la pauvre Yvette.
5. David voit Annette et Yvette et s'exclame: «Mais vous êtes deux!»

C. Mots apparentés. Before reading the ***Qu'est-ce qui se passe?*** section that follows, skim through it and list the cognates you see. You should find between twenty-five and thirty.

Qu'est-ce qui se passe?

NOTE
The textbook tape symbol indicates sections that are recorded on the textbook tape.

Qui est-ce?

Yvette Clark is visiting her twin sister, Annette, a student at the University of Nice. As she waits for her sister in front of the **musée Archéologique**, *a young man approaches. Since she does not speak French very well, Yvette is unsure what to say when he speaks to her.*

— Salut, Annette! Ça va?

Yvette hésite un moment avant de répondre. Elle pense en elle-même: «*He thinks I'm Annette. How do I tell him...?*»

— Non, non... euh, je veux dire oui, ça va, mais... euh... je regrette... je ne suis pas Annette. Je suis Yvette.

— Comment? Qu'est-ce que tu dis, Annette?

— Non, non, répond Yvette. Vous ne comprenez pas. Je ne suis pas Annette.

— Comment? Qu'est-ce que ça veut dire?

Décidément, ce jeune homme ne comprend rien! Yvette insiste encore une fois.

— Non, je ne suis pas Annette. Vous ne comprenez pas! Écoutez-moi bien! Je ne suis pas Annette! Je ne suis pas étudiante à l'Université de Nice.

— Mais qu'est-ce que tu dis? demande David. Tu es malade? C'est moi, David. Nous sommes dans le même cours de français. Nous ne sommes pas à la caméra invisible, non?

Yvette pense: «*I'm never going to get this guy to understand. He's so sure I'm Annette.*» C'est juste à ce moment qu'Annette arrive. La pauvre Yvette est sauvée.

— Bonjour, Annette! dit sa sœur jumelle.

David, très surpris de voir les deux sœurs jumelles, s'exclame:
— Mais, ce n'est pas possible! Vous êtes deux. Maintenant je comprends. Tu as une sœur jumelle, Annette.

— Mon pauvre David. Permets-moi de te présenter ma sœur, Yvette.
— Mademoiselle, enchanté. Excusez-moi pour la confusion.

Avez-vous compris?

A. Qui parle? Which character in the story would be most likely to make each of the following statements: **David**, **Yvette**, or **Annette**?

1. Monsieur, vous ne comprenez pas. Je ne suis pas Annette.
2. Mais je sais que tu es Annette parce que nous sommes dans le même cours.
3. Je ne suis pas étudiante à l'Université de Nice.
4. Excusez-moi. Je ne parle pas très bien français.
5. Je comprends... vous êtes des sœurs jumelles.
6. Permets-moi de te présenter ma sœur, Yvette.

B. D'abord... Which happens first, a or b?

1. a. David dit bonjour à Yvette.
   b. Yvette arrive au musée Archéologique.
2. a. David dit: «Bonjour Annette.»
   b. Yvette pense: «Il ne comprend pas.»
3. a. Yvette hésite à répondre parce qu'elle ne sait pas très bien parler français.
   b. Yvette répond: «Non, non, vous ne comprenez pas.»
4. a. David comprend qu'Annette et Yvette sont des sœurs jumelles.
   b. Annette arrive.
5. a. David dit: «Excusez-moi pour la confusion.»
   b. David comprend la situation.

Le musée Archéologique, Nice

Remarquez que...

Students in French secondary schools (**les lycées**) pursue their diploma (**le baccalauréat**) in a specific field. The five principal categories are **le bac littéraire, scientifique, économique, technique**, and **professionnel.**

In the United States and Canada, secondary education diplomas are generally earned based on credits given for classes taken. At the end of their studies at the **lycée**, French students must pass a series of difficult exams covering all the material they have studied in order to receive the **baccalauréat**. If they do not pass, they cannot go on to the university, unless they successfully retest. Some students choose to take competitive exams after receiving the **baccalauréat** in order to be admitted to special schools called **les grandes écoles**, which are prestigious institutions specializing in engineering, business, education, or the sciences.

Qu'en pensez-vous? What would be the advantages and disadvantages of a system in which students must pass a cumulative exam in order to receive a secondary education diploma?

le cerveau *brain* **l'élève** (*m/f*) *pupil, pre-university student* **la copie** *test paper*

Qu'est-ce qu'on dit?

TEXTBOOK TAPE

NOTE
Items accompanied by a tape symbol are recorded on the textbook tape.

How do you like these aspects of your university?

J'aime beaucoup... *J'aime assez...* *Je n'aime pas...*

l'université (*f*)	le laboratoire de langues
le restaurant universitaire	**le foyer des étudiants**
les professeurs (*m*)	les résidences universitaires (*f*)
les étudiant(e)s	**les salles de classe** (*f*)
les examens (*m*)	**les amphithéâtres** (*m*)
le campus	**les bâtiments** (*m*)

What is your university like?

Le campus est...	**grand** **joli** agréable **vieux**	Il n'est pas...	**petit** **laid** désagréable moderne
La bibliothèque est...	grande jolie agréable vieille	Elle n'est pas...	petite laide désagréable moderne
Les bâtiments sont...	grands jolis agréables vieux	Ils ne sont pas...	petits laids désagréables modernes
Les salles de classe sont...	grandes jolies agréables vieilles	Elles ne sont pas...	petites laides désagréables modernes

le foyer des étudiants *the student center* **les salles de classe** *the classrooms* **les amphithéâtres** *the lecture halls* **les bâtiments** *the buildings* **grand(e)** *big* **joli(e)** *pretty* **vieux (vieille)** *old* **petit(e)** *little* **laid(e)** *ugly*

Describing your university

A friend is asking Annette about the University of Nice.

— **Comment est** l'Université de Nice?
— J'aime beaucoup l'université. Les cours sont un peu difficiles mais intéressants.
— Et les étudiants, ils sont **sympathiques**?
— Oui, ils sont très sympa.
— Et comment sont les résidences?
— Elles sont vieilles mais assez agréables.

Comment est (sont)...? *What is (are) . . . like?* **sympathique (sympa)** *nice*

NOTE
The textbook tape symbol indicates sections that are recorded on the textbook tape.

A. L'université. Several students are talking. Make the following columns on a sheet of paper. Each time you hear a *positive* remark about one of the items, place a √ in the appropriate column. If the remark is *negative*, write X.

EXEMPLE VOUS ENTENDEZ: La bibliothèque est laide.

LA BIBLIOTHÈQUE	LE CAMPUS	LES PROFESSEURS	LES COURS
X			

B. Vrai ou faux? Are these statements generally **vrai** (*true*) or **faux** (*false*) for your university? If a statement is not applicable for your school, answer **faux**.

1. L'université est moderne.
2. Les bâtiments sont vieux.
3. Le campus est joli.
4. La bibliothèque est petite.
5. Les professeurs sont intéressants.
6. Les salles de classe sont agréables.
7. Le laboratoire de langues est moderne.
8. Les amphithéâtres sont grands.
9. Le foyer des étudiants est vieux.
10. Les résidences universitaires sont laides.

Voilà pourquoi!

L'article défini

SELF-CHECK
Self-check questions will be found throughout the book next to explanations of structures. Read the entire ***Voilà pourquoi!*** section before trying to answer the self-check questions. Check your answers in *Appendix B*.
(Continued on the next page)

The short word **le, la, l', les** before nouns is called the definite article.

le campus *la* bibliothèque *l'*université *les* cours

The form of the definite article you use depends on the noun's gender and whether it is singular or plural. The term *gender* refers to an arbitrary categorization of all nouns in French as masculine or feminine. Except for most words identifying people, you cannot guess a noun's gender from its meaning. Always learn the article with a noun in order to know its gender.

Use **le** before masculine singular nouns and **la** before feminine singular nouns. **Le** and **la** both change to **l'** when the following word starts with a vowel sound (including mute **h**). To pluralize a noun, add an **-s** to the end of it. Do not add an -s, however, if the noun ends in an **s**, **x**, or **z**. Use **les** as the definite article before all plural nouns.

	SINGULAR BEFORE CONSONANTS	SINGULAR BEFORE VOWEL SOUNDS	ALL PLURALS
MASCULINE	le livre	l'homme	les livres les hommes
FEMININE	la classe	l'étudiante	les classes les étudiantes

(Continued from the preceding page.)

1. What are the four forms of the word for *the* in French? When do you use each?
2. Besides meaning *the*, what is another use of the definite article in French?
3. When is the **-s** of the plural form **les** pronounced?

Use the definite article before nouns:

- To specify items, as when using the word *the* in English.

  Écoutez *les* questions et écrivez *les* réponses.
  *Listen to **the** questions and write **the** answers.*

- To say what you like, dislike, or prefer. In this case, English usually uses no article.

  Je n'aime pas *les* devoirs.
  I don't like homework.

Et ça se prononce comment?

L'article défini

The final **-s** of plural nouns is not pronounced. In conversations, one must usually rely on the article to determine whether a noun is singular or plural. Listen carefully as you repeat the following nouns. Notice the **z** sound of final -s pronounced in **liaison**.

le livre	**les livres**	**la cassette**	**les cassettes**
l'étudiant	**les‿ᶻétudiants**	**l'étudiante**	**les‿ᶻétudiantes**

Open your mouth wide to pronounce the **a** of **la**. Pucker your lips slightly when you pronounce the **e** in **le**, and spread the corners of your mouth apart when saying the **e** in **les**. Remember that this is the sound you will hear if something is plural.

NOTE
The textbook tape symbol indicates sections that are recorded on the textbook tape.

Savez-vous le faire?

A. Parlez bien. Listen as David talks about university life. In each sentence, you will hear the singular or plural form of one of the following nouns. Indicate which form you hear by writing the article on your paper.

1. le professeur — les professeurs
2. le cours — les cours
3. l'étudiant — les étudiants
4. l'examen — les examens
5. le livre — les livres
6. la cassette — les cassettes
7. la femme — les femmes
8. la bibliothèque — les bibliothèques
9. le cours — les cours
10. l'université — les universités

Now go back and pronounce one of the forms of each noun above. Ask another student to say whether you gave the singular (**singulier**) or the plural (**pluriel**) form.

B. Opinions. Tell how you feel about the following aspects of university life.

1. les cours dans les amphithéâtres
2. les étudiants
3. les examens
4. les professeurs
5. le cours de français
6. les devoirs
7. le restaurant universitaire
8. les résidences universitaires

> **J'aime beaucoup...**
> *J'aime assez...*
> JE N'AIME PAS (BEAUCOUP)...

C. Et vous? Tell how you feel about different aspects of your university by completing the following sentences.

1. J'aime...
2. Je n'aime pas beaucoup...
3. J'aime assez...
4. Je n'aime pas...

Voilà pourquoi!

SELF-CHECK

1. What are the two ways of saying *they are* in French? When do you use each? What do you say for a mixed group?
2. How do you negate a verb in French? When do you use **n'** instead of **ne**?

(Continued on the next page.)

Il est... Elle est... Ils sont... Elles sont...

To describe people and things, you can use the expressions **il est**, **elle est**, **ils sont**, and **elles sont** plus an adjective.

- Use **il est** to say *he is* or *it is*, when *it* stands for a noun that is masculine.

  David? *Il* est français. Le livre? *Il* est intéressant.

- Use **elle est** to say *she is* or *it is*, when *it* stands for a noun that is feminine.

  Annette? *Elle* est américaine. La bibliothèque? *Elle* est grande.

- Use **ils sont** to say *they are* to describe a group of men or a mixed group of both men and women, or when *they* refers to a group of masculine nouns or both masculine and feminine nouns.

  David et Annette? *Ils* sont sympathiques. **Les examens? *Ils* sont faciles.**

- Use **elles sont** to say *they are* to describe a group of all women or a group of all feminine things.

  Annette et Yvette? *Elles* sont américaines. **Les questions? *Elles* sont intéressantes.**

(Continued from the preceding page.)

3. What is the base form of an adjective? What do you add to make it plural? feminine? feminine plural?
4. What adjectives do you know that do not follow this pattern? What are their four forms?
5. What is the difference in pronunciation between the masculine and feminine forms of an adjective such as **petit**?

Ne... pas

To say what someone is not like or what one does not do, place **ne** before the verb in the sentence and **pas** after it. **Ne** changes to **n'** before a vowel sound.

Elles ne sont pas petites. *They are not small.*
Je ne travaille pas. *I don't work.*
Il n'est pas grand. *He is not tall.*

Les adjectifs

When you use an adjective to describe someone or something in French, match the gender (masculine or feminine) and number (singular or plural) of the adjective to the gender and number of the noun you are describing. The masculine form of the adjective will be your base form. To change the form to feminine, add an **-e** (unless it already ends in an *unaccented* **e**) to the masculine form. To make it plural, add an **-s**, unless it already ends in **s** or **x**.

SINGULAR		PLURAL	
MASCULINE	FEMININE	MASCULINE	FEMININE
facile	facile	faciles	faciles
petit	petite	petits	petites
français	française	français	françaises

Adjectives ending in **-ien** double the final **n** before adding **-e** in the feminine (**canadien / canadienne**).

Some adjectives are irregular.

SINGULAR		PLURAL	
MASCULINE	FEMININE	MASCULINE	FEMININE
beau	belle	beaux	belles
vieux	vieille	vieux	vieilles

Et ça se prononce comment?

Il et elle

Be careful to pronounce the vowels in **il/ils** and **elle/elles** distinctly. The letter **i** in French is pronounced similarly to the double *ee* in the English words *see* and *feed*, but it is said more quickly and the tongue is held tenser. The letter **e** in **elle/elles** is pronounced somewhat like the *e* in the English word *bet*.

Il est grand.	**Elle est grande.**
Ils sont beaux.	**Elles sont belles.**

Les adjectifs

Since most final consonants are silent, you will not hear or say the final consonant of masculine adjective forms, unless they end in **c**, **r**, **f**, or **l**. When the **-e** is added to make the feminine form, the consonant is no longer final and is pronounced.

grand	**grande**
français	**française**

The final **-s** of plurals is not pronounced.

Ils sont petits.	**Elles sont petites.**

Savez-vous le faire?

A. On parle de qui? You will hear some sentences. Determine who the sentence is about: **David**, **Annette**, or **les deux** (*both*).

B. Claude qui? In French, Claude is both a man's and a woman's name. As you hear sentence **a** or **b** below, determine whether it describes **Claude Bellon** or **Claude Lacoste**.

a. Claude Bellon

1. a. Claude n'est pas laid.
   b. Claude n'est pas laide.
2. a. Claude est grand.
   b. Claude est grande.
3. a. Claude n'est pas petit.
   b. Claude n'est pas petite.
4. a. Claude est intéressant.
   b. Claude est intéressante.
5. a. Claude est canadien.
   b. Claude est canadienne.

b. Claude Lacoste

Afterwards, go back and pronounce one sentence from each pair and have a classmate say whether you said **a** or **b**.

C. Opinions. Tell whether you think the word in parentheses describes the indicated item at your university.

EXEMPLES les salles de classe (agréables)
Oui, elles sont agréables.
OU: **Non, elles ne sont pas agréables.**

le campus (grand)
Oui, il est grand.
Non, il n'est pas grand.

1. l'université (jolie)
2. le campus (petit)
3. les bâtiments (modernes)
4. les étudiants (sympathiques)
5. les étudiantes (désagréables)
6. les professeurs (intéressants)
7. les cours (faciles)
8. les examens (difficiles)

D. Qui est-ce? Name someone in your class that each of these words describes. Be sure to use the correct form of the adjective.

EXEMPLE grand → **Anne est grande.**

1. grand 2. petit 3. intéressant 4. sympathique

Now, identify a pair of classmates that these adjectives describe.

EXEMPLE grand → **Anne et Alex sont grands.**

E. C'est-à-dire... French speakers have a tendency to understate. Where an English speaker might say *She's smart,* a French speaker might say *She's not dumb.* How might a French speaker choose to restate the following?

EXEMPLE Elle est grande.
Elle n'est pas petite.

1. Il est grand.
2. Elle est jolie.
3. Elle est petite.
4. Il est laid.
5. Les cours sont difficiles.
6. Le campus est désagréable.
7. Les examens de français sont faciles.
8. Les bâtiments sont vieux.

F. Situation. Imagine that you are studying for a year at the University of Nice and a classmate stops to ask how you like it. Create a conversation with a classmate where you talk about:

- the courses at the university
- the professors
- the residence halls
- the cafeteria

Des étudiants à l'Université de Nice

Remarquez que...

In France, higher education is free. Upon receipt of the **baccalauréat**, there is a wide range of educational possibilities.

You may:

- Take special STS courses (**sections de techniciens supérieurs**) at **un lycée** to prepare a BTS (**brevet de technicien supérieur**).
- Study the sciences, humanities, economics, or law at **une université**, receiving the following degrees after the indicated number of years of study.

two years: **un DEUG (diplôme d'études universitaires générales)**
un DEUST (diplôme d'études universitaires scientifiques et techniques)
three years: **une licence**
four years: **une maîtrise**
seven years: **un doctorat**

- Study dentistry, medicine, or pharmacy at **une université**.
- Attend **une école spécialisée** to get specific training in such fields as business, social, and paramedic work. For these studies, you receive **un diplôme d'école**.
- Attend **un IUT** (**institut universitaire de technologie**) to prepare **un DUT** (**diplôme universitaire de technologie**).
- After preparatory courses, pass a competitive exam (**un concours**) and enter into **une GE** (**grande école**) to take superior level courses in engineering, business, education, or the sciences. You receive **un diplôme grande école**.

Et vous? If you were in France, which of these study options would interest you the most?

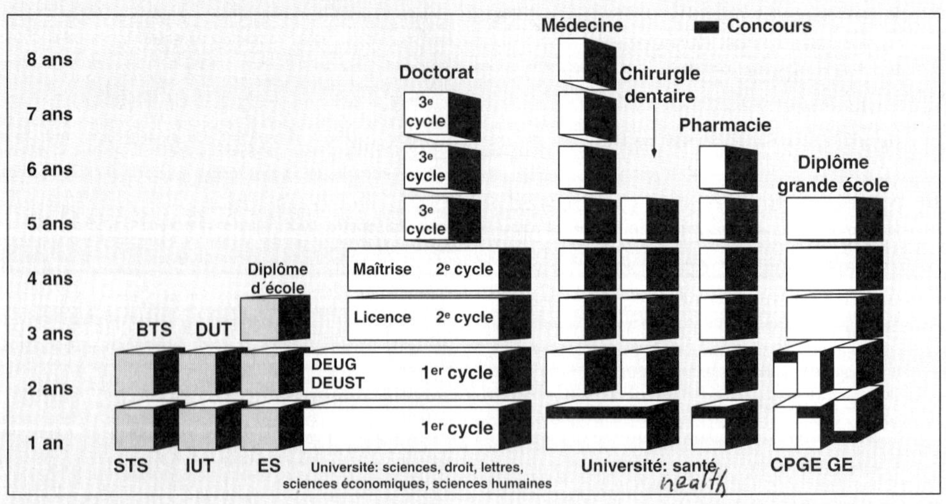

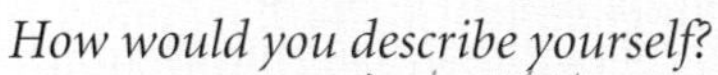

Qu'est-ce qu'on dit?

TEXTBOOK TAPE

How would you describe yourself?

Je suis (très, assez, un peu)... Je ne suis pas (**du tout**)...

optimiste / pessimiste

idéaliste / réaliste

timide / extroverti(e)

sympathique / méchant(e)

intelligent(e) / bête

amusant(e) / ennuyeux (ennuyeuse)

actif (active) / paresseux (paresseuse)

intellectuel(le) / sportif (sportive)

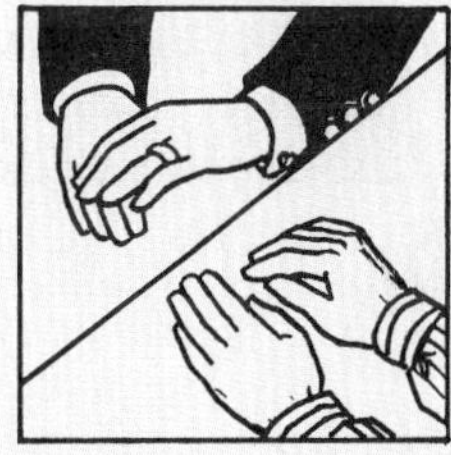

marié(e) / célibataire

ne... pas du tout *not at all*

David is asking Annette about her sister.

— Yvette et toi, vous êtes californiennes, n'est-ce pas?
— Oui, nous sommes de Los Angeles.
— Et Yvette, elle est mariée?
— Non, elle est célibataire.
— Elle est étudiante, **comme** toi?
— Non, **les études**, ce n'est pas son style. Elle travaille dans un club de gym.
— Elle aime le sport, **alors**?
— Ah oui, beaucoup. Elle est très sportive!
— Yvette et toi, vous êtes **plutôt** extroverties, n'est-ce pas?
— Moi, je suis assez extrovertie mais Yvette est **plutôt** timide.

comme *like* **les études** (*f*) *studies, going to school* **alors** *then* **plutôt** *rather*

A. Comment est-il? Yvette is going out on a blind date. Indicate by **oui** or **non** whether she would probably like to find out the things you hear said about her date.

B. Une personne ou deux? Annette is talking about Yvette and herself. If she is talking about herself, write **Annette** and if the statement is about her sister, write **Yvette**. If she is talking about both of them, write **les deux**.

C. Réponses. You overhear a conversation between David and an American in Nice. Give the logical response on the right to each question on the left.

1. Vous êtes canadien?
2. Vous êtes de Los Angeles, n'est-ce pas?
3. Est-ce que vous êtes marié?
4. Vous êtes étudiant?
5. Est-ce que vous êtes sportif?

a. Oui, j'étudie à l'Université de Nice.
b. Non, je suis célibataire.
c. Non, je suis américain.
d. Non, je suis de Seattle.
e. Oui, j'aime beaucoup le sport.

Voilà pourquoi!

SELF-CHECK

1. What pronoun would you use to address a child? two children? a salesclerk?
2. To make an adjective feminine, you usually add an **-e**. What are four slightly irregular patterns? How do you form the feminine for each?

Les pronoms sujets

Below are the subject pronouns in French. There are two ways to say *you* in French. Use **tu** to talk to a child, a friend, a family member, or a classmate. Use **vous** when you are addressing an adult stranger or someone to whom you wish to show respect. Always use **vous** when talking to more than one person.

je	*I*	nous	*we*
tu	*you* (sing. familiar)	vous	*you* (sing. formal, all second-person plurals)
il	*he, it* (masculine)	ils	*they* (masculine or mixed group)
elle	*she, it* (feminine)	elles	*they* (feminine)

Le verbe **être**

You have seen all of the forms of the verb **être** (*to be*). The word **être** is the infinitive, the form of the verb you would find if you looked up *to be* in an English / French dictionary. The following conjugation chart shows the forms you use with each of the subject pronouns.

ÊTRE (*TO BE*)	
je **suis**	nous **sommes**
tu **es**	vous **êtes**
il/elle **est**	ils/elles **sont**

With nouns, use the corresponding form of **il/elle** or **ils/elles.**

Le professeur *est* sympathique. **Les étudiants *sont* intelligents.**

L'accord des adjectifs (*reprise*)

A few adjectives double or change their final consonant before adding **-e** for agreement with feminine nouns. Note these patterns:

MASCULINE			FEMININE	
-ien	(canadien)	→	**-ienne**	(canadienne)
-if	(sportif)	→	**-ive**	(sportive)
-eux	(paresseux)	→	**-euse**	(paresseuse)
-el	(intellectuel)	→	**-elle**	(intellectuelle)

Et ça se prononce comment?

Les lettres **u** et **ou**

The letters **u** and **ou**, as in the subject pronouns **tu** and **vous**, have distinct pronunciations. The combination **ou** is similar to the *oo* in the English word *boot*, except it is shorter and the tongue is held firmer:

vous **beaucoup** **douze** **cours**

The sound corresponding to a single **u** has no similar English sound. To pronounce it, position your mouth to pronounce a French **i** with your tongue held high in the mouth. Then, round your lips:

tu **université** **une**

Savez-vous le faire?

TEXTBOOK TAPE

A. Littérature française. Listen and decide if each name should be spelled with **u** or **ou**. Write your choices on a sheet of paper.

1. Victor H__go
2. Marguerite D__ras
3. Sen__vo Agbota Zins__
4. Marguerite d'Ang__lême
5. Jean-Jacques R__sseau
6. Albert Cam__s

B. Compliments. Tell these people how nice they are.

EXEMPLES your sister → **Tu es très sympathique.**
your boss → **Vous êtes très sympathique.**

1. your roommate
2. a friend's father
3. a classmate
4. a stranger
5. a salesclerk
6. two friends
7. your father
8. your professor's child

C. Descriptions. Make a sentence describing the indicated people by combining one element from each column.

1. your best male friend
2. your best female friend
3. you and your family
4. yourself
5. the students in your class
6. the female students in your class
7. a classmate

		sportif(-ive)(s)
elles		**sympathique(s)**
nous	**suis**	**ennuyeux(-euse)(s)**
il	**est**	**amusant(e)(s)**
je	**sommes**	**marié(e)(s)**
elle	**sont**	**timide(s)**
ils		**extroverti(e)(s)**

D. Personnalités. Annette and Yvette look alike, but they have opposite personalities. How would Yvette complete these sentences?

EXEMPLE Je suis timide, mais... → **Je suis timide, mais Annette est extrovertie.**

1. Je suis idéaliste, mais...
2. Je suis optimiste, mais...
3. Je suis amusante, mais...
4. Je suis un peu paresseuse, mais...

E. Et vous? How much do these words describe you? (**Je suis... Je ne suis pas...**)

très ***assez*** ***un peu*** ***ne... pas du tout***

1. athletic 2. lazy 3. stupid 4. boring 5. intellectual 6. active

F. Annette et toi. Complete Yvette's answers to these questions.

1. — Annette et toi, vous êtes de Dallas, n'est-ce pas? → — Non, nous...
2. — Vous êtes mariées? → — Non, nous...
3. — Tu habites ici à Nice? → — Non, je (j')...
4. — Tu es en France pour étudier? → — Non, Annette est ici pour étudier, mais moi, je...
5. — Tu aimes les sports? → — Oui, je suis très...

Voilà pourquoi!

Les questions

There are several ways of asking a question that will be answered *yes* or *no.*

- You can ask a question with rising intonation, that is by raising the pitch of your voice at the end. A statement normally has falling intonation.

STATEMENT:	Tu es extrovertie. *You are outgoing.*	QUESTION:	Tu es extrovertie? *Are you outgoing?*

- You can also ask a question by adding **est-ce que** to the beginning of a statement. Your intonation will still need to rise.

STATEMENT:	Tu es sportif. *You are athletic.*	QUESTION:	Est-ce que tu es sportif? *Are you athletic?*

- If you are presuming that someone will probably answer ***yes*** to a question, you can use **n'est-ce pas** at the end of a question with rising intonation.

STATEMENT:	Il est marié. *He's married.*	QUESTION:	Il est marié, n'est-ce pas? *He's married, isn't he?*

Remember that to answer a *yes/no* question negatively, place **ne** before the verb and **pas** after. **Ne** changes to **n'** before vowel sounds.

— Est-ce que tu es française?
— Non, je ***ne*** suis ***pas*** française. Je suis canadienne.
— Ah, tu ***n'***es ***pas*** d'ici?
— Non, je suis de Montréal.

SELF-CHECK

1. What are three ways of forming a question that can be answered **oui** or **non**? What happens to your intonation in each case?
2. Of the boldfaced words in the following sentences, which rhyme with **le** and which with **les**? Ils **ne** sont pas ici. / Il **n'est** pas ici. / Tu **n'es** pas ici.

Et ça se prononce comment?

Ne, n'es et n'est

When negating the verb **être**, you must be careful to pronounce **ne** differently from **n'es** or **n'est**. **Ne** rhymes with **je** or **le**, and its vowel is pronounced with your lips slightly puckered. The vowel of **est** or **es** rhymes with **les**. Pronounce it with your lips spread in a tight smiling position. Compare:

Ils *ne* sont *pas* étudiants. **Il *n'*est *pas* étudiant.**

Savez-vous le faire?

A. **Au contraire.** Complete each sentence with the word or phrase that, in your opinion, does not describe the person(s) named. Pay attention to the pronunciation of **ne** and **n'est**.

EXEMPLE Tom Cruise n'est pas... (beau, laid) → **Tom Cruise n'est pas laid.**

1. Madonna n'est pas... (timide, extrovertie)
2. Moi, je ne suis pas... (optimiste, pessimiste)
3. Maintenant, nous ne sommes pas... (en classe, à la maison)
4. Jean-Claude Van Damme n'est pas... (grand, petit)
5. Les étudiants du cours de français ne sont pas... (bêtes, intelligents)

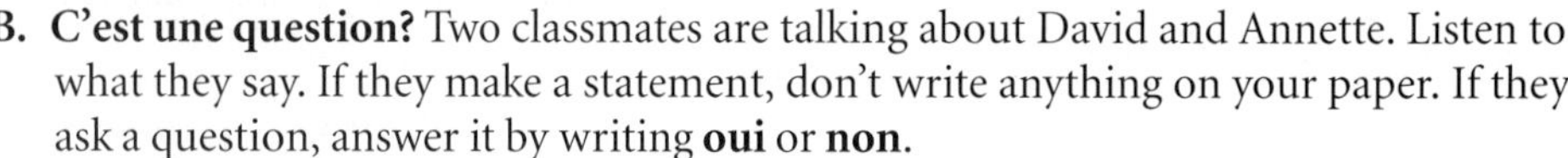

B. **C'est une question?** Two classmates are talking about David and Annette. Listen to what they say. If they make a statement, don't write anything on your paper. If they ask a question, answer it by writing **oui** or **non**.

C. **Qui êtes-vous?** Ask a classmate whether these words describe him/her. Your classmate will answer, then ask you the same question. When you see ???, you may ask about something of your choice. Afterwards, report what you have in common with your partner and how you are different. Be sure to use the correct form of the adjective.

EXEMPLE marié → — **Est-ce que tu es marié(e)?**
— **Non, je ne suis pas marié(e).** OU **Oui, je suis marié(e).**

1. timide
2. optimiste
3. idéaliste
4. marié
5. paresseux
6. sportif
7. intellectuel
8. ???

APRÈS, À TOUTE LA CLASSE: **Paul et moi, nous sommes idéalistes et actifs. Nous ne sommes pas paresseux. Je ne suis pas marié(e), mais Paul est marié...**

D. **Camarades de classe.** Find out the following information about a classmate.

1. what his/her name is
2. how he/she is doing
3. whether he/she is from here
4. if he/she is married
5. if he/she likes French class
6. if he/she is athletic

E. **Amis.** On a piece of paper, write four adjectives that describe you. Then go around the room asking your classmates if the same adjectives describe them. If an adjective is on their list, they answer **oui**, otherwise **non**. When you find someone who has three of the same four adjectives as you, write down his/her name. After everyone is through, explain to the class what you have in common.

actif *timide*
INTELLECTUEL
SPORTIF **réaliste**
grand extroverti
pessimiste *optimiste*
??? **???**

TEXTBOOK TAPE

Qu'est-ce qu'on dit?

What are you studying?

J'étudie la philosophie. Je n'étudie pas la littérature.

LES LANGUES (*f*)
l'allemand (*m*)
l'anglais (*m*)
l'espagnol (*m*)
le français

LES SCIENCES SOCIALES (*f*)
l'histoire (*f*)
la psychologie
les sciences politiques (*f*)

LES BEAUX-ARTS (*m*)
les cours de théâtre (*m*)
le dessin
la musique

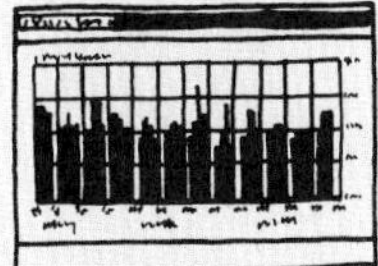

LES COURS DE COMMERCE (*m*)
la comptabilité
le marketing

LES COURS TECHNIQUES (*m*)
les mathématiques (*f*)
l'informatique (*f*)

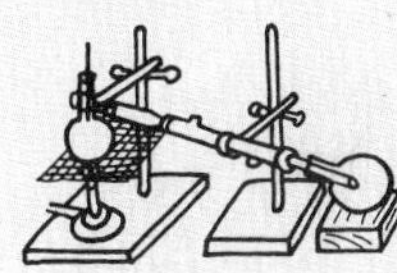

LES SCIENCES (*f*)
la biologie
la chimie
la physique

SUPPLEMENTAL VOCABULARY
LES LANGUES: l'arabe (*m*); le chinois; l'hébreu (*m*); le japonais; le russe
LES SCIENCES SOCIALES: la géographie; les sciences économiques (*f*); la sociologie
LES BEAUX-ARTS: la danse; la peinture (*painting*); la sculpture
LES COURS DE COMMERCE: la gestion (*management*)
LES COURS TECHNIQUES: le génie (*engineering*)
LES SCIENCES: l'astronomie (*f*); la géologie

You can use the following expressions to compare people and things.

Pour Annette, le français est **moins** compliqué **que** la chimie.
La chimie est **plus** difficile **que** le français.

Annette is telling David what she is like compared to her sister.

— Alors, vous êtes des sœurs jumelles?
— Oui, mais nous sommes très différentes. Moi, je suis plus sérieuse qu'Yvette. Elle est plus frivole que moi et elle est plus calme et plus patiente. Moi, je suis assez impatiente.
— Qui est la plus sportive?
— Yvette est beaucoup plus sportive. Et moi, je suis plus intellectuelle.

l'allemand *German* **la comptabilité** *accounting* **l'informatique** *computer science* **la physique** *physics* **moins... que** *less . . . than* **plus... que** *more . . . than*

A. Disciplines. As you hear the name of a course, indicate to which of these disciplines it belongs.

LES LANGUES — LES BEAUX-ARTS — LES SCIENCES SOCIALES — LES SCIENCES — LES COURS DE COMMERCE

B. À chacun ses goûts. Annette only likes languages and science courses. She really doesn't like anything else. Listen to the list of courses. If it is something Annette would like, respond **oui**, if not, answer **non**.

C. À quelle faculté? Universities in France are divided into **facultés.** Students who want to major in the natural sciences go to the **faculté des sciences.** The humanities and the social sciences are studied at the **faculté des lettres.** Tell whether one would major in the following subjects **à la faculté des lettres** or **à la faculté des sciences.**

EXEMPLE l'astronomie → **à la faculté des sciences**

1. la physique
2. l'histoire
3. l'allemand
4. la biologie
5. la philosophie
6. la littérature
7. la chimie
8. la psychologie

SELF-CHECK
What are the four uses of the definite article **le**, **la**, **l'**, **les**?

L'article défini (*reprise*)

As you may remember from *Sujet de conversation 1*, the definite article (**le, la, l', les**) is used to refer to a specific noun, like the word *the* in English, and to say what you like or prefer.

Faites les devoirs dans le cahier.
Do the homework in the workbook.

J'aime les langues.
I like languages.

You will also use the definite article in the following cases. Note that in these cases English uses no article.

- To talk about courses.

  J'aime le français. Les langues sont faciles pour moi.
  I like French. Languages are easy for me.

- To talk about something as a general category or an abstract noun.

  En général, les jeunes sont très actifs.
  Generally, young people are very active.

Savez-vous le faire?

A. Opinions. Tell how you feel about the following courses.

1. les cours de commerce
2. la philosophie
3. la comptabilité
4. les langues
5. les sciences politiques
6. l'histoire
7. la psychologie
8. les mathématiques

J'aime beaucoup...
J'AIME ASSEZ... **J'aime un peu...**
Je n'aime pas...
JE N'AIME PAS DU TOUT...

B. Est-ce que vous comprenez? Tell how well you understand the following subjects by using one of the expressions given.

Je comprends bien...
Je comprends assez bien...
Je ne comprends pas bien...
Je ne comprends pas du tout...

1. l'espagnol
2. la chimie
3. la psychologie
4. l'allemand
5. la philosophie
6. l'informatique
7. la physique
8. le français

C. Vos cours. Tell whether you are studying the following subjects.

EXEMPLE **Oui, j'étudie la chimie.** OU **Non, je n'étudie pas la chimie.**

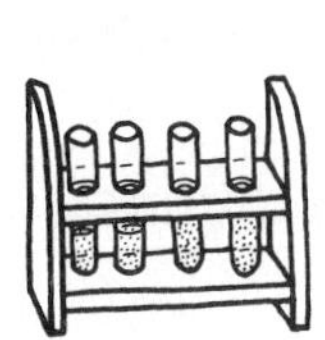

EXEMPLE

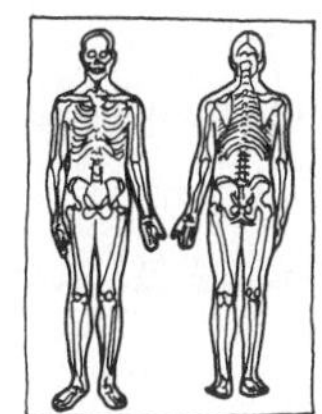

1.

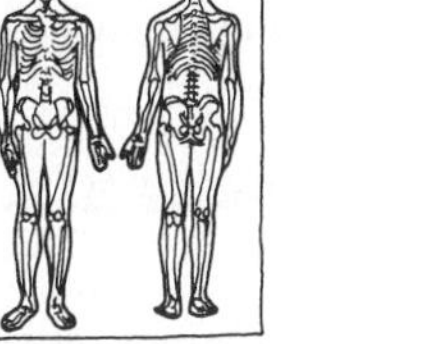

2.

3.

4.

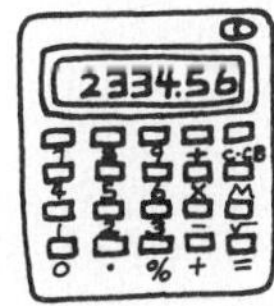

5.

6.

7.

D. L'université. Talk about your courses or other aspects of your university by completing the following sentences.

1. J'étudie...
2. J'aime beaucoup...
3. J'aime assez...
4. Je n'aime pas beaucoup...
5. Je n'aime pas du tout...
6. Je ne comprends pas...
7. Je comprends bien...
8. Je pense que les cours sont...

E. Quel cours? In what courses would you most likely study these famous French people?

1. Napoléon Bonaparte
2. Henri Matisse
3. Marie Curie
4. Blaise Pascal
5. Louis Pasteur
6. Sarah Bernhardt
7. Jean-Paul Sartre
8. Simone de Beauvoir
9. Claude Debussy

F. Camarades de classe. Engage a classmate in conversation by telling him/her what you are studying this semester. Your classmate will select a course and inquire about it and its instructor. Answer his/her questions. Then switch roles.

EXEMPLE — **J'étudie les maths, le français et la comptabilité.**
— **Comment est la comptabilité?**
— **La comptabilité est difficile.**
— **Et comment est le professeur?**
— **Il est sympathique, mais il est un peu ennuyeux.**

Voilà pourquoi!

SELF-CHECK
What two expressions can you use to compare people and things?

Les comparaisons

You can compare people and things by using **plus... que** (*more . . . than*) or **moins... que** (*less . . . than*). **Que** changes to **qu'** before a vowel sound.

David est *plus* grand *que* Jean-Luc.
David is taller than Jean-Luc.

Annette est *moins* sportive *qu'* Yvette.
Annette is less athletic than Yvette.

Savez-vous le faire?

A. À Nice. Look at these four photos of places and activities in and around Nice. Listen to the statements comparing places and decide if the information is **vrai** or **faux**.

Le casino Ruhl

La promenade des Anglais

Le village médiéval d'Èze

Le carnaval de Nice

D. Amis. Compare yourself to your best friend, using the following adjectives.

EXEMPLE **grand** → **Je suis plus grand(e).** OU **Je suis moins grand(e).**

1. patient	3. sérieux	5. timide	7. intellectuel	9. actif
2. extroverti	4. réaliste	6. sportif	8. pessimiste	10. ???

C. Cours difficiles. Use the indicated adjectives to compare each pair of courses.

EXEMPLE les maths / la chimie (facile)
Les maths sont plus (moins) faciles que la chimie.

1. le français / la chimie (difficile)
2. l'histoire / l'anglais (ennuyeux)
3. la littérature / la biologie (intéressant)
4. l'informatique / le dessin (compliqué)
5. le commerce / la musique (amusant)
6. la comptabilité / la psychologie (facile)

D. Les notes. Nathalie, a new friend of Annette's, is telling her about the French school system. Here is one of her old grade reports. What statements might she make about how much she likes certain courses? How would she compare them for interest and difficulty? In France, courses are scored on a scale of 20 instead of 100. (A 12 is average, and 18 or higher is rarely seen.)

COLLÈGE VICTOR GRIGNARD
177, Avenue Paul Santy
69008 LYON
Tél. : 74.30.45

NOM SANCHEZ
Prénom Nathalie
Date de naissance 15.05.66

1er TRIMESTRE 1979-1980
CLASSE 4e Redoub. ☐ Boursier ☐

DISCIPLINES	Types d'exercices	Notes sur 20	APPRÉCIATIONS ET RECOMMANDATIONS DES PROFESSEURS
FRANÇAIS — Comp. fran.		12,5	Bien -
FRANÇAIS — Grammaire, Orthographe	}	12	Doit faire des efforts de participation orale.
FRANÇAIS — Lect. expliq., Récitation (M)	}	13	
LATIN (M)			
HISTOIRE GÉOGRAPHIE (M AGNIEL)		12	A. Bien dans l'ensemble - Travail sérieux
ÉDUCATION CIVIQUE (M)			
LANGUE VIVANTE I Écrit / Oral — Anglais (M Pouillat)		12	Assez bons résultats à l'écrit. Participation active à l'oral -
LANGUE VIVANTE II Écrit / Oral — Espagnol (Mme Dubus)		/ 11,5	Assez bien à l'oral. Nathalie est en progrès -
MATHÉMATIQUES (M Germain)		10	Résultats en dents de scie. Il faut travailler régulièrement. Ensemble trop moyen
TECHNOLOGIE (M)			
SCIENCES NATURELLES (M)		14	Travail sérieux -
SCIENCES PHYSIQUES (M)		13	Assez bien
ÉDUCATION ARTISTIQUE — MUSIQUE (M)	12,5	11	A. Bien
ÉDUCATION ARTISTIQUE — DESSIN (M Callamard)		16	Satisfaisant
ÉDUCATION MANUELLE ET TECHNIQUE (Mme BONNEL)		13,5	Bon ensemble
ÉDUCATION PHYSIQUE (M)			

COMPORTEMENT

Appréciations globales et recommandations (conseil de classe)

Assez bon travail

du chef d'établissement

[signature]

COLLÈGE VICTOR GRIGNARD
177, Avenue Paul - Santy
69008 LYON

[signature]

E. **Camarades de chambre.** An acquaintance of your roommate has just found out that you are rooming together. Compare your personality traits to those of your roommate. If you do not have a roommate, imagine that you are rooming with one of your friends.

— Alors, Robert et toi, vous êtes camarades de chambre?
— Oui, mais nous sommes un peu (assez, très) différents...

Remarquez que...

In France, universities are run by the government and tuition is free. Many students live at home or at the **cité universitaire**, where the university residences are located.

La cité universitaire

At the university, students begin to concentrate on their field of specialization in the first year. Universities are divided into **facultés** and students attend courses at the **faculté** of their specialization.

Facultés. What courses would you expect to take at this **faculté**?

La faculté des lettres, Université de Nice

C'est à lire!

Here is an advertisement for French language classes for foreigners offered in the city of Montpellier in southern France. The following activities will help you understand the reading.

A. Vous savez déjà... If you were planning to study abroad, what sorts of information would you expect to find in advertisements for schools? Work with a partner to make a list of things that would probably be found in such ads.

B. Mots apparentés. Look at the ad that follows. Use cognates and your guessing ability to determine the following information.

1. What months are courses offered? From these months, what semester do you think **été** is: spring, summer, or fall?
2. What types of courses are offered and for whom?
3. What types of activities are named?

Avez-vous compris?

La publicité. Read the preceding ad and list all of the words that fit logically into the following categories. Use a separate piece of paper.

DATES	COURSES	STUDENT BODY	LODGING

Ça y est! C'est à vous!

A. **Organisez-vous!** You will be writing a short description of yourself. When you write in French, use and combine what you know and avoid translating from English. It is very difficult to translate correctly from one language to another. First organize your thoughts by completing these sentences in French.

1. Je m'appelle...
2. Je suis de (d')...
3. J'habite...
4. J'étudie...
5. J'aime... (Je n'aime pas...)
6. Je suis... (Je ne suis pas...)

B. **Rédaction: Autoportrait.** You are a new student at the **Université de Nice**. Write a short paragraph introducing yourself to your new roommate. Tell him or her your name, where you are from, what you are studying, how you feel about your classes, and what they are like. Then describe what kind of person you are. You can use the sentences you completed about yourself in ***A. Organisez-vous!*** to guide you. Feel free to add other information about yourself. Link sentences with words like **et**, **mais**, or **parce que** to make your paragraph flow better.

C. **Présentations.** After you have completed ***B. Rédaction: Autoportrait***, exchange papers with a classmate. Read each other's composition, then go around the room and introduce your partner to several classmates, telling them a few things that you learned about him or her. You may need to use the following verb forms to describe him or her: **il/elle s'appelle**, **il/elle étudie**, **il/elle aime**, **il/elle habite**.

D. **Comparaisons.** Now that you know your partner from ***C. Présentations*** better, work together to prepare at least five sentences comparing yourselves to each other. Later, you will take turns reading them to the class.

EXEMPLE ALEX: **Monique est plus sportive que moi.**
MONIQUE: **Alex est moins patient que moi.**

E. **Questions.** You have already become acquainted with most of your classmates. Choose five classmates you would like to know better and prepare a question for each. You can use the verb **être**, or you may wish to use **Est-ce que tu étudies...?** or **Est-ce que tu aimes...?** to find out whether they are studying or like something. (The final **-es** of these verb forms is silent.)

F. **Au café.** You overhear two people being introduced at the table next to you at the café. You will not be able to understand many things that are said, but you should be able to pick out the following details from the conversation.

- What are the first names of the two people being introduced?
- Where are they from?
- What are they studying?

Pour vérifier

Study the vocabulary on the facing page. Do the following exercises as a self-test, then check your answers in *Appendix C.*

Identifying people

A. **Qui est-ce?** Identify the following people, using **C'est un(e)... / Ce sont des...**

1.

2.

3.

Getting acquainted with and describing others

B. **Descriptions.** Write a sentence describing each of the people or groups of people in ***A. Qui est-ce?***

C. **Comparaisons.** Write two sentences comparing the boy and girl in ***A. Qui est-ce?***

D. **Questions.** You meet a French student at your university and he wants to know about you and your French class. How would he ask for the following information? How would you answer?

He wants to know if . . . you are . . . (married, from here, athletic)
the professor is . . . (difficult, French)
the students are . . . (intelligent, nice, fun)

Talking about university life

E. **J'étudie...** Write a short paragraph telling where you are a student and what you are studying. Tell which courses you do/do not like and do/do not understand. Compare your classes for difficulty and interest.

F. **L'Université de Nice.** Look back at the photo of the **faculté des lettres** at the **Université de Nice** on page 57. Imagine what this university is like. Use the following adjectives to compare it to your school: **moderne, vieux, beau, grand.**

G. **L'université.** Tell how much you like these aspects of your university. Then make two statements telling what each is or is not like.

1. la bibliothèque 2. les salles de classe 3. le campus 4. les cours

Vocabulaire

Identifying people

C'est...
- mon ami(e)
- une dame
- un(e) élève
- un(e) étudiant(e)
- une (jeune) femme
- une fille
- un garçon
- un (jeune) homme
- un monsieur
- ma sœur (jumelle)

Ce sont...
- des enfants (*m*)
- des gens (*m*)
- des jeunes (*m/f*)

Getting acquainted with and describing others

ADJECTIFS

actif(-ive)
agréable
américain(e)
amusant(e)
beau (belle, *pl.* beaux, belles)
bête
californien(ne)
calme
célibataire
compliqué(e)
désagréable
différent(e)
ennuyeux(-euse)
extroverti(e)
français(e)
frivole
grand(e)
idéaliste
impatient(e)
intellectuel(le)
intelligent(e)
introverti(e)
joli(e)
laid(e)
marié(e)
méchant(e)
même
moderne
optimiste
paresseux(-euse)
patient(e)
pessimiste
petit(e)
réaliste
sérieux(-euse)
sportif(-ive)
sympathique
timide
vieux (vieille)

DIVERS

alors
comme
Comment est (sont)...
est-ce que...
être: je suis (un peu, assez, très)...
- je ne suis pas (très, du tout)...
- tu es...
- il/elle est...
- nous sommes...
- vous êtes...
- ils/elles sont...

étudier
même
moins... que
n'est-ce pas
plus... que
plutôt
pour
voir

Talking about university life

J'aime (assez, beaucoup)...
Je n'aime pas (beaucoup)...
J'étudie...
Tu aimes...?
- l'allemand (*m*)
- l'amphithéâtre (*m*)
- l'anglais (*m*)
- les bâtiments (*m*)
- les beaux-arts (*m*)
- la bibliothèque
- la biologie
- le campus
- la chimie
- la comptabilité
- les cours de commerce (*m*)
- le cours de français
- les cours de théâtre (*m*)
- les cours techniques (*m*)
- le dessin
- l'espagnol (*m*)
- les études (*f*)
- les examens (*m*)
- le foyer des étudiants
- le français
- l'histoire (*f*)
- l'informatique (*f*)
- le laboratoire de langues
- les langues (*f*)
- la littérature
- le marketing
- les mathématiques (*f*)
- la musique
- la philosophie
- la physique
- les professeurs (*m*)
- la psychologie
- les résidences universitaires (*f*)
- le restaurant universitaire
- les salles de classe (*f*)
- les sciences (*f*)
- les sciences politiques (*f*)
- les sciences sociales (*f*)
- le sport
- l'université (*f*)

Santon
Nice, France
Photograph by Beryl Goldberg, 1993

The word **santon** means *little saint.* These figurines are placed in Christmas manger scenes in Provence.

Regional Overview
NICE
POPULATION: 346,000
DEPARTMENT: **Alpes-Maritimes**
PROVINCE: **Côte d'Azur**
MAJOR INDUSTRIES: horticulture, perfume production, tourism

Chapitre 2 Après les cours

By the end of this chapter, you should be able to do the following in French:

- Talk about leisure activities
- Order at a café
- Talk about what you and others do
- Ask who, what, when, where, and why

Nature morte aux grenades
Henri Matisse (1869–1954)
1947
Nice, Musée Matisse
Giraudon/Art Resource, New York

Nice was the subject of many of Matisse's paintings. He painted indoor scenes as well as outdoor scenes of the city he loved. This still life focuses on the contrast between the brilliant Mediterranean light and the shadowed interior of a room.

Pour commencer

Qu'est-ce que vous aimez **faire après** les cours?

Après les cours, j'aime... (je n'aime pas...)

sortir avec des amis...

aller prendre un verre au café

aller **voir** un film au cinéma

dîner au restaurant

rester à la maison...

dormir

écouter la radio

travailler sur ordinateur

qu'est-ce que *what* **faire** *to do, to make* **après** *after* **sortir** *to go out* **rester** *to stay* **aller** *to go* **voir** *to see*

faire du jogging

lire

jouer au tennis (au football, au basket-ball, à des jeux vidéo)

regarder la télévision

CULTURE NOTE

Le football (*soccer*) is one of the most popular sports in France. What is known as *football* in the United States and Canada is called **le football américain** in France.

David invite Annette à sortir.

— Tu es **libre ce soir**? **Tu voudrais** faire **quelque chose**?
— Oui, je voudrais bien. **Où** est-ce que tu voudrais aller?
— Je ne sais pas. Tu voudrais aller danser?
— Non, je préfère aller au cinéma. Tu voudrais voir un film?
— Oui, bien sûr! **On va** prendre un verre **avant**?
— **Pourquoi pas?** À quelle heure?
— À six heures, au café La Martinique. **D'accord?**
— Oui, d'accord. **Alors**, à tout à l'heure.
— Au revoir.

libre *free* **ce soir** *this evening* **tu voudrais** *would you like* **quelque chose** *something* **où** *where* **on va** *shall we go* **avant** *before* **pourquoi pas?** *why not?* **d'accord** *okay* **alors** *well, so*

Savez-vous le faire?

A. Mal au pied. You have hurt your foot. Accept or decline the invitations you hear by saying **Oui, bien sûr!** or **Non, merci.**

TEXTBOOK TAPE

EXEMPLE VOUS ENTENDEZ: Est-ce que tu voudrais faire du jogging?
VOUS RÉPONDEZ: **Non, merci.**

B. C'est amusant? Tell whether you think the following activities are fun or boring.

EXEMPLE regarder la télévision → **C'est amusant. / C'est ennuyeux.**

1. écouter la radio
2. travailler sur ordinateur
3. jouer au volley-ball
4. aller prendre un verre
5. lire le livre de français
6. voir un film au cinéma
7. faire les devoirs
8. parler français
9. aller danser

C. Des invitations. Invite a classmate to do the following activities. The person invited should either accept or propose something else. Then, decide on a time.

EXEMPLE jouer au tennis

— Est-ce que tu voudrais jouer au tennis?
— Oui, je voudrais bien. / Non, je préfère aller au cinéma.
— D'accord. À quelle heure?
— À sept heures. D'accord?
— Oui, d'accord. Alors, à tout à l'heure.
— À tout à l'heure.

1. dîner au restaurant
2. aller danser
3. aller prendre un verre
4. faire du jogging
5. aller voir un film
6. faire les devoirs

Comment s'y prendre?

It takes time and practice to understand a foreign language when you hear it. However, you can use some strategies that will help you learn to understand spoken French more quickly.

Listening for specific information

In everyday conversations, you usually do not need to comprehend everything you hear. Practice listening for specific details, such as times, places, or prices. Do not worry about understanding every word.

Savez-vous le faire?

TEXTBOOK TAPE

A. Quand? Listen to three scenes in which some friends make plans to go out. Indicate only the day and time they decide to meet.

SCÈNE A: le jour ______ l'heure ______

SCÈNE B: le jour ______ l'heure ______

SCÈNE C: le jour ______ l'heure ______

B. Qu'est-ce qu'elles font? Listen to Annette and Yvette making plans. Every time Annette suggests doing something, Yvette wants to do something else. Say what Yvette prefers to do in each case.

SCÈNE A: ______ SCÈNE B: ______ SCÈNE C: ______

Qu'est-ce qui se passe?

On sort ensemble

David, Yvette, and Annette run into two of David's friends. Listen to their conversation. Do not try to understand every word. The first time, listen only for the leisure activities they mention. Each time you hear one mentioned, write it down.

Avez-vous compris?

A. **Vous comprenez?** Listen again to the conversation between David and his friends and answer these questions.
   1. Do Thomas and Gisèle already know Annette and Yvette?
   2. Thomas and Gisèle find out several things about Annette and Yvette. Name two things they discover.

B. **Que savez-vous?** You picked up some information from listening to the conversation between David and his friends. Work in teams to list as many things as you can and see which team can list the most items.

Remarquez que...

The café is in many ways the center of French social life. Here the French entertain guests, visit with friends, or sit to watch the passersby. In Nice, **la rue Masséna** is a particularly popular pedestrian area. Tourists and citizens stroll from one café to another before selecting one in which to enjoy a drink or snack, to visit with friends, or to watch the crowd.

Au café à Nice

For those looking just for a quick snack, fast-food restaurants have become very popular.

Vous voudriez un hamburger et un Coca?

Vive la différence. Do you think there is an equivalent to the café in your culture?

SUJET DE CONVERSATION 1
Ordering at a café

Qu'est-ce qu'on dit?

A café is a convenient place to get a drink or something light to eat. What would you like?

TEXTBOOK TAPE

Je voudrais... Pour moi...

un express

un café au lait

un thé au citron

une eau minérale

un jus de fruits

un Coca

un verre de vin rouge
ou un verre de vin blanc

une bière

un demi

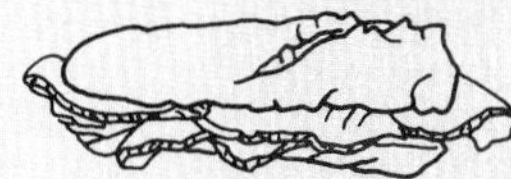
un sandwich
au jambon

un sandwich
au fromage

des frites

You will pay for your order in **francs.**

The **franc** is the monetary unit of France. The value of the **franc** varies, but it is usually worth between 20 and 30 U.S. cents. Each **franc** is divided into 100 **centimes**.

David and Annette are ordering at the café.

DAVID: Monsieur, s'il vous plaît.
LE GARÇON: Bonjour, monsieur, mademoiselle. Vous désirez?
ANNETTE: Pour moi, un chocolat **chaud.**
DAVID: Moi, je voudrais un demi.
LE GARÇON: Très bien, monsieur.

After they have finished, Annette pays the bill.

ANNETTE: S'il vous plaît, monsieur. C'est combien?
LE GARÇON: Ça fait 22 francs, mademoiselle.
ANNETTE: **Voilà** 30 francs.
LE GARÇON: Et **voici** votre **monnaie.**
ANNETTE: Merci, monsieur.
LE GARÇON: Je vous en prie.

chaud *hot* **voilà** *there are, there is* **voici** *here are, here is* **la monnaie** *change*

A. À votre santé. Which of each pair of drinks would be a healthier choice?

1. un café au lait / un jus de fruits
2. un verre de vin / une eau minérale
3. un jus de fruits / un express
4. une eau minérale / une bière
5. un Coca / un jus d'orange
6. un chocolat / une eau minérale
7. une bière / un thé au lait
8. un demi / un jus d'orange

B. C'est combien? Listen to what the waitperson says. If the bill is more than 20F, say **oui**, if not, say **non**.

C. Peu sucré. David likes all drinks except sweet ones. Name the drinks on page 69 he would probably order.

D. Je voudrais... A friend offers you the following foods and drinks. Use **je voudrais...** to say which one you would like.

1. un express / un thé au lait / un café au lait
2. un jus d'orange / un thé au citron / un Coca
3. un Coca / une bière / un chocolat / une eau minérale
4. un verre de vin blanc / une bière / un jus de fruits
5. un sandwich au fromage / un sandwich au jambon
6. des frites / un sandwich au fromage

Voilà pourquoi!

L'article indéfini

To identify an object or a person, use **un** or **une** to say *a*. Use **un** with masculine words and **une** with feminine words. Use **des** (*some*) with plural nouns. **Un** and **une** also mean *one*.

SELF-CHECK
What are the two forms of the word for *a*? When do you use each? How do you say *some*?

	MASCULIN	FÉMININ
SINGULIER	**un** café	**une** bière
PLURIEL	**des** verres	**des** frites

Annette est *une* jeune femme américaine.
***Un* demi pour moi, s'il vous plaît.**
Je voudrais *des* frites.

Learn nouns with **un** or **une** in front of them to help you remember their gender!

Et ça se prononce comment?

Un et une

Be careful to pronounce **un** and **une** differently. Use the very tight sound **u** with lips rounded, as in **tu**, to say **une**. The vowel sound of **un** is nasal. Pronounce the **n** in **un** only when there is liaison with a following noun beginning with a vowel sound.

TEXTBOOK TAPE

***une* bière**	***un* thé**
***une* eau minérale**	***un* express**

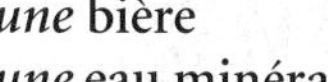

Savez-vous le faire?

A. Écoutez bien! Listen to the following orders at a café. On a separate piece of paper, write down the missing article (**un** or **une**) that you hear.

1. ______ bière, s'il vous plaît.
2. Je voudrais ______ express.
3. ______ jus de fruits, s'il vous plaît.
4. Pour moi, ______ Coca.
5. Pour moi, ______ sandwich au jambon.
6. ______ chocolat, s'il vous plaît.
7. Pour moi, ______ eau minérale.
8. ______ bière pour moi, s'il vous plaît.

Now go back and read a couple of orders you might place if you were at a café. Pronounce **un** and **une** distinctly.

B. Je voudrais... You are very thirsty and hungry. Order each of these items.

Je voudrais...

C. J'aime... Tell how well you like the food and drinks in the preceding activity. Remember that you use the definite article (**le, la, l', les**) to talk about likes, dislikes, and preferences. The first two are given as examples.

EXEMPLES **J'aime bien les sandwiches au jambon.**
Je n'aime pas du tout le café au lait.

D. Faites une liste. Divide into teams and, on a separate piece of paper, write as many names of drinks as you can remember under each category. See which team can think of the most names.

BOISSONS CHAUDES (*HOT DRINKS*)	**BOISSONS FROIDES (*COLD DRINKS*)**
un thé	

E. S'il vous plaît. Pretend that a classmate is working at a café. Call him/her over and order something to eat and drink.

EXEMPLE — **S'il vous plaît, monsieur (mademoiselle, madame).**
— **Oui, vous désirez?**
— **Je voudrais un sandwich au fromage et un Coca, s'il vous plaît.**

Voilà pourquoi!

Les chiffres

Here are the numbers 30–100. Notice how prices are given in **francs** and **centimes.**

— **Un café crème, c'est combien?**
— **10F50 (dix francs cinquante).**

30 trente	40 quarante	50 cinquante	60 soixante
31 trente et un	41 quarante et un	51 cinquante et un	61 soixante et un
32 trente-deux	42 quarante-deux	52 cinquante-deux	62 soixante-deux
33 trente-trois	43 quarante-trois	53 cinquante-trois	63 soixante-trois
34 trente-quatre	44 quarante-quatre	54 cinquante-quatre	64 soixante-quatre
35 trente-cinq	45 quarante-cinq	55 cinquante-cinq	65 soixante-cinq
36 trente-six	46 quarante-six	56 cinquante-six	66 soixante-six
37 trente-sept	47 quarante-sept	57 cinquante-sept	67 soixante-sept
38 trente-huit	48 quarante-huit	58 cinquante-huit	68 soixante-huit
39 trente-neuf	49 quarante-neuf	59 cinquante-neuf	69 soixante-neuf

70 soixante-dix	80 quatre-vingts	90 quatre-vingt-dix
71 soixante et onze	81 quatre-vingt-un	91 quatre-vingt-onze
72 soixante-douze	82 quatre-vingt-deux	92 quatre-vingt-douze
73 soixante-treize	83 quatre-vingt-trois	93 quatre-vingt-treize
74 soixante-quatorze	84 quatre-vingt-quatre	94 quatre-vingt-quatorze
75 soixante-quinze	85 quatre-vingt-cinq	95 quatre-vingt-quinze
76 soixante-seize	86 quatre-vingt-six	96 quatre-vingt-seize
77 soixante-dix-sept	87 quatre-vingt-sept	97 quatre-vingt-dix-sept
78 soixante-dix-huit	88 quatre-vingt-huit	98 quatre-vingt-dix-huit
79 soixante-dix-neuf	89 quatre-vingt-neuf	99 quatre-vingt-dix-neuf
		100 cent

SELF-CHECK
When is the only time you use **et** with numbers? Do you use **et** with 81 and 91?

Et ça se prononce comment?

Les chiffres

Some French numbers are pronounced differently, depending on what follows them.

deux̸ deux̸ cafés deux^{z}express trois̸ trois̸ cafés trois^{z}express

six^{s} six̸ cafés six^{z}express dix^{s} dix̸ cafés dix^{z}express huit^{t} huit̸ cafés huit^{t}express

Savez-vous le faire?

A. **Prononcez bien.** Place these orders for you and your friends, paying attention to the pronunciation of the numbers.

EXEMPLE un demi → **Pour moi, un demi, s'il vous plaît.**
trois demis → **Pour nous, trois demis, s'il vous plaît.**

un jus de fruits	deux express	six thés	huit express
un express	trois cafés au lait	six express	dix demis
deux demis	trois eaux minérales	huit chocolats	dix eaux minérales

B. **L'heure du thé.** Look at the café menu on the next page. As you hear an item named, tell its price.

EXEMPLE VOUS ENTENDEZ: Un café express, c'est combien?
VOUS RÉPONDEZ: **C'est 10 francs.**

C. **Numéros de téléphone.** French phone numbers are read in pairs. Which of the telephone numbers in the ads below would you call if you liked to do the following activities?

EXEMPLE faire du jogging → **Le quarante-trois, vingt-neuf, douze, trente-deux.**

1. faire du ski
2. jouer au golf
3. faire du judo
4. faire du skateboard
5. faire du camping
6. faire du karate

ECOLE DE GOLF DE PARIS 17

14 tapis - Vestiaires - Douches
Saunas - U.V.A. - Magasin conseil
Bar cafétéria - Parking
Cours - Stages - Voyages

UNIQUE
Renseignements :
(1) 47 63 06 54
5, avenue des Ternes PARIS 17e

AU VIEUX CAMPEUR
48, rue des Ecoles
75005 PARIS
(1) 43 29 12 32
3614 Vieuxcamp

25 disciplines sportives
grimpe, escalade, montagne, VTT, spéléo, parapente, randonnée, camping, jogging, équitation, tennis, squash, gym - danse, yachting, plongée, canoé - kayak, SKI.
Librairie cartothèque

JUDOGI

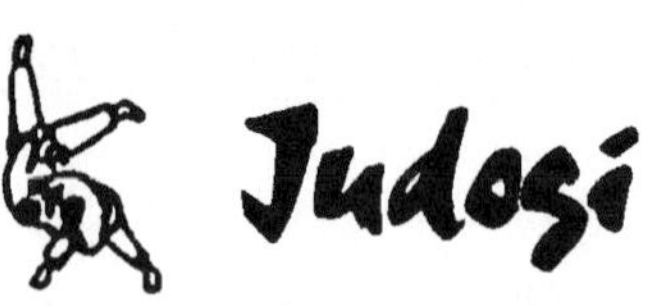

Kimonos - Articles Arts Martiaux et Tatamis Olympiques
Télex : 212714 F
107 bd Beaumarchais
75003 Paris - - - - - - - - (1) 42 72 95 59

5, rue Bailleul - 75001 PARIS (1) 49 27 91 60

D. Votre monnaie. You are at a café in Nice. Ask the waitperson what you owe. The first figure is your bill and the second is the amount you pay. Act out the scene with a classmate. Switch roles each time.

EXEMPLE 6F80 (10F)

— **C'est combien, monsieur?**
— **Six francs quatre-vingts, mademoiselle.**
— **Voilà dix francs.**
— **Et voici votre monnaie.**

1. 4F50 (5F) 2. 15F (20F) 3. 38F (40F)

E. Au café. In groups of three, prepare a scene in which you meet a friend at a café. One classmate will play the waitperson and take your orders. Decide what you are going to do together after leaving the café and call the waitperson back to pay the bill.

Remarquez que...

In France, the bill often will not be brought until it is asked for, leaving customers the freedom to sit as long as they wish. To ask for the bill, say, **L'addition, s'il vous plaît!** Normally, the tip is included in restaurant and café bills. One usually also leaves any small change. The menu will say **service compris** if the tip is included in the prices listed.

Le service est compris? Has the tip been included in the price of the items on this menu? How do you know?

L'heure du thé

Prix Service Compris [15%]

Café express	10
Double express	20
Café au lait	18
Infusions (*Tilleul, verveine, menthe, tilleul-menthe, verveine-menthe, camomille*)	18
Lait chaud	16
Café décaféiné	10
Double express avec pot de lait	21
Chocolat	18
Café ou Chocolat Viennois	20
Thé (*avec lait ou citron*)	18
Thé à la menthe	18
Thé aux fruits de la passion	18
Thé à la framboise	18
Cappuccino	23
Croissant	7
Confiture pot	6
Tartines beurrées	6
Viandox	10
Viandox avec vin	14
Grog au rhum	20
Vin chaud	12
Clacquesin chaud	25
Irish Coffee	46

SUJET DE CONVERSATION 2
Talking about what you and others do

Qu'est-ce qu'on dit?

Use these expressions to say how often you do things on the weekend.

En général, qu'est-ce que **vous faites** le week-end?

toujours	Je joue **toujours** au tennis.
souvent	J'invite **souvent** des amis à la maison.
quelquefois	Je **bricole quelquefois.**
rarement	Je regarde **rarement** la télévision.
ne... jamais	Je **ne** travaille **jamais.**

Use the following expressions to tell how well you do something.

très bien	Je joue très bien au tennis.
assez bien	Je joue assez bien au golf.
comme ci comme ça	Je parle français **comme ci comme ça.**
assez mal	Je danse assez mal.
très mal	Je **chante** très mal.

vous faites (**faire** *to do*) **toujours** *always* **souvent** *often* **bricoler** *to tinker around* **quelquefois** *sometimes* **rarement** *rarely* **ne... jamais** *never* **comme ci comme ça** *so-so* **chanter** *to sing*

David et Annette parlent au téléphone.

— Allô, Annette. C'est David.
— Ah, bonjour, David, comment ça va?
— Bien. Et toi?
— Moi, assez bien.
— Dis, Annette, mon ami Bruno et moi jouons au tennis ce week-end. Est-ce que tu voudrais jouer avec nous samedi matin?
— Je ne sais pas... Je joue très mal. Mais, je voudrais **venir** regarder **si** c'est possible.
— Oui, bien sûr. Et Yvette? Elle voudrait **peut-être** jouer avec nous?
— Oui, peut-être. Elle aime beaucoup le tennis et elle joue beaucoup **mieux** que moi... mais elle aime aussi dormir **tard** le samedi matin.
— Alors, pourquoi pas samedi après-midi?
— À quelle heure?
— **Vers** quatre heures?
— Oui, c'est **parfait**.
— Est-ce que vous voudriez aller **manger ensemble** au restaurant après?
— Oui, bonne idée!
— Bon, à samedi, alors.
— À samedi.

venir *to come* **si** *if* **peut-être** *perhaps* **mieux** *better* **tard** *late* **vers** *towards, around* **parfait** *perfect* **manger** *to eat* **ensemble** *together*

A. Célébrités. Name a famous person whom each description fits.

EXEMPLE Elle chante très bien. → **Barbra Streisand**

1. Il joue très bien au basket-ball.
2. Elle travaille beaucoup.
3. Il chante mal.
4. Ils habitent à Washington, D. C.
5. Elle danse très bien.
6. Ils jouent très mal au football américain.

B. Comment sont-ils? David is comparing himself to his friend Bruno. Read what he says, then choose an adjective to describe each of them.

EXEMPLE J'aime sortir avec des amis le samedi soir, mais Bruno préfère rester à la maison. (timide, extroverti)
David est plus extroverti et Bruno est peut-être plus timide.

1. J'aime jouer au basket-ball, mais Bruno préfère lire. (sportif, intellectuel)
2. J'aime danser et parler avec les gens. Bruno préfère regarder la télévision. (ennuyeux, amusant)
3. Bruno aime dormir le dimanche, mais je préfère bricoler. (paresseux, actif)
4. J'aime jouer au basket-ball avec des amis, mais Bruno préfère faire du jogging seul. (timide, extroverti)

Voilà pourquoi!

SELF-CHECK

1. What do you call the basic form of the verb that you find listed in the dictionary?
2. What are the three possible endings for infinitives in French?
3. If you have two verbs in a row, which one will be in the infinitive form?

L'infinitif

To name an activity in French, use the verb in the infinitive. The infinitive is the basic form of the verb that you find listed in the dictionary. Some examples of infinitives in English are *to play, to sleep, to be.* In French, infinitives are single words ending in **-er**, **-ir**, or **-re**: **jouer**, **dormir**, **être**. In French, whenever there are two or three verbs together in a sentence, the second and third verbs are in the infinitive.

— Qu'est-ce que tu *aimes faire*?
— J'*aime aller danser.*

— Est-ce que tu *voudrais sortir*?
— Je *préfère rester* à la maison.

Et ça se prononce comment?

La consonne r et l'infinitif

The consonant **r** is one of the few (CaReFuL) consonants that are normally pronounced at the end of words. There is one important exception, however. The final **r** of infinitives ending in **-er** is not pronounced. This ending is pronounced like the **é** in **café**.

parler inviter danser regarder jouer écouter

However, the **r** in infinitives ending in **-ir** or **-re** is pronounced. To pronounce a French **r**, hold the back of your tongue firmly arched upward in the back of your mouth and pronounce a very hard **h**-sound in your throat.

sortir dormir lire faire être prendre

Savez-vous le faire?

A. Infinitifs. Listen and fill in the infinitive ending that you hear.

EXEMPLE li___ / parl___ au téléphone
VOUS ENTENDEZ ET VOUS ÉCRIVEZ: **lire / parler au téléphone**

1. fai___ du jogging / dîn___ au restaurant
2. sort___ avec des amis / rest___ à la maison
3. prend___ un verre au café / invit___ des amis à la maison
4. dorm___ tard / jou___ au tennis
5. regard___ la télévision / écout___ la radio
6. all___ au cinéma / li___
7. êt___ à la maison / êt___ en classe

Now, ask a classmate which activity from each pair he/she likes better.

EXEMPLE **— Est-ce que tu préfères lire ou parler au téléphone?**
— Je préfère lire.

B. Préférences. Tell how well you like the following activities.

EXEMPLE **J'aime assez bricoler.**

EXEMPLE

1.

2.

3.

4.

5.

au

6. leisure

7.

8.

C. Loisirs. Complete the following sentences to describe your favorite pastimes.

1. À la maison, j'aime...
2. J'aime... avec des amis.
3. Je préfère jouer...
4. Après le cours de français, j'aime...
5. Demain, je voudrais...
6. Je n'aime pas du tout...

D. Une interview. Ask a classmate the following questions.

1. Qu'est-ce que tu aimes faire le week-end? le vendredi soir? le samedi matin? le samedi soir? le dimanche?
2. Quel sport est-ce que tu préfères? Le tennis? Le football? Est-ce que tu préfères jouer au tennis ou regarder un match de tennis à la télévision?
3. Quel jour est-ce que tu préfères regarder la télévision? Le lundi? Le mardi? Qu'est-ce que tu aimes regarder?
4. Est-ce que tu aimes aller au cinéma le week-end? Quel film est-ce que tu voudrais voir ce week-end?

E. Sondage. Here are the results of a survey of Canadian teenagers' favorite pastimes. Ask a partner questions to determine the order of his/her preferences.

EXEMPLE — **Est-ce que tu préfères faire du sport ou lire?**
— **Je préfère faire du sport.**

LOISIRS

Quels sont tes loisirs préférés?

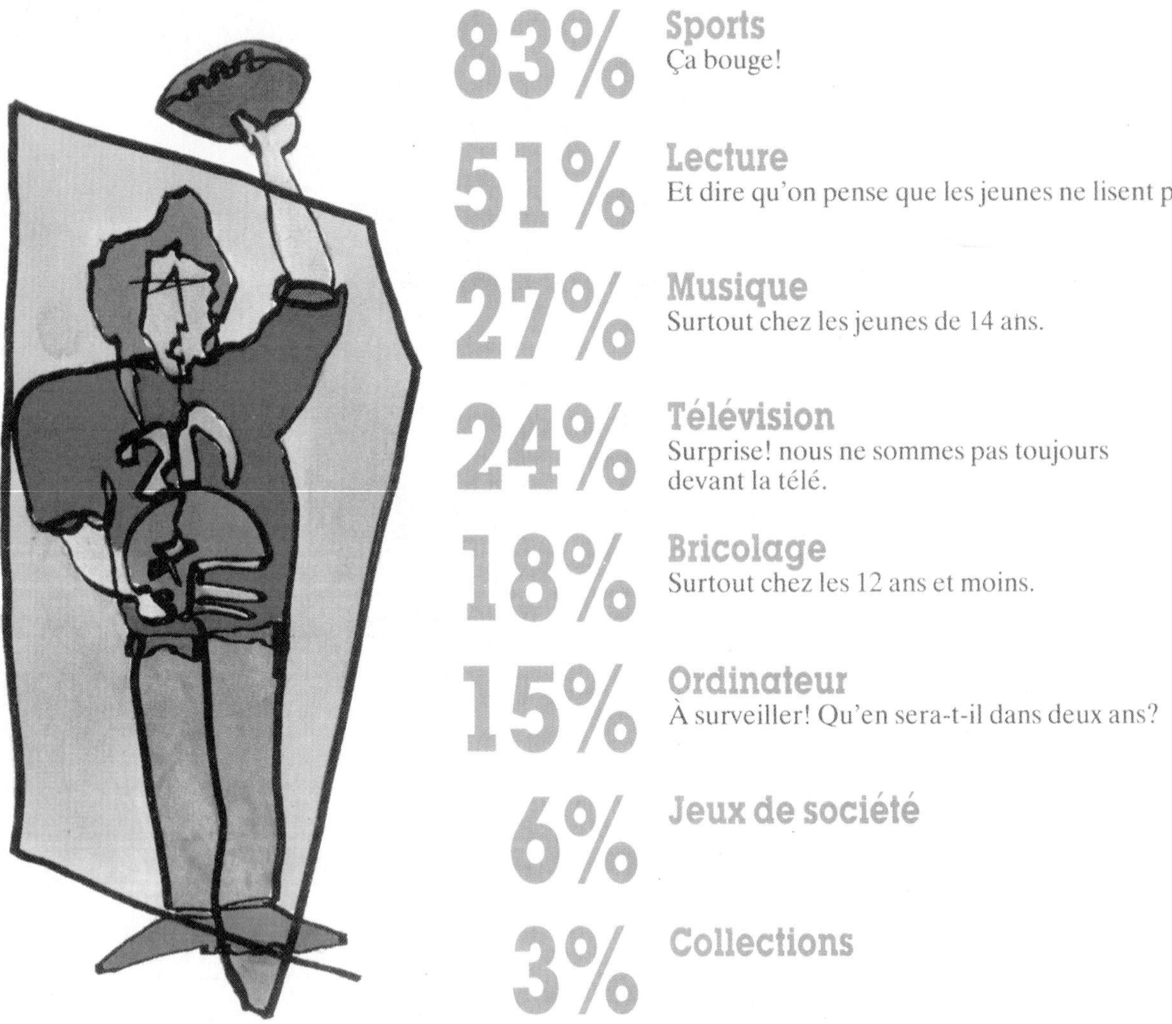

83% **Sports**
Ça bouge!

51% **Lecture**
Et dire qu'on pense que les jeunes ne lisent pas!

27% **Musique**
Surtout chez les jeunes de 14 ans.

24% **Télévision**
Surprise! nous ne sommes pas toujours devant la télé.

18% **Bricolage**
Surtout chez les 12 ans et moins.

15% **Ordinateur**
À surveiller! Qu'en sera-t-il dans deux ans?

6% **Jeux de société**

3% **Collections**

Julie marque un toucher.

lecture (*f*) *reading* **jeu** (*m*) **de société** *board game*

Voilà pourquoi!

> **SELF-CHECK**
> 1. How do you determine the root of an **-er** verb? What endings do you add to it?
> 2. When do you drop the final **-e** of words like **je**, **ne**, and **le**?
> 3. Which **-er** verb endings are silent?
> 4. Where do you generally place adverbs such as **bien**?

Les verbes en -er

To say what a person does or is doing, you must conjugate the verb. Regular verbs follow a predictable pattern, having the same set of endings. The largest group of regular verbs have infinitives ending in **-er**. All verbs ending in **-er** that you have learned, except **aller**, are conjugated by dropping the **-er** and adding the following endings. (For the time being, you will be able to use **aller** and verbs not ending in **-er** only in the infinitive.)

PARLER (*TO SPEAK, TO TALK*)	
je parl**e**	nous parl**ons**
tu parl**es**	vous parl**ez**
il/elle parl**e**	ils/elles parl**ent**

Just like the **e** of **ne** and **le**, the **e** of **je** drops before vowel sounds. All simple words consisting of a consonant sound and the letter **e** make this change. This is called elision.

j'habite / je n'habite pas **j'aime / je n'aime pas** **j'écoute / je n'écoute pas**

The present tense can be expressed in three ways in English, depending on the context. Express all three of the following English structures by a single verb form in French.

Je travaille. { *I work.* / *I am working.* / *I do work.* }

Il parle français. { *He speaks French.* / *He is speaking French.* / *He does speak French.* }

Here are the **-er** verbs that you have seen so far.

aimer	*to like, to love*	**habiter**	*to live*
bricoler	*to tinker around*	**inviter**	*to invite*
chanter	*to sing*	**jouer**	*to play*
compter	*to count*	**manger**	*to eat*
danser	*to dance*	**parler**	*to speak, to talk*
dîner	*to have dinner*	**penser**	*to think*
donner	*to give*	**regarder**	*to look at, to watch*
écouter	*to listen (to)*	**rester**	*to stay*
étudier	*to study*	**travailler**	*to work*
fermer	*to close*		

Quelques adverbes

Use the following adverbs to say how well, how often, or how much you do something. Unlike in English, such adverbs generally follow directly after the verb in French, except **quelquefois**, which can also be placed at the beginning or end of a sentence, or **comme ci comme ça**, which is placed at the end.

bien ≠ mal   **souvent ≠ rarement**   **beaucoup ≠ (un) peu**

Je *parle beaucoup* au téléphone.	*I* **talk** *on the phone* **a lot.**
Bruno *regarde assez souvent* la télévision.	*Bruno* **watches** *television* **fairly often.**
Je *joue* au tennis *comme ci comme ça.*	*I* **play** *tennis* **so-so.**
***Quelquefois,* je *joue* assez bien.**	*Sometimes I* **play** *fairly well.*

To say *never,* place **ne** before the verb and **jamais** after it.

Je *ne mange jamais* au restaurant.	*I* **never eat** *at a restaurant.*

Et ça se prononce comment?

Les verbes en -er

The present tense endings of **-er** verb forms are all silent except for those of the **nous** (**-ons**) and **vous** (**-ez**) forms.

je rest~~e~~   tu rest~~es~~   il rest~~e~~   elle rest~~e~~   il~~s~~ rest~~ent~~   elle~~s~~ rest~~ent~~

In conversation, you will be able to rely on context to distinguish between **il** and **ils**, or **elle** and **elles**. You will hear a difference only with verbs beginning with a vowel sound.

il travaill~~e~~ — il~~s~~ travaill~~ent~~   il aim~~e~~ — ils‿aim~~ent~~

The **-ons** ending of the **nous** form rhymes with the **bon** of **bonjour** and the **-ez** of the **vous** form rhymes with **les**. The **vous** form of **-er** verbs is pronounced like the infinitive. There is liaison of the **s** of **nous** and **vous** with verbs beginning with vowel sounds.

nou~~s~~ travaillo~~ns~~   vou~~s~~ travaille~~z~~   nous‿aimo~~ns~~   vous‿aime~~z~~

Savez-vous le faire?

A. **Le professeur ou les étudiants?** Complete these sentences so that they describe the students and the instructor in your class. The verb forms are pronounced the same, but you need to make liaison with the **s** of **ils** before vowels.

LES ÉTUDIANTS?	ET LE PROFESSEUR?
1. Ils parlent (beaucoup / peu) en classe.	Il/Elle parle (beaucoup / peu) en classe.
2. Ils écoutent (souvent / rarement) les cassettes.	Il/Elle écoute (souvent / rarement) les cassettes.
3. Ils travaillent (beaucoup / peu).	Il/Elle travaille (beaucoup / peu).
4. Ils aiment (beaucoup / assez / peu) le cours.	Il/Elle aime (beaucoup / assez / peu) le cours.

B. C'est l'infinitif? Since the **-ez** ending for the **vous** form and the infinitive ending of **-er** verbs sound alike, be careful not to confuse them when writing. As you hear each question, write the appropriate endings on your paper.

EXEMPLE: VOUS ENTENDEZ ET VOUS ÉCRIVEZ: **Est-ce que vous regard*ez* le football à la télévision?**

1. Est-ce que vous dîn___ souvent au restaurant?
2. Est-ce que vous aim___ dîn___ au restaurant?
3. Est-ce que vous mang___ quelquefois au restaurant universitaire?
4. Est-ce que vous travaill___ beaucoup?
5. Est-ce que vous aim___ travaill___?

Now, ask your professor these questions.

C. Entre amis. Say whether your best friend does the following.

EXEMPLE habiter seul(e)
Oui, il/elle habite seul(e). / Non, il/elle n'habite pas seul(e).

1. travailler
2. parler espagnol
3. parler beaucoup
4. danser bien
5. jouer au tennis
6. manger beaucoup
7. dîner souvent au restaurant
8. regarder souvent la télévision
9. rester toujours à la maison

D. Et toi? Working in pairs, ask your partner if he/she does the things listed in *C. Entre amis.*

EXEMPLE **— Est-ce que tu habites seul(e)?**
— Non, j'habite avec ma famille.

E. Vos amis et vous. What could you say about you and your friends, using the words given below?

EXEMPLE bien
Nous dansons bien.

1. bien
2. assez mal
3. quelquefois
4. souvent
5. ne... jamais
6. comme ci comme ça

L'IDÉAL

BAR — DANCING

29, rue Paul Cézanne
35400 CHÂTEAU-MALO
Tél. 99.81.08.48

SALLE POUR BANQUET AVEC SONO

DANCING EN MATINÉE: TOUS LES DIMANCHES APRÈS-MIDI

F. Sondage. A French marketing firm wants to know how often students at your school do the following things on the weekend. Ask four classmates if they do each of the following activities often. They will answer using one of the adverbs to the right. Score the number of points corresponding to each answer. Add up the number of points for the answers for each activity. The activity with the most points is the most popular.

toujours	*6 points*
très souvent	*5 points*
assez souvent	*4 points*
quelquefois	*3 points*
rarement	*2 points*
ne... jamais	*1 point*

regarder la télévision
dîner au restaurant
jouer à des jeux vidéo
écouter la radio
étudier
bricoler

EXEMPLE rester à la maison
— **Est-ce que tu restes souvent à la maison le week-end?**
— **Je reste rarement à la maison le week-end.**

Score two points and ask three other students.

Afterwards, report your findings to the class.

EXEMPLE **Les étudiants d'ici restent rarement à la maison.**

G. Présentations. If you introduced your best friend to a classmate, what would you say? Act out the scene with two other students. Make the introduction, then say at least five things about your best friend. Remember that you can use the verb **être**, as well as **-er** verbs.

H. Une boum. Working with a partner, imagine that you are at a party and an interesting stranger comes up and starts talking to you. First, you introduce yourselves, then you start to chat and you find out you have a lot in common. Finally, you offer your new friend something to drink.

Qu'est-ce qu'on dit?

Quand est-ce que vous êtes à l'université?

Tous les jours sauf le week-end?
Le week-end?
Le lundi, le mardi...?
Toute la journée (de 8 heures à 5 heures)?

Quand est-ce que vous préparez les cours?

Le matin?
L'après-midi?
Le soir?

Où est-ce que vous **aimez mieux** faire les devoirs?

À la bibliothèque?
À la maison?
Chez des amis?

Annette parle avec Bruno.

— David et toi, vous **passez** beaucoup de **temps** ensemble, n'est-ce pas?
— Oui, nous **déjeunons presque** toujours ensemble.
— Où est-ce que vous mangez **d'habitude**?
— Quelquefois nous préparons **quelque chose** à la maison et **d'autres fois** nous mangeons dans un fast-food.
— Qu'est-ce que vous aimez faire après les cours?
— Nous jouons souvent au tennis avec Philippe et Jean-Luc.
— Qui **gagne** généralement?
— David et moi, nous ne gagnons jamais, mais nous **commençons** à jouer un peu mieux.

---

quand *when* **tous les jours** *every day* **sauf** *except* **toute la journée** *the whole day* **aimer mieux** *to like better, to prefer* **chez...** *at . . . 's house* **passer** *to spend* **le temps** *time* **déjeuner** *to have lunch, to have breakfast* **presque** *almost* **d'habitude** *usually* **quelque chose** *something* **d'autres fois** *other times* **gagner** *to win* **commencer** *to begin*

A. Bruno et toi. Reread the preceding conversation between Annette and Bruno. What would Annette later say to David about his activities with Bruno?

1. Bruno et toi, vous passez (très peu de temps / beaucoup de temps) ensemble, n'est-ce pas?
2. Vous déjeunez (souvent / rarement) ensemble?
3. Vous déjeunez (quelquefois / toujours) à la maison?
4. Vous jouez au tennis avec Philippe et Jean-Luc (l'après-midi / toute la journée)?
5. Vous (ne gagnez jamais / gagnez souvent)?
6. Bruno joue (très bien / assez mal) au tennis?

B. C'est vrai? If a classmate said the following about your French class, would it be true? Indicate whether or not it is true by saying **C'est vrai** or **Ce n'est pas vrai.**

1. Nous passons beaucoup de temps au laboratoire de langues.
2. Quelquefois nous écoutons des cassettes en classe.
3. Généralement, le français est facile.
4. Nous sommes en classe tous les jours sauf le week-end.
5. Nous parlons toujours français en classe.
6. Nous travaillons souvent ensemble en classe.
7. D'habitude, nous préparons les examens ensemble après le cours.
8. Nous commençons le ***Chapitre huit*** demain.

C. Détails. David and his friends are having lunch tomorrow at Le Trapèze as soon as it opens. Read Annette's questions and select the logical response from the following list.

1. Quand est-ce que nous déjeunons ensemble?
2. À quelle heure?
3. Qui déjeune avec nous?
4. Pourquoi est-ce que tu n'invites pas Bruno?
5. Où est-ce que nous déjeunons?
6. Comment est Philippe?
7. Qu'est-ce que tu voudrais faire après?

a. Au restaurant Le Trapèze.
b. Philippe et Jean-Luc.
c. Demain.
d. Aller jouer au tennis.
e. Très sympa.
f. Parce qu'il travaille demain.
g. À midi.

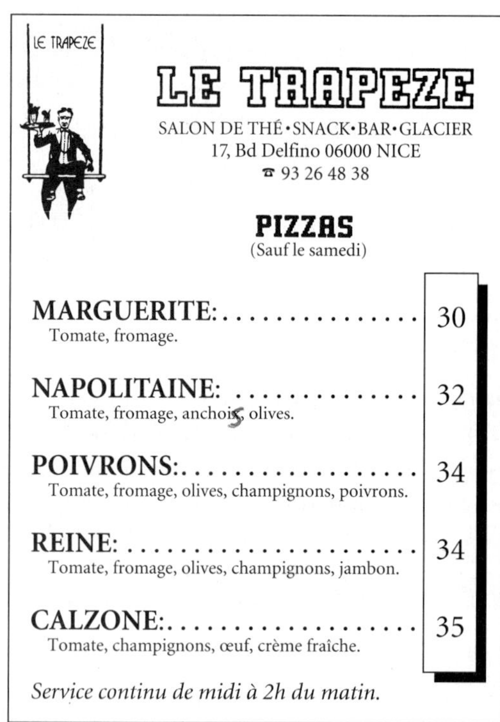

Voilà pourquoi!

Les questions

You have learned to ask whether someone is doing or does something by making questions with **est-ce que**. To ask for information such as *what, where, when,* or *why*, just add the appropriate question word before **est-ce que**, as in the following examples.

Est-ce que vous mangez?	*Are you eating? / Do you eat?*
*Qu'***est-ce que vous mangez?**	***What*** *are you eating? /* ***What*** *do you eat?*
Quand **est-ce que vous mangez?**	***When*** *are you eating? /* ***When*** *do you eat?*
À quelle heure **est-ce que vous mangez?**	***What time*** *are you eating? /* ***What time*** *do you eat?*
Où **est-ce que vous mangez?**	***Where*** *are you eating? /* ***Where*** *do you eat?*
Pourquoi **est-ce que vous mangez?**	***Why*** *are you eating? /* ***Why*** *do you eat?*
Comment **est-ce que vous mangez?**	***How*** *are you eating? /* ***How*** *do you eat?*
Avec *qui* **est-ce que vous mangez?**	***With whom*** *are you eating? /* ***With whom*** *do you eat?*

Do not use **est-ce que** with **qui** when it is the subject of the verb or with **où** when it is followed by **être**.

Qui mange? *Who is eating? / Who eats?* **Où est Philippe?** *Where's Philippe?*

Les verbes en -cer et -ger

With **-er** verbs ending in **-ger**, like **manger** and **voyager** (*to travel*), you must insert an **-e-** before the **-ons** ending in the **nous** form. With **-er** verbs ending in **-cer**, like **commencer**, the **c** changes to a **ç** before the **-ons** ending in the **nous** form.

nous mang*e*ons **nous voyag*e*ons** **nous commen*ç*ons**

SELF-CHECK

1. How do you form an information question? When are the two times you cannot use **est-ce que**?
2. When do you add an **-e-** before the **-ons** ending of the **nous** form of a verb? When do you change a **c** to **ç**?

Et ça se prononce comment?

Les lettres g, c, gu et qu

Verbs ending in **-cer** and **-ger** have spelling changes to indicate pronunciation. In French, a **g** or a **c** is pronounced hard before an **a, o,** or **u**. They are pronounced soft before **i** or **e**. A hard **c**-sound in English is released with a whispering puff of air. Avoid doing this in French.

Hard g:	**Gabrielle, Hugo, Marguerite**	Soft g:	**Georges, Gérard, Gilles**
Hard c:	**Catherine, Colette**	Soft c:	**Cécile, Maurice**

Sometimes it is necessary to indicate that a **g** or a **c** is soft before an **a, o,** or **u**. To do this, you insert an **-e-** after a **g** (**nous mang*e*ons**) and you add a **cédille** to a **c** (**nous commen*ç*ons**).

In French, **gu** is usually pronounced like a hard **g** and **qu** like a hard **c**. The **u** is generally not pronounced. You will hear a w-sound after **qu** when followed by **oi**, as in **pourquoi**.

Guillaume **qui** **que** **quand** **quelle heure**

Savez-vous le faire?

A. Ça s'écrit comment? American typewriters generally do not have a **ç**. Listen to a note that Annette sent to her friend, Cécile. First write down all the words where **c** is pronounced like **s**. Then decide which **c**'s should be changed to **ç**. Finally, reread the message aloud.

```
Cécile,
  Comment çа va? L'examen de francais est bien-
tôt, n'est-ce pas? David et moi, nous commençons
à préparer l'examen après le cours de commerçe
demain. Est-ce que tu voudrais travailler avec
nous?
                Annette
```

B. Comment s'appellent-ils? Say the names of these famous French-speaking people. First decide whether the **g** should be hard or soft.

1. Charles de Gaulle
2. Guillaume le Conquérant
3. Gabrielle Roy
4. Hubert de Givenchy
5. Georges Simenon
6. Gérard Depardieu
7. Victor Hugo
8. Marguerite Duras
9. Gilles Vigneault

C. Invitations. Some friends are making plans. Decide what words are needed to complete their conversation. The first blank has been completed as an example.

qui	*qu(e)*	où
quand	**comment**	*pourquoi*

1. — Est-ce que tu voudrais déjeuner avec nous?
   — **Quand** ?
   — Vers midi.
   — ______ est-ce que vous mangez?
   — Au café.
2. — Est-ce que tu voudrais dîner avec moi?
   — ______ est-ce que tu dînes?
   — À la maison.
   — ______ est-ce que tu prépares?
   — Une pizza.
3. — Est-ce que tu voudrais préparer l'examen de français avec nous?
   — ______ prépare l'examen?
   — Annette, Bruno et moi.
   — ______ est-ce que vous travaillez?
   — Ici.

4. — Est-ce que tu voudrais jouer au volley-ball avec nous?
   — Avec _____ est-ce que tu joues?
   — Avec des amis.
   — _____ est-ce que vous jouez?
   — Maintenant.

Now, using the preceding conversations as a model, create a conversation inviting a classmate to do something with you. Your classmate should ask at least two questions.

D. Et toi? Get to know another classmate better by asking the following questions. Remember your partner's answers so that you can tell the class what you find out.

1. Est-ce que tu joues au tennis (au volley-ball, au football, au golf)? Avec qui est-ce que tu joues? Quand est-ce que vous jouez généralement? Qui gagne d'habitude? Qui joue le mieux?
2. Est-ce que tu travailles? Où est-ce que tu travailles? Quand est-ce que tu travailles, le matin, le soir ou l'après-midi?
3. Est-ce que tu passes beaucoup de temps à l'université? Est-ce que tu aimes étudier à l'université? Pourquoi? Comment est le cours de français? Est-ce que nous commençons le ***Chapitre trois*** aujourd'hui?
4. Est-ce que tu aimes sortir avec des amis? Où est-ce que vous aimez aller ensemble? Qu'est-ce que vous n'aimez pas faire? Est-ce que vous mangez souvent ensemble?

E. Encore des questions. You want to find out more about your partner. Ask questions to find out the following information.

1. where he/she usually has lunch — with whom he/she likes to have lunch — whether he/she often prepares something at home
2. what he/she likes to do after class — whether he/she likes to sleep in the afternoon
3. whether he/she likes to spend the whole day at home — why he/she does or does not like to stay home in general
4. whether he/she studies every day — when he/she likes to study, in the morning, afternoon, or evening — what he/she does not like to study — whether he/she studies a lot

La plage à Nice

F. **Une soirée agréable.** Work with a classmate to look at the following ads from the newspaper *Nice Matin* and find a restaurant where you would like to have dinner. Then choose something to do afterwards. Decide what you are doing, when, where, and with whom. Then ask a third classmate if he/she would like to do it with you. He/She will ask for all the essential information before accepting or saying that he/she prefers to do something else. When done, switch roles.

LES BONNES TABLES

PUBLICITÉ

COCO BEACH (Depuis 1935). – Poissons grillés, langoustes, bouillabaisses. Cap de Nice, bord de mer, terrasse. Ouvert tous les soirs, à partir de 19 heures. Réservations: téléph. 93.89.39.26.

LA RÉSERVE DE NICE. – Toute la gastronomie de la mer dans son panorama exceptionnel, et toujours sa fameuse dunette à 75 F, vin et service compris. 60, boulevard F.-Pilatte. 93.89.31.70 (parking).

LA MADONETTE - NICE. – C'est pour rire. Dîner-spectacle unique sur la Côte. Service sur patin à roulettes. Ouvert tous les soirs, sauf le lundi. Réservations: tél. 93.86.92.92

POUPON ET MARINETTE (102, boulevard de la Madeleine, Nice. Téléph. 93.86.21.39). – Authentique cuisine niçoise. Depuis 25 ans. Fermé dimanche.

MIAMI PLAGE (197, pde des Anglais - 93.86.11.25). – À midi, mais le soir aussi, un bon restaurant sur la plage. Salades variées, saumon fumé maison, poissons grillés, fondue bourguignonne (le soir). Spécialités. Fermé le dimanche soir. Menu 78 F à midi en semaine.

A LA RIBOTE (Magnan, 93.86.56.26). – Menus, carte, cuisine faite par le patron.

PLAGE BEAU RIVAGE (quai des États-Unis, Nice). – Ouverte tous les jours. Petit déjeuner, snack, déjeuner avec suggestion du jour à partir de 80 F. Spécialité de poissons: langouste de vivier grillée à 190 F. Piano-bar tous les soirs. Pour les groupes, repas jusqu'à 300 personnes, cocktail jusqu'à 700 personnes. Réservation au 93.80.75.06 ou 93.80.80.70 poste 590.

C'est à lire!

By using cognates and your ability to make intelligent guesses, you should be able to find several choices to order from this Parisian café menu.

This exercise will guide you.

Vous savez déjà... What you already know about cafés and restaurants will help you determine the following information.

1. Under **Buffet chaud**, what would **une omelette jambon** be? **une omelette fromage? une omelette nature?**
2. What you see at the bottom of the menu indicates that checks are accepted under one condition. What usually is the condition for accepting checks?
3. At the bottom of the menu you see that the management claims they are not responsible for something. For what does management usually claim not to be responsible?

AUX TROIS OBUS

120, rue Michel-Ange
Paris

NOS SALADES

SALADE VERTE ______ 15
SALADE NIÇOISE ______ 43
(*Tomate, œuf, thon, olives, salade, anchois, riz, poivron*)
SALADE 3 OBUS ______ 43
(*Salade, choux-fleur, foies de volaille, jambon, œuf dur*)
SALADE POULET ______ 43
(*Émincé de poulet, maïs, riz, tomates, poivron, salade*)

SALADE MIXTE ______ 33
(*Tomates, œuf dur, salade*)
SALADE CHEF ______ 43
(*Tomates, pommes à l'huile, jambon, gruyère, salade, œuf dur*)
SALADE DE CRUDITÉS ______ 38
(*Concombres, tomates, carottes, choux*)

BUFFET CHAUD

ŒUFS AU PLAT NATURE (*3 œufs*) ______ 25
ŒUFS PLAT JAMBON (*3 œufs*) ______ 29
OMELETTE NATURE ______ 25
OMELETTE JAMBON ______ 29
OMELETTE FROMAGE ______ 29
OMELETTE MIXTE ______ 35
(*Jambon, fromage*)

OMELETTE PARMENTIER ______ 29
CROQUE-MONSIEUR ______ 25
CROQUE-MADAME ______ 32
HOT-DOG ______ 25
FRANCFORTS FRITES ______ 35
ASSIETTE DE FRITES ______ 15

MOULES MARINIÈRES	*43 F*
FRISÉE AUX LARDONS	*43 F*
RÔTI DE BŒUF PUREE	*45 F*
CASSOULET AU CONFIT	*70 F*
ST JACQUES PROVENÇALE	*90 F*

JAMBON DE PARIS ______ 14
SAUCISSON SEC ______ 14
SAUCISSON À L'AIL ______ 14
RILLETTES ______ 14
MIXTE (*Jambon, gruyère*) ______ 22
SANDWICH CRUDITÉS ______ 29

NOS SANDWICHES

JAMBON DE PAYS ______ 25
PÂTÉ ______ 14
TERRINE DU CHEF ______ 25
CLUB SANDWICH ______ 35
(*Pain de mie, poulet, jambon, tomates, œuf, laitue, mayonnaise*)
JAMBON À L'OS ______ 25
GRUYÈRE, CAMEMBERT ______ 14

Suppl. Pain mie __3__ Campagne __5__

FROMAGES

Camembert ______ 15
Roquefort ______ 18
Brie ______ 18
Cantal ______ 18
Chèvre ______ 18

Gruyère ______ 18
Assiette de fromages ______ 30

PRIX SERVICE COMPRIS (15%)
Les chèques sont acceptés sur présentation d'une pièce d'identité.

La Direction n'est pas responsable des objets oubliés dans l'Établissement.

Avez-vous compris?

A. Mots apparentés. Read over the menu and use cognates to help you identify these items.

1. Two kinds of sandwiches.
2. Three or four items used in the salads.
3. Two or three items you could order from the **buffet chaud**.

B. Bon appétit! What would you order at the Trois Obus? List all the dishes in French that you can identify on this menu, then number them in the order of your preference. Work with a partner, who will play the waitperson, and order something to eat and drink.

— S'il vous plaît, monsieur!
— Oui, vous désirez?

— À votre santé!

Ça y est! C'est à vous!

A. **Organisez-vous.** For a film class, you have decided to prepare a script for a French movie about a young foreign student's adventures abroad. Before beginning, check that you remember how to communicate the following in French.

- How do you greet a friend?
- How do you introduce that friend to someone you are with?
- How do you call the waitperson over and order a drink?
- How do you ask what your companions like to do and say what you do/do not like to do?
- How do you invite a friend to do something?
- How do you pay the bill?
- How do you say good-bye?

B. **Rédaction.** Using your answers from ***A. Organisez-vous***, write a scene where two college students are introduced by a common friend at a café. The three of them order a drink and start to chat about what they have in common. Also remember to add details, such as when they like to do some things or why they do not like to do other things. The group finally makes plans to do something later, they get the bill, and they pay.

C. **Scène: Au café.** Compare the conversation you prepared in ***B. Rédaction*** with those of two classmates and prepare a scene together to act out for the class.

D. **Et à l'université?** You are studying abroad and you have just moved in with your new French roommate. Find out the following information:

- Whether he/she is from there
- What he/she is studying; whether each course is interesting or difficult; what time each class begins; whether the classes are usually big at the university
- If he/she likes the cafeteria or other aspects of university life
- What he/she likes to do on the weekend; whether he/she likes to sleep late on Saturdays or Sundays; whether he/she likes to go out with friends and what they like to do together; whether he/she often invites friends over

E. **Camarades de chambre.** Guided by the questions in the previous activity, write a diary entry describing your roommate. If you do not have a roommate, imagine one. To say *my roommate* use **mon camarade de chambre** for a man and **ma camarade de chambre** for a woman. To say *his* or *her class* use **son cours.** In the plural, use **ses cours.**

F. **Rencontre au café.** Listen to the conversation between Annette and her friends at the café and answer the following questions.

1. How much time do Annette and Yvette spend at the café? Why?
2. What is the waitperson's name?
3. What does Yvette like to order at the café?

Pour vérifier

Study the vocabulary on the facing page. Do these exercises as a self-test, then check your answers in *Appendix C.*

Ordering and paying at a café

A. Au café. Write a conversation with a waitperson in a café. Call the waitperson over; he/she will ask what you want. Order something to eat and to drink.

B. L'addition, s'il vous plaît. Write a conversation in which you call the waitperson over and ask him/her how much it is for the items ordered in the preceding activity. After the waitperson tells you the price, you pay and receive your change.

Inviting friends to do something

C. J'aime... List three activities you like to do at home and three activities you like to do with friends. Finally, list three activities you do not like to do.

EXEMPLE **À la maison, j'aime lire... / Avec des amis, j'aime... / Je n'aime pas...**

D. Invitations. Imagine that you are close friends with these people. What would they probably like to do? Write a conversation inviting them to do something at the times indicated. Decide on an exact time.

EXEMPLE Michael Chang (demain matin)
— **Est-ce que tu voudrais jouer au tennis avec moi demain matin?**
— **D'accord! À quelle heure?**
— **Vers dix heures?**

1. Michael Jordan (demain après-midi)
2. Norm Peterson de *Cheers* (ce soir)
3. Jane Fonda (demain matin)
4. Gene Siskel (samedi soir)

Asking for information and telling how, how much, when, and how often

E. Questions. As friends tell you what they like to do, write a follow-up question asking for the indicated information. Then imagine their answers.

EXEMPLE — Je n'aime pas parler au téléphone. (*Why?*)
— **Pourquoi est-ce que tu n'aimes pas parler au téléphone?**
— **C'est ennuyeux!**

1. J'étudie beaucoup. (*What?*)
2. Je joue au tennis. (*How?*)
3. J'aime sortir le week-end. (*With whom?*)
4. Je dîne souvent au restaurant. (*Where?*)

F. On... Give the requested information, using the indicated subject pronoun.

EXEMPLE How often you play tennis (Je...) → **Je joue souvent au tennis.**

1. When your best friend likes to go out (Il/Elle...)
2. How often you invite friends over (J[e]...)
3. What your friends like to do on the weekend (Ils/Elles...)
4. How often you and your friends play video games (Nous...)

Vocabulaire

Ordering and paying at a café

ORDERING

un garçon
Vous désirez?
Je voudrais...
Pour moi... s'il vous plaît.
une bière
un café (au lait)
un chocolat (chaud)
un Coca
un demi
une eau minérale
un express
des frites (*f*)
un jus de fruits
un sandwich au jambon / au fromage
un thé (au citron)
un verre de vin blanc / rouge

PAYING

L'addition, s'il vous plaît.
C'est combien?
Ça fait... francs.
merci
Je vous en prie.
Voilà... francs.
Voici votre monnaie.
un centime
un franc

Pour les chiffres, voir la page 73.

Inviting friends to do something

INVITING

Est-ce que tu es libre ce soir?
Est-ce que tu voudrais...?
On va...?
Qu'est-ce que tu aimes faire?
aller au cinéma
bricoler
chanter
commencer
danser
déjeuner
dîner au restaurant
dormir tard
écouter la radio
faire du jogging
faire quelque chose
gagner
inviter des amis à la maison
jouer au tennis / au basket-ball / au football / à des jeux vidéo
lire
manger dans un fast-food
parler au téléphone
passer le temps ensemble
prendre un verre au café
préparer les cours
regarder la télévision
rester à la maison
sortir avec des ami(e)s
travailler sur ordinateur
venir
voir un film au cinéma
voyager

ACCEPTING

Bien sûr!
Bonne idée!
C'est parfait!
D'accord!
J'aime mieux...
Je préfère...
Je voudrais...
Pourquoi pas?

Asking for information and telling how, how much, when, and how often

QUESTION WORDS

à quelle heure
combien
comment
où
pourquoi → parce que
quand
qu'est-ce que
(avec) qui

HOW WELL

(très / assez) bien
comme ci comme ça
(très / assez) mal
mieux

HOW MUCH

assez
beaucoup
(un) peu

WHEN

après
l'après-midi
avant
le matin
le soir (ce soir)
tous les jours (sauf)
toute la journée (de... à... heures)
vers
le week-end (ce week-end)

HOW OFTEN

d'habitude
ne... jamais
quelquefois... d'autres fois
rarement
souvent
toujours

MISCELLANEOUS

alors
avec nous
chez des amis
en général
peut-être
presque
si

Unité 2 Au Québec

Regional Overview
Le Canada
AREA: 3,851,809 square miles (9,976,197 sq. km.)
POPULATION: 26,800,000
MAJOR INDUSTRIES: agriculture, forestry, mining, tourism
CAPITAL: Ottawa

Chapitre 3 Un nouvel appartement

By the end of this chapter, you should be able to do the following in French:

- Describe where you live
- Tell what you have
- Describe your house or apartment
- Exchange addresses and phone numbers

Tadoussac
Charles F. Comfort (1900–)
1935
The National Gallery of Canada
Vincent Massey Bequest, 1968

The town of Tadoussac (from the Montagnais Indian word *Tatoushak*) is located at the confluence of the Saguenay and Saint Lawrence rivers, in the province of **Québec**. It was the first fur trading post in the province, and has been a favorite vacation resort for many years.

Pour commencer

TEXTBOOK TAPE

Use these expressions to talk about where you live.

J'habite...

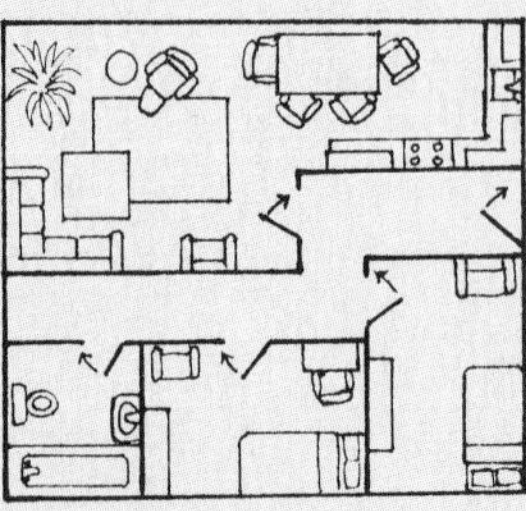

dans un appartement

dans une maison

dans une chambre à la résidence universitaire

Il/Elle est...	grand(e)	joli(e)	moderne	confortable
	petit(e)	laid(e)	vieux (vieille)	**cher (chère)**

Il/Elle se trouve...

en ville
dans un grand immeuble

en banlieue

à la campagne

J'habite... seul(e)
avec ma famille
avec **un(e) camarade de chambre**
avec **mon meilleur ami (ma meilleure amie)**

Note. In Canada, one might say **copain/copine de chambre** for *roommate*.

J'habite en ville.

cher (chère) *expensive* **Il/Elle se trouve** *It is located* **un(e) camarade de chambre** *a roommate* **mon meilleur ami (ma meilleure amie)** *my best friend*

Compare the French and French-Canadian method of counting floors with the method used in the United States.

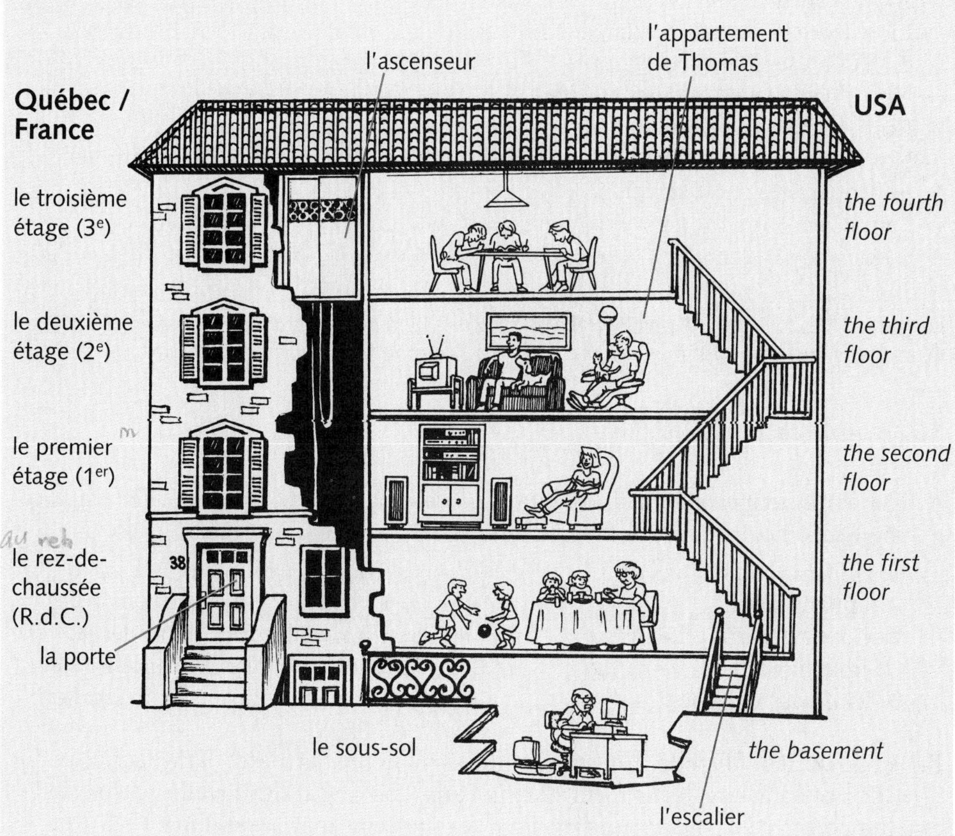

Est-ce que vous aimez mieux...?

monter l'escalier

prendre l'ascenseur

Robert, a young American, is about to start studying at Laval University in Quebec. He is talking on the phone to his friend Thomas, with whom he is thinking about living.

— Où est-ce que tu habites?
— J'habite dans un immeuble **au centre-ville.**
— À quel étage?
— Mon appartement est au deuxième étage.
— Tu habites seul?
— Non, j'habite avec mon ami Claude.
— L'université est **loin de chez toi**?
— Non, pas très loin. Et **il y a un arrêt d'autobus tout près**. C'est très **commode.**
— Et l'appartement est agréable?
— J'aime beaucoup mon appartement. Il est assez grand et pas **trop** cher.

au centre-ville *downtown* **loin de** *far from* **chez toi** *your house* **il y a** *there is* **un arrêt d'autobus** *a bus stop* **tout près** *right by, very near* **commode** *convenient* **trop** *too*

Savez-vous le faire?

A. L'appartement de Thomas. Look at Thomas's apartment on page 99. Tell whether these sentences are true or false. **(C'est vrai. / C'est faux.)** Correct the false ones.

1. Thomas habite dans un appartement.
2. L'appartement est dans un immeuble.
3. Thomas habite seul.
4. Thomas habite avec une amie.
5. L'appartement est au sous-sol.
6. L'immeuble est très moderne.
7. Thomas habite au troisième étage.
8. Il y a un ascenseur et un escalier.

B. Aux Galeries Lafayette. You are near the stairs in the basement of the famous **Galeries Lafayette** department store in Paris. Looking at the directory below, tell shoppers to go to the appropriate floor for the items they are seeking.

EXEMPLE les parfums → **Allez au rez-de-chaussée.**

1. le salon de beauté
2. les appareils électriques
3. les articles de sport
4. les vêtements Yves Saint-Laurent
5. l'agence de voyages
6. les vêtements de garçons
7. le magasin hommes
8. les appareils-photos

BIENVENUE AUX GALERIES LAFAYETTE!

REZ-DE-CHAUSSÉE	PREMIER ÉTAGE	DEUXIÈME ÉTAGE
Parfums	Appareils-photos	Agence de voyages
Magasin femmes	Articles de sport	Salon de beauté
Magasin hommes	Magasin enfants	Appareils électriques

C. Voisins indiscrets. Tell who lives on each floor of the apartment building on page 99.

EXEMPLE **La femme et les quatre enfants habitent au rez-de-chaussée.**

D. Camarades de chambre. You have answered an ad for a new roommate. Use these questions to ask your prospective roommate about the place. Play both roles with a classmate.

1. Où est-ce que vous habitez, dans un appartement ou une maison?
   J'habite...
2. Avec qui est-ce que vous habitez?
   J'habite...
3. Où se trouve l'appartement / la maison?
   Il/Elle se trouve...
4. Est-ce que l'appartement / la maison est près ou loin de l'université?
   Il/Elle est...
5. Comment est l'appartement / la maison?
   Il/Elle est...
6. Est-ce qu'il/elle est cher/chère?
   Il/Elle...

E. C'est vrai? Make a list of three things that are true about where you live and one that is not. Then read your list to the class, who will guess which is false.

EXEMPLE — **J'habite dans un appartement. Il se trouve au centre-ville. L'appartement est au troisième étage. J'habite avec cinq amis.**
— **Tu n'habites pas avec cinq amis.**

Comment s'y prendre?

Guessing from context

You can often guess the meaning of unknown words from the context in which they appear. Read each of these sentences in its entirety, then guess the meaning of the boldfaced words.

1. Le taxi arrive à l'immeuble et Robert **paie** le chauffeur. Il **entre** dans l'immeuble et monte l'escalier. Arrivé à l'appartement, il **sonne** à la porte. Une jeune femme arrive pour **ouvrir** la porte. **Après** un instant, elle commence à fermer la porte.
2. Robert ne comprend pas. Il est **confus** et **surpris**. La jeune femme parle, mais Robert **l'interrompt** et **s'exclame**: «Mais qui êtes-vous?»

Some words may have different meanings in different contexts. For example, the word **bien** can mean *well* or it can also be used for emphasis, in place of **très** for *very*. Read the following sentences and use the context to decide if **bien** means *well* or *very*.

C'est bien compliqué. **C'est une situation bien difficile!** **Je comprends bien.**

Savez-vous le faire?

A. **Selon le contexte.** The boldfaced words in the following sentences can have different meanings depending on the context. You should know what they mean in the first sentence of each group. See if you can guess what they mean in the others.

1. Écoutez **bien**!
   C'est **bien** bête ça!
   Bravo! C'est très **bien**!
2. J'habite au deuxième étage. Tu habites ici **aussi**?
   Claude est un nom de fille **aussi** bien qu'un nom de garçon.
3. Bravo! **Encore! Encore!**
   Ça, c'est **encore** plus compliqué.
   Je suis au premier étage, alors je monte **encore** un étage pour aller au deuxième?
4. Nous parlons **toujours** français en classe.
   Tu habites **toujours** la rue Dauphine?

B. **Vous savez déjà.** You already know the boldfaced word or words in sentence **a.** See if you can understand the boldfaced word or words in sentence **b** using the context.

1. a. Comment **dit**-on ça en français?
   b. Le chauffeur de taxi **dit**: «Voilà».
2. a. **Ouvrez** votre livre, **lisez** le paragraphe et **fermez** le livre.
   b. Robert **ouvre** la lettre de Thomas, **lit** les instructions et **referme** la lettre.
3. a. **Prenez** une feuille de papier.
   b. Elle **prend** la lettre.
4. a. **Donnez**-moi un café, s'il vous plaît.
   b. Thomas **donne** l'adresse de l'appartement à Robert.

Qu'est-ce qui se passe?

On cherche un nouvel appartement

Robert, an American, has come to study at Laval University in Quebec. His Canadian friend, Thomas, has invited Robert to share an apartment with him and his roommate, Claude. Robert is on his way to see the apartment and to meet Claude.

— Voilà, monsieur, le 38, rue Dauphine, dit le chauffeur de taxi.
Robert ouvre la lettre de Thomas, consulte les instructions et vérifie l'adresse. Il lit: «Mon appartement se trouve 38, rue Dauphine. C'est un grand immeuble avec une porte bleue. Je suis au deuxième étage.» «Oui, c'est bien là», pense-t-il. Il paie le chauffeur, entre dans l'immeuble et monte l'escalier. Arrivé à la porte de l'appartement, il sonne. Quelques instants après, une jolie jeune femme vient lui ouvrir.

— Euh... Bonjour, mademoiselle, je suis Robert. C'est bien ici que Claude et Thomas habitent? demande Robert.

— Claude, c'est moi. Mais...

Robert, bien surpris, l'interrompt et s'exclame:
— Claude, c'est vous? Euh... Mais vous êtes une femme!
— Eh oui, monsieur, je suis bien une femme! répond la jolie jeune femme.
— Euh... je veux dire que... C'est que, vous comprenez, en anglais, Claude, c'est un nom de garçon, dit Robert.
— En français, monsieur, le nom de Claude est utilisé aussi bien pour un garçon que pour une fille, répond la jeune femme.
— Ah, je comprends! Excusez-moi, mademoiselle. Je suis confus. Alors, vous êtes Claude. Moi, je suis Robert, Robert Martin. Est-ce que Thomas est ici?
— Thomas? répond-elle, d'un air surpris.
— Eh oui, Thomas, mon ami. Il habite ici avec vous.
— Mais certainement pas, monsieur! dit-elle d'un ton énervé.
Quand elle commence à fermer la porte, Robert s'exclame:
— Un instant, s'il vous plaît, mademoiselle. Regardez! C'est bien l'adresse que mon ami m'a donnée.
Elle prend la lettre, lit les instructions et commence à comprendre la situation.
— Oui, monsieur, c'est bien ici le 38, rue Dauphine, mais vous êtes au premier étage et votre ami habite au deuxième étage.
— Au premier étage? Ah! Oui, c'est ça. Je comprends maintenant. *First floor* c'est le rez-de-chaussée et *second floor* c'est le premier étage. Je monte encore un étage pour trouver l'appartement de mon ami.
— Voilà, monsieur Martin, c'est bien ça. Au revoir et bienvenue au Québec!
— Au revoir, mademoiselle, et merci.

Avez-vous compris?

A. Vrai ou faux? Répondez **vrai** ou **faux**.

1. Robert arrive en taxi à l'immeuble où habite Thomas.
2. Il monte directement au deuxième étage de l'immeuble.
3. Il sonne et Claude, la femme qui habite avec Thomas, ouvre la porte.
4. Claude est un nom de garçon et aussi un nom de fille en français.
5. Robert ne comprend pas très bien la manière de compter les étages en français.
6. En France et au Québec, le *first floor*, c'est le rez-de-chaussée et le *second floor*, c'est le premier étage.

B. Voilà pourquoi. Fill in the blanks to explain how Robert got confused.

Robert arrive en taxi pour trouver l'appartement de __1__. Thomas habite au __2__ étage avec Claude, un ami. Robert monte au __3__ étage et sonne. Une jeune femme ouvre la porte. C'est Claude, mais elle n'habite pas avec Thomas. Robert ne comprend pas, il pense que la jeune femme habite avec __4__. Voilà le problème: Robert est au __5__ étage et Thomas et Claude habitent au __6__ étage. C'est un autre Claude, un jeune __7__, pas une jeune femme, qui habite avec Thomas.

Remarquez que. . .

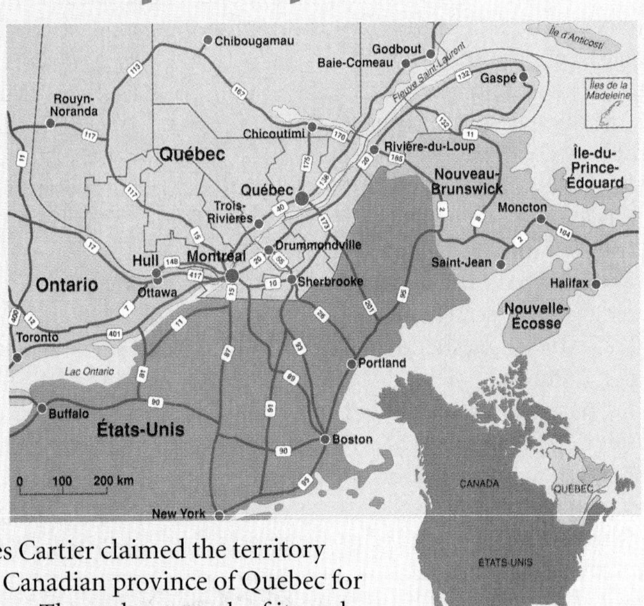

In 1534, Jacques Cartier claimed the territory that is now the Canadian province of Quebec for the French crown. Throughout much of its early history, Great Britain and France struggled for control of this vast land. Today, Quebec is inhabited by descendants of French and Anglo-Saxon settlers and native peoples, the Amerindians and the Inuit, as well as by an ethnically diverse immigrant population. About 80 percent of Quebec's population uses French as its first language.

Surrounded by English speakers, this francophone population has struggled to maintain its cultural and linguistic identity. In 1974, French was declared the official language of Quebec, and in 1977, a law was established requiring signs to be posted in French. Both anglophone and francophone public schools exist, but new immigrants are required to send their children to francophone schools.

This desire to be an independent culture has stirred great political debate. For many years, some factions have pushed for political autonomy from Canada, others for a special sovereignty relationship in which the national government would only have jurisdiction over limited matters, such as the monetary system. How Quebec can be both a part of Canada and yet a unique and independent culture has yet to be resolved.

Origines. **Quebec's history is evident in the names of its cities. Find three places on the above map with English names, three with French names, and three with Native American names.**

SUJET DE CONVERSATION 1
Telling what you have

Qu'est-ce qu'on dit?

TEXTBOOK TAPE

Here's how to tell what you have.

J'ai beaucoup de **choses.**

une voiture

un vélo

des vêtements (*m*)

un téléviseur

un magnétoscope et des cassettes vidéo (*f*)

une chaîne stéréo avec un lecteur de disques compacts et des disques compacts (*m*) de jazz

une affiche

un ordinateur

une chaise et un bureau

des plantes (*f*)

un chat et un chien

Before Robert's arrival, he and Thomas had discussed living together over the phone.

— Tu **cherches** un appartement ici à Québec? Écoute, tu sais, moi, je **partage** un appartement avec Claude, mon camarade de chambre. **Nous avons** trois chambres; tu voudrais habiter avec nous?
— C'est possible. Comment est **ton** appartement?
— Il est assez grand et confortable, mais pas trop cher. Tu aimes les animaux?
— Oui, pourquoi?
— Parce que Claude a un chien et un chat.
— Pas de problème. Vous **fumez**?
— Non, je ne fume pas et Claude **non plus**.
— Bon, et moi non plus. Alors ça va.

j'ai (**avoir** *to have*) **une chose** *a thing* **chercher** *to look for* **partager** *to share* **nous avons** (**avoir** *to have*) **ton (ta, tes)** *your* **fumer** *to smoke* **non plus** *neither*

Telling what you have

A. Où trouve-t-on...? Would you more commonly find these things in a bedroom (**dans une chambre**), in a classroom (**dans une salle de classe**), or in both (**dans les deux**)?

1. une plante
2. un tableau
3. des affiches
4. des disques compacts
5. des vêtements
6. un téléviseur
7. un chien
8. un bureau
9. un magnétoscope

B. Non, merci. If someone wanting you to share an apartment made these statements, would you want to or not? Answer **oui** or **non**.

1. J'ai un très petit appartement avec une chambre.
2. Je voudrais partager un joli appartement pas très cher.
3. Je fume, mais pas beaucoup.
4. Je partage l'appartement avec neuf chats et trois petits chiens.
5. L'appartement est très confortable et commode.
6. Je cherche un(e) camarade de chambre qui n'étudie pas beaucoup et qui aime sortir.
7. Je préfère habiter seul(e), mais l'appartement est très cher et je cherche un(e) camarade de chambre.

C. À qui est-ce? Here is Robert's bedroom at home and that of his 13 year-old brother, Paul. Say whether Robert or Paul has the items you hear named.

EXEMPLE VOUS ENTENDEZ: Il a un bureau.
VOUS RÉPONDEZ: **Robert**

la chambre de Robert

la chambre de Paul

Voilà pourquoi!

Le verbe **avoir**

To say what someone has, use the verb **avoir**. Its conjugation is irregular.

AVOIR (*TO HAVE*)	
j'**ai**	nous^z**avons**
tu **as**	vous^z**avez**
il/elle **a**	ils/elles^z**ont**

L'article pluriel **des**

You know to use **un** and **une** to identify an unspecified item. When there is more than one item, use **des**. This is the equivalent of *some* in English. In English, the word *some* is often omitted, but **des** is always used in French.

— Tu aimes les animaux?	*— Do you like animals?*
— Oui, pourquoi?	*— Yes, why?*
— Parce que j'ai *des* chats et *des* chiens.	*— Because I have* (**some**) *cats and dogs.*

Les pluriels en **-x**

The plural of most nouns and adjectives is formed by adding **-s**. However, words ending in **-u** usually form their plural with **-x**. Words ending in **-al** often change this ending to **-aux** in the plural.

un bureau → des bureaux un tableau → des tableaux un animal → des animaux

Ne... pas de...

After most negated verbs, **de (d')** is used instead of **un, une,** or **des**. One exception to this rule is after the verb **être**.

	AFFIRMATIVE	NEGATIVE
	J'ai *un* magnétoscope.	Je n'ai pas *de* magnétoscope.
	Tu as *une* voiture?	Tu n'as pas *de* voiture?
	Ils ont *des* cassettes vidéo.	Ils n'ont pas *de* cassettes vidéo.
BUT:	C'est *un* garçon.	Ce n'est pas *un* garçon.

SELF-CHECK

1. What does **avoir** mean? Why might one confuse the **tu** and **ils/elles** forms of **avoir** with those of **être** (*to be*)?
2. Is the plural indefinite article, **des**, used exactly like the English word *some*? Why not?
3. Which of these nouns and adjectives would have a plural ending with **-x** instead of **-s**: **un hôpital, une voiture, une affiche, une eau minérale?**
4. What do **un**, **une**, and **des** become after most negated verbs?

Et ça se prononce comment?

Avoir et **être**

Be careful to pronounce the forms of the verbs **avoir** and **être** distinctly. Open your mouth wide to pronounce the **a** in **tu as** and **il/elle a**. Remember that **es** and **est** are pronounced like the é in **café**. Pronounce **ils sont** with an s sound, and the liaison in **ils ont** with a z sound.

ÊTRE →	**Tu es professeur.**	AVOIR →	**Tu as beaucoup de cours.**
	Elle est professeur.		**Elle a beaucoup de cours.**
	Ils sont professeurs.		**Ils‿ont beaucoup de cours.**

Savez-vous le faire?

TEXTBOOK TAPE

A. **Avoir ou être?** You will hear different subject pronouns with either the verb avoir or être. Using a separate piece of paper, write down what you hear in the column corresponding to that verb.

EXEMPLE 1 VOUS ENTENDEZ: **elle est**
EXEMPLE 2 VOUS ENTENDEZ: **ils ont**

	AVOIR	ÊTRE
VOUS ÉCRIVEZ:	EXEMPLE 2: **ils ont**	EXEMPLE 1: **elle est**

Now, using the verbs you wrote, go back and write questions you could ask the instructor about various classmates.

EXEMPLE 1 **Susan, elle est mariée?**
EXEMPLE 2 **Éric et Anne, ils ont un ordinateur?**

AVOIR	ÊTRE
un chien	**marié(e)**
une voiture	*sérieux(-euse)*
DES ANIMAUX	SPORTIF(-IVE)
UN CHAT	TIMIDE
???	???
un appartement	**idéaliste**
un ordinateur	**optimiste**
???	d'ici
beaucoup de disques compacts	*californien(ne)*
beaucoup d'ami(e)s	INTELLECTUEL(LE)
	???

B. **Appareils électriques.** You do not realize that you are shopping at a store that sells only electronic equipment. Choose a classmate to play the salesperson and ask for these items.

EXEMPLE chats → — **Pardon, monsieur, vous avez des chats?**
— **Non, mademoiselle, nous n'avons pas de chats.**

1. téléviseurs
2. bureaux
3. livres
4. vélos
5. chaises
6. chiens
7. ordinateurs
8. plantes
9. chaînes stéréo
10. cassettes

C. **Vous avez quoi?** Robert is talking about what he and his roommates have at their apartment. Tell what he says, using the verb **avoir**.

EXEMPLE **Nous avons une chaîne stéréo et des disques compacts.**

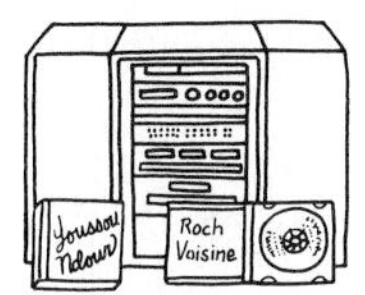

EXEMPLE Nous... 1. Thomas et Claude... 2. Claude...

3. J(e)... 4. Thomas, tu...? 5. Claude et toi, vous...?

Voilà pourquoi!

Combien de... Beaucoup de...

As with **ne... pas**, use **de (d')** instead of **des** after **beaucoup** and **combien** (*how much, how many*), when they are followed by a noun.

— J'ai *des* livres français. — *I have (some) French books.*
— *Combien de* livres est-ce que tu as? — ***How many** books do you have?*
— J'ai *beaucoup de* livres. — *I have **a lot of** books.*

SELF-CHECK
We have seen three cases where **de** is used instead of **un**, **une**, or **des** before nouns. They are after **combien**, after _____ and after _____.

Savez-vous le faire?

A. **Combien?** Ask a classmate how many of the items pictured in the preceding activity (*C. Vous avez quoi?*) he/she has.

EXEMPLE **— Combien de disques compacts est-ce que tu as?**
— J'ai un (deux, trois, beaucoup de...) disque(s) compact(s).
OU **— Je n'ai pas de disques compacts.**

B. Qu'est-ce que tu as? Go around the room and find someone who has each of the following things. Afterwards, tell the class what you found out.

EXEMPLE une chaîne stéréo
— **Éric, est-ce que tu as une chaîne stéréo?**
— **Oui, j'ai une chaîne stéréo. / Non, je n'ai pas de chaîne stéréo.**
APRÈS **Éric a une chaîne stéréo.**

1. un ordinateur
2. beaucoup de vêtements
3. des amis français
4. une voiture
5. un chien
6. des cassettes vidéo de Walt Disney
7. un chat
8. un magnétoscope
9. beaucoup de plantes
10. un vélo

C. Chez toi. Find out more about a classmate's home life by asking these questions.

1. Est-ce que tu habites dans un appartement, une maison ou une résidence universitaire? Est-ce que tu cherches un(e) camarade de chambre? Est-ce que tu as un(e) camarade de chambre? Est-ce qu'il/elle fume? Et toi, est-ce que tu fumes? Est-ce que tu préfères habiter seul(e) ou partager un appartement / une maison?
2. Est-ce que ta chambre est grande ou petite? Est-ce que tu as beaucoup de choses? Tu as beaucoup de vêtements?
3. Est-ce que tu aimes les animaux? Tu as des animaux? Est-ce que tu préfères les chiens ou les chats? Est-ce que tu préfères les grands chiens ou les petits chiens?

D. Camarades de chambre. You are thinking of becoming roommates with a classmate. Prepare a scene to role-play where you ask the following, as well as two other questions of your choice. Ask:

- if the apartment or house is big or small
- if your partner has a cat or dog
- if he/she smokes
- if he/she has a lot of things; what he/she has

Quebec City is perched atop a cliff overlooking the St. Lawrence River.

Qu'est-ce qu'on dit?

TEXTBOOK TAPE

Here's how to describe your home.

Chez moi, il y a six **pièces**. Il y a...

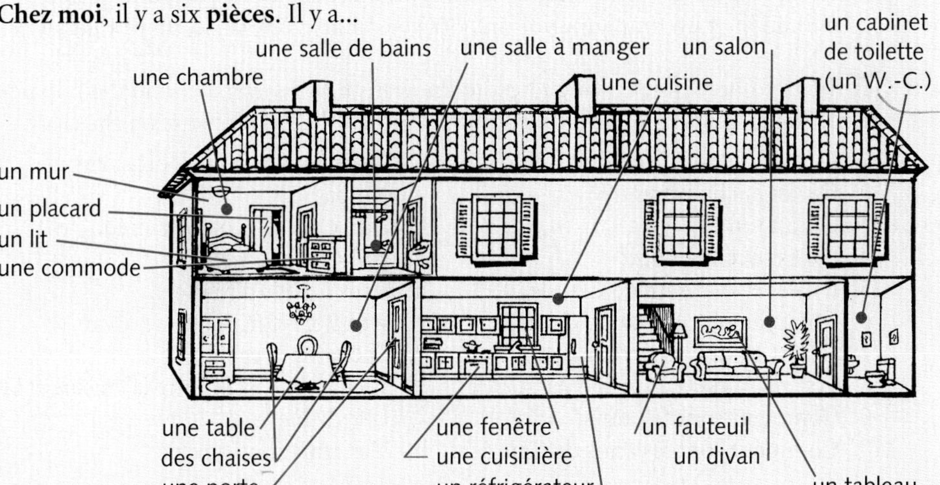

Use these expressions to tell a friend where to put his/her things.

Mets tes affaires...

When Robert finally arrives at the right apartment, Thomas shows him around.

— Mets **ta valise n'importe où** et **viens** voir l'appartement... Voici le salon.
— C'est ton chat?
— Non, c'est le chat de Claude. C'est un animal **embêtant**! Il aime dormir **partout**. Voilà le salon et la salle à manger... et voici ma chambre.
— Et la chambre de Claude?
— **Sa** chambre est **là** entre la cuisine et la salle de bains. Et voici ta chambre. Tu as une grande fenêtre avec une belle vue. C'est une chambre très agréable.

chez moi *at my house* **une pièce** *a room* **mets** *put* **ton, ta, tes** *your* **tes affaires** (*f*) *your things* **ta valise** *your suitcase* **n'importe où** (*just*) *anywhere* **viens** *come* **embêtant(e)** *annoying, bothersome* **partout** *everywhere* **son, sa, ses** *his* **là** *there*

A. Où? Which of the objects in parentheses might logically be in each location?

1. sur une étagère (des disques, un chat, une chaîne stéréo, un fauteuil)
2. dans une commode (un café, des vêtements, des livres, un chien, un vélo)
3. sous un lit (une voiture, un divan, un chat, une valise, une fenêtre)
4. devant une fenêtre (une porte, un tableau, un lit, une plante, un mur)
5. derrière un divan (une fenêtre, un chat, un mur, une cuisinière, une étagère)
6. entre un lit et un mur (une voiture, des vêtements, une valise, un réfrigérateur)

B. Que dit-il? Robert is still trying to get to know his new roommates and their apartment. For each question he asks Thomas, choose a logical response on the right.

1. Est-ce que c'est ta chaîne stéréo?
2. Où est ta chambre?
3. Où est ton lit?
4. Où est ma chambre?
5. Où est la chambre de Claude?
6. Comment est le chat de Claude?
7. Où est-ce que vous mangez?
8. Comment est la chambre de Claude?
9. Comment sont tes amis?
10. Comment sont les amis de Claude?

a. Ses amis sont un peu bizarres mais sympa.
b. Oui, c'est ma chaîne stéréo.
c. Voilà ma chambre.
d. Dans la salle à manger.
e. Je préfère dormir sur le divan.
f. Ta chambre est là.
g. Sa chambre est là entre la cuisine et la salle de bains.
h. Mes amis sont sympa.
i. Il est embêtant.
j. Sa chambre est petite mais jolie.

Voilà pourquoi!

SELF-CHECK

1. In what two ways can **il y a** be translated into English?
2. Where do you place **ne... pas** when negating **il y a**?

Il y a

To say *there is* or *there are* in French, use the expression **il y a**. The negative of **il y a un/une/des** is **il n'y a pas de**.

— *Il y a des* fenêtres dans ta chambre?
— Non, *il n'y a pas de* fenêtres.

Remember that **voilà** can also mean *there is* or *there are*. However, use **voilà** only when you are pointing out something. **Voici** means *here is* or *here are*.

***Voilà* la salle de bains, là, entre le salon et ma chambre.**
***Voici* ta chambre, ici, derrière la cuisine.**

Les prépositions

Use these prepositions to say where things are located.

sur	*on*	**devant**	*in front of*	**dans**	*in, into*
sous	*under*	**derrière**	*behind*	**entre**	*between*

Savez-vous le faire?

A. À vendre. Tell what rooms are found in this house.

EXEMPLE **Au rez-de-chaussée, il y a une cuisine... Au premier étage, il y a...**

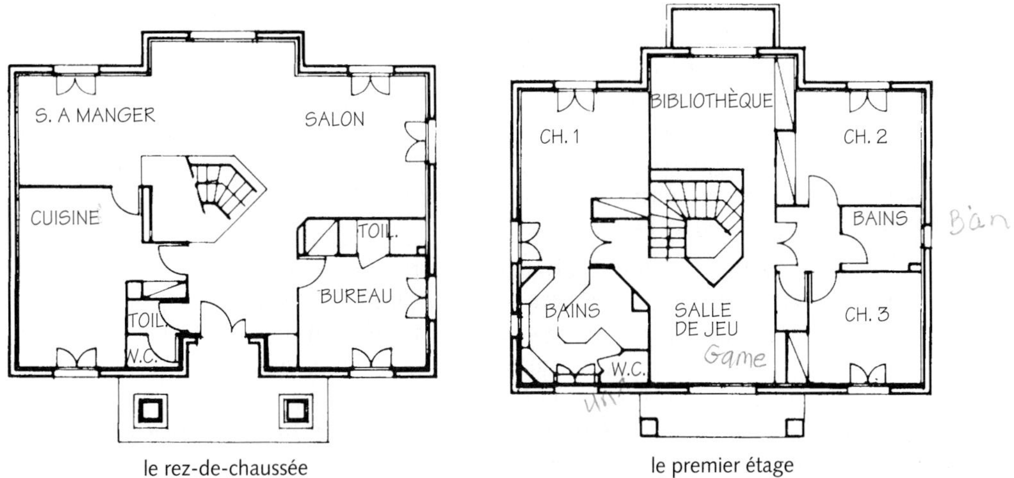

le rez-de-chaussée | le premier étage

B. Chez moi. Look at the drawing of the bedroom on page 111 and tell what there is in it. Then say if there are the same things in your room.

EXEMPLE **Dans la chambre, il y a un placard...**
Dans ma chambre, il y a...

C. Où est-ce que je mets ça? Thomas is helping Robert move in. Where does Robert tell him to put his things? Make logical sentences, using elements from each column.

EXEMPLE **Mets le téléviseur sur l'étagère.**

	le téléviseur	
	le lit	sur le bureau
	les vêtements	devant la fenêtre
	l'ordinateur	entre le lit et le mur
Mets	la chaîne stéréo	sous le lit
	les livres	dans le placard
	les cassettes	sur l'étagère
	la valise	entre la porte et la fenêtre
	la commode	
	la plante	

Voilà pourquoi!

SELF-CHECK

1. How would you say *John's house* and *Mary's dog* in French?
2. With which two forms of the definite article does **de** combine to form one word?
3. How would you say *his house* and *her house* in French? How would you say *his dog* and *her dog* in French? Does French have different words for *his* and *her*?

La possession avec **de**

In English, possession and relationship can be indicated by *'s*. In French, you will need to use a phrase with the word **de**.

Voilà la chambre *de Claude.*	**Yvette est la sœur *d'Annette.***
There is Claude's room.	*Yvette is Annette's sister.*

When **de** is followed by a definite article and a noun, it combines with the masculine singular **le** and the plural (masculine or feminine) **les** to form **du** and **des**. It does not change when followed by **la** or **l'**.

de + le	→	**du**	**C'est le livre *du* professeur.**
de + les	→	**des**	**C'est la résidence *des* étudiant(e)s.**
de + la	→	**de la**	**C'est la porte *de la* salle de bains.**
de + l'	→	**de l'**	**C'est la voiture *de l'*ami(e) de Claude.**

De is also used to indicate content or type. In this case, the definite article is not used with the following noun.

un verre *de* vin   une classe *de* français   une salle *de* bains   un disque *de* jazz

Les adjectifs possessifs: **mon, ton** et **son**

You can also indicate to whom something belongs by using the possessive adjectives. In English, these are *my, your, his, her*, etc. In French, these words agree in gender and number with the noun they precede. Note that the masculine form is used before feminine nouns that begin with a vowel sound.

	SINGULAR			PLURAL
	MASCULINE	FEMININE BEFORE CONSONANTS	FEMININE BEFORE VOWEL SOUNDS	
my	**mon** livre	**ma** cassette	**mon** amie	**mes** vêtements
your	**ton** livre	**ta** cassette	**ton** amie	**tes** vêtements
his/her/its	**son** livre	**sa** cassette	**son** amie	**ses** vêtements

The use of the forms **son/sa/ses** depends on the gender and number of the object possessed, not the person who owns it. They all can mean *his, her,* or *its.*

C'est **son** fauteuil.

C'est **son** fauteuil aussi.

Et c'est **son** fauteuil aussi.

Et ça se prononce comment?

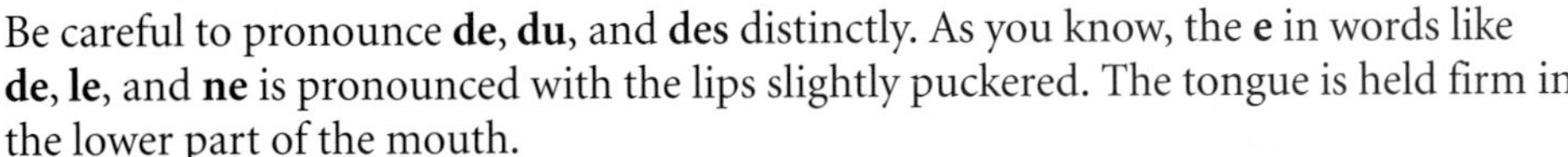

De, du et **des**

Be careful to pronounce **de**, **du**, and **des** distinctly. As you know, the **e** in words like **de**, **le**, and **ne** is pronounced with the lips slightly puckered. The tongue is held firm in the lower part of the mouth.

The **u** in **du**, as in **tu**, is pronounced with the tongue arched firmly near the roof of the mouth as when pronouncing the French vowel **i** in **il** but with the lips puckered.

The vowel in **des**, **mes**, **tes**, **ses**, and **les** is a sharp sound like the **é** in **café**, pronounced with the corners of the lips spread. This sound in articles and possessive adjectives indicates to the listener that the following noun is plural.

Savez-vous le faire?

A. De qui? As you hear each sentence, fill in the missing words being careful to distinguish the sounds of **du**, **de la**, **des**, and **de**. After you are through, go back and read each sentence saying whether it is *true* (**vrai**) or *false* (**faux**) based on your French class and your university. Correct those that are false.

1. Le livre ______ est sur son bureau.
2. Les étudiants ______ sont embêtants.
3. La salle ______ est agréable.
4. La porte ______ a une fenêtre.
5. Les chambres ______ sont modernes.
6. Les exercices ______ sont souvent amusants.
7. Les réponses ______ sont dans le cahier.
8. Les examens ______ sont faciles.

B. Où encore? A friend is helping you move into a new apartment. Complete these instructions by specifying the logical place in parentheses. Use the correct form of **de** + the definite article in your answers.

EXEMPLE Mets ma chaîne stéréo sur l'étagère. (la cuisine, le salon)
Mets ma chaîne stéréo sur l'étagère du salon.

1. Mets ma voiture devant la porte. (la salle de bains, l'immeuble)
2. Mets mes livres sur l'étagère. (la cuisine, le salon)
3. Mets mes disques compacts dans le placard. (le salon, la cuisine)
4. Mets mon thé et mon café dans le placard. (la chambre, la cuisine)
5. Mets ma cuisinière devant la fenêtre. (la cuisine, la salle de bains)

C. C'est comment? Ask five questions about a classmate's home and school life.

EXEMPLES — **Comment sont tes amis?**
— **Mes amis sont sympathiques. Ils sont intellectuels.**
— **Comment est ton appartement?**
— **Mon appartement est agréable.**

appartement MAISON
chambre **chat**
CAMARADE DE CHAMBRE ???
amis COURS
professeurs **???**
université **meilleur(e) ami(e)**

grand *petit*
SYMPATHIQUE
INTÉRESSANT
embêtant ennuyeux
??? *agréable*
SPORTIF **???**

D. À qui est-ce? Robert asks Thomas if these things belong to Claude. Say what questions he asks.

EXEMPLES

— **Ce sont les animaux de Claude?**

— **C'est le livre de Claude?**

1.

2.

3.

4.

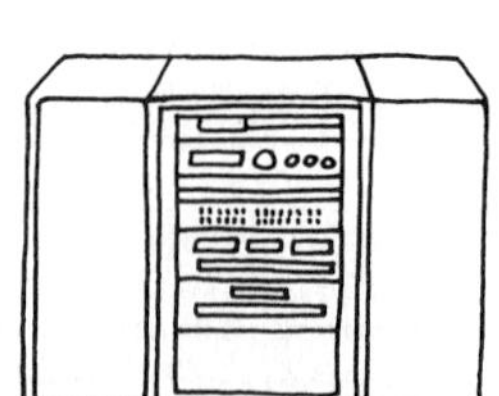

5.

6.

E. Selon ses goûts. It turns out that Claude loves animals and sports and is not at all interested in music. Answer Robert's questions in *D. À qui est-ce?* using **son/sa/ses.**

EXEMPLES **Oui, ce sont ses animaux.** **Non, ce n'est pas son livre.**

F. Et chez vous? Tell in which room you have the following items and where they are located. If you do not have an item, say so.

EXEMPLE table → **Ma table est dans ma cuisine devant une fenêtre.**
OU **Je n'ai pas de table.**

1. téléviseur 2. ordinateur 3. lit 4. commode 5. chaîne stéréo 6. livres

G. Camarades de chambre. Imagine that a classmate is moving in with you and you are showing him/her around your apartment. Act out the scene. Your partner should ask you at least three questions as you show the apartment.

Voilà pourquoi!

Les adjectifs possessifs: **notre, votre** et **leur**

You learned to use **mon/ma/mes, ton/ta/tes,** and **son/sa/ses** to indicate possession. The possessive adjectives for *your* (polite or plural), *our,* and *their* have only two forms, singular (**notre, votre,** and **leur**) and plural (**nos, vos,** and **leurs**).

SELF-CHECK
1. Why are there four columns in the chart showing the possessive adjectives?
2. Which three possessive adjectives have the same forms for masculine and feminine?

	SINGULAR			PLURAL
	MASCULINE	FEMININE BEFORE CONSONANTS	FEMININE BEFORE VOWEL SOUNDS	
my	**mon** lit	**ma** chambre	**mon** amie	**mes** livres
your (familiar)	**ton** lit	**ta** chambre	**ton** amie	**tes** livres
his/her/its	**son** lit	**sa** chambre	**son** amie	**ses** livres
our	**notre** lit	**notre** chambre	**notre** amie	**nos** livres
your (polite / plural)	**votre** lit	**votre** chambre	**votre** amie	**vos** livres
their	**leur** lit	**leur** chambre	**leur** amie	**leurs** livres

Et ça se prononce comment?

La voyelle **o**

Compare the **o** sounds in **notre/nos** and **votre/vos.** The lips are puckered to make both these sounds and the tongue is held firm, but the **o** in **nos/vos** is pronounced with the back of the tongue arched higher in the mouth than for the **o** in **notre** and **votre.** The letter **o** is pronounced with the sound of **nos** when it is the last sound in a syllable, when it is followed by an **s,** or when it is written **ô.** Otherwise, it is pronounced with the more open sound of **notre.**

notre chien / nos chiens **votre chat / vos chats**

Savez-vous le faire?

A. À l'université. Listen to the following sentences and fill in the missing words on a sheet of paper. When you have finished, read each sentence aloud and say whether it is **vrai** or **faux**. Pay attention to the pronunciation of **o**.

1. ______ est vieille.
2. ______ sont confortables.
3. ______ est belle.
4. ______ sont difficiles.
5. ______ est de Montréal.

B. Compliments. You are visiting a friend at his parents' home in Quebec and you want to pay them compliments. What might you say?

EXEMPLE **Votre salon est très agréable.**

fenêtres **cuisine**
chambres CHIENS
voiture **ENFANTS**
salon ???

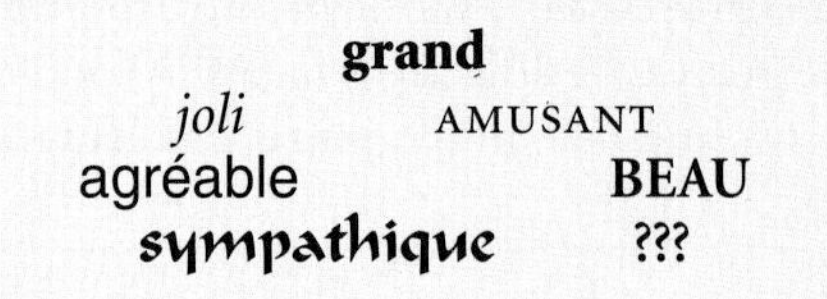

C. Chez nous. Two friends are trying to persuade a third to move in with them. How should they answer these questions if they want to impress him? Answer using **notre** or **nos**.

1. Votre appartement est très cher?
2. Vos chiens sont méchants?
3. Votre rue est belle?
4. Votre cuisine est grande?
5. Vos parents passent beaucoup de temps à l'appartement?
6. Votre appartement a beaucoup de fenêtres?
7. Comment est la vue de votre appartement?

D. Préférences. Say whether you like the following things, using **leur/leurs** or **son/sa/ses.**

EXEMPLES les films de Laurel et Hardy → **J'aime bien leurs films.**
les films d'Alfred Hitchcock → **Je n'aime pas beaucoup ses films.**

1. les films de Steven Spielberg
2. les films des Marx Brothers
3. la musique des Beatles
4. la musique de Prince
5. les disques de U2
6. les disques de Madonna

Qu'est-ce qu'on dit?

Travelers frequently have to give the following information. How would you answer?

Quel est votre nom?	Martin.
Quel est votre prénom?	Robert.
Quelle est votre adresse?	C'est le 214, Robinhood.
Quelle ville?	Atlanta.
Quel pays?	États-Unis.
Quelle est votre nationalité?	Américaine.

BUREAU DU REGISTRAIRE
Cité Universitaire
QC., Canada, G1K 7P4

UNIVERSITÉ LAVAL

DEMANDE D'ADMISSION

Appuyez fortement sur le stylo afin que tous les feuillets soient nettement marqués.

Répondez aux seules questions numérotées en rouge.

1 À QUEL TRIMESTRE DÉSIREZ-VOUS COMMENCER VOS ÉTUDES? ☐ HIVER 19____ ☐ ÉTÉ 19____ ☐ AUTOMNE 19____

2 NOM DU CANDIDAT
Nom: Martin
Prénom: Robert

3 SEXE: 1. ☑ MASC. 2. ☐ FEM.

4 DATE DE NAISSANCE: Année 76 Mois 02 Jour 28

5 ADRESSE DU CANDIDAT
numéro: 214 rue: Robinhood appartement:
municipalité: Atlanta comté province:
état-pays: Georgie USA Code postal: 30306
téléphone (résidence): IND. RÉG. 404 NO. 201-1284
téléphone (travail): IND. RÉG. ___ NO. ___-___

6 CODE PERMANENT DU MINISTÈRE DE L'ÉDUCATION: ____

SEULS LES CANDIDATS QUI ONT FRÉQUENTÉ UN COLLÈGE DU QUÉBEC RÉPONDENT À LA QUESTION 6.

7 N° D'ASS SOCIALE: 456 986 208

52 LIEU DE RÉSIDENCE: ____

8 LANGUE MATERNELLE: 1. ☐ Française 2. ☑ Anglaise 3. ☐ Autre

9 LANGUE D'USAGE: 1. ☑ Française 2. ☑ Anglaise 3. ☐ Autre

10 LIEU DE NAISSANCE
province: Atlanta état-pays: Georgie USA

53 CITOYENNETÉ: PAYS USA

11 STATUT AU CANADA: 1. ☐ Citoyen canadien 2. ☐ Résident permanent 3. ☑ Détenteur d'un Visa
USA
CITOYENNETÉ SI AUTRE QUE CANADIENNE

Robert is talking to a friend, telling how to get in touch with him at his new apartment.

— Quelle est ton adresse?
— C'est le 38, rue Dauphine.
— Et c'est quel appartement?
— C'est l'appartement numéro 131 (cent trente et un).
— Et le code postal?
— G1K 7X2.
— Quel est ton numéro de téléphone?

CULTURE NOTE
In Canada, they also read phone numbers using individual digits (**six**, **neuf**, **deux**, **deux**, **six**, **neuf**, **un**).

— C'est le 692-2691 (six cent quatre-vingt-douze, vingt-six, quatre-vingt-onze.)
— Et comment est **le quartier**?
— Il est agréable et près de **tout**.
— L'appartement n'est pas trop cher? C'est combien, **le loyer**?
— Je partage l'appartement avec deux amis, Thomas et Claude. C'est 825 dollars **par mois** partagés entre nous trois. Alors pour moi, c'est 275 dollars.

le quartier *neighborhood* **tout** *all, everything* **le loyer** *rent* **par mois** *per month*

A. **Numéros de téléphone.** Unlike phone numbers in Canada and the United States, phone numbers in France are composed of eight numbers read in pairs (**54 03 88 12 = le cinquante-quatre, zéro trois, quatre-vingt-huit, douze**). Look at these ads from the Paris yellow pages and tell what number you might call if you were looking for these items.

1. un téléviseur	3. un chien	5. un fauteuil	7. des livres
2. une voiture	4. un ordinateur	6. une cuisinière	8. un chat

ANIMAL CENTER

ANIMAL-CENTER
OISEAUX VOLAILLES CHIENS CHATS
POISSONS EAU DOUCE EAU MER + ACC.
Continent Chambourcy - - - (1) 39 65 07 91
70 rte Mantes-Chambourcy - (1) 39 65 08 59
46 av Gare
78310 Coignières - - - - - (1) 34 61 69 12

M.P.O.

Bernard CLAVREUIL, expert

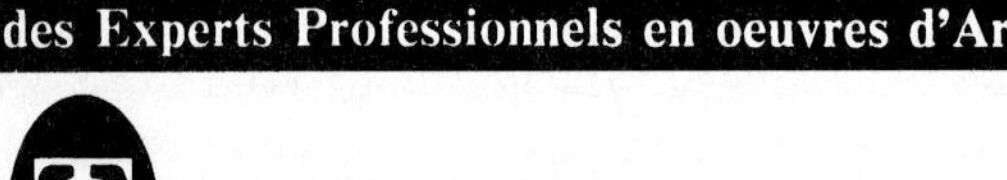

Expertises - Achat - Vente
Livres anciens et manuscrits
médecine, sciences voyages, littérature
Librairie Thomas Scheler
19, r. de Tournon Fax : (1) 40 46 91 46
75006 PARIS (1) 43 26 97 69

B. Quel indicatif? Look at this area code map from the front of a Quebec phone book and indicate where in Canada one finds each of the area codes you hear.

617 BOSTON, MASS.
413 MASSACHUSETTS
401 RHODE ISLAND
203 CONNECTICUT
516 LONG ISLAND, N.Y.
212 MANHATTAN – BRONX
718 BROOKLYN – QUEENS STATEN ISLAND
201 NEWARK, N.J.
908 NEW BRUNSWICK, N.J.
609 NEW JERSEY
410 BALTIMORE, MD.
302 DELAWARE
202 WASHINGTON, D.C.
312 CHICAGO, ILL.
708 AURORA, ILL.

LE CANADA ET LES ÉTATS-UNIS SE DIVISENT EN PLUS DE 100 RÉGIONS TÉLÉPHONIQUES CARACTÉRISÉES PAR UN INDICATIF RÉGIONAL FORMÉ DE TROIS CHIFFRES.

Voilà pourquoi!

SELF-CHECK

1. What verb can separate the adjective **quel** (*which, what*) from the noun it describes?
2. Before which two of these numbers do you never put **un**: **cent, mille, million?**

L'adjectif **quel**

The adjective **quel/quelle/quels/quelles** is used with a noun in a question to ask *which* or *what*? The form you use varies with the number and gender of the noun modified. It can be placed just before the noun:

Quel appartement **est-ce que tu préfères? C'est dans** *quelle rue*?

Or, it may be separated from the noun by the verb **être**:

Quel est *ton quartier* préféré? *Quels* sont *les devoirs* pour demain?

Les chiffres au-dessus de 100

Once you have learned to count to 100, you can count as high as you want with these words.

100	**cent**	1 000	**mille**	1 000 000	**un million**
101	**cent un**	1 001	**mille un**	1 234 692	**un million deux cent trente-quatre mille six cent quatre-vingt-douze**
102	**cent deux**	1 352	**mille trois cent cinquante-deux**		
199	**cent quatre-vingt-dix-neuf**	2 000	**deux mille**		
200	**deux cents**				
201	**deux cent un**				

Note the following about numbers:

- **Cent** means *one hundred* and **mille** means *one thousand*. Never put **un** before them. On the other hand, you do say ***un* million**.
- **Cent** has an **s** in numbers like **deux cents** and **trois cents** only when no other number follows the word **cent**. For example, there is no **s** in **deux cent un**. Never add an **s** to **mille** in numbers like **deux mille** and **trois mille**.
- There is no hyphen between **cent**, **mille**, or **un million** and another number.

Savez-vous le faire?

A. Préférences. Ask about a classmate's favorite places and things.

EXEMPLE restaurant → — **Quel est ton restaurant préféré?**
— **Je préfère** *Chez André.*

1. cours
2. rue
3. quartier
4. cassettes vidéo
5. sports
6. université
7. livre
8. voiture

B. À quelle distance? Robert is planning to visit all of Quebec province. Look at the diagram and tell how far these cities are from the city of Quebec.

EXEMPLE **Montréal** → **— Quelle est la distance entre Montréal et Québec?**
— 253 kilomètres.

1. Joliette	3. Trois-Rivières	5. Hull	7. Gaspé
2. Rimouski	4. Saint-Georges	6. Chicoutimi	8. Sainte-Agathe-des-Monts

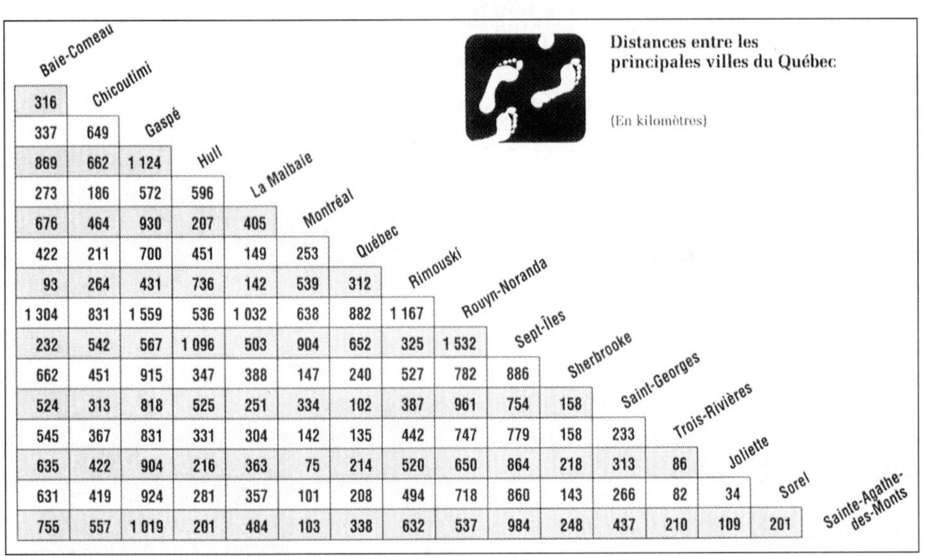

Distances entre les principales villes du Québec

(En kilomètres)

	Baie-Comeau	Chicoutimi	Gaspé	Hull	La Malbaie	Montréal	Québec	Rimouski	Rouyn-Noranda	Sept-Îles	Sherbrooke	Saint-Georges	Trois-Rivières	Joliette	Sorel
Chicoutimi	316														
Gaspé	337	649													
Hull	869	662	1 124												
La Malbaie	273	186	572	596											
Montréal	676	464	930	207	405										
Québec	422	211	700	451	149	253									
Rimouski	93	264	431	736	142	539	312								
Rouyn-Noranda	1 304	831	1 559	536	1 032	638	882	1 167							
Sept-Îles	232	542	567	1 096	503	904	652	325	1 532						
Sherbrooke	662	451	915	347	388	147	240	527	782	886					
Saint-Georges	524	313	818	525	251	334	102	387	961	754	158				
Trois-Rivières	545	367	831	331	304	142	135	442	747	779	158	233			
Joliette	635	422	904	216	363	75	214	520	650	864	218	313	86		
Sorel	631	419	924	281	357	101	208	494	718	860	143	266	82	34	
Sainte-Agathe-des-Monts	755	557	1 019	201	484	103	338	632	537	984	248	437	210	109	201

Perce, Québec

C. C'est combien? You are going to move into a new apartment and you and your roommate are looking through a catalog for various things you will need. For each pair of ads, discuss which item you prefer.

EXEMPLE — **Quel téléviseur est-ce que tu préfères?**
— **Je préfère le téléviseur à 3 490 francs.**

1.

DEPUIS
995F.

- AMPLIFICATION DES BASSES
- DOUBLE CASSETTE

La mini-chaîne compacte PO/FM stéréo avec système Bass Booster (suramplification des basses). Platine tourne-disque manuelle, arrêt automatique. Cellule céramique. Capot de protection avec hublot. **Tuner analogique PO/FM. Ampli.** Sélecteur de fonctions. Prise jack 3,5 mm. Sortie 2 HP. **Lecteur enregistreur double cassette.** Lecture en continu. Ejection amortie. Avance/retour rapide. Prise jack 3,5 mm. **2 enceintes** amovibles. Bass Reflex. Dim. de la chaîne : prof. 30 cm, larg. 30,2 cm, haut. 30,7 cm.
Livraison normale : 743.0233. 995 F
En 24 H. chez vous : 743.0253. 1195 F

2.

D. Renseignements. If you were going to move in with a classmate, what information would you need to know?

EXEMPLE — **Quelle est ton adresse?**
— **Mon adresse est le 2114, rue Duval.**

son adresse	*son numéro de téléphone*
LE NUMÉRO DE SON APPARTEMENT	
SON CODE POSTAL	???

E. Questions. Find out more about a classmate by asking these questions.

1. Quelle est ton adresse? Est-ce que c'est loin d'ici ou près d'ici?
2. Comment est ton appartement (ta maison, ta résidence)? Comment est le quartier? Est-ce que l'arrêt d'autobus est loin?
3. Est-ce que tu habites seul(e) ou est-ce que tu partages ton appartement (ta maison, ta chambre) avec un(e) ami(e)? Comment est ton/ta camarade de chambre?
4. Est-ce que tu as un bureau? un ordinateur? Qu'est-ce que tu voudrais avoir pour ta chambre? pour ton salon? pour ta cuisine?

F. Un abonnement. You are selling subscriptions for *Brune* magazine and you have just sold your first one. Ask the customer for the information you need to fill out the form. Play both roles with a classmate.

EXEMPLE — **Quel est votre nom?**
— **Mon nom? C'est Sodji.**
— **Quel est votre prénom?**

BULLETIN D'ABONNEMENT

Je désire m'abonner pour un an (4 numéros) à BRUNE.

TARIFS (par avion, sauf France)

7 000 F CFA	**Afrique Zone CFA**	**88 FF**	**France**
10 000 F CFA	**Afrique Hors Zone CFA**	**140 FF**	**CEE**
40 $	**USA-Canada**	**120 FF**	**Dom-Tom**

Règlement exclusivement par mandat international libellé en francs français. France et Dom-Tom: paiement par chèque ou mandat-lettre à l'ordre de BRUNE.

Découper et retourner ce formulaire d'abonnement accompagné de votre réglement à:

BRUNE - SERVICE ABONNEMENTS
10, rue Charles-Divry - 75014 PARIS - FRANCE

NOM ....
PRÉNOM ....
ADRESSE ....
....
CODE POSTAL..........
VILLE ....
PAYS ....

C'est à lire!

The poetry and songs of such stars as Gilles Vigneault, Diane Dufresne, Félix Leclerc, and Robert Charlebois have internationalized the **chanson québécoise**, the poetic expression of the thoughts and dreams of the people of Quebec. In the following excerpt, Gilles Vigneault celebrates the warmth and hospitality of the people of Quebec.

As you begin to read literary selections in another language, you may sometimes be aided by glosses of unknown words. However, you will still need to use your abilities to guess unfamiliar words and structures in order to fully understand. The following exercises will help you read this excerpt from *Mon pays.*

A. Mots apparentés. Find a line of the poem containing a cognate that provides the indicated information.

1. In which line does the poet say he is crying out?
2. In which line does he describe his country?
3. In which lines does he say how he prepares for his guests?
4. Which line indicates for whom he is making preparations?
5. Which line indicates that the poet believes in the brotherhood of all men?

B. Sentiments. Find the line(s) of the poem where the poet expresses these ideas.

1. Le Québec est grand et isolé.
2. Je parle à toute l'humanité.
3. Vous êtes les bienvenus dans mon pays.
4. Je passe mon temps à préparer ma maison pour des visiteurs.
5. Tous les humains sont des amis.

Mon pays

De ce grand pays solitaire
Je crie **avant que de me taire**
À tous les hommes de **la terre**
Ma maison, c'est votre maison.

Entre mes quatre murs de **glace**
Je mets mon temps et mon espace
À préparer le **feu**, la place
Pour les humains de l'horizon
Et les humains sont de ma race.

avant que de me taire *before growing silent* **la terre** *earth* **la glace** *ice* **le feu** *fire*

Gilles Vigneault

Avez-vous compris?

Interprétation. Read the poem by Gilles Vigneault, then answer these questions.

1. Comment est-ce que Vigneault trouve son pays?
2. Qu'est-ce que le poète dit à tous les hommes de la terre pour indiquer son hospitalité?
3. Comment est-ce qu'il prépare sa maison pour ses visiteurs?
4. Qu'est-ce que le poète dit pour indiquer qu'il aime tous les hommes?

Ça y est! C'est à vous!

A. Organisez-vous. Organizing your thoughts before you begin a writing assignment can greatly simplify your task. Imagine that you are responding to a roommate ad in Quebec. What would you want to know about the apartment and its occupant? Jot down as many words and phrases in French as you can under each heading, using a separate piece of paper.

LOCATION	ROOMS AND FURNISHINGS	ROOMMATE'S PERSONALITY

B. Rédaction: Une lettre. You are moving to Quebec and respond to an ad in the newspaper for a roommate. Write a letter in which you introduce yourself and tell the sort of place you are looking for. Then, write three paragraphs asking about the apartment's location, the rooms and furnishings, and what the roommate is like. Begin the letter by **Cher monsieur / Chère madame / Chère mademoiselle.** End the letter with **En attendant votre réponse, je vous prie d'agréer mes sentiments respectueux**, and sign your name.

C. Une petite annonce. Listen to this phone conversation where a student answers a want ad for a roommate. See if you can answer these questions.

1. L'appartement a combien de chambres?
2. C'est combien pour le loyer?
3. Il est près de l'université?
4. Quelle est l'adresse?

D. Agent immobilier. Imagine the interior of the house pictured below. Draw and label a floor plan, using *A. À vendre* on page 113 as a model. Then imagine that you are a real estate agent showing a customer around the home. Role-play the situation with a classmate. Your classmate should ask at least four questions.

Pour vérifier

Study the vocabulary on the facing page. Do the following exercises as a self-test, then check your answers in *Appendix C.*

Describing where and with whom you live

A. Mon appartement. Robert 's friend, Marc, is describing his apartment and his roommate. Complete his description with vocabulary from the facing page.

J'ai un appartement pas loin de l'université. J(e) ______ l'appartement avec mon camarade de chambre Jean-Paul. Le ______ est de 600 $ par mois. L'appartement est joli, mais mon camarade de chambre est très ______ . Il ______ des cigarettes et il aime passer tout son temps sur le divan du ______ . Je préfère habiter seul mais le ______ est trop cher.

B. Quel...? Robert is still talking to Marc about the apartment. What questions with **quel** did Robert ask to get these answers from Marc?

1. C'est le 835, rue Lanson.
2. C'est le 692-6554.
3. C'est le G1K 7X2.

C. Le loyer. You are making out checks for one month's rent for the apartments in these ads. Write out the numbers.

6095 HUTCHISON
1½ chauffé meublé éclairé
305 $
271-6566

AHUNTSIC: Bas duplex 5½, 640 $, 10,206 St-Charles, 385-9222.

AHUNTSIC, H. Bourassa, 1½ neuf, TRANQUILLE, 250 $, 594-0094.

Talking about what you have

D. Une chambre d'hôtel. Robert, Thomas, and Claude are staying in a hotel in **Montréal**. Robert is talking about what they have or do not have in their room. Complete the sentences with the correct form of **avoir** and **un/une/des** or **de**.

Nous ______ ______ chaises mais nous n' ______ pas ______ table. Claude ______ beaucoup ______ valises. «Combien ______ vêtements est-ce que tu ______ , Claude?» Nous ______ ______ grande commode et ______ grand placard. Claude et Thomas ______ ______ lits. J(e) n'______ pas ______ lit, mais ça va, j'aime bien dormir sur le divan. «Est-ce que vous ______ ______ lits confortables, Claude et Thomas?»

E. La Maison Blanche. Imagine how the residents of the White House might answer these questions.

1. Combien de chambres est-ce qu'il y a dans votre maison?
2. Est-ce que vos chambres sont grandes?
3. Est-ce que votre quartier est joli? vieux?

F. Chez Claude et Thomas. Refer to the drawing of Thomas's and Claude's apartment on page 99 and write at least five sentences describing their apartment and their belongings.

Vocabulaire

Describing where and with whom you live

NOMS

une adresse
un(e) ami(e)
un appartement
un arrêt d'autobus
un ascenseur
un cabinet de toilette
un(e) camarade de chambre
une chambre
un code postal
une cuisine
un escalier
un étage
une fenêtre
un immeuble
un loyer
une maison
un mur
une nationalité
un nom
un numéro de téléphone
un pays
une pièce
un placard
une porte
un prénom
un quartier
un rez-de-chaussée
une rue
une salle à manger
une salle de bains
un salon
un sous-sol
une ville
un W.-C.

ADJECTIFS

cher (chère)
commode
confortable
embêtant(e)
meilleur(e)
moderne
préféré(e)
quel(le)

VERBES

chercher
fumer
monter (l'escalier)
partager
prendre (l'ascenseur)

PRÉPOSITIONS

dans
derrière
devant
entre
loin (de)
(tout) près (de)
sous
sur

DIVERS

à la campagne
au centre-ville
au premier (deuxième...) étage
cent
en banlieue
en ville
il y a
là
mille
n'importe où
Où se trouve(nt)...?
par mois
partout
trop
un million (de)
Viens voir!
voici
voilà

Talking about what you have

NOMS

des affaires (*f*)
une affiche
un animal
un bureau
une cassette vidéo
une chaîne stéréo
une chaise
un chat
un chien
une chose
une commode
une cuisinière
un disque compact de jazz
un divan
une étagère
un fauteuil
un lecteur de disques compacts
un lit
un magnétoscope
un ordinateur
un placard
une plante
un réfrigérateur
une table
un tableau
un téléviseur
une valise
un vélo
des vêtements (*m*)
une voiture
une vue

ADJECTIFS POSSESSIFS

mon/ma/mes
ton/ta/tes
son/sa/ses
notre/nos
votre/vos
leur/leurs

DIVERS

avoir
beaucoup de
chez moi / chez toi
combien de
mets (mettre)
non plus
tout

Regional Overview
Le Québec
AREA: 594,860 square miles (1,500,000 sq. km.)
POPULATION: 6,600,000
CAPITAL: Quebec City
MAJOR INDUSTRIES: forestry, hydroelectric energy, manufacturing, technology, tourism

Carved pine weathervane from Bécancour, Québec
1875
Courtesy of the Royal Ontario Museum
Toronto, Canada

This beaver weathervane typifies the folk art of **Québec**. Other familiar creatures often found on such weathervanes are horses, cows, roosters, and fish.

Chapitre 4 Chez les parents

By the end of this chapter, you should be able to do the following in French:

- Introduce your family
- Describe people
- Describe your possessions
- Say where you go in your free time

Paysage à Hochelaga
Marc-Aurèle Fortin (1881–1970)
1931
National Gallery of Art, Ottawa
Vincent Massey Bequest, 1968

Hochelaga is a working-class neighborhood of Montreal. It is named after the Indian village where Montreal originated.

Pour commencer

TEXTBOOK TAPE

SUPPLEMENTAL VOCABULARY
un beau-père *a stepfather, a father-in-law*
une belle-mère *a stepmother, a mother-in-law*
des beaux-parents *stepparents, in-laws*
un beau-frère *a stepbrother, a brother-in-law*
une belle-sœur *a stepsister, a sister-in-law*
un frère jumeau *a twin brother*
une sœur jumelle *a twin sister*
un demi-frère *a half-brother*
une demi-sœur *a half-sister*
un petit-fils *a grandson*
une petite-fille *a granddaughter*
des petits-enfants *grandchildren*
un(e) fiancé(e)

Robert va passer le week-end chez la famille de Thomas et il regarde des photos de la famille de Thomas.

Voilà des photos de ma famille...

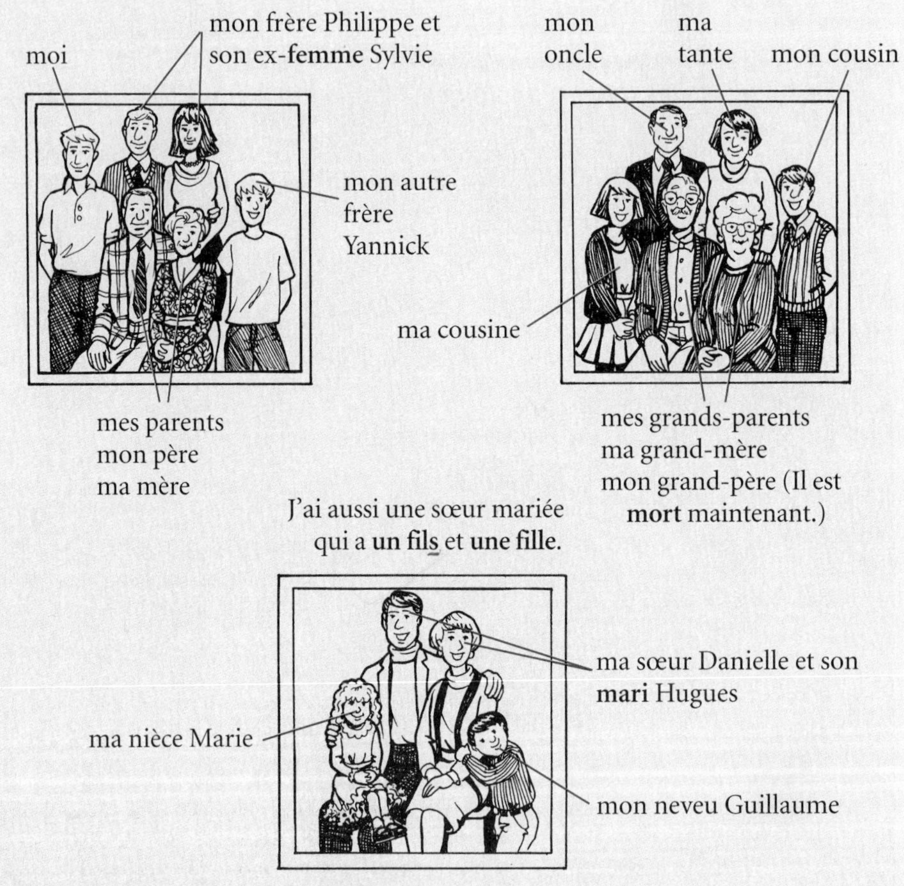

Thomas présente Robert à sa famille.

THOMAS: Papa, maman, je vous présente mon **nouveau** camarade de chambre, Robert Martin.
ROBERT: Bonjour, monsieur. Bonjour, madame.
LES ROCCO: Bonjour, Robert.
THOMAS: Ah tiens, voilà Philippe! Philippe, je te présente mon nouveau camarade de chambre. Robert, Philippe, mon frère.
PHILIPPE: Salut, Robert.
ROBERT: Bonjour, Philippe.
THOMAS: Et où est Yannick?
PHILIPPE: Il est dans le salon, **je crois**. Il **est en train de** jouer à des jeux vidéo.

une femme *wife* **mort(e)** *dead* **un fils** *son* **une fille** *daughter* **un mari** *husband* **nouveau (nouvelle)** *new* **je crois** *I believe* **être en train de** + infinitive *to be busy* + verb (*-ing* form)

Savez-vous le faire?

A. À qui parle-t-il? Écoutez ces conversations et indiquez si Thomas présente Robert **à un ami** ou **à un professeur**.

B. Présentations. Avec deux ou trois camarades de classe qui joueront les rôles indiqués, présentez un(e) de vos camarades de classe aux personnes indiquées. Utilisez **Je te présente...** ou **Je vous présente...**

Présentez un(e) camarade de classe à...

1. vos parents 2. un(e) ami(e) 3. votre professeur 4. votre frère ou votre sœur

C. Qui est-ce? Qui est probablement plus âgé(e) (*older*)?

1. la sœur / la tante
2. la nièce / la tante
3. la tante / le frère
4. le grand-père / l'oncle
5. le neveu / l'oncle
6. le mari / la fille
7. le père / le fils
8. la mère / la grand-mère
9. le cousin / l'oncle

D. C'est logique. Lisez ces listes à haute voix (*aloud*). Après, indiquez pour chaque liste le mot qui ne va pas de façon logique avec les autres.

1. ma sœur, mon frère, mes parents, mon mari
2. ma tante, ma mère, mon oncle, mes cousins
3. ma sœur, ma mère, mon père, mes parents
4. ma femme, mon mari, mon grand-père, mon ex-femme
5. mes grands-parents, mon grand-père, mon oncle, ma grand-mère

E. La généalogie. Thomas explique la parenté *(kinship)* à sa petite sœur. Complétez ses phrases.

EXEMPLE **Le père de notre père, c'est notre grand-père.**

1. Les parents de notre père, ce sont ______ .
2. Le mari de notre tante, c'est ______ .
3. Notre grand-père est marié avec ______ .
4. Le fils de notre sœur, c'est ______ .
5. La fille de notre sœur, c'est ______ .
6. Les enfants de notre oncle, ce sont ______ . Sa fille, c'est ______ et son fils, c'est ______ . Sa femme, c'est ______ .

F. Je vous présente... Présentez les membres de votre famille à la classe.

EXEMPLE **Je vous présente mes parents: mon père, Richard, ma mère...**

Je te présente mon ami, Jean-Claude.

Comment s'y prendre?

Asking for clarification

When you do not understand something that is key to your comprehension, it is useful to be able to ask for clarification. You already know three ways to do this: by asking for something to be repeated or by asking what a word means or how it is spelled.

— **Comment? Répétez, s'il vous plaît.**
— **Je ne comprends pas. Qu'est-ce que ça veut dire *belle-sœur*?**
— **Ça s'écrit comment?**

Savez-vous le faire?

TEXTBOOK TAPE

A. Je ne comprends pas. Listen to three conversations. In each, which method of requesting clarification does Robert use when he does not understand: **a**, **b**, or **c**?

a. asking for something to be repeated (**Comment? Répétez, s'il vous plaît.**)
b. asking the meaning of a word (**Qu'est-ce que ça veut dire?**)
c. asking the spelling of a word (**Ça s'écrit comment?**)

SCÈNE A

SCÈNE B

SCÈNE C

B. Comment? Listen to these three other scenes, in which one of the speakers is having difficulty understanding. In each case, what could he or she say to ask for clarification?

Qu'est-ce qui se passe?

Ma famille

Listen as Robert describes his family. Use what you know and your ability to guess logically to help you understand.

The first time listen only for the number of times someone asks for clarification.

Avez-vous compris?

A. La famille de Robert. Écoutez encore une fois (*again*) la description de la famille de Robert et complétez l'arbre généalogique (*family tree*) avec les prénoms des membres de sa famille.

B. C'est qui? Robert parle de sa famille. Complétez ses phrases. (Pour certaines phrases, il y a plusieurs [*several*] possibilités.)

1. Ma sœur Sarah...	habite à New York.
2. Mes parents...	habite à Atlanta.
3. Mes deux frères...	est mariée.
4. Mon frère Paul...	habitent avec ma mère et ma grand-mère.
5. Mon père...	est pharmacienne.
6. Ma grand-mère...	sont divorcés.
7. Ma mère Julie...	travaille.
	danse très bien.

Remarquez que...

CULTURE NOTE
The metropolitan population of Quebec City is about 650,000. It was founded in 1608. The Amerindian word **Kebec** means "a narrowing of the waters."

For historical reasons, the population of the province of Quebec is concentrated around a few large cities in the south. Quebec City, the capital and the only walled city in North America, is perched on a promontory overlooking the St. Lawrence River. In **vieux Québec** you can visit houses built in the 17th and 18th centuries and meander through galleries, cafés, restaurants, boutiques, and inns, all surrounded by stone walls and all with a distinct French flavor. Modern Quebec offers skyscrapers, business and industrial centers, and a busy port. Many foreign students come to Quebec each year to study French at Laval University, which is in Sainte-Foy, just outside the city. Founded in 1663 as the Seminary of Quebec, Laval University is the oldest university in Canada.

Québec

Montreal, the metropolis located on a large island in the St. Lawrence River, is the largest city in Quebec, and is second only to Paris in number of French-speakers. Here culture lovers can enjoy theater, jazz, dance, opera, symphony, and art galleries. In **vieux Montréal** you can appreciate the charm of the historic districts and visit restaurants and boutiques. The University of Montreal is the largest university outside of France where all classes are taught in French.

S'il fallait choisir... If you were going to study French at a Canadian university in the province of Quebec, where would you choose to go, Montreal or Quebec City? Why?

Montréal

Qu'est-ce qu'on dit?

Voici comment décrire un(e) ami(e) ou un membre de votre famille.

Comment s'appelle-t-il/elle? → Il/Elle s'appelle...

Quel âge a-t-il/elle? → Il/Elle a 21 (37, 60) ans.

Comment est-il/elle? → Il/Elle est
- jeune / âgé(e)
- grand(e) / petit(e) / **de taille moyenne**
- marié(e) / divorcé(e) / célibataire

Il/Elle **porte** des lunettes.

Il a
- une barbe
- une moustache

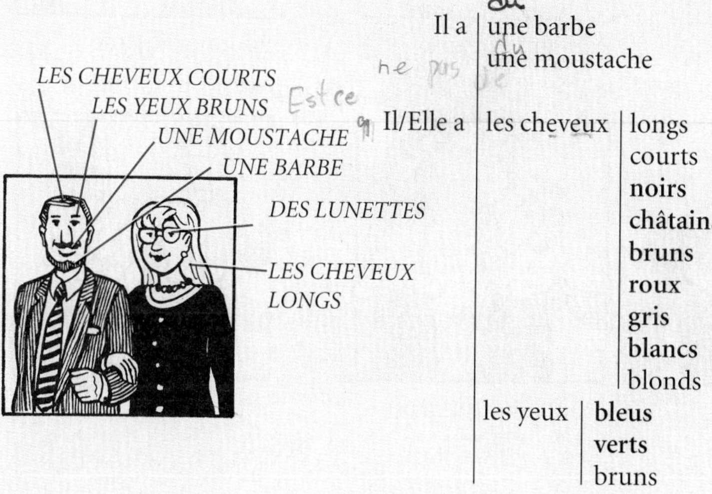

Il/Elle a
- les cheveux: longs, courts, **noirs**, **châtains**, **bruns**, **roux**, **gris**, **blancs**, blonds
- les yeux: **bleus**, **verts**, bruns

Comment va-t-il? / Comment va-t-elle? → Aujourd'hui, il/elle **a l'air**
- **fatigué(e)**
- content(e)
- **triste**
- **malade**

SUPPLEMENTAL VOCABULARY

MARITAL STATUS
fiancé(e) *engaged*
séparé(e) *separated*
remarié(e) *remarried*
veuf (veuve) *widowed*

APPEARANCE
les yeux noirs *very dark brown eyes*
les yeux couleur noisette *hazel eyes*
les cheveux mi-longs *shoulder-length hair*
des lentilles *(f)* de contact *contact lenses*
mince *thin*
gros(se) *fat*

---

de taille moyenne *medium-sized* **porter** *to wear* **noir(e)** *black* **châtain(e)** *light-brown* **brun(e)** *dark-brown* **roux (rousse)** *red* **gris(e)** *grey* **blanc (blanche)** *white* **bleu(e)** *blue* **vert(e)** *green* **avoir l'air** *to look, to seem* **fatigué(e)** *tired* **triste** *sad* **malade** *sick* omit indef article

Quelle est sa profession? → Il/Elle est...

médecin

secrétaire

avocat(e)

infirmier / infirmière

serveur / serveuse

homme / femme d'affaires

musicien(ne)

chanteur / chanteuse

acteur / actrice

SUPPLEMENTAL VOCABULARY

architecte
assistant(e) social(e) *social worker*
banquier *banker*
cadre *executive*
caissier (caissière) *cashier*
charpentier *carpenter*
coiffeur / coiffeuse *hair stylist*
dentiste
dessinateur / dessinatrice (de publicité) *graphic artist*
écrivain *writer*
employé(e)
fonctionnaire *government employee*
informaticien(ne) *computer scientist*
ingénieur *engineer*
journaliste
mécanicien(ne) *mechanic*
ouvrier (ouvrière) *manual worker*
père / mère de famille
plombier *plumber*
programmeur(-euse)
technicien(ne)
retraité(e) *retired*
vendeur / vendeuse *salesclerk*
vétérinaire

Robert parle de sa famille avec la mère de Thomas.

— Vous êtes combien dans votre famille?
— Nous sommes six. J'ai une sœur et deux frères.
— Et vos parents, ils habitent où?
— Mon père est danseur à New York mais maintenant il est **au chômage.** Ma mère est pharmacienne. Elle habite à Atlanta. Ils sont divorcés.
— Et vos frères et votre sœur, ils sont plus grands ou plus petits que vous?
— Ma sœur est plus âgée. Elle est mariée et elle habite à Chicago. Mes deux frères ont 13 et 15 ans.
— Et vous? Vous ressemblez à votre père ou à votre mère?
— Je ressemble plutôt à ma mère. Mon père a les yeux verts et les cheveux châtains.

au chômage *unemployed*

A. C'est logique? Répétez toutes les possibilités logiques.

1. avoir les cheveux (roux, noirs, bruns, bleus, blonds, gris)
2. avoir les yeux (bleus, blonds, gris, verts, bruns)
3. avoir une barbe (noire, rousse, verte, blonde, grise)

B. Insulte ou compliment? Dites si chaque phrase est une insulte ou un compliment. Transformez les insultes en compliments.

1. Votre père a l'air sympathique.
2. Votre frère a l'air bête.
3. Votre mère a l'air jeune.
4. Votre oncle a l'air méchant.
5. Votre grand-mère a l'air très âgée.
6. Vous avez l'air content.

C. Qui est-ce? Voilà des descriptions. Indiquez le nom d'une personne célèbre *(famous)* qui correspond à chaque *(each)* description.

1. Il est mort.
2. Elle est morte.
3. Elle est musicienne.
4. Il a les cheveux longs.
5. Ils sont divorcés.
6. Ils sont mariés.
7. Il a une barbe.
8. Elle est divorcée.
9. Il porte des lunettes.

D. Quelle profession? Qui est mieux payé?

1. un acteur / un serveur
2. un médecin / un infirmier
3. une avocate / un professeur
4. une pharmacienne / une secrétaire
5. un danseur / une personne au chômage
6. une femme d'affaires / un homme d'affaires

Voilà pourquoi!

C'est... Ce sont...

Use **Qui est-ce?** to ask *who* someone is and **Qu'est-ce que c'est?** to ask *what* something is.

Use **c'est...** and **ce sont...** to answer these questions.

> ***C'est* mon neveu. / *Ce sont* mes neveux.**
> ***C'est* notre voiture. / *Ce sont* nos voitures.**

C'est and **ce sont** are used instead of **il est / elle est** and **ils sont /elles sont** when you are identifying *who* or *what* someone or something is. In other cases, you will generally use **il(s)** and **elle(s)** to talk about people and things.

***Ce n'est pas* Robert.**	***Ce ne sont pas* les amies de Robert.**
***C'est* Thomas.**	***Ce sont* les amies de Thomas.**
***Il est* de Montréal.**	***Elles sont* au café.**
***Il est* intelligent.**	***Elles sont* intelligentes.**

SELF-CHECK

1. What question do you ask if you want someone to identify something in French? To identify someone?
2. What are two ways of saying *He's a doctor.* in French? When do you not translate the word *a*?
3. What six adjective / profession endings have slightly irregular patterns in the feminine form?

Les adjectifs, les professions et les nationalités

To tell someone's profession or nationality, you can use **c'est / ce sont** *with* an article or **il est / elle est / ils sont / elles sont** *without* an article.

C'est un acteur. / Il est acteur. **C'est un Canadien. / Il est canadien.**

You must use **c'est / ce sont** if the word for the profession or nationality is modified.

C'est un acteur intéressant. / C'est un étudiant du cours de français.

Most professions have masculine and feminine, singular and plural forms like adjectives. Many form the feminine by adding **-e** to the masculine form.

Il est avocat. Il est intelligent. **Il est étudiant. Il est petit.**
Elle est avocate. Elle est intelligente. **Elle est étudiante. Elle est petite.**

Note the patterns in the agreement of adjectives and professions with the following endings.

			MASCULINE	FEMININE
-eux	→	-euse	paresseux	paresse**use**
-eur	→	-euse	danseur	dans**euse**
-en	→	-enne	moyen pharmacien	moy**enne** pharmaci**enne**
-er	→	-ère	cher infirmier	ch**ère** infirmi**ère**
-el	→	-elle	intellectuel	intellectu**elle**
-if	→	-ive	sportif	sport**ive**

Form the plural of adjectives and professions by adding **-s**, unless they already end in **s** or **x**.

Il est sportif. Il est sérieux. **Ils sont sportifs. Ils sont sérieux.**

A few names of professions like **médecin** and **professeur** exist only in the masculine form.

Il est médecin. / C'est un médecin. **Elle est médecin. / C'est *un* médecin.**
Il est professeur. / C'est un professeur. **Elle est professeur. / C'est *un* professeur.**

If you need to indicate that the person in one of these professions is a woman, you can add **femme** in front of the name of the profession.

C'est une femme médecin.

Et ça se prononce comment?

La combinaison **eu**

TEXTBOOK TAPE

Many words describing friends and family members contain the letter combination **eu**. To pronounce **eu** in words like **chanteur** and **sœur,** pronounce the **è** in **mère** or **père** and pucker your lips. When **eu** is the last sound of a syllable, or if it is followed by **s**, pronounce it with the tongue arched a little higher. Compare the following:

chanteur   neuf   sœur   chanteuse   paresseux   vieux

Savez-vous le faire?

TEXTBOOK TAPE

A. Comme chanteur ou comme chanteuse? Écoutez et décidez si on prononce chaque **eu** comme **chanteur** ou comme **chanteuse.**

deux neveux	des professeurs ennuyeux	un acteur préféré
les cheveux roux	des sœurs paresseuses	neuf vieux chiens
les yeux bleus	des disques de chanteurs canadiens	des amis sérieux

Maintenant dites si vous avez les choses ou les personnes nommées sur la liste.

B. Qu'est-ce que c'est? ou Qui est-ce? La petite nièce de Thomas pose beaucoup de questions. Comment est-ce que Thomas répond? Jouez les deux rôles.

EXEMPLE — Qui est-ce?
— **C'est mon camarade de chambre, Claude.**

EXEMPLE

1.

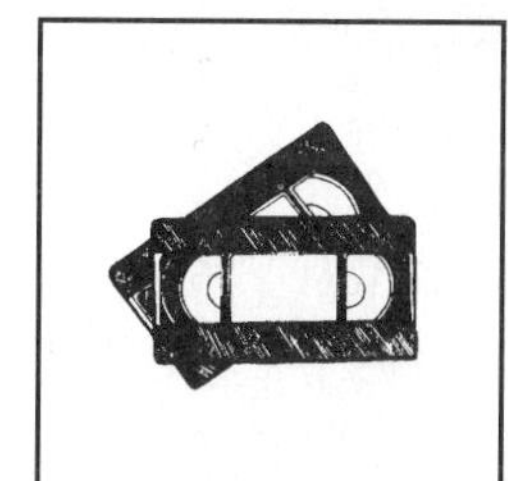
2.

3.

4.

5.

C. Qui est-ce? Écrivez le prénom de trois membres de votre famille sur une feuille de papier. Donnez la feuille à un(e) camarade de classe qui va deviner *(will guess)* l'identité de chaque personne sur votre liste. Faites la même chose *(do the same)* pour sa liste. Finalement, parlez de la famille de votre partenaire à la classe.

EXEMPLE Tracy / Susie / Felipe

— **Tracy? Est-ce que c'est ta mère?**
— **Non, ce n'est pas ma mère.**
— **Est-ce que c'est ta tante?**
— **Oui, c'est ma tante.**

Après, à la classe: **Sa tante s'appelle Tracy, sa mère s'appelle Susie...**

D. Quelle profession? Quelle est une profession ou une situation logique pour les personnes suivantes?

EXEMPLES Mon cousin travaille dans un hôpital. → **Il est infirmier (médecin).**

Ma cousine travaille dans un hôpital. → **Elle est infirmière (médecin).**

1. Ma mère travaille dans une clinique.
2. Ma sœur travaille dans un théâtre.
3. Son mari travaille aussi dans un théâtre.
4. Mes cousines travaillent dans le commerce.
5. Mon père joue dans un orchestre.
6. Mes grands-parents travaillent à l'université.
7. Mon oncle ne travaille pas maintenant mais il cherche un travail.
8. Sa femme travaille dans un restaurant.

E. Camarades de classe. Parlez à un(e) camarade de classe pour obtenir ces renseignements. Ensuite, décrivez votre partenaire à la classe.

Find out . . .
- if he/she is married.
- if he/she has any children.
- how many people are in his/her family.
- how many brothers / sisters he/she has.
- what his/her mother's name is.
- what his/her father's name is.
- where his/her parents live.
- if his/her parents work and what their professions are.
- if his/her grandparents are deceased.

F. On rend visite à la famille. Vous invitez votre camarade de chambre ou un(e) ami(e) chez vous pour le week-end et il/elle vous pose (*asks you*) des questions pour mieux connaître (*to know*) votre famille. Jouez la scène avec un(e) partenaire. Parlez de votre famille ou d'une famille imaginaire, si vous préférez. Faites une description physique et parlez de leur travail.

Voilà pourquoi!

Les descriptions avec **avoir**

Avoir is used in many expressions describing people.

J'ai les yeux bleus. **Elles ont les cheveux noirs.** **Il a une barbe.**

Use the following expressions to ask and say how old someone is.

Quel âge avez-vous? → **J'ai vingt ans.**
Quel âge as-tu?
Quel âge a ton frère? → **Il a trente et un ans.**

To say that someone *seems / looks* + adjective, use **avoir l'air** + adjective.

Tu as l'air fatigué(e) aujourd'hui. **Ta sœur a l'air contente.**

SELF-CHECK

1. How do you ask how old someone is? How do you tell your age?
2. How would you tell a friend that he/she looks sick?

Savez-vous le faire?

A. Quel âge ont-ils? Devinez (*Guess*) l'âge des gens suivants. Chaque fois, le professeur va répondre si la personne est plus âgée ou moins âgée que vous pensez.

EXEMPLE Meryl Streep → — **Elle a trente ans?**
— **Non, elle est plus âgée que ça.**
— **Elle a cinquante ans?**
— **Non, elle est moins âgée.**
— **Elle a quarante-cinq ans?...**

1. Connie Chung
2. John Candy
3. Bill Cosby
4. Gérard Depardieu
5. Carol Burnett
6. Madonna

Maintenant, décrivez l'apparence physique de ces gens.

EXEMPLE **Meryl Streep est grande et jolie. Elle a les cheveux blonds et...**

B. Qui est-ce? Écrivez votre nom sur une feuille de papier. Le professeur va redistribuer (*will redistribute*) les feuilles de papier. Le reste de la classe va poser des questions pour deviner le nom qui est écrit sur votre feuille de papier. Répondez **oui** ou **non** à leurs questions.

EXEMPLE — **Est-ce que c'est une femme?** → — **Oui.**
— **Est-ce qu'elle a les cheveux bruns?** → — **Non.**
— **Est-ce qu'elle est devant Susan?** → — **Oui.**
— **Est-ce qu'elle est derrière Lewis?** → — **Oui.**
— **C'est Alisha, n'est-ce pas?** → — **Oui.**

C. Ça va? Utilisez l'expression **avoir l'air** pour décrire l'apparence de ces gens.

EXEMPLE **Elle a l'air malade.**

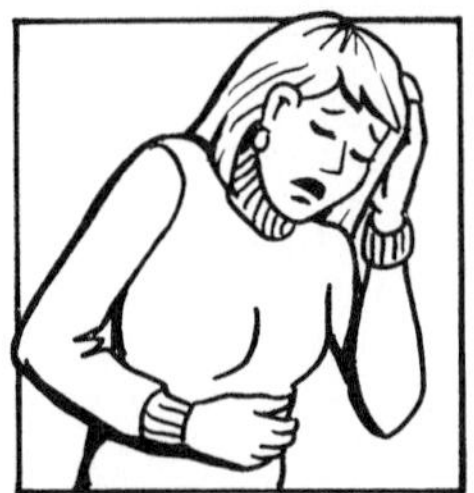

EXEMPLE

1.

2.

3.

4.

5.

D. Au festival de la neige. Chaque année (*Each year*), il y a un festival de la neige (*snow*) au Québec. Regardez la photo et donnez vos impressions. Utilisez **Ça a l'air...**

amusant	*bête*	**ENNUYEUX**
INTÉRESSANT	**agréable**	**désagréable**
super	*sensationnel*	BIZARRE

Au festival de la neige

SUJET DE CONVERSATION 2
Describing possessions

Qu'est-ce qu'on dit?

Vous **achetez** des nouveaux **rideaux** pour votre chambre. Quelle couleur préférez-vous?

Je préfère le...

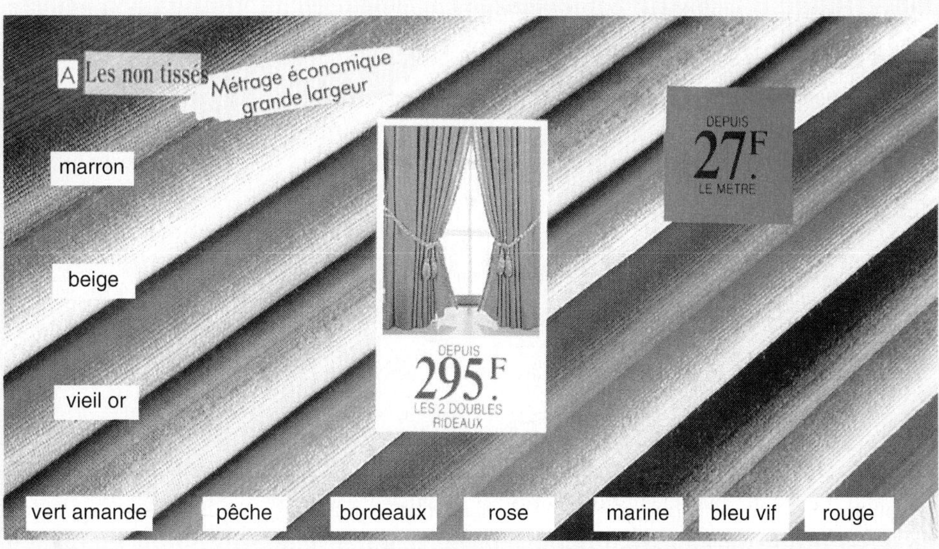

Et quelle sorte de voiture est-ce que vous avez?

J'ai une	**grosse** voiture.	J'ai une voiture	américaine.	J'ai une voiture	noire.
	petite		anglaise		blanche
	nouvelle		allemande		rouge
	vieille		française		bleue
	bonne		japonaise		**jaune**
	mauvaise				orange

Thomas et Robert **font un tour** au **jardin.**

— Voici le garage. Mon père passe beaucoup de temps ici.
— Quelle belle voiture!
— Elle est **des années trente**. Mon père adore les vieilles voitures européennes.
— Moi, j'aime mieux les nouvelles voitures. **Surtout** les petites voitures de sport italiennes.
— Tu voudrais aller voir le jardin? Ma mère a beaucoup de jolies **fleurs**.
— Elle passe beaucoup de temps dans le jardin?
— Oui, c'est sa passion!

acheter *to buy* **des rideaux** (*m pl*) *curtains* **gros(se)** *big, fat* **bon(ne)** *good* **mauvais(e)** *bad* **jaune** *yellow* **font un tour (faire un tour)** *take a walk around* **un jardin** *a garden* **des années trente** *from the thirties* **surtout** *especially* **une fleur** *a flower*

A. Quels objets? Trouvez les noms (*nouns*) de la liste suivante que les adjectifs indiqués pourraient (*could*) décrire. Faites attention à la forme de l'adjectif.

un homme, une femme, un divan, des fleurs, une voiture, une plante, un vélo, des vêtements, un chat, une barbe, des chaises

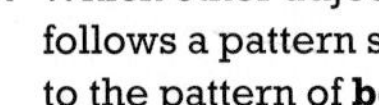

1. rousse	3. rouge	5. bleues	7. blonde	9. brun	11. blanches
2. roux	4. blond	6. bleus	8. blanc	10. brune	12. verte

B. Opinions. Nommez une chose ou une personne pour chacune des descriptions suivantes.

EXEMPLE une voiture chère → **une Mercedes**

1. une voiture américaine
2. une grosse voiture
3. une petite voiture
4. une mauvaise voiture
5. une bonne voiture
6. un acteur européen
7. un bon acteur
8. un mauvais acteur
9. un acteur roux

Voilà pourquoi!

Quelques adjectifs irréguliers

The following adjectives have irregular forms.

MASCULINE		FEMININE	
SINGULAR	PLURAL	SINGULAR	PLURAL
beau	beaux	belle	belles
nouveau	nouveaux	nouvelle	nouvelles
vieux	vieux	vieille	vieilles
bon	bons	bonne	bonnes
gros	gros	grosse	grosses
roux	roux	rousse	rousses
long	longs	longue	longues
blanc	blancs	blanche	blanches
tout	tous	toute	toutes

SELF-CHECK

1. Which other adjective follows a pattern similar to the pattern of **beau** and **vieux**?
2. Which adjectives double their final consonant before adding **-e** in the feminine form? What other adjectives have you learned that do this?
3. Which two adjectives add a different letter before adding **-e**?
4. Which adjectives have plurals ending in **-x**?

Et ça se prononce comment?

La lettre l

In English, there are two pronunciations of the letter *l*. Some words have a light *l*, pronounced with the tongue held up in the front-central part of the mouth: *lift, lack, leap*. Other words have a heavier sounding *l*, pronounced with the tongue held low in the back of the mouth: *full, pill, file*. The French **l** is pronounced more like the light *l* of *lift* or *leap*. It is never pronounced like the heavy *l* of *full* or *file*.

nouvelle belle blanc intellectuelle longue il s'appelle elle

When the letters **ll** are preceded by an **i**, they are generally pronounced like the *y* in *yes.*

famille **fille** **travaille** **vieille**

The words **mille, million, tranquille, ville,** and their derivatives do not follow this rule. Also note that the **l** in **fils** (*son*) is not pronounced, but the **s** is.

Savez-vous le faire?

A. Préférences. Complétez les phrases suivantes avec les mots que vous entendez. Ensuite, répondez à chaque question.

Est-ce que vous préférez avoir...

1. une grande ______ ou une petite ______?
2. une ______ voiture ou une ______ voiture?
3. une fille ______ ou une fille ______?
4. une ______ ou un ______?
5. une maison dans une petite ______ tranquille ou dans une grande ______ intéressante?

B. Tout le contraire! L'oncle et la tante de Thomas sont très différents. D'après la description de son oncle, jouez le rôle de Thomas et décrivez sa tante.

EXEMPLE Mon oncle est petit. → **Ma tante n'est pas petite. Elle est grande.**

1. Mon oncle est mince.
2. Mon oncle est laid.
3. Mon oncle est plus jeune.
4. Mon oncle a les cheveux longs.
5. Mon oncle est pessimiste.
6. Mon oncle est embêtant.
7. La voiture de mon oncle est vieille.
8. La voiture de mon oncle est mauvaise.

C. Interview. Posez les questions suivantes à un(e) camarade de classe.

1. À qui est-ce que tu ressembles dans ta famille?
2. Comment sont tes parents? Est-ce qu'ils sont grands, petits ou de taille moyenne? Est-ce qu'ils ont les cheveux blonds, roux, bruns, noirs, blancs ou gris? Est-ce qu'ils ont les yeux verts, bruns, gris bleus ou noirs? Est-ce que ton père a une barbe ou une moustache? des lunettes?
3. Quel âge ont-ils? Est-ce qu'ils ont l'air encore (*still*) jeunes? Quel âge as-tu?
4. Quel(le)s acteurs / actrices est-ce que tu trouves beaux / belles? Pourquoi? Quel(le)s acteurs / actrices ont l'air intelligent(e)s? bêtes?
5. Qui dans la classe a l'air fatigué? Qui a l'air content?

D. Tu voudrais sortir? Vous proposez à un(e) ami(e) canadien(ne) de sortir avec votre cousin(e). Votre ami(e) vous pose (*asks you*) beaucoup de questions et vous lui décrivez votre cousin(e). Inventez une conversation avec un(e) partenaire.

Voilà pourquoi!

SELF-CHECK

1. How do you ask what color something is? Where are adjectives of color placed with respect to nouns they describe?
2. Which of the following adjectives are placed before the noun they describe: **grand**, **moderne**, **beau**, **laid**, **sympathique**, **bon**, **mauvais?**
3. When do you use the forms **bel**, **nouvel**, and **vieil**?
4. Is the adjective **tout/toute/tous/toutes** placed directly before the noun it describes?

Les couleurs

To ask what color something is, use **De quelle couleur est/sont...?** When colors describe a noun, they must agree with it, except for **orange** and **marron** (*reddish-brown*), which have only one form, and do not agree. Note the irregular feminine forms of **blanc(he)** and **violet(te)**.

— De quelle couleur sont vos vêtements? → — **Ils sont bleus et orange.**
— De quelle couleur sont ces fleurs? → — **Elles sont blanches et violettes.**
— De quelle couleur est ta voiture? → — **Elle est rouge.**

La place des adjectifs

In French, most adjectives are placed after the noun they describe.

Nous avons une voiture *rouge.*
Je préfère les appartements *modernes.*
Ma mère a les cheveux *roux* et les yeux *verts.*

A few adjectives go before the noun. They include:

beau	jeune	bon	grand	autre
joli	vieux	mauvais	petit	même
	nouveau		gros	

J'ai un *petit* appartement *laid.* Je voudrais un *autre* appartement.
Est-ce que tu as des *bons* amis?
Nous avons une *grosse* voiture *américaine.* C'est une *belle* voiture.
Mes parents ont une *nouvelle* maison en banlieue.

The adjectives **beau, nouveau,** and **vieux** have alternate masculine forms, **bel, nouvel,** and **vieil**, which are used before nouns beginning with a vowel sound.

MASCULINE BEFORE CONSONANTS	MASCULINE BEFORE VOWELS
un *beau* quartier	un *bel* appartement
un *nouveau* quartier	un *nouvel* appartement
un *vieux* quartier	un *vieil* appartement

The adjective **tout** (*all, whole*) is placed before a noun's article. It means *the whole* before singular nouns and *all* before plural nouns. A useful expression with **tout** is **tout le monde** (*everybody*).

Tout le quartier est calme.	*The whole neighborhood is calm.*
Toute la classe est ici.	*The whole class is here.*
Tous mes amis parlent français.	*All my friends speak French.*
Toutes les maisons sont très belles.	*All the houses are very pretty.*
Tout le monde est content.	*Everyone is happy.*

F. Une famille idéale. Dites quelle sorte de famille et de maison vous voudriez avoir.

EXEMPLE une fille → **Je voudrais avoir une fille intelligente.**

1. un mari / une femme
2. un fils
3. un chien
4. une chambre
5. une maison
6. une cuisine
7. un jardin
8. une voiture

grand *actif* SPORTIF
NOUVEAU **européen**
JOLI ***INTELLIGENT***
beau **PETIT**
SYMPATHIQUE **???**
bon vieux
??? **INTÉRESSANT**

G. Tous. Dites si les phrases suivantes décrivent tous vos amis, toute votre famille ou toutes vos affaires.

EXEMPLE Mes amis sont d'ici. → **Oui, tous mes amis sont d'ici.**
Non, tous mes amis ne sont pas d'ici.

1. Mes amis sont sympathiques.
2. Ma famille habite ici.
3. Mes cours sont intéressants.
4. Mes cousins sont petits.
5. Les murs de ma chambre sont blancs.
6. Mes professeurs sont intelligents.

H. Une nouvelle voiture. Vous cherchez une nouvelle voiture et vous dites à un(e) ami(e) quelle sorte de voiture vous voudriez avoir. Préparez la scène avec un(e) autre étudiant(e).

Vous cherchez...

- une grosse voiture?
- une voiture chère?
- une voiture de sport?
- une voiture américaine?

AUDI 80
Dans le genre allemand, l'Audi est construite pour durer. Finition impeccable, fantaisie exclue et coffre assez petit signalent une belle réalisation. Le 5-cylindres n'offre que 133 ch, et la suspension trop souple n'en fait sûrement pas une sportive. Prix: 221 000 F.

Rover 200
Amélioration de la rigidité, poignée de maintien et possibilité de rabattre les dossiers arrière sont les atouts particuliers de cette anglaise. Pas très chère, la 216 (122 ch) a en série une capote électrique et une alarme fonctionnant, aussi toit rabattu. Souple et plaisante, c'est le bon rapport qualité/prix. Prix: 131 200 F.

Remarquez que...

French speakers generally do not say **merci** when complimented. To them, this would sound rather conceited. They tend to make little of what is being complimented and respond: **Vous trouvez (Tu trouves)** (*find*)?, or **Vous pensez (Tu penses)**?

Compliments. Compliment one of your classmates, who will respond in the French manner.

Saying where people go in their free time

SUPPLEMENTAL VOCABULARY
à la discothèque
aux matchs de football (de hockey, de basket-ball, de base-ball)
au stade
à la synagogue
à la mosquée

Qu'est-ce qu'on dit?

Où est-ce qu'**on va pendant** son **temps libre** où vous habitez?

On aime faire du shopping...

dans les petits magasins

au centre commercial

On achète des livres...

à la librairie

De temps en temps, on **assiste aux** activités culturelles...

au musée

au théâtre

à un concert

Pour retrouver des amis, on va...

au bar

au restaurant

à l'église

Si on aime les activités **de plein air**, on va peut-être...

au parc

à la plage

à la piscine

---

on va *one goes* **pendant** *during* **le temps libre** *free time* **de temps en temps** *from time to time* **assister à** *to attend* **pour** *in order to* **retrouver** *to meet* **de plein air** *outdoor*

— Et vous? Qu'est-ce que **vous allez faire** le week-end **prochain**?
— **Je vais** | aller **nager** au **lac**
| rester à la maison
| **louer** des cassettes vidéo
| aller voir des amis

C'est vendredi après-midi et Robert et Thomas parlent de leurs projets pour le week-end.
— Je voudrais louer une cassette vidéo ce soir. **Qu'en penses-tu?**
— C'est une bonne idée. Qu'est-ce que tu vas faire demain?
— **D'abord**, je vais déjeuner en ville avec la famille de **ma petite amie. Ensuite**, nous allons voir une exposition au musée des Beaux-Arts. Et toi? Tu vas travailler demain?
— Je vais travailler demain matin. Je vais **rentrer** vers midi et **puis** je vais passer le reste de l'après-midi chez des amis.

vous allez faire *you are going to do* **prochain(e)** *next* **je vais** *I am going to* **nager** *to swim* **le lac** *the lake* **louer** *to rent* **Qu'en penses-tu?** *What do you think?* **d'abord** *first* **mon/ma petit(e) ami(e)** *my boyfriend /girlfriend* **ensuite** *next* **rentrer** *to return, to come home* **puis** *then*

A. On y va pour... En équipes (*teams*), faites une liste des activités que vous associez avec les endroits suivants. Vous avez trente secondes pour chaque endroit. L'équipe avec la liste la plus complète gagne.

EXEMPLE une bibliothèque → Pour lire, étudier...

1. un restaurant
2. un cinéma
3. un magasin de musique
4. un café
5. un centre commercial
6. une piscine
7. un parc
8. une plage
9. une librairie

nager **???** *déjeuner* **lire** **dormir** DANSER
ÉTUDIER ACHETER DES LIVRES
acheter des vêtements **jouer au football**
acheter des disques ÉCOUTER DES DISQUES
manger voir un film *dîner* PARLER ???
retrouver des amis **faire du shopping**

B. Et ensuite? Qu'est-ce que Robert dit qu'il va faire d'abord et qu'il va faire ensuite?

EXEMPLE manger / préparer le dîner
D'abord, je vais préparer le dîner et ensuite, je vais manger.

1. rentrer à la maison / dormir
2. dîner au restaurant avec elle / retrouver ma petite amie en ville
3. travailler tout l'après-midi / aller prendre un verre avec des amis
4. rentrer à la maison / jouer au tennis avec Claude
5. acheter des vêtements / sortir danser avec des amis ce soir
6. passer toute la journée à la maison / louer des cassettes vidéo

Voilà pourquoi!

> **SELF-CHECK**
> 1. When do you use the pronoun **on**? What form of the verb do you use with **on**?
> 2. What are the forms of **aller**?
> 3. With which forms of the definite article does **à** contract? With which forms does it not contract?

Le pronom sujet **on**

Use **on** as the subject when you are referring to people in general (*one, people, they*). Consider the difference between these sentences.

Mes parents? Ils parlent français.	*My parents? They speak French.*	(specific people)
À Paris, on parle français.	*In Paris they speak French.*	(general group)

On always takes the same form of the verb as **il** and **elle**.

Le verbe **aller**

To talk about going places, you will use the irregular verb **aller** (*to go*).

ALLER (*TO GO*)	
je **vais**	nous‿**allons**
tu **vas**	vous‿**allez**
il/elle/on **va**	ils/elles **vont**

Je vais souvent au parc.
Vous allez au centre commercial?

Remember that you also use **aller** when greeting someone.

— Comment allez-vous?	**— Comment ça va?**
— Je vais bien, merci.	**— Ça va. Et toi, ça va?**

La préposition **à**

To talk about where you are or where you are going, use **à** (*to, at, in*). When **à** falls before **le** or **les**, the two words contract to **au** or **aux**.

CONTRACTIONS WITH À			
à + le	→	au	Je vais **au** cinéma.
à + la	→	à la	Je vais **à la** librairie.
à + l'	→	à l'	Je vais **à** l'église.
à + les	→	aux	Je vais **aux** matchs de football.

You can also use **à** to say whom you are talking to or phoning.

Je parle *à l'*ami de Sylvie.
Tu téléphones *aux* parents de Thomas?

Et ça se prononce comment?

Les lettres **a** et **au**

Pronounce the letters **a** and **au** distinctly.

- Pronounce **a** or **à** with the mouth wide open as in the word *father*.

Ton *a*mi v*a* *à* l*a* pl*a*ge. **Tu v*a*s *à* P*a*ris *a*vec t*a* c*a*m*a*r*a*de.**

- Pronounce **au** like the **o** in **nos.**

Paul va *au* rest*au*rant? **Les *au*tres vont *au*ssi avec Paul?**

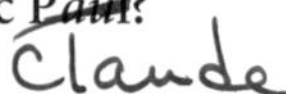

Savez-vous le faire?

A. Où va Thomas? Thomas parle des endroits (*places*) qu'il aime visiter. Écoutez et complétez les mots avec **a** ou **au**.

Je vais souvent...

1. au musée d'Art de Saint-L___rent
2. au Parc S___f___ri
3. au restaurant L'___berge
4. à la g___lerie Le Ch___riot
5. à la bibliothèque municip___le
6. au café Cent___r

B. Pourquoi ça? Expliquez pourquoi Thomas va à chacun des endroits indiqués dans l'exercice précédent. Faites attention à la prononciation.

EXEMPLE **Il va au musée d'Art de Saint-Laurent pour voir une exposition.**

C. Assez souvent? Demandez si vos camarades de classe vont souvent aux endroits indiqués.

EXEMPLE le restaurant → **— Tu vas souvent au restaurant?**
— Je vais rarement au restaurant.

souvent ***quelquefois*** ***rarement*** ***ne... jamais***

1. le lac
2. la plage
3. la bibliothèque
4. l'église
5. le musée
6. la piscine
7. le centre commercial
8. les expositions d'art

D. Tout le monde sort. Thomas parle de sa famille et de ses amis. Où est-ce qu'ils vont? Complétez ses phrases.

Robert et moi

mes parents

Claude

Philippe et Yannick

mon professeur de français

le chien de Claude

EXEMPLE **Moi, je vais à la piscine.**

1. Robert et moi, nous...
2. Mes parents...
3. Claude...
4. Philippe et Yannick, vous...?
5. Mon professeur de français...
6. Le chien de Claude...

E. Ici on... Dites deux choses qu'on fait souvent dans votre région et deux autres choses qu'on ne fait pas souvent.

EXEMPLE **On aime aller à la plage... On ne va pas souvent au lac...**

F. **Des touristes.** Ces touristes lisent le *Guide touristique de Montréal.* Où est-ce qu'ils vont?

EXEMPLE **Maria Elena va au cinéma.**

Cinéma Imax
Au Vieux-Port de Montréal, angle boulevard Saint-Laurent et rue de la Commune
(514) 496-4629 (Renseignements)
(514) 496-1799 (Réservations de groupes)
(514) 522-1245 (Achats téléphoniques, RÉSEAU ADMISSION)
1-800-361-4595 (Achats ext. de Montréal)
Place-d'Armes

Des images d'une précision et d'une qualité à couper le souffle, projetées sur un écran haut comme un immeuble de 7 étages. IMAX, c'est le cinéma grandeur nature, le nouveau standard de perfection. Pendant l'été, IMAX est combiné avec l'exposition EXPOTEC.

EXEMPLE Maria Elena...

Maisons de la Culture (514) 872-6211
On compte à Montréal douze maisons de la Culture dont la plupart se composent d'une section bibliothèque aussi bien que d'une section diffusion culturelle (salles d'exposition et de spectacles, ateliers, cinéma, et rencontres conférences). Spectacles (cirque, magie, clownerie, marionnettes) pour surtout plaire aux enfants.
Horaire: Du mardi au jeudi: de 13h à 21 h; du vendredi au dimanche: de 13h à 17h; lundi: fermé. **Entrée gratuite.**

1. Chester et Ruth...

Université McGill
Centre d'accueil
805, rue Sherbrooke Ouest, Salle Burnside, Bureau 105
(514) 398-6555 McGill

James McGill (1744-1813), négociant et homme politique canadien, fit fortune dans le commerce des fourrures. À sa mort, il légua à l'institution royale pour l'avancement des sciences la somme de dix mille livres sterling et son domaine Burnside pour qu'on y érige une université ou un collège. En 1821, l'institution reçut sa première charte des mains du roi George IV et le Collège McGill fut ainsi créé. Les cours débutèrent en 1829, année où fut annexé le collège de médecine de Montréal. À noter, la stèle marquant le site du village amérindien Hochelaga ainsi que le musée Peter Redpath des sciences naturelles, le premier édifice conçu comme musée au Canada.
Horaire: On peut visiter le musée Redpath ((514) 398-4086)) de 9h à 17h du lundi au vendredi, de septembre à juin, et du lundi au jeudi, du 24 juin à la fête du Travail.
Visites commentées du campus sur préavis de 24 heures. (514) 398-6555

2. Lin Chen...

Parc Olympique ★
4141, avenue Pierre-De Coubertin (514) 252-8687
Pie-IX ou Viau

Site des Jeux Olympiques d'été de 1976, le parc est d'une architecture très avant-gardiste. Il compte la plus haute **tour inclinée** au monde, et ses installations, comme le Stade et les **piscines**, sont accessibles au public. Le guide Michelin donne trois étoiles—la plus haute cote possible pour un attrait touristique—à la tour, pour sa vue panoramique et son complexe sportif. Le Parc olympique est aussi relié, par un passage en contrebas, au **parc Maisonneuve**. Des visites commentées ainsi qu'un spectacle audiovisuel sont disponibles. Une navette, durant la saison estivale, relie gratuitement le Parc au **Jardin botanique** à partir du hall touristique. **Visites commentées du Parc**: de septembre à mai: tous les jours à 11h et à 14h; de juin à août: tous les jours de 9h à 17h. **Funiculaire**: d'octobre à avril, tous les jours de 10h à 18h; de mai à septembre incl., de 10h à 23h; fermé de la mi-janvier à la mi-février et ouvre à midi tous les lundis de l'année.
Entrée: Adultes: 5,50$; enfants: 3,75$.

3. Daniel et Sarah...

Voilà pourquoi!

Le futur immédiat

To talk about what you are going to do, use **aller** followed by an infinitive.

Qu'est-ce que tu *vas faire* aujourd'hui?

Il y a becomes **il va y avoir** when you want to say what *there is going to be / there are going to be.*

***Il va y avoir* beaucoup de choses à faire.**

In the negative, put the **ne... pas** around the conjugated form of **aller.**

Je *ne* vais *pas* rester à la maison.
Il *ne* vont *pas* être là.

SELF-CHECK

1. How do you say what you are going to do? How do you negate **aller** + infinitive?
2. When do you use **le** with **matin**, **après-midi**, **soir**, **week-end**, or a day of the week?

Here are some expressions you can use to tell when you are going to do something.

maintenant	*now*	**plus tard**	*later*
aujourd'hui	*today*	**demain**	*tomorrow*
ce matin	*this morning*	**demain matin**	*tomorrow morning*
cet après-midi	*this afternoon*	**demain après-midi**	*tomorrow afternoon*
ce soir	*tonight*	**demain soir**	*tomorrow evening*
ce week-end	*this weekend*	**le week-end prochain**	*next weekend*
cette semaine	*this week*	**la semaine prochaine**	*next week*
lundi	*Monday*	**lundi prochain**	*next Monday*
ce mois-ci	*this month*	**le mois prochain**	*next month*
cette année	*this year*	**l'année prochaine**	*next year*

To say that you do something at the same time each day or week, use the definite article **le.**

Je travaille le week-end. *I work on weekends.*
Nous sommes en classe le matin. *We are in class in the morning.*

Savez-vous le faire?

A. Leurs projets. Thomas parle à Robert de ses projets et des projets de ses amis pour le week-end prochain. Qu'est-ce qu'il dit?

EXEMPLE **Claude va dormir tard.**

EXEMPLE Claude...

1. Je...

2. Tu...?

3. Ta petite amie et toi, vous...?

4. Nous...

5. Nos amis...

B. Projets. Demandez à un(e) camarade de classe ce qu'il/elle va faire aux moments indiqués.

EXEMPLE ce soir → — **David, qu'est-ce que tu vas faire ce soir?**
— **Je vais sortir avec des amis.**
OU **Je n'ai pas de projets pour ce soir.**

1. demain après-midi
2. vendredi soir
3. samedi matin
4. la semaine prochaine
5. dimanche soir
6. plus tard, après les cours

C. Quel jour? Demandez quel jour votre camarade de classe préfère faire les choses suivantes. Ensuite, demandez-lui s'il /si elle va faire cette activité cette semaine.

EXEMPLE aller au cinéma

— **Quel jour est-ce que tu vas au cinéma d'habitude?**
— **Je vais au cinéma le vendredi soir ou le dimanche.**
— **Est-ce que tu vas aller au cinéma ce week-end?**
— **Non, je ne vais pas aller au cinéma cette semaine.**

1. louer une cassette vidéo
2. rester à la maison
3. parler à ses parents
4. aller au centre commercial
5. regarder la télévision
6. aller danser

D. Votre ville. La semaine prochaine, un groupe d'étudiants français va visiter votre ville. Vous êtes leur guide. Dites où vous allez aller et ce que vous allez faire.

EXEMPLE **Lundi, nous allons visiter l'université. Nous allons voir le campus et...**

Voilà pourquoi!

Ce (cet)/cette/ces

SELF-CHECK
When do you use the alternate masculine form **cet**?

To say both *this/these* and *that/those,* use the adjective **ce (cet)/cette/ces.** Use **ces** with all plural nouns, both masculine and feminine. The masculine singular **ce** becomes **cet** before nouns beginning with a vowel sound.

	SINGULAR	PLURAL
MASCULINE BEFORE CONSONANTS	**ce** film	**ces** films
MASCULINE BEFORE VOWELS	**cet** appartement	**ces** appartements
FEMININE	**cette** université	**ces** universités

If you need to distinguish *this* from *that,* you can add the suffixes **-ci** and **-là.**

Est-ce que tu préfères *cet* appartement-*ci* ou *cet* appartement-*là*?
*Do you prefer **this** apartment or **that** apartment?*

Et ça se prononce comment?

La voyelle e

You already know that a final **e** is usually not pronounced in French, except in short words like **je**. As you notice in **ce/cette/ces**, unaccented **e** has three different pronunciations, depending on what follows it.

- In short words like **ce**, **que** or followed by a single consonant within a word . . . → pronounce it as in **j*e***, **l*e***, **r*e*garder**, **vendr*e*di**.
- When, as in **ces**, it is followed by an unpronounced consonant at the end of a word . . . → pronounce it as in **l*e*s**, **m*e*s**, **parl*ez***, **mang*er***, **premi*er***
- In words like **cette** and **cet**, where it is followed by two consonants within a word, or a single pronounced consonant at the end of a word . . . → pronounce it as in **m*è*re**, ***e*lle**, **ch*e*rcher**.

Savez-vous le faire?

A. Prononcez bien! D'abord, écoutez ces phrases. Est-ce qu'elles décrivent bien votre vie à l'université? Ensuite, lisez les phrases à haute voix et répondez **C'est vrai!** ou **C'est faux!**

1. Ce livre est court.
2. Cette classe est grande.
3. Cette université est assez petite.
4. Cet exercice est facile.
5. Ces phrases sont longues.
6. Cette page est jolie.
7. Ce soir, il y a des devoirs.
8. Cette semaine, il va y avoir un examen.

B. Préférences. Robert parle de ce qu'il aime et de ce qu'il n'aime pas dans son appartement. Écoutez et décidez s'il parle d'une chose ou de plus d'une chose. Écrivez vos réponses sur une feuille de papier.

EXEMPLE VOUS ENTENDEZ: **J'aime ce quartier.**

	UNE CHOSE	PLUS D'UNE CHOSE
VOUS ÉCRIVEZ:	**ce quartier**	

C. C'est un compliment? Utilisez un élément de chaque colonne pour composer deux groupes de phrases. D'abord, faites une liste de compliments, et ensuite, faites une liste de critiques.

ce (cet)	homme	agréable
cette	femme	désagréable
ces	université	joli
	vêtements	laid
	centre commercial	beau
	restaurant	grand
	exposition	petit
	appartement	intéressant
		ennuyeux
		cher
		???

D. Dis-moi! Thomas parle à Robert de ses projets et Robert lui pose des questions. Utilisez **ce (cet)/cette/ces** pour compléter logiquement les questions de Robert.

EXEMPLE — Je vais faire du shopping au nouveau centre commercial.
— Où est *ce centre commercial*?

1. — Demain après-midi, je vais sortir avec des étudiants en ville.
   — Qui sont...?
2. — Demain soir, nous allons dîner au restaurant Le Petit Berger.
   — Où se trouve...?
3. — Ensuite, nous allons voir un film.
   — Comment s'appelle...?
4. — Vendredi, je vais jouer au tennis avec un ami.
   — Qui est...?
5. — Il habite dans la rue Belleville.
   — Où est...?

E. Préférences. Nommez votre personne préférée ou votre endroit (*place*) préféré pour chacune des catégories suivantes. Un(e) autre étudiant(e) va dire s'il/si elle est d'accord (*is in agreement*) avec vous.

EXEMPLE un magasin
— J'aime *Montgomery Ward.*
— J'aime aussi ce magasin. / Je n'aime pas ce magasin.

1. un restaurant
2. un film
3. une ville
4. une chanteuse
5. un parc
6. un acteur
7. une actrice
8. une voiture

C'est à lire!

The Canadian magazine *Vidéo-Presse* interviewed a group of francophone school children to find out what role their grandparents played in their lives. Before you read the article "Quelle place occupent tes grands-parents dans ta vie?," do this activity to help you understand it .

Sens différents. Certains mots ont un sens (*meaning*) un peu différent dans différents contextes. Est-ce que vous pouvez deviner (*can guess*) le sens différent des mots en caractères gras dans ces phrases?

1. a. Je travaille **comme** serveur dans un café.
   b. **Comme** j'habite près de mes grands-parents, nous dînons souvent ensemble.
2. a. Mon père travaille dans le **même** café.
   b. Mon grand-père est quelquefois sévère, mais j'aime mes grands-parents **quand même**.
   c. Ma grand-mère a l'air très jeune, elle n'a **même** pas de cheveux gris.
3. a. J'aime **manger**.
   b. Ma grand-mère fait bien **à manger**.

Quelle place occupent tes grands-parents dans ta vie?

***Vidéo-Presse* a rencontré un groupe de jeunes francophones de Hammond, village situé dans l'est de l'Ontario.**

Aniclaude
Mes grands-parents sont très importants dans ma vie. Comme j'habite près de la maison de ma grand-mère Gindon, nous nous voyons souvent. Je pense que ça favorise l'amitié.

France
Dans ma famille, nous sommes 27 petits-enfants. Alors, je ne peux pas toujours être avec ma grand-mère. Je l'aime quand même.

Tina
Ma grand-mère a l'air d'une vraie grand-mère. Ses cheveux sont blancs, elle est grassette un peu, porte des lunettes et fait bien à manger. Elle est très belle pour son âge et n'a même pas de rides.

Brigitte
C'est difficile d'imaginer nos grands-parents sévères. Ma grand-mère est tellement fine. C'est plus facile d'être amie avec des grands-parents qui jouent avec nous.

Extraits de *Vidéo-Presse* Vol. XX No. 9 mai 1991, pages 6-9.

Avez-vous compris?

A. C'est qui? Lisez l'article et décidez quel enfant parle dans ces phrases.

EXEMPLE Ma grand-mère a beaucoup de petits-enfants.
C'est France qui parle.

Aniclaude France Tina Brigitte

1. Il est facile d'aller voir très souvent ma grand-mère.
2. J'aime beaucoup jouer avec mes grands-parents.
3. Je voudrais voir mes grands-parents plus souvent, mais ce n'est pas possible.
4. Mes grands-parents ne sont pas sévères.
5. J'ai une grande famille.
6. J'habite tout près de la maison de mes grands-parents.
7. J'aime beaucoup la cuisine de ma grand-mère.
8. Ma grand-mère est très jolie.

B. Et vous? Écrivez une description d'un de vos grands-parents. Si vous n'avez pas de grands-parents, décrivez une autre personne qui est importante dans votre vie.

Ça y est! C'est à vous!

A. **Organisez-vous!** Vous voulez présenter un(e) ami(e) à votre famille. D'abord, lisez ***B. Rédaction: En famille*** et décidez à l'avance quelles expressions sont nécessaires pour cette situation. Ensuite, répondez aux questions suivantes.

Qu'est-ce qu'on dit pour...

- demander combien de personnes ils sont?
- dire (*to say*) combien vous êtes dans votre famille?
- demander le nom de quelqu'un (*someone*)?
- dire le nom de quelqu'un?
- demander l'âge de quelqu'un?
- dire l'âge de quelqu'un?
- décrire (*to describe*) quelqu'un?
- présenter quelqu'un?
- répondre à une présentation?

B. **Rédaction: En famille.** Écrivez cette scène. Après, avec un(e) partenaire, présentez la scène à la classe. Jouez les deux rôles.

Vous voulez présenter un(e) ami(e) à votre famille. En allant (*On the way*) chez vos parents, vous décrivez votre famille. Votre ami(e) pose des questions et parle un peu de sa famille. Quand vous arrivez, présentez votre ami(e) à un membre de votre famille.

C. **Un sondage.** Devinez les réponses aux questions suivantes. Écrivez vos prédictions sur une feuille de papier.

1. Quel est l'âge moyen des étudiants du cours?
2. Quel est l'âge moyen des parents des étudiants du cours de français?
3. En moyenne, combien de personnes est-ce qu'il y a dans les familles des étudiants du cours de français?
4. En moyenne, combien de cousins ont les étudiants du cours de français?

Maintenant, prenez quatre petites feuilles de papier et écrivez la réponse à chacune des questions suivantes sur une des feuilles. Après, quatre groupes vont prendre les feuilles avec les réponses à une des questions pour calculer la moyenne pour la classe.

1. Quel âge avez-vous?
2. Quel âge a votre mère? Et votre père?
3. Vous êtes combien dans votre famille?
4. Combien de cousins est-ce que vous avez?

D. **La famille de Claude.** Claude présente sa famille à Robert. Faites une liste des membres présentés et donnez deux détails que vous comprenez au sujet de sa sœur Chantal.

Pour vérifier

Étudiez la liste de vocabulaire. Après avoir fini (*After finishing*) ces exercices, vérifiez vos réponses dans *Appendix C.*

Identifying and describing people and things

A. Conversations. Robert parle avec un oncle de Thomas. Complétez logiquement leur conversation. Utilisez des mots du vocabulaire de la page suivante.

— Vous ______ combien dans votre famille?
— Nous ______ quatre: ma femme, mon ______ et ma ______ .
— Comment ______ vos enfants?
— Ils ______ Luc et Christine.

B. Professions. Donnez une profession logique.

1. Ma femme travaille dans un hôpital. Elle est...
2. Mes amis travaillent au théâtre. Ils sont...
3. Ma cousine travaille dans un restaurant. Elle est...
4. Mes frères jouent dans un orchestre. Ils sont...

C. Quel adjectif? Complétez ces phrases avec un adjectif ou une expression logique de la page suivante.

1. Est-ce que tu voudrais dormir? Tu as l'air ______ .
2. Une personne qui a cent ans est ______ . Elle a probablement les cheveux ______ .
3. Je ne suis pas grand et je ne suis pas petit non plus. Je suis ______ .

D. Personnages. Décrivez ces personnages imaginaires.

1. le père Noël 2. la Belle et la Bête (*Beast*) 3. Papa Stroumpf (*Smurf*)

E. Jamais content. Aujourd'hui, Thomas se plaint (*is complaining*) de tout. Complétez ses phrases avec la forme correcte de **ce** et l'adjectif le plus logique.

EXEMPLE *Ce* **parc est très** ***laid.*** (beau, laid)

1. ______ magasin est très ______ . (mauvais, bon)
2. ______ cassette vidéo est très ______ . (intéressant, ennuyeux)
3. ______ acteur est très ______ . (bête, sympa)
4. ______ vieux films sont toujours ______ . (amusant, mauvais)

Talking about your free time

F. Devinette. Est-ce que vous comprenez les devinettes (*riddles*) suivantes?

1. maintenant + quelques heures = p_ _ _ t_ _ _
2. cet après-midi + vingt-quatre heures = d_ _ _ _ _ a_ _ _ _-_ _ _ _
3. dimanche + soixante-douze heures = m_ _ _ _ _ _ _.
4. ce mois + trente jours = l_ m_ _ _ p_ _ _ _ _ _ _
5. jeudi + deux jours = c_ w_ _ _-_ _ _

G. Projets. Dites quelque chose que vous allez faire à chacun des moments mentionnés dans l'activité précédente. Écrivez cinq phrases.

Vocabulaire

Identifying and describing people and things

FAMILLE ET AMIS

Comment s'appelle(nt)...
Je vous/te présente...
Quel âge a...?
Vous êtes combien?
un(e) cousin(e)
une femme
une fille
un fils
un frère
une grand-mère
un grand-père
des grands-parents (*m*)
un mari
une mère
un neveu
une nièce
un oncle
des parents (*m*)
un père
un(e) petit(e) ami(e)
une sœur
une tante

AUTRES NOMS

une barbe
une fleur
un garage
un jardin
des lunettes (*f*)
une moustache
une photo

PROFESSIONS

un(e) acteur / actrice
un(e) avocat(e)
un(e) chanteur / chanteuse
un(e) danseur / danseuse
un(e) homme / femme d'affaires
un(e) infirmier / infirmière
un médecin
un(e) musicien(ne)
un(e) pharmacien(ne)
un(e) secrétaire
un(e) serveur / serveuse

COULEURS

De quelle couleur est / sont...?
beige
blanc(he)
bleu(e)
blond(e)
brun(e)
châtain(e)
gris(e)
jaune
marron
noir(e)
orange
rose
rouge
roux/rousse
vert(e)
violet(te)

ADJECTIFS ET EXPRESSIONS

âgé(e)
autre
beau (bel) / belle
bon(ne)
content(e)
court(e)
des années
de taille moyenne
divorcé(e)
européen(ne)
fatigué(e)
gros(se)
italien(ne)
japonais(e)
long(ue)
malade
mauvais(e)
mort(e)
nouveau (nouvel) / nouvelle
tout / tous / toute / toutes
triste
vieux (vieil) / vieille

VERBES ET EXPRESSIONS

avoir... ans
avoir l'air + *adjectif*
avoir les cheveux / les yeux...
être au chômage
monter
porter
ressembler à

Talking about your free time

NOMS

une activité culturelle
un bar
un centre commercial
une église
une exposition
une idée
un lac
une librairie
un magasin
un musée
un parc
une passion
une piscine
une plage
des projets (*m*)
le temps libre
un théâtre

VERBES

acheter
adorer
aller
faire (du shopping)
louer
nager
rentrer
retrouver

ADVERBES

d'abord
ensuite
puis
surtout

Pour des expressions temporelles, voir la page 158.

DIVERS

ce/cet/cette/ces
en plein air
on
prochain(e)
Qu'en penses-tu?
tout le monde

Unité 3 À Paris

Regional Overview
Paris
AREA: 41 square miles (105 sq. km.; 479 sq. km. with its suburbs)
POPULATION: 2,200,000 (approximately 9 million with its suburbs)
DEPARTMENT: Ville de Paris
PROVINCE: Île-de-France
MAJOR INDUSTRIES: manufacturing, technology, tourism

Chapitre 5 Des projets

By the end of this chapter, you should be able to do the following in French:

- Describe the weather
- Suggest activities
- Tell when you did something
- Tell where you went

La Tour Eiffel
Robert Delaunay (1885–1941)
1910–1911
Basel Kunstmuseum
Giraudon/Art Resource, New York

Between 1909 and 1911, Delaunay produced a series of thirty cubist paintings of the Eiffel Tower. To Delaunay, the Eiffel Tower symbolized modernity. It also provided him an opportunity to explore on canvas the way light distorts form and color.

Pour commencer

Alice Pérez travaille pour une grande compagnie américaine. Elle est transférée à Paris pour deux ans. La voilà à Paris avec sa famille. Elle décide **donc** de **suivre des cours** pour **améliorer** son français. Ses activités dépendent souvent du **temps.**

À Paris, le temps est variable. Et chez vous? **Quel temps fait-il?**

SUPPLEMENTAL VOCABULARY
Il fait bon. *The weather's nice.*
Le ciel est couvert. *The sky is overcast.*
Le temps est nuageux. *It's cloudy.*
Il y a un orage. *There's a storm.*
Il y a du verglas. *It's icy.*
Il fait du brouillard. *It's foggy.*

En été...

il fait chaud.

il fait du soleil et il fait beau.

En automne...

il fait frais.

quelquefois, il fait mauvais.

En hiver...

il fait froid.

il neige.

Au printemps...

il fait du vent.

il pleut.

donc *thus, so, therefore* **suivre des cours** *to take courses* **améliorer** *to improve* **le temps** *weather* **Quel temps fait-il?** *How's the weather?* **en été** *in the summer* **en hiver** *in the winter* **au printemps** *in the spring*

S'il fait beau ce week-end, qu'est-ce que vous avez l'intention de faire?

J'ai l'intention de (d')... / Je n'ai pas l'intention de (d')...

quitter l'appartement tôt samedi matin.

partir pour le week-end.

visiter une autre ville.

passer la journée à la plage.

faire du bateau.

faire du ski nautique.

passer la soirée avec des amis.

aller boire quelque chose au café.

rentrer tard.

Alice Pérez parle à son fils du week-end.

— Alors, qu'est-ce que tu as l'intention de faire demain?
— S'il fait beau, je voudrais aller au parc.
— Et s'il fait mauvais?
— Je ne sais pas. Je vais probablement aller au café avec des amis.

Savez-vous le faire?

A. Temps impossible. Quelle description du temps ne s'accorde pas logiquement avec les autres dans les phrases suivantes?

1. Il fait beau, il fait du soleil, il neige et il fait chaud.
2. Il neige, il fait chaud, il fait froid et il fait du vent.
3. Il fait du soleil, il pleut, il fait mauvais et il fait gris.
4. Il fait mauvais, il fait beau, il fait chaud et il fait du soleil.
5. Il pleut, il fait du soleil, il fait chaud et il fait beau.

B. Projets. Est-ce que vous avez l'intention de faire les choses suivantes demain?

EXEMPLE aller danser → **Oui, j'ai l'intention d'aller danser.**
OU **Non, je n'ai pas l'intention d'aller danser.**

1. rester à la maison
2. dormir tard
3. sortir avec des amis
4. acheter des vêtements
5. passer la soirée seul(e)
6. visiter une autre ville
7. quitter la maison tôt
8. nager
9. rentrer tard

C. Quel temps fait-il? Quel temps fait-il aujourd'hui dans ces régions francophones? Utilisez au moins deux expressions pour chaque (*each*) photo.

Dans les Alpes, en Suisse

En Normandie, en France

En Martinique

D. Ça dépend du temps! Qu'est-ce que vous aimez faire...

1. quand il fait beau?
2. quand il pleut?
3. quand il fait chaud?
4. quand il neige?

E. Qu'est-ce que tu voudrais faire ce week-end? Un(e) ami(e) passe le week-end chez vous et vous parlez de ce que (*what*) vous allez faire. Préparez la scène avec un(e) autre étudiant(e). Décidez de ce que vous allez faire s'il fait beau et s'il fait mauvais.

Comment s'y prendre?

Recognizing the prefix re-

Recognizing certain prefixes will help you to understand more verbs. Read the following sentences and decide what the prefix **re-** means.

Elle part tôt le matin, elle rentre pour le déjeuner et elle ***re*part** l'après-midi. Elle ouvre l'enveloppe et elle lit des instructions sur une feuille de papier, mais elle ne comprend pas. Alors, elle ***re*lit** les instructions et elle ***re*met** la feuille de papier dans l'enveloppe.

Using the sequence of events to make logical guesses

You can often guess the meaning of unfamiliar verbs in a narrative by imagining what the logical order of actions would be. For example, if you take the bus, you usually wait for the bus first and you have to get on the bus before you get off. Learn to read a whole paragraph, rather than one word at a time.

Use the sequence of events in this passage to guess the meaning of the boldfaced words.

Alice **attend** l'autobus devant l'appartement. Quand l'autobus arrive, elle **monte** dedans, et elle **descend** quand elle arrive à l'université.

Dans son appartement, Alice ouvre une enveloppe. Elle **sort** une feuille de papier de l'enveloppe et **lit** les instructions sur la feuille.

Elle **quitte** son appartement et va directement au café. Elle entre dans le café et commande un verre de vin rouge. Elle **boit** son verre, **paie l'addition** et **repart**.

Elle entre dans la station de métro et elle achète un ticket **au guichet**, mais elle ne **prend** pas le métro.

Understanding infinitives after prepositions

To understand most narratives, you will need to recognize certain prepositions that are followed by infinitives. **Pour** means *in order to* when it is followed by a verb. **Sans** (*without*) can also be followed by an infinitive. What do these sentences mean?

Alice demande l'addition au serveur. Elle quitte le café **sans boire** son café. Elle entre dans la station et elle va au guichet **pour acheter** un billet. Elle repart **sans prendre** le métro.

Savez-vous le faire?

A. L'ordre chronologique. Voilà les activités d'Alice d'aujourd'hui. Mettez-les (*Put them*) dans l'ordre logique. La première et la dernière (*last*) sont indiquées.

1. Alice voit une enveloppe sur la table.

__7__ Elle va à la porte.
__5__ Elle lit les instructions sur la feuille de papier.
__4__ Elle sort une feuille de papier de l'enveloppe.
__3__ Elle ouvre l'enveloppe.
__2__ Elle prend l'enveloppe.
__1__ Elle regarde un instant l'enveloppe.
__6__ Elle remet la feuille dans l'enveloppe.

9. Elle ouvre la porte et elle sort.

B. Quel verbe? Choisissez l'expression qui complète logiquement chaque phrase.

1. Alice quitte l'appartement sans... (boire son café, ouvrir la porte).
2. Elle prend l'autobus pour... (rester à la maison, aller en ville).
3. Elle retrouve des amis pour... (passer le week-end seule, aller au cinéma).
4. Elle va au guichet pour... (acheter des billets, boire une bière).
5. Après, elle va au café avec des amis pour... (boire quelque chose, danser).
6. Elle rentre à la maison sans... (quitter le café, prendre l'autobus).

Qu'est-ce qui se passe?

Qu'est-ce qu'elle fait?

Seule dans son appartement, Alice Pérez a l'air un peu agitée. Elle prend l'enveloppe qui se trouve sur la table et en sort une feuille de papier. Elle lit les instructions, remet la feuille dans l'enveloppe et quitte son appartement.

Alice entre dans un café où elle commande un verre de vin rouge et ensuite, demande l'addition. Quand l'addition arrive, elle la prend et paie le garçon. Elle ouvre l'enveloppe, relit les instructions, met l'addition dans l'enveloppe et quitte le café sans boire son verre de vin. Quelle femme bizarre! Qu'est-ce qu'elle fait? Pourquoi a-t-elle l'air si agitée?

Maintenant, Alice va directement à la station de métro. Elle entre dans la station et sans regarder le plan, va au guichet et demande un ticket. Quand on lui donne son ticket, elle le met dans l'enveloppe, remonte l'escalier et quitte la station de métro. Pourquoi est-ce qu'elle achète un ticket sans prendre le métro? Tout ça est très bizarre!

Elle continue sa route jusqu'à ce qu'elle arrive devant un cinéma. Elle vérifie l'adresse qu'il y a sur sa feuille de papier, va au guichet et achète un billet. Mais, comme avant, elle met le billet dans l'enveloppe, relit encore les instructions et repart, sans entrer dans le cinéma.

Elle va au coin de la rue pour attendre l'autobus. Quand l'autobus arrive, elle monte dedans. Elle descend à l'université. Elle semble plus calme maintenant. Elle a même l'air plutôt contente. Qu'est-ce qui se passe? Pourquoi est-ce qu'elle a fait tout ça?

Maintenant... c'est à vous! Qu'est-ce que vous en pensez? Est-ce que vous trouvez aussi les actions d'Alice plutôt bizarres? Qu'est-ce qu'elle fait? Elle est agent de police? espionne comme James Bond? détective privé? lunatique? Ou bien... est-ce qu'il y a une explication simple et logique? Faites les exercices de la section *Avez-vous compris?* pour connaître l'explication.

Avez-vous compris?

A. Comprenez-vous? Indiquez par **oui** ou par **non** si Alice fait ces choses.

1. Alice ouvre une enveloppe, sort une feuille de papier et lit les instructions.
2. Elle quitte son appartement et va directement à l'université en autobus.
3. Elle va au café pour prendre un café.
4. Elle boit un verre de vin rouge au café.
5. Elle refuse de payer l'addition.
6. Elle va à la station de métro pour acheter un ticket.
7. Elle va au cinéma pour voir un nouveau film.
8. Elle met l'addition du café, le billet de cinéma et le ticket de métro dans l'enveloppe.
9. Après, elle prend le métro pour aller à l'université.
10. Elle prend l'autobus pour aller à l'université.

B. Voilà pourquoi... Imaginez une explication pour le comportement (*behavior*) d'Alice. Ensuite, lisez l'explication ci-dessous (*below*).

Est-ce qu'elle...

est agent de police?	est détective privé?
travaille pour la CIA?	collectionne des souvenirs de Paris?
fait un exercice pour son cours de français?	souffre d'amnésie?

Alice est étudiante. Elle suit un cours de français pour étrangers (*foreigners*) à Paris. Ses devoirs, dans l'enveloppe, consistent à prouver au professeur qu'elle est capable de commander quelque chose à boire au café, d'acheter un billet au cinéma et un ticket de métro. Elle doit rapporter (*must bring back*) l'addition, le billet d'entrée et le ticket de métro comme preuves (*proof*).

CULTURE NOTE
The Celtic people who settled on the island in the Seine were called the **Parisii**, from which the name of **Paris** developed. The greater metropolitan area around Paris covers 185 square miles (479 sq. kilometers) and has a population of approximately nine million.

Remarquez que...

Modern Paris, covering 41 square miles with a population of more than two million people, developed from a settlement on an island in the Seine River beginning in about 300 B.C. The Seine flows through the center of Paris, dividing it into the Right and Left Banks. You can wander along its banks to browse the bookstores, watch the boats, admire the buildings, and visit the cafés and watch passersby.

Paris is divided into **arrondissements**, the districts of Parisian local government. However, people still tend to think in terms of **quartiers** (*neighborhoods*), many of which retain their historical atmosphere. Praised as "the City of Light," "a movable feast," and "an outdoor museum," Paris has something for everyone. The biggest problem for a visitor to Paris is how to see and do it all. Besides movies, dances, concerts, and theatrical productions, there are many art galleries and museums. One can spend the day shopping, enjoying the finest or simplest food, strolling in a park, visiting a zoo, or watching a sporting event. And in the evening, bars and clubs offer an exciting nightlife. Weekly publications such as *L'Officiel des spectacles* and *Pariscope* keep visitors and Parisians informed of what's going on in the capital.

SOMMAIRE

Les informations que nous publions nous sont communiquées par les organisateurs sous réserve de changements de dernière minute.

À chacun ses goûts. Look at the table of contents for this issue of *L'Officiel des spectacles.* To what page would you turn to find a swimming pool to go to? if you wanted to go dancing? to see a first-run movie? to find out the days and hours the Louvre is open?

Qu'est-ce qu'on dit?

Les expressions suivantes sont utiles pour inviter **quelqu'un** et pour suggérer une activité.

— **Qu'est-ce qu'on fait** aujourd'hui?
— On mange quelque chose? J'**ai faim**.
— D'accord. **Allons** au Macdo!

— On fait quelque chose ce soir?
— **Ne** faisons **rien** ce soir!
— D'accord. Restons à la maison.

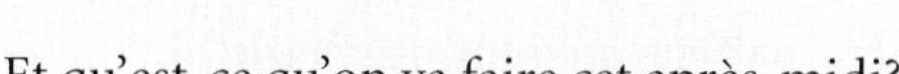

Et qu'est-ce qu'on va faire cet après-midi?

J'ai envie de...

faire une promenade.

faire un tour à vélo.

faire la cuisine.

J'ai besoin de...

faire des courses.

faire le ménage.

faire la lessive.

SUPPLEMENTAL VOCABULARY

faire de l'alpinisme *to go mountain climbing*
faire du patinage (sur glace) *to go (ice) skating*
faire de la marche à pied *to go walking*
faire du cheval *to go horseback riding*
faire du vélo *to go bike-riding*
faire des haltères *to lift weights*
aller à la chasse *to go hunting*
aller à la pêche *to go fishing*

---

quelqu'un *someone* **Qu'est-ce qu'on fait?** *What shall we do?* **avoir faim** *to be hungry* **allons...!** *let's go...!* **ne... rien** *nothing* **avoir envie de** *to feel like* **avoir besoin de** *to need* **faire des courses** *to run errands*

Suggesting activities

Alice et son mari, Vincent, **font des projets** après les cours.

— Qu'est-ce qu'on fait maintenant?
— Moi, j'ai envie d'aller au café. Et toi?
— Bonne idée, **j'ai soif.** Qu'est-ce qu'on fait après?
— Moi, je vais rentrer. J'ai besoin de préparer un examen.
— Tu as l'intention de travailler ce soir aussi?
— Oui, **malheureusement**! Mais faisons quelque chose demain, après l'examen!
— D'accord! C'est une bonne idée.

faire des projets *to make plans* **avoir soif** *to be thirsty* **malheureusement** *unfortunately*

A. Suggestions. Choisissez la réponse la plus logique dans la colonne **B** pour chaque suggestion donnée dans la colonne **A.**

A	B
1. Tu as faim?	a. On va au cinéma?
2. Vous avez soif?	b. Allons boire quelque chose!
3. Nous avons envie de sortir ce soir!	c. Restons à la maison aujourd'hui!
4. J'ai besoin d'exercice.	d. Invitons des amis à dîner chez nous!
5. J'ai besoin de vêtements pour l'été.	e. On va au centre commercial?
6. Tu as l'air fatigué.	f. Faisons une promenade!
7. J'ai envie de faire la cuisine ce soir.	g. On va au lac ou à la piscine?
8. Vous avez envie d'aller nager?	h. On va manger un hamburger?

B. Où? Suggérez à vos amis un endroit pour faire les choses suivantes.

EXEMPLE Nous avons envie de faire une promenade. → **On va au parc?**

1. Tu voudrais faire du bateau?
2. Nous avons besoin de faire des devoirs.
3. Je vais faire du shopping cet après-midi.
4. Tu as envie de faire du jogging?
5. Tu as besoin de faire des courses?

à la bibliothèque *au lac*
EN VILLE AU PARC
au centre commercial
???

C. Activités préférées. Sur une feuille de papier, écrivez ces activités par ordre de préférence. Après, posez des questions comme dans l'exemple pour déterminer l'ordre de préférence établi par un(e) camarade de classe.

faire du jardinage
faire un tour à vélo
faire du ski
faire des courses
faire du shopping
faire la cuisine
faire du sport
ne rien faire

EXEMPLE **— Est-ce que tu préfères faire du sport ou faire une promenade?**
— Je préfère faire une promenade.

Voilà pourquoi!

Le pronom on et les suggestions

The pronoun **on** is often used instead of **nous** to say *we*, especially when making plans.

Qu'est-ce qu'*on* va faire ce soir?	*What are **we** going to do tonight?*
***On* a besoin de faire la lessive.**	***We** need to do the laundry.*

You can invite someone to do something with you by asking a question with **on**.

***On* va au cinéma?**	*Shall **we** go to the movies?*

To make a suggestion with *let's*, use the **nous** form of the verb without the pronoun **nous**.

***Allons* au cinéma.**	***Let's go** to the movies.*
***Ne rentrons pas* trop tard.**	***Let's not return** too late.*

SELF-CHECK

1. What are two ways of suggesting an activity in French?
2. How is the ending of the **vous** form of **faire** different from the usual **vous** form verb ending?
3. How do you say that you are doing *nothing*?

Le verbe **faire**

To say *to make* or *to do*, use the irregular verb **faire.**

FAIRE (*TO MAKE, TO DO*)	
je **fais**	nous **faisons**
tu **fais**	vous **faites**
il/elle/on **fait**	ils/elles **font**

— Qu'est-ce que tu fais ce soir?
— Je regarde la télévision.

— Qu'est-ce que Papa fait pour le dîner?
— Il fait des sandwiches.

Faire can also have a variety of meanings in idiomatic expressions.

faire du shopping	*to go shopping*
faire du camping	*to go camping*
faire des projets	*to make plans*
faire de l'exercice	*to exercise*
faire une promenade	*to go for a walk*
faire un tour (à vélo, en voiture)	*to go for a ride (on a bike, in a car)*
faire un voyage	*to take a trip*
faire du jogging	*to go jogging*
faire du ski (nautique)	*to go (water) skiing*
faire du sport (du basket-ball, du golf, du football, du tennis, du hockey)	*to play sports (basketball, golf, soccer, tennis, hockey)*
faire des courses	*to run errands*
faire la cuisine - unchanged	*to cook*
faire la lessive -	*to do laundry*
faire le ménage -	*to do housework*
faire du jardinage	*to do gardening*
faire des devoirs	*to do homework*

Faire is also used in many, but not all, weather expressions.

— **Quel temps *fait*-il aujourd'hui?**
— **Il *fait* mauvais. Il pleut beaucoup.**

To tell what the weather is going to be like, you will also need to know the infinitives **pleuvoir** (*to rain*) and **neiger** (*to snow*).

— **Quel temps est-ce qu'il va faire demain? Il va *pleuvoir*?**
— **Il va faire mauvais et il va peut-être *neiger*.**

La négation et **ne... rien**

The **un, une, des, du,** and **de la** in the expressions with **faire** become **de** when the verb is negated. The definite article (**le, la, les**) does not change.

	Ils font *du* bateau aujourd'hui.	→	**Ils ne font pas *de* bateau aujourd'hui.**
	Je fais toujours *une* promenade.	→	**Je ne fais jamais *de* promenade.**
BUT	**Nous faisons *la* cuisine.**	→	**Nous ne faisons pas *la* cuisine.**

To say you do *nothing*, use **ne... rien**. Place it around the verb, like **ne... pas** or **ne... jamais**. When negating an infinitive, place both parts of the negative expressions before it.

Nous *ne* faisons *rien* ce soir. **Vous *n'*allez *rien* faire?** **Je préfère *ne rien* faire.**

Et ça se prononce comment?

La combinaison **ai**

Listen to the sound of the letters **ai** in the conjugation of the verb **faire**. In which three forms does it sound the same? How does it sound in the other two? Generally, the letters **ai** are pronounced with a more open sound, as in **j'aime**, when they are followed by a pronounced consonant at the end of a syllable. They have a tighter sound, as in **j'ai**, when there is no following consonant sound. Compare these pairs of phrases:

j'ai / j'aime **je fais / vous faites** **français / française**

The form **nous faisons** is an exception; the **ai** is pronounced like the **e** in **le**.

Savez-vous le faire?

A. **Prononcez bien!** Écoutez et écrivez les questions. Ensuite, posez les questions à votre professeur. Faites attention à la prononciation.

1. Qu'est-ce que vous ______ après le cours de ______?
2. Qu'est-ce que vous pensez quand nous ne ______ rien en classe?
3. Qu'est-ce que vous ______ souvent avec vos amis?
4. Est-ce que vous ______ souvent la cuisine ensemble?
5. Est-ce que vos amis ______ la cuisine ______?

B. Que font-ils? Le fils d'Alice Pérez parle des projets de sa famille aujourd'hui. Complétez les phrases avec une expression avec **faire**.

1. Maman, est-ce que tu... ce matin?

2. Nous... cet après-midi.

3. Papa...

4. Papa et toi, vous...

5. Mon frère et ma sœur...

6. Moi, je...

C. Souvent ou rarement? Demandez à un(e) camarade de classe si les personnes indiquées font souvent les choses suivantes pendant leur temps libre.

EXEMPLE tu (faire du shopping)
— **Est-ce que tu fais souvent du shopping pendant ton temps libre?**
— **Je ne fais pas souvent de shopping.**

1. Tu... (faire de l'exercice)
2. Tu... (faire une promenade)
3. Ton/Ta camarade de chambre... (faire la cuisine)
4. Tes amis... (faire du camping)
5. Ta famille... (faire un voyage)
6. Tes amis et toi... (faire du sport ensemble)

D. Qui fait ça? Demandez à un(e) camarade de classe qui dans sa famille fait le plus souvent les choses suivantes.

EXEMPLE faire du jardinage
— **Qui fait le plus souvent du jardinage dans ta famille?**
— **Mon père fait le plus souvent du jardinage.**
OU **Nous ne faisons pas de jardinage dans ma famille.**

1. faire du ski
2. faire de l'exercice
3. faire le ménage
4. faire la cuisine
5. faire du jogging
6. faire du camping

E. Quel temps fait-il? Choisissez une ville française et demandez à un(e) camarade de classe quel temps il y fait d'après la carte de prévision du temps.

EXEMPLE — **Quel temps fait-il à Paris?**
— **Il fait mauvais à Paris.**

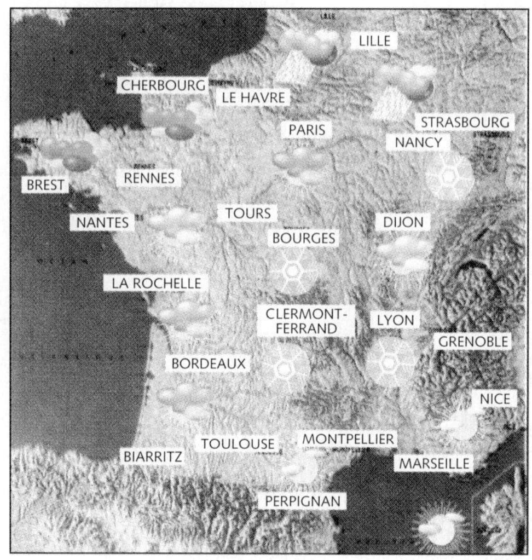

F. Sortons! Alice n'aime pas rester à la maison. Comment répond-elle à ces suggestions?

EXEMPLE On fait le ménage ce matin? → **Ne faisons pas le ménage ce matin!**
On va en ville? → **Oui, allons en ville!**

1. On loue une cassette vidéo?
2. On fait une promenade?
3. On invite des amis à la maison?
4. On fait du camping ce week-end?
5. On fait du jardinage cet après-midi?
6. On va nager à la piscine?

G. Qu'est-ce qu'on fait? Suggérez une activité d'après le temps indiqué. Un(e) camarade de classe va accepter ou suggérer une autre activité.

EXEMPLE Il va pleuvoir cet après-midi.
— **Il va pleuvoir cet après-midi. On va au cinéma?**
— **Oui, allons voir un film.**
OU **Louons une cassette vidéo et restons à la maison.**

1. Il va faire du soleil ce matin.
2. Il va faire mauvais ce soir.
3. Il va neiger ce week-end.
4. Il va pleuvoir demain.
5. Il va faire chaud samedi prochain.
6. Il va faire beau la semaine prochaine.

aller au cinéma *aller au lac*
LOUER UNE CASSETTE VIDÉO
rester à la maison
FAIRE DU SKI ???
FAIRE DU CAMPING *faire un voyage*
jouer au tennis **???**

H. On fait des projets. Des amis passent le week-end chez vous et chacun voudrait faire quelque chose de différent. Soudain *(Suddenly)*, le temps change et vous décidez de rester à la maison. Préparez une scène avec deux ou trois camarades de classe.

Voilà pourquoi!

Les expressions avec avoir

Below are a few useful expressions with **avoir** in French that do not translate directly into English. Many of these expressions describe feelings.

avoir faim	*to be hungry*	**avoir raison**	*to be right*
avoir soif	*to be thirsty*	**avoir tort**	*to be wrong*
avoir sommeil	*to be sleepy*	**avoir envie de**	*to feel like, to want to*
avoir peur	*to be afraid*	**avoir besoin de**	*to need*
avoir froid	*to be cold*	**avoir l'intention de**	*to intend to*
avoir chaud	*to be hot*	**avoir l'air**	*to look, to seem*
avoir... ans	*to be . . . years old*	+ adjective	+ adjective

SELF-CHECK
Will these expressions with **avoir** be translated by *to have* in English?

Avoir envie de and **avoir besoin de** can be followed by an infinitive or a noun.

J'ai envie de sortir. *J'ai envie d'*un Coca.
J'ai besoin de travailler. *J'ai besoin d'*un stylo.

Savez-vous le faire?

A. **Qu'est-ce qu'ils ont?** Alice est à la fête d'anniversaire (*birthday party*) de l'enfant d'un ami. Qu'est-ce qu'elle dit? Utilisez une expression avec **avoir**.

1. Les enfants...

2. Vincent et moi, on...

3. Elle..

4. Je(J')...

5. Le chien...

6. Tu... de faire ça au chien!

B. Qu'est-ce qu'il y a? Un ami vous dit les choses suivantes. Utilisez une expression avec **avoir** pour lui demander pourquoi.

EXEMPLE Allons manger quelque chose. → **Pourquoi? Tu as faim?**

1. J'ai besoin de café si je vais faire tous ces devoirs.
2. Allons boire quelque chose.
3. Ferme la fenêtre s'il te plaît.
4. Allons dormir!
5. Attention! Ce chien a l'air méchant.
6. J'ai peut-être un peu de température.

C. Et vous? Complétez les phrases suivantes d'une façon originale.

1. Quand j'ai très faim, j'aime...
2. Quand j'ai très soif, j'aime...
3. Quand j'ai sommeil, j'aime...
4. J'ai souvent tort quand je...
5. Généralement, j'ai raison quand je...
6. Quand j'ai froid, j'aime boire...
7. Quand j'ai chaud, j'aime boire...
8. J'ai peur quand...
9. Ce soir, j'ai besoin de...
10. Maintenant, j'ai envie de...

D. Des excuses. Invitez un(e) autre étudiant(e) à faire les choses suivantes. Il/Elle va accepter ou trouver une excuse.

EXEMPLE aller prendre un verre
— **Tu as envie d'aller prendre un verre avec moi?**
— **Oui, allons au café.**
OU **Malheureusement, j'ai besoin d'aller faire des courses.**

1. faire du jogging 2. aller à l'église 3. aller danser 4. faire une promenade

E. Après le cours. Faites des projets pour après le cours avec un(e) camarade de classe. Utilisez le dialogue entre Alice et Vincent à la page 176 comme exemple.

Remarquez que...

Temperatures in France are indicated in degrees Celsius (centigrade). To convert to Fahrenheit, multiply the Celsius temperature by nine, then divide by five and add thirty-two degrees.

Quelle est la température? Voici les températures minimales et maximales en Celsius pour quelques villes en France. Choisissez une ville et donnez la température maximale et minimale en Celsius et ensuite, en Fahrenheit.

FRANCE							
Ajaccio	N	15	22	Lyon	N	14	22
Biarritz	N	15	25	Marseille	N	13	22
Bordeaux	N	15	23	Nancy	N	10	23
Brest	N	11	22	Nantes	N	14	22
Cherbourg	N	13	20	Nice	N	15	20
Clermont-F	N	11	24	Paris	N	13	24
Dijon	N	11	22	Pau	N	16	26
Dinard	N	12	23	Perpignan	N	15	20
Embrun	N	8	21	Rennes	N	13	22
Grenoble	N	11	21	Rouen	N	13	22
La Rochelle	N	16	24	St-Étienne	N	11	23
Lille	N	12	23	Strasbourg	N	12	22
Limoges	N	14	23	Toulouse	N	15	21
Lorient	N	12	20	Tours	N	14	23

Qu'est-ce qu'on dit?

Alice explique pourquoi elle a décidé d'étudier le français. Et vous, quand est-ce que vous avez décidé de faire du français?

MOINS RÉCEMMENT

il y a deux ans	J'ai commencé à travailler avec notre **succursale**.
l'année ***dernière***	J'ai décidé d'étudier le français.
l'été dernier	J'ai visité la France avec ma famille.
il y a trois mois	J'ai loué un appartement à Paris.
la semaine dernière	J'ai ouvert un nouveau bureau ici.
le week-end dernier	J'ai travaillé tout le week-end.
il y a ***quelques*** *jours*	J'ai passé deux jours à Bruxelles.
hier	J'ai décidé d'ouvrir un bureau en Belgique aussi.

PLUS RÉCEMMENT

Une amie d'Alice remarque qu'elle a l'air fatiguée.

— Tu as l'air fatiguée! Tu as beaucoup de travail?
— Lundi j'ai fait un voyage à Bruxelles et après, j'ai **été** malade.
— Qu'est-ce que tu as fait à Bruxelles?
— J'ai parlé avec des gens d'une succursale.
— Qu'est-ce que tu as pensé de Bruxelles?
— J'ai **trouvé** les Belges très sympathiques mais il a **plu** tout le temps.

il y a deux ans *two years ago* **une succursale** *a branch (of the company)* **dernier**(**-ère**) *last*
quelques *a few* **hier** *yesterday* **été** (**être** *to be*) **trouvé** (**trouver** *to find*) **plu** (**pleuvoir** *to rain*)

Paris, le Quartier latin

A. Et vous? Complétez ces phrases pour dire quand vous avez fait les choses indiquées.

1. J'ai décidé d'étudier le français (le semestre / trimestre dernier, l'année dernière, il y a deux ans, ???).
2. Ce semestre / trimestre a commencé (il y a quelques mois, il y a deux mois, le mois dernier, ce mois-ci, ???).
3. J'ai commencé mes études universitaires (cette année, l'année dernière, il y a deux ans, il y a trois ans, ???).
4. J'ai parlé à ma famille (aujourd'hui, hier, il y a quelques jours, la semaine dernière, le mois dernier, ???).
5. J'ai dîné au restaurant (hier soir, il y a deux jours, il y a quelques jours, le week-end dernier, la semaine dernière, le mois dernier, ???).
6. J'ai fait une promenade (ce matin, hier, il y a quelques jours, le week-end dernier, le mois dernier, l'année dernière, ???).

B. La journée d'Alice. Hier, Alice n'est pas sortie de l'appartement. Est-ce qu'elle a peut-être fait les choses suivantes? Répondez **peut-être** ou **non.**

1. Elle a passé la journée au lit.
2. Elle a fait une promenade.
3. Elle a parlé au téléphone.
4. Elle a travaillé sur ordinateur.
5. Elle a visité une exposition d'art.
6. Elle a fait des courses en ville.
7. Elle a dormi tard.
8. Elle a regardé une cassette vidéo.
9. Elle a été malade.
10. Elle a fait un tour à la campagne.

Voilà pourquoi!

SELF-CHECK

1. How do you say that you did something yesterday? How many parts does the **passé composé** have?
2. How do you form the past participle of most **-er** and **-ir** verbs? Which verbs that you know have irregular past participles?
3. How do you negate verbs in the **passé composé?**

Le passé composé avec avoir

To say what someone did or what happened in the past, use the **passé composé**. The **passé composé** is composed of two parts, the auxiliary verb and the past participle. The auxiliary verb, usually **avoir**, is conjugated with the subject. Note how the past participle is formed for most verbs ending in **-er** or **-ir**.

PARLER → PARLÉ	
j'**ai parlé**	nous **avons parlé**
tu **as parlé**	vous **avez parlé**
il/elle/on **a parlé**	ils/elles **ont parlé**

DORMIR → DORMI	
j'**ai dormi**	nous **avons dormi**
tu **as dormi**	vous **avez dormi**
il/elle/on **a dormi**	ils/elles **ont dormi**

Also learn the past participles of these irregular verbs.

avoir → **j'ai eu, tu as eu...**
boire → **j'ai bu, tu as bu...**
lire → **j'ai lu, tu as lu...**
pleuvoir → **il a plu**
voir → **j'ai vu, tu as vu...**
être → **j'ai été, tu as été...**
faire → **j'ai fait, tu as fait...**
prendre → **j'ai pris, tu as pris...**

In the negative, **ne... pas, ne... jamais,** and **ne... rien** go around the auxiliary.

Je *n'*ai *pas* eu d'accident. **Ils *n'*ont *rien* fait.**

Adverbs indicating how often (**toujours, souvent...**) and how well (**bien, mal, assez bien...**) are usually placed between the auxiliary and the past participle.

J'ai *bien* mangé. **Ils ont *toujours* téléphoné le week-end.**

The **passé composé** can be translated in a variety of ways in English.

J'ai pris l'autobus. { *I took the bus.* / *I have taken the bus.* / *I did take the bus.* }

The following expressions are useful when talking about the past. Note that you use the word **an** instead of **année**, to say *year* after a number.

hier (matin, après-midi, soir) *yesterday (morning, afternoon, evening)*
lundi (mardi, mercredi, jeudi, vendredi, samedi, dimanche) dernier
last Monday (Tuesday, Wednesday, Thursday, Friday, Saturday, Sunday)
le week-end dernier *last weekend*
la semaine dernière *last week*
le mois dernier *last month*
l'année dernière *last year*
la dernière fois *the last time*
récemment *recently*
il y a (quelques minutes, trois jours) *(a few minutes, three days) ago*
pendant (deux heures, longtemps) *during, for (two hours, a long time)*

Savez-vous le faire?

A. Un peu d'histoire. Dites quelles personnes célèbres dans la colonne de gauche ont fait chacune des choses dans la colonne de droite.

EXEMPLES **Pascal a étudié les mathématiques.**
Berlioz et Ravel ont composé des symphonies.

Pascal...
Berlioz et Ravel...
Pierre et Marie Curie...
Les frères Lumière...
Charles de Gaulle...
Gustave Eiffel...
Auguste Rodin et Camille Claudel...
François Mitterrand...
Jacques Cousteau...
Simone de Beauvoir...

participer à la construction de la statue de la Liberté
faire des sculptures
être élu président de la République française en 1981
étudier les mathématiques
faire le premier film
être président de la République française pendant les années cinquante
composer des symphonies
faire des travaux sur les effets de la radioactivité
faire des voyages sous-marins
parler de la situation de la femme

B. Quand? Indiquez la dernière fois que vous avez fait les choses suivantes?

EXEMPLE dîner au restaurant → **J'ai dîné au restaurant vendredi dernier.**
OU **Je n'ai pas dîné au restaurant récemment.**

1. voir un bon film
2. visiter un musée
3. faire du shopping
4. lire un bon livre
5. danser
6. manger seul(e)
7. être chez vos parents
8. jouer au volley-ball
9. travailler

hier matin *ce matin* ???
L'ANNÉE DERNIÈRE **il y a trois ans**
il y a quelques minutes *???* LE MOIS DERNIER
lundi dernier *le week-end dernier* **la semaine dernière**

C. Une vie active. Alice parle des activités de sa famille depuis (*since*) qu'ils sont en France.

EXEMPLE **À Chamonix, les enfants ont fait du ski.**

EXEMPLE À Chamonix, les enfants...

il a fait

1. À Deauville, toute la famille...

y

2. Vendredi dernier, Vincent et moi...

nous avon joué au tennis

plu

3. Hier, je(j')... lu

4. Hier, Vincent...

5. Ce matin, Vincent et Éric...

D. **Quel temps a-t-il fait?** Pour chaque dessin de l'activité précédente, dites le temps qu'il a fait ce jour-là.

EXEMPLE **À Chamonix, il a fait froid et il a neigé.**

E. **Meilleurs amis.** Demandez si un(e) camarade de classe a fait les choses suivantes avec son/sa meilleur(e) ami(e) hier.

EXEMPLE parler au téléphone
— Est-ce que vous avez parlé au téléphone hier?
— Oui, on a parlé au téléphone hier.
OU **Non, on n'a pas parlé au téléphone hier.**

1. déjeuner ensemble
2. jouer au tennis ensemble
3. prendre un verre
4. étudier
5. faire la cuisine ensemble
6. être ensemble

F. **Un jeu.** Pour chaque catégorie, travaillez en équipes de trois ou quatre étudiants et faites des listes en remontant (*going back*) aussi loin que possible dans le passé. L'équipe avec la liste la plus longue gagne. Vous avez une minute pour chaque catégorie. Écrivez vos listes sur une feuille de papier.

EXEMPLE Qui a gagné les élections présidentielles des États-Unis *(United States)*?
En 1992, Clinton a gagné.
En 1988, Bush a gagné.
En 1984...

1. Qui a joué au Superbowl?
2. Quelles équipes (*teams*) ont participé à la Série mondiale de base-ball?
3. Quel film a gagné l'Oscar du meilleur film?

G. **Interview.** Posez les questions suivantes à un(e) autre étudiant(e).

1. Quel temps est-ce qu'il a fait le week-end dernier? Est-ce que tu as travaillé? Est-ce que tu as fait du sport? Est-ce que tu as dormi tard samedi matin? Et dimanche?
2. Est-ce que tu as été malade récemment? Pendant combien de jours est-ce que tu as été malade? Est-ce que tu as beaucoup dormi? Est-ce que tu as regardé la télé? Est-ce que tu as lu?
3. Quel film récent est-ce que tu as aimé? Quel film est-ce que tu n'as pas aimé?
4. Est-ce que tu as eu un accident de voiture récemment? Il y a combien de temps?

Qu'est-ce qu'on dit?

La dernière fois que **vous êtes parti(e)** en week-end, où est-ce que vous êtes allé(e)? Qu'est-ce que vous avez fait?

Je suis parti(e)	~~le~~ vendredi après-midi. ~~le~~ samedi matin. ???	Je suis arrivé(e)	~~le~~ vendredi soir. ~~le~~ samedi après-midi. ???
Je suis allé(e)	à Denver. à New York. ???	Je suis resté(e)	trois jours. **une nuit.** le week-end.
J'**y** suis allé(e)	**en avion.** en voiture. en train. **en autocar.**	**Je suis descendu(e)**	dans un hôtel. dans un camping. chez des amis.
Je suis allé(e)	à la plage. à un concert. dans un club.	Je suis rentré(e)	le dimanche soir. le lundi matin.

VOCABULARY NOTE
The word **autobus** refers to a bus that runs within a city. **Autocar** refers to a bus that goes from one city to another, like a Greyhound bus.

Alice parle avec son amie Claire.

— Alors, tu as passé un bon week-end?
— Oui, très bon. On est allé à Deauville.
— Quand est-ce que vous êtes partis?
— Nous sommes partis samedi matin et nous sommes rentrés hier soir.
— Vous avez trouvé un bon hôtel?
— Nous sommes descendus dans un petit hôtel confortable, pas trop loin de la plage.
— **Quelle chance!** Tu as l'air bien **reposée.**

vous êtes parti(e) (**partir** *to leave, to go away*) **une nuit** *one night* **y** *there* **en avion** *by plane* **en autocar** *by bus* **je suis descendu(e)** (**descendre** *to go/come down, to stay [in a hotel]*) **Quelle chance!** *What luck!* **reposé(e)** *rested*

Une plage en Normandie

A. En week-end. Décrivez la dernière fois que vous êtes parti(e) en week-end en complétant les phrases suivantes.

1. Je suis allé(e) à (Santa Fé, Kansas City, Montréal, Miami, ???).
2. J'y suis allé(e) (en avion, en voiture, en train, en autocar).
3. Je suis parti(e) (le matin, l'après-midi, le soir, la nuit).
4. Je suis arrivé(e) (une heure, deux heures, trois heures, ???) plus tard.
5. Je suis descendu(e) (dans un hôtel, chez des amis, dans un camping, ???).
6. Je suis resté(e) (un jour, deux jours, trois jours, ???).

B. Et le week-end dernier? Qu'est-ce que vous avez fait le week-end dernier? Choisissez la phrase qui vous décrit le mieux.

1. Je suis resté(e) à la maison ce week-end. / Je ne suis pas resté(e) à la maison.
2. Je suis sorti(e) samedi soir. / Je ne suis pas sorti(e) samedi soir.
3. J'ai invité des amis chez moi. / Je n'ai pas invité d'amis chez moi.
4. Je suis allé(e) au cinéma. / Je ne suis pas allé(e) au cinéma.
5. J'ai dîné au restaurant samedi. / Je n'ai pas dîné au restaurant samedi.
6. Je suis allé(e) danser samedi soir. / Je ne suis pas allé(e) danser samedi soir.
7. Je suis rentré(e) tard samedi soir. / Je ne suis pas rentré(e) tard samedi soir.
8. J'ai dormi tard dimanche matin. / Je n'ai pas dormi tard dimanche matin.

C. Elle est sortie? Vous allez entendre une description de ce que Claire, l'amie d'Alice, a fait la semaine dernière. Sur une feuille de papier, indiquez quand elle est sortie et quand elle est restée à la maison.

EXEMPLE VOUS ENTENDEZ: Samedi après-midi, elle est allée au cinéma.

	ELLE EST SORTIE	ELLE EST RESTÉE À LA MAISON
VOUS ÉCRIVEZ:	**samedi après-midi**	

Voilà pourquoi!

Le passé composé avec **être**

A few verbs in French have **être** as their auxiliary in the **passé composé**.

> **SELF-CHECK**
> 1. What is similar about the meaning of most verbs taking **être** in the **passé composé?**
> 2. What do you have to remember to do with the past participle of these verbs?

ALLER → ALLÉ		SORTIR → SORTI	
je **suis allé(e)**	nous **sommes allé(e)s**	je **suis sorti(e)**	nous **sommes sorti(e)s**
tu **es allé(e)**	vous **êtes allé(e)(s)**	tu **es sorti(e)**	vous **êtes sorti(e)(s)**
il/on **est allé**	ils **sont allés**	il/on **est sorti**	ils **sont sortis**
elle **est allée**	elles **sont allées**	elle **est sortie**	elles **sont sorties**

Unlike the past participle of verbs that use **avoir** as the auxiliary, the past participle of these verbs must agree with the subject in number and gender.

Alice est allé*e* en ville hier mais aujourd'hui elle n'est pas sorti*e*.

Here are some verbs that use **être** as their auxiliary. Notice that most of them are verbs of movement.

aller	*to go*	**je suis allé(e), tu es allé(e)...**
arriver	*to arrive*	**je suis arrivé(e), tu es arrivé(e)...**
descendre (de)	*to go down, to get off*	**je suis descendu(e), tu es descendu(e)...**
entrer (dans)	*to enter*	**je suis entré(e), tu es entré(e)...**
monter (dans)	*to go up, to get on/in*	**je suis monté(e), tu es monté(e)...**
partir (de)	*to go away, to leave*	**je suis parti(e), tu es parti(e)...**
rentrer	*to return, to come home*	**je suis rentré(e), tu es rentré(e)...**
rester	*to stay*	**je suis resté(e), tu es resté(e)...**
retourner	*to return, to come back, to go back*	**je suis retourné(e), tu es retourné(e)...**
sortir (de)	*to go out, to leave*	**je suis sorti(e), tu es sorti(e)...**

Use **rentrer** to talk about returning home or going back to the place where you are staying. Use **retourner** in other cases. Note that **partir** means *to leave* in the sense of *to go away.* It is the opposite of **arriver. Sortir** means *to leave* in the sense of *to go out.* It is the opposite of **rentrer** or **entrer. Quitter** also means *to leave.* It takes **avoir** as its auxiliary and will always have a direct object: **Elle a quitté la maison à huit heures.**

Et ça se prononce comment?

Avoir et **être** *(reprise)*

Be careful to pronounce the forms of the auxiliaries **avoir** and **être** distinctly. Practice the difference in these forms.

tu as parlé	**tu es parti(e)**
il a parlé	**il est parti**
ils‿ont parlé	**ils sont partis**

Savez-vous le faire?

A. ***Avoir* ou *être*?** Complétez les questions suivantes avec l'auxiliaire que vous entendez.

1. Est-ce que vos parents ______ allés à l'université?
2. Est-ce qu'ils ______ étudié le français?
3. Est-ce qu'ils ______ fait du sport?
4. Est-ce qu'ils ______ retournés à l'université pour faire une maîtrise ou un doctorat?
5. Est-ce que votre meilleur(e) ami(e) ______ entré(e) à l'université avec vous?
6. Est-ce que cet(te) ami(e) ______ téléphoné récemment?
7. Est-ce que cet(te) ami(e) ______ sorti(e) avec vous récemment?

Ensuite, répondez aux questions. Faites attention à la prononciation de l'auxiliaire.

EXEMPLE **Ma mère est allée à l'université mais mon père n'est pas allé à l'université.**

B. Mardi dernier. Voilà ce qu'a fait Alice mardi dernier. Complétez les phrases avec le passé composé du verbe entre parenthèses. (Après, cette illustration vous aidera [*will help you*] à apprendre les verbes conjugués avec **être** au passé composé.)

EXEMPLE **Alice *est sortie* de son appartement vers midi. (sortir)**

1. Mardi dernier, Alice ______ à l'appartement. (ne pas rester)
2. Elle ______ vers midi. (sortir)
3. Elle ______ dans un autobus. (monter)
4. L'autobus ______ en ville. (arriver)
5. Alice ______ de l'autobus. (descendre)
6. Elle ______ dans un restaurant. (entrer)
7. Elle ______ une heure au restaurant. (rester)
8. Elle ______ vers deux heures. (partir)
9. Elle ______ à l'arrêt d'autobus. (retourner)
10. Elle ______ à son appartement vers trois heures. (rentrer)

C. Le week-end dernier. Demandez à un(e) autre étudiant(e) s'il/si elle a fait les choses suivantes le week-end dernier. Attention! Certains verbes prennent **avoir** au passé composé et d'autres prennent **être**.

EXEMPLE sortir → **— Est-ce que tu es sorti(e) le week-end dernier?**
— Oui, je suis sorti(e). / Non, je ne suis pas sorti(e).

1. aller en ville
2. faire du shopping
3. aller danser samedi
4. rentrer tard samedi soir
5. travailler
6. regarder la télévision

D. Le dernier cours. Vous avez été malade et vous demandez à un(e) camarade de classe si on a fait les choses suivantes pendant le dernier cours de français.

EXEMPLE parler français → — **Est-ce que vous avez parlé français?**
— **Oui, nous avons beaucoup parlé.**
OU **Oui, on a beaucoup parlé.**

1. commencer un nouveau chapitre
2. écouter une cassette
3. aller à la bibliothèque
4. faire beaucoup d'exercices dans le livre
5. partir avant l'heure
6. avoir un examen

E. Questions. Alice parle à son fils Éric de son week-end. Elle désire toujours plus de détails. Trouvez une question logique en vous basant sur les phrases d'Éric.

EXEMPLE ÉRIC: — **Je suis sorti avec des amis hier soir.**
ALICE: — **Avec qui est-ce que tu es sorti?**
OU **Où est-ce que vous êtes allés?**

1. — Nous sommes allés en ville.
— ______________________
2. — Nous avons fait du shopping.
— ______________________
3. — Après, nous sommes allés au cinéma.
— ______________________
4. — Ensuite, nous avons fait une promenade.
— ______________________
5. — Je suis rentré assez tard.
— ______________________

où **quand**
avec qui
POURQUOI
QUEL **qu'est-ce que**
à quelle heure
combien de *???*
COMMENT

F. Tu as passé un bon week-end? Demandez à votre partenaire s'il/si elle a passé un bon week-end. Il/Elle va dire ce qu'il/elle a fait samedi matin, samedi soir et dimanche après-midi. Pour chaque chose qu'il/elle dit, demandez plus de détails.

Voilà pourquoi!

SELF-CHECK
1. What does the word **y** often mean?
2. Where do you place **y** in a sentence in the present? in the **passé composé**? when there is a verb followed by an infinitive?

Le pronom y

Use the pronom **y** to replace a prepositional phrase to say *there.*

Je suis allé(e) *à Paris* l'année dernière. → **J'*y* suis allé(e) l'année dernière.**

In the present, **y** is placed just before the verb, in the **passé composé** before the auxiliary, and when there is a conjugated verb + an infinitive, it goes before the infinitive.

Je passe beaucoup de temps *à Paris*. → **J'*y* passe beaucoup de temps.**
J'ai passé beaucoup de temps *à Paris*. → **J'*y* ai passé beaucoup de temps.**
Je vais passer beaucoup de temps *à Paris*. → **Je vais *y* passer beaucoup de temps.**

In French, y is often used where *there* is understood.

On *y* va? *Shall we go (there)?* **J'*y* vais!** *I'm going (there)!*

Savez-vous le faire?

A. Vous y allez souvent? Dites si vous allez souvent (quelquefois, rarement, ne... jamais) aux endroits suivants. Indiquez la dernière fois que vous y êtes allé(e).

EXEMPLE à la plage → **J'y vais quelquefois. J'y suis allé(e) l'été dernier.**

1. au théâtre
2. au musée
3. chez vos parents
4. au bureau du professeur
5. à New York
6. aux matchs de football

B. En week-end. Pensez à une ville où vous avez passé un week-end magnifique. Préparez une conversation dans laquelle votre partenaire vous pose des questions pour obtenir des renseignements (*information*) sur les sujets suivants.

- où vous êtes allé(e)
- quand vous y êtes allé(e)
- avec qui vous y êtes allé(e)
- comment vous y êtes allé(e)
- combien de temps vous y avez passé
- si vous êtes descendu(e) dans un hôtel ou chez des amis
- ce que vous y avez fait
- si vous avez l'intention d'y retourner un jour

C'est à lire!

There is much to do in Paris. How do the Parisians themselves prefer to spend their free time? On page 194, you will find a survey from *Le Figaro* magazine. You can understand what the survey found out by using your ability to recognize verbs and to guess from words that you already know.

A. Mots apparentés. Dites un mot en anglais qui ressemble aux verbes en caractères gras. Ensuite devinez leur sens.

1. Trente pour cent des Français **se reposent** pendant le week-end.
2. Quels moyens de transport **utilisez**-vous?
3. Beaucoup de Français **s'évadent** à la campagne.
4. L'ambiance du week-end **favorise** cette activité.
5. Beaucoup de Français **possèdent** une résidence secondaire.
6. Combien de kilomètres faites-vous pour **vous rendre** à votre destination?

B. Selon le contexte. Utilisez le contexte pour deviner le sens des mots en caractères gras dans la conversation suivante:

— Est-ce que vous partez souvent en week-end?
— Assez souvent, mais pas toutes les semaines.
— Vous partez **en famille**?
— Oui, je n'aime pas beaucoup voyager seul.
— Quand est-ce que vous partez d'habitude?
— Généralement, le samedi mais pas très tôt. **En fin de matinée** ou **en début** d'après-midi, vers midi.

Les week-ends des Français

Beaucoup de Français préfèrent rester chez eux plutôt que de partir en week-end. Et 90% de ceux qui s'évadent utilisent leur voiture personnelle. La maison, la voiture: ce sont les refuges rassurants de la société du «cocooning». Voilà le principal renseignement de notre sondage «Sofres-Figaro-Magazine» sur les week-ends des Français.

Quand partez-vous en week-end?

Toutes les semaines	**4%**
Une ou deux fois par mois	**13**
Quelquefois dans l'année	**26**
Rarement	**24**
Sans réponse	**33**

Quelles sont vos activités préférées du week-end?

Vous promener	**48%**
Voir des amis	**39**
Voir la famille	**36**
Vous reposer	**30**
Regarder la télévision	**22**
Bricoler	**21**
Lire un livre	**20**
Faire du sport	**20**
Jardiner	**19**
Aller au restaurant	**16**
Aller voir un spectacle	**13**
Assister à une manifestation sportive	**11%**
Aller à la chasse ou à la pêche	**11**
Aller au cinéma	**10**
Lire des revues ou des magazines	**9**
Aller visiter un musée, un monument	**9**
Faire des courses	**7**
Sans réponse	**3**

Le total des pourcentages est supérieur à 100, les personnes interrogées ayant donné plusieurs réponses.

Le plus souvent, comment partez-vous?

Seul(e)	**7%**
En couple	**38**
En famille	**50**
Avec des amis	**21**
Sans réponse	**0**

En règle générale, quel moyen de transport utilisez-vous?

Voiture personnelle	**90%**
Train	**11**
Autocar	**4**
Avion	**3**
Voiture de location	**1**
Sans réponse	**2**

En règle générale, où allez-vous lorsque vous partez en week-end?

Dans votre résidence secondaire	**10%**
Chez des **parents**	**55**
Chez des amis	**43**
À l'hôtel	**13**
En camping	**16**
Autres réponses	**4**
Sans réponse	**0**

Quand partez-vous en week-end?

Le vendredi après-midi	**7%**
Le vendredi soir	**23**
Le samedi matin tôt	**24**
Le samedi en fin de matinée ou en début d'après-midi	**33**
Sans réponse	**13**

Combien de kilomètres faites-vous pour vous rendre sur votre lieu de séjour lorsque vous partez en week-end?

Moins de 100 kilomètres	**28%**
Entre 100 et 200 kilomètres	**34**
Entre 200 et 500 kilomètres	**26**
Plus de 500 kilomètres	**8%**
Sans réponse	**4**

les parents (*m*) *relatives*

Avez-vous compris?

A. Résultats. Regardez la case (*box*) à la page 194 où sont indiquées les activités préférées des Français et répondez aux questions suivantes.

1. Trouvez au moins (*at least*) une activité pour les catégories suivantes: activités culturelles / activités à la maison / activités sportives / activités sociales.
2. Est-ce que les Français préfèrent les activités de plein air ou les activités qu'on fait à la maison? Quelles sont les trois activités de plein air qu'ils préfèrent?

B. Quand on part... Utilisez les renseignements du sondage (*poll*) pour compléter ces phrases.

1. La majorité des Français ne partent pas en week-end toutes les semaines. Ils partent...
2. En général, ils ne partent pas seuls. Ils préfèrent partir...
3. Quand ils partent en week-end, ils ne descendent pas toujours à l'hôtel. Le plus souvent, ils vont...
4. Généralement, ils ne partent pas le vendredi, ils partent...

C. Et vous? Utilisez les questions dans chaque case du sondage du *Figaro* pour faire un sondage sur les passe-temps de vos camarades de classe.

Ça y est! C'est à vous!

A. Organisez-vous! Vous allez décrire un voyage imaginaire à Paris. Regardez les photos à la page suivante et imaginez ce qu'on peut (*can*) faire aux endroits suivants.

EXEMPLE au Quartier latin
parler avec des étudiants, acheter des vieux livres

1. au musée d'Orsay
2. au Forum des Halles
3. au bois de Boulogne

B. Rédaction: Une semaine à Paris. Vous avez passé une semaine à Paris. Écrivez un journal (*diary*) où vous décrivez ce que vous avez fait chaque jour. Parlez des choses suivantes:

- à quelle heure vous êtes parti(e) d'ici
- à quelle heure vous êtes arrivé(e) à Paris
- dans quelle sorte d'hôtel vous êtes descendu(e)
- combien vous avez payé par nuit
- combien de temps vous avez passé à l'hôtel
- ce que vous avez fait lundi, mardi... à quelle heure vous êtes sorti(e) et rentré(e)
- ce que vous avez beaucoup aimé
- si vous avez l'intention d'y retourner et quand

C. Ressemblances. Échangez votre journal avec un(e) camarade de classe. Lisez l'exercice précédent et faites une liste des différences et des ressemblances entre son journal et le vôtre. Ensuite, comparez votre liste avec la liste de votre partenaire pour voir si vous avez trouvé les mêmes ressemblances et différences. Finalement, comparez votre semaine à Paris avec celle de votre camarade et décrivez-les aux autres étudiants.

D. La journée d'Éric. Alice parle avec son fils Éric de sa journée. Écoutez pour déterminer ce qu'il a fait ce matin et cet après-midi.

Le Quartier latin

Le musée d'Orsay

Le Forum des Halles

Le bois de Boulogne

Pour vérifier

Étudiez la liste de vocabulaire. Après avoir fini ces exercices, vérifiez vos réponses dans *l'Appendix C.*

Talking about the weather

A. Quel temps fait-il? Utilisez deux expressions pour décrire le temps qu'il fait dans ces endroits pendant la saison indiquée.

1. en Alaska en hiver
2. en Arizona en été
3. à Londres (*London*) au printemps
4. en Californie en automne

B. Et cette semaine? Imaginez: 1. Quel temps il va faire demain dans les endroits indiqués dans l'activité précédente. 2. Quel temps il a fait hier.

Suggesting leisure activities

C. Moi, j'ai... Utilisez une expression avec **avoir** pour dire la même chose.

EXEMPLE Je voudrais boire quelque chose. → **J'ai soif.**

1. Éric a envie de dormir.
2. Alice et moi avons besoin de manger.
3. Je pense que je vais faire un voyage cet été.

D. Suggestions. Suggérez quelque chose à faire dans les situations suivantes.

EXEMPLE J'ai besoin d'exercice. → **On fait du jogging? / Faisons du jogging.**

1. Regarde! Il neige!
2. Tous mes vêtements sont vieux!
3. J'ai faim.
4. Le chien a besoin de sortir de l'appartement.

E. Activités. Indiquez une activité souvent faite par les personnes indiquées. Utilisez une expression avec **faire**.

EXEMPLE Mon frère... → **Mon frère fait souvent du camping.**

1. Moi, je...
2. Mes amis et moi, nous...
3. Mon ami _____...
4. Mon amie _____...
5. Les jeunes Américains...

Saying where you went and what you did there

F. La dernière fois. Indiquez la dernière fois que vous avez fait les choses suivantes.

1. rentrer après minuit
2. partir en week-end
3. passer toute la journée à la maison
4. aller à la plage
5. être malade
6. avoir un examen

Vocabulaire

Talking about the weather

LES SAISONS
l'automne (*m*)
(en automne)
l'été (*m*) (en été)
l'hiver (*m*) (en hiver)
le printemps
(au printemps)

LE TEMPS
Quel temps fait-il?
Il fait beau / mauvais.
Il fait chaud / frais / froid.
Il fait du soleil.
Il fait du vent.

Il neige. (neiger)
Il pleut. (pleuvoir)

Suggesting leisure activities

EXPRESSIONS AVEC AVOIR
avoir besoin de
avoir chaud
avoir envie de
avoir faim
avoir froid
avoir l' intention de
avoir peur (de)
avoir raison
avoir soif
avoir sommeil
avoir tort

D'AUTRES VERBES
améliorer
boire
décider
dépendre de
suivre un cours
take

EXPRESSIONS AVEC FAIRE
faire de l'exercice
faire des courses
faire des projets
faire du bateau
faire du camping
faire du jardinage
faire du shopping
faire du ski (nautique)
faire du sport (du tennis...)
faire la cuisine
faire la lessive
faire le ménage
faire une promenade
faire un tour (à vélo,
en voiture)
faire un voyage

SUGGESTIONS
On y va?
Qu'est-ce qu'on fait?

DIVERS
c'est dommage
la chance
confortable
un fast-food
malheureusement
ne... rien
une nuit
quelques
quelqu'un
reposé(e)
si
une soirée
tard
tôt

Saying where you went and what you did there

EXPRESSIONS VERBALES
arriver
descendre
entrer (dans)
monter
partir de...
partir pour...
partir pour le (en) week-end
passer
quitter
rentrer
rester
retourner
sortir (de)
trouver
visiter

NOMS
une activité (de plein air)
un accident
des affaires (*f*)
un camping
un club
une fois
un hôtel
une succursale
le travail

DIVERS
dernier (dernière)
donc therefore
en autocar
en avion
en train
passé(e)
pendant
y

Pour les expressions qui indiquent le passé, voir la page 185.
Pour les participes passés, voir les pages 184 et 190.

Le Baiser
Constantin Brancusi (1876–1957)
Circa 1911
Paris, Musée National d'Art Moderne
Giraudon/Art Resource

Although Brancusi was Romanian, he lived in Paris for most of his career. **Le Baiser** (*The Kiss*) is one of a series of sculptures, all bearing the same name. A full-length version of **Le Baiser** was installed in Montparnasse Cemetery in Paris.

Chapitre 6 Les invitations

By the end of this chapter, you should be able to do the following in French:

- Issue and accept invitations
- Plan activities
- Ask about acquaintances
- Offer something to eat and drink

Notre-Dame
Henri Rousseau (1844–1910)
1909
The Phillips Collection

This painting of **Notre-Dame de Paris** was executed only a year before Rousseau's death. Many artists, including Robert Delaunay and Paul Signac, have painted **Notre-Dame** from this same spot on the **Quai Henri IV**.

Pour commencer

Éric, le fils d'Alice, invite sa petite amie Michèle au cinéma ce soir.

Et vous, quel genre de film est-ce que vous avez envie de voir?

une comédie

une comédie musicale

un film policier

un film d'épouvante

un film d'aventures

un drame

un film de science-fiction

un film d'amour

un dessin animé

Éric téléphone à sa petite amie Michèle pour parler de leurs projets pour ce soir.

MME THIBAULT: Allô? Qui est à l'appareil?
ÉRIC: Allô? Bonjour, madame Thibault. C'est Éric Pérez. Est-ce que je peux parler avec Michèle?
MME THIBAULT: Un moment. Ne quittez pas.
MICHÈLE: Allô?
ÉRIC: Salut, Michèle. C'est moi, Éric. Comment ça va?
MICHÈLE: Ça va. Et toi?
ÉRIC: Ça va. Écoute, tu es libre ce soir? Tu veux sortir?
MICHÈLE: Oui. Qu'est-ce que tu as envie de faire?
ÉRIC: On **passe le** nouveau **film** de John Carpenter.
MICHÈLE: Ah non, pas ça, je déteste les films d'épouvante. Je trouve ça horrible. Je préfère voir un film d'amour.
ÉRIC: Non, moi, **ça ne me plaît pas tellement.** Que penses-tu d'une comédie?
MICHÈLE: D'accord. Allons voir une comédie. Tu veux voir ce nouveau film au Gaumont?
ÉRIC: Oui, d'accord! À quelle heure?
MICHÈLE: Allons à **la séance** de vingt heures quarante-cinq.
ÉRIC: Alors, je passe chez toi vers huit heures?
MICHÈLE: D'accord. À tout à l'heure.
ÉRIC: Au revoir, Michèle.

passer un film *to show a movie* **ça ne me plaît pas** *I don't like that* **tellement** *so much*
la séance *showing*

Savez-vous le faire?

A. Quels sont vos goûts? Comment trouvez-vous ces genres de films?

EXEMPLE les comédies → **Je trouve les comédies amusantes.**

1. les comédies
2. les films policiers
3. les films d'aventures
4. les films de science-fiction
5. les comédies musicales
6. les films d'épouvante
7. les drames
8. les dessins animés

intéressant *amusant*
???
ENNUYEUX
mauvais bête
désagréable *horrible*

B. Préférences. Demandez à un(e) partenaire s'il/si elle aime les genres de films mentionnés dans l'exercice précédent. Ensuite, expliquez les préférences de votre partenaire à la classe.

EXEMPLE une comédie
— Est-ce que tu aimes les comédies?
— Oui, j'aime les comédies. / Non, je n'aime pas les comédies.
APRÈS, À LA CLASSE: **Robert aime les comédies, mais il n'aime pas...**

C. Quel genre de film est-ce? Voilà la liste des films dont on parle dans le *Pariscope* de cette semaine. Trouvez un titre correspondant à chaque genre de film mentionné dans *A. Quels sont vos goûts?* à la page précédente.

EXEMPLE les comédies → ____________, **c'est une comédie.**
OU **Il n'y a pas de comédie cette semaine.**

SIGNIFICATION DES LETTRES PRÉCÉDANT LES TITRES DES FILMS : AV □ aventure ; CD □ comédie dramatique ; CM □ comédie musicale ; CO □ comédie ; CT □ court métrage ; DA □ dessin animé ; DC □ documentaire ; DP □ drame psychologique ; EP □ film d'épouvante ; ER □ érotique ; ES □ espionnage ; FA □ fantastique ; FC □ film catastrophe ; FH □ film historique ; FM □ film musical ; FP □ film politique ; GC □ grand classique ; GR □ guerre ; GS □ grand spectacle ; HO □ horreur ; KA □ karaté ; PO □ policier ; SF □ science fiction ; WS □ western. ▶ Interdits aux – 18 ans.

1 les halles

1 LES FORUMS CINEMAS ORIENT EXPRESS rue de l'Orient-Express, niveau-4. 42.33.42.26 - 36.65.70.67 (Ciné Fil). M° Châtelet Les Halles. Perm de 11h15 (sf dim et jours fériés) à 24 h. Pl: 34, 35, 36 et 38 F: de 13h30 à 18h30 Pl: 33 F;Mer tarif unique 28 et 29 F. Etud, CV, militaires, pl: 28 et 29 F. Séances de 12 h, pl: 28 F, Carte UGC Privilège 1: 116 F (4 entrées); Carte UGC Privilège 2: 174 F (6 entrées). Rens: 3615 UGC.

PO ***L'arme fatale 3*** v.o.
Séances: 11h40 (sf Dim). 14h10, 16h30, 19h10, 21h40. Film 20 mn après.

CO ***Boomerang*** v.o.
Séances: 11h20, 13h50, 16h20, 18h50, 21h20. Film 25 mn après.

CD ***The player*** v.o.
Séances: 11h50 (sf Dim). 14h20, 16h50, 19h20, 21h50. Film 25 mn après.

CD ***Talons aiguilles*** v.o.
Séances: 11h30 (sf Dim), 14h, 16h30, 19h, 21h30. Film 35 mn après.

HO ***La nuit déchirée*** v.o. Int - 16 ans.
Séances: 12h (sf Dim). 14h, 16h, 18h, 20h, 22h. Film 20 mn après.

CO ***Delicatessen***
Séances: 12h (sf Dim), 14h, 16h, 18h, 20h, 22h. Film 15 mn après.

2 FORUM HORIZON 7, place de la Rotonde, Nouveau Forum. 45.08.57.57 - 36.65.70.83 (Ciné Fil). M° Châtelet Les Halles. Perm de 11h à 24h. Pl: 39, 42, 44 et 48 F; Mer 34 et 37 F. Etud, milit., C.V, tlj : 34 et 37 F. Séances: de 12h: 28 F. Carte UGC Privilège 1: 116 F (4 entrées); Carte UGC Privilège 2: 174 F (6 entrées). Rens.: 3615 UGC.. **Salles accessibles aux handicapés.**

CD ***L. 627***
Séances: 12h, 15h, 18h, 21h. Film 30 mn après.

DP ***La main sur le berceau*** v.o. Int - 12 ans. Dolby stéréo.
Séances: 11h, 13h10, 15h20, 17h30, 19h40, 21h50. Film 25 mn après.

AV ***Le dernier des Mohicans*** v.o. Dolby stéréo.
Séances: 11h05, 13h15, 15h25, 17h35, 19h45, 21h55. Film 15 mn après.

CD ***Un cœur en hiver*** Dolby stéréo.
Séances: 11h15, 13h25, 15h35, 17h45, 19h55, 22h05. Film 20 mn après.

CM ***Ballroom dancing*** v.o.
Séances: 12h05, 14h05, 16h05, 18h05, 20h05, 22h05. Film 20 mn après.
Grande salle: (Pl: 48 et 42 F)

AV ***Horizons lointains*** v.o. 70mm. Dolby THX.
Séances: 12h15, 15h15, 18h15, 21h15. Film 30 mn après.

3 GAUMONT LES HALLES 1, 3 rue Pierre Lescot, Forum des Halles. Niveau-3. 40.26.12.12. M° Châtelet Les Halles. Pl: 41 F. Mer tarif unique: 33 F. Etud, C.V, F.N (du Dim 20h au Ven 18h), - 18 ans (du Dim 20h au Mar 18h): 32 F. De 11h à 12h45, pl: 28 F. Carte bleue acceptée. Réservation possible le jour même. Rens: 3615 Gaumont. 5 salles accessibles aux handicapés.

CD ***Léolo***
Séances: 11h10, 13h20, 15h30, 17h40, 19h50, 22h. Film 20 mn après.

DP ***JF partagerait appartement*** v.o. Int - 12 ans.
Séances: 11h45, 14h15, 16h45, 19h15, 21h45. Film 30 mn après.

WS ***Impitoyable*** v.o. Dolby stéréo. Scope. (Pl: 44 et 33 F).
Séances: 11h20, 13h55, 16h30, 19h20, 21h55. Film 15 mn après.

SF ***Alien 3*** v.o. Int - 12 ans.
Séances: 12h, 14h20, 16h40, 19h, 21h20. Film 20 mn après.

CO ***Albert souffre***
Séances: 11h05, 13h15, 15h25, 17h40, 19h50, 22h05. Film 15 mn après.

DP ***La peste*** version anglaise
Séances: 11h10 (film), 13h35, 16h15, 18h55, 21h35. Film 10 mn après.

D. Possibilités. Dites le genre de film que chacun a probablement envie de voir.

EXEMPLE Vincent adore les livres d'Agatha Christie.
Il a envie de voir un film policier.

1. Éric adore les livres de Jules Verne et de Ray Bradbury.
2. Sa petite amie adore les Trois Stooges et Chevy Chase.
3. Vincent et Alice aiment beaucoup les livres d'Agatha Christie.
4. Les amis de Vincent aiment la musique et la danse.
5. Les amis d'Éric aiment louer la cassette vidéo *Halloween Trois.*
6. La petite amie d'Éric adore les films de Steven Spielberg.
7. Alice aime beaucoup les films de Walt Disney.

E. On fait des projets. Téléphonez à un(e) camarade de classe. Invitez votre camarade à aller voir un film ce soir. Choisissez un film, une séance et décidez à quelle heure vous allez passer chez votre ami(e). Jouez les rôles avec un(e) camarade de classe.

Remarquez que...

The French do not use A.M. and P.M. To indicate this information, you may use:

du matin	**Nous allons partir à huit heures et demie *du matin.***
de l'après-midi	**Il est une heure *de l'après-midi.***
du soir	**J'aime préparer mes cours vers neuf heures *du soir.***

In official schedules, and more and more in conversation, the French use the 24-hour clock. With the 24-hour clock, you continue counting 13 to 24, instead of beginning with 1 to 12 o'clock again during the P.M. hours. Also, you do not use **et quart**, **et demie**, or **moins**, but rather the number of minutes after the hour. To convert from the 24-hour clock, just subtract twelve hours:

13h45 (**treize heures quarante-cinq**) = 1h45 (**deux heures moins le quart de l'après-midi**)
22h30 (**vingt-deux heures trente**) = 10h30 (**dix heures et demie du soir**)

À la télé. Invitez un(e) camarade de classe chez vous pour regarder la télé. Choisissez trois émissions (*programs*) que vous allez regarder et dites à quelle heure commence chaque émission.

télévision

MERCREDI **29 JUILLET**

TF1

12h : Tournez manège. — **12h30** : Le juste prix. — **13h** : Journal. — **13h40** : Les feux de l'amour. — **14h30** : Côte Ouest. — **15h30** : Hemingway. — **17h05** : Club Dorothée. — **17h40** : Loin de ce monde. — **18h** : Premiers baisers. — **18h20** : Une famille en or. — **18h50** : Santa Barbara. — **19h15** : La roue de la fortune. — **19h45** : Pas folles les bêtes. — **20h** : Journal. — **20h50** : «Le secret de château Valmont », téléfilm de Charles Jarrot, avec Michael York, Lucy Gutteridge, Hugh Grant, Mia Sara (1ère partie). — **22h55** : Club olympique. — **0h35** : Journal.

A2

12h25 : Que le meilleur gagne. — **13h** : Journal. — **13h40** : Jeux olympiques. — **20h** : Journal. — **20h50** : Jeux sans frontières. — **22h15** : «Coiffure pour dames », pièce de Robert Harlinq, mise en scène de Stéphane Hillel, avec Marthe Villalonga, Françoise Christophe. — **24h** : Journal. — **0h20** : Musiques au cœur de l'été.

FR3

12h45 : Journal. — **13h** : Jeux olympiques. — **13h25** : Les vacances de Monsieur Lulo. — **14h50** : L'homme de Vienne. — **15h40** : La grande vallée. — **16h30** : Les vacances de M. Lulo. — **18h30** : Questions pour un champion. — **19h** : Le 19/20. — **20h** : Jeux olympiques. — **22h30** : Journal. — **22h50** : Les incorruptibles. — **23h40** : Spécial francophonie. — **0h35** : Mélomanuit.

M6

12h : Lassie. — **12h30** : Ma sorcière bien aimée. — **13h** : Roseanne. — **13h30** : Madame est servie. — **14h** : Les années FM. — **14h25** : EM6. — **14h50** : Culture Pub. — **15h20** : La tête de l'emploi. — **15h45** : Fréquenstar. — **16h50** : Zygomachine. — **17h15** : Nouba. — **17h35** : Brigade de nuit. — **18h30** : L'étalon noir. — **19h** : La petite maison dans la prairie. — **20h** : Madame est servie. — **20h40** : «La panthère contre le crime », téléfilm américain de Brian Trenchard-Smith, avec Edward John Stazak, John Stanton, Jim Richards. — **22h30** : « Les complices », téléfilm allemand de Michael Lahn, avec Alexander Radazum, Gudrun Landgrebe, Angelika Bender. — **23h55** : Vénus. — **0h20** : Boulevard des clips.

Comment s'y prendre?

Noting the important information

When making plans, we often jot down important information for later reference. If a friend invited you to do something, what sort of information would you want to remember? Look at the following invitation and think about what information is given.

Nous vous attendons

le Samedi 18 novembre

à 19 *heures.*

Notre adresse:

85 boulevard St Michel

Téléphone 43.29-69.50

R.S.V.P.

Savez-vous le faire?

A. Prenez des notes. Des amis invitent Éric à faire quelque chose. Écoutez leurs invitations et prenez des notes en français. Qu'est-ce qu'ils vont faire? Où? Quand? Vous allez entendre trois invitations.

B. À vous. Éric demande à Michèle si elle veut bien l'accompagner (*accompany him*). Utilisez vos notes de l'exercice précédent pour jouer le rôle d'Éric. Donnez les détails de l'invitation à Michèle. Un(e) camarade de classe va jouer le rôle de Michèle et va accepter ou refuser l'invitation.

EXEMPLE — **Je vais jouer au tennis avec Marc demain à...**
Est-ce que tu voudrais jouer avec nous?
— **Je veux bien!**

Qu'est-ce qui se passe?

On va au cinéma?

Alice demande à son mari s'il veut aller au cinéma. Lisez les questions de l'exercice suivant. Ensuite, écoutez leur conversation et notez les détails importants.

Avez-vous compris?

A. Quel film? Répondez aux questions suivantes d'après la conversation entre Alice et son mari.

1. Quels genres de films est-ce qu'ils mentionnent?
2. Comment est-ce que Vincent trouve les films de science-fiction avec Arnold Schwarzenegger?
3. Quel genre de film est-ce qu'ils décident d'aller voir?
4. Où est-ce qu'on passe ce film?
5. À quelle séance est-ce qu'ils vont aller?

B. Vos notes. Utilisez vos notes pour recréer (*re-create*) la conversation entre Alice et Vincent avec un(e) camarade de classe.

C. Allons au cinéma. Regardez les affiches. Avec un(e) camarade de classe, parlez des films qui passent au cinéma. Décidez quel film vous préférez aller voir, parlez des séances et choisissez une heure pour aller voir le film.

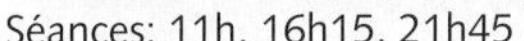
Séances: 11h, 16h15, 21h45

Séances: 13h30, 19h

Remarquez que...

Since Auguste and Louis Lumière devised the early motion picture camera, the **cinématographe** which gave us the word **cinéma**, France has played a great role in the history of film. The Lumière brothers showed the first real movie depicting scenes of life in Paris in 1895. Georges Méliès was the first filmmaker to create fictional narratives and to use special effects like slow motion and double exposure. After World War II, filmmakers of **la nouvelle vague** such as Claude Chabrol, Jean-Luc Godard, Éric Rohmer, Louis Malle, and François Truffaut continued this spirit of innovation. The dedication of the French to the film industry continues today and is evident in events such as the annual film festival at Cannes, which attracts actors and filmmakers from all over the world. The **césar** is the French equivalent of the Hollywood Oscar.

Qu'en savez-vous? Can you match these films to their actors and directors (**metteurs en scène**)?

1. *Jules et Jim*
2. *Chocolat*
3. *La Rue cases nègres* (*Sugar Cane Alley*)
4. *La Femme Nikita*
5. *Indochine*
6. *Le Retour de Martin Guerre*
7. *Vagabond*
8. *Au Revoir les enfants*
9. *À Bout de souffle* (*Breathless*)
10. *Trois Hommes et un couffin* (*Three Men and a Baby*)

a. Jean-Luc Godard (metteur en scène), Jean-Paul Belmondo (acteur), Jean Seberg (actrice)
b. Louis Malle (metteur en scène), Gaspard Manesse (acteur)
c. Régis Wargnier (metteur en scène), Catherine Deneuve (actrice)
d. Agnès Varda (metteur en scène), Sandrine Bonnaire (actrice)
e. Coline Serreau (metteur en scène), Roland Giraud (acteur)
f. Claire Dennis (metteur en scène), Cécile Ducasse (actrice)
g. Euzhan Palcy (metteur en scène), Jarry Cadenat (acteur)
h. Luc Besson (metteur en scène), Anne Parillaud (actrice)
i. François Truffaut (metteur en scène), Jeanne Moreau (actrice)
j. Daniel Vigne (metteur en scène), Gérard Depardieu (acteur), Nathalie Baye (actrice)

Qu'est-ce qu'on dit?

Pour inviter **quelqu'un, vous pouvez** dire...

À UN(E) AMI(E)	À UNE AUTRE PERSONNE À UN GROUPE DE PERSONNES
Est-ce que tu es libre ce soir?	Est-ce que vous êtes libre(s) ce soir?
Tu veux...?	**Vous voulez...?**
Est-ce que tu voudrais...?	Est-ce que vous voudriez...?
Est-ce que tu as envie de...?	Est-ce que vous avez envie de...?
Je t'invite à...	Je voudrais vous inviter à...

CULTURE NOTE
The expression **je t'invite** / **je vous invite** implies that you will pay.

Si quelqu'un vous invite, vous pouvez répondre...

POUR DIRE **OUI**	POUR SUGGÉRER UNE AUTRE ACTIVITÉ
Oui, je veux bien.	Je préfère...
Quelle bonne idée!	J'aime mieux...
Avec plaisir!	Allons **plutôt** à...
D'accord	

POUR DIRE **NON**

Je regrette, mais...
Malheureusement...
Je ne peux pas parce que...
Je voudrais bien, mais...
  je suis **occupé(e)**.
  je ne suis pas libre.
  je dois travailler.

Éric fait des projets avec Michèle.
— Je pense aller voir la nouvelle exposition au Grand Palais demain. **Ça te dit?**
— Je regrette mais, moi, je ne peux pas. Mes parents travaillent **jusqu'à** huit heures demain et je dois rester avec ma petite sœur. On peut y aller samedi si tu veux.
— Samedi? Oui, d'accord. À quelle heure?
— Rendez-vous devant le musée vers dix heures?
— D'accord.

quelqu'un *someone* **vous pouvez** (**pouvoir** *can, to be able*) **tu veux, vous voulez** (**vouloir** *to want*) **plutôt** *instead, rather* **je peux** (**pouvoir** *can, to be able*) **occupé(e)** *busy* **je dois** (**devoir** *must, to have to*) **Ça te dit?** *How does that sound to you?* **jusqu'à** *until*

A. Oui, volontiers. On invite Alice à faire beaucoup de choses. Écoutez ses réponses et écrivez **oui** si elle accepte. Si elle n'accepte pas, écrivez **non.**

B. Qu'est-ce qu'elle veut faire? Écoutez les projets d'Alice. Dites si elle invite quelqu'un **à manger quelque chose, à boire quelque chose** ou **à faire quelque chose d'autre.**

EXEMPLE VOUS ENTENDEZ: Je voudrais vous inviter à dîner chez nous.
VOUS RÉPONDEZ: **à manger quelque chose**

Le Grand Palais

Le Petit Palais

The **Grand Palais** and **Petit Palais** are museums built for the 1900 World's Fair. The **Grand Palais** holds important temporary exhibits and houses the Science Museum. The **Petit Palais** houses the Museum of Fine Arts of the City of Paris.

Voilà pourquoi!

Les verbes **devoir**, **pouvoir** et **vouloir**

Use the irregular verb **devoir** followed by an infinitive to say what you *must do* or *have to do*. **Devoir** can also mean *to owe*.

DEVOIR (*TO HAVE TO, MUST, TO OWE*)	
je **dois**	nous **devons**
tu **dois**	vous **devez**
il/elle/on **doit**	ils/elles **doivent**
PASSÉ COMPOSÉ: **j'ai dû**	

Je *dois* travailler demain. *I have to work tomorrow.*
Je *dois* 100 dollars à mon frère. *I owe my brother 100 dollars.*

In the **passé composé**, **devoir** can mean that someone *had to do something* or *must have done something*. Context will clarify the meaning.

Michèle n'est pas chez elle. Elle *a dû* partir. *Michèle isn't home. She **must have** left.*
Ils *ont dû* aller en ville. *They **had to** go downtown. / They **must have** gone downtown.*

The irregular verbs **pouvoir** (*can, to be able*) and **vouloir** (*to want*) have similar conjugations.

VOULOIR (*TO WANT*)	
je **veux**	nous **voulons**
tu **veux**	vous **voulez**
il/elle/on **veut**	ils/elles **veulent**
PASSÉ COMPOSÉ: **j'ai voulu**	

POUVOIR (*CAN, TO BE ABLE*)	
je **peux**	nous **pouvons**
tu **peux**	vous **pouvez**
il/elle/on **peut**	ils/elles **peuvent**
PASSÉ COMPOSÉ: **j'ai pu**	

Je *veux* y aller, mais je ne *peux* pas.
*I **want** to go, but I **can't**.*

Il *n'a* pas *pu* sortir parce qu'il *a dû* travailler.
*He **wasn't able** to go out because he **had to** work.*

SELF-CHECK

1. What are three possible meanings of **devoir**? What are two meanings of **pouvoir**? What does **vouloir** mean?
2. The **nous** and **vous** forms have the same vowel in the stem as the infinitive. What vowels do the other forms have?
3. How is the pronunciation of the **ils/elles** forms different from the pronunciation of the **il/elle** forms for these verbs?

Et ça se prononce comment?

Le son **oi**

The combination **oi** is pronounced similarly to the *wa* sound at the start of the English word *water*. Practice this sound in these words:

m*oi* t*oi* je d*oi*s dev*oi*r ils d*oi*vent fr*oi*d pourqu*oi* voul*oi*r au rev*oi*r

Savez-vous le faire?

A. Prononcez bien! Complétez la conversation avec les mots logiques de la liste suivante. Ensuite, écoutez la conversation pour vérifier vos réponses.

pourquoi moi soir voir moi dois soif voiture

— Tu veux faire quelque chose avec ______ ?
— Tu as ______ ?
— Oui, allons au café! On y va dans ma ______ ?
— ______ pas? Après, tu veux aller ______ un film?
— Je regrette, ______ , je ______ travailler ce ______ .

Maintenant, jouez la scène avec un(e) partenaire. Faites attention à la prononciation.

B. On doit... Aujourd'hui les Pérez ne peuvent pas faire ce qu'ils veulent. Jouez le rôle d'Alice qui explique ce que chacun doit faire.

EXEMPLE Moi...
Moi, je dois faire de l'exercice.

1. Le chien et moi, nous...

2. Éric et Cathy...

3. Vincent...

4. Nos amis...

5. Louis...

C. On aimerait... Regardez les illustrations de l'exercice précédent. D'après Alice, qu'est-ce que chacun veut faire?

EXEMPLE Moi, je **veux dormir.**

D. Pourquoi ça? Alice explique pourquoi ils ne peuvent pas faire ce qu'il veulent dans l'exercice *B. On doit...* à la page précédente. Regardez encore les illustrations et décidez ce qu'elle dit.

EXEMPLE **Moi, je ne peux pas dormir parce que je dois faire de l'exercice.**

E. Encore des explications. Deux jours plus tard, Alice explique encore pourquoi la famille n'a pas pu faire ce qu'ils voulaient (*wanted*).

EXEMPLE **Moi, je n'ai pas pu dormir parce que j'ai dû faire de l'exercice.**

F. Invitations. Éric invite des amis à un festival de dessins animés. Complétez leur conversation logiquement avec la forme correcte de **vouloir, devoir** ou **pouvoir**. Dans certains cas, il y a plus d'une réponse possible.

— Michèle, est-ce que tu ______ aller au festival de dessins animés avec moi ce soir?
— Malheureusement, je ne ______ pas. J'ai un examen important demain et je ______ étudier.
— Jean-Luc et Marc, est-ce que vous ______ y aller?
— Ça dépend. Nous ne ______ pas si c'est avant 18h parce que nous travaillons aujourd'hui.
— Ça commence à 20h, alors nous ______ partir vers 19h30.
— Alors oui, nous ______ bien.
— Est-ce que tu ______ inviter tes frères, Marc?
— Ils ne ______ pas sortir ce soir. Ils ______ aider mes parents à la maison.

G. Ça dépend. Imaginez que des amis vous invitent (*invite you*) à faire les choses suivantes. Acceptez ou refusez leurs invitations.

1. Tu as envie de sortir ce soir? Tu veux aller au cinéma?
2. Tu voudrais sortir avec moi ce week-end? J'ai envie d'aller voir un match de football.
3. Tu es libre ce soir? Je t'invite au restaurant.
4. Est-ce que tu es libre demain? Je voudrais aller au parc pour jouer au volley-ball.
5. Est-ce que tu voudrais regarder un match de basket à la télé ce soir?

Oui, je veux bien. *Je regrette, mais...* **Je préfère...**

MALHEUREUSEMENT... **JE SUIS OCCUPÉ(E).**

Je ne suis pas libre. **Quelle bonne idée!**

Je ne peux pas parce que...

Avec plaisir. JE VOUDRAIS BIEN, MAIS...

D'accord. *Je dois...*

H. Questions personnelles. Posez les questions suivantes à un(e) camarade de classe pour savoir (*to know*) ce qu'il/elle fait pendant son temps libre.

1. Ask if he/she is free this afternoon or has to do something.
2. Ask what he/she wants to do this weekend, whether he/she wants to go out, and with whom he/she likes to go out.
3. Ask when he/she likes to go out with his/her friends, and what they all like to do together.
4. Ask if he/she has to study for this course this weekend and if he/she has to study a lot for this course.
5. Ask if he/she often invites his/her friends to a restaurant.
6. Ask what his/her friends often like to do on the weekend and if they often have to study.

I. Non, merci. Albert, un camarade de classe de Michèle, veut sortir avec elle, mais elle ne veut pas sortir avec lui (*him*). Albert téléphone à Michèle pour l'inviter à sortir. Elle refuse. Albert continue avec ses invitations mais elle continue à refuser. Jouez les deux rôles avec un(e) camarade de classe. Albert doit insister. Michèle doit être très imaginative avec ses excuses.

— Chaque année, il y a un célèbre festival de cinéma à Cannes. Voudriez-vous y aller?

Qu'est-ce qu'on dit?

Comment est-ce que vous aimez **fêter** votre **anniversaire**?

J'aime...

faire une boum.

passer une soirée tranquille entre amis.

SUPPLEMENTAL VOCABULARY

un anniversaire de mariage *a wedding anniversary*
Joyeux Noël! *Merry Christmas!*
Bon anniversaire! *Happy Birthday!*
Bonne année! *Happy New Year!*

CULTURE NOTE

Since France is traditionally a Catholic country, many holidays are based on the Catholic calendar. You may also want to know these holidays:
la pâque *Passover*
Yom Kippur
Hanukkah
Ramadan

Quelle est la date de votre anniversaire?

C'est le premier...	le deux...	le trois...	le quatre...
janvier	avril	juillet	octobre
février	mai	août	novembre
mars	juin	septembre	décembre

Voici quelques **fêtes** françaises. Quelle est votre fête préférée?

le jour de l'an (le premier janvier)

Pâques (*f pl*) (en mars ou avril)

la fête du travail (le premier mai)

la fête nationale (le quatorze juillet)

la Toussaint (le premier novembre)

Noël (le vingt-cinq décembre)

fêter *to celebrate* **un anniversaire** *birthday* **une fête** *holiday*

Éric et sa petite amie Michèle ont décidé de **faire une boum.**

— Alors, c'est décidé! C'est pour samedi, la boum!
— Samedi, c'est le premier ou le deux?
— C'est le deux.
— Alors samedi vers quelle heure?
— Disons... vers 8h, 8h30?
— Bon, alors, moi je vais arriver un peu **en avance.** Et je vais **apporter** mon fameux **gâteau** au chocolat.
— Bonne idée! Ton gâteau est délicieux. Tu peux aussi apporter ta collection de disques compacts?
— Oui, bien sûr!... Alors, on va inviter les **copains** de **l'école** et qui d'autre? Je veux inviter ma **voisine** Karima.
— C'est qui Karima? Je ne **la connais** pas.
— **Mais si** tu la connais! C'est l'Algérienne qui habite **à côté.**
— Je sais qu'une famille algérienne habite là, mais je ne **les** connais pas.
— Alors, je vais l'inviter et tu vas pouvoir **faire sa connaissance.**

faire une boum *have a party* **en avance** *early* **apporter** *to bring* **un gâteau** *cake* **un(e) copain / copine** *friend* **l'école** *(f) school* **un(e) voisin(e)** *neighbor* **la** *her* **je connais (connaître** *to know, to be acquainted with)* **mais si** *but yes* **à côté** *next door* **les** *them* **faire sa connaissance** *to meet him/her*

A. Quel temps fait-il? Quel temps fait-il dans votre ville pendant ces mois?

1. en janvier
2. en juillet
3. en avril
4. en octobre
5. en décembre
6. en août
7. en novembre
8. en mai

B. D'autres fêtes. Voici d'autres jours importants en France. Est-ce que vous pouvez choisir la date correspondante dans la colonne de droite?

1. les poissons d'avril	a. le 14 février
2. la Saint-Valentin	b. le 15 août
3. l'Assomption	c. le dernier dimanche de mai
4. la fête de l'Armistice (1918)	d. le 1er avril
5. le jour du débarquement en Normandie (1944)	e. le 11 novembre
6. la fête des Mères	f. le 6 juin

C. Une boum. Vous parlez avec des amis à une boum. Donnez votre opinion en complétant les phrases suivantes.

EXEMPLE L'acteur Arnold Schwarzenegger? Je le trouve... → **Je le trouve sympa.**

1. Mes voisins? Je les trouve...
2. Les amis de mes parents? Je les trouve...
3. Les vêtements populaires en ce moment? Je les trouve...
4. Le groupe U2? Je le trouve...
5. Les films d'Alfred Hitchcock? Je les trouve...
6. La chanteuse Madonna? Je la trouve...

bon **mauvais**
intéressant ENNUYEUX
JOLI laid *???*
SUPER *bête*
DIFFICILE **???**
sympa

Voilà pourquoi!

La date

Dates in French are expressed using the cardinal numbers (**deux, trois...**) except when saying it is the *first* of the month. For the *first*, use **le premier**. You can use either of the following questions to ask the date.

— **Quelle est la date aujourd'hui?**
— **C'est le quinze novembre.**
— **Quelle date sommes-nous?**
— **Nous sommes le premier avril.**

Note that the day goes before the month in French.

14/8/1957 = **le 14 août mille neuf cent cinquante-sept**
12/10/1989 = **le 12 octobre mille neuf cent quatre-vingt-neuf**

There are two ways of expressing years in French.

1995 → **mille neuf cent quatre-vingt-quinze**
1895 → **dix-huit cent quatre-vingt-quinze**

Use **en** to say in what month or year.

J'y suis allé(e) ***en*** **1993.** **Nous sommes parti(e)s** ***en*** **juin.**

Dates are often used with the verbs **naître** (*to be born*) and **mourir** (*to die*). Use the auxiliary **être** with these verbs in the **passé composé**, and remember that the past participle must agree with the subject in gender and number.

Je ***suis né(e)*** **en 1975.** **Sa mère** ***est morte*** **en 1993.**

SELF-CHECK

1. How do you express the first of the month? And the other days?
2. How do you say that someone was born or died?

Savez-vous le faire?

A. Activités logiques. Qu'est-ce que vous faites d'habitude les jours suivants?

EXEMPLE 25/12
Le 25 décembre, j'aime passer la journée avec ma famille et nous mangeons beaucoup.

1. 24/12 2. 4/7 ou 1/7 3. 31/12 4. 1/1 5. 14/2

Maintenant, dites ce que vous avez fait à ces dates l'année dernière.

EXEMPLE 25/12
L'année dernière, je n'ai rien fait le 25 décembre. Je suis resté(e) à la maison.

B. Ils sont nés... Travaillez en groupes de trois ou quatre personnes. Chaque groupe doit deviner en quelle année ces gens sonts nés. S'ils sont morts, donnez cette date aussi. Le groupe qui devine la date la plus proche de la date correcte gagne.

EXEMPLE Henri Matisse
Il est né en 1869 et il est mort en 1954.

1. Napoléon 2. Marie-Antoinette 3. François Mitterrand

C. Des excursions. Éric invite des amis à partir ou à sortir avec lui. Suivez l'exemple.

EXEMPLE 10 jours à Nice / le 2 août
— Tu veux venir passer dix jours à Nice avec nous?
— Quand est-ce que vous allez partir?
— On va partir le 2 août et on va rentrer le 12 août.

1. trois semaines à Cannes / le 5 juillet
2. cinq jours à la campagne / le 1er septembre
3. trois heures au musée / à 1h30
4. dix jours à Chamonix / le 10 février

D. Interview. Posez les questions suivantes à un(e) camarade de classe.

1. Quelle est la date aujourd'hui? Quelle est la date de ton anniversaire? En quelle année est-ce que tu es né(e)? Quel temps fait-il d'habitude le jour de ton anniversaire? Qu'est-ce que tu aimes faire ce jour-là?
2. Quelle est la date de l'anniversaire de ton père? de ta mère? Est-ce que vous faites quelque chose ensemble pour leur anniversaire? Quelles sont d'autres dates importantes pour toi? Pourquoi?
3. Quelle est ta fête préférée? Quelle est la date de cette fête? Est-ce que tu restes à la maison ce jour-là? Qu'est-ce que tu fais?

E. Une boum. Imaginez que vous allez faire une boum chez vous pour votre anniversaire. Avec un(e) camarade de classe, préparez une conversation où vous invitez un(e) ami(e) à votre boum. N'oubliez pas de parler de l'heure et de la date de la boum.

Voilà pourquoi!

Le verbe **connaître**

Connaître means *to know someone, someplace,* or *something* in the sense of *to be acquainted with.* In the **passé composé**, it often means *met.*

CONNAÎTRE (*TO KNOW, TO BE ACQUAINTED WITH*)

je **connais**	nous **connaissons**
tu **connais**	vous **connaissez**
il/elle/on **connaît**	ils/elles **connaissent**

PASSÉ COMPOSÉ: j'**ai connu**

Reconnaître (*to recognize*) is conjugated like **connaître**.

— Est-ce que tu *connais* mes parents?
— Oui, mais je ne les *reconnais* pas toujours.

To say *to make the acquaintance of* or *to meet,* use **faire la connaissance de.**

Je voudrais *faire la connaissance de* cette femme là-bas.

SELF-CHECK

1. How is the pronunciation of **il connaît** different from **ils connaissent**?
2. How do you say the direct objects *him, her, it,* and *them* in French? Where do you place these words in the present? Where do you place **ne... pas** with relation to these words?
3. Where do you place the direct object pronoun when there is a conjugated verb followed by an infinitive? Where do you place it in the **passé composé**?

Les pronoms **le, la, l', les**

Use **le, la, l'**, and **les** to replace a person, animal, or thing that is the direct object of the verb. Use **le** (*him, it*) for masculine singular nouns and **la** (*her, it*) for feminine singular nouns. **Les** (*them*) replaces all plural nouns. **Le** and **la** become **l'** when the following word begins with a vowel sound.

— Tu connais *mon voisin*?
— Oui, je *le* connais.

— Tu trouves *cette musique* agréable?
— Non, je *la* trouve ennuyeuse.

— Tu as *mon disque compact*?
— Oui, je *l'*ai.

— Tu invites *tes amis*?
— Oui, je *les* invite.

If there is a conjugated verb followed by an infinitive in a sentence, place the direct object pronoun before the infinitive.

— Vous voulez voir *ce film*?
— Oui, nous voulons *le* voir.

— Tu vas inviter *mes parents*?
— Non, je ne vais pas *les* inviter.

If there is no infinitive, place it directly before the conjugated verb, including when the verb is negated.

— Tu invites *tes cousins*?
— Oui, je *les* invite. / Non, je ne *les* invite pas.

— Vous avez *ma cassette*?
— Oui, nous *l'*avons. / Non, nous ne *l'*avons pas.

— Tu as vu *ce film*?
— Oui, je *l'*ai vu. / Non, je ne *l'*ai pas vu.

— Il a acheté *ce disque compact*?
— Oui, il *l'*a acheté. / Non, il ne *l'*a pas acheté.

Whenever the direct object comes before the verb in the **passé composé**, the past participle must agree with it in gender and number.

— Tu as invité *mes voisins*?
— Oui, je *les* ai invités.

— Vous avez vu cette *cassette vidéo*?
— Oui, nous *l'*avons vu*e*.

Savez-vous le faire?

A. **Le quartier.** Éric dit à ses amis que sa famille connaît bien différents endroits de leur quartier. Qu'est-ce que chacun connaît bien?

EXEMPLE Maman aime aller voir des films. Elle...
Elle connaît bien les cinémas du quartier.

1. J'aime bien aller prendre un verre avec mes amis. Je...
2. Cathy et Louis aiment bien faire du shopping. Ils...
3. Mes amis et moi aimons bien manger. Nous...
4. Papa aime aller aux expositions d'art. Il...
5. Martine et toi, vous aimez aller nager, n'est-ce pas? Alors, vous...?
6. Martine, tu aimes faire des promenades? Alors, tu...?

B. **Vous les reconnaissez?** Dites si vous reconnaissez ces sites parisiens.

EXEMPLE Cette avenue? → **Oui, je la reconnais. C'est les Champs-Élysées.**
OU **Non, je ne la reconnais pas.**

EXEMPLE Cette avenue

1. Cette église?

2. Ce musée?

3. Ce parc?

C. Tu le connais? Demandez à un(e) camarade de classe s'il/si elle connaît bien différents endroits de votre ville. Donnez un nom précis. Utilisez le pronom **le, la, l'** ou **les** dans la réponse.

EXEMPLE la rue... → **— Est-ce que tu connais la rue Canyon?**
— Oui, je la connais. / Non, je ne la connais pas.

1. le magasin...
2. la librairie...
3. le parc...
4. le musée...
5. la rue...
6. les appartements...
7. le centre commercial...
8. le cinéma...
9. le restaurant...

D. **Votre ville.** Un ami français vous pose des questions au sujet de (*about*) votre ville. Dites comment vous trouvez les choses et les personnes suivantes. Utilisez le pronom **le, la, l'** ou **les.**

EXEMPLE les restaurants → **Je les trouve excellents.**

1. les théâtres	3. votre quartier	5. vos voisins	7. les rues
2. l'université	4. le temps	6. votre appartement	8. les parcs

excellent embêtant *agréable* ??? PETIT

MAUVAIS bon **HORRIBLE** **joli** laid **sympa**

E. **Une boum.** Vous êtes à une boum et vous faites la connaissance d'un(e) autre étudiant(e). Vous commencez à parler et vous apprenez que vous habitez dans le même immeuble et que vous connaissez les mêmes personnes. Parlez des connaissances que vous avez en commun.

Voilà pourquoi!

SELF-CHECK

1. Which verb meaning *to know* do you use to say that you are familiar with people or places? Which verb do you use to say that you know facts such as when, where, or why?
2. How do you say that you know how to do something?

Les verbes **savoir** et **connaître**

You already can use **connaître** to say that you know a person or a place. **Savoir** also means *to know*. In the **passé composé, savoir** means that someone *found out* something.

SAVOIR (*TO KNOW*)

je **sais**	nous **savons**
tu **sais**	vous **savez**
il/elle/on **sait**	ils/elles **savent**

PASSÉ COMPOSÉ: **j'ai su**

Use **connaître** to say you know people, places, or things with the meaning *to be acquainted with, to be familiar with,* or *to know of.*

Est-ce que tu *connais* bien le quartier?
Vous *connaissez* ma sœur, n'est-ce pas?
Tu *connais* un bon restaurant dans le quartier?

You have been using **je ne sais pas** to say that you do not know an answer. Use **savoir** to say you know facts, information, or a language. how to / can memorize

Est-ce que tu *sais* mon adresse et mon numéro de téléphone?
Je *sais* le français mais je ne *sais* pas l'allemand.

Savoir is often followed by **si** or question words like **où**, **quand**, **pourquoi**, **qui**, **quel**, and **comment.** Instead of **qu'est-ce que**, use **ce que** after **savoir. Je sais ce que...** means *I know what...* **Je sais que...** means *I know that...*

> **Tu *sais* si elle va y aller?**
> **Ils ne *savent* pas ce qu'ils veulent faire.**
> **Ils ne *savent* pas que nous arrivons ce soir.**

Use an infinitive after **savoir** to say you know how to do something.

> **Je *sais* nager mais je ne *sais* pas faire du ski nautique.**
> **Tu *sais* parler français?**

Savez-vous le faire?

A. Qui sait faire ça? Dites qui sait faire ces choses dans votre famille.

EXEMPLE nager → **Tout le monde sait nager dans ma famille.**
OU **Moi, je sais nager mais les autres ne savent pas nager.**
OU **Nous ne savons pas nager dans ma famille.**

1. faire de la cuisine italienne
2. faire du ski
3. jouer au tennis
4. bien danser
5. bien chanter
6. parler français

Maintenant demandez à un(e) autre étudiant(e) et à votre professeur s'ils savent faire ces mêmes choses.

EXEMPLE nager → **— Marc, tu sais nager? / Monsieur Grant, vous savez nager?**
— Non, je ne sais pas nager.

B. Que savent-ils faire? Dites ce que ces personnes savent bien faire.

1. Mes camarades de classe et moi, nous...
2. Le professeur...
3. Mon/Ma meilleur(e) ami(e)...
4. Tous mes amis...
5. Moi, je...
6. Ma mère...

C. Un bon film. Après le dîner, Vincent et Alice décident d'aller au cinéma. Avec un(e) partenaire, préparez sept questions logiques en combinant un élément de chaque colonne. Ensuite, utilisez les questions pour créer la conversation entre Vincent et Alice.

	où	tu veux faire ce soir?
	qui	il y a un cinéma?
	quel	il y a un bon film ce soir?
Est-ce que tu sais	à quelle heure	a fait ce film?
	ce que (qu')	acteur joue le rôle principal dans ce film?
	que (qu')	j'ai fait la connaissance de cet acteur?
	si (s')	le film commence?

D. ***Savoir* ou *connaître?*** Vous voulez faire quelque chose d'intéressant. Complétez les questions suivantes avec **Est-ce que tu sais...** ou **Est-ce que tu connais...** Ensuite, posez les questions à un(e) camarade de classe.

1. ______ les cinémas du quartier?
2. ______ s'il y a un film français qui passe en ce moment?
3. ______ bien le cinéma français?
4. ______ les films de Gérard Depardieu?
5. ______ quel âge il a?
6. ______ quel jour de la semaine les films changent?

Remarquez que...

Since France is traditionally a Catholic country, many holidays are related to the calendar of Catholic holy days. One important day of celebration is a person's saint's day or **fête**. Many French first names are taken from the saints' day calendar, and each person celebrates the date of the saint whose name he/she bears. In some families, saints' day celebrations are considered almost as important as birthdays.

Et votre fête? Est-ce que votre fête est indiquée sur le calendrier?

1994 JANVIER		
1	**S**	**Jour de l'AN**
2	**D**	**Epiphanie**
3	L	S^e Geneviève
4	M	S. Odilon
5	M	S. Èdouard
6	J	S. Mélaine
7	V	S. Raymond
8	S	S. Lucien
9	**D**	S^e Alix
10	L	S. Guillaume
11	M	S. Paulin
12	M	S^e Tatiana
13	J	S^e Yvette
14	V	S^e Nina
15	S	S. Remi
16	**D**	S. Marcel
17	L	S^e Roseline
18	M	S^e Prisca
19	M	S. Marius
20	J	S. Sébastien
21	V	S^e Agnès
22	S	S. Vincent
23	**D**	S. Barnard
24	L	S. Fr. de Sales
25	M	*Conv. S. Paul*
26	M	S^e Paule
27	J	S^e Angèle
28	V	S. Th. d'Aquin
29	S	S. Gildas
30	**D**	S^e Martine
31	L	S^e Marcelle

FÉVRIER		
1	M	S^e Ella
2	M	*Présentation*
3	J	S. Blaise
4	V	S^e Véronique
5	S	S^e Agathe
6	**D**	S. Gaston
7	L	S^e Eugénie
8	M	S^e Jacqueline
9	M	S^e Apolline
10	J	S. Arnaud
11	V	*N.-D Lourdes*
12	S	S. Félix
13	**D**	S^e Béatrice
14	L	S. Valentin
15	M	**Mardi-Gras**
16	M	**Cendres**
17	J	S. Alexis
18	V	S^e Bernadette
19	S	S. Gabin
20	**D**	**Caréme**
21	L	S. P. Damien
22	M	S^e Isabelle
23	M	S. Lazare
24	J	S. Modeste
25	V	S. Roméo
26	S	S. Nestor
27	**D**	S^e Honorine
28	L	S. Romain

Epacte 17 / Lettre dominicale B Cycle solaire 15 / Nbre d'or 19 indiction romaine 2

MARS		
1	M	S. Aubin
2	M	S. Charles le B.
3	J	S. Guénolé
4	V	S. Casimir
5	S	S. Olive
6	**D**	S^e Colette
7	L	S^e Félicité
8	M	S. Jean de D.
9	M	S^e Françoise
10	J	S. Vivien
11	V	S^e Rosine
12	S	S^e Justine
13	**D**	S. Rodrigue
14	L	S^e Mathilde
15	M	S^e Louise
16	M	S^e Bénédicte
17	J	S. Patrice
18	V	S. Cyrille
19	S	S. Joseph
20	**D**	PRINTEMPS
21	L	S^e Clémence
22	M	S^e Léa
23	M	S. Victorien
24	J	S^e Cath. de Su.
25	V	**Annonciation**
26	S	S^e Larissa
27	**D**	**Rameaux**
28	L	S. Gontran
29	M	S^e Gwladys
30	M	S. Amédée
31	J	S. Benjamin

AVRIL		
1	V	S. Hugues
2	S	S^e Sandrine
3	**D**	**PAQUES**
4	L	S. Isidore
5	M	S^e Irène
6	M	S. Marcellin
7	J	S. J.-B. de la S.
8	V	S^e Julie
9	S	S. Gautier
10	**D**	S. Fulbert
11	L	S. Stanislas
12	M	S. Jules
13	M	S^e Ida
14	J	S. Maxime
15	V	S. Paterne
16	S	S. Benoit-J.
17	**D**	S. Anicet
18	L	S. Parfait
19	M	S^e Emma
20	M	S^e Odette
21	J	S. Anselme
22	V	S. Alexandre
23	S	S. Georges
24	**D**	**Jour du Souvenir**
25	L	S. Marc
26	M	S^e Alida
27	M	S^e Zita
28	J	S^e Valérie
29	V	S^e Cath. de Si.
30	S	S. Robert

MAI		
1	**D**	**FÊTE du TRAVAIL**
2	L	S. Boris
3	M	SS. Phil., Jacq.
4	M	S. Sylvain
5	J	S^e Judith
6	V	S^e Prudence
7	S	S^e Gisèle
8	**D**	**VICT. 1945/F.J.-d'Arc**
9	L	S. Pacôme
10	M	S^e Solange
11	M	S^e Estelle
12	**J**	**ASCENSION**
13	V	S^e Rolande
14	S	S. Matthias
15	**D**	S^e Denise
16	L	S. Honoré
17	M	S. Pascal
18	M	S. Eric
19	J	S. Yves
20	V	S. Bernardin
21	S	S. Constantin
22	**D**	**PENTECÔTE**
23	L	S. Didier
24	M	S. Donatien
25	M	S^e Sophie
26	J	S. Bérenger
27	V	S. Augustin
28	S	S. Germain
29	**D**	**Fête des Mères**
30	L	S. Ferdinand
31	M	*Visitation*

JUIN 1994		
1	M	S. Justin
2	J	S^e Blandine
3	V	S. Kévin
4	S	S^e Clotilde
5	**D**	**Fête Dieu**
6	L	S. Norbert
7	M	S. Gilbert
8	M	S. Médard
9	J	S^e Diane
10	V	S. Landry
11	S	S. Barnabé
12	**D**	S. Guy
13	L	S. Antoine de P.
14	M	S. Elisée
15	M	S^e Germaine
16	J	S. J.F. Régis
17	V	S. Hervé
18	S	S. Léonce
19	**D**	S. Romuald
20	L	S. Silvère
21	M	ÉTÉ
22	M	S. Alban
23	J	S^e Audrey
24	V	S. Jean-Bapt.
25	S	S. Prosper
26	**D**	S. Anthelme
27	L	S. Fernand
28	M	S. Irénée
29	M	SS. Pierre, Paul
30	J	S. Martial

1994 JUILLET		
1	V	S. Thierry
2	S	S. Martinien
3	**D**	S. Thomas
4	L	S. Florent
5	M	S. Antoine
6	M	S^e Mariette
7	J	S. Raoul
8	V	S. Thibaut
9	S	S^e Amandine
10	**D**	S. Ulrich
11	L	S. Benoit
12	M	S. Olivier
13	M	SS. Henri, Joël
14	J	**FÊTE NATIONALE**
15	V	S. Donald
16	S	*N.D.Mt-Carmel*
17	**D**	S^e Charlotte
18	L	S. Frédéric
19	M	S. Arsène
20	M	S^e Marina
21	J	S. Victor
22	V	S^e Marie-Mad.
23	S	S^e Brigitte
24	**D**	S^e Christine
25	L	S. Jacques
26	M	SS. Anne, Joa.
27	M	S^e Nathalie
28	J	S. Samson
29	V	S^e Marthe
30	S	S^e Juliette
31	**D**	S. Ignace de L.

AOÛT		
1	L	S. Alphonse
2	M	S. Julien-Ey.
3	M	S^e Lydie
4	J	S. J.M. Vianney
5	V	S. Abel
6	S	*Transfiguration*
7	**D**	S. Gaétan
8	L	S. Dominique
9	M	S. Amour
10	M	S. Laurent
11	J	S^e Claire
12	V	S^e Clarisse
13	S	S. Hippolyte
14	**D**	S. Evrard
15	**L**	**ASSOMPTION**
16	M	S. Armel
17	M	S. Hyacinthe
18	J	S^e Hélène
19	V	S. Jean Eudes
20	S	S. Bernard
21	**D**	S. Christophe
22	L	S. Fabrice
23	M	S^e Rose de L.
24	M	S. Barthélemy
25	J	S. Louis
26	V	S^e Natacha
27	S	S^e Monique
28	**D**	S. Augustin
29	L	S^e Sabine
30	M	S. Fiacre
31	M	S. Aristide

SEPTEMBRE		
1	J	S. Gilles
2	V	S^e Ingrid
3	S	S. Grégoire
4	**D**	S^e Rosalie
5	L	S^e Raïssa
6	M	S. Bertrand
7	M	S^e Reine
8	J	*Nativité N.D.*
9	V	S. Alain
10	S	S^e Inès
11	**D**	S. Adelphe
12	L	S. Apollinaire
13	M	S. Aimé
14	M	*La S^e Croix*
15	J	S. Roland
16	V	S^e Edith
17	S	S. Renaud
18	**D**	S^e Nadège
19	L	S^e Emilie
20	M	S. Davy
21	M	S. Matthieu
22	J	S. Maurice
23	V	AUTOMNE
24	S	S^e Thècie
25	**D**	S. Hermann
26	L	SS. Côme, Dam.
27	M	S. Vinc. de Paul
28	M	S. Venceslas
29	J	S. Michel
30	V	S. Jérôme

OCTOBRE		
1	S	S^e Th. de l'E.J.
2	**D**	S. Léger
3	L	S. Gérard
4	M	S. Fr. d'Assise
5	M	S^e Fleur
6	J	S. Bruno
7	V	S. Serge
8	S	S^e Pélagie
9	**D**	S. Denis
10	L	S. Ghislain
11	M	S. Firmin
12	M	S. Wilfried
13	J	S. Géraud
14	V	S. Juste
15	S	S^e Th. D'Avila
16	**D**	S^e Edwige
17	L	S. Baudouin
18	M	S. Luc
19	M	S. René
20	J	S^e Adeline
21	V	S^e Céline
22	S	S^e Elodie
23	**D**	S. Jean de C.
24	L	S. Florentin
25	M	S. Crépin
26	M	S. Dimitri
27	J	S^e Emeline
28	V	SS. Sim., Jude
29	S	S. Narcisse
30	**D**	S^e Bienvenue
31	L	S. Quentin

NOVEMBRE		
1	**M**	**TOUSSAINT**
2	M	**Défunts**
3	J	S. Hubert
4	V	S. Charles
5	S	S^e Sylvie
6	**D**	S^e Bertille
7	L	S^e Carine
8	M	S. Geoffroy
9	M	S. Théodore
10	J	S. Léon
11	**V**	**ARMISTICE 1918**
12	S	S. Christian
13	**D**	S. Brice
14	L	S. Sidoine
15	M	S. Albert
16	M	S^e Marguerite
17	J	S^e Elisabeth
18	V	S^e Aude
19	S	S. Tanguy
20	**D**	S. Edmond
21	L	*Prés. Marie*
22	M	S^e Cécile
23	M	S. Clément
24	J	S^e Flora
25	V	S^e Catherine L.
26	S	S^e Delphine
27	**D**	**Avent**
28	L	S. Jacq. de la M.
29	M	S. Saturnin
30	M	S. André

DÉCEMBRE 1994		
1	J	S^e Florence
2	V	S^e Viviane
3	S	S. Xavier
4	**D**	S^e Barbara
5	L	S. Gérald
6	M	S. Nicolas
7	M	S. Ambroise
8	J	*Imm. Concept.*
9	V	S. P. Fourier
10	S	S. Romaric
11	**D**	S. Daniel
12	L	S^e Jeanne F.C.
13	M	S^e Lucie
14	M	S^e Odile
15	J	S^e Ninon
16	V	S^e Alice
17	S	S. Gaël
18	**D**	S. Gatien
19	L	S. Urbain
20	M	S. Abraham
21	M	S. Pierre C.
22	J	HIVER
23	V	S. Armand
24	S	S^e Adèle
25	**D**	**NOËL**
26	L	S. Etienne
27	M	S. Jean
28	M	*SS. Innocents*
29	J	S. David
30	V	S. Roger
31	S	S. Sylvestre

Qu'est-ce qu'on dit?

Quand vous invitez des amis à une boum chez vous, qu'est-ce que vous aimez servir?

TEXTBOOK TAPE

J'aime servir... Je n'aime pas servir...

des **boissons** (non-)alcoolisées (*f*)
de la **viande**
des fruits (*m*)
des desserts (*m*)

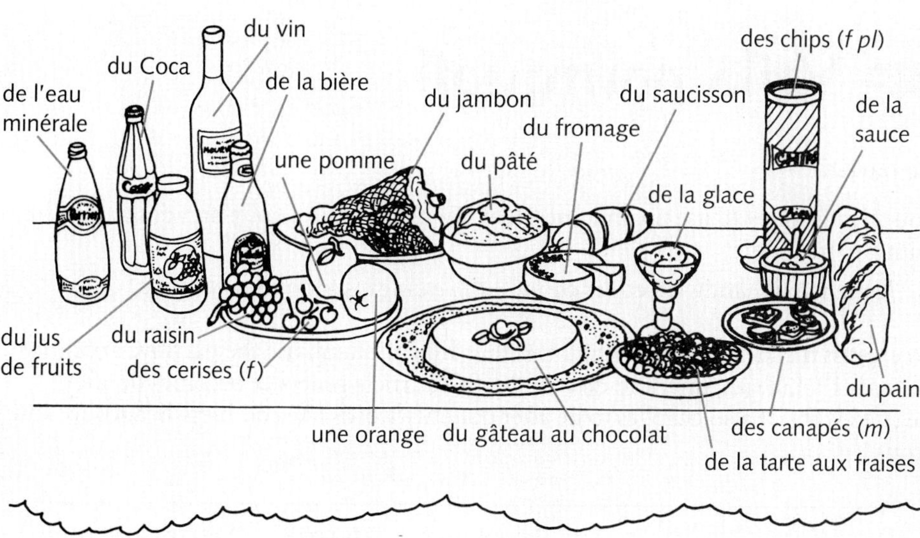

Éric parle à son amie Martine à la boum.

— Tu as faim? Il y a **plein de** choses à manger dans la cuisine.
— Pas **trop**. Mais je voudrais bien quelque chose à boire.
— Qu'est-ce que tu veux? Du Coca? Du jus de fruits? Du vin?
— Du Coca, s'il te plaît.
— Voilà!
— Merci.
— Je t'en prie... Qu'est-ce que tu penses de cette musique?
— Je la trouve super. J'aime beaucoup le rock. Quelle sorte de musique est-ce que tu préfères?
— Moi, j'aime toutes sortes de musique, sauf l'opéra. J'aime la musique classique, le blues, le jazz, la musique pop, le folk, la musique country...
— Tu écoutes souvent du hard rock?
— Pas trop.

une boisson *a drink* **la viande** *meat* **plein de** *all sorts of* **trop** *too much*

A. Ni faim ni soif. Des amis vous offrent quelque chose à boire ou à manger, mais vous n'avez envie de rien. Répondez par **Non merci, je n'ai pas faim** ou par **Non merci, je n'ai pas soif.**

EXEMPLE VOUS ENTENDEZ: Tu voudrais de l'eau minérale?
VOUS RÉPONDEZ: **Non merci, je n'ai pas soif.**

B. Quelle catégorie? Écoutez encore *A. Ni faim ni soif* et placez chaque chose offerte dans la catégorie logique. Écrivez la lettre de la catégorie sur une feuille de papier.

a. une viande b. un dessert c. un fruit d. une boisson

EXEMPLE VOUS ENTENDEZ: Tu voudrais de l'eau minérale?
VOUS RÉPONDEZ: **d**

Voilà pourquoi!

SELF-CHECK

1. How do you express the idea of *some* in French?
2. When do you use **du**, **de la**, **de l'**, and **des**? When do you use **de** instead?
3. What article do you generally use after verbs expressing likes or preferences?

Le partitif

You already know to use **un** and **une** to say *a* with a singular noun and **des** to say *some* with a plural noun.

Je mange *un* sandwich et *des* chips. *I'm eating a sandwich and (some) chips.*

To express the idea of *some* with nouns that are not plural, use the partitive article (**du, de la, de l'**). Like **un, une,** and **des,** the partitive article generally becomes **de** after negated verbs. It also changes to **de** after quantity words like **combien, beaucoup,** and **trop.**

	AFFIRMATIVE	NEGATIVE	AFTER QUANTITIES
MASCULINE BEFORE CONSONANTS	**du** Coca	**pas de** Coca	**beaucoup de** Coca
FEMININE BEFORE CONSONANTS	**de la** tarte	**pas de** tarte	**beaucoup de** tarte
ALL NOUNS BEFORE VOWELS	**de l'**eau	**pas d'**eau	**beaucoup d'**eau

Although the word *some* may be left out in English, **du, de la, de l',** and **des** may not be left out in French.

Tu veux écouter *de la* musique?
Do you want to listen to (some) music?

On va écouter *du* jazz.
We're going to listen to (some) jazz.

Note the difference between the use of the partitive and indefinite articles in these sentences.

Vous voulez *une* tarte?
You want a pie?
(This refers to a whole pie.)

Vous voulez *de la* tarte?
You want (some) pie?
(This refers to a portion or serving.)

After verbs of liking, disliking, and preference, use the definite article (**le, la, l', les**) instead of the partitive. The definite article does not change to **de**. Compare the following:

J'*aime* bien *le* jambon.	**Je mange souvent *du* jambon.**
Ma mère *aime la* tarte.	**Nous mangeons souvent *de la* tarte.**
Je *n'aime pas le* fromage.	**Je *ne* mange *pas de* fromage.**

Also use the definite article in general descriptions of nouns. In this case, English uses no article.

***Le* fromage français est célèbre.**	*French cheese is famous.*
***Le* gâteau au chocolat, c'est délicieux.**	*Chocolate cake is delicious.*

Le verbe **servir**

The verb **servir** is irregular.

SERVIR (*TO SERVE*)	
je **sers**	nous **servons**
tu **sers**	vous **servez**
il/elle/on **sert**	ils/elles **servent**
PASSÉ COMPOSÉ: j'ai servi	

Savez-vous le faire?

A. **Une fête d'anniversaire.** C'est l'anniversaire de votre neveu qui a cinq ans. Dites si on sert les choses suivantes aux enfants qui sont à sa fête d'anniversaire.

EXEMPLES du gâteau → **Oui, on sert du gâteau.**
du pâté → **Non, on ne sert pas de pâté.**

1. de la glace
2. de la bière
3. du Coca
4. du jus de fruits
5. du vin
6. du café

B. **Chez vous.** Est-ce que ces personnes servent souvent (quelquefois, rarement, ne... jamais) les choses indiquées?

EXEMPLE (pâté) Moi, je...
Moi, je sers souvent du pâté. / Moi, je ne sers jamais de pâté.

1. (jambon) Ma grand-mère...
2. (vin) Mes parents...
3. (eau minérale) Moi, je...
4. (glace) Mon/Ma camarade de chambre...
5. (jus de fruits) Mes amis...
6. (fraises) Moi, je...
7. (tarte aux fraises) Mes parents...
8. (cerises) Le restaurant universitaire...

C. Sur la table. Il y a beaucoup à manger à la boum d'Éric. Voici la table de la salle à manger et la table de la cuisine. Est-ce que vous pouvez trouver neuf différences entre les deux tables?

EXEMPLE **Il y a du vin dans la cuisine mais il n'y a pas de vin dans la salle à manger.**

la salle à manger　　　　la cuisine

D. À l'université. Est-ce que vos amis et vous faites ces choses **peu, beaucoup, trop** ou **pas du tout**?

EXEMPLE faire du sport → **On fait beaucoup (peu) de sport.**
OU **On ne fait pas du tout de sport.**

1. écouter de la musique classique
2. passer du temps au café
3. faire des devoirs
4. faire des boums
5. servir des canapés aux boums
6. manger de la glace
7. passer du temps au lac
8. manger de la pizza

E. Au lac. Quand vous passez la journée au lac avec des amis, qu'est-ce que vous aimez faire?

EXEMPLE **On aime bien faire du bateau...**

manger
SERVIR boire
FAIRE **???**
??? *apporter*
écouter

ski nautique
MUSIQUE *eau minérale*
sauce Coca *chips* **vin**
bateau SANDWICHES ???
promenade ??? *fromage*
CASSETTES

F. Préférences. Posez ces questions à un(e) camarade de classe.

1. Est-ce que tu préfères le Coca, le jus d'orange ou le jus de pomme? Est-ce que tu aimes boire du Coca avec le déjeuner? Est-ce que tu aimes bien la bière? Est-ce que tu aimes boire du vin avec le dîner?
2. Est-ce que tu préfères le gâteau ou la tarte? Est-ce que tu aimes la glace? Est-ce que tu manges généralement un dessert quand tu vas au restaurant? Du gâteau? De la tarte? De la glace?
3. Quel genre de musique est-ce que tu préfères? Est-ce que tu écoutes souvent du jazz? de la musique classique? du rock? Quelle sorte de musique est-ce que tu écoutes quand tu prépares tes cours? Est-ce que tu écoutes de la musique quand tu fais de l'exercice?

G. Préparatifs. Avec un(e) camarade de classe, vous voulez faire une boum pour la classe de français. Discutez ensemble les choses suivantes:

- Quand et où vous allez faire la boum.
- La musique (Imaginez que vos amis aiment toutes sortes de musique.)
- Ce que vous allez servir (Imaginez que vous n'aimez pas les mêmes choses.)

C'est à lire!

Specialized fields (cinema, business, music, math) require specific vocabulary. In this excerpt from *Jeune et Jolie* magazine, you will read about the discovery of projection techniques and the early troubled history of the cinema. Keeping in mind the type of words you expect to find in such an article will help you guess the meaning of unknown words.

Devinez! Keeping the indicated topics in mind, guess the meaning of the boldfaced words.

LE CINÉMA

1. J'aime louer des cassettes vidéo, mais pour voir des films d'aventures, je préfère aller au cinéma parce que **l'écran** est plus grand.
2. Je préfère aller au cinéma l'après-midi parce que **l'entrée** est moins chère.
3. Le cinéma vient de la **projection d'images** par un projecteur.
4. Quand le projecteur ne fonctionne pas bien, les **spectateurs** ne peuvent pas voir le film et ils ne sont pas contents.

LA SCIENCE

1. Un homme ou une femme qui fait de la recherche doit avoir beaucoup de **curiosité scientifique.**
2. Pierre et Marie Curie ont découvert le radium. Cela a été une **découverte** importante.
3. On peut travailler longtemps dans un **laboratoire** sans faire de grandes découvertes.
4. Une **expérience** scientifique mal **réglée** peut avoir de graves conséquences.

Un peu d'histoire

En 1895, les frères Lumière, Louis et Alphonse, font une découverte sur la projection d'images. Très vite, cette découverte **devient** une curiosité scientifique... Ainsi, le cinéma est né à Paris **lors de** sa projection officielle le 28 décembre 1895 dans un sous-sol du Grand-Café, **à deux pas de** l'Opéra de Paris, 14, boulevard des Capucines. L'écran faisait un mètre de **haut** et l'entrée un franc: **il y eut** 35 spectateurs. Le cinéma quitte alors le cercle académique pour des salles toutes simples, des cafés ou des **chapiteaux**. Malheureusement l'histoire commence mal! En 1897, plus de 150 personnes **meurent carbonisées** lors d'une séance, un projecteur mal réglé au Bazar de la Charité **prend feu**... **La classe aisée** est choquée et se réfugie vers le music-hall.

Les frères Lumière

devient *becomes* **lors de** *at the time of* **à deux pas de** *a short distance from* **haut** *high* **il y eut** *there were* **chapiteaux** *(m) tents* **meurent carbonisées** *burned to death* **prendre feu** *to catch fire* **la classe aisée** *the upper class*

Avez-vous compris?

A. Vrai ou faux? Lisez l'article sur l'histoire du cinéma et décidez si ces phrases sont vraies ou fausses.

1. Le cinéma est né avec une découverte sur la projection d'images par les frères Lumière.
2. La première projection officielle est en 1895 au sous-sol du Grand-Café à Paris.
3. Le cinéma est immédiatement populaire et on commence tout de suite à construire (*build*) des salles de cinéma.
4. En 1897, un accident choque les spectateurs et tout le monde décide d'abandonner le cinéma pour retourner au music-hall.

B. Un peu d'histoire. Complétez les phrases avec un mot de la liste. Après, changez l'ordre des lettres initiales de chacun de ces mots pour trouver un nom qu'on associe avec l'histoire du cinéma. (Il est nécessaire de changer certains accents aussi!)

entrée Lumière écran images mètre réglé un franc

En 1895, les frères ______ font une découverte sur la projection d' ______ et voilà que le cinéma est né. La première projection officielle est le 28 décembre 1895 au sous-sol d'un café à Paris. L' ______ coûte ______ et l' ______ n'est pas grand: il mesure un ______ de haut. Pendant un certain temps, les Parisiens ont la possibilité de voir ces «projections» dans les cafés ou d'autres salles simples. En 1897, un projecteur mal ______ prend feu et 150 spectateurs meurent carbonisés. L'histoire du cinéma ne commence pas bien!

Mot trouvé: __ __ __ __ __ __ __

Ça y est! C'est à vous!

A. Organisez-vous! Vous allez faire une boum. D'abord, complétez la liste de possibilités pour chacune des catégories suivantes.

- Quand est-ce que vous allez faire la boum?
  Ce week-end, le jour de mon anniversaire...
- Où est-ce que vous pouvez la faire?
  À la piscine de mon appartement, au lac...
- Qui est-ce que vous allez inviter?
  Les voisins, la famille...
- Qu'est-ce que vous allez servir?
  Du Coca, du gâteau...
- Qu'est-ce que vous voulez faire?
  Danser, faire des jeux...
- Quel genre de musique est-ce que vous allez écouter?
  Du rock...

B. Situation: Une boum. Maintenant, comparez vos listes de l'exercice précédent avec les listes d'un(e) autre étudiant(e). Utilisez vos idées pour préparer une conversation où vous faites des préparatifs pour la boum.

C. Une lettre d'invitation. Écrivez une lettre où vous invitez un(e) ami(e) à la boum que vous avez préparée dans l'exercice précédent.

> Cher/Chère...
> Je t'invite à une boum...
>
> Ton ami(e),

D. Excuses. Avec un(e) partenaire, faites une liste d'excuses pour ne pas aller à la boum d'un(e) camarade de classe. Ensuite, lisez son invitation préparée dans l'exercice précédent et répondez que vous ne pouvez pas y aller.

> **Je regrette mais je ne peux pas parce que...** **Je dois...**
> **Ce n'est pas possible ce week-end parce que...**

E. À la boum. Pendant votre boum, un(e) ami(e) veut faire la connaissance d'un(e) étudiant(e) de la classe de français. Préparez une conversation où votre ami(e) décrit ce(tte) camarade et où vous dites comment il/elle s'appelle et si vous le/la connaissez bien. Ensuite, votre ami(e) vous pose trois autres questions.

F. La boum d'Éric. Deux amies d'Éric, Martine et Sophie, sont à sa boum. Écoutez leur conversation et répondez aux questions suivantes.

1. Pourquoi est-ce que Sophie ne reconnaît pas le frère de Martine?
2. Comment est-ce que Martine le trouve avec sa barbe? Et Sophie?

Pour vérifier

Étudiez la liste de vocabulaire. Après avoir fini ces exercices, vérifiez vos réponses dans *l'Appendix C.*

Issuing an invitation

A. Invitations. Complétez ces conversations avec la forme correcte du verbe logique.

1. pouvoir, vouloir, devoir

   — Est-ce que tu ______ aller à la boum d'Éric samedi soir?
   — Je ne ______ pas. Je ______ travailler samedi soir.

2. connaître, vouloir, avoir envie, faire

   — Martine et Sophie, est-ce que vous ______ Jean-Luc?
   — Nous ______ sa connaissance la semaine dernière.
   — Jean-Luc et moi allons au parc. Est-ce que vous ______ de venir avec nous?
   — Oui, on ______ bien.

B. Casse-tête. Vous savez déjà que la fête nationale française est le 14 juillet. Lisez ce casse-tête (*riddle*) pour apprendre quand a lieu la fête nationale d'autres nations francophones et complétez ces phrases.

1. La fête nationale canadienne est ______ .
2. La fête nationale du Zaïre est ______ .
3. La fête nationale de la Suisse est ______ .
4. À Haïti on célèbre la fête nationale ______ .
5. En Belgique, à Bruxelles par exemple, on célèbre ______ .

À Haïti, la fête nationale est en hiver. C'est le jour de l'an. Les Canadiens célèbrent six mois après les Haïtiens et deux semaines avant les Français. Au Zaïre, c'est exactement un mois avant les Canadiens, et en Suisse c'est exactement deux mois après les Zaïrois. Les Belges font leur célébration une semaine après les Français et trois semaines après les Canadiens.

Offering something to eat or drink

C. À la boum. Nommez trois choses que vous aimez manger ou boire. Ensuite, offrez ces choses à un(e) ami(e).

Discussing movies and music

D. Ça te dit? Écrivez une conversation où vous invitez un(e) ami(e) à voir cette cassette vidéo et où vous parlez de ce genre de film.

Un film de René Goscinny, Albert Uderzo et Georges Dargaud. Musique de Gérard Calvi. Une production des Dargaud Films-Paris.

Nous sommes en 50 avant Jésus-Christ. Le général romain Caius Bonus et ses puissantes troupes font le siège d'un village gaulois. Mais c'est sans compter sur la vitalité du vaillant guerrier gaulois Astérix et de son généreux ami Obélix qui, aidés de l'astucieux druide Panoramix, auront tôt fait de semer la panique chez les Romains! Que fera Astérix quand le général romain kidnappera le druide gaulois pour s'approprier le secret de la potion magique qui donne une force surhumaine? Partez à l'aventure avec Astérix dans ce film d'animation original et hilarant!

Vocabulaire

Issuing an invitation

FÊTES ET CÉLÉBRATIONS
un anniversaire
une boum
une fête
la fête nationale
le jour de l'an
Noël
Pâques *(f pl)*
la Saint-Valentin
la Toussaint

EXPRESSIONS VERBALES
apporter
connaître
devoir
faire la connaissance de
faire une boum
fêter
inviter quelqu'un
mourir (Il/Elle est mort[e].)
naître (Il/Elle est né[e].)
passer chez
pouvoir
reconnaître
regretter
savoir
vouloir

LA DATE
Quelle date sommes-nous?
  Nous sommes le...
Quelle est la date aujourd'hui?
  C'est le...
    janvier
    février
    mars
    avril
    mai
    juin
    juillet
    août
    septembre
    octobre
    novembre
    décembre

DIVERS
algérien(ne)
allô
Avec plaisir!
Ça me plaît! / Ça ne me plaît pas!
Ça te dit?
un(e) copain/copine d'école
d'accord
en avance
Je t'invite à...
Je voudrais vous inviter à...
jusqu'à
libre
Mais si!
Un moment!
Ne quittez pas!
occupé(e)
Qui est à l'appareil?
un rendez-vous
tranquille
vers
un(e) voisin(e) (d'à côté)

Offering something to eat or drink

CHOSES À MANGER ET À BOIRE
les boissons ([non-]alcoolisées) *(f)*
les canapés *(m)*
les cerises *(f)*
les chips *(f pl)*
le dessert
le fromage
les fruits *(m)*
le gâteau (au chocolat)
la glace
le jambon
les oranges *(f)*
le pain
le pâté
les pommes *(f)*
le raisin
la sauce
le saucisson
la tarte (aux fraises)
la viande

DIVERS
délicieux(-euse)
fameux(-euse)
Je t'en prie.
plein de
plutôt
servir
s'il te plaît
tellement
trop

Discussing movies and music

LES FILMS
une comédie
une comédie musicale
un dessin animé
un drame
un film d'amour
un film d'aventures
un film d'épouvante
un film de science-fiction
un film policier

LA MUSIQUE
le blues
le folk
le jazz
la musique classique
la musique country
la musique pop
le (hard) rock

DIVERS
une collection de
un genre
horrible
passer un film
une séance
super
toutes sortes de... sauf...

Unité 4 Aux Antilles

Regional Overview
La Guadeloupe
AREA: 687 square miles (1,780 sq. km.)
POPULATION: 387,000 (including the dependencies)
CAPITAL: **Basse-Terre**
MAJOR INDUSTRIES: agriculture, tourism
(**La Guadeloupe** has several nearby island dependencies: **Marie-Galante, la Désirade, Petite-Terre** and **les Saintes. Saint-Martin** and **Saint-Barthélemy** are 150 miles [240 km.] to the northwest.)

La Martinique
AREA: 425 square miles (1,100 sq. km.)
POPULATION: 360,000
CAPITAL: **Fort-de-France**
MAJOR INDUSTRIES: agriculture, tourism

Haïti
AREA: 10,714 square miles (27,740 sq. km.)
POPULATION: 6,300,000
CAPITAL: **Port-au-Prince**
MAJOR INDUSTRY: agriculture

Chapitre 7 En vacances

By the end of this chapter, you should be able to do the following in French:

- Choose vacation activities
- Decide where to go on vacation
- Prepare for a trip
- Make travel arrangements

Man in Orange Hat
Joseph-Jean Laurent (1893–1976)
1970
Milwaukee Art Museum
Gift of Richard and Erna Flagg

Laurent was a tailor in **Port-au-Prince, Haïti,** who began painting when he was sixty-eight years old. The colors in this painting of a voodoo figure named Legba reflect the brilliant hues of the Antilles.

Pour commencer

TEXTBOOK TAPE

NOTE
Items accompanied by a tape symbol are recorded on the textbook tape.

Luc, un jeune Parisien, va passer ses vacances en Guadeloupe.

Et vous? Où est-ce que vous aimez passer vos vacances?

dans **un pays étranger** ou exotique

sur une île tropicale

dans une grande ville

à la campagne

à la mer

à la montagne

Qu'est-ce que vous aimez mieux faire pendant les vacances?

admirer les **paysages**

visiter des sites historiques et touristiques

profiter des activités culturelles

un pays étranger *a foreign country* **un paysage** *a landscape*

faire de la plongée sous-marine

courir le long des plages

faire de la planche à voile

goûter la cuisine locale

faire un pique-nique **assis(e) par terre**

passer des vacances **reposantes** à la maison et ne rien faire

Luc parle à son ami Alain de ses vacances en Guadeloupe.

— Je vais bientôt partir en vacances.
— Et tu vas où?
— À Basse-Terre, en Guadeloupe.
— Quelle chance! Tu pars quand?
— Je vais partir le 20 juillet et je **compte** passer cinq semaines en vacances.
— C'est **chouette**, ça!

La Guadeloupe

goûter *to taste* **assis(e)** *seated, sitting* **par terre** *on the ground* **reposant(e)** *restful* **compter** *to count (on), to plan* **chouette** *great, neat*

Savez-vous le faire?

A. Préférences. Qu'est-ce que vous aimez mieux faire pendant les vacances?

EXEMPLE faire du camping ou descendre dans un hôtel de luxe
J'aime mieux faire du camping.

1. nager ou faire du ski
2. visiter une île tropicale ou visiter une grande ville
3. faire du shopping ou faire de la planche à voile
4. visiter des musées ou aller au théâtre
5. faire de l'exercice ou goûter la cuisine locale
6. courir le long des plages ou passer l'après-midi assis(e) sur la plage
7. faire un pique-nique à la campagne ou faire un pique-nique sur la plage
8. aller voir des amis ou rester à la maison

B. Tourisme. Regardez les extraits suivants de guides touristiques et dites pourquoi Luc va aller à chacun des endroits indiqués. Complétez chaque phrase avec une des activités suivantes:
visiter un parc naturel / goûter la cuisine locale / voir des fleurs et des animaux locaux nager et courir / profiter des activités culturelles / faire de la plongée sous-marine

EXEMPLE Il téléphone au Conseil Général parce qu'il veut **profiter des activités culturelles.**

LE CONSEIL GENERAL POUR UNE POLITIQUE DU PATRIMOINE

Par le biais des musées départementaux dont il est propriétaire,
- le musée Edgar Clerc au Moule,
- le musée Shœlcher à Pointe-à-Pitre,
- l'éco-musée de Marie-Galante (le Château Murat),

le Conseil Général assure le sauvetage, la protection de notre patrimoine. Il garantit ainsi la transmission aux Guadeloupéens de ce que l'histoire et la tradition leur ont légué.

Conseil Général: 1, Bd du gouverneur Félix Eboué
97109 Basse-Terre
Tél : 81 15 60 — Télex : 914 418 GL — Fax : 81 68 79

EXEMPLE

RESTAURANT
LA NOVA
Spécialités Antillaises
Fruits de mer - Ouassous Langoustes
Crabes farcis - Palourdes
Ouvert tous les jours
(sauf le Mardi)
RIFLET (Face à la plage)
DESHAIES Tél. 28.40.74

1. Il va au restaurant La Nova pour...

PROMENADE EN MER AVEC ERICK

Déjeuner en mer - Plongée sous-marine - connaissance des îlets.
Réservations Tél. ***91.59.19***

2. Il téléphone à Promenade en Mer avec Érick parce qu'il a envie de...

BALLADES AVEC JACQUES

Visite complète

*** Parc naturel B.T.S**

Chutes du Carbet - Soufrière etc...

***GRANDE TERRE**

Pointe des Chateaux : Porte d'enfer etc...

Renseignements
7 lot Montout
Montauban
97190 GOSIER

Tél : 84.10.42

3. Il téléphone à Ballades avec Jacques parce qu'il veut...

4. Il va à l'Alizéa parce qu'il a envie de...

5. Luc va au parc zoologique et botanique pour...

C. **On fait des projets.** Faites des projets pour vos prochaines vacances (vraies ou imaginaires). Où est-ce que vous allez aller? Avec qui est-ce que vous allez voyager? Qu'est-ce que vous allez faire? Qu'est-ce que vous n'allez pas faire?

Comment s'y prendre?

Using your knowledge of the world

What you already know about the world can help you determine the meaning of unknown words. Below is a description of **la Soufrière,** an active, but dormant, volcano that is part of the **petites Antilles** mountains, and overlooks the city of **Basse-Terre.** What kind of words would you expect to find in an article about volcanoes? Keeping this topic in mind, determine the meaning of the boldfaced words in the brochure excerpt below.

Le volcanisme

La Soufrière, appelée familièrement «la Vieille Dame», **domine** la Basse-Terre de ses 1467 mètres. Ce volcan **encore actif** est **le plus haut sommet** des petites Antilles et permet la découverte de **panoramas uniques**.

Depuis la ville de Basse-Terre, il suffit de 30 minutes en voiture pour gagner la «Savane à Mulets», **vaste esplanade au pied du dôme**. La route laisse Sainte-Claude, sa fraîcheur, ses belles maisons créoles et ses jardins exubérants pour grimper en serpentant à travers l'épaisse forêt tropicale. De la Savane à Mulets la vue englobe toute la rade de Basse-Terre, les monts Caraïbes et les îles voisines qui semblent flotter dans l'air. Les plus courageux peuvent gravir le dôme par un sentier balisé et découvrir au sommet **des paysages irréels** et envoûtants, des fumerolles qui jaillissent du sol, des gouffres grondants et des chaos rocheux dramatisés par le silence total et **l'odeur du soufre**.

Recognizing past time

You have already learned how to tell what someone did in the past, using the **passé composé.** When reading a story about the past, you will also encounter **l'imparfait** (*the imperfect*). It is a single word with one of these endings: **-ais, -ait, -ions, -iez,** or **-aient**. You will learn how to use the imperfect tense in the next unit. In the meantime, learn to recognize it when reading. It has several possible meanings.

Je parlais.	*I was speaking.* *I used to speak.* *I spoke.*	**Il allait.**	*He was going.* *He used to go.* *He went.*

Can you understand these sentences in the past?

Près de Basse-Terre, il y *avait* un volcan qui *dominait* un grand parc. Je *montais* au sommet du volcan quand j'ai vu des jets de vapeur qui *sortaient* du cratère. J'ai immédiatement pensé que le volcan *allait* entrer en éruption.

Savez-vous le faire?

A. Devinez. Vous comprenez déjà les mots entre parenthèses. Est-ce que vous pouvez utiliser ces mots pour deviner le sens des mots en caractères gras dans les phrases qui suivent?

1. (goûter) Je trouve la Guadeloupe parfaitement à mon **goût**.
2. (reposant) La Soufrière est un volcan actif, mais **en repos**.
3. (par terre) Touchez **la terre** d'un volcan. Elle est chaude.
4. (malheureusement) **Heureusement**, il y avait quelqu'un de plus calme dans ce groupe.
5. (une explosion) J'ai pensé que le volcan allait **exploser**.
6. (des aventures) Après les vacances, j'aime **raconter mes aventures** à mes amis.
7. (assis) Je **me suis assis** par terre.

B. Manifestations volcaniques. Utilisez vos connaissances (*knowledge*) des volcans pour deviner le sens de ces phrases.

1. La Soufrière est un volcan en repos, mais pas si en repos que ça. Il y a souvent des manifestations volcaniques: des jets de vapeur, l'odeur de soufre, de la lave rouge.
2. Ces manifestations sont tout à fait normales. Il n'y a pas de danger. Le volcan n'entre pas en éruption.
3. En montant vers le sommet, on apprécie des vues spectaculaires. C'est magnifique!
4. Arrivé au sommet du volcan, j'ai eu l'impression d'être sur une autre planète.

C. Le passé. Avant de lire la lettre qui suit, cherchez-y les verbes au passé composé et à l'imparfait. Sur une feuille de papier, faites deux listes et écrivez l'infinitif de chaque verbe.

	PASSÉ COMPOSÉ			IMPARFAIT		
EXEMPLE	**j'ai trouvé**	→	**trouver**	**il y avait**	→	**avoir**

Qu'est-ce qui se passe?

NOTE
The textbook tape symbol indicates sections that are recorded on the textbook tape.

Quelle aventure!

Luc, un jeune Parisien qui passe ses vacances en Guadeloupe, raconte ses aventures dans une lettre à son ami Alain.

Cher Alain, le 10 août

Je passe des vacances formidables ici en Guadeloupe! Les gens sont très sympa et tout le reste est parfaitement à mon goût... la cuisine, le paysage, le climat, les femmes!

J'ai trouvé un petit hôtel pas trop cher à Basse-Terre. La chambre n'est pas grande, mais j'ai une vue splendide sur la mer. Je nage presque tous les jours mais je ne passe pas tout mon temps à la plage. Je fais aussi des promenades magnifiques et je commence à bien connaître l'île.

La semaine dernière, je suis allé au parc naturel. Le parc est dominé par un énorme volcan en repos... mais comme j'ai bien vu, pas si «en repos» que ça! En montant vers le volcan, j'ai remarqué qu'il y avait un peu de vapeur qui sortait du cratère, mais je n'ai pas fait trop attention. Quand j'étais presque au sommet du volcan, je me suis assis par terre pour me reposer un peu. C'est là que j'ai remarqué que la terre était toute chaude, mais vraiment chaude! Alors, j'ai regardé le sommet du volcan et j'ai pensé voir des jets de vapeur qui sortaient! Le volcan allait exploser!

J'ai commencé à crier aux autres touristes: «Attention! Attention! Le volcan entre en éruption, il va exploser! Sauvez-vous!» Tout le monde a commencé à courir. Heureusement, il y avait quelqu'un de plus calme parmi le groupe. Une jeune Guadeloupéenne a dit: «Mais non, mais non... calmez-vous! C'est tout à fait normal. Le volcan est en repos. Il n'y a pas de danger!»

Sur le moment, j'ai eu l'impression d'être complètement ridicule! Mais cette impression a passé presque immédiatement. Nous avons commencé à parler, elle s'appelle Micheline et elle est super sympa. Nous avons continué l'escalade du volcan ensemble. Arrivés tout en haut, nous avons trouvé une vue impressionnante... la lave... les fissures... l'odeur... C'était un paysage presque irréel. Pour un instant, j'ai eu l'impression d'être sur une autre planète!

Mais, tout est bien qui finit bien. Micheline et moi, nous sortons ensemble presque tous les soirs depuis. Tu vois, la Guadeloupe c'est vraiment extra!

À bientôt,

Luc

Avez-vous compris?

Nouvelles de Luc. Répondez en français.

1. Comment est-ce que Luc trouve la Guadeloupe? Et les Guadeloupéens?
2. Où est-ce que Luc a trouvé un hôtel? Comment est l'hôtel? Comment est sa chambre?
3. Qu'est-ce que Luc fait en Guadeloupe?
4. Une fois arrivé au sommet du volcan, pourquoi est-ce que Luc a commencé à crier aux autres touristes de se sauver?
5. Qui est Micheline?

Remarquez que...

Les Antilles françaises (*the French West Indies*), comprising **Martinique** and the **Guadeloupe** archipelago, are a favorite vacation spot. They are known for their friendly people, beautiful countryside, unique cuisine, and water sports. The **Guadeloupe** archipelago is made up of the larger island of **Guadeloupe** itself and the surrounding smaller islands of **Marie-Galante, les Saintes, la Désirade, Petite-Terre, Saint-Martin,** and **Saint-Barthélemy**.

A. Ici on s'amuse bien. Voilà un plan des Antilles et des activités qui y sont populaires. Mettez ces activités dans l'ordre de vos préférences.

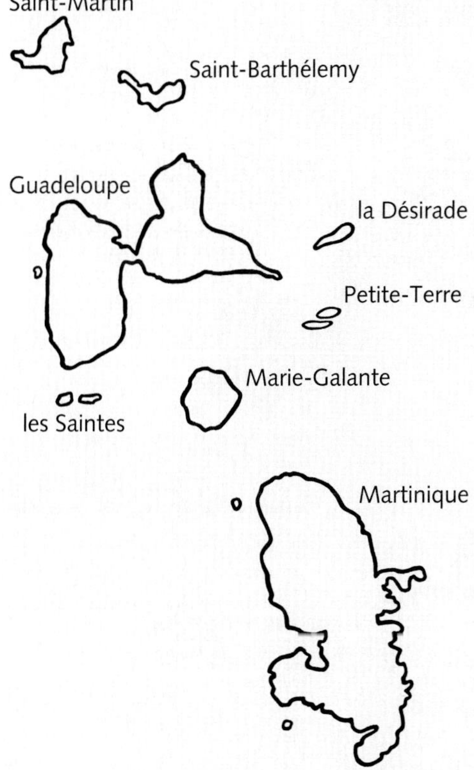

B. Les dépendances proches. Les îles de Saint-Martin et de Saint-Barthélemy sont à 240 kilomètres au nord de la Guadeloupe. La Désirade, Petite-Terre, Marie-Galante et les Saintes, au contraire, sont visibles des plages guadeloupéennes et on peut facilement y faire un voyage d'un seul jour. Regardez la description suivante de trois de ces îles et proposez au moins une chose que vous voudriez voir sur chacune. Quelle île vous semble la plus intéressante?

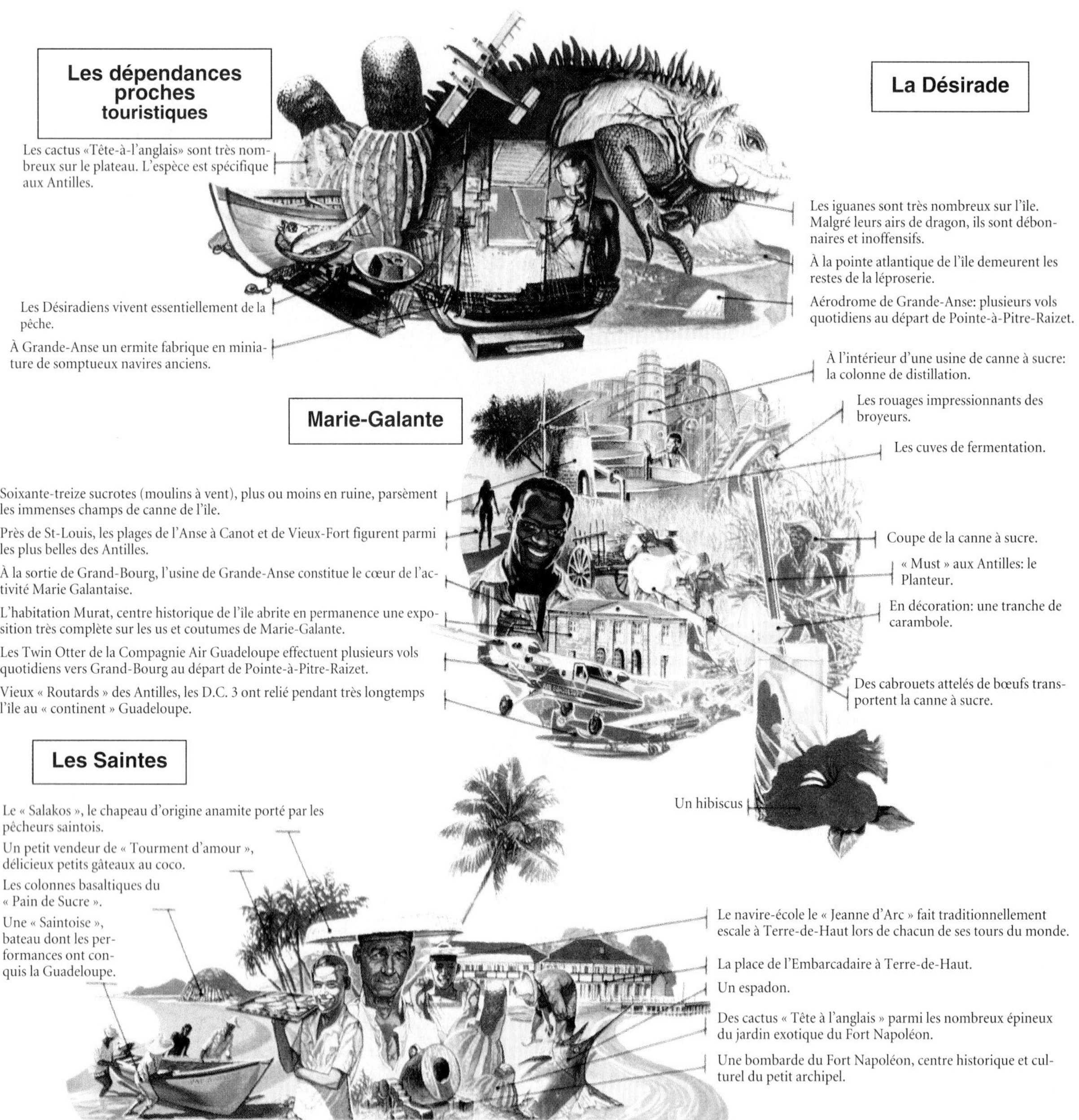

NOTE
Items accompanied by a tape symbol are recorded on the textbook tape.

Qu'est-ce qu'on dit?

Imaginez le voyage de vos **rêves**! Où voudriez-vous aller? Voudriez-vous visiter...

L'AFRIQUE
l'Algérie
l'Égypte
le Sénégal
le Zaïre

L'ASIE
l'Arabie Saoudite
la Chine
Israël
le Japon
le Viêt-nam

L'AMÉRIQUE DU NORD OU L'AMÉRIQUE CENTRALE
les Antilles
le Canada
les États-Unis
le Mexique

L'AMÉRIQUE DU SUD
l'Argentine
le Brésil
la Colombie
le Pérou

L'AUSTRALIE

L'EUROPE
l'Allemagne
la Belgique
l'Espagne
la France
la Grèce
la Grande-Bretagne
l'Italie
la Russie
la Suisse

SUPPLEMENTAL VOCABULARY[1]
EN AFRIQUE
la Côte-d'Ivoire
le Maroc
EN ASIE
l'Inde
l'Indochine
l'Iran
l'Iraq
la Turquie
EN EUROPE
le Danemark
la Norvège
la Pologne
la Suède

Quelles villes voudriez-vous visiter? Londres? Moscou? Mexico? Bruxelles? Dakar?

Avant ses vacances, Luc a parlé de ses projets de vacances avec un agent de voyages.
— Je voudrais partir le mois prochain.
— Vous avez **déjà** décidé où vous voudriez aller?
— Non, **pas encore**. Je **ne** parle **que** français et je préfère visiter un pays francophone, mais pas en Europe.
— Alors, que pensez-vous d'aller...

à Tahiti? À HAÏTI? *aux Antilles?* **en Louisiane?** AU QUÉBEC? **au Zaïre?** **en Algérie?**

— **J'aimerais** bien visiter les Antilles.
— Bonne idée. Mes parents **viennent** de Guadeloupe. Les Antillais sont connus pour leur **chaleur**. Quand est-ce que vous voulez partir?
— Le 20 juillet.
— Et quand est-ce que vous voudriez rentrer?
— Le 25 août.
— **Le billet** le moins cher est à 3 545 francs. Voulez-vous faire vos réservations maintenant?
— Oui, je voudrais réserver mon billet. Est-ce que j'ai besoin d'un passeport?
— Non, mais n'**oubliez** pas votre carte d'identité.

un rêve *a dream* **avant** *before* **déjà** *already* **pas encore** *not yet* **ne... que** *only* **j'aimerais** *I would like* **ils viennent (venir** *to come***)** **la chaleur** *warmth* **le billet** *the ticket* **oublier** *to forget*

[1]Supplemental vocabulary enables you to personalize the material. It is not tested in the Testing Program.

A. Quel continent? Indiquez sur quel continent se trouvent ces pays.

EXEMPLE la Chine
La Chine se trouve en Asie.

1. les États-Unis
2. l'Algérie
3. le Viêt-nam
4. l'Allemagne
5. le Japon
6. Israël
7. la Grande-Bretagne
8. le Zaïre

en Europe *en Asie*
EN AMÉRIQUE DU SUD
en Amérique du Nord
en Australie
en Afrique

B. La francophonie. Vous voulez visiter une région francophone pendant vos vacances. Pour chaque paire d'endroits proposée, choisissez celui où on parle français. Un(e) camarade de classe va jouer le rôle de l'agent de voyages.

EXEMPLE en Suisse ou en Allemagne
— Est-ce que vous préférez aller en Suisse ou en Allemagne?
— Je préfère passer mes vacances en Suisse.

1. au Japon ou au Zaïre
2. en Belgique ou en Espagne
3. au Québec ou au Mexique
4. en Égypte ou en Algérie
5. au Sénégal ou en Colombie
6. en Guadeloupe ou aux Bahamas
7. à Londres ou à Genève
8. à Montréal ou à Toronto
9. au Québec ou en Alberta
10. en Californie ou en Louisiane

C. Célébrités. Nommez quelqu'un de célèbre qui est des endroits suivants.

1. de France 2. de Grande-Bretagne 3. d'Afrique 4. des États-Unis

SELF-CHECK

Self-check questions will be found throughout the text next to explanations of structures. Read through these questions before reading the ***Voilà pourquoi!*** section to preview what you are going to learn. Read the whole ***Voilà pourquoi!*** section before answering the questions. Check your answers in ***Appendix B***.

1. When do you use the definite article with the name of a country?
2. How do you say *to* or *in* with a city? With a feminine country? With a masculine country beginning with a consonant? With a masculine country beginning with a vowel sound?
3. How do you say *from* with a city? With a feminine country? With a masculine country beginning with a consonant? With a masculine country beginning with a vowel sound?

Voilà pourquoi!

Les régions géographiques

Continents, countries, provinces, and states are either masculine or feminine in French. Most of those ending in **e** are feminine and the rest are masculine. A few places, such as **les États-Unis** and **les Antilles**, are plural. Note these exceptions: **Tahiti** is feminine and **le Mexique**, **le Zaïre**, and **le Maine** are masculine. See page 121 for a map of the United States and Canada in French.[1]

When used as the subject or object of a verb, you need to use the appropriate definite article with continents, countries, states, and provinces. **Israël** and **Tahiti** are exceptions. Do not use an article with them.

J'adore *l'*Europe. *La* France est très belle.
Je voudrais visiter *le* Canada, surtout *le* Québec.
J'aimerais aussi voir *les* États-Unis: *la* Californie, *le* Texas, *la* Floride, *le* Maine.

BUT: **Mes parents visitent Israël. Moi, je visite Tahiti.**

[1] Most states of the United States are masculine. All those ending in -e are feminine except **le Maine**, **le Nouveau-Mexique**, and **le New Hampshire**.

Do not use an article with names of cities: **Paris, Londres, Rome, Mexico.** Two notable exceptions are **La Nouvelle-Orléans** and **Le Caire.**

Cette année nous allons visiter *Miami, Atlanta* et *La Nouvelle-Orléans.*

The prepositions you use to say *to* or *in* and *from* a place depend on the type of place.

- For cities, use **à** to say *to* or *in* and **de** to say *from.*

Je vais *à* Paris.	**J'habite *à* Paris.**	**Je viens *de* Paris.**

- For plural countries or regions, use **aux** to say *to* or *in* and **des** to say *from.*

Je vais *aux* États-Unis.	**J'habite *aux* États-Unis.**	**Je viens *des* États-Unis.**
Je vais *aux* Antilles.	**J'habite *aux* Antilles.**	**Je viens *des* Antilles.**

- For feminine countries, states, provinces, or continents (those ending in **e**), use **en** to say *to* or *in* and **de** (**d'**) to say *from.* Also use **en** and **d'** for masculine countries beginning with a vowel sound.

Je vais *en* France.	**J'habite *en* France.**	**Je suis *de* France.**
Je vais *en* Californie.	**J'habite *en* Californie.**	**Je suis *de* Californie.**
Je vais *en* Europe.	**J'habite *en* Europe.**	**Je suis *d'*Europe.**
Je vais *en* Normandie.	**J'habite *en* Normandie.**	**Je suis *de* Normandie.**

Exceptions: **au Mexique / du Mexique, au Zaïre / du Zaïre.**

- For masculine countries and provinces (those not ending in **e**) beginning with a consonant sound, use **au** to say *to* or *in* and **du** to say *from.*[1]

Je vais *au* Canada.	**J'habite *au* Canada.**	**Je suis *du* Canada.**
Je vais *au* Japon.	**J'habite *au* Japon.**	**Je suis *du* Japon.**
Je vais *au* Québec.	**J'habite *au* Québec.**	**Je suis *du* Québec.**

Savez-vous le faire?

A. C'est connu. Quels pays sont connus pour ces choses?

EXEMPLE Quel pays est connu pour ses pyramides?
L'Égypte ou le Mexique.

Quel pays est connu pour...

1. le café
2. le fromage et le vin
3. le chocolat
4. les spaghetti
5. la musique rock
6. le carnaval
7. le thé
8. la chaleur de son peuple

[1] Usage varies with names of masculine states. Generally, use **dans le** (**l'**) to say *to* or *in*, and **du** (**de l'**) to say *from.* Exception: **au Texas / du Texas.** Use **dans l'état de** to distinguish a state from a city with the same name (**dans l'état de New York**).

B. Paris-Dakar. Chaque année, il y a une course automobile (*car race*) de Paris à Dakar. Décrivez la route de cette course.

EXEMPLE **On commence à Rouen. De Rouen, on va à... De... on va à...**

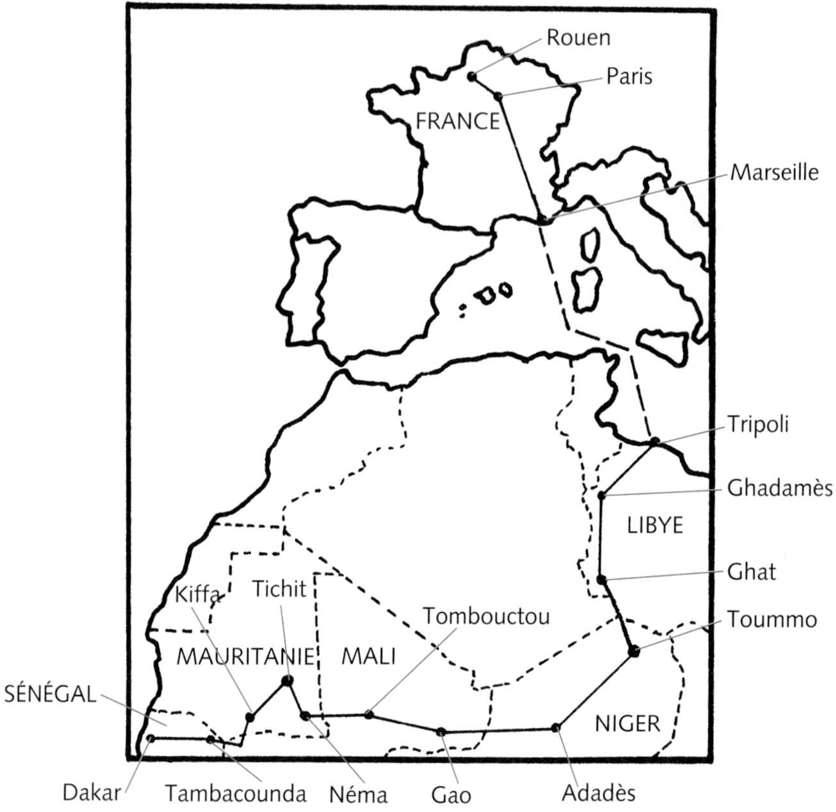

C. Leçon de géographie. Dans quels pays se trouvent ces villes?

EXEMPLE Londres → **Londres se trouve en Grande-Bretagne.**

1. Tokyo
2. Mexico
3. Moscou
4. Berlin
5. Hanoi
6. Alger
7. Le Caire
8. Dakar
9. La Nouvelle-Orléans
10. Beijing

D. Conseils. Un(e) ami(e) veut savoir ce que vous aimeriez faire pendant les vacances. Choisissez l'activité que vous préférez de chaque paire. Ensuite, votre ami(e) doit suggérer un des endroits entre parenthèses à visiter.

EXEMPLE visiter des musées / faire de la plongée sous-marine (Antilles, France)

— Qu'est-ce que tu voudrais faire pendant les vacances?
— J'aimerais faire de la plongée sous-marine.
— Alors, allons aux Antilles!

1. visiter des musées / passer du temps sur la plage (New York, Basse-Terre)
2. faire du ski / faire de la planche à voile (Suisse, Antilles)
3. étudier une autre langue / étudier Shakespeare (Grande-Bretagne, Japon)
4. aller à l'opéra / voir des animaux exotiques (Italie, Zaïre)

5. visiter une île tropicale / aller dans une grande ville (Londres, Guadeloupe)
6. acheter des nouveaux vêtements / visiter des pyramides aztèques (Mexique, France)
7. écouter du jazz / écouter de la musique country (Nashville, La Nouvelle-Orléans)
8. faire du ski / visiter Disney World (Floride, Colorado)

E. À vous de choisir. Votre ami(e) va vous acheter un cadeau (*gift*). Répondez à ses questions. Un(e) camarade de classe va jouer le rôle de votre ami(e).

EXEMPLE le café (Colombie, Mexique)
— Tu préfères le café de Colombie ou du Mexique?
— Je préfère le café de Colombie.

1. le champagne (France, Californie)
2. la bière (Allemagne, États-Unis)
3. le chocolat (Belgique, Suisse)
4. les voitures (Japon, États-Unis)
5. le thé (Grande-Bretagne, Chine)
6. les vins (France, Allemagne)
7. les vêtements (France, Afrique)
8. les films (Japon, France)

F. Jeu géographique. Divisez la classe en quatre groupes. Le premier groupe choisit dans le tableau ci-dessous (*below*) un continent et une valeur (*value*). Le deuxième groupe doit nommer (*name*) l'endroit décrit. Si le deuxième groupe répond correctement, il gagne les points, sinon (*otherwise*), le premier groupe peut essayer (*try*) de les gagner. Après, le deuxième groupe choisit une question pour le troisième groupe.

EXEMPLE PREMIER GROUPE: **En Europe pour 25 points.**
DEUXIÈME GROUPE: **Les Basques habitent en France et en Belgique.**
PROFESSEUR: **Non, ce n'est pas correct.**
PREMIER GROUPE: **Les Basques habitent en France et en...**

POINTS	EN AMÉRIQUE DU NORD OU EN AMÉRIQUE DU SUD	EN AFRIQUE OU EN ASIE	EN EUROPE
5	New York est la plus grande ville de ce pays.	Tel-Aviv est une ville importante de ce pays.	Les Beatles sont de ce pays.
10	Ce pays a une grande province francophone.	C'est la capitale de la Chine.	Ce pays est connu pour l'opéra et Michel-Ange.
15	Après Paris, c'est la plus grande ville francophone.	Cléopâtre vient d'ici.	Bruxelles est sa capitale.
20	Quel état des États-Unis est une «montagne verte»?	C'est un grand pays francophone à côté du Maroc.	On y parle français, italien, allemand et romanche.
25	On y parle portugais.	Dakar est sa capitale.	Les Basques habitent en France et ici aussi.
30	La capitale de cet état est l'expression française pour *red stick*.	C'est l'ancien (*former*) Congo belge.	Ce pays a la forme d'un hexagone.

Voilà pourquoi!

> **SELF-CHECK**
> 1. How do you say *to come? to become?*
> 2. What is the difference in pronunciation between **il vient** and **ils viennent**?
> 3. What auxiliary is used with **venir**, **revenir**, and **devenir** in the **passé composé**? What is the past participle of each?

Le verbe **venir**

To tell where someone comes from, you may use the verb **venir** (*to come*).

VENIR (*TO COME*)

je **viens**	nous **venons**
tu **viens**	vous **venez**
il/elle/on **vient**	ils/elles **viennent**

PASSÉ COMPOSÉ: je **suis venu(e)**

Mes parents *viennent* de Guadeloupe. Ils *sont venus* habiter en Floride en 1971. Tu *viens* en vacances avec nous? Nous allons à la plage.

Devenir (*to become*) and **revenir** (*to come back*) are conjugated like **venir. Devenir, revenir,** and **venir** all use the auxiliary **être** in the **passé composé.**

Je *viens* d'Haïti. Beaucoup d'Haïtiens *deviennent* canadiens. Je *suis devenue* canadienne en 1989. Je *reviens* voir ma famille ici de temps en temps.

Savez-vous le faire?

A. D'où viennent-ils? Luc fait la connaissance d'autres touristes à son hôtel. Complétez les phrases avec la ville logique pour expliquer d'où ils viennent.

EXEMPLE Je m'appelle Yoshiko. Je suis japonaise. **Je viens de Tokyo.**

Berlin | Londres | MEXICO | MOSCOU | Tokyo | Genève | Bruxelles

1. Ce sont Philippe et Yamilé. Ils sont belges. Ils...
2. Joan et moi, nous sommes anglais. Nous...
3. Hans, tu es allemand, n'est-ce pas? Tu...?
4. Je m'appelle Tamara. Je suis russe. Je...
5. Georges et Véronique, vous êtes suisses, n'est-ce pas? Est-ce que vous...?
6. Ça, c'est Raquel. Elle est mexicaine. Elle...

B. Les vacances. Luc et sa mère parlent des vacances. Dites quand chacun est revenu.

EXEMPLE **J'ai passé cinq semaines en Guadeloupe. Je suis parti le 20 juillet et je suis revenu le 25 août.**

1. Papa et moi avons passé trois semaines à Cannes. Nous sommes partis le cinq août...
2. Les voisins ont passé cinq jours à la campagne. Ils sont partis le dix juillet...
3. Ta sœur a passé un mois au Canada. Elle est partie le premier août...
4. Nous avons passé dix jours à Chamonix à Pâques. Nous sommes partis le dix avril...
5. Tante Colette a passé deux mois chez des amis à Nice. Elle est partie le quinze mai...
6. *Et maintenant, décrivez vos dernières vacances.*

C. Interview. Posez les questions suivantes à un(e) camarade de classe.

1. D'où est-ce que tu viens? Et tes parents? Et tes grands-parents?
2. Pourquoi est-ce que tu es venu(e) à cette université? Est-ce que tes parents sont venus ici aussi? Est-ce que tu as l'intention de revenir ici l'année prochaine? Qu'est-ce que tu voudrais devenir après les études?
3. Quels jours est-ce que tu viens à l'université? Est-ce que tu es venu(e) à l'université hier? Est-ce que tu reviens quelquefois à l'université le week-end?
4. Est-ce que le cours de français devient plus difficile au deuxième semestre / trimestre? Quand est-ce que tu deviens nerveux / nerveuse en classe?

D. Des vacances. Vous allez passer vos vacances **en Europe**, **en Afrique** ou **en Amérique**. Choisissez le continent que vous préférez et préparez une conversation avec votre agent de voyages. Dans la conversation, parlez des choses suivantes:

- trois pays ou trois régions que vous aimeriez visiter sur ce continent et pourquoi
- les choses qu'on peut faire dans chaque endroit
- combien de temps vous allez rester dans chaque endroit
- si vous voulez faire vos réservations
- quand vous voulez partir et rentrer

Remarquez que...

The Guadeloupe archipelago and nearby Martinique are French **départements d'outre-mer** (**DOM**). They are part of France, and their people have the political rights and responsibilities of all French citizens. This relationship has its advantages and disadvantages. The people of the region must form an identity that recognizes their roots and history, as well as their nationality.

Gros titres. Quels problèmes sociaux ou politiques est-ce que ces gros titres (*headlines*) suggèrent? Est-ce qu'on a les mêmes problèmes dans votre société?

L'ÉGALITÉ SOCIALE
ET
LE DÉVELOPPEMENT ÉCONOMIQUE
DANS LES DOM

PROMOUVOIR L'ÉGALE DIGNITÉ DES POPULATIONS D'OUTRE-MER ET RESPECTER LEUR IDENTITÉ PARTICULIÈRE

Qu'est-ce qu'on dit?

TEXTBOOK TAPE

Avant de faire un voyage **à l'étranger, il faut** faire beaucoup de **préparatifs.**

Avant **le départ**, il faut...

écrire à l'office de tourisme pour **obtenir des renseignements.**
lire des guides touristiques et faire un itinéraire.
téléphoner à l'hôtel pour réserver une chambre.
dire à un(e) ami(e) ou à vos parents où vous allez.
demander à un(e) ami(e) de passer chez vous pour donner à manger à vos animaux.
faire vos valises (en avance ou au dernier moment).

Pour payer le voyage, vous pouvez...

faire des économies.
emprunter de l'argent à un(e) ami(e) ou à la banque.
payer par carte de crédit.

À votre **arrivée**, vous devez...

montrer votre passeport et passer à **la douane.**
changer de l'argent ou des chèques de voyage.
acheter **un plan** de la ville.

Des amis de Luc, Alain et sa femme Catherine, parlent de la lettre qu'il **leur** a écrite.

— Qu'est-ce que tu lis?
— C'est une lettre de Luc. Il écrit de Guadeloupe.
— Alors, **ça lui plaît**, la Guadeloupe? Qu'est-ce qu'il **raconte**?
— Ça lui plaît beaucoup! Il **décrit** un volcan actif au parc naturel. Il dit aussi qu'il a **rencontré** une nouvelle amie guadeloupéenne qui **lui** montre l'île.
— La Guadeloupe doit être magnifique. Les plages, la mer, les paysages tropicaux... Pourquoi ne pas aller le rejoindre? On a des vacances ce mois-ci, toi et moi.
— Tu **rêves**! Partir pour la Guadeloupe au dernier moment... c'est bien trop cher!
— On ne sait jamais! Je vais téléphoner à l'agence de voyages demain pour leur **demander les prix.** Et je vais aussi écrire à l'office de tourisme de la Guadeloupe pour obtenir des renseignements.

à l'étranger *abroad* **il faut** *one must, it is necessary to* **des préparatifs** (*m*) *preparations* **le départ** *departure* **obtenir** *to get, to obtain* **des renseignements** (*m*) *information* **faire ses valises** (*f*) *to pack one's suitcases* **faire des économies** (*f*) *to save money* **emprunter de l'argent** (*m*) *to borrow money* **une arrivée** *an arrival* **montrer** *to show* **la douane** *customs* **un plan** *a map* **leur** (*to*) *them* **Ça lui plaît?** *Does he like it?* **raconter** *to tell* **décrit** (**décrire** *to describe*) **rencontrer** *to meet* **lui** (*to*) *him* **rêver (de)** *to dream (about)* **demander les prix** (*m*) *to ask for prices*

A. **On rêve.** Complétez la conversation entre Alain et Catherine avec les mots suivants: **plaît, rêves, écrit, obtenir des renseignements, des vacances, y, lui.** Écrivez vos réponses sur une feuille de papier.

— Voilà une lettre de Luc. Il ______ de Guadeloupe.
— La Guadeloupe lui ______ ?
— Oui, ça ______ plaît beaucoup.
— Nous avons ______ ce mois-ci. Pourquoi ne pas ______ aller aussi?
— Tu ______ ! C'est beaucoup trop cher!
— On ne sait jamais! Je vais téléphoner à l'office de tourisme pour ______ .

B. **Visiteurs.** Des Français viennent passer leurs vacances dans votre région. Qu'est-ce que vous leur dites? Complétez ces phrases logiquement.

1. Je leur écris de venir au mois d(e)...
2. Je leur dis qu'il fait... ce mois-là.
3. Je leur dis qu'on peut...
4. Je leur décris...
5. Je leur demande combien de temps...
6. Je dis que je vais leur montrer...

Voilà pourquoi!

Les verbes **dire, lire** et **écrire**

You have already seen the verbs **dire**, **lire**, and **écrire**, either in the infinitive or in classroom expressions (**Lisez, Écrivez, Comment dit-on?**). Here are their full conjugations. The verb **décrire** (*to describe*) is conjugated like **écrire**.

SELF-CHECK
1. What is unusual about the **vous** form of **dire**?
2. Which two of these verbs have similar past participles? What is the past participle of **lire**?

DIRE (*TO SAY, TO TELL*)

je **dis**	nous **disons**
tu **dis**	vous **dites**
il/elle/on **dit**	ils/elles **disent**

PASSÉ COMPOSÉ: j'**ai dit**

ÉCRIRE (*TO WRITE*)

j'**écris**	nous **écrivons**
tu **écris**	vous **écrivez**
il/elle/on **écrit**	ils/elles **écrivent**

PASSÉ COMPOSÉ: j'**ai écrit**

LIRE (*TO READ*)

je **lis**	nous **lisons**
tu **lis**	vous **lisez**
il/elle/on **lit**	ils/elles **lisent**

PASSÉ COMPOSÉ: j'**ai lu**

Here are some things you might like to read or write.

un article	*an article*
une carte postale	*a postcard*
une rédaction	*a composition*
une histoire	*a story*
un journal	*a newspaper*
une lettre	*a letter*
un poème	*a poem*
une revue	*a magazine*
un roman	*a novel*

Savez-vous le faire?

A. **Revues françaises.** Quelle revue est-ce que ces personnes lisent le plus probablement?

1. Mes parents sont dans les affaires. Ils...
2. Vous aimez voyager. Est-ce que vous...?
3. Tu aimes la musique. Est-ce que tu...?
4. Moi, j'aime le rock. Je...
5. Micheline travaille dans le tourisme. Elle...
6. Alain est homme d'affaires. Il...

B. **Qu'est-ce qu'on dit?** Vous expliquez à des amis quand on dit les expressions suivantes. Complétez les phrases avec la forme correcte du verbe ***dire*** et l'expression logique.

Enchanté, madame.
Répétez, s'il vous plaît!
BON VOYAGE! **JE VEUX BIEN.**
À tout à l'heure! À demain!
Salut!

EXEMPLE Vos amis vont partir en voyage. Vous leur **dites «Bon voyage»**.

1. Nous n'avons pas compris le professeur. Nous lui...
2. Tes camarades de classe et toi allez voir le prof demain. Vous lui...
3. Tu vas voir tes camarades de classe plus tard, à la bibliothèque. Tu leur...
4. Un ami fait la connaissance de ta mère. Il lui...
5. J'accepte une invitation au cinéma avec des amis. Je leur...
6. Mes amis retrouvent d'autres amis au cinéma. Ils leur...

C. **Des lettres.** Vos parents reçoivent des lettres où chacun décrit ses vacances. De quel pays est-ce que chacun leur écrit?

EXEMPLE Nos voisins leur décrivent les ruines de Pompéi. Ils leur **écrivent d'Italie.**

1. Ma tante leur décrit l'Amazone. Elle leur...
2. Mon frère et moi leur décrivons le Quartier latin. Nous leur...
3. Des amis de mon père lui décrivent le vieux Montréal. Ils lui...
4. Je leur décris le palais de Buckingham. Je leur...
5. Mes cousins leur décrivent la statue de la Liberté. Ils leur...
6. Une amie de ma mère lui décrit les pyramides. Elle lui...

D. **Interview.** Posez les questions suivantes à un(e) camarade de classe.

1. Est-ce que tu écris beaucoup de lettres? À qui? Est-ce que tu écris des cartes postales quand tu es en vacances?
2. Est-ce que tu lis le journal tous les jours? Est-ce que tu l'as lu ce matin? Quelle revue est-ce que tu lis le plus souvent? Est-ce que tu l'as lue ce mois-ci?
3. Est-ce que tu lis beaucoup de romans? Qui écrit des romans intéressants? Est-ce que tu as lu des romans français? Qui a écrit ces romans? Est-ce que tu lis plus de romans d'aventures ou d'amour? Est-ce que tu préfères lire des romans policiers ou des romans d'épouvante? Est-ce que tu voudrais écrire un roman? Pour quel cours est-ce que tu écris beaucoup?

E. **Préparatifs.** Vous allez partir en vacances avec un(e) ami(e) qui veut savoir si vous avez tout préparé. Préparez une conversation avec un(e) autre étudiant(e) où vous dites si vous avez fait les choses suivantes.

- écrire pour réserver une chambre
- faire un itinéraire
- acheter des billets
- acheter des chèques de voyage
- dire à quelqu'un où vous allez
- demander à quelqu'un de donner à manger à vos animaux
- faire vos valises

Voilà pourquoi!

Les compléments d'objet indirect

When using verbs indicating giving and receiving (**donner, emprunter...**) or communication (**dire, parler...**), the person you are giving something to or communicating with is generally an indirect object. Indirect objects are preceded by **à** or **pour** in French. The verbs that follow often have indirect objects.

SELF-CHECK

1. What types of verbs are frequently followed by indirect objects?
2. What words generally precede a noun that is an indirect object?
3. What two pronouns can be used for indirect objects?

VERBS OF GIVING AND RECEIVING

acheter pour	J'**achète** des souvenirs **pour mes amis.**
apporter à	Notre chien **apporte** le journal **à mon père.**
donner à	L'office de tourisme **donne** des renseignements **aux touristes.**
emprunter à	Je vais **emprunter** de l'argent **à mes parents.**
prêter à *to lend*	Mes parents **prêtent** de l'argent **à mon frère.**
servir à	Je **sers** du vin **à mes amis.**

VERBS OF COMMUNICATION

décrire à	Luc **décrit** la Guadeloupe **à Alain** dans sa lettre.
demander à	Je vais **demander** les prix **à l'agent de voyages.**
dire à	Luc **dit à ses amis** qu'il aime la Guadeloupe.
écrire à	Luc **écrit à Alain et Catherine.**
lire à	Alain **lit** la lettre de Luc **à sa femme.**
montrer à	Micheline **montre** l'île **à Luc.**
parler à	Catherine **parle à Alain** d'aller en Guadeloupe.
poser (une question) à	Luc **pose** beaucoup de questions **à Micheline.**
téléphoner à	Il **téléphone** toujours **à ses parents** le dimanche après-midi.

With verbs of communication, **de** is used before an infinitive when asking or telling someone to do something.

Je *dis à* mes amis *de* venir en juin.	*I tell my friends to come in June.*
Je vais *demander à* mon frère *de* faire ça.	*I'm going to ask my brother to do that.*

Also use indirect objects with **plaire** (*to please*) to say that somebody likes something. Use the auxiliary **avoir** with the past participle of **plaire** (**plu**) in the **passé composé.**

La Guadeloupe plaît à Luc.	*Luc likes Guadeloupe. (Guadeloupe is pleasing to Luc.)*
Les plages plaisent à Luc.	*Luc likes the beaches. (The beaches are pleasing to Luc.)*
Le volcan aussi a plu à Luc.	*Luc liked the volcano, too. (The volcano pleased Luc, too.)*

Les pronoms **lui** et **leur**

Use the pronouns **lui** (*him, her*) and **leur** (*them*) to replace **à** or **pour** and an indirect object that is either a person or an animal. Like direct object pronouns (**le, la, l', les**), **lui** and **leur** go just before the conjugated verb, unless there is an infinitive. If there is an infinitive, they generally precede it.

Luc écrit *à sa grand-mère.*	**Luc *lui* écrit.**
Il ne téléphone pas *à ses parents.*	**Il ne *leur* téléphone pas.**
Ça plaît *à ses parents.*	**Ça *leur* plaît.**
Il va acheter quelque chose *pour son père.*	**Il va *lui* acheter quelque chose.**
Il a envie de parler *à son père et à sa mère.*	**Il a envie de *leur* parler.**
Ça doit plaire *à sa mère.*	**Ça doit *lui* plaire.**

Savez-vous le faire?

A. **Quel accueil!** Des amis viennent passer leurs vacances chez vous. Dites si vous faites les choses suivantes pour vos invités.

EXEMPLE présenter vos amis → **Bien sûr que je leur présente mes amis!**
OU **Mais non, je ne leur présente pas mes amis!**

1. dire de faire le lit
2. prêter votre voiture
3. parler de vos problèmes
4. montrer la ville
5. emprunter de l'argent
6. prêter de l'argent
7. préparer le dîner
8. dire de partir

Maintenant, dites si vous faites toujours (souvent, quelquefois, rarement, ne... jamais) ces choses pour votre camarade de chambre ou votre meilleur(e) ami(e).

EXEMPLE présenter vos amis → **Je lui présente toujours mes amis.**
OU **Je ne lui présente jamais mes amis!**

B. **Souvenirs.** Vous visitez l'Europe et vous rapportez (*bring back*) des cadeaux pour tout le monde. Qu'est-ce que vous apportez aux personnes suivantes?

des disques compacts
du chocolat belge ???
DU VIN FRANÇAIS
du thé anglais ???
des vêtements italiens
des cartes postales

EXEMPLE à votre mère
Je lui rapporte du thé anglais.

1. à vos parents
2. à votre meilleur(e) ami(e)
3. aux étudiants du cours de français
4. au professeur de français

C. **Vos amis.** Posez les questions suivantes à un(e) camarade de classe.

1. Comment s'appelle ton (ta) meilleur(e) ami(e)? Est-ce que tu lui parles de tes problèmes? Tu lui décris tes rêves? Est-ce que tu peux tout lui dire? Est-ce que tu lui parles souvent de ta famille? Qu'est-ce que tu ne peux pas lui dire? Est-ce que tu lui téléphones tous les jours? Est-ce que tu lui écris quand tu es en vacances? Est-ce que vous passez quelquefois les vacances ensemble?
2. Est-ce que tu parles souvent à tes voisins? Est-ce qu'ils sont sympathiques? Est-ce que tu leur prêtes quelquefois des choses? Est-ce que tu leur empruntes des choses? Quand ils sont en vacances, est-ce que tu donnes à manger à leur chien ou à leur chat? Est-ce que tu lis leur journal?

Qu'est-ce qu'on dit?

TEXTBOOK TAPE

Si vous allez dans une agence de voyages ou à l'aéroport pour acheter un billet, **on vous posera peut-être** les questions suivantes. Regardez l'itinéraire de Luc et imaginez comment il a répondu.

- Est-ce que vous voulez un billet **aller-retour** ou **un aller simple**?
- À quelle date est-ce que vous voulez partir?
- Quand est-ce que vous voudriez rentrer?
- Préférez-vous un **vol** du matin, de l'après-midi ou du soir?
- Préférez-vous être en première classe ou en classe touriste?
- Préférez-vous la section fumeur ou non-fumeur?

ITINÉRAIRE

À l'intention de: Moreau/Luc

ALLER Mardi 20 juillet: Départ de Paris Orly Air France-Vol 506	16h25 Classe touriste/Vol direct Non-fumeur	Boeing 747
Mardi 20 juillet: Arrivée à Pointe-à-Pitre	18h50	
Un repas et une collation seront servis en vol.		
RETOUR Mercredi 25 août: Départ de Pointe-à-Pitre Air France-Vol 521	16h55 Classe touriste/Vol direct Non-fumeur	Boeing 747
Jeudi 26 août: Arrivée à Paris Orly	7h00	
Un repas et un petit déjeuner seront servis en vol.		
		Prix du billet aller-retour: 3545 F

Prévoyez d'arriver à l'aéroport deux heures avant l'heure de départ et n'oubliez pas de reconfirmer votre retour 72 heures avant le départ.

BON VOYAGE!

Qu'est-ce que vous demandez à l'agent? Imaginez comment l'agent a répondu à Luc.

- C'est combien pour le billet?
- À quelle heure est le départ de Paris Orly?
- Est-ce qu'on sert **le petit déjeuner** (le déjeuner, le dîner) pendant le vol?
- Est-ce que l'avion fait des **escales** ou est-ce que c'est un vol direct?

Quelle est votre réaction si...

vous devez **attendre** votre vol **à cause d'**un délai?
l'avion commence à descendre rapidement?
le vol arrive en avance (à l'heure, en retard)?
on **perd** vos bagages à l'aéroport?

---

on vous posera *someone will ask you* **peut-être** *maybe* **aller-retour** *round-trip* **un aller simple** *a one-way ticket* **un vol** *a flight* **le petit déjeuner** *breakfast* **une escale** *a stopover* **attendre** *to wait (for)* **à cause de** *due to, because of* **perd** (**perdre** *to lose*)

Luc téléphone à Alain de Guadeloupe pour lui demander s'il a **toujours** l'intention de venir avec sa femme.

— Alain, tu m'**entends**? Il y a du **bruit** ici dans l'hôtel.
— Oui, je t'entends bien.
— Catherine et toi, vous venez toujours passer quinze jours en Guadeloupe?
— Oui, on pense descendre au même hôtel que toi. Ta chambre te plaît?
— Oui, c'est un petit hôtel pas cher, mais très agréable. Si tu veux, je peux venir vous **chercher** à l'aéroport à Pointe-à-Pitre.
— Non, non, **il ne faut pas perdre** ton temps à nous attendre à l'aéroport. L'avion peut arriver en retard.
— Non, j'insiste! Quand est-ce que vous arrivez?
— Nous arrivons samedi le huit, avec le vol 578 à 19h30.
— Bon, si ça change, téléphonez-moi. La Guadeloupe va vous plaire. Les gens sont très sympa. Dites, Micheline nous invite à dîner chez elle dimanche. Ça vous dit?
— Bien sûr! Alors, à samedi à l'aéroport vers 19h30!
— D'accord! Alors, bon voyage! À samedi! Au revoir!
— Au revoir!

toujours *still* **entends (entendre** *to hear*) **le bruit** *noise* **venir (aller) chercher** *to pick up*
il ne faut pas *you shouldn't* **perdre** *to lose, to waste*

A. Et vous? Choisissez la phrase qui vous décrit le mieux quand vous êtes en vacances.

1. a. Je préfère les vols du matin. b. Je préfère partir le soir. c. Ça ne me plaît pas de voyager en avion.
2. a. J'arrive à l'aéroport bien en avance. b. J'arrive au dernier moment. c. Je manque (*miss*) mon vol.
3. a. À mon arrivée, je loue une voiture à l'aéroport. b. Je prends un taxi. c. Des amis viennent me chercher à l'aéroport.
4. a. Je réserve une chambre d'hôtel bien à l'avance. b. Je passe la nuit dans l'aéroport. c. Je cherche une chambre à mon arrivée.
5. a. D'habitude, je descends dans un hôtel pas trop cher. b. Je descends dans un hôtel de luxe. c. Ça dépend de qui va payer.
6. a. Je perds beaucoup de temps à l'hôtel. b. Je quitte l'hôtel tôt le matin et je rentre tard le soir. c. Ça dépend du temps.

B. Mon dernier vol. Décrivez votre dernier vol en complétant les phrases suivantes.

1. J'ai dû attendre le vol à l'aéroport pendant (une heure, trente minutes, ???).
2. Je suis allé(e) de (Los Angeles, Dallas, ???) à (Omaha, La Nouvelle-Orléans, ???).
3. J'ai passé (quarante-cinq minutes, trois heures, ???) en avion.
4. J'ai trouvé les hôtesses et les stewards (excellents, bons, médiocres, mauvais, ???).
5. À l'arrivée, j'ai attendu mes valises pendant (cinq minutes, quinze minutes, ???).

C. **Des préparatifs.** Votre ami parle de son vol. Dites s'il parle **de son billet, de son ami, de ses valises, de l'avion, de l'aéroport** ou **du film.**

1. Je l'ai pris de Paris à New York.
2. Je les ai faites le matin du vol.
3. Je l'ai acheté un mois à l'avance.
4. J'y suis arrivé une heure en avance.
5. Je ne l'ai pas vu. J'ai préféré dormir.
6. Je lui ai téléphoné à mon arrivée.

Voilà pourquoi!

SELF-CHECK

1. Which of these **-re** verbs is conjugated with **être** in the **passé composé**?
2. What four pronouns are used for both direct and indirect objects? Where are they usually placed in a sentence with an infinitive? Where are they placed otherwise?
3. When is an unaccented **e** silent? When must you pronounce it?

Les verbes en -re

The verb **attendre** (*to wait for*) is useful when making arrangements for meeting someone. Note that you do not use **pour** after **attendre** to say whom you are waiting *for*.

ATTENDRE (*TO WAIT FOR*)

j'**attends**	nous **attendons**
tu **attends**	vous **attendez**
il/elle/on **attend**	ils/elles **attendent**

PASSÉ COMPOSÉ: **j'ai attendu**

— Vous attendez quelqu'un?
— Oui, j'attends des amis.

The following verbs are conjugated like **attendre**. They all are conjugated with the auxiliary **avoir** in the **passé composé** except **descendre** (**je suis descendu[e], tu es descendu[e]...**).

dépendre (de) *to depend (on)*
descendre *to go down, to get off, to stay* (at a hotel)
entendre *to hear*
perdre *to lose, to waste*
rendre quelque chose à quelqu'un *to return/turn in something to someone*
rendre visite à quelqu'un *to visit someone*
répondre à *to answer*
(re)vendre *to sell (back)*

Les pronoms **me, te, nous, vous**

You already know the third-person direct object pronouns (**le, la, l', les**) and indirect object pronouns (**lui, leur**). In the first and second persons, the same pronouns are used for both direct and indirect objects: **me, te, nous, vous. Me** and **te** become **m'** and **t'** before vowel sounds. Remember that object pronouns will go before the conjugated verb, unless it is followed by an infinitive. In that case, they will go before the infinitive.

DIRECT OBJECTS		INDIRECT OBJECTS	
me (m')	**nous**	**me (m')**	**nous**
te (t')	**vous**	**te (t')**	**vous**
le/la/l'	**les**	**lui**	**leur**

Tu ne *m'*entends pas?
Nous *l'*avons attendu(e) deux heures.
Je peux *vous* attendre.

Et ça se prononce comment?

Le e caduc

Unaccented e's are usually not pronounced if you can drop them without bringing three pronounced consonants together. When there are two unaccented e's in a row, usually the second one is dropped.

NOTE
Items accompanied by a tape symbol are recorded on the textbook tape.

Tu m~~e~~ parles? Je n~~e~~ veux pas d~~e~~ vin. Vous n~~e~~ voulez pas m~~e~~ donner d~~e~~ l'argent?

An unaccented **e** is pronounced when dropping it would create a group of three pronounced consonants.

Le professeur me parle. Luc te connaît. Karim le veut.

Savez-vous le faire?

A. **Ça se prononce?** Imaginez que vous parlez à votre meilleur(e) ami(e). D'abord, écoutez chaque paire de phrases et décidez si on prononce chaque **e**. Ensuite, lisez la phrase que vous diriez (*would say*) le plus probablement à votre ami(e).

1. a. Tu me parles trop de tes problèmes. b. Tu ne me parles pas trop de tes problèmes.
2. a. Je te prête souvent de l'argent. b. Je ne te prête presque jamais d'argent.
3. a. Tu peux me téléphoner après minuit. b. Tu ne peux pas me téléphoner après minuit.
4. a. Tu me rends souvent visite. b. Tu ne me rends pas souvent visite.
5. a. Je vais venir te voir ce week-end. b. Je ne vais pas venir te voir ce week-end.

B. **À l'université.** Dites si vous faites souvent (quelquefois, rarement, ne... jamais) les choses suivantes.

EXEMPLE perdre vos devoirs → **Je ne perds jamais mes devoirs.**
OU **Je perds quelquefois mes devoirs.**

1. rendre vos devoirs au professeur
2. répondre aux questions du professeur
3. entendre d'autres langues à l'université
4. revendre vos livres après les examens
5. attendre l'autobus
6. descendre en ville
7. perdre du temps
8. répondre aux lettres de vos amis

C. **Mes amis et moi.** Complétez les phrases suivantes.

1. Dans mon magasin préféré, on vend...
2. J'attends toujours... avec impatience.
3. Je rends souvent visite à...
4. Récemment, j'ai rendu visite à...
5. Je perds beaucoup de temps quand...
6. Je perds souvent patience avec... parce que...
7. Récemment, j'ai perdu patience avec...
8. Mes amis perdent patience avec moi quand...

D. **Un voyage.** Complétez les questions suivantes avec la forme correcte du verbe logique. Après, posez les questions à un(e) camarade de classe. Vous pouvez utiliser ces verbes plus d'une fois: **rendre**, **perdre**, **attendre**, **descendre**, **vendre**, **entendre**.

1. À qui est-ce que tu ______ souvent visite?
2. Quand des amis te ______ visite de loin, est-ce que tu les ______ à l'aéroport?
3. Est-ce que tu ______ patience quand ils ______ tes bagages à l'aéroport?
4. Est-ce qu'on doit souvent ______ des avions en retard à l'aéroport ici?
5. Qu'est-ce qu'on ______ généralement dans les boutiques à l'aéroport?
6. Quand tu voyages avec ta famille, est-ce que vous ______ souvent dans un hôtel de luxe?
7. Est-ce qu'on ______ bien quand on téléphone d'un avion?
8. Est-ce que tu deviens nerveux / nerveuse si l'avion monte ou ______ rapidement?

E. **Disputes.** Une de vos amies se dispute (*is arguing*) avec son petit ami. Quels reproches se font-ils?

EXEMPLE **Tu ne me téléphones pas assez souvent!**

Je	**(ne... pas)**	**te**	**attendre pendant des heures**
Tu	**(ne... jamais)**	**me**	**rendre l'argent que tu empruntes**
			écouter
			parler de tes projets
			écrire des poèmes
			téléphoner
			préparer le dîner
			oublier
			???

F. **Professeurs et étudiants.** Dites au professeur trois choses que les autres étudiants et vous faites pour lui/elle et trois choses que le professeur fait pour vous. Faites deux listes sur une feuille de papier.

EXEMPLES **Nous vous écoutons.** **Vous nous donnez beaucoup d'examens.**

G. **À l'agence de voyages.** Vous achetez un billet pour aller dans un autre pays. Utilisez les expressions de la section ***Qu'est-ce qu'on dit?*** à la page 258 pour préparer la scène avec un(e) camarade de classe, qui va jouer le rôle de l'agent de voyages.

H. **À l'aéroport.** Des amis viennent vous rendre visite. Vous leur téléphonez pour leur dire que vous allez venir les chercher à l'aéroport. Demandez-leur des renseignements sur le vol, la date et l'heure de leur arrivée. Dites-leur aussi ce que vous allez faire ensemble dans votre région.

Voilà pourquoi!

Les pronoms au passé composé

In *Chapitre cinq*, you learned to use the **passé composé** to talk about the past. Review the explanations on pages 184–185 and 189–190. Since then, you have learned the **-re** verbs.

J'ai perdu mes bagages. **Je suis descendu(e) dans un petit hôtel.**

You have also learned these verbs.

WITH AVOIR			WITH ÊTRE		
connaître	→	j'ai connu...	descendre	→	je suis descendu(e)...
courir	→	j'ai couru...	devenir	→	je suis devenu(e)...
devoir	→	j'ai dû...	revenir	→	je suis revenu(e)...
dire	→	j'ai dit...	venir	→	je suis venu(e)...
écrire	→	j'ai écrit...			
lire	→	j'ai lu...			
plaire	→	ça m'a plu			
prendre	→	j'ai pris...			
pouvoir	→	j'ai pu...			
vouloir	→	j'ai voulu...			

Object pronouns, as well as y, go before the auxiliary in the **passé composé**.

Tu as vu *ce film?* **Non, je ne *l'*ai pas encore vu.**
Vous avez écrit *à vos amis?* **Oui, nous *leur* avons écrit hier.**
Vos parents sont allés *en Guadeloupe?* **Oui, ils *y* sont allés l'été dernier.**

The past participle agrees with a *direct object* that precedes a verb in the **passé composé**.

Vous avez fait *les valises?* **Oui, nous *les* avons fait*es*.**
Tu as vu *ma sœur?* **Non, je ne *l'*ai pas vu*e*.**

However, past participles do not agree with indirect object pronouns or with y.

Tu as écrit *à ma sœur?* **Non, je ne *lui* ai pas écrit.**
Tu as dîné *chez ma sœur?* **Non, je n'*y* ai pas dîné.**

Use a direct object pronoun when the noun it replaces is what is being acted upon. Use an indirect object pronoun to replace **pour** or **à** + person or animal after a verb of communication or exchange, or when saying for whom something is done. Y replaces a prepositional phrase indicating location.

DIRECT OBJECT	**Luc a invité *Micheline?***	**Oui, il *l'*a invité*e*.**
INDIRECT OBJECT	**Il a parlé *à Micheline?***	**Oui, il *lui* a parlé.**
	Il a prêté de l'argent *à ses amis.*	**Il *leur* a prêté de l'argent.**
Y	**Il a passé un mois *en Guadeloupe?***	**Oui, Luc *y* a passé un mois.**

SELF-CHECK

1. Besides **descendre**, **venir**, **devenir**, and **revenir**, what other verbs learned earlier are conjugated with **être** in the **passé composé**?
2. Where are object pronouns and **y** placed in the **passé composé**? Does the past participle agree with direct or indirect object pronouns?
3. Nouns that are indirect objects are preceded by what prepositions?

Savez-vous le faire?

A. **Votre dernier voyage.** Pensez aux dernières vacances où vous avez pris l'avion. Dites quand vous avez fait les choses suivantes. Remplacez les mots en caractères gras par un pronom complément d'objet direct.

au dernier moment	ne... jamais	*le jour de mon départ*	**ne... pas**
UN MOIS À L'AVANCE		???	**tous les jours**
deux fois		*une fois*	???
le jour de mon arrivée		*longtemps en avance*	

EXEMPLE réserver **la chambre d'hôtel**
Je l'ai réservée longtemps à l'avance.

1. acheter **les billets d'avion**
2. faire **vos valises**
3. faire **les réservations d'hôtel**
4. perdre **vos bagages**
5. prendre **le petit déjeuner** dans votre chambre
6. regarder **la télé dans votre chambre**
7. quitter **l'hôtel** tôt le matin
8. acheter **le journal**

Maintenant, dites si vous avez fait les choses suivantes. Remplacez les mots en caractères gras par un pronom complément d'objet indirect ou y.

EXEMPLE arriver **à l'aéroport** en avance
Oui, j'y suis arrivé(e) en avance.

1. écrire **à votre meilleur(e) ami(e)**
2. passer beaucoup de temps **à l'hôtel**
3. aller **en Europe**
4. téléphoner **à vos parents**
5. acheter des souvenirs **pour vos amis**
6. passer beaucoup de temps **à l'aéroport**
7. donner votre itinéraire **à vos parents**
8. aller **à votre hôtel** en taxi

B. **Les mêmes choses.** Suivez (*follow*) l'exemple pour découvrir si votre camarade de classe a fait les mêmes choses que vous récemment. Si votre camarade de classe a fait la même chose, demandez-lui si ça lui a plu.

EXEMPLE louer une cassette vidéo
— Quelle cassette vidéo est-ce que tu as louée récemment?
— J'ai loué *Indochine.* Tu l'as louée aussi?
— Je l'ai louée samedi dernier. Ça t'a plu?
— Ça m'a beaucoup plu.

1. voir un film 2. lire un livre 3. acheter une revue 4. acheter un disque compact

C. **En contact.** Indiquez la dernière fois que vous avez fait les choses suivantes pour les personnes nommées. Utilisez un pronom complément d'objet direct ou indirect.

EXEMPLE vos parents (voir, écrire)
Je les ai vus il n'y a pas trop longtemps.
Je leur ai écrit la semaine dernière.

1. vos parents (parler, rendre visite, emprunter de l'argent)
2. votre meilleur(e) ami(e) (inviter chez vous, prêter de l'argent, téléphoner)
3. votre professeur (poser une question, chercher dans son bureau, donner une excuse)
4. votre voisin (entendre dans son appartement, voir, demander un service)

ne... jamais
il y a longtemps
il n'y a pas trop longtemps
récemment
hier
aujourd'hui
???

Remarquez que...

Comme tous les pays et toutes les régions du Nouveau Monde, la Guadeloupe a une histoire de colonisation et d'immigration.

Dates importantes. Voici quelques événements (*events*) importants de l'histoire de la Guadeloupe. Est-ce que vous pouvez deviner la date de chaque événement?

- Christophe Colomb est arrivé en Guadeloupe en...
- Deux Français, Léonard de l'Olive et Jean Duplessis d'Ossonville ont établi une colonie en Guadeloupe en...
- La Guadeloupe est devenue un territoire français en...
- Jean-Baptiste Labat a armé des esclaves (*slaves*) africains pour lutter (*fight*) contre les Anglais en...
- Les Anglais ont occupé la Guadeloupe deux fois entre... et...
- La France a aboli l'esclavage (*slavery*) dans ses colonies en...
- La Guadeloupe est devenue un département français d'outre-mer en...

1946
1635
1759
1703
1794
1674
1848
1493

C'est à lire!

What kind of information would you find in an ad for a vacation package? Read the advertisement for "Jet Tours en Martinique" on the next page, and decide if this sort of trip would appeal to you. The following activity will help prepare you for the reading.

En contexte. Devinez le sens des mots en caractères gras dans le contexte.

1. Ces îles s'appellent la Martinique et la Guadeloupe. Elles sont aussi **appelées** les Antilles.
2. Les plages sont magnifiques: l'eau bleue et transparente et le **sable** fin et blanc.
3. Aux Antilles on peut faire de la planche à voile et il y a toujours des **voiliers** visibles à l'horizon.
4. Les hôtels à Fort-de-France offrent deux avantages: on peut profiter des activités d'une grande ville et on peut être **en bord de** mer.

JET TOURS EN MARTINIQUE

Fascinante par la diversité de ses paysages et de ses habitants, cette île est aussi appelée «île aux fleurs».
La capitale, Fort-de-France, avec sa baie aux horizons sans limites, parsemée de centaines de voiliers, est une ville toujours animée.
La Martinique, ce sont de charmants villages typiques, aux petits marchés aux odeurs épicées, ce sont des jardins, et surtout, des plages immenses de sable blond et fin.
Au Sud, le plus beau site : la baie du Diamant.

La Batelière :

Deux avantages importants pour ce charmant hôtel, c'est d'être à la fois très proche du centre-ville de Fort-de-France, et en même temps de se trouver en bord de plage.
Tous les sports nautiques y sont à l'honneur : voile, planche à voile.
Une salle de gymnastique ainsi que 6 courts de tennis permettent une remise en forme parfaite.
9 jours/7 nuits à partir de 5 180 F avec petits déjeuners américains.

Les voyages Jet Tours sont en vente dans toutes les agences de voyages, agences Air France et agences Jet Tours.
Paris : Tél. : 47.05.01.95
Marseille : Tél. : 91.22.19.19
Lyon : Tél. : 78.42.80.77
Mulhouse : Tél. : 89.66.20.02
Nice : Tél. : 93.80.88.66.

Bon à découper et à envoyer à Jet Tours AIR FRANCE SOTAIR, 22, rue de la Mégisserie, 75001 Paris. RÊVE PROMIS RÊVE TENU!

Prière de m'envoyer votre prochaine brochure Jet Tours à l'adresse ci-dessous: .... Réf Naf Naf

Nom ....

Prénom ....

Numéro .... Rue ....

Code postal ....

Ville ....

Avez-vous compris?

Vrai ou faux? Lisez la publicité "Jet Tours en Martinique" et indiquez si ces phrases sont vraies ou fausses. Corrigez les phrases qui sont fausses.

1. Il y a une diversité de paysages en Martinique.
2. La Martinique s'appelle aussi «l'île aux marchés».
3. Pointe-à-Pitre est la capitale de la Martinique.
4. Fort-de-France est un petit village tranquille.
5. L'hôtel La Batelière est loin de la ville, à côté de la mer.
6. À l'hôtel La Batelière, on peut profiter des sports nautiques et d'une salle de gymnastique.

Ça y est! C'est à vous!

Brainstorming will help you approach a writing task. Working alone or with a group, brainstorming involves listing everything that comes to mind on a given topic. Put all your ideas together on paper, then look over them to determine what you want to say and how you want to organize it.

You are going to create an advertisement for your town or for another place that you like. Decide on the place, then list everything that comes to mind about it, using nouns, verbs, and adjectives. When you have finished, decide how you want to organize your ideas.

A. **Organisez-vous.** Sur une feuille de papier, faites une liste de noms, adjectifs et verbes que vous associez avec votre ville ou un endroit (*place*) que vous aimez. Ensuite, organisez toutes vos idées en catégories logiques.

les choses à voir *???*
LES CHOSES À FAIRE **LES JOLIS ENDROITS**
la cuisine ???

B. **Rédaction: Une publicité.** Préparez le texte d'une publicité pour un voyage dans votre ville ou dans un autre endroit que vous aimez. Imaginez qu'on va publier cette publicité dans une revue française.

C. **Viens me rendre visite!** Vous invitez un(e) ami(e) français(e) à venir vous rendre visite. Préparez une conversation avec un(e) camarade de classe où vous parlez des choses que vous pouvez faire après son arrivée.

D. **À la radio.** Vous entendez une publicité à la radio pour "Jet Tours en Martinique". Écoutez la publicité et faites sur une feuille de papier une liste d'au moins trois raisons de visiter la Martinique.

Pour vérifier

Étudiez la liste de vocabulaire. Après avoir fini ces exercices, vérifiez vos réponses dans l'*Appendix C.*

Making vacation plans

A. **Associations.** Faites une liste des mots que vous associez avec un aéroport. Ensuite, faites une autre liste des choses à faire sur une île tropicale.

B. **Une famille internationale.** C'est très curieux. La ville d'origine de tous les membres de ma famille commence par la même lettre de l'alphabet que le pays ou l'état dans lequel elle se trouve. D'abord, complétez les phrases suivantes avec le verbe **venir**. Ensuite, répondez à ces devinettes (*riddles*) en disant la ville et le pays d'origine de chacun.

EXEMPLE Ma femme vient de la capitale d'un pays en Amérique du Sud.
Elle vient de Brasilia, au Brésil.

1. Je ______ de la capitale d'un pays francophone en Europe.
2. Le mari de ma sœur ______ de la capitale d'un état des États-Unis.
3. Mes cousins ______ de la ville la plus peuplée du monde (*in the world*).

C. **Les dernières vacances.** Lisez les phrases de l'exercice *A. Préférences* à la page 238. Dites si vous avez fait ces choses pendant vos dernières vacances.

EXEMPLE **J'ai fait du camping. Je ne suis pas descendu(e) dans un hôtel de luxe.**

Contacting others and making arrangements

D. **Qui?** Complétez les phrases suivantes de façon logique avec **dire**, **lire**, **écrire** ou un verbe en **-re**.

EXEMPLE Je lis toujours deux ou trois fois les lettres que ma petite amie m'écrit.

1. Les étudiants ______ beaucoup de rédactions pour ce cours. Le professeur les ______ pendant des heures et il les ______ aux étudiants après un ou deux jours.
2. Nous ______ les articles de ce journaliste tous les jours. Il ______ pour un journal local et il ______ toujours quelque chose d'intéressant.
3. Est-ce que vous ______ les romans de Stephen King? Mes amis ______ qu'il ______ les meilleurs romans d'épouvante.

E. **Conversations.** Complétez les conversations suivantes avec un complément d'objet direct ou indirect.

1. — Vous allez ______ attendre à l'aéroport à notre arrivée?
— Oui, nous pouvons venir ______ chercher.
2. — Tu ______ entends? Il y a du bruit sur la ligne.
— Oui, je ______ entends.
3. — Isabelle a besoin d'argent. Tu vas ______ prêter 500 francs?
— Non! Elle ne ______ a pas encore rendu l'argent que je ______ ai prêté le mois dernier.

Vocabulaire

Making vacation plans

NOMS
un aéroport
une agence de voyages
un agent de voyages
un aller simple
l'arrivée (*f*)
des bagages (*m*)
une banque
un billet (aller-retour)
un bruit
une carte de crédit
une carte d'identité
la chaleur
un chèque de voyage
le déjeuner
un délai
un départ
le dîner
la douane
un guide (touristique)
un hôtel (de luxe)
une île (tropicale)
un itinéraire
la mer
une montagne
un office de tourisme
un passeport
un pays
un paysage
le petit déjeuner
un plan
des préparatifs (*m*)
le prix
une réservation
un rêve
une section (non-)fumeur
un site (historique)
une valise
un vol (direct)
un volcan

EXPRESSIONS VERBALES
admirer
changer de l'argent (*m*)
compter (sur)
courir
devenir
donner à manger à
faire de la planche à voile
faire de la plongée sous-marine
faire des économies (*f*)
faire les valises (*f*)
faire une escale
faire un pique-nique
goûter
obtenir des renseignements (*m*)
payer
perdre
plaire
réserver (à l'avance)
revenir
rêver (de)
vendre (revendre)
venir

Pour les participes passés, voir la page 263.

ADJECTIFS
assis(e)
connu(e)
étranger (étrangère)
exotique
francophone
guadeloupéen(ne)
local(e) (*m pl* locaux)
magnifique
reposant(e)

DIVERS
à cause de
à l'étranger
à l'heure
au dernier moment
avant
C'est chouette!
déjà
en avance
en classe touriste
en première classe
en retard
en vacances
il faut (il ne faut pas)
J'aimerais...
le long de
(ne...) pas encore
ne... que
par terre
toujours

Pour les pays, voir la page 245. Pour les états des États-Unis et les provinces du Canada, voir la page 121.

Contacting others and making arrangements

NOMS
un article
une carte postale
une escale
une histoire
un journal
une lettre
un poème
une rédaction
une revue
un roman

VERBES
aller / venir chercher quelqu'un
attendre
décrire
demander
dépendre (de)
descendre
dire
écrire
emprunter
entendre
insister
lire
montrer
oublier
perdre
poser une question
prêter
raconter
rejoindre
rencontrer
rendre (visite à)
répondre
téléphoner (à)

Pour les pronoms compléments d'objet direct et indirect, voir la page 260.

Window Detail, Caribbean house
Photo by Gilles de Chabaneix in *Caribbean Style*, S. Slesin et al., © 1985
Reproduced permission of Clarkson Potter, Inc.

Like those in the painting on page 235 of ***Chapitre Sept***, the colors in this window detail typify the natural colors of the Antilles.

Chapitre 8 À l'hôtel

By the end of this chapter, you should be able to do the following in French:

- Get a hotel room
- Talk about travel
- Ask for and give directions
- Buy clothes

Coumbite
Gérard Valcin (1923–1988)
1971
Milwaukee Art Museum
Gift of Richard and Erna Flagg

Agriculture is one of the principal industries on many of the islands in the Antilles. In this painting, the drummer sets the rhythm for the laborers as they work the fields.

TEXTBOOK TAPE

Pour commencer

Alain et Catherine ont décidé de descendre dans un petit hôtel en Guadeloupe. Et vous, où est-ce que vous aimez mieux descendre quand vous êtes en vacances?

dans un hôtel pas cher

dans un hôtel de luxe

dans **une auberge de jeunesse**

dans **une station estivale**

dans un chalet de ski

Aimez-vous mieux louer une chambre...?

à deux lits ou avec un grand lit

avec ou sans salle de bains et W.-C.

avec une douche

avec un bidet

Comment préférez-vous **régler la note?**

en espèces *(f)*

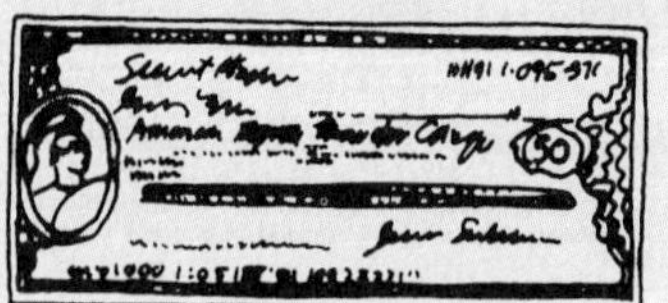
par chèques de voyage *(m)*

par carte *(f)* de crédit

une auberge de jeunesse *a youth hostel* **une station estivale** *a summer resort* **régler la note** *to pay the bill*

Alain et Catherine arrivent à la réception de l'hôtel à Basse-Terre.

ALAIN: Bonjour, monsieur.
L'HÔTELIER: Bonjour, monsieur. Bonjour, madame.
ALAIN: Vous avez une chambre pour deux personnes avec un grand lit?
L'HÔTELIER: Vous avez réservé?
ALAIN: Non, nous n'avons pas de réservations.
L'HÔTELIER: C'est pour **une seule nuit**?
CATHERINE: Non, c'est pour quatre nuits.
L'HÔTELIER: Très bien. Nous avons une chambre avec salle de bains et W.-C. privés.
CATHERINE: C'est combien la nuit?
L'HÔTELIER: 350 francs, madame.
ALAIN: Vous avez quelque chose de moins cher?
L'HÔTELIER: Voyons... nous avons une chambre avec douche et **lavabo** à 250 francs si vous préférez.
CATHERINE: Le petit déjeuner est **compris**?
L'HÔTELIER: Non, madame. Il y a un supplément de 40 francs par personne. Il est servi entre sept heures et neuf heures dans la salle à manger.
ALAIN: Eh bien, on prend la chambre avec douche. Vous préférez que je vous paie maintenant?
L'HÔTELIER: Non, monsieur. Vous pouvez régler la note à votre départ.
ALAIN: Vous acceptez les chèques de voyage?
L'HÔTELIER: C'est comme vous voulez. Vous pouvez payer par chèques de voyage, par carte de crédit ou en espèces bien sûr! C'est à quel nom, s'il vous plaît?
CATHERINE: Monsieur et madame Lebourg. L-E-B-O-U-R-G.
L'HÔTELIER: Très bien. Voici **la clé**, madame. C'est la chambre 210. Prenez l'ascenseur **jusqu'au** deuxième étage. Tournez **tout de suite à droite** en sortant de l'ascenseur. Votre chambre est **au bout du couloir. Bon séjour!**

---

une seule nuit *a single night* **un lavabo** *a sink* **compris(e)** *included* **la clé** *the key* **jusqu'à** *up to, as far as, until* **tout de suite** *immediately* **à droite** *to the right* **au bout du couloir** *at the end of the hall* **Bon séjour!** *Have a nice stay!*

Savez-vous le faire?

A. Conseils. En vous servant des indications données dans chaque phrase, dites où ces personnes devraient aller. Dans certains cas, il y a plusieurs possibilités.

un petit hôtel pas cher	*une auberge de jeunesse*
UN HÔTEL DE LUXE	**un chalet de ski**
une station estivale	*un parc naturel*

EXEMPLE Le frère de Luc est jeune, il voyage seul et il n'a pas beaucoup d'argent.
Il peut descendre dans une auberge de jeunesse.

1. Catherine aime les hôtels qui ont un bon restaurant et une piscine.
2. Les amis de Luc sont des étudiants qui ont très peu d'argent.
3. Alain veut une chambre privée, mais il ne veut pas payer très cher.
4. Les parents de Catherine aiment mieux aller où ils peuvent faire du golf et du tennis.
5. La sœur de Catherine aime passer tout son temps à faire du ski.
6. Luc adore faire du camping.
7. Quand il descend dans un hôtel, Luc préfère ne pas payer très cher.
8. Micheline adore les activités de plein air.

B. Réponses. Votre meilleur(e) ami(e) et vous allez passer six jours dans un petit hôtel à Basse-Terre. Vous arrivez sans réservations à la réception. Répondez aux questions de l'hôtelier selon vos besoins et vos goûts.

— Vous avez réservé?
— ???
— Vous voulez une chambre pour une seule personne?
— ???
— C'est pour combien de nuits?
— ???
— Vous voulez une chambre avec un grand lit?
— ???
— Vous préférez une chambre avec salle de bains?
— ???
— Nous avons une chambre à 200 francs. Vous voulez régler la note maintenant ou à votre départ?
— ???
— Comment voulez-vous payer?
— ???
— C'est à quel nom?
— ???
— Très bien. Vous avez la chambre 143. Voici votre clé. Bon séjour!
— ???

C. **On dit...** Deux touristes arrivent au même hôtel qu'Alain. Ils ne parlent pas français et Alain joue le rôle de traducteur à la réception. Comment est-ce qu'il demande les renseignements suivants?

1. Whether there is a room for two with a double bed and a bath.
2. How much it costs per night.
3. If there is anything cheaper.
4. If breakfast is included.
5. When and where it is served.
6. If one pays now or at departure.
7. If credit cards are accepted.

D. **Réservations.** Votre meilleur(e) ami(e) et vous allez passer six jours dans un petit hôtel en Guadeloupe. Téléphonez à l'hôtel pour réserver votre chambre. Obtenez aussi tous les renseignements importants (le prix, le petit déjeuner, comment vous allez payer...). Jouez les deux rôles avec un(e) camarade de classe.

EXEMPLE **—Allô? C'est bien l'hôtel Écotel? Je voudrais réserver...**

Remarquez que...

Les hôtels en France et dans ses départements d'outre-mer sont réglés (*regulated*) par le gouvernement. Il y a cinq catégories d'hôtel: les hôtel une, deux, trois ou quatre étoiles (*stars*) et les hôtels de luxe. Le prix pour chaque catégorie d'hôtel est fixé, sauf pour les hôtels de luxe. En général, les hôtels une étoile sont petits et simples, les chambres ont un bidet et un lavabo et la salle de bains est à l'étage. Les hôtels deux et trois étoiles ont généralement des chambres avec salle de bains et d'autres sans. Dans les hôtels quatre étoiles et les hôtels de luxe, toutes les chambres ont normalement une salle de bains.

Les hôtels français servent souvent un petit déjeuner qui consiste de pain ou d'un croissant accompagné de beurre (*butter*), de confiture (*jam*) et de quelque chose à boire (du café, du thé ou du chocolat). En général, les Français ne mangent pas de petit déjeuner à l'américaine avec des œufs au bacon (*bacon and eggs*) ou des saucisses.

Un choix d'hôtels. Regardez les publicités suivantes pour des hôtels en Guadeloupe. Vous êtes touriste. Qu'est-ce que vous pensez trouver dans ces hôtels? Dans lequel est-ce que vous préférez descendre? Pourquoi?

Choisissez un moulin pour vos vacances en Guadeloupe !

Derrière ce moulin à sucre se cache...
Une étape gourmande...
Un village hôtel charmant...
Une base de randonnées tropicales ...

Le Relais du Moulin

Forfait AVION + HOTEL : SVP, consultez votre agent de voyage habituel - catalogue *jumbo*, *Jet tours*.

INFORMATIONS : RELAIS DU MOULIN Châteaubrun Ste-Anne 97180 Guadeloupe - Tél. : 19 (590) 88.23.96/88.13.78 Fax : 19 (590) 88.03.92 - Télex : 919 913 REMOUL.

HOTEL RESTAURANT ★★NN, 40 chambres ★★ et ★★★, piscine, tennis, tir à l'arc, centre équestre, base VTT, bar, restaurants (2), randonnées tropicales. Plage (600 m).

C'est aussi une base de loisirs d'évasion en vélo, à cheval, à pied, en voilier et bien d'autres découvertes.

Comment s'y prendre?

Anticipating a response

When you cannot understand everything you hear, use what you can understand, as well as nonverbal cues such as circumstances, tone of voice and appearance to guess how people will respond. Written materials such as guidebooks or signs on the wall can also help you anticipate what people will say in a particular situation.

Savez-vous le faire?

A. Le ton de la voix. Écoutez le début de ces trois conversations. Pour chaque conversation, écoutez le ton de la voix (*tone of voice*) pour deviner ce qu'ils disent ensuite, a ou b.

1. a. C'est bien. Nous allons prendre la chambre.
   b. Est-ce que vous avez quelque chose de moins cher?
2. a. Nous préférons une chambre avec salle de bains.
   b. Bon, c'est bien. Je vais prendre la chambre.
3. a. Voici votre clé monsieur. Vous avez la chambre numéro 385.
   b. Je regrette monsieur, mais nous n'avons pas de réservations à votre nom.

Maintenant écoutez les conversations en entier pour vérifier vos réponses.

B. Dans le guide. Il est plus facile d'anticiper ce qu'on vous dira à la réception si vous lisez un guide avant d'arriver. Familiarisez-vous avec la description de l'hôtel Concorde La Fayette et de l'hôtel de Weha dans le *Guide Michelin.* Pour chaque phrase que vous entendez, décidez dans quel hôtel se trouve la personne qui parle. Une explication des symboles se trouve ci-dessous (*below*).

EXEMPLE VOUS ENTENDEZ: Non monsieur, le petit déjeuner n'est pas compris. Il y a un supplément de 32 francs.
VOUS RÉPONDEZ: **C'est l'hôtel de Weha.**

de Weha sans rest, 205 av. Choisy (13e) ✆ 45 86 06 06, Télex 206898, Fax 43 31 06
TV ☎ AE ⓓ E VISA
32 – **34 ch** 490.

Concorde La Fayette Ⓜ, 3 pl. Gén.-Koenig 40 68 50 68, Télex 650892, Fax 40 68 50 43, « Bar panoramique au 34e étage ≤ Paris » – TV ☎ – 40, AE ⓓ E VISA E6
R voir rest. **Étoile d'Or** ci-après - **L'Arc-en-Ciel R** 215/235 , enf. 100 – **Les Saisons** (Coffee shop) **R** carte 170 à 240 – 85 – **935 ch** 1350/2100, 44 appart.

L'INSTALLATION

30 ch	Nombre de chambres
	Ascenseur
	Air conditionné
TV	Télévision dans la chambre
	Établissement en partie réservé aux non-fumeurs
	Téléphone dans la chambre relié par standard
☎	Téléphone dans la chambre, direct avec l'extérieur
	Chambres accessibles aux handicapés physiques
	Repas servis au jardin ou en terrasse
	Salle de remise en forme
	Piscine : de plein air ou couverte
	Plage aménagée – Jardin de repos
	Tennis à l'hôtel
25 à 150	Salles de conférences : capacité des salles
	Garage dans l'hôtel (généralement payant)
P	Parking réservé à la clientèle
	Accès interdit aux chiens (dans tout ou partie de l'établissement)
Fax	Transmission de documents par télécopie
mai-oct.	Période d'ouverture, communiquée par l'hôtelier
sais.	Ouverture probable en saison mais dates non précisées. En l'absence de mention, l'établissement est ouvert toute l'année.

REPAS

enf. 55	Prix du menu pour enfants
	Établissement proposant un menu simple à moins de **70 F**
R 65/120	**Menus à prix fixe** : minimum 65 maximum 120
65/120	Menu à prix fixe minimum 65 non servi les fins de semaine et jours fériés
bc	Boisson comprise
	vin de table en carafe
R carte 120 à 285	**Repas à la carte** – Le premier prix correspond à un repas normal comprenant : hors-d'œuvre, plat garni et dessert. Le 2e prix concerne un repas plus complet (avec spécialité) comprenant : deux plats, fromage et dessert.
30	Prix du petit déjeuner (généralement servi dans la chambre)

CHAMBRES

ch 155/360	Prix minimum 155 pour une chambre d'une personne, prix maximum 360 pour une chambre de deux personnes
29 ch 165/370	Prix des chambres petit déjeuner compris

Qu'est-ce qui se passe?

À la réception

Deux jeunes Guadeloupéennes viennent passer leurs vacances à Paris. Elles descendent à l'hôtel Empire. D'abord, lisez ce que le *Guide Michelin* dit de cet hôtel, et ensuite, écoutez la conversation pour déterminer le prix de leur chambre.

Empire H. sans rest, 3 r. Montenotte 43 80 14 55, Télex 643232, Fax 47 66 04 33 TV AE E VISA
38 – **49 ch** 380/630.

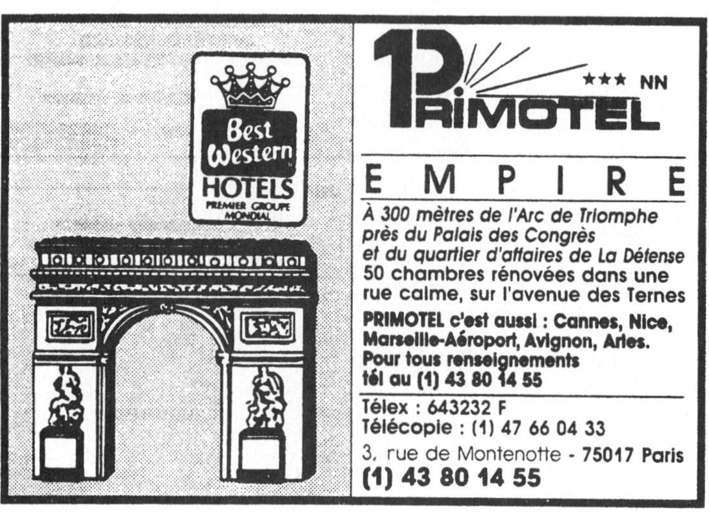

Avez-vous compris?

A. L'hôtel Empire. Écoutez la conversation une seconde fois et répondez à ces questions.

1. Est-ce que les touristes ont des réservations?
2. Est-ce que l'hôtel a beaucoup de chambres libres?
3. Pourquoi est-ce que les touristes ne veulent pas la première chambre?
4. Quel est le prix de la chambre qu'elles prennent?
5. Combien est le petit déjeuner? Où est-ce qu'il est servi?
6. Est-ce que la chambre est avec ou sans salle de bains?
7. Quel est le numéro de leur chambre?

B. À la réception. Imaginez que vous êtes à la réception de l'hôtel de Weha, de l'hôtel Concorde La Fayette ou de l'hôtel Empire. Selon les renseignements du *Guide Michelin*, préparez avec un(e) autre étudiant(e) une conversation logique où vous demandez une chambre. Ensuite, présentez votre conversation à la classe qui va deviner dans quel hôtel vous vous trouvez.

Remarquez que...

Les visiteurs en Guadeloupe peuvent goûter une grande variété de plats (*dishes*) antillais. Un mélange (*mix*) d'éléments africains, français et indigènes, la cuisine créole de la Guadeloupe et de la Martinique utilise beaucoup de fruits de mer (*seafood*) et ressemble beaucoup à la cuisine créole de la Louisiane. Chaque année au mois d'août, des gens viennent de l'île entière pour la célèbre fête des cuisinières (*Festival of Cooks*).

La fête des cuisinières

Vos goûts. Aimez-vous la cuisine créole? Dites si vous avez déjà (*already*) mangé chacun des plats nommés. Ensuite, donnez-en votre opinion. Avez-vous trouvé ça: délicieux, bon, assez bon, mauvais, très mauvais?

EXEMPLE Oui, j'ai déjà mangé du boudin et j'ai trouvé ça assez bon.
OU Non, je n'ai jamais mangé de boudin.

le boudin

la langouste

les bananes flambées au rhum

le crabe farci

le sorbet

l'ananas

la noix de coco

Qu'est-ce qu'on dit?

TEXTBOOK TAPE

Quelle phrase de chaque groupe vous décrit le mieux quand vous voyagez?

— Où allez-vous?
— Je reste dans mon **propre** pays.
— Je voyage à l'étranger.
— Je **fais une croisière.**
— Je **fais le tour du monde.**

— Comment voyagez-vous?
— Je prends ma voiture. / l'autocar. / l'avion. / le train. / le bateau.

— Vous arrivez à l'aéroport d'une grande ville. Quel moyen de transport préférez-vous pour aller en ville?
— Je loue une voiture.
— Je prends le métro. / l'autobus. / un taxi.
— J'y vais à pied.

— Préférez-vous passer des vacances reposantes ou animées?
— Je quitte l'hôtel tôt le matin.
— Je dors tard.
— Je ne fais rien le soir.
— Je sors tous les soirs.

— Où mangez-vous?
— Je mange dans les meilleurs restaurants.
— Je mange dans les **endroits** les moins chers possibles.
— Je mange à l'hôtel.
— On me sert **mes repas** dans ma chambre.

C'est **déjà la fin** de leur séjour et Alain et Catherine font des projets pour **le lendemain.**

— Tu dors déjà?
— Non, pas encore, mais j'ai très sommeil. Pas toi?
— Ah si, je suis **épuisé.** Mais **avant de** dormir, faisons des projets pour demain.
— Moi, j'aimerais dormir tard. Je sais que tu n'aimes pas perdre du temps à l'hôtel quand on est en vacances, mais je suis **tellement** fatiguée.
— D'accord, on dort tard demain matin mais demain après-midi, on visite la ville.
— Et demain soir, on sort? C'est notre dernière **soirée** à Basse-Terre. Nous partons **après-demain.**
— Je voudrais trouver un bon restaurant qui sert les spécialités de la région.
— Bonne idée! On peut inviter Luc et Micheline à nous accompagner.

propre *own* **faire une croisière** *to take a cruise* **faire le tour du monde** *to take a trip around the world* **un endroit** *a place* **un repas** *a meal* **déjà** *already* **la fin** *the end* **le lendemain** *the next day* **épuisé(e)** *exhausted* **avant (de faire)** *before (doing)* **tellement** *so* **une soirée** *an evening* **après-demain** *the day after tomorrow*

TEXTBOOK TAPE

A. Qui est fatigué? Indiquez, selon le sens de la phrase que vous entendez, si la personne qui parle est **fatiguée** ou **pas fatiguée**.

EXEMPLE VOUS ENTENDEZ: On sort ce soir?
VOUS RÉPONDEZ: **pas fatiguée**

B. Moi, je... Complétez ces phrases pour décrire vos habitudes (*habits*).

1. Je dors mal quand...
2. Je dors bien quand...
3. Le week-end, je dors jusqu'à...
4. Je sors souvent avec...
5. Pour arriver à l'université à l'heure, je pars de la maison à...
6. Quand j'ai sommeil, j'aime...
7. Quand je suis épuisé(e), j(e)...

C. Moyens de transport. Luc parle à Micheline des moyens de transport qu'il utilise à Paris. Choisissez la phrase entre parenthèses qui complète logiquement ce qu'il dit.

EXEMPLE Pour aller à Nice (je prends le métro, je prends le train).
Pour aller à Nice, je prends le train.

1. Mes amis et moi prenons le bateau quand (nous allons en ville, nous allons à Londres).
2. Quand je vais en ville (je prends l'autobus, je prends l'avion).
3. Quand je vais voir mes parents à Lille (je prends le métro, je prends l'autocar).
4. Pour aller à l'aéroport (je prends un taxi ou le métro, je prends le bateau).
5. Pour retourner à Paris de Guadeloupe (je vais prendre le train, je vais prendre l'avion).

Voilà pourquoi!

Les verbes comme **dormir** et **sortir**

The verbs **partir**, **sortir**, and **dormir** are conjugated like **servir**. **Partir** and **sortir** are conjugated with **être** in the **passé composé**. **Dormir** is conjugated with **avoir**.

PARTIR (*TO GO AWAY, TO LEAVE*)

je **pars**	nous **partons**
tu **pars**	vous **partez**
il/elle/on **part**	ils/elles **partent**

PASSÉ COMPOSÉ: je **suis parti(e)**

SORTIR (*TO GO OUT, TO LEAVE*)

je **sors**	nous **sortons**
tu **sors**	vous **sortez**
il/elle/on **sort**	ils/elles **sortent**

PASSÉ COMPOSÉ: je **suis sorti(e)**

DORMIR (*TO SLEEP*)

je **dors**	nous **dormons**
tu **dors**	vous **dormez**
il/elle/on **dort**	ils/elles **dorment**

PASSÉ COMPOSÉ: j'**ai dormi**

SELF-CHECK

1. Compare the endings of verbs like **dormir** with the endings of **lire**, **écrire**, **venir**, and the **-re** verbs. Do they follow a similar pattern?
2. What auxiliary is used with **sortir** and **partir** in the **passé composé**? And with **dormir**?
3. What prepositions are used after **partir** and **sortir**?
4. What is the difference between the pronunciations of **il sort** and **ils sortent**?

Note the prepositions used after **partir** and **sortir**.

partir de... pour...	**Je *pars de* l'hôtel *pour* l'aéroport à huit heures.**
sortir de...	**Il faut *sortir de* la chambre et aller au bout du couloir.**
sortir à...	**Est-ce que Micheline *sort au* restaurant avec nous?**

The conjugation of **courir** is similar in the present, but its past participle is **couru.**

COURIR (*TO RUN*)

je **cours**	nous **courons**
tu **cours**	vous **courez**
il/elle/on **court**	ils/elles **courent**

PASSÉ COMPOSÉ: j'**ai couru**

Et ça se prononce comment?

Les verbes comme **dormir** et **sortir**

Although you often cannot distinguish aurally the difference between singular and plural third-person forms of **-er** verbs (**il parle** sounds like **ils parlent**), you can distinguish between these forms of verbs like **sortir** and **dormir**, as well as those of **-re** verbs. Compare the following sentences.

ALAIN	ALAIN ET CATHERINE
Il dort tard.	**Ils dorment tard.**
Il sort ce soir.	**Ils sortent ce soir.**
Il part après-demain.	**Ils partent après-demain.**
Il descend dans un petit hôtel.	**Ils descendent dans un petit hôtel.**
Il rend visite à des amis.	**Ils rendent visite à des amis.**

When a word ends with a pronounced consonant sound in French, it must be released. Notice that when you pronounce the non-italicized consonants in these English phrases, the tongue or lips do not have to move back releasing them.

*What par*t*?* *What sor*t*?* *In the dor*m.

Compare how the italicized consonants in these plural verb forms are released.

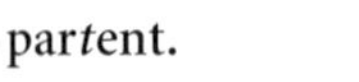

Ils par*t*ent. **Ils sor*t*ent.** **Ils dor*m*ent.**

Savez-vous le faire?

A. Vos amis. On vous pose des questions sur vos amis. Décidez si on parle de **a.** votre meilleur ami ou de **b.** vos amis en général.

EXEMPLE **a.** Est-ce qu'il dort souvent tard? **b.** Est-ce qu'ils dorment souvent tard?
VOUS ENTENDEZ: Est-ce qu'il dort souvent tard?
VOUS RÉPONDEZ: **a. mon meilleur ami**

MON MEILLEUR AMI	MES AMIS EN GÉNÉRAL
1. a. Est-ce qu'il sort le vendredi soir?	b. Est-ce qu'ils sortent le vendredi soir?
2. a. Est-ce qu'il part souvent en week-end?	b. Est-ce qu'ils partent souvent en week-end?
3. a. Est-ce qu'il dort beaucoup?	b. Est-ce qu'ils dorment beaucoup?
4. a. Est-ce qu'il sert souvent du vin?	b. Est-ce qu'ils servent souvent du vin?
5. a. Est-ce qu'il perd souvent patience?	b. Est-ce qu'ils perdent souvent patience?

Maintenant, répondez à ces questions pour décrire **a.** votre meilleur ami et **b.** vos amis en général.

B. Les meilleurs étudiants. Dites si les meilleurs étudiants font les choses indiquées.

EXEMPLE dormir en classe / écouter en classe
Les meilleurs étudiants ne dorment pas en classe, ils écoutent en classe.

1. dormir au laboratoire de langues / faire attention
2. partir tôt pour arriver en classe en avance / dormir trop tard pour arriver à l'heure
3. sortir tous les soirs jusqu'à minuit / rester à la maison pour préparer les cours
4. écouter le professeur / dormir en classe

Maintenant demandez à un(e) camarade de classe s'il/si elle fait ces choses.

C. Camarades de classe. Posez des questions avec les éléments donnés pour mieux connaître un(e) camarade de classe. Ensuite, expliquez à la classe ce que vous avez appris.

EXEMPLE dormir: beaucoup / peu
— D'habitude, est-ce que tu dors beaucoup ou peu?
— D'habitude je dors beaucoup.
APRÈS, À LA CLASSE: **Robert dort beaucoup.**

1. servir aux boums: du Coca / de la bière / des jus de fruits
2. sortir plus souvent: le week-end / pendant la semaine
3. partir pour l'université: le matin / l'après-midi / le soir
4. partir pour l'université: en avance / à l'heure / en retard
5. dormir mieux: dans son lit / dans un hôtel / en classe
6. sortir le plus souvent: pour voir un film / pour danser / pour dîner

D. Qui? Recopiez ces cases (*boxes*) sur une feuille de papier. Circulez parmi (*among*) vos camarades de classe et demandez-leur s'ils font les choses indiquées ou s'ils les ont faites récemment. Si vous trouvez quelqu'un qui répond **oui**, notez son nom. La première personne à compléter une ligne horizontale, verticale ou diagonale avec des noms gagne.

dormir tard d'habitude	sortir le week-end dernier	sortir d'habitude le vendredi soir	partir de la maison avant six heures du matin le lundi
dormir tard le week-end dernier	partir souvent en week-end	dormir jusqu'à midi le samedi	sortir hier au cinéma
courir tous les jours	partir en week-end le week-end dernier	dormir jusqu'à midi samedi dernier	déjà courir dix kilomètres
courir le week-end dernier	servir quelquefois du vin au dîner	servir du vin au dîner hier	dormir moins de six heures d'habitude

E. Ils partent. Alain parle de ce que Catherine et lui font le jour de leur départ de Pointe-à-Pitre. Complétez ses phrases avec les verbes **courir**, **dormir**, **servir**, **sortir** ou **partir** et l'heure indiquée.

EXEMPLE Catherine... jusqu'à... mais je... pour courir.
Catherine **dort** jusqu'à six **heures et demie** mais je **sors** pour courir.

1. Je... jusqu'à...

2. L'hôtel... le petit déjeuner à...

3. Nous... pour l'aéroport à...

4. L'avion... pour Paris à...

5. Les stewards et les hôtesses... le déjeuner à...

6. Catherine... de... à...

F. **De retour.** De retour (*back*) à Paris, Alain parle de ce que Catherine et lui ont fait le jour de leur départ. Regardez les illustrations de l'exercice précédent et indiquez ce qu'il dit.

EXEMPLE **Catherine a dormi jusqu'à 6h30 mais je suis sorti pour courir.**

G. **Un voyage à deux.** Vous pensez faire un voyage avec un(e) ami(e) et vous voulez savoir si vous avez les mêmes habitudes (*habits*). Qu'est-ce que vous lui demandez? Avec un(e) camarade de classe, préparez une conversation dans laquelle vous parlez des choses suivantes:

- Jusqu'à quelle heure vous dormez quand vous êtes en vacances.
- À quelle heure vous sortez le matin et comment vous passez le temps.
- Si vous sortez le soir, où vous allez et à quelle heure vous rentrez.

Voilà pourquoi!

Le verbe **prendre**

The conjugation of **prendre** (*to take*) is irregular. **Prendre** can also be translated as *to have* when talking about having a drink or something to eat.

PRENDRE (*TO TAKE*)

je **prends**	nous **prenons**
tu **prends**	vous **prenez**
il/elle/on **prend**	ils/elles **prennent**

PASSÉ COMPOSÉ: j'**ai pris**

On prend la voiture, n'est-ce pas?
Ça prend combien de temps?
Je prends une eau minérale et un sandwich.

Comprendre (*to understand*) and **apprendre** (*to learn*) are conjugated like **prendre**. When **apprendre** is followed by an infinitive, the infinitive is preceded by **à**.

SELF-CHECK

1. How many **n**'s are there in the **nous** and **vous** form of **prendre**? And in the **ils/elles** form (besides the ending)? How is the preceding **e** pronounced in each case?
2. If **j'ai pris** is the **passé composé** of **prendre**, what is the **passé composé** of **comprendre** and **apprendre**?

Tous mes amis apprennent le français. Moi, j'apprends à parler japonais aussi.
Est-ce que tu comprends toujours le professeur?

Les moyens de transport

You can either use **prendre** to say that you are *taking* a particular means of transportation, or you can say that you are *going by* a particular vehicle, using **aller** and the preposition **en.** To say you are going *on foot* use **à pied.**

Je prends la voiture. / J'y vais en voiture.
Je prends l'autobus. / J'y vais en autobus.
J'y vais à pied.

Et ça se prononce comment?

Le verbe **prendre**

The **e** in the root of the verb **prendre** has three different pronunciations.

- When it is the last sound of the word, it is nasal: **je prends / tu prends / il prend.**
- When it is followed by a single **n**, it rhymes with **le: vous prenez / nous prenons.**
- When it is followed by two **n**'s, it sounds like the **è** of **mère: ils prennent / elles prennent.**

Savez-vous le faire?

A. Combien de personnes? Luc parle de ses amis. Indiquez s'il parle d'**une personne** ou de **plus d'une personne.**

EXEMPLE VOUS ENTENDEZ: Ils prennent le métro à l'université.
VOUS RÉPONDEZ: **plus d'une personne**

B. Prononcez bien. Dites si ces phrases décrivent mieux **le professeur, les étudiants** ou **tout le monde** dans votre classe. Attention à la prononciation du verbe.

EXEMPLE bien comprendre les cassettes
Tout le monde comprend bien les cassettes.

1. prendre des notes en classe
2. bien comprendre la grammaire
3. apprendre des conjugaisons
4. apprendre beaucoup de vocabulaire
5. comprendre tout le vocabulaire
6. prendre beaucoup de temps pour lire

C. Le dernier cours. Dites si les autres étudiants et vous avez fait les choses données dans l'exercice précédent pendant le dernier cours.

EXEMPLE bien comprendre les cassettes
Nous avons bien compris les cassettes.

D. Air Gabon. Vous voulez faire un tour d'Afrique. Regardez la publicité suivante pour Air Gabon et dites combien de temps ça prend pour aller de Libreville, la capitale gabonaise, à chacune des villes indiquées. Les villes avec un astérisque sont francophones. Savez-vous dans quel pays chacune se trouve?

EXEMPLE Lomé* → **Pour aller de Libreville à Lomé, ça prend une heure quarante-cinq.**

1. Dakar*
2. Abidjan*
3. Cotonou*
4. Bangui*
5. Luanda
6. Pointe-Noire*
7. Lagos
8. Kinshasa*

POUR ALLER PLUS VITE EN AFRIQUE.

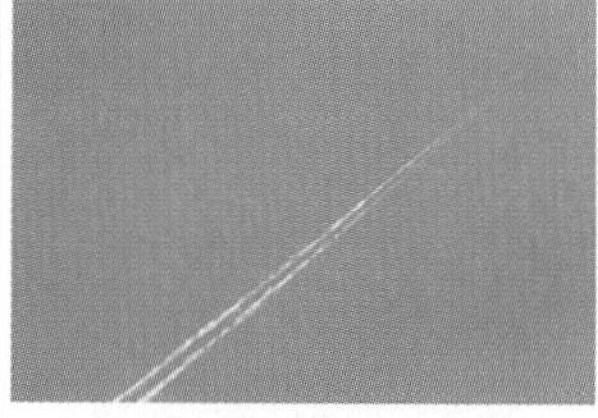

LIBREVILLE/DAKAR : 7h30

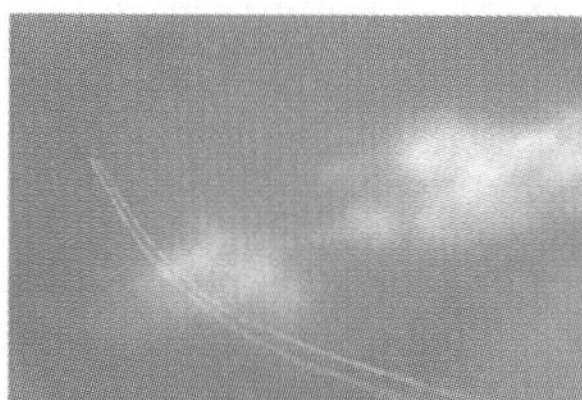

LIBREVILLE/ABIDJAN : 3h35

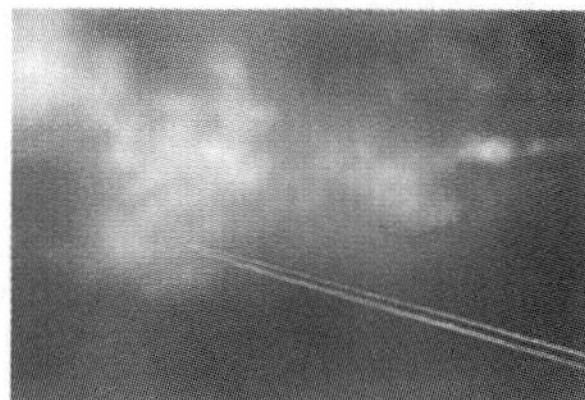

LIBREVILLE/LOME : 1h45

LIBREVILLE/COTONOU : 1h30

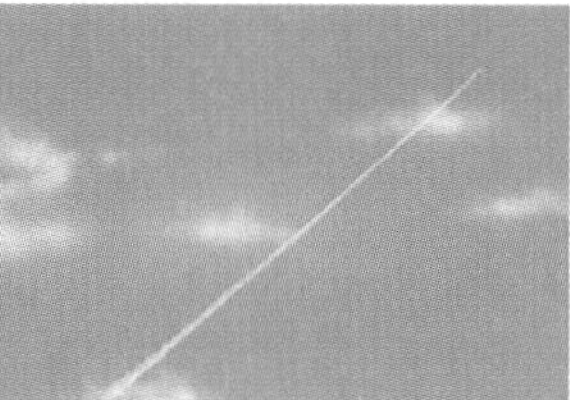

LIBREVILLE/BANGUI : 1h40

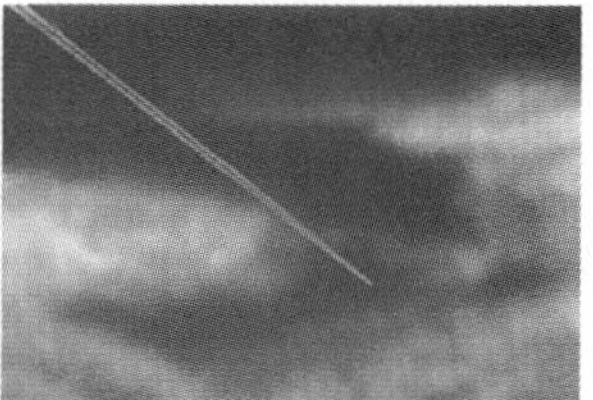

LIBREVILLE/LUANDA : 1h45

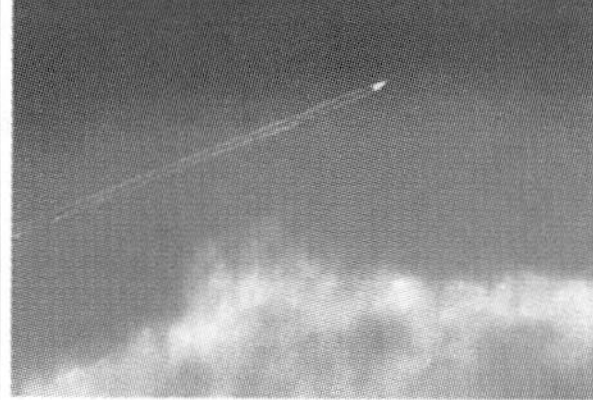

LIBREVILLE/POINTE NOIRE : 1h10

LIBREVILLE/LAGOS : 1h40

LIBREVILLE/KINSHASA : 1h30

AIR GABON est la ligne "express" pour voyager en Afrique. Au départ de l'aéroport International Leon M'Ba (Libreville), véritable plaque tournante du continent, AIR GABON dessert aujourd'hui 41 villes en Afrique et en Europe.

Sans oublier un service à bord au sol efficace car la grande tradition des affaires et du commerce du pays tout entier a appris à AIR GABON à connaître les besoins, donc apporter les services à tous ses passagers.

E. Au café. Luc est au café avec Micheline et ses petits frères. Micheline demande à chacun ce qu'il va prendre. Complétez leur conversation avec le verbe **prendre** et choisissez une boisson pour chacun. Il fait très chaud et chacun va prendre quelque chose de froid.

— Les enfants, vous __1__ un chocolat chaud ou un Coca?
— Nous __2__ .
— Et toi Luc, tu __3__ un café ou une eau minérale?
— Je __4__ . Et toi, Micheline, tu vas prendre un thé ou un verre de vin blanc?
— Je vais __5__ .

Maintenant, elle commande ce qu'ils vont boire. Qu'est-ce qu'elle dit au garçon?

6. Les enfants...
7. Mon ami...
8. Et moi, je...

F. Moyens de transport. Répondez aux questions suivantes.

EXEMPLE Comment est-ce que vous allez à l'université?
Je prends l'autobus ou j'y vais à pied.

1. Comment est-ce que vous rentrez après les cours?
2. Comment est-ce que vous allez d'un cours à l'autre?
3. En général, comment est-ce que les étudiants vont à l'université?
4. Comment est-ce que vous rentrez chez vos parents?
5. Comment est-ce que les Américains aiment voyager? Et les Français?

G. Questions personnelles. Posez les questions suivantes à un(e) camarade de classe.

1. Qu'est-ce que tu étudies ce semestre? Dans quels cours est-ce que tu prends beaucoup de notes? Dans quels cours est-ce que tu ne prends pas de notes?
2. Dans quels cours est-ce que tu apprends beaucoup? Dans quels cours est-ce que tu n'apprends pas beaucoup?
3. Est-ce que tu poses des questions quand tu ne comprends pas? Est-ce que le professeur comprend toujours les questions des étudiants?
4. Qu'est-ce que tu voudrais apprendre à faire? Est-ce que tu as appris à faire quelque chose récemment? Est-ce que tu voudrais apprendre une autre langue étrangère? Est-ce que ça prend beaucoup de temps?

H. Un voyage. Vous avez décidé, avec deux autres camarades de classe, de visiter une ville francophone. Choisissez une ville et décidez comment vous préférez y aller. Parlez aussi du moyen de transport que vous allez utiliser dans cette ville. Est-ce que vous préférez prendre l'autobus, louer une voiture ou prendre le métro (si c'est possible)?

Qu'est-ce qu'on dit?

Micheline va rendre visite à Luc en France. Il lui décrit un petit hôtel pas trop loin de chez lui. Où se trouve cet hôtel?

un parking
au bout de la rue
au coin de la rue
une école privée
un supermarché
une pharmacie
une cathédrale
dans la rue Lorraine
de l'autre côté de la place
une place
un stade
une banque
dans la rue Deschamps
en face de l'hôtel
un bureau de poste
un marché
l'hôtel Molière
un hôpital
un lycée
sur le boulevard La Fayette
un bureau de tabac
une station-service
sur l'avenue Duclos
à gauche de l'hôtel
à droite de l'hôtel
à côté de l'hôtel

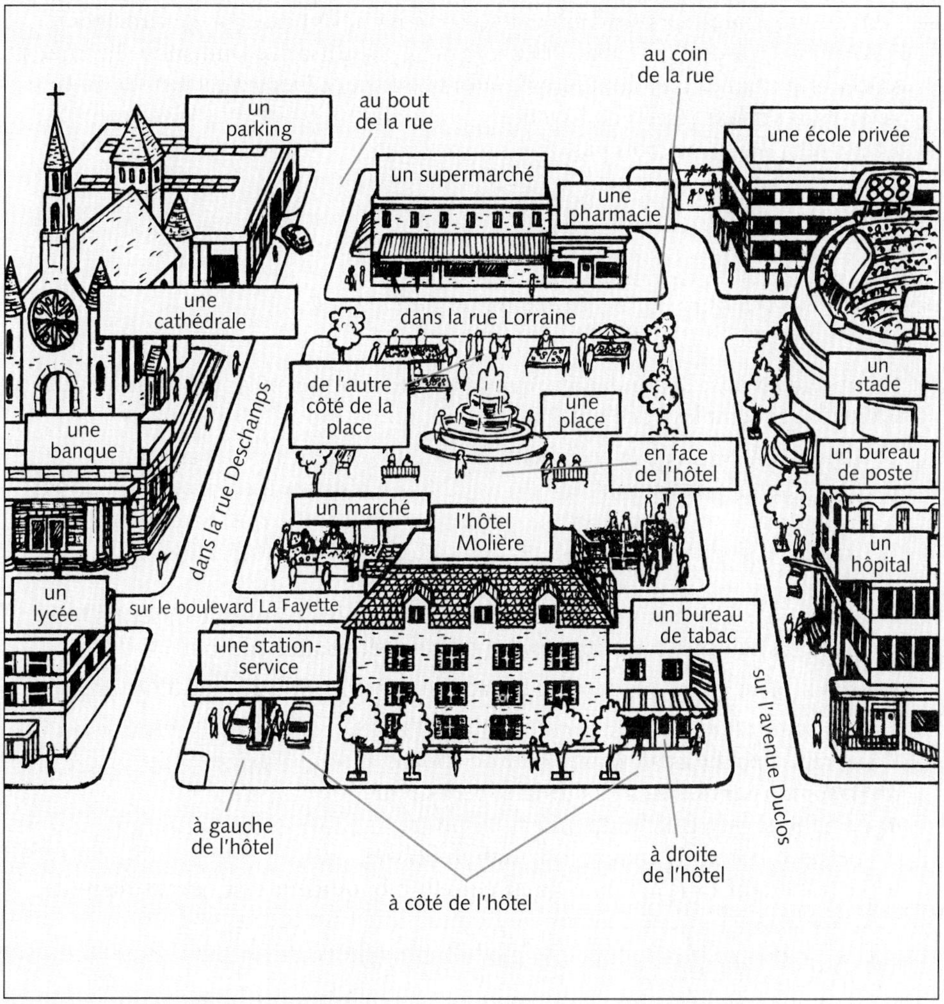

Les expressions suivantes sont utiles quand on **indique le chemin**.

Prenez la rue...	Descendez la rue...
Continuez **tout droit** jusqu'à...	Montez la rue...
Tournez à gauche (à droite).	**Traversez** la place...

indiquer le chemin *to explain the way, to give directions* **tout droit** *straight (ahead)* **traverser** *to cross*

C'est leur dernière soirée à Basse-Terre et Alain et Catherine ont invité Luc et Micheline à dîner. Ils cherchent un bon restaurant et ils demandent des suggestions à la réception de l'hôtel.

— S'il vous plaît, monsieur, savez-vous s'il y a un bon restaurant dans le quartier?
— Je vous recommande *Le Tropical.*
— Servent-ils de la cuisine régionale?
— Oui, et les prix ne sont pas trop **élevés.**
— C'est loin d'ici?
— Non, c'est tout près. Ça prend cinq minutes s'il n'y a pas beaucoup de **circulation.** Descendez la rue du Père Labat. Allez tout droit jusqu'à la rue Dumanoir. Tournez à gauche et continuez tout droit jusqu'à la rue Boudet. *Le Tropical* est juste là, au coin.
— Savez-vous s'il faut réserver à l'avance?
— À cette heure-ci, **je ne crois pas.**
— Merci, monsieur.
— Je vous en prie.

élevé(e) *high* **la circulation** *traffic* **je ne crois pas** *I don't believe so*

A. Comprenez-vous? Répondez aux questions suivantes selon la conversation entre Catherine et l'employé de l'hôtel.

1. Alain et Catherine, que cherchent-ils?
2. Y a-t-il un bon restaurant dans le quartier?
3. Comment s'appelle-t-il?
4. Comment sont les prix?
5. Le restaurant est-il près de l'hôtel?
6. Dans quelle rue se trouve-t-il?
7. Faut-il des réservations?

B. C'est où? Vous sortez de votre hôtel pour aller faire des courses. Utilisez les renseignements suivants pour déterminer l'adresse de chaque endroit.

EXEMPLE Le bureau de poste est en face de l'hôtel. → **33, rue d'Orléans**

1. La piscine est au bout de la rue, à côté de l'hôtel.
2. Le supermarché est de l'autre côté de l'hôtel.
3. La station-service est à droite du supermarché.
4. La banque est à gauche du bureau de poste.
5. La bibliothèque est en face de la station-service.
6. Le restaurant *La Petite Auberge* est entre la bibliothèque et le bureau de poste.

29	33	37	41
	rue d'Orléans		
28	32 *l'hôtel*	36	40

C. Après le cours. Un ami français passe quelques jours chez vous et il veut vous retrouver après le cours de français aujourd'hui. Dites-lui comment faire.

1. Pour aller au campus, descends la rue...
2. Sur le campus, viens au bâtiment...
3. Va au... étage.
4. Attends-moi devant...

Voilà pourquoi!

L' inversion

To ask for information, you can form a question using **est-ce que**, **n'est-ce pas**, or intonation. You can also form a question by inverting the subject pronoun and verb. With inversion, subject pronouns are attached to the end of the verb by a hyphen. Questions formed with **est-ce que** and inversion have the same meaning.

Savez-vous l'adresse? = **Est-ce que vous savez l'adresse?**
Faut-il des réservations? = **Est-ce qu'il faut des réservations?**

Generally, the pronoun **je** is not inverted. Use **est-ce que** with it or ask a question with rising intonation.

Est-ce que je fais des réservations? OR **Je fais des réservations?**

When a verb ends in a vowel, a **-t-** is inserted before the pronouns **il**, **elle**, and **on** for easier pronunciation. The inverted form of **il y a** is **y a-t-il**.

Mange-*t*-il souvent ici?	BUT:	**Est-il cher?**
Où va-*t*-on ce soir?		**Sert-on le dîner maintenant?**
Y a-*t*-il un bon restaurant près d'ici?		**Attend-elle devant le restaurant?**

When there is a conjugated verb followed by an infinitive or a verb in the **passé composé**, only the first verb or auxiliary is inverted.

Va-t-il venir avec nous? **Ont-ils réservé à l'avance?**

In *yes/no* questions and longer information questions, you usually do not invert nouns or proper names. Instead leave them before the verb and add an extra inverted pronoun.

***Alain et Catherine*, pourquoi vont-*ils* à la réception?**
***Luc* va-t-*il* inviter Micheline aussi?**

Est-ce que is not usually used after question words when the verb is **être**. Use inversion with both nouns and pronouns.

Où est le restaurant? **Qui sont Catherine et Alain?**

SELF-CHECK

1. When do you insert a **-t-** between a verb and an inverted subject pronoun?
2. Generally, you can only invert pronouns. When can you sometimes invert nouns and names?

Et ça se prononce comment?

La liaison

In questions with inversion, the final consonant of the verb is pronounced when followed by pronouns beginning with a vowel (**il, elle, on, ils, elles**). Remember that when the verb ends in a vowel you must add an extra **-t-** between the verb and **il, elle,** or **on.** Note that **d** is pronounced like a **t** in liaison.

Veut‿-il venir? **Prend‿-il l'autobus?** **Alain et Catherine parlent‿-ils français?**

Remember that **s** and **x** are pronounced like **z** in **liaison.**

les‿États‿Unis **les vieux‿hôtels** **deux‿étoiles ou trois‿étoiles**

Savez-vous le faire?

A. Que demandent-ils? Écoutez chaque question et écrivez les mots qui manquent (*that are missing*) sur une feuille de papier. Ensuite, posez les questions à un(e) camarade de classe qui doit baser les cinq premières réponses sur la conversation de la section *Qu'est-ce qu'on dit?*

1. Alain et Catherine ______ un café?
2. ______ manger dans le quartier?
3. ______ un bon restaurant dans le quartier?
4. Quelle rue ______ pour aller au *Tropical*?
5. Les prix au *Tropical* ______ élevés?
6. ______ les restaurants chers ou pas chers?
7. Ton restaurant préféré, comment ______ ?
8. Quelle sorte de cuisine ______ ?

B. À la réception. Vous travaillez à la réception d'un hôtel dans votre ville et un(e) touriste québecois(e) vous demande des renseignements. Préparez la scène avec un(e) camarade de classe. Dans la conversation posez les questions suivantes en utilisant l'inversion.

EXEMPLE Est-ce que vous connaissez bien le quartier?
— Connaissez-vous bien le quartier?
— Oui, je connais assez bien le quartier.

1. Est-ce que vous connaissez un bon restaurant italien ou chinois?
2. Est-ce que ce restaurant est loin d'ici?
3. Est-ce que nous pouvons y aller à pied?
4. Où est-ce qu'on peut trouver un taxi?
5. Est-ce que vous avez déjà mangé dans ce restaurant?
6. Est-ce que les prix sont élevés?
7. Est-ce qu'il faut réserver à l'avance?
8. Est-ce que vous savez à quelle heure ils commencent à servir le dîner?

C. Des vacances. Vous invitez un(e) ami(e) à partir en vacances avec vous. Posez les questions suivantes à un(e) camarade de classe en utilisant l'inversion. Il/Elle va vous répondre.

EXEMPLE Qu'est-ce que tu veux faire pendant les vacances?
— Que veux-tu faire pendant les vacances?
— Je veux faire du ski dans le Nouveau-Mexique.

1. Où est-ce que tu veux aller?
2. Est-ce que tu as déjà visité cet endroit?
3. En quelle saison est-ce que tu préfères y aller? Quel temps est-ce qu'il y fait d'habitude?
4. Qu'est-ce qu'on peut faire dans cet endroit?
5. Est-ce qu'il y a souvent beaucoup de touristes?
6. Est-ce que les hôtels sont chers?
7. Est-ce qu'il faut réserver longtemps à l'avance?
8. Quand est-ce que tu préfères partir?
9. Est-ce que les billets d'avion pour y aller sont chers?
10. Est-ce que tu as assez d'argent pour le voyage?

D. Un hôtel. Voici une liste d'hôtels du *Guide Michelin.* Faites une liste de cinq questions avec inversion pour votre agent de voyages et posez-les à un(e) camarade de classe. Une explication des symboles se trouve à la page 277.

EXEMPLE **— Y a-t-il une piscine à l'hôtel Novotel?**
— Oui, il y a une piscine.

Novotel M , 8-10 esplanade du Parvis de l'Europe ✆ 93 13 30 93, Télex 460243, Fax 93 13 09 04, – TV ☎ — 90. AE E VISA JX **v**
R carte environ 140 , enf. 50 – 46 – **173 ch** 495/560.

La Malmaison, 48 bd V. Hugo ✆ 93 87 62 56, Télex 470410, Fax 93 16 17 99, – ch TV ☎ AE E VISA rest FYZ **e**
R *(fermé 2 juil. au 1er août, dim. soir et lundi)* 120/240 – 35 – **50 ch** 455/810 – ½ P 520/565.

Atlantic, 12 bd V. Hugo ✆ 93 88 40 15, Télex 460840, Fax 93 88 68 60 – ch TV ☎ P – 30 à 80. AE E VISA FY **d**
R 110/120 – 50 – **123 ch** 600/900 – ½ P 970/1140.

Park, 6 av. de Suède ✆ 93 87 80 25, Télex 970176, Fax 93 82 29 27, – TV ☎ – 100. AE E VISA FZ **x**
Le Passage *(fermé dim.)* – 75 – **130 ch** 750/900.

Victoria sans rest, 33 bd V. Hugo ✆ 93 88 39 60, Télex 461337, – TV ☎ AE E VISA FYZ **z**
39 ch 510/590.

Voilà pourquoi!

SELF-CHECK
1. With which forms of the definite article does **de** contract?
2. How do you say *on a street*?

Les prépositions

In French, some prepositions are just one word, others are composed of two or more words.

sur	*on*	**près de**	*near*
sous	*under*	**loin de**	*far from*
devant	*in front (of)*	**à côté de**	*next to*
derrière	*behind*	**de l'autre côté de**	*on the other side of*
dans	*in, into*	**à droite de**	*to the right of*
entre	*between*	**à gauche de**	*to the left of*
		en face de	*across from*
		au coin de	*on the corner of*
		au bout de	*at the end of*

The final **de** of the prepositions on the right combines with **le** and **les** to become **du** and **des**.

Le cinéma est *en face du* restaurant et *à côté des* appartements où tes amis habitent.

Although prepositions generally have the meanings listed above, there are often exceptions.

Note that one says the following:

sur une avenue	*on an avenue*	BUT: **dans une rue**	*on a street*
sur un boulevard	*on a boulevard*		
sur une place	*on a square*		

Savez-vous le faire?

A. Chez moi. Choisissez les mots entre parenthèses qui décrivent le mieux l'endroit où vous habitez.

1. J'habite (près de / loin de / ???) l'université.
2. J'habite (dans une rue calme / sur une grande avenue / sur un boulevard avec beaucoup de circulation / ???).
3. En face de chez moi, il y a (un parking / une autre maison / un parc / un grand immeuble / ???).
4. Ma chambre est (en face de / à droite de / à gauche de / loin de / ???) la salle de bains.
5. Si vous entrez chez moi et que vous prenez le couloir, ma chambre est (à droite / à gauche / au bout / ???).
6. À droite de mon lit, il y a (un mur / une table / une commode / une étagère / ???) et de l'autre côté il y a (une étagère / une chaîne stéréo / une porte / ???).
7. Quand je suis au lit, en face de moi il y a (un mur / une fenêtre / un téléviseur / ???).

B. **Mon restaurant préféré.** Décrivez où se trouve votre restaurant préféré, une phrase à la fois. Vos camarades de classe vont deviner le nom du restaurant. Continuez votre description jusqu'à ce que quelqu'un devine juste.

EXEMPLE — **Mon restaurant préféré est dans la rue Lamar.**
— **Est-ce que c'est Casa Monterrey?**
— **Non. Il est à côté du cinéma Lincoln Village...**

C. **Je voudrais...** Un ami français qui vous rend visite veut faire les choses suivantes. Il veut savoir où se trouve l'endroit le plus près de l'université. Jouez les rôles avec un(e) camarade de classe.

EXEMPLE jouer au football
— **Je voudrais jouer au football. Est-ce qu'il y a un parc près d'ici?**
— **Il y a un parc dans la 45e rue. C'est de l'autre côté de l'université.**

1. prendre un verre
2. lire *Paris Match*
3. aller voir un film
4. aller dîner
5. jouer au volley-ball
6. aller danser

D. **Votre propre rue.** Regardez l'illustration de la rue d'Orléans à la page 290. Imaginez que vous habitez 32, rue d'Orléans. Décidez où se trouvent les endroits suivants: **un lycée**, **une banque**, **un café**, **un parc**, **un cinéma**, **une école**, **un bureau de tabac.** Ensuite, décrivez votre rue à la classe et les autres étudiants vont essayer (*to try*) de dessiner (*to draw*) votre rue.

E. **Agent immobilier.** Vous êtes agent immobilier et vous voulez vendre votre maison / appartement. Votre client(e) vous pose beaucoup de questions sur le quartier. Préparez la scène avec un(e) autre étudiant(e). D'abord, parlez du plan de la maison / l'appartement. Ensuite, dites où se trouvent l'université, les parcs, les supermarchés et d'autres endroits qui sont importants pour vous.

Pointe-à-Pitre est la plus grande ville de la Guadeloupe.

Voilà pourquoi!

SELF-CHECK

1. With which verbs do you drop the final **-s** in the **tu** form in the imperative?
2. Where do you place direct and indirect object pronouns in affirmative commands? What happens to the pronoun **me**?
3. Where do you place object pronouns in negative commands?
4. Which two verbs have irregular command forms?

L'impératif

You already know how to make suggestions (*Let's . . .*), using the **nous** form of a verb without the pronoun **nous**. To give directions, or to tell someone to do something, use the **tu** or the **vous** form of the verb without the pronoun **tu** or **vous**.

Allons au cinéma!	*Let's go to the movies!*
N'oubliez pas votre billet!	*Don't forget your ticket!*
Viens avec nous.	*Come with us.*

In **tu** form commands, drop the final **-s** of **-er** verbs and of **aller**, but not of other verbs.

	Regarde ça!	*Look at that!*
	Va demander à ton père!	*Go ask your father!*
BUT:	**Sors avec moi ce soir!**	*Go out with me tonight!*
	Fais quelque chose!	*Do something!*

The verbs **être** and **avoir** have irregular command forms.

Sois calme!	*Be calm!*	**Aie de la patience!**	*Have patience!*
Soyons gentils!	*Let's be nice!*	**Ayons confiance!**	*Let's have confidence.*
Soyez à l'heure!	*Be on time!*	**Ayez pitié!**	*Have pity!*

Les pronoms avec l'impératif

In negative commands, direct and indirect object pronouns and **y** have their usual place before the verb.

Ne les oublie pas!	*Don't forget them!*
Ne me regardez pas!	*Don't look at me!*
N'y va pas!	*Don't go there!*

In affirmative commands, however, these pronouns are attached to the end of the verb with a hyphen.

Dis-*lui* que nous insistons! *Tell **her** that we insist!*

When **me** follows the verb, it becomes **moi**.

Attendez-*moi* devant le restaurant! *Wait for **me** in front of the restaurant!*

When **y** follows the **tu** command **va**, the final **-s** is reattached to the end of the verb for easier pronunciation.

Vas-y! *Go ahead!*

Savez-vous le faire?

A. Le succès. Votre petit frère va entrer à l'université. Donnez-lui des conseils (*advice*). Dites-lui s'il faut faire les choses suivantes ou pas.

EXEMPLE habiter seul → **Habite seul.** OU **N'habite pas seul.**

1. aller à tous les cours
2. dormir en classe
3. être à l'heure
4. avoir confiance
5. lire les livres
6. sortir tous les soirs
7. faire toujours les devoirs
8. oublier les examens
9. prendre des notes

B. On part en vacances. Votre famille va partir en vacances. Utilisez un élément de chaque groupe pour leur dire ce qu'ils doivent ou ne doivent pas faire.

EXEMPLE **Faites les valises!**

ne pas oublier RÉSERVER *prendre un taxi* NE PAS ARRIVER **???** **faire** ne pas fumer lire **???** *aller*	**à l'aéroport** *en retard* ***les chambres d'hôtel*** ??? **les guides** les valises à l'hôtel en taxi **les billets ???** *dans l'avion*

C. Suggestions. Suggérez à un(e) ami(e) comment faire les choses suivantes.

EXEMPLE Pour être en bonne forme (*shape*)...
Pour être en bonne forme, mange bien, fais de l'exercice et dors assez.

1. Pour avoir beaucoup d'amis...
2. Pour être un bon parent...
3. Pour apprendre le français...
4. Pour préparer un long voyage...
5. Pour plaire aux hommes / femmes...
6. Pour plaire aux professeurs...

D. La première fois. Votre frère va sortir avec une fille pour la première fois. Répondez à ses questions. Dites-lui de faire ou de ne pas faire chaque chose.

EXEMPLE Est-ce que je l'invite au cinéma? → **Oui, invite-la au cinéma.**
OU **Non, ne l'invite pas au cinéma.**

1. Est-ce que je l'invite à dîner avant le film?
2. Est-ce que je lui achète des fleurs?
3. Combien de temps est-ce que je l'attends si elle est en retard?
4. Est-ce que je lui parle pendant le film?
5. Est-ce que je l'invite à la maison après?
6. Est-ce que je lui montre ma collection de cartes postales?
7. Est-ce que je l'accompagne chez elle après?
8. Qu'est-ce que je lui dis avant de partir?

E. À Pointe-à-Pitre. Regardez le plan de Pointe-à-Pitre, la plus grande ville de la Guadeloupe. Des touristes demandent des directions à la gare routière dans la rue Dubouchage. (Cherchez le petit autobus.) Lisez les explications qui suivent et décidez où ils vont.

EXEMPLE Montez la rue Dubouchage jusqu'à la rue Duplessis et tournez à gauche. Allez tout droit et tournez à droite juste après la place de la Victoire. C'est sur votre gauche à côté du poste de police.
Ils vont à l'office de tourisme.

1. Montez la rue Dubouchage jusqu'à la rue Duplessis et tournez à droite. Continuez tout droit dans la rue Massabielle. C'est sur votre gauche, juste après l'école.
2. Montez la rue Dubouchage, traversez la place de la Victoire et tournez à droite dans la rue Bébian. Tournez à gauche dans la rue Alsace-Lorraine. C'est juste devant vous.
3. Montez la rue Dubouchage, tournez à gauche dans la rue Duplessis et continuez tout droit dans la rue Thiers. Tournez à droite dans la rue Frébault. C'est tout de suite sur la gauche.

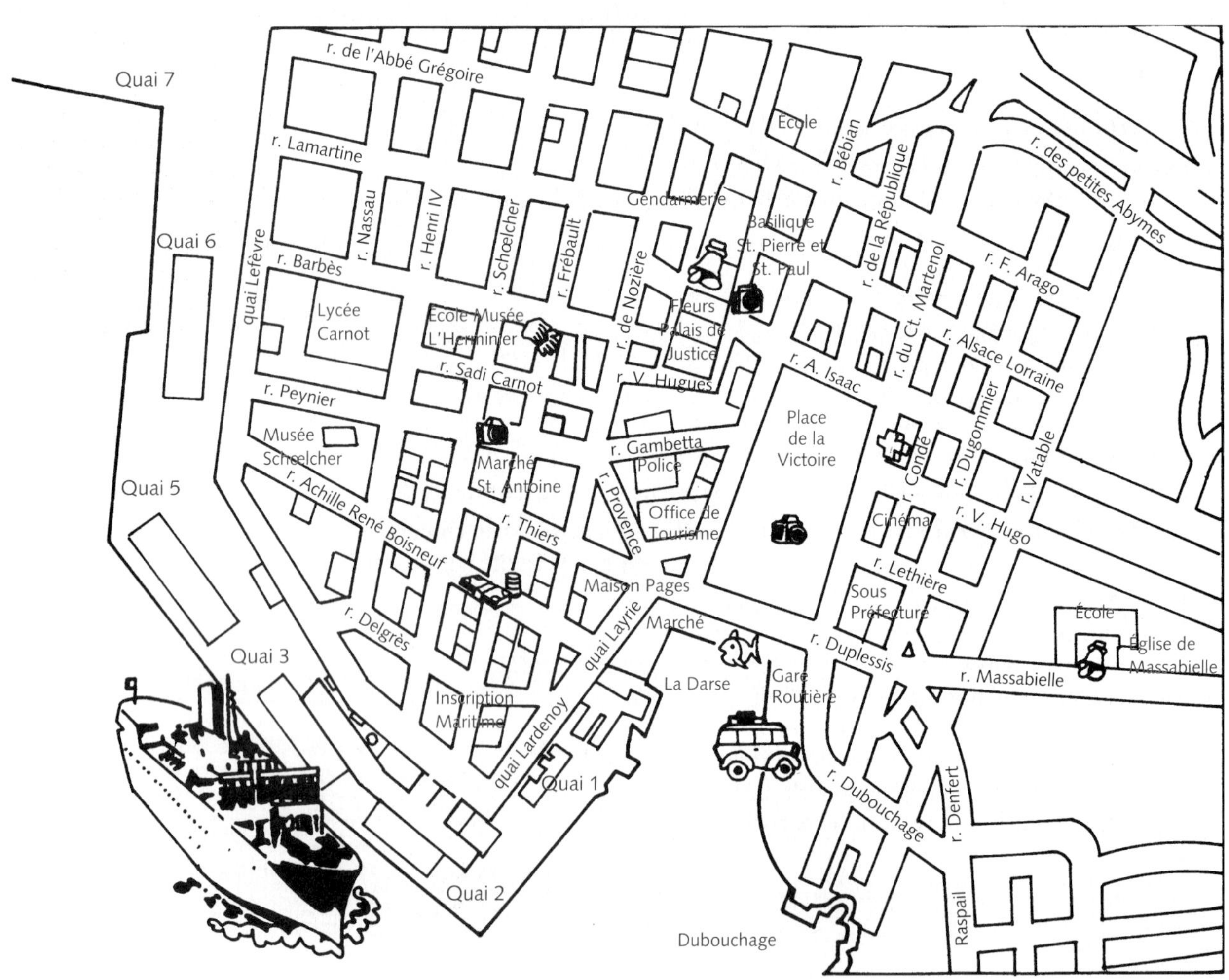

F. **Comment y aller.** Regardez le plan de Pointe-à-Pitre à la page précédente et expliquez à un(e) camarade de classe comment aller...

1. de l'office de tourisme à la gendarmerie (*police station*)
2. de la gendarmerie au musée Schœlcher
3. du musée Schœlcher à la sous-préfecture

G. **Directions.** Un(e) camarade de classe va venir étudier chez vous après les cours. Expliquez à la classe comment aller chez vous de l'université.

Remarquez que...

Basse-Terre est la capitale de la Guadeloupe mais Pointe-à-Pitre est sa plus grande ville. Voilà des sites à visiter.

D'autres sites. Regardez le plan de la ville à la page précédente et dites s'il y a d'autres sites que vous aimeriez visiter.

Le marché St-Antoine

CULTURE NOTE

Pointe-à-Pitre is named for a Dutch Jewish sailor named *Peter* who was chased from Brazil by the Portuguese in the 1600s. The place where he settled in **Guadeloupe** became known as **Pointe à Peter**, which later was spelled **Pointe-à-Pitre**. **Pointe-à-Pitre** soon became an important port and is now the largest port in Guadeloupe.

Les quais

Qu'est-ce qu'on dit?

Alain et Catherine sont de retour chez eux et ils **défont** leurs **valises**. Quels vêtements **sont à lui**? Quels vêtements sont à elle? De quels vêtements ont-ils eu besoin en Guadeloupe?

À lui...

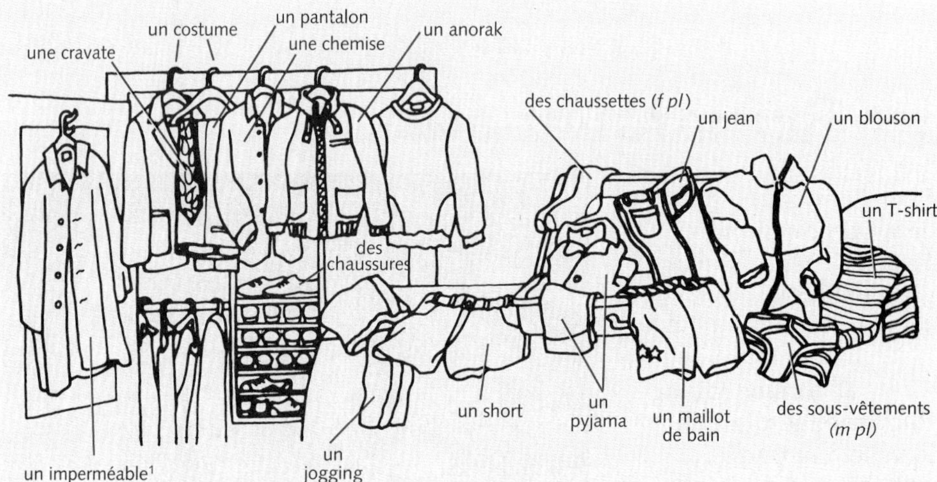

À elle...

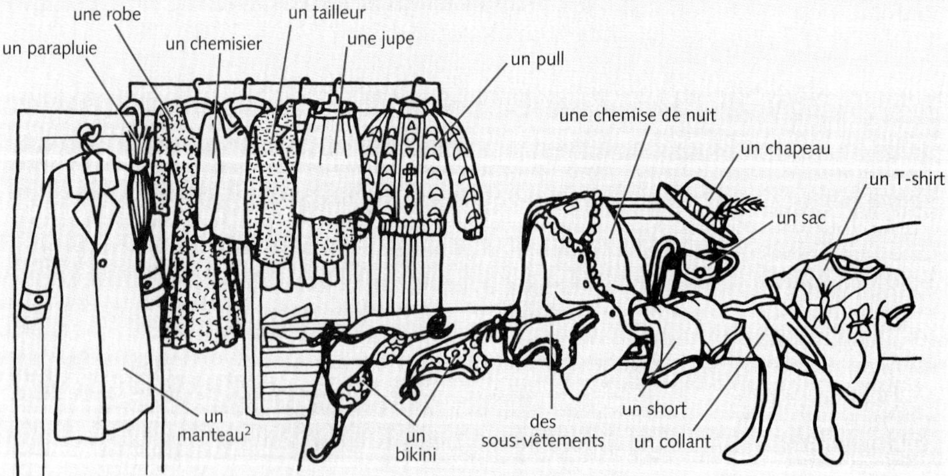

Quels vêtements est-ce que vous **mettez** en vacances?

défaire une valise *to unpack a suitcase* **être à** *to belong to* **lui** *him* **mettre** *to put on*

SUPPLEMENTAL VOCABULARY

une bague *a ring*
des baskets (*f*) *tennis shoes*
des bijoux (*m*) *jewelry*
des boucles d'oreilles (*f*) *earrings*
un bracelet
une ceinture *a belt*
un collier *a necklace*
une écharpe *a winter scarf*
un foulard *a dress scarf*
des gants (*m*) *gloves*
un slip *briefs, panties*
une combinaison *a slip*
un soutien-gorge *a bra*
en or *gold*
en argent *silver*
en cuir *leather*
en jean délavé *stonewashed denim*
en laine *wool*
en polyester
en velours *velvet*
bleu clair *light blue*
vert foncé *dark green*
rouge vif *bright red*
à pois *polka-dotted*
écossais(e) *plaid*
à fleurs *floral*
imprimé(e) *print*
rayé(e) *striped*
uni(e) *solid-colored*
à manches courtes *short-sleeved*
à manches longues *long-sleeved*
sans manches *sleeveless*

[1]Both a woman's *raincoat* and a man's *raincoat* are called **un imperméable.**
[2]Many people refer to a woman's overcoat as **un manteau** and a man's overcoat as **un pardessus.**

Avant de partir pour la Guadeloupe, Catherine a acheté des nouveaux vêtements.

LA VENDEUSE: Bonjour, madame. Comment est-ce que je peux vous servir?
CATHERINE: Je cherche une nouvelle robe. Je préfère quelque chose en jaune pastel.
LA VENDEUSE: Ces robes en **soie** sont très jolies.
CATHERINE: Vous n'avez pas quelque chose d'un peu moins cher?
LA VENDEUSE: Ces robes en coton sont plus simples mais elles sont **en solde.**
CATHERINE: Est-ce que je peux **essayer** cette robe-ci?
LA VENDEUSE: Mais bien sûr! Quelle **taille** est-ce qu'il vous faut?
CATHERINE: Je fais du 42.

Catherine met la robe, elle sort de **la cabine d'essayage** et parle à Alain.

CATHERINE: Alors, qu'en penses-tu Alain?
ALAIN: Elle **te va très bien**! Tu es très jolie comme ça.
CATHERINE: Elle n'est pas trop **étroite**?
ALAIN: Non, pas du tout!
CATHERINE: Bon, alors je vais la prendre.

la soie *silk* **en solde** *on sale* **essayer** *to try (on)* **la taille** *size* **la cabine d'essayage** *fitting room* **aller très bien à quelqu'un** *to look good on someone* **étroit(e)** *tight*

A. Préférences. Complétez les phrases suivantes pour exprimer vos préférences.

1. J'aime acheter mes vêtements (en solde, dans les meilleurs magasins, au centre commercial, ???).
2. Pour sortir le week-end, j'aime mettre (une robe, un costume, un jean, ???).
3. (Le noir, Le bleu, Le rouge, ???) me va bien.
4. Je ne mets jamais de (cravates, robes, jeans, shorts, ???).

B. En vacances. Vous achetez des vêtements pour les vacances. Regardez la page 300 et dites ce que vous achetez si vous allez faire les choses suivantes.

1. Vous allez à la plage en Guadeloupe.
2. Vous allez faire du ski dans les Alpes.
3. Vous allez à New York où vous avez l'intention d'aller au théâtre tous les jours.

C. L'armoire ou la commode. Alain et Catherine défont leurs valises et Catherine dit à Alain où il faut mettre les affaires: **dans la commode** (*dresser*) ou **dans l'armoire** (*wardrobe*). Qu'est-ce qu'elle lui dit?

EXEMPLE robe → — **Où est-ce que je mets cette robe?**
— **Mets-la dans l'armoire.**

1. chaussures
2. chaussettes
3. costume
4. tailleur
5. pull
6. T-shirts
7. short
8. jupe

Voilà pourquoi!

SELF-CHECK
What is the **passé composé** of **mettre**, **permettre**, and **promettre**?

Le verbe **mettre**

You know **mettre** (*to put, to put on, to place, to set*) in the infinitive. Here is its conjugation.

METTRE (*TO PUT* [ON], *TO PLACE, TO SET*)	
je **mets**	nous **mettons**
tu **mets**	vous **mettez**
il/elle/on **met**	ils/elles **mettent**
PASSÉ COMPOSÉ: j'ai **mis**	

Que *mettez*-vous pour sortir? **Pourquoi *as*-tu *mis* ton costume?**

Promettre (de) (*to promise*) and **permettre (de)** (*to allow*) are also conjugated like **mettre.**

Savez-vous le faire?

A. Que mettre? Dites quels vêtements vous mettez pour faire les choses suivantes.

EXEMPLE pour aller au lac → **Je mets un maillot de bain.**

1. pour faire du ski
2. pour aller à une interview importante
3. pour aller en classe
4. pour aller à un concert de rock
5. pour aller à l'opéra
6. pour dormir

B. Quels vêtements? À quelle occasion est-ce que les personnes suivantes mettent un costume ou une robe / un tailleur?

EXEMPLE Mon père... → **Mon père met un costume pour aller au travail.**
OU **Mon père ne met presque jamais de costume.**

1. Ma mère...
2. Mes ami(e)s...
3. Je...
4. [*Demandez au professeur.*] Quand est-ce que vous...
5. [*Demandez à un(e) autre étudiant(e).*] Quand est-ce que tu...
6. [*Décrivez votre classe.*] Nous...

Indiquez la dernière fois que vous avez mis un costume ou une robe?

C. Que mettent-ils? Qu'est-ce que les individus suivants mettent pour aller au travail?

1. Martina Navratilova
2. Richard Simmons
3. Barbara Walters
4. David Letterman
5. Astérix
6. Superman
7. le père Noël
8. vos professeurs

D. Ma semaine. Mettez la forme correcte du verbe **mettre** dans le blanc et choisissez les mots entre crochets (*in square brackets*) qui vous décrivent le mieux ou donnez une autre réponse.

1. En semaine, je ______ mon réveil (*alarm clock*) pour [7, 8, ???] heures. Le week-end je le ______ pour [7, 8, ???] heures. Ce matin, je l' ______ pour [7, 8, ???] heures.
2. Si je prends le petit déjeuner, je ______ [du sucre (*sugar*), de la crème, du lait, ne... rien] dans mon café.
3. Quand mon/ma camarade de chambre prend le petit déjeuner, il/elle ______ [la radio, la télé, une cassette, un disque compact, ne... rien].
4. Généralement, quand je passe la journée à la maison, je ______ [un T-shirt, un short, un jean, ???]. Samedi dernier, j' ______ [un jean, un T-shirt, un short, ???].

Voilà pourquoi!

Les pronoms disjoints

The following stressed pronouns have a variety of uses in French.

LES PRONOMS DISJOINTS	
moi	nous
toi	vous
lui/elle	eux/elles

SELF-CHECK
1. What are seven uses of stressed pronouns?
2. When talking about women, you use **elle/elles**. What do you use to talk about men or mixed groups?

Use the stressed pronouns:

- after prepositions → **avec toi   à côté de lui   chez eux**
- when there is no verb → **— Et toi?   — Moi aussi.**
- in compound subjects → **Mes amis et moi partons demain.**
- to emphasize whom you are talking about → **Lui, il préfère le coton mais moi, je préfère la soie.**
- after **c'est...** → **— C'est toi?** **— Oui, c'est moi.**
- after **être à** to say to whom something belongs → **— À qui sont ces valises?** **— Ces valises sont à eux.**
- with **même(s)** to say *self/selves* → **Je vais le faire moi-même.**

Savez-vous le faire?

A. À qui est-ce? Dites si ces vêtements sont à Alain ou à Catherine. Utilisez **lui** ou **elle**.

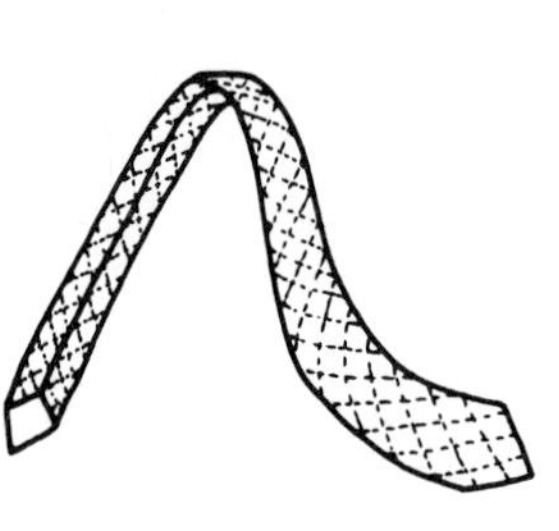

EXEMPLE
Cette cravate est à lui.

1.

2.

3.

4.

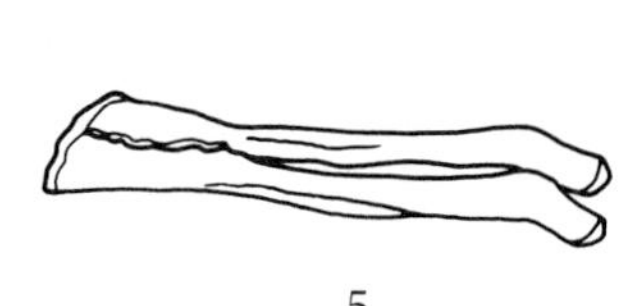

5.

B. Avec eux. Dites ce que vous faites souvent avec ces personnes.

EXEMPLE avec votre frère → **Lui et moi, nous jouons souvent au golf ensemble.**
OU **Lui et moi, nous ne faisons presque rien ensemble.**
OU **Je n'ai pas de frère.**

1. avec votre meilleur(e) ami(e)
2. avec votre mère
3. avec vos grands-parents
4. avec votre professeur
5. avec votre cousine préférée
6. avec votre tante préférée
7. avec vos voisins
8. avec vos amis

C. Des cadeaux. Vous avez fait le tour du monde et vous avez acheté des cadeaux pour les personnes nommées dans l'exercice précédent. Qu'est-ce que vous leur avez acheté?

EXEMPLE pour votre frère → **Pour lui, j'ai acheté du thé au Japon.**
OU **Pour lui, je n'ai rien acheté.**
OU **Je n'ai pas de frère.**

chocolat *livres* VÊTEMENTS **fromage** *café* **???** disques compacts ??? CARTES POSTALES	**Japon** *Grande-Bretagne* FRANCE ??? **ALLEMAGNE** **Suisse** Belgique Sénégal *Égypte* ??? **Mexique** **Brésil**

D. Qui est-ce? Qu'est-ce que vous avez fait d'intéressant au cours des dernières années? Écrivez une liste de trois choses sans écrire votre nom. Donnez votre liste au professeur, qui va redistribuer toutes les listes. Lisez la liste que votre professeur vous donne et devinez qui a fait les choses que vous lisez. Après, l'étudiant(e) qui a fait ces choses doit s'identifier.

EXEMPLE VOUS LISEZ: **Je suis allée au Japon en 1992.**
J'ai appris à faire du ski récemment.
J'ai fait du camping le mois dernier.
VOUS DEVINEZ: **C'est toi, Rachelle?**
RACHELLE DIT: **Oui, c'est moi.**
OU **Non, ce n'est pas moi.**
UNE AUTRE ÉTUDIANTE DIT: **Non, ce n'est pas elle, c'est moi.**

E. Connaissances. Posez les questions suivantes à un(e) camarade de classe. Répondez en utilisant un pronom complément d'objet direct ou indirect ou un pronom disjoint.

1. Habites-tu chez tes parents? Est-ce que tu leur parles tous les jours? Est-ce que tu vas les voir ce week-end? Prends-tu quelquefois des vacances avec eux?
2. Est-ce que tu rends souvent visite à tes amis de l'école secondaire? Passes-tu beaucoup de temps avec eux? Qu'est-ce que tu as fait récemment avec eux?
3. Connais-tu bien tes voisins? Vas-tu quelquefois chez eux? Est-ce que tu les invites souvent chez toi?

Remarquez que...

Si vous achetez des vêtements en Guadeloupe ou en Europe, il faut savoir votre taille. Quelle taille est-ce qu'il vous faut? En Guadeloupe, on peut trouver des jolis vêtements en batik ou madras et des chapeaux ou sacs de paille (*straw*). Pour voir les vêtements traditionnels guadeloupéens, regardez la photo des participantes à la fête des cuisinières à la page 279.

Au magasin de vêtements. Vous êtes en vacances en Guadeloupe et vous achetez une robe ou une chemise en batik avant de partir. Utilisez la conversation de la section ***Qu'est-ce qu'on dit?*** pour préparer une scène avec un(e) autre étudiant(e).

TABLE DE COMPARAISON DE TAILLES

Robes et chemisiers							
F	36	38	40	42	44	46	48
USA	6	8	10	12	14	16	18
Chaussures femmes							
F	36½	37	37½	38	38½	39	39½
USA	5	5½	6	6½	7	7½	8
Chaussures hommes							
F	39	40	41	42	43	44	45
USA	6	7	7½	8½	9	10	11
Costumes hommes							
F	44	46	48	51	54	56	59
USA	34	36	38	40	42	44	46
Chemises hommes							
F	36	37	38	39	40	41	42
USA	14	14½	15	15½	16	16½	17

C'est à lire!

Vous allez lire un poème qui parle d'Haïti. Avant de lire le poème, familiarisez-vous un peu avec ce pays francophone qui se trouve à quelques centaines de kilomètres de la Floride. Contrairement à la Guadeloupe et la Martinique, qui sont des départements français, Haïti est un pays indépendant. Comme beaucoup de pays aux Antilles, Haïti, avec ses belles plages, est un endroit très attirant. Malheureusement, ce pays est aussi un des pays les plus pauvres (*poor*) du monde. Le Haïtien moyen gagne l'équivalent d'un peu plus de 300$ américains par an. Avant de lire le poème *À qui*, travaillez avec un(e) ou deux autres étudiant(e)s pour faire une liste de tout ce que vous savez sur Haïti.

Images. Écrivez les trois premiers mots qui vous viennent à l'esprit (*come to mind*) en regardant les photos suivantes prises à Haïti.

À qui

Tiré d'*Haïti blues Echopoèmes*
J. F. Ménard

À qui
Devine
Qui devine
Au bord de mer
L'hôtel de touristes **plein**
À qui
Dis
Qui **dira**
La compagnie sur le port
Les cargos
L'avion **particulier**
Sur l'avenue
Les **devantures** le journal
À qui
Le compte en banque
Secret
Devine
Qui devine
Quelques-uns
Tous les autres grand goût
Pieds nus sur les asphaltes
Et sur la route **crevassée**
Les **lourdes** limousines
Dans les hauts les villas piscine
L'autre côté de la ravine
Qui
Sait lire compter **mentir**
Et qui ne **pourra** plus **courber**
   l'échine
Davantage
Lambi!

à qui *whose* **au bord de** *at the edge of* **plein**(e) *full* **dira** = **va dire** **particulier** (**particulière**) *private* **les devantures** (*f*) *shop windows* **pieds nus** (*m*) *barefoot* **crevassé**(e) *cracked* **lourd**(e) *heavy* **mentir** *to lie* **pourra** = **va pouvoir** **courber** *to bend* **l'échine** (*f*) *backbone* **davantage** = **plus** **lambi** *a type of shell commonly sold to tourists*

Les deux-tiers (⅔) des Haïtiens travaillent dans l'agriculture.

Avez-vous compris?

A. Qui? Répondez aux questions suivantes d'après le poème.

1. Où sont les touristes?
2. À votre avis, à qui sont les possessions mentionnées dans le poème? Quelle sorte de compte en banque est mentionnée? Qu'est-ce que ces gens savent faire?
3. Qui devine à qui sont ces choses? Que font les autres?

B. Questions. Le poème *À qui* pose des questions en répétant le mot interrogatif **qui** et le verbe **deviner.** Est-ce qu'il y a une question que vous vous posez souvent? Choisissez un mot interrogatif (**pourquoi, quand, où, comment, que, qui**) et un verbe et composez un poème qui exprime votre question. Utilisez *À qui* comme modèle.

EXEMPLE Pourquoi
Apprendre
Le français
Les verbes irréguliers
Je suis, tu es, il est
Pourquoi
Apprendre
Où se trouvent
Haïti, la Martinique, la Guadeloupe
J'apprends
Pour comprendre
Pourquoi
Apprendre

OÙ? *POURQUOI?*
QUAND?
COMMENT?
QUE?
QUI?

TRAVAILLER *AIMER*
FAIRE ???
ÉTUDIER
ÊTRE écouter
???

Ça y est! C'est à vous!

A. Organisez-vous. Vous allez écrire une lettre pour réserver une chambre d'hôtel. D'abord, organisez-vous! À la page suivante, vous trouverez un formulaire d'un guide touristique. Imaginez que vous voulez faire des réservations dans un hôtel en Guadeloupe. Recopiez le formulaire sur une autre feuille de papier et complétez-le.

B. Rédaction: Une lettre de réservation. En vous basant sur le formulaire de l'activité précédente, écrivez une lettre pour réserver une chambre d'hôtel. N'oubliez pas de dire quand vous allez arriver, quand vous allez partir et quelle sorte de chambre vous désirez. Commencez la lettre avec **Monsieur/Madame,** et terminez-la avec **Je vous remercie de votre obligeance, et je vous prie de croire, Monsieur/Madame, à l'assurance de mes sentiments distingués.**

C. À la réception. Vous êtes arrivé(e) à la réception de l'hôtel où vous avez envoyé (*sent*) la lettre de réservation de l'exercice précédent. Vous dites à l'hôtelier que vous avez des réservations et l'hôtelier vérifie quelle sorte de chambre vous avez réservée. Avec un(e) camarade de classe, préparez une conversation logique que vous allez présenter à la classe.

D. Ils se plaignent. Deux touristes ne sont pas contents de leur hôtel. Écoutez leur conversation et répondez aux questions suivantes.

1. Comment est leur chambre?
2. Pourquoi ne dorment-ils pas bien?
3. Qu'est-ce qu'on leur a servi au petit déjeuner?
4. Que vont-ils faire demain?

Monsieur,

Je me propose de séjourner dans votre établissement:

DU ....

AU ....

☐ EN CHAMBRE ET PETIT DÉJEUNER

☐ DEMI-PENSION ☐ PENSION

Je vous serais donc obligé(e) de bien vouloir me confirmer vos prix, par personne, service et taxes compris, pour:

☐ CHAMBRE 1 PERSONNE
☐ CHAMBRE 2 PERS. (1 lit double)
☐ SALLE(S) DE BAINS
☐ CHAMBRE 2 PERS. (2 lits)

☐ LIT(S) SUPPLÉMENTAIRE(S) POUR ENFANT(S)

Dès réception de vos conditions, je ne manquerai pas, si elles me conviennent, de vous confirmer ma réservation.

Je vous remercie de votre obligeance, et je vous prie de croire, Monsieur, à l'assurance de mes sentiments distingués.

Signature:

P.J. Coupon réponse international

Nom ....
Adresse ....
Ville .... État ....
Pays ....

Pour vérifier

Après avoir fait les exercices suivants, vérifiez vos réponses dans l'*Appendix C.*

Talking about travel and selecting a place to stay

A. À la réception. C'est l'hôtelier qui parle. Complétez ses phrases. Ensuite, imaginez que vous voyagez dans un pays francophone et utilisez les phrases que vous avez complétées pour inventer une conversation entre un hôtelier et vous.

1. Préférez-vous une chambre à deux lits ou ______? Et avec ou sans ______?
2. C'est pour une ______ nuit?
3. Le petit déjeuner n'est pas ______ dans le prix. Il y a un ______ de douze francs par personne. Le petit déjeuner est ______ entre sept heures et neuf heures.
4. Vous avez la chambre dix. Voilà votre ______. Votre chambre est au premier ______.
5. Vous pouvez payer maintenant ou vous pouvez ______ la note à votre ______. On accepte les ______ et les ______ ou vous pouvez payer en ______.
6. Bon ______.

B. Une journée comme les autres. D'abord, dites si vos amis et vous faites souvent les choses indiquées. Ensuite, dites si vous avez fait ces choses le week-end dernier.

EXEMPLE Moi, je... (dormir tard, courir le matin)
Moi, je dors tard quelquefois mais je ne cours jamais le matin.
Le week-end dernier, je n'ai pas dormi tard et je n'ai pas couru non plus.

1. Moi, je... (sortir le vendredi soir, prendre un taxi)
2. Mes amis... (sortir le dimanche soir, dormir en classe le lendemain)
3. Mon (Ma) meilleur(e) ami(e)... (partir en week-end, aller à la plage)
4. Chez moi, nous... (servir le dîner après huit heures, sortir au restaurant)

Asking for and giving directions

C. Directions. Regardez le plan de Pointe-à-Pitre à la page 298 et expliquez à un touriste que vous ne connaissez pas comment aller de la sous-préfecture à la gendarmerie.

Buying clothes

D. Que portent-ils? Regardez le dessin d'Alain, Catherine et l'hôtelier à la page 273 et dites ce que chacun porte. Et les deux touristes devant l'ascenseur, que portent-ils?

E. Un vol. Qu'est-ce que les personnes suivantes mettent d'habitude pour prendre l'avion?

1. Une hôtesse...
2. Un homme d'affaires...
3. Moi, je...
4. Les étudiants...

Vocabulaire

Talking about travel and selecting a place to stay

NOMS
une auberge de jeunesse
l'autocar (*m*)
l'avion (*m*)
le bateau
le bidet
une carte de crédit
un chalet de ski
une chambre (à deux lits / avec un grand lit / avec salle de bains / sans salle de bains)
un chèque de voyages
une clé
le couloir
une douche
une étoile
la fin
un hôtel (de luxe / pas cher)
un lavabo
le lendemain
le métro
le monde
le moyen de transport
une (seule) nuit
une personne
le petit déjeuner
un prix (élevé)
la réception
un repas
une soirée
une station estivale
un supplément
un taxi
les toilettes (*f*)
le train
les W.-C. (*m*)

EXPRESSIONS VERBALES
accepter
apprendre
comprendre
courir
descendre
dormir
être servi(e)
faire le tour du monde
faire une croisière
partir (de... pour...)
payer (en espèces)
prendre
recommander
régler (la note)
réserver
servir
sortir (de... à...)

DIVERS
animé(e)
après-demain
Bon séjour!
compris(e)
épuisé(e)
le moins
par (personne)
propre

Asking for and giving directions

LES ENDROITS
un bureau de poste
un bureau de tabac
une cathédrale
la circulation
une école (privée)
un hôpital
un lycée
un marché
un parking
une pharmacie
une place
un stade
une station-service
un supermarché

LES DIRECTIONS
à côté (de)
à droite (de)
à gauche (de)
au bout (de)
au coin (de)
dans la rue...
de l'autre côté de
en face (de)
juste là
loin (de)
près (de)
sur l'avenue (*f*)... / sur le boulevard... / sur la place...
tout droit (jusqu'à)

EXPRESSIONS VERBALES
(y) aller à pied
continuer
descendre
indiquer le chemin
monter
prendre
tourner
traverser

DIVERS
avant de (+ *infinitif*)
je ne crois pas
tellement
tout de suite

Buying clothes

EXPRESSIONS VERBALES
aller très bien à quelqu'un
défaire (une valise)
essayer
être à
mettre
porter

DIVERS
en coton
en soie
en solde
étroit(e)
une cabine d'essayage
une taille

Pour les vêtements, voir la page 300.
Pour les pronoms disjoints, voir la page 303.

Unité 5 En Normandie

Regional Overview
Rouen, 123 km. northwest of Paris
POPULATION: 105,000 (over 380,000 with its suburbs)
MAJOR INDUSTRIES: textiles, agriculture, mining, seaport

Chapitre 9 La vie ensemble

By the end of this chapter, you should be able to do the following in French:

- Talk about relationships
- Describe your daily routine
- Say what you did with or for others
- Say what you used to do

Port de Rouen
Camille Pissarro (1830–1903)
1896
Paris, Musée d'orsay

Pissarro was born on the Caribbean island of St. Thomas. His French parents sent him to boarding school in Paris in 1841, where he was exposed to the art world. He first visited Rouen in 1883, and its bustling waterfront inspired many great paintings.

Pour commencer

Depuis un certain temps, on redéfinit la notion traditionnelle du couple et de la famille. Aujourd'hui en France, 27 pour cent des **ménages comprennent** une seule personne (célibataire, divorcée ou **veuve**) et 30 pour cent des **naissances ont lieu hors** mariage. Voici les résultats de **sondages** récents sur les opinions des Français au sujet de **l'amour** et de **la vie**. Quelles sont vos opinions?

L'AMOUR

Croyez-vous au grand amour?

OUI	NON	SANS OPINION
66%	27%	7%

Croyez-vous au **coup de foudre?**

OUI	NON	SANS OPINION
70%	28%	2%

À votre avis, peut-on aimer quelqu'un sans avoir de relations sexuelles avec lui?

OUI	NON	SANS OPINION
71%	28%	1%

Si on **espère rencontrer** quelqu'un, où est-ce qu'on a la plus grande possibilité de succès?

FRÉQUENTER LES **BALS** OU LES DISCOTHÈQUES	66%
DEVENIR MEMBRES DE CLUBS OU D'ASSOCIATIONS	57%
S'ADRESSER À UNE AGENCE MATRIMONIALE	17%
PASSER **UNE PETITE ANNONCE**	16%

depuis *since* un ménage *a household* comprennent (comprendre *to be made up of*) veuf (veuve) *widowed* une naissance *a birth* avoir lieu *to take place* hors *outside* un sondage *a survey* l'amour (*m*) *love* la vie *life* croyez-vous au (croire à *to believe in*) le coup de foudre *love at first sight* à votre avis *in your opinion* espérer *to hope* rencontrer *to meet* un bal *a dance* une petite annonce *a classified ad*

LE COUPLE

Est-il normal qu'un couple **se dispute de temps en temps?**

OUI	NON
50%	50%

Pour être un couple heureux, faut-il partager le maximum de choses (loisirs, sorties, revenus, relations, logement) ou préférez-vous conserver une large autonomie?

TOUT PARTAGER	CONSERVER UNE AUTONOMIE	SANS OPINION
80%	16%	4%

Pour être heureux ensemble, lesquelles de ces conditions sont les plus importantes? (Indiquez les trois conditions les plus importantes.)

être à l'écoute de l'autre
avoir des enfants
la fidélité sexuelle
l'harmonie sexuelle
la patience
partager **les tâches domestiques**
avoir les mêmes intérêts, idées et amis

La liste indique l'ordre d'importance selon les réponses.

Quelle est votre réaction **envers** l'infidélité?

Est-ce une cause de rupture?

36% DES HOMMES / 44% DES FEMMES ONT DIT OUI

Est-ce que ça peut arriver sans forcément **remettre** le couple **en cause**?

49% DES HOMMES / 47% DES FEMMES ONT DIT OUI

Est-ce une liberté réciproque qu'on **s'accorde** dans le couple?

12% DES HOMMES / 4% DES FEMMES ONT DIT OUI

---

se disputer *to argue* **de temps en temps** *from time to time* **les tâches domestiques** *(f) housework*
envers *towards* **remettre en cause** *to challenge or threaten* **s'accorder** *to grant (each other)*

À cause du **SIDA** et d'autres **MST**, doit-on:

Limiter le nombre de rapports sexuels?

OUI	NON	SANS OPINION
44%	49%	7%

Limiter le nombre de partenaires?

OUI	NON	SANS OPINION
57%	37%	6%

Utiliser systématiquement **un préservatif**?

OUI	NON	SANS OPINION
81%	16%	3%

Rose, une jeune Américaine, parle à sa grand-mère de sa vie avec son grand-père.

— Est-ce que grand-papa et toi étiez heureux quand vous étiez jeunes?
— Oui, très. J'aimais beaucoup ton grand-père. Nous faisions tout ensemble.
— Même les tâches domestiques?
— Bon, on ne faisait pas tout ensemble. Il n'aidait pas beaucoup à la maison. Il rentrait souvent tard et il était fatigué... mais nous avions les mêmes intérêts et quand il avait du temps libre, on s'**amusait** beaucoup.

le SIDA *AIDS* **une MST (une maladie sexuellement transmissible)** *a sexually transmitted disease* **un préservatif** *a condom* **s'amusait (s'amuser)** *to have fun*

Savez-vous le faire?

A. **C'est vrai?** Est-ce que les phrases suivantes sont vraies ou fausses?

1. Les idées des Français sur le couple ont changé depuis un certain temps.
2. La majorité des Français croient au coup de foudre et au grand amour.
3. Pour les Français, l'acte sexuel n'est pas la chose la plus importante pour être heureux en couple.
4. En France, on pense qu'on a plus de chances de trouver quelqu'un à un bal que par une agence ou une annonce.
5. Les Français trouvent que la vie conjugale n'est pas sans difficultés. La moitié (*half*) trouve qu'il est normal de se disputer de temps en temps.
6. Selon les Français, pour être heureux en couple, il est plus important de conserver la liberté individuelle que de partager beaucoup de choses.
7. Pour les Français, la fidélité est importante si on espère être heureux en couple.
8. Le SIDA influence la vie sexuelle française.

B. **Résultats.** Utilisez les questions du sondage pour demander l'opinion de votre classe. Demandez aussi quelles sont les caractéristiques les plus importantes d'un couple heureux. Quels sont les plus grands problèmes pour un couple?

Comment s'y prendre?

Using word families

Recognizing words that belong to the same word family can make reading easier. Can you fill in the missing meanings below?

le jardin *garden*	**jardiner** *to garden*	**se marier** *to get married*	**le mariage** *marriage*
la vie *life*	**vivre** *???*	**espérer** *to hope*	**l'espoir** *???*
un arrêt (d'autobus) *a (bus)stop*	**s'arrêter** *???*	**habiter** *to live*	**un habitant** *???*

Faux amis

Using cognates and word families can make reading much easier. However, beware of **faux amis**, words that look like cognates but have different meanings. For example, you already know that **attendre** means *to wait*, not *to attend*; and **rester** does not mean *to rest*, but *to stay* or *to remain*. Use cognates to help you, but if a word does not seem right in the context, you will need to look it up.

Savez-vous le faire?

A. **Faux amis.** Les mots en caractères gras dans le paragraphe suivant ressemblent à des mots anglais, mais ce sont des faux amis. Essayez de déterminer leur sens selon le contexte.

M. Dupont est assis au jardin quand une jolie jeune fille qui passe **attire** son attention. Il la **salue** et lui dit: «Bonjour, mademoiselle.» Elle lui répond: «Bonjour, monsieur.» Cette fille ressemble à quelqu'un qu'il connaissait dans le passé et il commence à rêver. Il a des beaux **souvenirs** du temps où il était jeune. Il aimait une jeune fille et il **garde** toujours l'espoir de la revoir un jour.

B. **Familles de mots.** Servez-vous des mots connus dans la liste de gauche pour deviner le sens des mots en caractères gras dans les phrases de droite.

habiter	M. Dupont est un **habitant** de Rouen.
une rose	Il adore les roses et il plante des **rosiers** partout.
assis	L'après-midi, il **s'assied** au jardin pour admirer ses fleurs.
un arrêt	Aujourd'hui, trois filles **s'arrêtent** pour admirer son jardin et pour le saluer.
espérer	Il a un seul **espoir**: il veut revoir la femme qu'il aimait quand il était jeune.
l'amour	Il était **amoureux** de cette fille mais il était trop timide pour le lui dire.

C. **Le présent ou le passé?** Trouvez tous les verbes dans le texte qui suit: «Il n'est jamais trop tard!» Décidez si on parle du présent ou du passé et sur une feuille de papier, mettez les verbes dans un des groupes suivants. N'oubliez pas que l'imparfait décrit aussi le passé. Les formes de l'imparfait se terminent par: **-ais, -ais, -ait, -ions, -iez, -aient.**

MAINTENANT	AU PASSÉ
il aime passer des heures	**il a toujours eu**
	il connaissait

Qu'est-ce qui se passe?

TEXTBOOK TAPE

Il n'est jamais trop tard!

Rosalie Toulouse Richard, une Française qui habite à Atlanta depuis 1945, retourne à Rouen avec sa petite-fille pour rendre visite à son frère. Son vieil ami, André Dupont, ne sait pas encore qu'elle est à Rouen.

André Dupont, habitant de Rouen depuis longtemps, aime passer des heures à travailler dans son jardin. Il a toujours eu une passion pour les roses et depuis des années, il plante des rosiers de toutes les variétés et de toutes les couleurs! Souvent l'après-midi, il s'assied dans un fauteuil de jardin pour admirer la beauté de toutes ses fleurs.

Ses rosiers font l'admiration de tous les gens du quartier et beaucoup d'entre eux passent devant chez lui pour le saluer et pour regarder son beau jardin. Aujourd'hui, ce sont trois jeunes filles qui s'arrêtent lui dire bonjour. Il reconnaît deux d'entre elles, ce sont les petites-filles de Jean Toulouse, mais c'est la troisième qui attire son attention. Il ne l'a jamais vue, et pourtant il a l'impression de la connaître! Elle ressemble à quelqu'un... quelqu'un qu'il connaissait il y a très longtemps.

Les souvenirs lui reviennent, comme si c'était hier. C'était en 1945, il n'avait que dix-huit ans mais il était amoureux fou d'une jolie jeune fille de son âge. Elle s'appelait Rosalie...! Il voulait lui dire combien il l'aimait, mais il n'en avait pas le courage. Il était trop timide et quand il s'approchait d'elle, il ne pouvait même pas lui parler. Un beau jour, il s'est décidé à tout lui dire. Il a choisi des fleurs du jardin de ses parents pour en faire un bouquet, il a pris son vélo et il est allé chez Rosalie. Mais en arrivant, il a trouvé Rosalie en compagnie d'un soldat américain et elle regardait ce jeune soldat d'un regard de femme amoureuse. André, lui, est rentré chez lui sans jamais parler à Rosalie.

Quelques mois après, Rosalie s'est mariée avec l'Américain et ils sont partis vivre aux États-Unis. De temps en temps, André avait des nouvelles parce que le frère de Rosalie et lui étaient de bons amis. Il savait qu'elle habitait à Atlanta, qu'elle avait trois enfants, et il y a trois ans, il a appris que son mari était mort. Il gardait toujours l'espoir de la revoir, mais les années passaient et elle ne revenait toujours pas.

— Vos rosiers sont magnifiques, monsieur!

C'est Rosalie qui parle! En un instant, André Dupont revient au présent et ouvre les yeux. C'est la jeune fille qui parle... celle qu'il ne connaît pas.

— Rosalie???

— Moi, monsieur? Non, je m'appelle Rose. Rosalie, c'est ma grand-mère.

— Ta grand-mère?

— Oui. Vous connaissez ma grand-mère?

— Rosalie Toulouse? Oui, je la connais, mais...

— Eh bien, venez la voir, elle est chez son frère Jean! Je suis sûre qu'elle sera contente de revoir un ami d'ici! Allez, venez avec nous!

Quoi? C'est trop beau! Est-ce qu'il rêve? Rosalie, ici à Rouen! Comme la vie est à la fois belle et bizarre! Va-t-elle le reconnaître? A-t-il le courage de lui dire qu'il l'aime toujours, après toutes ces années? André Dupont choisit les plus belles roses de son jardin et en fait un magnifique bouquet. Il va enfin pouvoir les offrir à la femme pour qui il a planté tous ces rosiers au cours des années.

Avez-vous compris?

Qui parle? Qui dirait (*would say*) les choses suivantes: André, Rosalie ou Rose?

1. J'habite à Rouen depuis très longtemps. J'adore les fleurs et j'aime faire du jardinage.
2. J'ai eu trois enfants, et mon mari est mort il y a trois ans.
3. Je suis passée devant la maison d'un monsieur qui avait des roses splendides dans son jardin.
4. Ce monsieur m'a parlé. Il connaît ma grand-mère mais il ne l'a pas vue depuis longtemps.
5. Je l'ai invité à venir nous voir.
6. En 1945, je me suis mariée avec un Américain et je suis allée vivre aux États-Unis.
7. Ma grand-mère s'appelle Rosalie.
8. Quand j'étais jeune, j'étais très timide avec les filles.
9. En 1945, j'étais amoureux de Rosalie mais je n'ai jamais eu le courage de le lui dire. Un jour, elle s'est mariée avec un autre.
10. Je garde toujours l'espoir de dire à Rosalie que je l'aime.

Remarquez que...

Cimetière américain, Omaha Beach, Normandie, France

Pendant la Seconde Guerre mondiale (*Second World War*), les Allemands ont occupé le nord de la France (les deux-tiers du pays). Un gouvernement français a été créé à Vichy entre 1940 et 1944. Le chef du gouvernement de Vichy, le maréchal Philippe Pétain, a largement coopéré avec les Allemands. Après l'invasion allemande, le général Charles de Gaulle s'est enfui (*fled*) à Londres, où il a établi la Résistance française. Des membres de la Résistance se trouvaient dans les quatre coins de la France, où ils luttaient (*fought*) contre les Allemands. Le matin du Jour J, le 6 juin 1944, les forces alliées ont débarqué sur la côte du Calvados, en Normandie, soutenues par des bombardements aériens et par la deuxième division blindée (*armored*) française. Une grande partie de la province a été dévastée. Presque tout a depuis été reconstruit.

La France et les Amériques. La France et les pays des continents américains se sont beaucoup influencés. Trouvez le nom ou les noms qui correspondent à chaque description.

a. le traité de Versailles, le débarquement en Normandie
b. Montesquieu, Rousseau, Voltaire, Diderot
c. le marquis de La Fayette
d. Frédéric Bartholdi, Gustave Eiffel
e. Samuel de Champlain, le Cavelier de La Salle
f. Napoléon Ier
g. l'*Alabama* et le *Kearsage*
h. Napoléon III
i. Jacques Cartier
j. la Guyane française

1. Cet explorateur a réclamé le Canada pour la France en 1534–1535. Le Canada s'appelait alors la Nouvelle-France.
2. Ces Français ont joué un rôle important dans la découverte, l'exploration et la colonisation du continent nord-américain. Le premier a établi la ville de Québec en 1608.
3. En partie, les idées de la démocratie qui ont servi de fondation à la constitution des États-Unis ont eu comme source les idées de ces philosophes français du 18e siècle (*century*).
4. Pendant la guerre d'Indépendance américaine, ce Français a donné une aide militaire et financière aux forces révolutionnaires. Le succès des colonies américaines a influencé le développement de la Révolution française.
5. Il a conquis le Mexique en 1863 et y a établi son frère Maximilien comme empereur.
6. Autrefois, la France déportait des prisonniers dans cette région sud-américaine. Aujourd'hui, c'est un département d'outre-mer.
7. Il a vendu toute la région de la Louisiane aux États-Unis.
8. Les Français ont donné aux USA un de ses plus grands symboles de la liberté: la statue de la Liberté, créée par ces hommes.
9. En juin 1864, près de la côte de Cherbourg, ces deux navires (*ships*) — un des états confédérés et un navire Yankee—se sont engagés dans une violente bataille. Le navire confédéré repose encore au fond de la mer au large de Cherbourg.
10. Alliés pendant les deux guerres mondiales, les Français, les Canadiens et les Américains partagent ces deux grands événements historiques.

Qu'est-ce qu'on dit?

Quelles sont vos activités **quotidiennes**? À quelle heure est-ce que vous **vous réveillez**? Comment passez-vous la journée?

TEXTBOOK TAPE

D'habitude le matin...

je me lève facilement.

je me lève avec difficulté.

je me lave la figure et les mains (*f*).

je prends un bain.

je prends une douche.

je me brosse les dents.

je m'habille rapidement.

je me brosse les cheveux.

quotidien(ne) *daily* **se réveiller** *to wake up*

SUPPLEMENTAL VOCABULARY

se maquiller *to put on make-up*
se peigner *to comb one's hair*
se raser *to shave*
une brosse à dents *a toothbrush*
du dentifrice *toothpaste*
du maquillage *make-up*
un peigne *a comb*
un réveil *an alarm clock*
un radio-réveil *a clock radio*
du savon *soap*
une serviette *a towel*
du shampooing *shampoo*

Généralement, quand je rentre le soir...

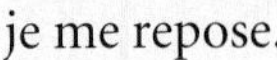
je me repose.

je m'amuse avec des amis.

je m'ennuie.

La nuit...

je me couche tôt / tard.

je m'endors **tout de suite** / avec difficulté.

Patricia Trentin, la cousine de Rose, se lève et réveille son mari.

— Henri! Henri! Lève-toi! Lève-toi **vite**! On est en retard!
— Mais quelle heure est-il?
— Il est déjà 7h30 et je dois être au bureau dans une heure.
— Mais calme-toi! Tu as le temps. Va prendre ton bain et je vais m'occuper des enfants. Après, tu peux préparer le petit déjeuner **pendant que** je prends ma douche.
— Hortense! Yannick! Levez-vous tout de suite! **Dépêchez-vous**! On est **pressés**!

tout de suite *right away* **vite** *quickly* **pendant que** *while* **se dépêcher** *to hurry* **pressé(e)** *in a hurry*

A. **D'abord...** Indiquez si l'ordre des activités que vous entendez est logique.

EXEMPLE VOUS ENTENDEZ: D'abord, je prends mon petit déjeuner et puis je me brosse les dents.
VOUS INDIQUEZ: **C'est logique.**

B. **Moi, je...** Est-ce que vous faites les choses suivantes: **tous les jours, une (deux, trois...) fois par jour (par semaine), de temps en temps, rarement?**

EXEMPLE Je me lève tout de suite. → **Je me lève *rarement* tout de suite.**

1. Je prends un bain.
2. Je me brosse les dents.
3. Je me lave la figure.
4. Je m'habille vite.
5. Je me lave les cheveux.
6. Je me lève tout de suite.
7. Je prends une douche le soir.
8. Je me couche tôt.
9. Je m'endors tout de suite.

Voilà pourquoi!

Les verbes réfléchis

A verb can be used to say that you are doing something to or for yourself or that you are doing something to or for another person or thing. For example, Patricia can dress herself and she can also dress her children. Compare the differences depicted here.

Je m'habille.

J'habille les enfants.

Je me lave les mains.

Je lave la voiture.

SELF-CHECK

1. What is the difference in usage between the reflexive verb **se laver** and the non-reflexive verb **laver**?
2. Where do you place **ne... pas** when negating reflexive verbs?
3. In which forms do verbs like **se lever**, **préférer**, **s'appeler**, and **s'ennuyer** have spelling changes? Which two forms do not have spelling changes?

When someone performs the action of a verb on or for himself/herself, a reflexive verb is generally used in French. The infinitive of reflexive verbs is found in a dictionary preceded by the reflexive pronoun **se**. When you conjugate these verbs, you will vary the reflexive pronoun with the subject.

SE LAVER (*TO WASH* [*ONESELF*])

je **me** lave	nous **nous** lavons
tu **te** laves	vous **vous** lavez
il/elle/on **se** lave	ils/elles **se** lavent

Note that **me**, **te**, and **se** change to **m'**, **t'**, and **s'** before a vowel sound: **je m'habille, tu t'habilles, elle s'habille, ils s'habillent.**

The placement rules for reflexive pronouns are the same as those for the direct and indirect object pronouns. In the negative, place **ne** before the reflexive pronoun and **pas** after the verb.

Je *ne* me couche *pas* avant minuit. **Nous *ne* nous levons *pas* facilement.**

Here are some reflexive verbs you can use to talk about your daily life:

s'amuser	*to have fun*	**s'habiller**	*to get dressed*
s'appeler	*to be named*	**se laver (les mains, la figure)**	*to wash (one's hands, one's face)*
se brosser (les cheveux, les dents)	*to brush (one's hair, one's teeth)*	**se lever**	*to get up*
se calmer	*to calm down*	**s'occuper de**	*to take care of*
se coucher	*to go to bed*	**se promener**	*to go walking*
se dépêcher	*to hurry*	**se reposer**	*to rest*
s'endormir[1]	*to fall asleep*	**se réveiller**	*to wake up*
s'ennuyer	*to be / get bored*	**se souvenir de**[1]	*to remember*

SUPPLEMENTAL VOCABULARY

s'acheter quelque chose *to buy something for oneself*
se déshabiller *to get undressed*
se rendormir[1] *to fall back asleep*
se fâcher *to get angry*

[1]**S'endormir** and **se rendormir** are conjugated like **dormir**. **Se souvenir** (**de**) is conjugated like **venir.**

Les verbes à changements orthographiques

A few **-er** verbs have spelling changes in their stems when they are conjugated. When the next to last syllable has an **e** or **é**, it often changes to **è** in the **je, tu, il, elle, on, ils,** and **elles** forms (those with silent endings). The stem for the **nous** and **vous** forms, and the past participle, are like the infinitive.

SE LEVER (*TO GET UP*)		PRÉFÉRER (TO PREFER)	
je me lève	nous nous levons	je préfère	nous préférons
tu te lèves	vous vous levez	tu préfères	vous préférez
il/elle/on se lève	ils/elles se lèvent	il/elle/on préfère	ils/elles préfèrent

Some other verbs that follow this pattern are: **acheter, se promener, répéter,** and **espérer.**

In a small number of verbs with a stem ending in **e** followed by a consonant and **-er**, you will double the final consonant of the stem when the verb ending is silent.

S'APPELER (*TO BE NAMED*)	
je m'appe**lle**	nous nous appe**lons**
tu t'appe**lles**	vous vous appe**lez**
il/elle/on s'appe**lle**	ils/elles s'appe**llent**

Verbs ending in **-yer**, like **s'ennuyer**, have spelling changes in the stem of the verb.

S'ENNUYER (*TO BE / GET BORED*)	
je m'enn**uie**	nous nous enn**uyons**
tu t'enn**uies**	vous vous enn**uyez**
il/elle/on s'enn**uie**	ils/elles s'enn**uient**

Essayer (*to try*) and **payer** follow this pattern.

Et ça se prononce comment?

Les verbes comme **préférer** et **se lever**

Compare the pronunciation of the **é** and **è** in the conjugated forms of **préférer.** Remember that the letter **é** (**e accent aigu**) sounds like the vowel of **les.** Say these sentences.

Nous préférons nous lever tard. **Préférez-vous préparer le petit déjeuner?**

The letter **è** (**e accent grave**) is a less tight sound. It sounds like the *e* in the English word *belt.* An **è** frequently occurs in the final syllable of words ending in silent **e: bière, chère, mère.** Say these sentences.

Je me lève à six heures. **Je préfère partir tôt.**

Savez-vous le faire?

A. **Quelle(s) lettre(s)?** Complétez les verbes dans les questions suivantes avec les lettres convenables. Ensuite, posez ces questions à un(e) camarade de classe en faisant attention à la prononciation de la voyelle **e**. Écrivez ses réponses pour faire un rapport à la classe.

1. Comment t'appe___es-tu? Comment s'appe___e ton/ta meilleur(e) ami(e)? Comment s'appe___ent tes parents?
2. Est-ce que tu te l___ves facilement ou avec difficulté? Est-ce que tes parents se l___vent tôt ou tard d'habitude?
3. Qu'est-ce que ton/ta meilleur(e) ami(e) préf___re faire le samedi matin? À quelle heure est-ce qu'il/elle se l___ve le week-end? Est-ce que vous vous ennu___ez souvent ensemble? Quand est-ce que tu t'ennu___es?
4. Qu'est-ce que tu esp___res faire l'année prochaine?

B. **Et vous?** Exprimez vos sentiments en complétant les phrases suivantes.

1. Je m'amuse beaucoup quand...
2. Je m'ennuie quand...
3. Je me dépêche quand...
4. Je m'occupe le plus de...
5. Je me souviens très bien des vacances que j'ai passées...

C. **Un samedi typique.** Voilà un samedi typique chez Patricia et son mari Henri. Regardez ce qu'ils font et formez des phrases en utilisant un verbe réfléchi.

EXEMPLE Patricia se **lève à six heures.**

1. Henri et Patricia...

2. Patricia...

3. Henri et Patricia...

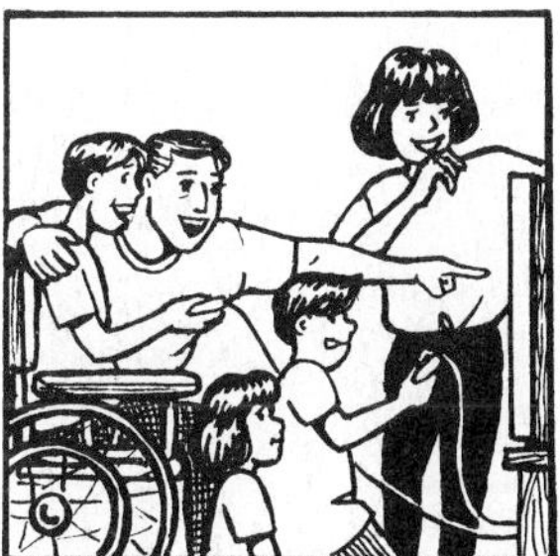

4. Henri et les enfants...

TOURNEZ S.V.P.

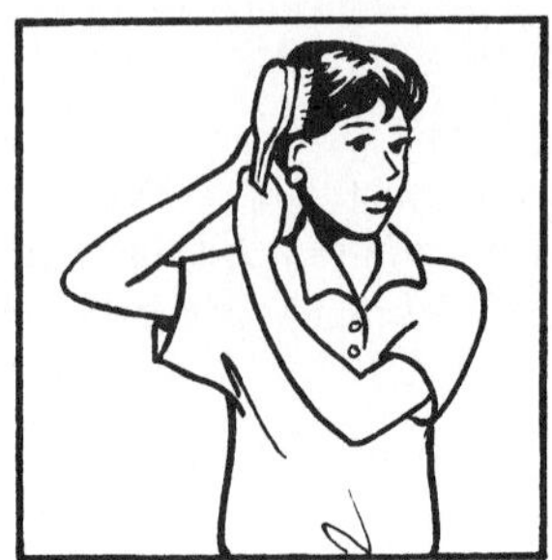

5. Patricia...

6. Patricia...

7. Henri et Patricia...

8. Henri... mais Patricia...

D. **Chez Patricia.** Regardez les illustrations de *C. Un samedi typique* et jouez le rôle de Patricia qui décrit son samedi typique.

EXEMPLE **Je me lève à six heures. Après, Henri et moi, nous...**

E. **Le week-end.** Demandez à un(e) camarade de classe s'il/si elle fait les choses suivantes le week-end.

EXEMPLE se lever tôt ou tard le samedi matin
— Est-ce que tu te lèves tôt ou tard le samedi matin?
— En général, je me lève tôt (tard).

1. se réveiller tôt ou tard le dimanche matin
2. se lever tout de suite
3. prendre un bain ou une douche
4. se laver les cheveux le week-end
5. sortir ou se reposer le samedi soir
6. s'amuser ou s'ennuyer le week-end
7. s'occuper d'un petit frère ou d'une petite sœur
8. se coucher tôt ou tard le samedi soir

F. **Camarades de chambre.** Vous cherchez un(e) camarade de chambre et vous allez interviewer quelqu'un qui répond à votre annonce dans le journal. Écrivez cinq questions que vous voudriez lui poser en utilisant au moins trois verbes réfléchis. Ensuite, interviewez un(e) autre étudiant(e) pour savoir si vous aimeriez être camarades de chambre.

EXEMPLE **Vous vous couchez tôt?**

G. **Votre emploi du temps.** Complétez votre emploi du temps pour une journée entière du matin jusqu'au soir. Décrivez votre emploi du temps à un(e) camarade de classe. (Il/Elle ne doit pas regarder votre feuille de papier!) Il/Elle va essayer de le dessiner (*to draw*). Ensuite, changez de rôles. Finalement, comparez vos emplois du temps pour voir si vous avez bien compris.

LUNDI **5**	14
8	15
9	16
10	17
11	18
12	19
13	20
MARDI **6**	14
8	15
9	16
10	17
11	18
12	19
13	20
MERCREDI **7**	14
8	15
9	16
10	17
11	18
12	19
13	20
JEUDI **8**	14
8	15
9	16
10	17
11	18
12	19
13	20

Le vieux quartier de Rouen

Voilà pourquoi!

SELF-CHECK
1. When using a reflexive verb in the infinitive, does the reflexive pronoun change with the subject?
2. Where do you attach reflexive pronouns in affirmative commands? What happens to the pronoun **te** in affirmative commands?
3. Where do you place reflexive pronouns in negative commands?

L'infinitif et le futur immédiat des verbes réfléchis

When you use a reflexive verb in the infinitive, the reflexive pronoun varies with the subject.

Nous ne voulons pas *nous* lever très tôt demain.
À quelle heure vas-tu *te* lever?
Je préfère *me* lever tard.

L'impératif des verbes réfléchis

When using a reflexive verb to ask or tell someone to do something, form the *affirmative* imperative by attaching the reflexive pronoun to the end of the verb with a hyphen. In this position, **te** changes to **toi**.

Lève-toi. **Marions-nous en juin.** **Occupez-vous de vos enfants.**

In *negative* commands, the reflexive pronoun goes before the verb, and **te** does not become **toi**.

Ne te lève pas tout de suite. **Ne nous couchons pas trop tard.**

Savez-vous le faire?

A. **Tu dois te reposer!** C'est samedi et Patricia est épuisée (*exhausted*). Henri va s'occuper des enfants parce qu'il veut qu'elle se repose. Lesquelles (*Which ones*) des choses suivantes lui dit-il de faire? Lesquelles lui dit-il de ne pas faire?

EXEMPLES se lever tout de suite → **Ne te lève pas tout de suite.**
se lever plus tard → **Lève-toi plus tard.**

1. se calmer
2. se reposer
3. se dépêcher
4. s'occuper des tâches domestiques
5. se coucher tard
6. se coucher tôt

B. **Tu as raison!** Patricia dit à Henri qu'elle va suivre ses conseils (*follow his advice*) de l'exercice précédent. Que dit-elle?

EXEMPLES **Tu as raison. Je ne vais pas me lever tout de suite.**
Je vais me lever plus tard.

C. **Baby-sitters.** Vous vous occupez de deux enfants d'un couple français et vous devez les réveiller et les aider à se préparer pour aller à l'école. Dites-leur ce qu'ils doivent ou ne doivent pas faire. Si vous le leur dites correctement, ils vous obéissent (*obey*) et ils continuent. Si vous ne le leur dites pas correctement, ils retournent au lit et vous êtes obligé(e) de tout recommencer.

EXEMPLES **Réveillez-vous.** **Ne vous recouchez pas.**

se lever *se (re)coucher*
s'endormir à table
aller à l'arrêt d'autobus SE BROSSER LES DENTS
s'habiller ***se brosser les cheveux*** *sortir de la maison*
se laver les mains *prendre le petit déjeuner*
se réveiller **prendre un bain**

D. **E.T. chez vous.** Un extra-terrestre est arrivé chez vous et il vous demande ce qu'il faut faire pour être accepté en tant qu'être humain (*as a human*). Dites-lui ce qu'il faut ou ne faut pas faire.

EXEMPLE Je m'habille avant de prendre une douche?
Non, ne t'habille pas avant de prendre une douche. Habille-toi après.

1. Je m'endors par terre?
2. Je m'habille dans la cuisine?
3. Je me brosse les mains?
4. Je me lève à minuit?
5. Je me couche à midi?
6. Je me couche dans le jardin?

E. **Faisons du camping.** Vous allez faire du camping à la mer avec un groupe d'amis ce week-end. Travaillez avec un petit groupe d'étudiants et faites des projets.

EXEMPLES **Levons-nous tôt.**
Ne nous couchons pas tard.

se lever tôt / tard
SE PROMENER **???**
DORMIR PAR TERRE
faire un tour en vélo
se coucher tôt / tard
faire un pique-nique
faire du bateau
se laver les cheveux **???**

Pour les campeurs qui souhaitent à la fois être près de la mer (2,5 km) et profiter des plaisirs de la campagne bretonne, le camping des «7 Saints» est idéal. Grâce au confort du camping et à la qualité de ses équipements, les campeurs trouvent sur place toutes les possibilités de vacances actives. Erdeven exprime son charme par sa plage de 8 km dont une partie est réservée aux naturistes. Golf 18 trous à proximité. Ouverture: du 1er mai au 15 septembre.

F. **Projets du week-end.** En utilisant des verbes réfléchis, faites une liste de cinq choses que vous allez ou n'allez pas faire ce week-end.

EXEMPLE **Ce week-end, je vais me reposer...**

Maintenant, circulez dans la classe et trouvez quelqu'un qui va faire au moins trois des choses que vous allez faire aussi.

EXEMPLE **Vas-tu te reposer?...**

G. **Dépêchez-vous!** Imaginez que vous êtes père ou mère de famille et que vous vous levez en retard. Avec deux camarades de classe, préparez une scène où vous dites à vos enfants de se lever et de se préparer pour l'école.

Qu'est-ce qu'on dit?

Où est-ce que vous avez fait la connaissance de votre meilleur(e) ami(e)? Qu'est-ce que vous faites l'un(e) pour l'autre?

Nous **nous sommes rencontré(e)s** la première fois | quand nous étions enfants.
au lycée.
à l'université.
chez un(e) autre ami(e).
???

Nous nous sommes rencontré(e)s il y a | quelques mois.
un (deux, trois...) ans.
longtemps.
???

Nous nous parlons | tous les jours.
une fois par semaine.
de temps en temps.
???

Nous **nous entendons** | toujours bien.
bien **la plupart du** temps.
???

Nous **nous disputons** | tout le temps.
de temps en temps.
rarement.
???

Pour nous amuser, nous aimons | aller danser.
passer la journée au lac.
???

À l'invitation de Rose, André **s'est rendu chez** les Toulouse pour retrouver Rosalie mais malheureusement elle n'était pas là. **Pourtant**, le lendemain, **tout à fait par hasard**, Rosalie et André se sont rencontrés. Voilà **ce qui s'est passé**.

Rosalie et André se sont rencontrés par hasard dans un café. Ils ne se sont pas vus tout de suite. Mais après quelques instants, ils se sont regardés et ils se sont reconnus.

se rencontrer *to meet* **s'entendre** *to get along* **la plupart de** *the majority of, most of* **se disputer** *to argue* **se rendre à / chez** *to go to* **pourtant** *however* **tout à fait** *completely* **par hasard** *by accident* **ce qui** *what* **se passer** *to happen*

Ils se sont embrassés. Et ils ont passé le reste de l'après-midi à se parler. Ça a été le coup de foudre! Ils se sont **enfin** quittés vers sept heures.

Depuis ce jour-là, ils se téléphonent et ils essaient de se retrouver en ville tous les jours, où ils passent des heures à se promener. Ils s'entendent très bien et ils ne se disputent presque jamais. Un soir, Rosalie rentre chez son frère et sa petite-fille Rose lui pose des questions sur sa journée.

— Salut, mamie. Tu as passé une bonne journée?
— Oui, très. André et moi, nous avons visité le Mont-Saint-Michel. On s'est promenés partout et on s'est bien amusés.
— Alors, vous vous entendez bien?
— Oui, très, très bien et **devine...**! Nous avons décidé de nous marier!

enfin *finally* **deviner** *to guess*

Selon la légende, l'archange saint Michel est apparu au huitième siècle sur cette île sur laquelle a été construit un oratoire. Celui-ci a été remplacé par une série d'abbayes et d'églises, chacune plus spectaculaire que la précédente. Les pèlerins (*pilgrims*) sont venus en foule (*in droves*) au Mont-Saint-Michel au cours de l'histoire. La construction d'une digue reliant (*a causeway connecting*) l'île à la côte a facilité la traversée rendue dangereuse par les marées (*tides*) et les sables mouvants (*quicksand*).

A. **Test: Êtes-vous romantique?** Passez ce test pour savoir si vous êtes romantique.

ÊTES-VOUS ROMANTIQUE?

I. Indiquez vos opinions sur ces sujets.

1. Pensez-vous que le vrai amour...
   a. arrive une fois dans la vie?
   b. n'existe pas?
   c. est sans importance?
2. Pensez-vous qu'un couple peut s'aimer pour toujours?
   a. Certainement.
   b. Je ne sais pas, on peut essayer.
   c. Probablement pas: la vie est trop longue.
3. Au restaurant, vous voyez des amoureux qui se regardent dans les yeux pendant tout le dîner. Vous trouvez ça...
   a. un peu bête mais charmant.
   b. ridicule.
   c. adorable.
4. Deux personnes doivent **surtout**...
   a. s'occuper de leurs enfants.
   b. essayer de se faire plaisir l'une à l'autre.
   c. s'efforcer de garder leur amour.

II. Comment êtes-vous en couple?

1. Vous vous rencontrez par hasard et c'est le coup de foudre, que pensez-vous?
   a. Ce n'est probablement que le désir sexuel.
   b. C'est peut-être l'amour.
   c. Je dois partir.
2. Vous vous disputez. Quelle est la meilleure manière de vous calmer?
   a. Nous devons nous embrasser.
   b. Nous devons essayer de parler calmement du problème.
   c. Nous devons nous quitter pendant quelque temps.
3. Vous vous adorez. Vous voulez...
   a. essayer de vous voir tous les jours.
   b. vous téléphoner tous les jours et vous voir quatre ou cinq fois par semaine.
   c. vous retrouver le week-end, si vous n'avez pas d'autres projets.

SCORE: Partie I. 1. a–2 points 2. a–2 points, b–1 point 3. c–2 points, a–1 point 4. c–2 points, b–1 point. Partie II. 1. b–2 points, a–1 point 2. a–2 points, b–1 point 3. a–2 points, b–1 point. Si vous avez 11–14 points, vous êtes une personne très (peut-être même un peu trop?) romantique. Attention! Ne perdez pas votre temps à attendre un amour parfait. Essayez d'être un peu plus réaliste, quand même. Si vous avez 6–10 points, vous êtes romantique, mais vous n'exagérez pas. Vous êtes prêt(e) à aimer quand le bon moment arrive, mais vous ne perdez pas votre temps à chercher l'amour idéal partout. Si vous avez 0–5 points, vous êtes réaliste, cynique même! Ne voulez-vous pas avoir un peu plus de poésie dans votre vie? Sinon, vous risquez de rester seul(e)!

---

surtout *especially*

B. **D'abord.** Indiquez la phrase qui décrit ce qui s'est passé en premier entre André et Rosalie quand ils se sont rencontrés au café.

EXEMPLE a. Ils se sont embrassés. b. Ils se sont vus.
b. Ils se sont vus.

1. a. Ils se sont rencontrés par hasard. b. Ils se sont reconnus.
2. a. Ils se sont quittés. b. Ils ont passé trois heures ensemble.
3. a. Ils se sont parlé. b. Ils se sont vus.
4. a. Ils se sont vus. b. Ils se sont embrassés.
5. a. Ils se sont dit bonjour. b. Ils se sont parlé pendant des heures.

Voilà pourquoi!

SELF-CHECK
1. When do you use a reciprocal verb?
2. Are the forms of reciprocal verbs different from the forms of reflexive verbs?
3. What verbs can be made into reciprocal verbs? How would you say *to look at each other*, *to listen to each other*, or *to know each other*?

Les verbes réciproques

You have seen that reflexive verbs are used when someone is doing something to or for himself / herself. You use similar verbs to describe reciprocal actions, that is, to indicate that people are doing something to or for each other. Here are some verbs commonly used to describe such actions. Note that although **se marier** is reflexive/reciprocal, **divorcer** is not.

s'aimer	*to like / to love each other*	**se marier (avec)**	*to get married (to)*
se détester	*to hate each other*	**se quitter**	*to leave each other*
se disputer	*to argue*	**se rencontrer**	*to meet each other (by chance)*
s'embrasser	*to kiss each other, to embrace*	**se retrouver**	*to meet each other (by design)*
s'entendre (bien, mal)	*to get along (well, badly)*		

Most verbs indicating actions done to other people can be made into reciprocal verbs.

téléphoner à quelqu'un *(to phone someone)* → **se téléphoner** *(to phone each other)*
Je téléphone à Bill. → **Nous nous téléphonons.**

aider quelqu'un *(to help someone)* → **s'aider** *(to help each other)*
Il faut aider tes amis. → **Il faut s'aider.**

Savez-vous le faire?

A. **Meilleur(e)s ami(e)s.** Complétez les phrases suivantes pour décrire vos rapports avec votre meilleur(e) ami(e).

1. Nous nous parlons...
2. On s'entend bien sauf quand...
3. Nous nous disputons quand...
4. On s'amuse quand...
5. On se retrouve souvent à...
6. On se téléphone...

B. Questions. Rose a beaucoup de questions pour sa grand-mère au sujet de ses rapports avec André. Utilisez les verbes donnés pour poser des questions logiques à Rosalie. Un(e) camarade de classe imaginera (*will imagine*) les réponses de Rosalie.

EXEMPLE se parler → **— Est-ce que vous vous parlez tous les jours?**
— Oui, nous nous parlons tous les jours.

1. se téléphoner
2. se retrouver
3. se disputer
4. s'embrasser
5. s'entendre
6. s'aimer

C. Les amoureux. Voilà les activités quotidiennes de Rosalie et André. Que font-ils?

EXEMPLE **Ils se téléphonent.**

se téléphoner	*se promener*
SE PARLER	***se regarder***
S'AIMER	
se retrouver	
s'embrasser	*bien s'entendre*
SE QUITTER	**se dire**

1. 

2. 

3. 

4. 

5. 

6. 

D. Rosalie parle. Rosalie décrit à Rose ses activités quotidiennes avec André. Utilisez les illustrations dans l'exercice précédent et jouez le rôle de Rosalie.

EXEMPLE **D'habitude, nous nous téléphonons le matin.**

Voilà pourquoi!

SELF-CHECK
1. Do you use **être** or **avoir** as the auxiliary with reflexive and reciprocal verbs in the **passé composé**?
2. Where are reflexive pronouns placed with respect to the auxiliary? Where do you place **ne... pas** in the negative?
3. When does the past participle agree with the subject?

Les verbes réfléchis et réciproques au passé composé

All reflexive and reciprocal verbs use **être** as the auxiliary verb in the **passé composé**. Always place the reflexive pronoun directly before the auxiliary, even in the negative.

je *me* suis levé(e)	je *ne me* suis *pas* levé(e)
tu *t'*es levé(e)	tu *ne t'*es *pas* levé(e)
il *s'*est levé	il *ne s'*est *pas* levé
elle *s'*est levée	elle *ne s'*est *pas* levée
nous *nous* sommes levé(e)s	nous *ne nous* sommes *pas* levé(e)s
vous *vous* êtes levé(e)(s)	vous *ne vous* êtes *pas* levé(e)(s)
ils *se* sont levés	ils *ne se* sont *pas* levés
elles *se* sont levées	elles *ne se* sont *pas* levées

Je *me* suis levé(e) tôt ce matin. **Ils *ne se* sont *pas* vus tout de suite.**

In the **passé composé**, the past participle will agree in gender and number with the reflexive pronoun (and the subject) if this pronoun is the direct object of the verb, but not if it is an indirect object. Since the reflexive pronoun is a direct object with most verbs, there is usually agreement.

Rose *s'*est lavé*e*. **André et Rosalie *se* sont rencontré*s*.**

With the following verbs, the pronoun is an indirect object, and there is no agreement: **se dire**, **se parler**, **se téléphoner**, **s'écrire**.

Ils se sont parlé. **Nous nous sommes téléphoné.**

Savez-vous le faire?

A. Hier. Dites si vous avez fait les choses suivantes hier.

EXEMPLE se lever tôt → **Oui, je me suis levé(e) tôt hier.**
OU **Non, je ne me suis pas levé(e) tôt hier.**

1. se lever avant huit heures
2. se laver les cheveux
3. s'ennuyer
4. s'amuser
5. se coucher tard
6. s'endormir tout de suite

B. Hier chez Patricia. Regardez les illustrations pour l'exercice *C. Un samedi typique* aux pages 325 et 326. Dites ce que Patricia et sa famille ont fait hier.

EXEMPLE **Patricia s'est levée à six heures.**

C. **Le week-end dernier.** Travaillez avec un(e) camarade de classe. Faites une liste de cinq choses que vous avez faites tou(te)s les deux le week-end dernier.

se lever tôt ou tard	**SE LAVER**	*se promener*
S'AMUSER	S'ENNUYER	**se dépêcher**
???	*se coucher*	S'OCCUPER DE
s'acheter **???**	*se reposer*	**s'endormir** ???

EXEMPLE **Samedi matin, nous nous sommes levé(e)s tard.**

D. **Pour continuer la conversation.** Chaque paire d'étudiants va écrire au tableau la liste préparée pour l'exercice précédent. Travaillez avec votre partenaire et écrivez des questions pour obtenir plus de renseignements.

EXEMPLE ILS ONT ÉCRIT: Samedi matin, nous nous sommes levé(e)s tard.
VOUS DEMANDEZ: **À quelle heure est-ce que vous vous êtes levé(e)s?**
ILS ONT ÉCRIT: Nous nous sommes promené(e)s.
VOUS DEMANDEZ: **Où est-ce que vous vous êtes promené(e)s?**

E. **Rosalie et André.** Regardez les illustrations pour l'exercice *C. Les amoureux* à la page 335. Ce sont les choses qu'André et Rosalie ont faites hier. Dites ce qu'ils ont fait.

EXEMPLE **André et Rosalie se sont téléphoné.**

F. **La première sortie.** Pensez à un couple célèbre et imaginez la première fois qu'ils sont sortis ensemble. Vous êtes l'ami(e) d'une de ces personnes et vous voulez tout savoir après. Préparez la scène avec un(e) autre étudiant(e). Utilisez des verbes réfléchis ou réciproques.

EXEMPLE — **Vous vous êtes amusés?**
— **Oui, nous nous sommes retrouvés à... et nous...**

Qu'est-ce qu'on dit?

TEXTBOOK TAPE

Comment était votre **jeunesse?**

La période la plus agréable de ma jeunesse était quand
- j'avais ____ ans.
- j'étais à l'école primaire.
- j'habitais à ____________ .

Quand j'étais petit(e),
- j'habitais avec ____________ .
- à ____________ .

j'avais
- beaucoup d'amis.
- beaucoup de problèmes.
- un chien et un chat.
- ???

je **me sentais**
- heureux / heureuse.
- **malheureux / malheureuse.**
- seul(e).
- ???

je **m'intéressais**
- aux animaux.
- au sport.
- aux études.
- à la musique.
- ???

je n'avais **aucun** talent pour
- la musique.
- le sport.
- les études.
- ???

En général, comme enfant,
- j'étais **sage** / insupportable / ???.
- j'écoutais **les conseils** de mes parents.
- je travaillais bien à l'école.
- je faisais mes devoirs.

Pour m'amuser,
- je regardais la télé.
- j'écoutais de la musique.
- je jouais au football / à des jeux vidéo.
- j'allais chez des amis.
- je lisais.

la jeunesse *youth* **se sentir** (conjugated like **dormir**) *to feel* **malheureux(-euse)** *unhappy*
s'intéresser à *to be interested in* **ne... aucun(e)** *no, not any* **sage** *good, well-behaved*
insupportable *impossible, intolerable* **les conseils** (*m*) *advice*

Rosalie parle à sa petite-fille de sa jeunesse en Normandie.

— La meilleure époque de ma vie ici, c'était avant la **guerre**, quand j'avais neuf ou dix ans. J'habitais avec ma famille à la campagne tout près de Rouen. Papa travaillait pour la ville et maman travaillait comme professeur de musique. Elle **enseignait** la musique à presque tous les enfants du village. J'avais **donc** toujours beaucoup d'amis. Je ne me sentais jamais seule.

— Toi aussi, tu t'intéressais à la musique?

— Oui, je jouais du piano et je **chantais**. J'aimais surtout jouer du jazz.

— Et **tonton** Jean?

— Lui, le pauvre, il n'avait aucun talent pour la musique! Lui, c'était un sportif. Il passait tout son temps **dehors** à jouer au foot et à faire du vélo. Moi, par contre j'étais **nulle** en sport.

— Tu étais heureuse?

— Ah, oui, très heureuse.

la guerre *the war* **enseigner** *to teach* **donc** *therefore, then* **chanter** *to sing* **tonton** *uncle* **dehors** *outside* **nul(le)** *zero, really bad*

A. **Et vous?** Complétez ces phrases pour parler de votre jeunesse.

1. La meilleure époque de ma jeunesse était quand j'avais ___ ans.
2. Mon père travaillait ___ .
3. Ma mère travaillait ___ .
4. J'avais beaucoup d(e) ___ .
5. J'étais ___ .
6. Je m'intéressais à la/au/à l'/aux ___ .
7. Je me sentais souvent ___ .
8. Je ne me sentais presque jamais ___ .
9. Je n'avais aucun talent pour ___ .

B. **Musiciens.** Vos parents et vos grands-parents parlent de la musique de leur jeunesse. Dites le genre de musique pour lequel chaque musicien(ne) est célèbre.

du jazz	*du rock*	du folk	DE LA MUSIQUE CLASSIQUE
du hard	du country-western	**du soul**	**du blues**

1. Led Zeppelin jouait...
2. Muddy Waters jouait...
3. Louis Armstrong jouait...
4. Janis Joplin chantait...
5. Woody Guthrie chantait...
6. Patsy Cline chantait...
7. James Brown chantait...
8. Elvis Presley chantait...

Voilà pourquoi!

SELF-CHECK

1. Which form of the present tense do you use to create the stem for all verbs in the imperfect, except for **être**?
2. You use the **passé composé** to talk about a specific occurrence in the past. What do you use the imperfect to express?
3. Which four imperfect endings are pronounced alike?
4. What single letter distinguishes the **nous** and **vous** forms of the imperfect from the present?

La formation de l'imparfait

To tell what things used to be like, you will use the imperfect (**l'imparfait**). All verbs except **être** form this tense by dropping the **-ons** from the present tense **nous** form and adding the endings **-ais**, **-ais**, **-ait**, **-ions**, **-iez**, and **-aient**.

PARLER nous parl~~ons~~ → parl–		FAIRE nous fais~~ons~~ → fais–		VENDRE nous vend~~ons~~ → vend–	
je	parl**ais**	je	fais**ais**	je	vend**ais**
tu	parl**ais**	tu	fais**ais**	tu	vend**ais**
il/elle/on	parl**ait**	il/elle/on	fais**ait**	il/elle/on	vend**ait**
nous	parl**ions**	nous	fais**ions**	nous	vend**ions**
vous	parl**iez**	vous	fais**iez**	vous	vend**iez**
ils/elles	parl**aient**	ils/elles	fais**aient**	ils/elles	vend**aient**

Je travaillais pour IBM. — *I used to work for IBM.*
Qu'est-ce que tu faisais d'habitude? — *What did you usually do?*
Il me rendait visite tous les jours. — *He visited me every day.*

Notice the irregular imperfect stem of **être** and the special forms that follow.

ÊTRE	
j'**étais**	nous **étions**
tu **étais**	vous **étiez**
il/elle/on **était**	ils/elles **étaient**

C'était en 1939. J'étais très jeune. Nous étions en Normandie.

il y a	→	**il y avait**	**Il n'y avait pas d'école au village.**
il neige	→	**il neigeait**	**Il neigeait souvent en hiver.**
ça plaît	→	**ça plaisait**	**Ça me plaisait beaucoup.**
il pleut	→	**il pleuvait**	**Il pleuvait beaucoup au mois de mai.**
il faut	→	**il fallait**	**Il fallait partir tôt pour aller à l'école.**

Verbs with a spelling change in the present tense **nous** form, like **manger** and **commencer**, retain the spelling change in all forms of the imperfect, except the **nous** and **vous** forms.

nous mange~~ons~~ → **je mang*e*ais, tu mang*e*ais, on mang*e*ait, elles mang*e*aient**
BUT: **nous mangions, vous mangiez**

nous commenç~~ons~~ → **je commen*ç*ais, tu commen*ç*ais, on commen*ç*ait, ils commen*ç*aient**
BUT: **nous commencions, vous commenciez**

L'emploi de l'imparfait

In *Chapitre dix*, you will learn more about when to use the **imparfait** and when to use the **passé composé** to talk about the past. Generally, use the **passé composé** to talk about an action that took place at a specific time in the past. Use the **imparfait** to:

- Tell what things used to be like.

  J'avais dix ans et j'étais très timide. *I was ten and I was very shy.*

- Tell what someone did or what happened over and over in the past.

  Je passais tous les après-midi dehors. *I spent every afternoon outside.*

These time expressions are often used with the imperfect:

fréquemment *frequently*
chaque lundi / semaine...
le lundi, le matin...
tous les jours / les étés...
autrefois *formerly*
à cette époque-là *at that time*
d'habitude *generally*
quand j'étais jeune
quand j'avais... ans

Jouer à / de

The verb **jouer** is useful for talking about childhood pastimes. After **jouer**, use the preposition **à** with sports or games, and use the preposition **de** with music types or musical instruments. Did you do any of the following when you were younger?

Je jouais		Je jouais aussi	
	du piano.		*au* base-ball.
	de la guitare.		*au* basket-ball.
	de la batterie (*drums*).		*au* hockey.
	de la trompette.		*au* tennis.
	du clavier (*keyboard*).		*au* football (américain).
	du saxophone.		*aux* cartes.

SUPPLEMENTAL VOCABULARY
jouer de la clarinette
jouer de la flûte
jouer du trombone
jouer au billard

Et ça se prononce comment?

Les terminaisons de l'imparfait

All the endings of the imperfect are pronounced alike, except the endings of the **nous** and **vous** forms. Note that the **nous** and **vous** forms of the imperfect are distinguished from the present only by the vowel **i** in the ending, which is pronounced like a **y**. Compare:

PRESENT: **Où est-ce que vous habitez?** *Where do you live?*
IMPERFECT: **Où est-ce que vous habitiez?** *Where did you used to live?*

Savez-vous le faire?

A. **Présent ou passé?** Vous allez entendre une des deux questions de chaque paire. La première question concerne le présent et la seconde fait allusion à quand vous étiez petit(e). Sur une feuille de papier, écrivez **maintenant** ou **quand j'étais petit(e)** pour indiquer la question entendue.

EXEMPLE Tu habites dans un appartement? / Tu habitais dans un appartement?
VOUS ENTENDEZ: Tu habitais dans un appartement?
VOUS ÉCRIVEZ: **quand j'étais petit(e)**

1. Est-ce que tu joues au basket? / Est-ce que tu jouais au basket?
2. Tes amis et toi, vous sortez souvent? / Tes amis et toi, vous sortiez souvent?
3. Où aimez-vous aller souvent ensemble? / Où aimiez-vous aller souvent ensemble?
4. Parles-tu souvent avec tes parents? / Parlais-tu souvent avec tes parents?
5. Est-ce que vous vous entendez bien? / Est-ce que vous vous entendiez bien?
6. Où est-ce que tes parents travaillent? / Où est-ce que tes parents travaillaient?
7. Est-ce que tu regardes les dessins animés le samedi? / Est-ce que tu regardais les dessins animés le samedi?
8. Qu'est-ce que tu aimes à la télé? / Qu'est-ce que tu aimais à la télé?

Maintenant, posez les deux questions ci-dessus (*above*) à un(e) camarade de classe. Ajoutez **maintenant** à la première question et **quand tu étais petit(e)** à la deuxième.

EXEMPLE **— Tu habites dans un appartement maintenant?**
— Oui, j'habite dans un appartement.
— Tu habitais dans un appartement quand tu étais petit(e)?
— Non, j'habitais dans une maison.

B. **La jeunesse.** Interviewez un(e) camarade de classe pour savoir ce qu'il/elle faisait quand il/elle était au lycée (*high school*). Après, dites à la classe les choses que votre camarade faisait ou ne faisait pas au lycée.

EXEMPLE fumer → **— Fumais-tu quand tu étais au lycée?**
— Non, je ne fumais pas.
APRÈS, À LA CLASSE: **Roger ne fumait pas. Il travaillait...**

être heureux (heureuse)
aller toujours en cours
s'amuser beaucoup **AVOIR BEAUCOUP D'AMIS**
jouer du piano faire du sport ***s'ennuyer***
perdre souvent patience avec ses parents
jouer de la musique *apprendre facilement*
??? *???*

C. **Et le prof?** Avec un(e) camarade de classe, préparez six questions pour votre professeur. Demandez ce qu'il/elle faisait quand il/elle était à l'université.

EXEMPLE — **Quand vous étiez étudiant(e), où habitiez-vous?**

???	*étudier*	**habiter**	AIMER	plaire
FALLOIR	**AVOIR**	**fumer**	*danser*	sortir
???	*faire*	ALLER		**être**
pouvoir	*vouloir*	jouer		**???**

D. **Ils jouaient.** Divisez la classe en groupes. Chaque groupe choisit la catégorie du groupe suivant. Si les membres du deuxième groupe peuvent nommer quelqu'un pour cette catégorie, ils reçoivent un point. Sinon, les membres du groupe qui a choisi la catégorie doivent le faire et ils reçoivent un point s'ils y réussissent (*are successful*). Autrement (*Otherwise*), ils perdent deux points.

EXEMPLE GROUPE 1: **Quelqu'un Qui jouait de la trompette pendant les années soixante.**
GROUPE 2: **Herb Alpert jouait de la trompette pendant les années soixante.**

	GENRE DE MUSIQUE (le rock, le jazz...)	INSTRUMENT (la guitare, la batterie...)	SPORT (le tennis, le football...)
LES ANNÉES 60			
LES ANNÉES 70			
LES ANNÉES 80			

E. **Au passé.** Demandez à votre partenaire ce qu'il/elle faisait en général aux moments décrits.

EXEMPLE pour son anniversaire quand il/elle était petit(e)
— Que faisais-tu pour ton anniversaire quand tu étais petit(e)?
— J'invitais des amis chez moi et nous jouions et nous mangions.

1. pendant les étés quand il/elle était petit(e) et quand il/elle était au lycée
2. pour les vacances quand il/elle était petit(e)
3. le week-end quand il/elle avait dix ans et quand il/elle était au lycée
4. quand il/elle restait à la maison et n'allait pas à l'école
5. quand il faisait mauvais quand il/elle était petit(e)

F. **Autrefois.** Imaginez que c'est l'an 2022 et votre fils/fille vous demande comment ça se passait quand vous étiez à l'université. Avec un(e) partenaire, imaginez les questions de votre fils/fille et vos réponses. Préparez une conversation.

G. **Vacances en Bretagne.** Patricia et ses amis passaient souvent les vacances en Bretagne quand ils étaient jeunes. Regardez les descriptions des endroits qu'ils visitaient et décrivez au moins quatre choses qu'ils faisaient probablement en vacances.

EXEMPLE Chaque année, Marie-Claude et Louise...
Chaque année, Marie-Claude et Louise allaient à la ferme camping du Vieux-Chêne. Elles nageaient, elles jouaient au tennis...

La Ferme Camping du Vieux-Chêne ★★★★ ①

Baguer-Pican - 35120 DOL-DE-BRETAGNE - Tél. 99.48.09.55

■ En pleine campagne à 7 km de la mer, à égale distance du Mont-Saint-Michel, Saint-Malo, Dinard, la ferme camping du Vieux-Chêne offre le charme de la vie champêtre dans un cadre verdoyant avec de vastes plans d'eau qui font le bonheur des pêcheurs. Il est possible de se ravitailler en produits à la ferme. Vivez vos vacances au naturel!
Ouverture: Pâques et du 1er mai au 30 septembre.

1. Au printemps, Patricia...

Camping du Port de Plaisance ★★★ ⑬

29118 BÉNODET - Tél. 98.57.02.38

■ Situé à l'entrée de Bénodet, station balnéaire renommée pour son port de plaisance, ses plages exposées sud-ouest, ses écoles de voile, tennis, casino, night clubs, etc.
Ce camping familial, tranquille, vous propose, dans un cadre verdoyant, fleuri, de 4 hectares, toutes les commodités garantissant d'agréables vacances.
À proximité: golf de l'Odet à 5 minutes et un mini-golf à 100 mètres.
Ouverture: du 15 avril au 30 septembre.

2. Henri et sa famille...

Remarquez que...

Vous vous êtes peut-être demandé pourquoi il y a tant de similarité entre l'anglais et le français. Leurs similarités sont dues en partie à un événement historique important.

En 1066, un duc normand nommé Guillaume a attaqué l'Angleterre et après sa victoire s'est nommé roi (*king*) d'Angleterre. (On l'appelait ensuite Guillaume le Conquérant.) Jusqu'en 1204, la Normandie ne faisait pas partie de la France mais de l'Angleterre et c'étaient les Normands (et non pas les Anglo-Saxons, habitants d'Angleterre à cette époque-là) qui contrôlaient le pays. Ces 136 ans de contrôle normand ont beaucoup changé la langue anglaise.

L'origine des mots. Comme les conquérants normands ont surtout remplacé la haute classe sociale, ce sont les mots associés avec cette classe qui ont été influencés le plus par le français. Lisez les mots anglais suivants et devinez s'ils viennent plutôt de l'ancien français ou de l'ancien anglais.

Une maison normande

manor	*estate*	*to dine*	*pork*	*mutton*
house	*field*	*to eat*	*pig*	*sheep*

C'est à lire!

Vous levez-vous facilement? Comment est-ce que vous passez votre matinée? La revue *Vogue Hommes* a interviewé dix Français de professions diverses au sujet de leur journée. Vous allez lire trois des interviews. Avant de commencer, faites l'exercice suivant.

Familles de mots. Servez-vous des mots connus dans la liste de gauche pour deviner le sens des mots en caractères gras dans les phrases de droite.

penser	Cette phrase résume bien ma **pensée**.
s'endormir	Je me réveille tôt mais j'aime **me rendormir** quelques minutes.
avoir sommeil	De combien d'heures de **sommeil** est-ce que vous avez besoin?
se réveiller	L'heure du **réveil** chez nous est entre sept et huit heures.
une discussion	Je passe trois heures au téléphone à **discuter** avec des amis.
rêver	Quand je suis d'humeur **rêveuse**, j'aime prendre un bain chaud.
la banque	Mon ami est **banquier**. Il travaille dans une banque en ville.
un homme d'affaires	J'aime bien les **petits déjeuners d'affaires**.

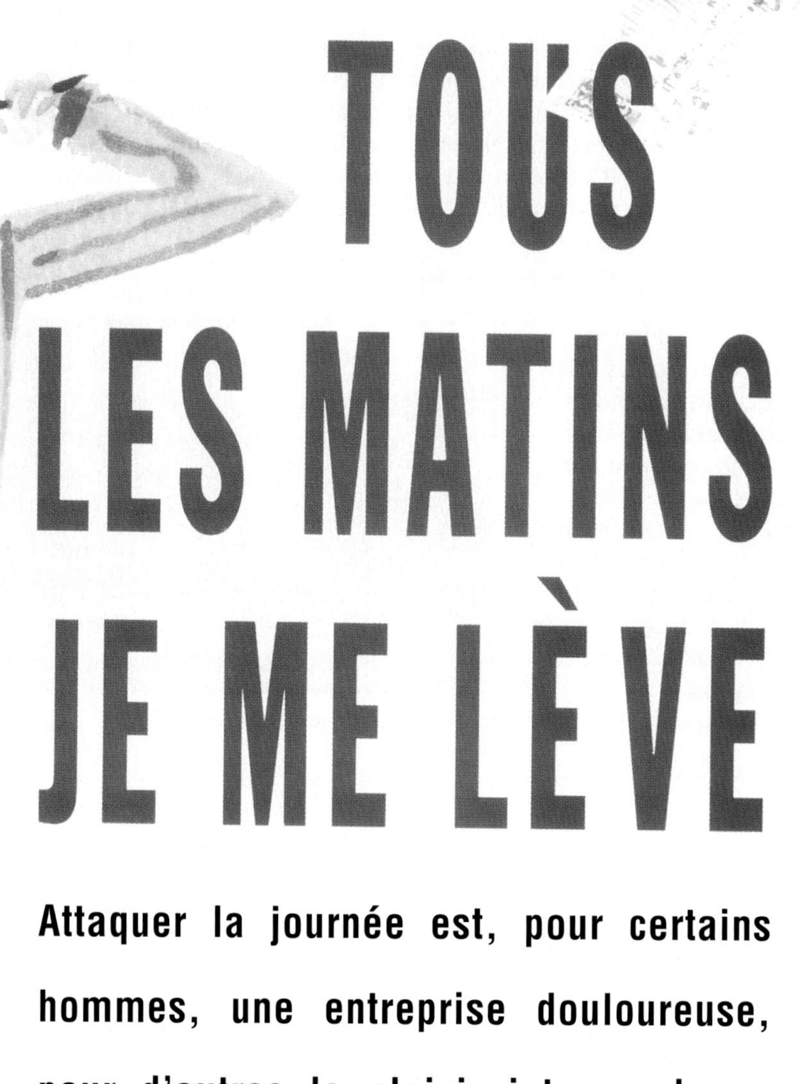

TOUS LES MATINS JE ME LÈVE

Attaquer la journée est, pour certains hommes, une entreprise douloureuse, pour d'autres le plaisir intense de se sentir chaque matin bien vivant. Trois d'entre eux racontent leur réveil. Bonjour les habitudes !

NICOLAS SARKOZY

Profession: député-maire de Neuilly-sur-Seine. **Prêt** en trente-cinq minutes.

Heure du réveil? Entre 6h30 et 6h45. J'adore me lever tôt parce que j'ai l'impression de gagner du temps dans la journée.

Nombre d'heures de sommeil? Sept heures.

Quelle est la première chose que vous faites en vous levant? Je vais dans ma salle de bains.

La radio? J'adore écouter la radio et **zapper**, je passe d'Europe 1 à RTL ou France Inter.

Le petit déjeuner? Jamais de petit déjeuner à la maison. Je suis un adepte des petits déjeuners d'affaires dans les grands hôtels, mon préféré est le Georges-V, ou dans les restaurants. J'aime **traîner** le matin dans les grands hôtels parisiens. Et puis un petit déjeuner, c'est mieux qu'un déjeuner, parce qu'en une heure on a généralement terminé. J'ai beaucoup d'appétit. J'**avale** une omelette au fromage et je bois du thé.

Vêtements? Je choisis mes vêtements en fonction de mes activités du jour. On ne s'habille pas de la même manière pour une cérémonie ou pour présider un match de football.

Comment vous rendez-vous à votre travail? De préférence à pied, **puisque** la mairie n'est qu'à dix minutes de mon domicile. Si je vais à un rendez-vous, c'est le chauffeur qui me **conduit**. J'écoute **volontiers** la radio, mais je suis incapable de lire en voiture.

ALAIN DE POUZHILAC

Profession: directeur d'EURO RSCG. Prêt en une heure et demie.

Heure du réveil? 6h45, et je passe trois quarts d'heure dans ma salle de bains. Je suis une véritable «**cocotte**». Deux fois par semaine, je me lève à 5h pour prendre l'avion.

Nombre d'heures de sommeil? Entre six et sept heures par nuit. Malheureusement je me réveille, je **réfléchis**, j'**angoisse**, je rêve et je finis par me rendormir.

Le petit déjeuner? Tous les matins, j'ai un petit déjeuner d'affaires avec mes collaborateurs ou des clients. Je ne mange pas, je prends juste un café. Nous nous retrouvons souvent à l'hôtel Bristol. J'adore cet endroit parce que je peux m'y rendre à pied, le salon et le jardin sont très agréables. Sinon, nous les organisons directement au bureau.

Bain ou douche? Si j'ai l'**humeur** dynamique, je prends une douche; si elle est plutôt rêveuse, c'est un bain assez chaud.

Vêtements? Jacques Séguéla a l'habitude de dire à mon sujet que je m'habille comme «un banquier de province». Mais, en vérité, je choisis mes vêtements selon mon instinct du matin, la couleur du temps et mon humeur.

Comment vous rendez-vous à votre travail? Tous les matins, un chauffeur vient me chercher en voiture de fonction équipée d'un téléphone que je n'utilise jamais.

Le moment préféré? Celui où je me réveille, où je découvre que je suis en vie, avec **des tas de** projets à **réaliser**; mais j'apprécie beaucoup le petit déjeuner en famille. Je n'aime pas la solitude, j'adore m'amuser et **rire**.

JEAN-PAUL DUBOIS

Profession: écrivain, auteur de *Tous les matins je me lève*—écrit pour ***le Nouvel Observateur***.

Heure du réveil? Comme je travaille chez moi la nuit, je n'ai pas vraiment d'heure. Cela peut être très tôt comme très tard. D'une manière générale, je suis quelqu'un qui n'aime pas dormir. Le matin, j'ai l'impression d'avoir devant moi un **tapis** qui **se déroule** lentement avec de bons et de mauvais moments.

Nombre d'heures de sommeil? Je dors quand j'ai sommeil et je me réveille quand je suis bien.

De quelle manière vous réveillez-vous et de quelle humeur? J'attends un moment dans mon lit, j'écoute s'il pleut. Je ne pense strictement à rien. Je suis plutôt angoissé le matin et toujours très **étonné** d'être encore en vie. Pour moi, le matin c'est un peu comme *Le Désert des tartares*, j'attends. Le matin, on n'est jamais que ce que l'on est le reste de la journée. D'ailleurs Cioran résume bien ma pensée: «Si l'on avait une perception infaillible de ce qu'on est, on **aurait** juste le courage de se coucher, mais certainement pas celui de se lever.» Je dois pourtant **avouer** que je **vis à l'écart des** rythmes sociaux.

Toilette? Rasoir électrique tous les trois jours; je n'utilise aucun produit de beauté.

Vêtements? Tous les matins, j'**enfile hâtivement** un jean, un tee-shirt, un pull ou une chemise selon le temps. Je ne me préoccupe pas beaucoup de mon aspect extérieur.

Téléphone? Je passe environ trois heures tous les matins au téléphone à discuter avec un ami.

---

prêt(e) *ready* **zapper** *to switch back and forth* **traîner** *to hang around* **avaler** *to swallow (eat quickly)* **puisque** = **parce que** **conduire** *to drive* **volontiers** *gladly* **cocotte** *primper* **réfléchir** *to think* **angoisser** *to agonize* **l'humeur** *(f) mood* **des tas de** *lots of* **réaliser** *to carry out* **rire** *to laugh* **le Nouvel Observateur** *a French newsmagazine* **un tapis** *a carpet* **se dérouler** *to unroll* **étonné(e)** *surprised* **aurait** *would have* **avouer** *to admit* **vivre à l'écart de** *to live apart from* **enfiler** *to slip on* **hâtivement** *hastily*

Avez-vous compris?

A. **Qui est-ce?** Lisez l'article et décidez si Nicolas Sarkozy, Alain de Pouzhilac ou Jean-Paul Dubois dirait les choses suivantes.

1. Je me lève quand ça me plaît.
2. Je dois voyager pour mon travail.
3. J'habite à dix minutes de mon bureau.
4. Je travaille à la maison.
5. Je mets un jean et un tee-shirt le matin.
6. Au petit déjeuner, je prends juste un café.

B. **Et vous?** Imaginez qu'on vous interviewe pour le même article. Répondez aux questions suivantes.

1. Quelle est votre profession? Comment vous rendez-vous au travail ou en classe?
2. À quelle heure vous réveillez-vous? Combien d'heures dormez-vous? De combien d'heures de sommeil avez-vous besoin? Quelle est la première chose que vous faites en vous levant? Écoutez-vous la radio ou regardez-vous la télé?
3. Où prenez-vous le petit déjeuner? Que mangez-vous? Buvez-vous du café?
4. Préférez-vous prendre un bain ou une douche? Quels vêtements mettez-vous?

Ça y est! C'est à vous!

A. **Organisez-vous.** Vous allez écrire une petite annonce (*personal ad*). Souvent, il est plus difficile d'écrire dans un style abrégé (*abbreviated*) que d'écrire un long paragraphe. Pour écrire un court message clairement, il faut s'organiser et le réviser. D'abord, organisez-vous en écrivant un bref profil de vous-même. Servez-vous du profil de Marie-Laure Augry, journaliste à la télévision française, comme modèle.

Nom: *AUGRY*

Prénom: *Marie-Laure*

Âge: *40 ans*

Profession: *Journaliste*

Animal Favori: *Mon chat Armand*

DÉTENTE: *Le lit et l'herbe verte*
MUSIQUE: *Le Rock and Roll*
LIVRE DE CHEVET: Une chaîne sur les bras *(Hervé Bourges)*
SPORTS: *Tennis, Rugby, Cyclisme*
PLAISIRS DE LA TABLE: *Tous, sauf les yaourts et les huîtres*
VACANCES: *À Fondettes (en Touraine)*
LOISIRS: *Le tennis et la chaise longue*
AIME: *La bonne cuisine*
DÉTESTE: *L'intolérance*

B. **Rédaction: Une annonce.** Vous avez décidé de mettre une petite annonce dans le journal. D'abord, lisez les annonces de *Rouen Poche* à la page suivante. Ensuite, utilisez votre autoportrait de l'exercice précédent pour écrire votre propre annonce.

C. **Évasion club.** Une manière de chercher l'homme ou la femme de vos rêves dans des agences comme l'Évasion club est d'échanger des cassettes avec des petits autoportraits. Écoutez les quatre portraits et décidez si chacun devrait (*should*) répondre à l'annonce 419, 420, 422, 423, 455 ou 456.

D. **Votre propre cassette.** En utilisant ce que vous avez préparé dans l'exercice ***A. Organisez-vous*** et ***B. Rédaction: Une annonce***, préparez l'autoportrait que vous allez enregistrer (*record*) sur cassette.

E. **La première rencontre.** Vous venez de répondre à une annonce personnelle. Imaginez votre première rencontre. Préparez la scène avec un(e) autre étudiant(e). Dans la conversation, parlez des choses suivantes.
- votre travail ou vos études
- vos loisirs préférés
- comment se passe une journée typique de votre vie

F. **Questions indiscrètes.** Après votre premier rendez-vous avec quelqu'un que vous avez rencontré grâce à une petite annonce, un(e) de vos ami(e)s veut tout savoir. Avec un(e) camarade de classe, faites une liste de questions. Vous pouvez poser des questions indiscrètes, si vous voulez.

se reconnaître tout de suite
où se retrouver ???
s'embrasser ???
S'AMUSER **???**

RENCONTRES

ÉVASION CLUB

RENCONTRES SÉLECTIONNÉES
HOMMES—FEMMES—COUPLES
CONTACTS IMMÉDIATS DE QUALITÉ. TÉL: 35.73.52.18
Discrétion assurée

419
Homme, la trentaine, seul, recherche femme, sympa, câline, pour passer moments agréables. Écrire au journal qui transmettra.

420
Dame, souhaite rencontrer monsieur, 60, 65 ans pour sorties et voyages. Écrire au journal qui transmettra.

422
Homme, 36 ans, sensible au charme et à l'humour, recherche femme sportive, jolie et dotée d'un heureux caractère. Écrire au journal qui transmettra.

423
Robert, 27 ans, ambitieux et sentimental, souhaite rencontrer blonde, 25, 30 ans pour sorties + si affinités. Écrire au journal qui transmettra.

455
Cadre, 45 ans, grand, mince, souhaite rencontrer femme distinguée, vive, sensuelle, peu attachée aux valeurs matérielles, pour partager loisirs, et vivre une relation tendre et sincère. Écrire au journal qui transmettra.

456
Si vous désirez partir avec moi en Espagne du 25 août au 30 septembre, prenez dès maintenant contact avec moi. Écrire au journal qui transmettra.

BIENVENUE DANS LA RONDE

23, RUE SAINT-ÉTIENNE DES TONNELIERS 76000 ROUEN

UNE FORMULE CHOC POUR VOUS QUI ÊTES SEULS OU NOUVEAUX DANS LA RÉGION DÎNERS DANSANTS, SORTIES EN GROUPE AU CINÉMA, JEUX DE SOCIÉTÉ, ETC... RENSEIGNEZ-VOUS.

☎ 35 36 04 95 ou 35 88 79 77

Personnes mariées, s'abstenir.

Après avoir fait les exercices suivants, vérifiez vos réponses dans l'*Appendix C*.

Describing your daily life and activities

A. **Les enfants sages.** Servez-vous d'un verbe choisi de la liste de vocabulaire pour former cinq phrases qui décrivent ce que les enfants sages font ou ce qu'ils ne font pas.

EXEMPLES **Les enfants sages se lavent les mains avant de manger.**
Les enfants sages ne se disputent pas.

B. **Un examen important.** Votre camarade de chambre a un examen important demain. Dites-lui de faire ou de ne pas faire les choses suivantes: **se coucher tôt, se calmer, s'endormir pendant l'examen, se dépêcher pendant l'examen.**

EXEMPLE se coucher tôt → **Couche-toi tôt.**

C. **Demain.** Utilisez des verbes de la liste de vocabulaire pour écrire six phrases qui décrivent ce que vous allez faire demain.

D. **Hier.** Rose parle à Henri de ce que chacun a fait hier. Indiquez l'ordre le plus logique.

EXEMPLE Mamie et moi... se promener / se lever tôt
Mamie et moi, nous nous sommes levées tôt et nous nous sommes promenées.

1. André... se lever vers quatre heures / se reposer pendant l'après-midi
2. André et Mamie... se retrouver en ville / s'embrasser
3. Moi, je... s'endormir tout de suite / se coucher

Talking about relationships

E. **Un bon rapport.** Dites si votre petit(e) ami(e) et vous faites souvent les choses suivantes quand vous vous entendez parfaitement: **s'embrasser, se disputer, se téléphoner.**

F. **En classe.** Dites si vos camarades de classe et vous avez fait les choses suivantes pendant le dernier cours: **se disputer, s'embrasser, s'amuser, se parler, se voir, s'ennuyer.**

Telling how life used to be

G. **À cette époque-là.** Complétez la première phrase pour parler de votre vie maintenant. Ensuite, complétez la seconde phrase pour parler de votre vie quand vous aviez dix ans.

EXEMPLE Maintenant, j'habite **à Denver.**
Quand j'avais dix ans, **j'habitais à Miami.**

1. Maintenant, chez moi, il y a... Quand j'avais dix ans...
2. Maintenant, la musique que je préfère, c'est... Quand j'avais dix ans...
3. Maintenant, je sais... très bien. Quand j'avais dix ans...
4. Maintenant, ma famille habite... Quand j'avais dix ans...
5. Maintenant, le samedi soir, mes amis et moi aimons... Quand j'avais dix ans...
6. Maintenant, je joue... Quand j'avais dix ans...

Vocabulaire

Describing your daily life and activities

NOMS
un bain
les cheveux (*m*)
les dents (*f*)
une douche
la figure
les mains (*f*)
les tâches domestiques (*f*)
la vie

VERBES
s'amuser (à faire)
s'appeler
se brosser
se calmer
se coucher
se dépêcher (de faire)
deviner
s'endormir
s'ennuyer (de faire)
s'habiller
s'intéresser à
se laver
se lever
s'occuper de
se passer
se promener
se rendre (à/chez)
se reposer
se réveiller
se sentir
se souvenir (de)

DIVERS
avec difficulté
enfin
facilement
pendant que
pressé(e)
quotidien(ne)
tout à fait
vite

Talking about relationships

NOMS
l'amour (*m*)
une annonce
un avis
un bal
un conseil
le coup de foudre
un couple
un ménage
une MST
une naissance
un préservatif
le SIDA
un sondage
la vie

VERBES
s'accorder
s'aimer
croire
se détester
deviner
se disputer (avec)
divorcer
s'embrasser
s'entendre (bien, mal)
espérer
essayer (de faire)
se marier (avec)
se parler
se quitter
se reconnaître
se regarder
remettre en cause
se rencontrer
se retrouver
se téléphoner

DIVERS
Ça peut arriver!
compris(e)
hors mariage
la plupart de
par hasard
sexuel(le)

Telling how life used to be

INSTRUMENTS DE MUSIQUE
la batterie
le clavier
la guitare
le piano
le saxophone
la trompette

AUTRES NOMS
la guerre
la jeunesse
un talent

VERBES
chanter
enseigner
jouer à (+ *sport ou jeu*)
jouer de (+ *musique, instrument de musique*)

EXPRESSIONS TEMPORELLES
à cette époque-là
autrefois
chaque lundi / été...
de temps en temps
d'habitude
fréquemment
tous les jours / les étés...

DIVERS
autrement
dehors
depuis
donc
envers
insupportable
malheureux / malheureuse
ne... aucun(e)
nul(le)
pourtant
sage

La tapisserie de la reine Mathilde
11th century
Bayeux, Musée de la Tapisserie
Erich Lessing/Art Resource

Called the "Bayeux Tapestry" in English (after the town of Bayeux in Normandy), this seventy-foot embroidered linen cloth depicts the Norman conquest of England in fifty-eight scenes.

Chapitre 10 La bonne cuisine

By the end of this chapter, you should be able to do the following in French:

- Order at a restaurant
- Say how much you need at the market
- Choose what to eat and drink
- Narrate what happened in the past

Les affiches à Trouville
Raoul Dufy (1877–1953)
1906
Paris, Musée National d'Art Moderne

Born in Le Havre, Dufy frequently painted scenes of the Norman coast, including regattas and seascapes, and the resort towns of Trouville, Deauville, and Honfleur.

Pour commencer

TEXTBOOK TAPE

En France, le petit déjeuner est un repas **léger**. On prend...

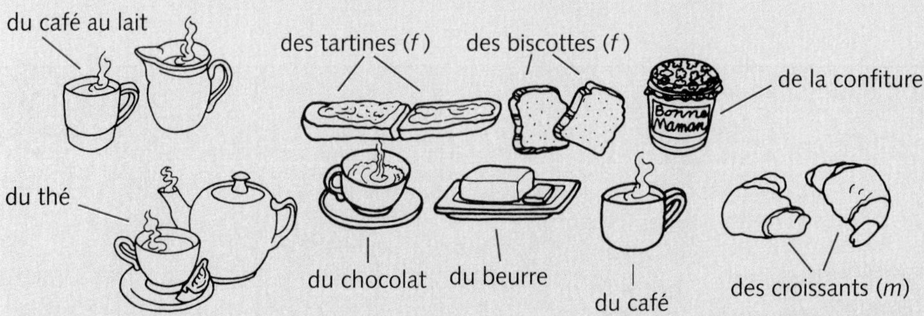

De plus en plus de Français, surtout les jeunes, mangent aussi des céréales le matin, mais ils ne prennent pas de petit déjeuner **copieux** comme les Américains et les Canadiens qui préfèrent prendre...

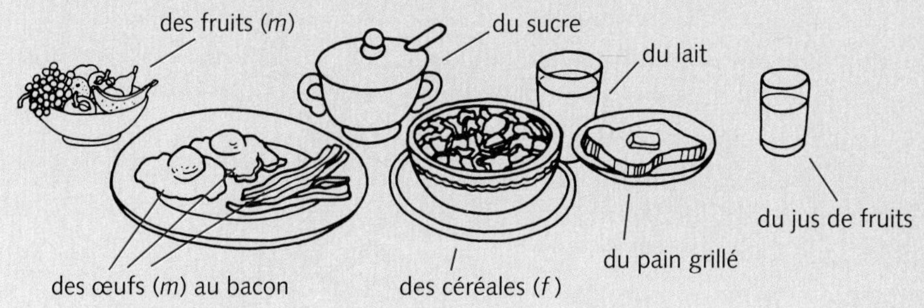

À midi, **certains** prennent un repas rapide dans les nombreux restaurants fast-food, les self-services et les cafés où on peut prendre...

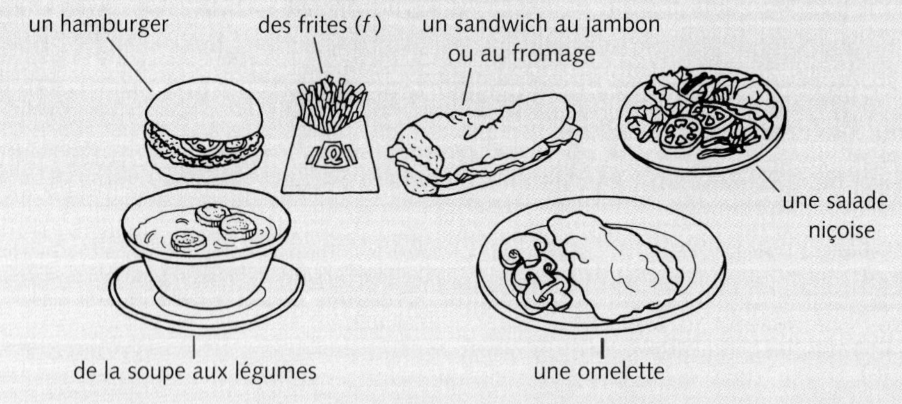

léger(-ère) *light* **copieux(-euse)** *copious, large* **certains** *some*

Beaucoup de Français préfèrent un repas traditionnel.

On commence par une entrée (un hors-d'œuvre):

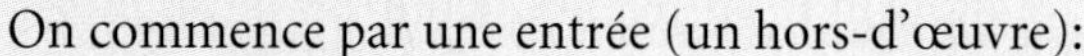

Après, on sert le plat principal:

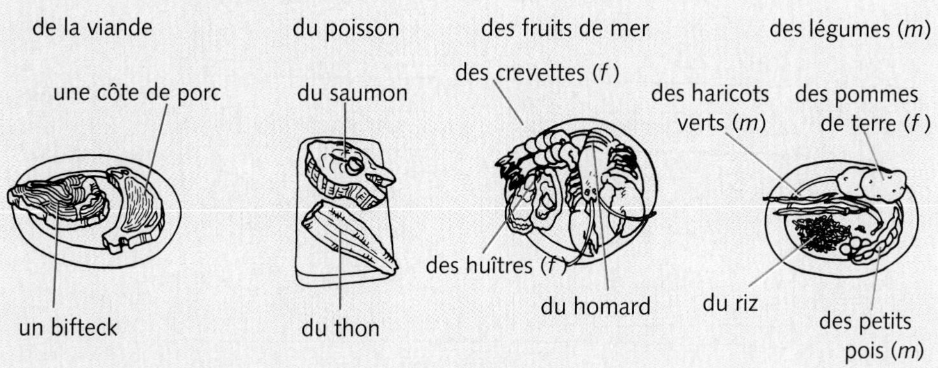

On finit le repas avec...

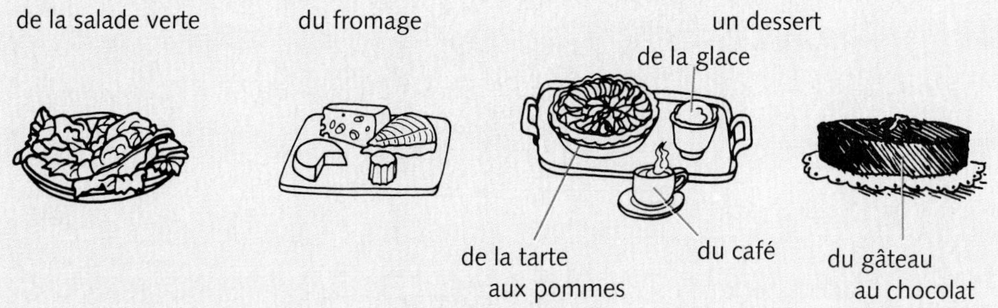

Avec le repas, on prend aussi des boissons et du pain.

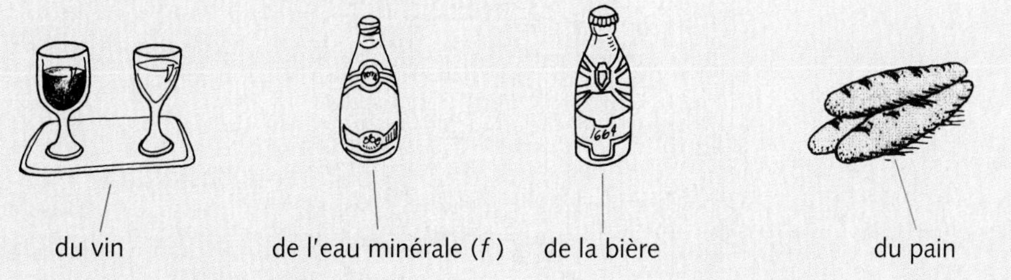

Quelquefois, on prend aussi...

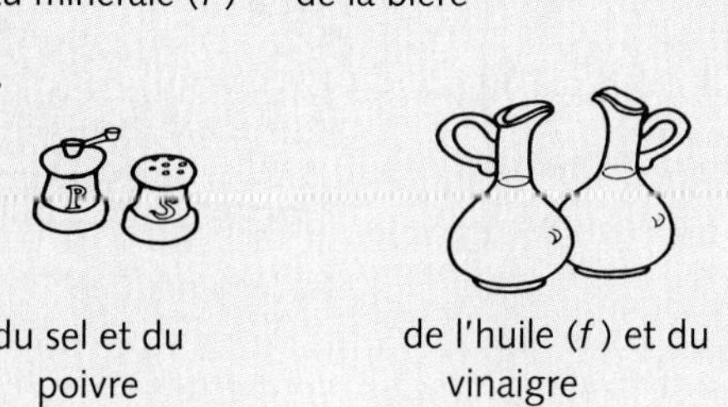

SUPPLEMENTAL VOCABULARY

du rôti de porc *pork roast*
de la dinde *turkey meat*
une brioche
un chausson aux pommes *an apple turnover*
un éclair
un mille-feuille
un napoléon

En France, la façon de **faire les courses** a aussi changé. De plus en plus de Français font les courses dans un supermarché où on vend de tout. Certains préfèrent aller chez les petits **commerçants** du quartier où le service est plus personnel.

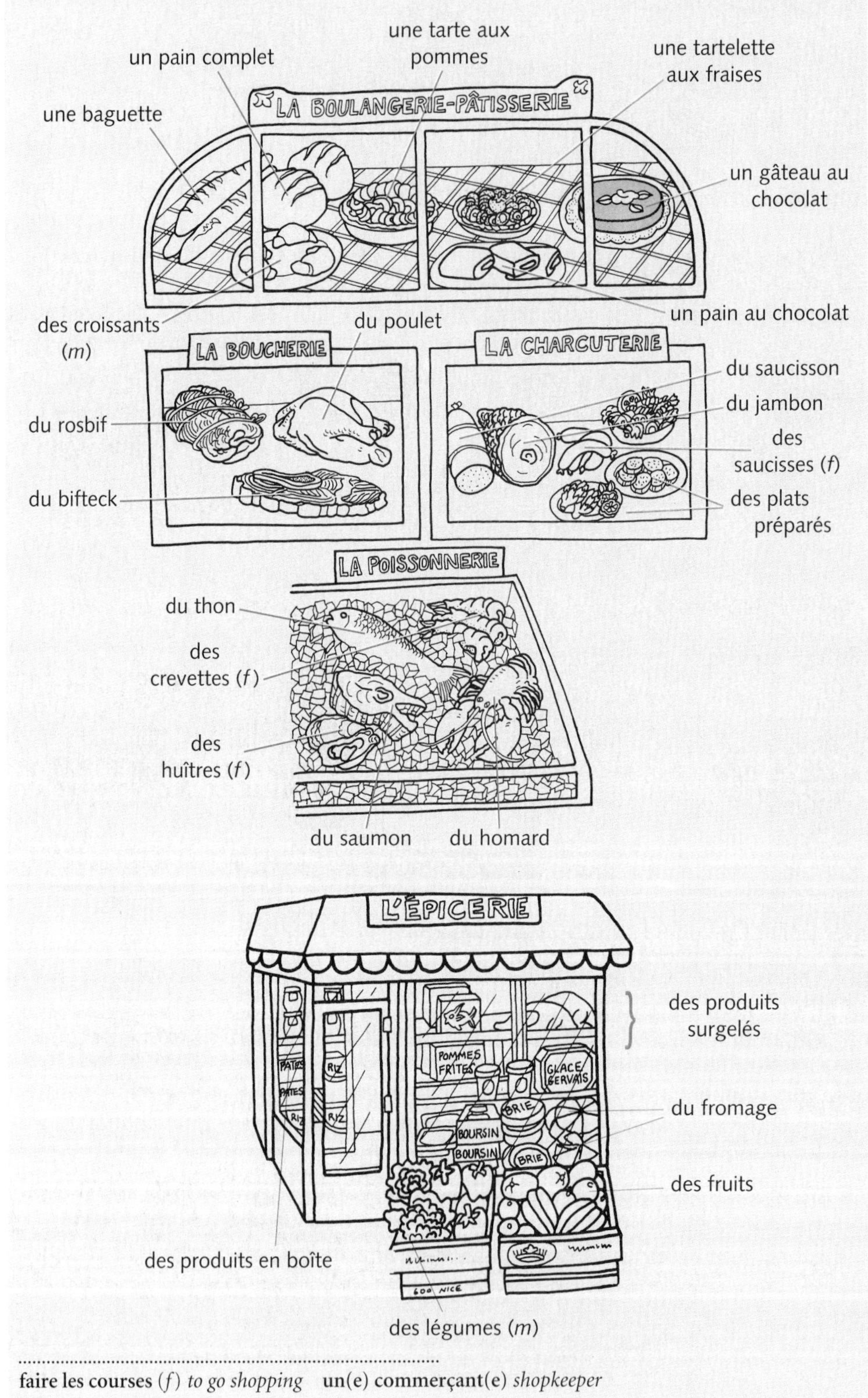

faire les courses (*f*) *to go shopping* **un(e) commerçant(e)** *shopkeeper*

André a invité Rosalie au restaurant Maraîchers. Avant d'écouter leur conversation, regardez la carte à la page suivante.

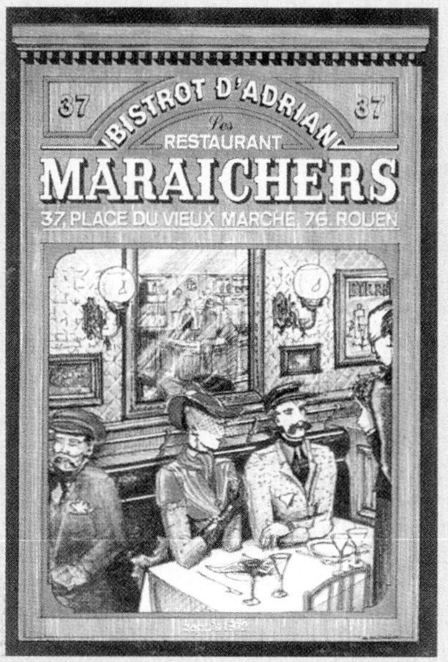

LE GARÇON: Bonsoir, monsieur. Bonsoir, madame. Une table pour deux?
ANDRÉ: Oui, s'il vous plaît.
LE GARÇON: Préférez-vous la terrasse ou l'intérieur?
ROSALIE: La terrasse.
LE GARÇON: Alors, c'est par ici.

André et Rosalie **s'asseyent** et le garçon leur apporte le menu. Quelques minutes après, il revient.

LE GARÇON: Aimeriez-vous **un apéritif** avant de **commander**?
ANDRÉ: Rosalie?
ROSALIE: Non, merci, pas ce soir.
ANDRÉ: Pour moi non plus.
LE GARÇON: Et pour dîner? Est-ce que vous avez décidé?
ANDRÉ: Nous allons prendre le menu à 135 francs.
LE GARÇON: Très bien, monsieur. Et qu'est-ce que vous désirez **comme** entrée?
ROSALIE: Moi, je vais prendre le saumon fumé.
LE GARÇON: Très bien. Et pour monsieur?
ANDRÉ: Les huîtres, s'il vous plaît.
LE GARÇON: Et comme plat principal?
ROSALIE: **La raie** pour moi, s'il vous plaît.
ANDRÉ: Et pour moi, le filet **de canard**.
LE GARÇON: Bien, monsieur. Et comme boisson?
ANDRÉ: Une carafe de vin rouge et une bouteille d'eau minérale.
LE GARÇON: De l'Évian ou de la Vittel?
ROSALIE: De la Vittel, s'il vous plaît.
LE GARÇON: Très bien, madame.

s'asseoir *to sit (down)* **un apéritif** *a before-dinner drink* **commander** *to order* **comme** *for, as* **la raie** *skate* **le canard** *duck*

37 BISTROT D'ADRIAN 37

RESTAURANT

MARAICHERS

Servis Jusqu'à 23 H.

Le Bistrot - 87 F.

Service 15% Compris

Adrian vous propose son petit Menu Bistrot composé uniquement de produits frais de saison

Première Assiette

9 Huîtres "Fines de claires no3" Sur lit de glace
Assiette de Coquillages farcis à l'ail
Cocotte de moules marinières
Salade aux lardons, Oeuf poché
Terrine de canard maison, au poivre vert
Plateau de fruits de mer "l'écailler" +50 Frs

Deuxième Assiette

Brochette de poissons, beurre blanc
Moules de pays, frites
Sardines grillées aux herbes
Langue de boeuf, sauce piquante
Poêlée de Rognon de bœuf, flambée au cognac
Bavette Poêlée à la fondue d'oignons

Troisième Assiette

Crème Caramel
fraises au vin ou fraises au sucre
feuillantine aux pommes
Glace et sorbet artisanaux
île flottante
Coupe normande

Les Maraîchers - 135 F.

Service 15% Compris

Les plus beaux produits du Terroir sélectionnés et cuisinés dans la grande tradition des Maraîchers

Première Assiette

12 Huîtres "Fines de claires n°3" Sur lit de glace
Saumon fumé par nos soins, Toasts chauds
Poêlon de 12 Escargots de Bourgogne à l'ail
Beignets de langoustines, Sauce tartare
Salade de cervelle d'agneau poêlée
Plateau de fruits de mer "l'écailler" +50 Frs

Deuxième Assiette

Aile de Raie capucine
Daurade entière au lard fumé
Pavé de Saumon Rôti, beurre de moules
filet de Canard à la Rouennaise
Andouillette à la ficelle "du Père Tafournel"
Faux-filet grillé ou Sauce Poivre

Troisième Assiette

Salade de Saison, ou plateau de fromages

Quatrième Assiette

Tarte tatin chaude, crème fraîche
Bavarois ananas coco
Symphonie aux trois chocolats
feuillantine aux fraises ou fraises Melba
Glace et Sorbet artisanaux
Crème Brûlée

Arrivage Journalier de Poissons, d'Huîtres et de Fruits de Mer

depuis 1912

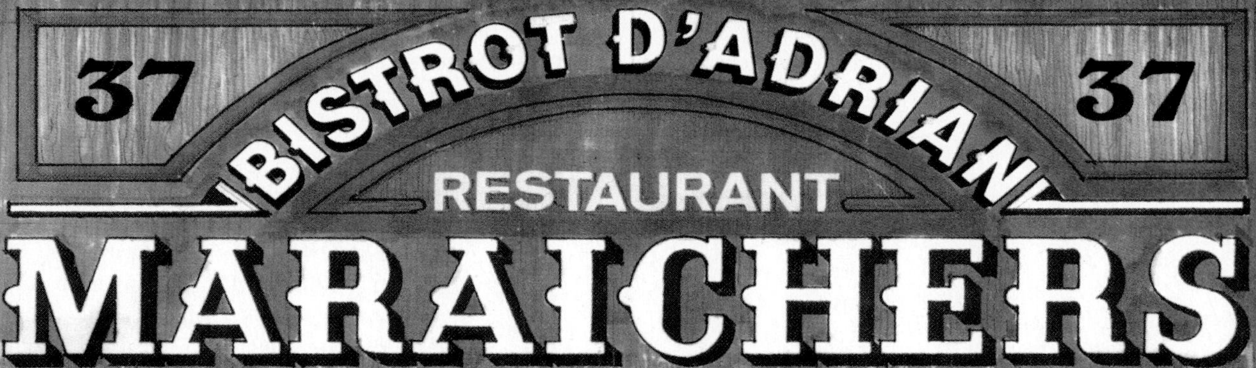

La Carte

Service 15% Compris

Servie Jusqu'à Minuit

Nos Huîtres et Fruits de Mer (Arrivage Journalier)

12 Huîtres "Fines de claires" Sur lit de glace n° 3 72 Frs n° 2 82 Frs
12 Huîtres "Spéciales St Vaast" Sur lit de glace n° 3 75 Frs n° 2 84 Frs
Plateau de fruits de mer "l'écailler" 95 Frs – "le marayeur" 160 Frs – "le Royal" 395 Frs 1 ou 2 personnes avec 1 Homard frais

Fraîcheur du Marché & Préparations Maison

Soupe de poissons maison, sa rouille et ses croûtons, 38 Frs – Assiette de coquillages farcis 38 Frs
Moules à la crème 45 Frs – Salade aux lardons, œuf poché 38 Frs – Terrine de canard maison au poivre 38 Frs
Salade de cervelle d'agneau poêlée 52 Frs – Beignets de langoustines, Sauce Tartare 65 Frs
Saumon fumé par nos soins toasts chauds 65 Frs – Poêlon de 12 Escargots de Bourgogne à l'ail 65 Frs

Poissons Frais d'Arrivage

– Brochette de poissons frais, beurre blanc 49 Frs – Moules de pays frites 49 Frs
– Sardines grillées aux herbes 49 Frs – Pavé de Saumon Rôti, Beurre de Moules 69 Frs
– Aile de Raie capucine 69 Frs – Daurade entière au lard fumé 69 Frs –
– Sole Meunière ou Sole Normande 120 Frs –

Traditionnels & Spécialités

Langue de Bœuf, sauce piquante 49 Frs – Tête de veau ravigote 49 Frs – Bavette poêlée à la fondue d'oignons 49 Frs – Poêlée de Rognon de bœuf flambée au cognac 49 Frs – Faux-filet Grillé ou Sauce Poivre 69 Frs – Filet de canard à la Rouennaise 69 Frs – Andouillette à la ficelle 69 Frs
Cœur de filet au Poivre flambé au calvados 95 Frs – Chateaubriand Grillé Beurre Persillé 92 Frs

Desserts

Plateau de Fromages 35 Frs

île flottante au caramel 25 Frs – Crème au Caramel 25 Frs – Baiser de vierge 30 Frs – Glace et Sorbet artisanaux 30 Frs – Fraises au vin ou sucrées 30 Frs – After eight 30 Frs – Coupe normande 30 Frs – Feuillantine aux Pommes 35 Frs – Tarte Tatin crème fraîche 35 Frs – Crème Brûlée 35 Frs – Bavarois ananas coco 35 Frs
Feuillantine aux fraises 38 Frs – Fraises Melba 38 Frs – Symphonie aux trois chocolats 42 Frs

depuis 1912

Savez-vous le faire?

A. **Aujourd'hui on sert...** Voilà ce qu'on sert aujourd'hui. Indiquez ce qu'il y a par catégorie.

EXEMPLE viande
Comme viande, il y a du rosbif, des côtes de porc...

1. viande
2. poisson
3. dessert
4. légume
5. boisson

du rosbif	**du café**
de la tarte	*du vin*
DES PETITS POIS	*de l'eau minérale*
du thé	**du thon**
des haricots verts	du jambon
du gâteau	**du saumon**
des côtes de porc	
des pommes de terre	

B. **Quel magasin?** Expliquez dans quel magasin on va pour acheter les produits dans l'exercice précédent.

EXEMPLE du rosbif → **On achète du rosbif à la boucherie.**

C. **Catégories logiques.** Cherchez le mot qui ne va pas logiquement avec les autres. Expliquez votre réponse.

EXEMPLE le thé, le jus de fruits, le sel, le lait, le vin
Le sel parce que ce n'est pas une boisson.

1. la tarte, les petits pois, les pommes de terre, les haricots verts
2. le gâteau au chocolat, le riz, la tarte aux pommes, les fruits, la glace
3. la salade de tomates, le pâté, la soupe à l'oignon, le rosbif
4. le déjeuner, le dîner, le petit déjeuner, la charcuterie
5. le homard, le rosbif, les crevettes, les huîtres

D. **On commande.** Regardez le menu à la page 358 et commandez un repas.

Que prenez-vous...
comme entrée? comme plat principal? comme dessert? comme boisson?

E. **Repas.** Voici ce que Rosalie a mangé au petit déjeuner et au dîner hier. Comparez votre petit déjeuner et votre dîner aux siens (*to hers*).

le petit déjeuner   le dîner

Remarquez que...

Pour commander dans un restaurant français, il est bon de savoir certaines choses. Par exemple, on peut commander «à la carte», ce qui permet de choisir les plats qu'on préfère, ou on peut choisir un menu «à prix fixe». Dans ce cas, on a un choix plus limité mais à un prix plus raisonnable.

Qu'est-ce que vous voulez? Regardez la carte à la page 358. Choisissez une entrée, un plat principal et un dessert et faites le total. Maintenant choisissez un plat de chaque catégorie du menu à 87 ou à 135 francs. Comparez le total. Lequel est le moins cher?

Selon la loi (*law*), les restaurants doivent afficher les menus et les prix à l'extérieur de l'établissement. Les clients peuvent donc lire les différents menus avant de choisir où dîner.

Comment s'y prendre?

Planning and predicting

Since no two cultures are identical, you may sometimes find yourself lacking the cultural knowledge to understand what you hear in French. For example, if the waiter asks **de l'Évian ou de la Vittel?**, you will not be able to answer unless you recognize that these are brand names of French mineral waters. In such situations, try to infer what is being asked from what has just been said. Also, when possible, prepare and predict from previous experiences what might be asked or said. (For example, before ordering mineral water, glance at the menu to see what kinds are sold.)

Savez-vous le faire?

A. **Pendant le repas.** Écoutez ces choses qu'on vous dirait (*would say*) au restaurant. Décidez si on vous dirait ces choses avant le repas ou à la fin du repas.

B. **Questions.** Faites une liste de cinq questions qu'un client pose souvent au garçon ou à la serveuse dans un restaurant.

Qu'est-ce qui se passe?

Au restaurant

Deux touristes se trouvent dans un restaurant français. Écoutez leur conversation et déterminez quelle sorte de soupe et quelle boisson ils choisissent.

Avez-vous compris?

A. **Que demandent-ils?** Écoutez encore une fois la conversation au restaurant et faites une liste de quatre questions que les deux clients ont posées à la serveuse.

B. **Qu'allez-vous choisir?** Avec un(e) camarade de classe, jouez une scène au restaurant entre un garçon / une serveuse et un(e) client(e). Jouez les deux rôles. Commandez une entrée, un plat principal, un légume, un dessert et une boisson.

Les fast-foods deviennent de plus en plus populaires en France.

Qu'est-ce qu'on dit?

Pour **remercier** André **de** l'avoir invitée au restaurant, Rosalie décide de l'inviter à diner chez elle. Elle va faire ses courses au marché parce que les produits y sont plus **frais**.

Au marché, elle trouve **un** bon **choix** de légumes et de fruits. Il y a...

SUPPLEMENTAL VOCABULARY

une aubergine *an eggplant*
du brocoli
du céleri
du chou *cabbage*
du chou-fleur *cauliflower*
un concombre *a cucumber*
une courgette *a zucchini*
des épinards (*m*) *spinach*
des abricots (*m*) *apricots*
un melon
une nectarine
un pamplemousse *a grapefruit*
des prunes (*f*) *plums*
des pruneaux (*m*) *prunes*

— Bonjour, monsieur.
— Bonjour, madame, vous désirez?
— Euh... voyons... un kilo de pommes de terre, **une livre** de tomates... Vous avez des haricots verts?
— Non, madame, pas aujourd'hui. Mais j'ai des petits pois. Regardez comme ils sont beaux.
— Non, merci, pas de petits pois aujourd'hui.
— Alors, qu'est-ce que je peux vous offrir d'autre?
— Donnez-moi aussi 300 grammes de cerises.
— Et voilà, 300 grammes. Et avec ça?
— C'est tout, merci. C'est combien?
— Voilà... Alors, un kilo de pommes de terre, 6F, une livre de tomates, 4F40 et 300 grammes de cerises, 7F50. Ça fait 17F90.
— Voici 20 francs.
— Et voici votre **monnaie**. Merci, madame.
— Merci. Au revoir, monsieur.

---

remercier (de) *to thank (for)* **frais (fraîche)** *fresh* **un choix** *a choice* **une livre** *a pound* **la monnaie** *change*

A. De quelle couleur? De quelle couleur sont ces fruits et légumes?

1. les pommes
2. les oranges
3. les cerises
4. les oignons
5. le raisin
6. les bananes
7. les citrons
8. les petits pois
9. les poires
10. les fraises
11. les carottes
12. les pommes de terre

B. Aimez-vous...? Demandez à un(e) camarade de classe ce qu'il/elle aime dans chaque catégorie.

EXEMPLE comme poisson → **— Qu'est-ce que tu aimes comme poisson?**
— J'aime le saumon. / Je n'aime pas le poisson.

1. comme entrée
2. comme viande
3. comme poisson
4. comme légume
5. comme fruit
6. comme dessert
7. comme boisson
8. comme fruits de mer

C. Ingrédients. De quoi a-t-on besoin pour préparer les plats indiqués?

EXEMPLE Rose va préparer un sandwich au jambon.
Elle a besoin de pain, de beurre et de jambon.

1. Rosalie va préparer une salade de fruits.
2. André va préparer un chocolat chaud, un thé et un café au lait.
3. Henri va préparer une salade verte.
4. Patricia va préparer un sandwich au fromage.
5. Rose va préparer une soupe aux légumes.

Voilà pourquoi!

SELF-CHECK

1. What word follows quantity expressions before nouns?
2. What pronoun do you use to replace a noun preceded by a partitive article, a number, or a quantity expression?

Les expressions de quantité

In French, words that tell or ask *how much* are followed by **de (d')** before a singular or a plural noun.

Combien de **cerises voulez-vous?** **Je voudrais *cent grammes de* cerises.**

Learn these quantity expressions. You already know some of them.

combien de
(un) peu de
assez de *enough*
beaucoup de
trop de *too much*
beaucoup trop de
une douzaine de *a dozen*
un kilo de
cent grammes de
un (demi-)litre de *a (half-)liter of*
une livre de *a pound of*
une tranche de *a slice of*
un morceau de *a piece of*
une cuillerée de *a spoonful of*
une (demi-)bouteille de *a (half-)bottle of*
une carafe de *a decanter of*
un verre de *a glass of*

Le pronom **en**

To avoid repetition, use the pronoun **en** to replace a noun preceded by a partitive article, by an expression of quantity, or by a number.

— **Tu veux** *du café*?
— **Non, merci, je n'***en* **veux pas. (Je ne veux pas** *de café.***)**

— **Vous voulez** *un kilo de cerises*?
— **Non, j'***en* **voudrais** *une livre*, **s'il vous plaît. (Je voudrais** *une livre de cerises*, **s'il vous plaît.)**

— **Tu as mangé** *une tartelette*?
— **Non, j'***en* **ai mangé** *deux*! **(J'ai mangé** *deux tartelettes.***)**

Et ça se prononce comment?

Le **h** aspiré

You have learned that **h** is never pronounced in French and that there usually is liaison and elision before it.

J'aime les herbes. **Il y a beaucoup** *d'***huile dans la salade.**

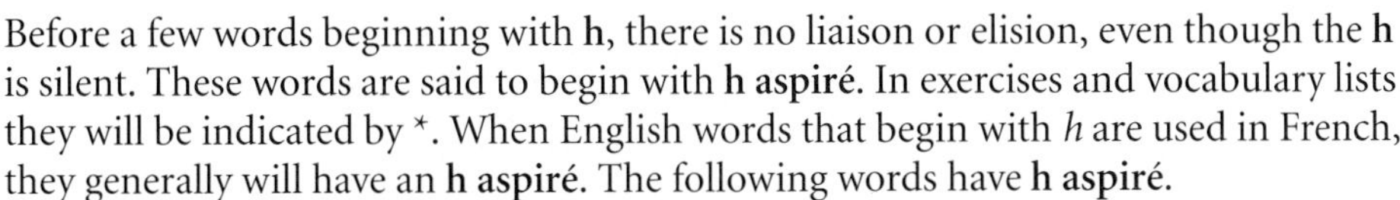

Before a few words beginning with **h**, there is no liaison or elision, even though the **h** is silent. These words are said to begin with **h aspiré**. In exercises and vocabulary lists they will be indicated by *. When English words that begin with *h* are used in French, they generally will have an **h aspiré**. The following words have **h aspiré**.

le homard **les haricots** **les hot-dogs**
les hors-d'œuvre **les hamburgers**

Je mange beaucoup *de* **hot-dogs.** **J'aime les hamburgers.**

Savez-vous le faire?

A. **Préférences.** Dites si vous aimez les choses suivantes. Ensuite, demandez à un(e) camarade de classe s'il/si elle en mange beaucoup. Faites attention au **h aspiré**.

EXEMPLE les *hot-dogs
— **J'aime les hot-dogs.**
Paul, est-ce que tu manges beaucoup de hot-dogs?
— **Oui, j'en mange beaucoup.** OU **Non, je n'en mange pas beaucoup.**

1. le *homard 2. les huîtres 3. les *hamburgers 4. les herbes

B. **Des recettes.** Voilà quelques recettes du livre de cuisine *La cuisine pour tous.* Indiquez ce qu'il faut pour faire ces plats.

EXEMPLE **Pour faire une compote d'abricots, il faut un kilo d'abricots...**

976. — *Compote d'abricots.*

Préparation: 10 mn. Cuisson: 10 mn.

1 kg d'abricots. 2 verres d'eau. 200 g de sucre.

Préparer un sirop au lissé avec le sucre et l'eau. Laver les abricots, les couper en deux, retirer les noyaux. Laisser bouillir 10 à 12 minutes dans le sirop. Dresser sur un compotier. Arroser avec le jus.

977. — *Compote d'abricots secs.*

Préparation: 24 h d'avance. Cuisson: 1 h.

300 g d'abricots. 125 g de sucre. 1/2 litre d'eau.

Laver, faire tremper les abricots 24 heures d'avance. Mettre cuire avec l'eau et le sucre pendant une heure, à feu assez doux.

1032. — *Pommes sur canapé.*

Préparation: 15 mn. Cuisson: 40 mn.

6 belles pommes. 125 g de beurre (on peut réduire à 75 g). 6 tranches de pain. 60 g de sucre en poudre. 1 pincée de vanille. 2 cuillerées d'eau.

Choisir de belles pommes si possible de même taille. Les éplucher, les vider soigneusement au vide-pommes, sans les briser. Couper le pain rassis en tranches minces que l'on beurre des 2 côtés. Garnir un plat à four avec le pain. Poser une pomme sur chaque tranche. Mettre au centre de chacune d'elles un petit morceau de beurre. Saupoudrer le tout de sucre et d'une pincée de vanille en poudre. Ajouter 2 cuillerées d'eau. Mettre à four doux pendant 40 minutes. Servir chaud dans le plat de cuisson.

292. — *Raie frite.*

Préparation: 10 mn. Cuisson: 25 mn.

1 kg de raie. 1/2 litre de marinade. 50 g de farine. 75 g de beurre. 1 citron.

Couper la raie en filets. Les faire macérer dans une marinade crue à l'huile. Les passer dans la farine. Faire fondre du beurre dans une poêle, y faire dorer les morceaux de poisson sur les deux faces (5 minutes de chaque côté), puis mettre la poêle au four et laisser cuire doucement pendant 1/4 d'heure. Servir avec citron.

★ Préparer la raie en petits filets, les faire macérer. Faire, d'autre part, une pâte à frire (1118). Y plonger les morceaux de raie et faire de petits beignets cuits dans l'huile bien chaude. Servir avec sauce tomate en saucière et garniture de persil et de citron.

C. C'est assez? Est-ce que la quantité indiquée dans chaque cas est suffisante?

EXEMPLE Vous déjeunez seul(e) le matin et il y a un verre de lait dans le réfrigérateur.
C'est assez. / Ce n'est pas assez. / C'est trop.

peu	beaucoup	TROP	trop peu	assez
	beaucoup trop		**ne... pas assez**	

1. Vous êtes quatre au restaurant et il y a une demi-bouteille de vin.
2. Vous allez préparer une salade de tomates pour deux personnes. Vous avez un kilo de tomates.
3. Vous allez faire une omelette pour deux personnes et vous avez un œuf.
4. C'est le matin et il y a un verre de lait dans le réfrigérateur chez vous.
5. Vous dînez seul(e) au restaurant et on vous sert six carafes de vin.
6. Il faut préparer des carottes pour six personnes et vous avez une seule carotte.

D. Quantités. Dites que vous voudriez les choses suivantes. Utilisez une expression de quantité.

EXEMPLE **Je voudrais un verre de vin blanc, s'il vous plaît.**

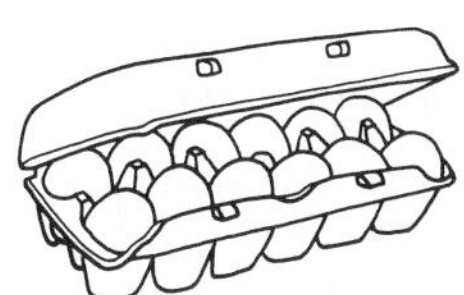

1.

2.

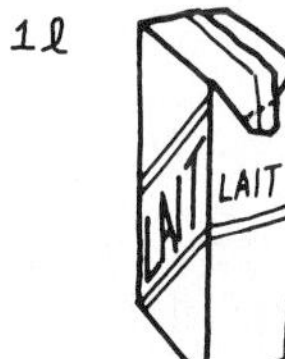

3.

4.

5.

6.

E. **Et vous?** Faites-vous attention à votre santé (*health*)? Répondez à ces questions pour décrire ce que vous faites. Employez le pronom **en** avec une quantité ou une négation.

EXEMPLE Vous mangez des desserts? → **Oui, j'en mange beaucoup (peu). Non, je n'en mange jamais.**

1. Vous mangez de la viande rouge?
2. Vous mangez des œufs?
3. Vous mangez des légumes?
4. Vous mangez des fruits?
5. Vous mangez du poisson?
6. Vous avez des problèmes?
7. Vous fumez des cigarettes?
8. Vous faites de l'exercice?

F. **Fruits et légumes.** En groupes, faites une liste pour chaque catégorie sur une feuille de papier. Écrivez autant de fruits ou de légumes que possible dans chacune des catégories. Le groupe avec la liste la plus longue gagne.

FRUITS	LÉGUMES
rouges:	rouges:
verts:	verts:
jaunes:	jaunes:
orange:	orange:
mauves:	bruns:

G. **Au marché.** Imaginez que vous préparez un dîner pour quatre amis. Décidez ce que vous voulez servir et allez acheter les provisions au marché. Un(e) camarade de classe va jouer le rôle du/de la marchand(e).

Remarquez que...

En France, on utilise le système métrique pour mesurer. Apprenez les équivalents:

1 kilo (kg) = 1000 grammes = 2.2 *pounds*

1 litre (l) = 1.057 *quarts*

Équivalents.
Trouvez un équivalent approximatif pour chaque quantité.

½ kilo = _____ gramme(s)
¼ kilo = _____ gramme(s)
1 *pound* = _____ gramme(s)
2.2 *pounds* = _____ kilo(s)
1 *quart* = _____ litre(s)
1 *gallon* = _____ litre(s)

Qu'est-ce qu'on dit?

Pensez-vous souvent à votre **santé**? Est-ce que les **conseils** suivants sont bons? Pouvez-vous en donner d'autres?

Pour rester en bonne santé, il faut
- manger beaucoup de fruits et de légumes.
- dormir assez.
- se reposer suffisamment.
- **éviter** le stress, l'alcool, le tabac et le sucre.

Pour devenir plus **fort**(e), il faut
- manger plus de protéines et de produits laitiers.
- prendre des vitamines.
- **faire des haltères**.
- faire de l'aérobic.

Quand on **fait attention à sa ligne** ou quand on veut **maigrir**, il faut
- manger des plats **sains** et légers.
- boire beaucoup d'eau.
- faire de l'exercice.

Rosalie parle à Rose du dîner qu'elle prépare pour ce soir.

— Qu'est-ce que je fais comme dessert ce soir? André adore la tarte aux pommes. Tu aimes ça aussi?
— Oui, mais je ne vais pas manger de dessert. Je **suis au régime**.
— Mais tu n'as pas besoin de maigrir.
— Si, si. J'**ai grossi** un peu depuis que nous sommes en France. Je passe trop de temps dans les cafés et je mange trop de pâtisseries.
— Alors, si tu veux **perdre du poids**, mange plus de yaourt, de fruits et de légumes. Et évite les sauces, ça fait grossir et c'est mauvais pour la santé. Et essaie aussi de manger plus **lentement**. Comme ça, tu manges moins.
— J'essaie de boire moins de boissons alcoolisées.
— Oui, et il faut boire plus d'eau. Si tu bois huit verres d'eau par jour, tu vas maigrir plus **vite**.

penser à *to think about* **la santé** *health* **des conseils** (*m*) *advice* **éviter** *to avoid* **fort(e)** *strong* **faire des haltères** *to lift weights* **faire attention (à)** *to pay attention (to), to be careful (with)* **la ligne** *figure* **maigrir** *to slim down* **sain(e)** *healthy* **être au régime** *to be on a diet* **grossir** *to gain weight* **perdre du poids** *to lose weight* **lentement** *slowly* **vite** *quickly*

A. **C'est bon pour la santé?** Sur une feuille de papier, faites une liste des boissons et des aliments (*foods*) qui sont bons pour la santé et une autre de ceux qui sont mauvais pour la santé.

	BON POUR LA SANTÉ	MAUVAIS POUR LA SANTÉ
EXEMPLES	l'eau	la bière

B. **Il faut...** Utilisez les listes que vous avez préparées dans l'exercice précédent pour compléter les phrases suivantes.

1. Pour maigrir, il faut éviter...
2. Pour perdre du poids, il faut manger... Il faut boire...
3. Pour grossir, il faut manger... Il faut boire...

Voilà pourquoi!

SELF-CHECK

1. In which forms of **-ir** verbs do you insert an **-iss-** before the ending?
2. What is the conjugation of **-ir** verbs in the imperfect?
3. How do you pronounce a single **s** between vowels? How do you pronounce double **ss**?

Les verbes en -ir

Many verbs that describe a change in physical appearance (*to get thinner, to turn red...*) end in -**ir**. Many are based on the feminine forms of corresponding adjectives.

gros(se)	*fat*	→	**grossir**	*to grow fatter*
grand(e)	*tall*	→	**grandir**	*to grow up/to grow taller*
vieux (vieille)	*old*	→	**vieillir**	*to grow older*
maigre	*thin*	→	**maigrir**	*to get thinner*
rouge	*red*	→	**rougir**	*to blush, to turn red*

Here are some other common -**ir** verbs.

choisir (de faire)	*to choose (to do)*	**(ré)agir (à)**	*to (re)act (to)*
finir (de faire)	*to finish (doing)*	**réfléchir (à)**	*to think (about)*
obéir (à quelqu'un)	*to obey (somebody)*	**réussir (à)**	*to succeed (at), to pass [a test]*

Regular -**ir** verbs are conjugated as follows. All -**ir** verbs presented in this chapter take **avoir** as the auxiliary in the **passé composé**.

CHOISIR (*TO CHOOSE*)	
je choisi**s**	nous choisi**ssons**
tu choisi**s**	vous choisi**ssez**
il/elle/on choisi**t**	ils/elles choisi**ssent**

PASSÉ COMPOSÉ: j'**ai choisi...**

IMPARFAIT: je **choisissais...**

Can you complete the rest of the conjugation of **choisir** in the **passé composé** and **imparfait**?

Le pronom y (*reprise*)

In addition to being used to replace prepositions of location to say *there*, the pronoun **y** is used to replace the preposition **à** and a noun that is not a person or an animal.

Je réfléchis ***à mes problèmes.***	→	**J'*y* réfléchis.**
Nous réussissons ***aux examens.***	→	**Nous *y* réussissons.**
J'obéis ***aux conseils de mon médecin.***	→	**J'*y* obéis.**

Like **en** and other object pronouns, **y** is placed before an infinitive, if there is one, otherwise, it goes before the conjugated verb. It is attached to the end of an affirmative command, but it precedes the verb in negative commands.

Je veux réfléchir ***à la situation.***	→	**Je veux *y* réfléchir.**
J'ai réfléchi ***à la situation.***	→	**J'*y* ai réfléchi.**
Réfléchissez ***à la situation.***	→	**Réfléchissez-*y*.**
Ne réfléchissez pas ***à la situation.***	→	**N'*y* réfléchissez pas.**

Et ça se prononce comment?

La lettre s et les verbes en -ir

TEXTBOOK TAPE

Sometimes it is difficult to remember whether to use one **s** or two when spelling forms of **-ir** verbs such as **choisir** or **réussir.** If you keep in mind that a single **s** between vowels is pronounced like a **z** and **ss** is pronounced like an **s**, it will help your spelling. At the beginning of a word, **s** is always pronounced like **s**.

ils choisissent (z, s) **nous réussissons** (s, s) **je grossis** (s)

When talking about the present, an **s** sound in the ending of **-ir** verbs indicates that you are talking about more than one person.

il rougit / ils rougissent **elle finit / elles finissent**

Savez-vous le faire?

A. **En classe.** Un ami parle de son cours de français. Est-ce qu'il parle du professeur ou des étudiants? Sur une feuille de papier, écrivez ses phrases dans la liste logique.

	IL PARLE DU PROFESSEUR	IL PARLE DES ÉTUDIANTS
EXEMPLE		**Ils réussissent toujours à comprendre.**

B. **Et notre classe.** Relisez les phrases écrites dans l'exercice précédent. Cette fois-ci, dites si ces choses sont vraies pour votre classe de français.

EXEMPLE **Dans notre classe aussi, les étudiants réussissent toujours à comprendre.**
OU **Les étudiants ne réussissent pas toujours à comprendre.**

C. **Il faut bien choisir.** Rosalie dit ce que chacun choisit de manger pour le dîner. Imaginez ce qu'elle dit.

EXEMPLE Rose veut maigrir. Elle...
Elle **choisit de la salade, des légumes et des fruits.**

des légumes ???
DES FRUITS **DE LA SALADE**
du fromage de la sauce
??? *de la viande rouge*
DU POISSON **des desserts**

1. Moi, je veux avoir un régime sain. Je...
2. Rose et moi, nous voulons maigrir. Nous...
3. André veut grossir. Il...
4. Henri veut être plus fort. Il...
5. Et toi, Patricia, tu veux avoir plus d'énergie? Tu...?
6. Et vous, les enfants, vous voulez grandir vite? Vous...?
7. André et Henri veulent des vitamines C dans leur régime. Ils...

D. **Qu'est-ce qu'on doit faire?** Les enfants de Patricia veulent savoir ce qu'ils doivent faire. Jouez le rôle de Patricia, qui répond à leurs questions.

EXEMPLE Nous devons finir notre lait? → **Oui, finissez votre lait.**

1. Nous devons réfléchir avant de parler?
2. Nous devons réussir aux examens?
3. Nous devons obéir à Papa?
4. Nous devons finir nos devoirs?

E. **Nous avons bien fait.** Les enfants disent à Patricia qu'ils ont fait ce qu'elle leur a dit de faire dans l'exercice précédent. Que disent-ils?

EXEMPLE **Nous avons fini notre lait.**

F. **La santé.** Répondez aux questions suivantes en utilisant le pronom y.

1. Est-ce que vous réfléchissez parfois *(sometimes)* à votre régime?
2. Est-ce que vous faites attention à votre ligne?
3. Est-ce que vous pensez souvent à votre santé?
4. Est-ce que vous obéissez toujours aux conseils de votre médecin?

Voilà pourquoi!

Le verbe **boire**

You have already used **boire** (*to drink*) in the infinitive. Here is how you conjugate it.

BOIRE (*TO DRINK*)

je **bois**	nous **buvons**
tu **bois**	vous **buvez**
il/elle/on **boit**	ils/elles **boivent**

PASSÉ COMPOSÉ: j'ai **bu...**

IMPARFAIT: je **buvais...**

SELF-CHECK

1. Which two forms of **boire** have **u** in the stem instead of **oi**?
2. How do you say *more fruit than meat, as many fruits as vegetables*, and *less coffee than water*?

La comparaison des noms

Use these expressions to compare how much.

plus de... (que)(de) *more... (than)*
autant de... (que)(de) *as much... (as), as many... (as)*
moins de... (que)(de) *less... (than)*

Tu dois manger *plus de* légumes *que de* desserts.
Je bois *moins de* bière *qu'*avant.
André mange *plus de* desserts *que* Rose.

As with other quantities, use the pronoun **en** to replace nouns after these expressions.

— Je bois beaucoup *moins de café* maintenant. Et toi?
— J'*en* bois *moins* aussi. (Je bois *moins de café* aussi.)

Savez-vous le faire?

A. **Et les autres?** Posez des questions à un(e) camarade de classe au sujet de ses habitudes alimentaires. Demandez...

EXEMPLE s'il/si elle boit des boissons alcoolisées
— Bois-tu des boissons alcoolisées?
— Oui, je bois des boissons alcoolisées de temps en temps.
OU **— Non, je n'en bois jamais.**

1. ce qu'il/elle boit avec le dîner
2. ce qu'il/elle boit le matin
3. s'il/si elle est au régime
4. s'il/si elle grossit à Thanksgiving
5. ce qu'il/elle aime choisir comme dessert
6. s'il/si elle mange vite ou lentement
7. ce qu'il/elle ne boit presque jamais
8. ce qu'il/elle mange pour maigrir

B. **Comparaisons.** Comparez ce que vous faites avec vos amis et avec les membres de votre famille. Nommez quelqu'un qui fait ces choses **plus / autant / moins que** vous.

EXEMPLE boire du vin

Mon camarade de chambre boit plus de vin que moi. Mes parents boivent autant de vin que moi. Mon ami Luc boit moins de vin.

1. boire du Coca
2. manger des pâtisseries
3. faire de l'exercice
4. choisir des plats légers
5. avoir de l'énergie
6. boire de l'eau

C. **Au passé et maintenant.** Aimez-vous les boissons suivantes? Dites combien vous en buviez quand vous étiez au lycée. Ensuite, faites une comparaison avec ce que vous faites maintenant, en vous servant du pronom **en**.

EXEMPLE du Coca → **Quand j'étais au lycée, je buvais trop (peu...) de Coca. Maintenant, j'en bois moins (autant, plus).**

1. du café
2. de l'eau
3. de la bière
4. du lait
5. du jus de fruits
6. du thé

D. **Un bon régime.** Un(e) ami(e) veut améliorer son régime. Donnez-lui des conseils sur ce qu'il/elle doit et ne doit pas faire.

EXEMPLE **Évite les sauces. Ne bois pas trop de boissons alcoolisées...**

Remarquez que...

La cuisine normande est saine et simple, basée sur les produits régionaux: les fruits de mer, les pommes et les produits laitiers. Beaucoup de plats régionaux normands sont préparés avec du beurre ou de la crème. Les spécialités régionales (la terrine de canard, la sole normande et les tripes à la mode de Caen) montrent la variété gastronomique trouvée en Normandie. Les nombreux fromages normands comme le camembert, le neufchâtel, le pont-l'évêque aussi bien que des plats à base de pommes comme la tarte aux pommes, le sucre de pommes et les pâtes de pommes sont surtout appréciés par les gens de la région. En Normandie, il faut aussi essayer le cidre bouché et le calvados.

Quels plats? Quels plats normands voudriez-vous goûter? Lesquels n'aimeriez-vous pas goûter?

Avez-vous goûté du fromage normand?

Qu'est-ce qu'on dit?

La dernière fois que vous avez dîné chez des ami(e)s, comment était la soirée? Qu'est-ce qui s'est passé?

Il faisait beau... Il faisait mauvais...	quand...	j'ai quitté la maison.
Il était six (sept, ???) heures...	quand...	je suis arrivé(e) chez mes amis.
On avait très faim... On n'avait pas très faim...	et/mais...	on a mangé tout de suite. on n'a pas mangé tout de suite.
Le repas était délicieux... assez bon... médiocre... mauvais...	et/mais...	j'ai beaucoup mangé. j'ai peu mangé.
La conversation était animée... intéressante... ennuyeuse...	et/mais...	j'ai beaucoup parlé. j'ai peu parlé.
Après le repas, nous étions fatigué(e)s... nous avions envie de continuer la soirée...	et/mais...	je suis parti(e). je suis resté(e).
Il était **environ** dix (10, 11, ???) heures...	quand...	je suis rentré(e).
J'étais fatigué(e)... Je n'étais pas fatigué(e)...	et...	je me suis couché(e) tout de suite. je ne me suis pas couché(e) tout de suite.
Le lendemain, c'était dimanche (lundi, ???)...	et...	je me suis levé(e) tôt. je me suis levé(e) tard.

environ *about, around*

Tri, un ami d'Henri, parle avec Rose pendant le dîner.

— Vous avez trouvé cela difficile de vous adapter à la vie en France?

— Pas vraiment. Généralement, la vie ici n'est pas très différente de la vie chez nous. Mais ce sont les petites choses de tous les jours qui m'**étonnent** le plus. Je suis **parfois** surprise par des petits détails culturels que, malheureusement, je ne comprends pas encore très bien.

— Racontez-moi un peu.

— Eh bien, le jour de notre arrivée en France, nous avons pris le train de Paris à Saumur, parce que nous voulions visiter les célèbres châteaux de la Loire. Quand nous sommes arrivées, il était déjà dix heures du soir et nous étions très fatiguées. Nous avons trouvé un hôtel près de la gare et **comme** nous avions faim nous avons décidé d'aller dîner dans un restaurant du coin. Il n'y en avait pas beaucoup dans le quartier mais nous avons cherché partout et enfin nous en avons trouvé un qui était **encore** ouvert. Nous **venions de** nous asseoir à table quand la serveuse est arrivée. Elle avait l'air **gênée**, et elle nous a demandé tout de suite: «**Le patron** vous a parlé? Il sait que vous êtes ici?» Je me suis demandé ce qui se passait, le restaurant était pourtant encore ouvert. Alors je lui ai répondu: «Non, **qu'est-ce qu'il y a?**» La serveuse hésitait: «Madame... je regrette, mais il **n'**y a **plus** de pain.» Nous étions assez surprises par cette réaction, mais... Mamie lui a dit que nous pouvions dîner sans pain et après elle m'a expliqué qu'en France un repas sans pain, **ça ne se faisait pas.**

— Vous savez, ici nous avons même un proverbe à ce sujet... un jour sans pain est un jour sans soleil.

étonner *to astonish* **parfois** *sometimes* **comme** *as, since* **encore** *still* **venir de (faire)** *to have just (done)* **gêné(e)** *embarrassed* **le/la patron(ne)** *the owner, manager* **qu'est-ce qu'il y a?** *what's the matter?* **ne... plus** *no more, no longer* **ça ne se faisait pas** *that wasn't done*

A. **Le voyage de Rose.** Complétez ces phrases selon ce que Rose a dit dans la section *Qu'est-ce qu'on dit?*.

1. Rose et sa grand-mère sont allées de Paris à ___ .
2. Elles voulaient voir ___ .
3. Quand elles sont arrivées, il était ___ heures.
4. Elles se sentaient ___ .
5. Elles ont trouvé un hôtel près de ___ .
6. Comme elles avaient faim, elles ont cherché ___ .
7. La serveuse avait l'air ___ .
8. La serveuse n'était pas à l'aise parce qu'il n'y avait plus de ___ .

B. **Et vous?** Répondez à ces questions en vous basant sur votre dernière sortie au restaurant. Si la question est au passé composé, répondez au passé composé. Si la question est à l'imparfait, répondez à l'imparfait.

1. À quel restaurant êtes-vous allé(e)?
2. Quelle heure était-il quand vous êtes arrivé(e)?
3. Qu'est-ce que vous avez commandé?
4. Comment était la serveuse/le serveur?
5. Est-ce que vous avez mangé vite?
6. Est-ce que le repas était bon?
7. Qu'est-ce que vous avez fait après?

C. **Dans ma famille.** Choisissez l'adverbe entre parenthèses qui décrit le mieux votre famille quand vous étiez petit(e).

1. (Généralement, Quelquefois), toute la famille mangeait ensemble.
2. Mes parents faisaient (souvent, rarement) des plats que j'aimais.
3. (Heureusement, Malheureusement), nous commandions (souvent, rarement) une pizza.
4. (Normalement, De temps en temps), je prenais le petit déjeuner à la maison.
5. Quand j'étais petit(e), je mangeais (vite, lentement).

La vallée de la Loire est connue pour la beauté de son paysage et pour ses nombreux châteaux. Le château de Chambord (ci-dessus), construit par François Ier en 1519, est un des chefs-d'œuvre architecturaux de la Renaissance.

Voilà pourquoi!

SELF-CHECK

1. Do you generally use the **passé composé** or the **imparfait** to say what happened? To describe how things were?
2. What are the three main uses of the **passé composé**? What are the three main uses of the **imparfait**?

Le passé composé et l'imparfait

When talking about the past in French, you send a different message, depending on whether you put the verb in the **passé composé** or the **imparfait**. In English, the use of different past tenses also sends different messages. Consider the difference between these two sentences. Do you get a different message in each? What is the difference?

When her husband came home, they kissed.
When her husband came home, they were kissing.

When you are narrating what happened in the past, you will generally use the **imparfait** to set the scene or describe the background (*what was going on*). You will use the **passé composé** to tell the sequence of events of the story (*what happened*).

Consider these uses of the **passé composé** and the **imparfait**.

USE THE **PASSÉ COMPOSÉ** TO SAY:

1. WHAT HAPPENED: a completed action or an event with a beginning and end, no matter how long the duration.

   Il s'est levé tôt.
   He got up early.
   Ils ont dansé toute la nuit.
   They danced all night.

2. WHAT CHANGED: a change in a condition or state of being at a precise moment in time. Watch for expressions like **tout à coup** (*all at once*), **soudain** (*suddenly*), and **à ce moment-là**.

   Soudain, elle est devenue furieuse.
   Suddenly, she became furious.
   Tout à coup, j'ai compris la situation.
   All at once, I understood the situation.

3. WHAT HAPPENED NEXT: the sequence of events in a narration.

   Elles ont décidé d'aller dîner. Elles sont sorties. Elles ont trouvé un restaurant et elles y sont entrées.
   They decided to go eat. They went out. They found a restaurant and went in.

USE THE **IMPARFAIT** TO SAY:

1. HOW THINGS USED TO BE: repeated or habitual actions.

   J'allais en France chaque été.
   I used to go to France each summer.
   Nous allions toujours en Normandie.
   We always went to Normandy.

2. WHAT SOMEONE OR SOMETHING WAS LIKE: physical or mental conditions and states.

   Il avait faim.
   He was hungry.
   Elle était furieuse.
   She was furious.
   Je ne savais pas nager.
   I didn't know how to swim.

3. WHAT WAS GOING ON: description or setting.

   Il pleuvait.
   It was raining.
   Elle dormait.
   She was sleeping.
   Il était deux heures.
   It was two o'clock.

In a sentence describing an interrupted past action, you will use both the **imparfait** and the **passé composé.** Use the **imparfait** to say what was going on when something else occurred. To say what happened, interrupting the first activity, use the **passé composé.**

Quand son mari est rentré, ils s'embrassaient.
When her husband came home, they were kissing.

If you used the **passé composé** in each clause, you would be talking about two sequenced actions rather than one action going on when another occurred.

Quand son mari est rentré, ils se sont embrassés.
When her husband came home, they kissed.

Et ça se prononce comment?

Le passé composé et l'imparfait

The difference in pronunciation between the two past tenses may sometimes seem very subtle to you, but since they are used differently and impart different messages, it is essential that you learn to differentiate what you hear and that you try to pronounce them both correctly. Listen to these sentences. Where do you hear a difference?

J'ai travaillé. / Je travaillais.
Elle a mangé. / Elle mangeait.
Tu as été étonné(e). / Tu étais étonné(e).
Il est allé. / Il allait.

Construit entre 1515 et 1522, Chenonceaux traverse le Cher, un affluent (*tributary*) de la Loire.

Savez-vous le faire?

A. **Quand?** Rose parle avec André de ce qu'elle a fait hier et elle parle aussi des choses qu'elle faisait quand elle était petite. Sur une feuille de papier, écrivez chaque phrase que vous entendez dans la colonne appropriée.

	HIER	QUAND J'ÉTAIS PETITE
EXEMPLES	**J'ai mangé de la pizza.**	**Je jouais du piano.**

Maintenant, dites si vous avez fait les choses écrites dans la première liste, *hier*. Ensuite, dites si vous faisiez les choses dans la seconde liste *quand vous étiez petit(e)*.

B. **André et Rosalie.** André parle à Rosalie du jour où il l'a vue avec le soldat américain. Reliez les phrases des deux colonnes pour recréer une histoire logique.

EXEMPLE **C'était une belle journée d'automne. Il faisait du soleil. Je suis sorti de la maison vers huit heures...**

LA SCÈNE/LA SITUATION

C'était une belle journée d'automne.
Il faisait du soleil.

Je me sentais bien.
Les roses étaient très belles.
J'étais amoureux.
Tu embrassais un jeune soldat américain.
J'étais très triste.
Je voulais pleurer.
Je n'avais pas envie de manger ou de parler avec mes amis.

LES ACTIONS

Je suis sorti de la maison vers huit heures.
J'ai cueilli (*picked*) des roses dans le jardin.
Je suis allé au café.
J'ai lu le journal pendant quelques minutes.
Je suis allé te chercher.
Je suis arrivé chez toi.
Je t'ai vue.
Je suis parti sans rien dire.
Je suis rentré chez moi.
Je suis resté seul dans ma chambre pendant plusieurs jours.

C. **Et vous?** Parlez de votre vie en répondant à ces questions.

1. Où et quand êtes-vous né(e)?
2. Quel âge avait votre mère quand vous êtes né(e)?
3. Comment était votre vie quand vous aviez dix ans?
4. Dans quelle ville avez-vous grandi? Comment était cette ville à cette époque-là? Quel âge aviez-vous quand vous êtes parti(e) seul(e) en voyage pour la première fois?
5. Qu'est-ce que vous aimiez faire quand vous étiez jeune?
6. Quand avez-vous commencé vos études universitaires?

D. **Quand ils sont rentrés...** Patricia, Henri et leurs amis, Tri et Hanh, ont laissé leurs enfants avec une nouvelle baby-sitter le week-end dernier. Quand ils sont rentrés, voilà ce qu'ils ont vu. Décrivez la scène.

EXEMPLE **Annick descendait l'escalier dans les vêtements de sa mère, la baby-sitter, Alice, et son petit ami...**

E. **Hier.** Faites une liste de sept choses que vous avez faites hier.

EXEMPLES **Je me suis levé(e) tôt.**
J'ai pris mon petit déjeuner à sept heures...

Ensuite, récrivez les phrases. Cette fois, décrivez la scène autour de vous quand vous avez fait chaque chose.

EXEMPLES **Quand je me suis levé(e) hier matin, il faisait frais.**
Quand j'ai pris mon petit déjeuner, mon/ma camarade de chambre dormait, l'appartement était calme, le chat jouait...

F. **Il était une fois...** Lisez le commencement de l'histoire de *La Belle et la Bête.* Récrivez l'histoire au passé, en mettant les verbes en caractères gras à l'imparfait ou au passé composé.

EXEMPLE **Il y avait un marchand très riche...**

Il y **a** un marchand (*merchant*) très riche qui **a** trois filles. Ils **habitent** tous ensemble dans une belle maison en ville. Mais un jour, le marchand **perd** toute sa fortune, et ses filles et lui **sont** obligés d'aller habiter dans une petite maison à la campagne.

Ses deux filles aînées (*older*) **sont** très malheureuses. Elles **parlent** constamment des choses dont elles **ont** envie: des vêtements, de l'argent... La plus jeune de ses filles **s'appelle** Belle à cause de sa grande beauté. Non seulement **est**-elle très jolie mais elle **est** très douce (*sweet*). Elle **accepte** sa nouvelle vie et elle **est** heureuse.

Un jour, le marchand **part** en voyage d'affaires. Il **neige** et il **fait** très froid et en route il **se perd** dans la forêt. Le marchand **pense** qu'il **va** mourir quand, soudain, il **trouve** un château. La porte du château **est** ouverte et il **décide** d'entrer. Il **remarque** une grande table couverte de plats délicieux. Il **mange** puis il **s'endort.**

Il **est** vers huit heures du matin quand il **se réveille.** Il **entre** dans le jardin où il **trouve** une jolie rose qu'il **veut** apporter à Belle. À ce moment-là, un monstre horrible **arrive** et **commence** à crier (*shout*). Il **dit** au marchand qu'il **veut** que Belle vienne habiter chez lui. Sinon (*Otherwise*) le monstre **va** manger le marchand.

G. **La Belle et la Bête.** Continuez l'histoire de *La Belle et la Bête* en complétant les phrases par la forme correcte du verbe à l'imparfait ou au passé composé.

Quand le marchand ______ (rentrer) il ______ (raconter) ses aventures à ses filles et Belle ______ (décider) d'aller habiter chez le monstre. Quand elle ______ (arriver) chez lui, elle ______ (trouver) tout ce dont elle ______ (avoir) besoin. Chaque jour, elle ______ (avoir) tout ce qu'elle ______ (vouloir). Mais pendant plusieurs jours, elle ______ (ne pas voir) le monstre.

Un jour, elle ______ (se promener) dans le jardin quand le monstre ______ (venir) lui parler. Elle l(e) ______ (trouver) horrible et elle ______ (crier). Le monstre lui ______ (dire) de ne pas avoir peur et de venir se promener avec lui.

Tous les jours, les deux ______ (faire) une promenade et ______ (se parler). Petit à petit, ils ______ (devenir) amis. Après un certain temps, Belle ______ (savoir) qu'elle ______ (aimer) le monstre et un jour elle l' ______ (embrasser). Tout à coup, le visage du monstre ______ (changer). Ce ______ (ne plus être) un monstre. C(e) ______ (être) un beau jeune prince.

Voilà pourquoi!

Les adverbes: formation et position

SELF CHECK

1. How can you form adverbs from some adjectives?
2. Where do you place adverbs telling when or where? Where do you place most others?

You already know many adverbs that tell when (**demain**), where (**partout**), how (**vite**), how much (**beaucoup**), or how often (**souvent**) something is done. To form the French equivalent of most English adverbs ending in *-ly*, add **-ment** to the end of the masculine form of the adjective if it ends in a vowel, and to the feminine form if the masculine form ends in a consonant.

vrai	→	**vraiment**	*truly, really*
attentif	→	**attentivement**	*attentively*
(mal)heureux	→	**(mal)heureusement**	*(un)fortunately*

With adjectives ending in **-ent** or **-ant**, replace **-ent** by **-emment** and **-ant** by **-amment.**

différent	→	**différemment**	*differently*
constant	→	**constamment**	*constantly*

Adverbs telling *when* or *where* generally go at the beginning or the end of sentences or clauses. **Évidemment** (*obviously*), **généralement**, **heureusement**, and **malheureusement** are also placed at the beginning or end.

Je suis allé(e) en Normandie ***récemment.***
J'ai vu des choses magnifiques ***partout.***
Malheureusement, **j'ai dû rentrer.**

Most other adverbs are placed after the verb they modify in the present or imperfect. In the **passé composé**, adverbs ending in **-ment** are usually placed after the past participle and most other adverbs are placed between the auxiliary and the past participle.

PRÉSENT/IMPARFAIT	PASSÉ COMPOSÉ
Nous attendons **patiemment** à l'aéroport.	Nous avons attendu **patiemment** à l'aéroport.
Je descendais **rapidement** de l'avion.	Je suis descendu(e) **rapidement** de l'avion.
Je comprends **bien** la question.	J'ai **bien** compris la question.
Mes amis parlaient **beaucoup** de leur voyage.	Mes amis ont **beaucoup** parlé de leur voyage.

Un détail de la tapisserie de la reine Mathilde.

Savez-vous le faire?

A. **Au lycée.** Comment étiez-vous quand vous étiez à l'école secondaire? Ajoutez un adverbe à chaque phrase pour vous décrire.

EXEMPLE Je dansais. → **Je dansais assez bien.**

(assez) bien	???	*souvent*	LE SOIR
(très) mal	rarement	**le week-end**	
vite	facilement	???	*quelquefois* PARTOUT
lentement	*constamment*	**???**	

1. Je parlais au téléphone.
2. Je sortais avec des amis.
3. Je faisais mes devoirs.
4. J'apprenais mes leçons.
5. J'avais des problèmes.
6. J'écoutais de la musique.
7. J'obéissais à mes parents.
8. Je rougissais.

B. **Et toi?** Complétez les questions suivantes avec l'adverbe qui correspond à l'adjectif entre parenthèses et posez-les à un(e) camarade de classe qui y répondra.

EXEMPLE Est-ce que tu te lèves _________ (facile) le matin?
— Est-ce que tu te lèves facilement le matin?
— Oui, je me lève facilement le matin.

1. À midi, est-ce que tu manges ______ (lent) ou ______ (rapide)?
2. Peux-tu préparer tes cours ______ (tranquille) à la maison?
3. Est-ce que ton/ta meilleur(e) ami(e) parle ______ (constant) de ses problèmes? Quand il/elle parle de ses problèmes, l'écoutes-tu ______ (patient)?
4. Es-tu sorti(e) ______ (récent) avec ton/ta meilleur(e) ami(e)?
5. ______ (Général), est-ce que tu t'habilles tout de suite le dimanche matin?

C. **Traits nécessaires.** Choisissez l'adverbe qui correspond à l'adjectif en caractères gras pour décrire ce que chacune de ces personnes fait.

EXEMPLE Les bons professeurs sont **patients**.
Les bons professeurs répètent patiemment leurs questions.
OU **Les bons professeurs écoutent patiemment leurs étudiants.**
OU **Les bons professeurs attendent patiemment les réponses des étudiants.**

1. Les bons étudiants sont **attentifs**.
2. Les bons athlètes sont **rapides**.
3. Les bons professeurs sont **intelligents**.
4. Les bons parents sont **calmes**.
5. Les bons petits amis sont **amoureux**.
6. Les bons présidents sont **honnêtes**.

(se) parler	expliquer	**???**
COURIR	***répondre***	(SE) REGARDER
réagir AGIR	**penser**	**???**
attendre	**???**	
ÉCOUTER		

Remarquez que...

Ce qui est considéré normal ou poli (*polite*) diffère d'une culture à l'autre. Les plats qu'on mange, l'ordre dans lequel on les mange et la façon de les manger peuvent varier d'une société à l'autre.

Différences. Regardez ces photos. Qu'est-ce que vous remarquez?

C'est à lire!

Jacques Prévert est l'un des plus célèbres poètes français du vingtième siècle. Dans ses poèmes, il aime parler de la vie de tous les jours. Vous allez lire son poème *Déjeuner du matin.* Avant de commencer, faites l'exercice qui suit.

En contexte. Devinez le sens des mots en caractères gras dans le paragraphe suivant.

Il a pris mon paquet de cigarettes qui était sur la table. Il en a sorti une cigarette qu'il a **allumée. La fumée** grise a rempli la cuisine d'une odeur désagréable. Il a fini sa cigarette, il a mis **les cendres** dans **le cendrier** et il **a reposé** le paquet de cigarettes sur la table.

Déjeuner du matin

Il a mis le café
Dans **la tasse**
Il a mis le lait
Dans la tasse de café
Il a mis le sucre
Dans le café au lait
Avec la petite cuiller
Il a tourné
Il a bu le café au lait
Et il a reposé la tasse
Sans me parler
Il a allumé
Une cigarette
Il a fait **des ronds**
Avec la fumée
Il a mis les cendres
Dans le cendrier
Sans me parler
Sans me regarder
Il s'est levé
Il a mis
Son chapeau sur sa tête
Il a mis
Son manteau de **pluie**
Parce qu'il pleuvait
Et il est parti
Sous la pluie
Sans **une parole**
Sans me regarder
Et moi j'ai pris
Ma tête dans ma main
Et j'ai pleuré.

Jacques Prévert

la tasse *the cup* **des ronds** (*m*) *rings* **la pluie** *rain* **une parole** *a word*

Avez-vous compris?

A. **Qu'est-ce qui s'est passé?** Lisez le poème *Déjeuner du matin* et nommez dix choses que l'homme dans le poème a faites. Nommez aussi deux choses qu'il n'a pas faites d'après le poème.

B. **Analyse du texte.** Selon vous, qui sont les personnages (*characters*) dans le poème? Pourquoi est-ce qu'ils ne se parlent pas?

C. **Leur vie ensemble.** Imaginez le passé des personnages dans le poème. Où est-ce qu'ils se sont connus? Parlaient-ils plus avant? Est-ce qu'ils étaient plus heureux? Qu'est-ce qu'ils faisaient ensemble? Qu'est-ce qui s'est passé? Pourquoi ne se parlent-ils plus? Écrivez une rédaction qui explique leur passé ensemble.

Ça y est! C'est à vous!

A. **Organisez-vous!** Vous allez préparer de la jambalaya pour des amis. Lisez la liste d'ingrédients qu'il vous faut dans la recette de droite et faites les choses suivantes.

- Faites une liste des choses que vous devez acheter pour le dîner.
- Soulignez les choses que vous pouvez acheter dans une épicerie.
- Décidez combien vous voulez en acheter.

JAMBALAYA

Pour 6 à 8 personnes
Préparation 30 mn - Cuisson 35 mn

500 g de riz long dit «de luxe», un poivron vert, un poivron rouge, un demi-concombre, un petit bol de petits pois écossés, un petit bol de petits haricots verts coupés en dés, un petit bol de céleri en branches très tendre et finement émincé, 2 tomates, 3 oignons, ciboule et ciboulette, 2 gousses d'ail.
Pour la garniture:
300 g de talon de jambon cuit en un seul morceau, une boîte de crabe, 6 œufs, un dl d'huile, 2 cuillerées à soupe de sauce de soja, une pincée de poivre de Cayenne, quelques gouttes de jus de citron, persil haché, sel et poivre.

La jambalaya: recette simple à réaliser en 1 h 5 mn.

B. **Scène: À l'épicerie.** Utilisez vos réponses dans *A. Organisez-vous!* pour écrire une conversation entre un épicier et vous. D'abord, dites-lui bonjour et ensuite, expliquez-lui que vous voulez acheter une petite bouteille d'huile, une petite bouteille de sauce de soja, 500 grammes de riz long... N'oubliez pas de payer!

C. **Chez les petits commerçants.** Écoutez trois conversations entre un(e) commerçant(e) et un(e) client(e) et répondez aux questions suivantes pour chacune des conversations.

- Dans quel magasin se trouvent-ils?
- Qu'est-ce que le/la client(e) achète?
- Quel est le total?

D. **À la pâtisserie.** Vous êtes dans la pâtisserie ci-dessous (*below*) et vous voulez acheter deux choses. Avec un(e) camarade de classe, inventez une conversation entre le/la commerçant(e) et vous.

Pour vérifier

Après avoir fait les exercices suivants, vérifiez vos réponses dans l'*Appendix C.*

Shopping for food and talking about diet and health

A. **Questions?** Répondez aux questions suivantes.

1. En France, que mange-t-on pour le petit déjeuner? Et aux États-Unis ou au Canada?
2. Que vend-on dans une pâtisserie? Dans une charcuterie? Dans une épicerie?
3. Généralement, qu'est-ce qu'on peut commander dans un fast-food?

B. **Ingrédients.** Voilà la liste des ingrédients pour les plats que Rosalie va préparer. Dites ce dont elle a besoin et quel plat elle va préparer avec ces ingrédients: **de la soupe à l'oignon, une tarte aux pommes ou du bœuf bourguignon.**

EXEMPLE 1 kg pommes / 1 douz œufs / 500 g sucre
Elle a besoin d'un kilo de pommes, d'une douzaine d'œufs et de cinq cent grammes de sucre pour faire une tarte aux pommes.

1. 250 g oignons / 60 g beurre / 1 l bouillon
2. 700 g bœuf / 1 b vin rouge / 50 g beurre / 100 g oignons

C. **À la boucherie.** Vous faites les courses et vous passez à la boucherie. Écrivez une conversation logique entre le (la) boucher(-ère) (*butcher*) et vous. Ensuite, imaginez que vous êtes dans une boulangerie et inventez une conversation entre le (la) boulanger(-ère) (*baker*) et vous.

D. **C'est-à-dire...** Patricia parle avec ses enfants. Récrivez leurs phrases en choisissant un synonyme dans la liste de vocabulaire pour remplacer les mots en caractères gras.

1. Quand on mange trop, on **prend du poids.**
2. Tu **as perdu du poids**, maman?
3. Le temps passe et nous **devenons vieux.**
4. Je **pense** trop à mes problèmes.
5. Les enfants **deviennent plus grands.**
6. Vous **devenez** facilement **rouges.**

Narrating how things happened

E. **La jeunesse.** André parle avec Rose de sa jeunesse. Mettez les verbes entre parenthèses au passé composé ou à l'imparfait.

Quand j' _____ (être) jeune, mes parents n' _____ (habiter) pas très loin de la maison des parents de Rosalie. Elle et moi, nous _____ (se voir) assez souvent. Je _____ (la trouver) si belle, j' _____ (être) fou d'amour pour elle. Mais je crois que pour elle, je _____ (ne être) qu'un ami. Et moi je _____ (ne pas avoir) le courage de lui parler de mon amour. Un jour, j(e) _____ (décider) de lui dire que je _____ (l'aimer). J(e) _____ (aller) chez elle. Mais quand j(e) _____ (arriver), je _____ (la voir) avec un jeune soldat américain. Ils _____ (s'embrasser). À ce moment, j(e) _____ (savoir) que ce _____ (ne pas être) moi qu'elle _____ (aimer).

Vocabulaire

Shopping for food and talking about diet and health

LES MAGASINS
la boucherie
la boulangerie
la charcuterie
un(e) commerçant(e)
l'épicerie (*f*)
le marché
la pâtisserie
la poissonnerie
le supermarché

LES REPAS ET LES RESTAURANTS
un apéritif
une carte
un choix
le déjeuner
un dessert
le dîner
une entrée
un hors-d'œuvre (*inv.*)
un menu à... francs / à prix fixe
la monnaie
le/la patron(ne)
le petit déjeuner
un plat (principal)

LES QUANTITÉS
assez de
autant de... (que)
beaucoup de
une bouteille de
une carafe de
cent grammes de
combien de
une cuillerée de
une douzaine de
un kilo de
un (demi-)litre de
une livre de
moins de... (que)
un morceau de
(un) peu de
plus de... (que)
une tasse de
une tranche de
trop de
un verre de

QUELQUES ALIMENTS
du canard
des produits laitiers (*m*)
des protéines (*f*)
de la soupe à l'oignon
des vitamines (*f*)
du yaourt

Pour d'autres aliments, voir les pages 354–356, 363.

VERBES
s'asseoir (à l'intérieur, sur la terrasse)
boire
choisir (de faire)
commander
être au régime
éviter
faire attention (à)
faire de l'aérobic
faire des haltères
faire les courses
grossir
maigrir
offrir
perdre du poids

DIVERS
l'alcool (*m*)
certains
des conseils (*m*)
copieux(-euse)
frais (fraîche)
fort(e)
léger(-ère)
la ligne
médiocre
par ici
sain(e)
la santé
le stress

Narrating how things happened

ADVERBES
à ce moment-là
comme
constamment
différemment
encore
environ
évidemment
généralement
lentement
parfois
soudain
suffisamment
tout à coup
vite
vraiment

VERBES
s'adapter à
étonner
finir (de faire)
grandir
obéir (à)
penser (à)
(ré)agir (à)
réfléchir (à)
remercier (de)
réussir (à)
rougir
venir de (+ *infinitif*)
vieillir

DIVERS
Ça ne se faisait pas.
un château
gêné(e)
ne... plus
une parole
la pluie
Qu'est-ce qu'il y a?

Unité 6 Au Zaïre

Regional Overview
L'Afrique
AREA: 11,683,000 square miles (30,259,000 sq. km.)
POPULATION: 646,000,000 (About 140,000,000 live in the African countries where French is an official language; 60,000,000 live in Algeria, Morocco, and Tunisia, where Arabic is the official language, and French is widely used.)
MAJOR INDUSTRIES: agriculture, manufacturing, mining

Le Zaïre
AREA: 905,563 square miles (2,345,000 sq. km.)
POPULATION: 37,800,000
CAPITAL: **Kinshasa**
MAJOR INDUSTRIES: agriculture, mining

Chapitre 11 La vie à l'avenir

By the end of this chapter, you should be able to do the following in French:

- Talk about the future
- Share observations and beliefs
- Give details about observations
- Discuss options

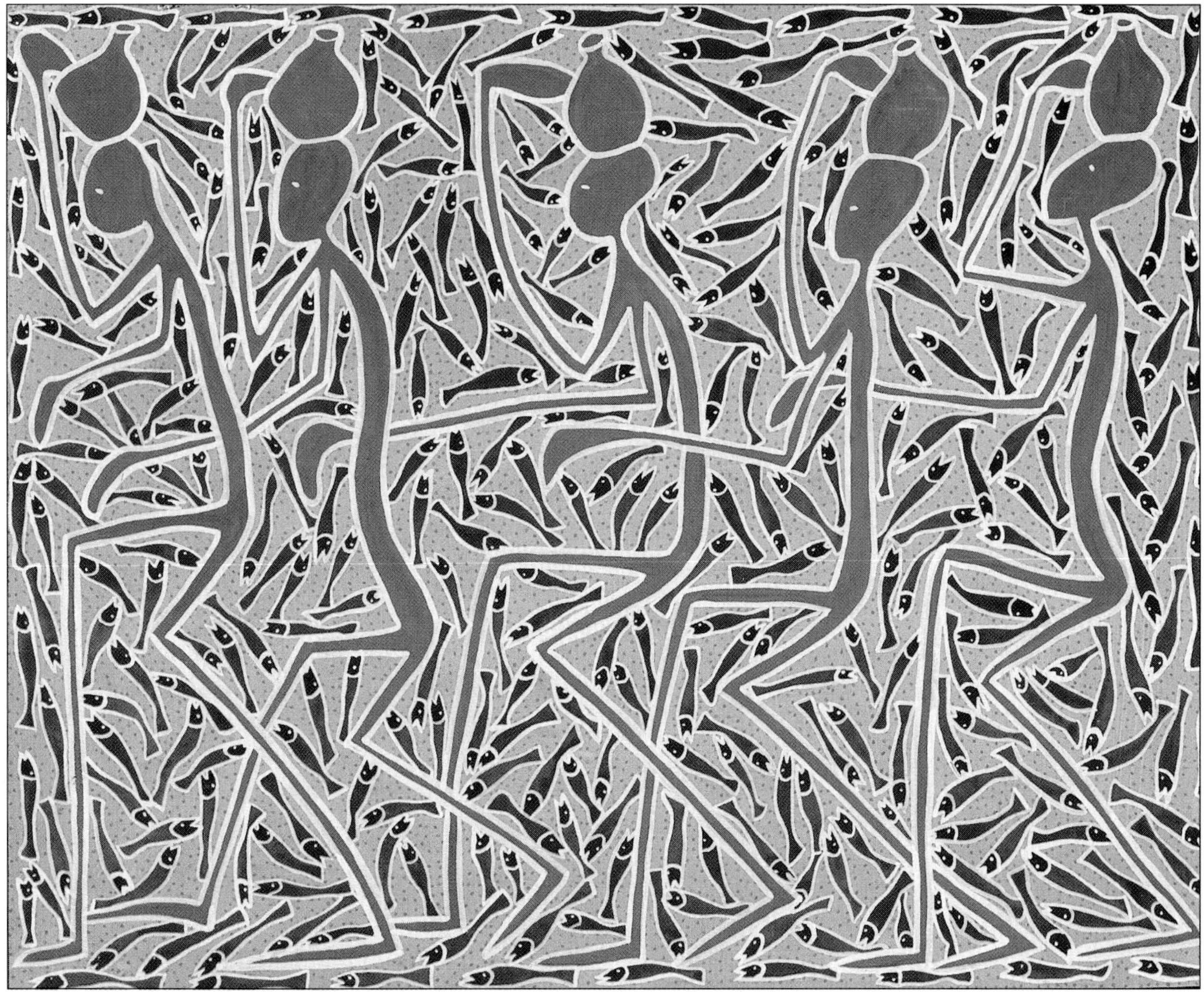

Figures Carrying Water
Mode Muntu (circa 1950–1986)
1973
Collection: Bogumil Jewsiewicki
The Museum for African Art, New York

Rhythmic repetition is one aesthetic characteristic of African art, found in painting as well as in music and poetry. The paintings of Mode Muntu, an artist from Zaïre, clearly display this trait; they often contain figures that are repeated in similar positions.

Pour commencer

Daniel Turquin, un jeune Américain, est médecin **bénévole** pour Humanité internationale, une association qui **protège les droits** de l'homme. Voici quelques problèmes **mondiaux** qui **préoccupent** Daniel. À votre avis, **lequel** est le plus grave dans votre région? Lequel est le plus **répandu**?

la pauvreté

le chômage et le problème **des sans domicile fixe** (SDF)

la pollution

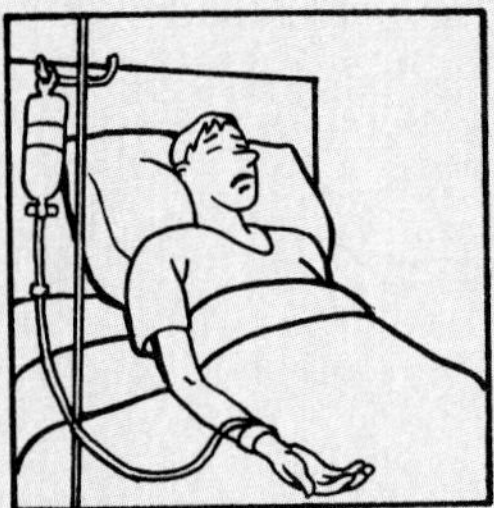

la maladie
(le cancer, le SIDA, la malnutrition, la dépression, l'alcoolisme)

la criminalité
(la violence domestique, le meurtre, **le viol**, les gangs, **le vol**, la drogue)

Êtes-vous plutôt conservateur (conservatrice) ou libéral(e)? Quelles solutions sont possibles?

Le gouvernement doit-il...
- aider les pauvres?
- **dépenser** plus d'argent pour l'éducation?
- dépenser plus d'argent pour **la recherche** médicale?
- **gaspiller** moins de ressources naturelles / moins d'argent?
- protéger l'environnement?
- développer l'économie?
- créer des **lois** plus sévères?

Et vous? Qu'est-ce que vous pouvez faire pour combattre ces problèmes?

bénévole *volunteer* **protéger** *to protect* **les droits** (*m*) *rights* **mondial(e)** *worldwide* **préoccuper** *to worry* **lequel (laquelle)** *which one* **répandu(e)** *widespread* **le chômage** *unemployment* **les sans domicile fixe** *the homeless* **le viol** *rape* **le vol** *theft* **dépenser** *to spend* **la recherche** *research* **gaspiller** *to waste* **une loi** *a law*

Daniel, en tournée en Afrique avec Humanité internationale, parle avec un nouvel ami africain, Mukala. Mukala parle de ses impressions des États-Unis.

— Quand j'ai visité les États-Unis l'année dernière, dans chaque ville où j'allais, je **ne** voyais **rien que** des crimes à la télé.
— Oui, c'est vrai qu'on en voit beaucoup dans toutes les grandes villes. Sous certains aspects, la société américaine est très violente.
— Pourquoi est-ce qu'il y a **tant de** violence?
— Je **crois** que c'est à cause des inégalités économiques. Je pense que l'égalité politique existe plus ou moins aux États-Unis, mais certains Américains n'ont pas les mêmes possibilités que d'autres à cause de leur situation économique.
— Alors, ils se tournent **vers** le crime?
— Certains se tournent vers la drogue et plus tard vers le crime.
— Qu'est-ce que le gouvernement a proposé pour **lutter contre** la criminalité?
— Il y en a qui croient que la solution, c'est l'éducation. D'autres disent qu'il faut changer la situation dans les prisons. On voit quelquefois des criminels violents comme les **meurtriers** sortir de prison après très peu de temps.
— Est-ce que les Américains croient à **la peine de mort**?
— Certains oui, d'autres n'y croient pas. Mais c'est permis dans **la plupart des** états.

ne... rien que *nothing but* **tant de** *so much, so many* **crois (croire** *to believe)* **vers** *towards* **lutter contre** *to fight against* **un meurtrier** *a murderer* **la peine de mort** *the death penalty, capital punishment* **la plupart (de)** *most (of)*

Savez-vous le faire?

A. Actualités. Est-ce que vous lisez le journal tous les jours? Choisissez la réponse qui complète correctement les phrases suivantes. Si vous ne savez pas, devinez.

1. Ici, il y a plus de (3, 4, 5, 6, 7, ???) pour cent de chômage.
2. Il y a plus de chômage chez les gens qui ont (moins de 30, de 30 à 50, plus de 50) ans.
3. (Le cancer, Le SIDA, La dépression) est parfois causé(e) par la pollution.
4. Il y a plus de criminalité (dans les grandes villes, dans les petites villes, à la campagne).
5. Le crime le plus répandu ici c'est (le meurtre, le vol, la violence domestique, le viol).
6. Il y a (plus de, moins de, autant de) criminalité en France qu'ici.
7. Il y a plus de pauvreté (en Europe, en Amérique du Nord, en Afrique, en Asie).
8. À mon avis, le problème le plus grave pour l'humanité, c'est (la malnutrition, le chômage, la pollution, la maladie, la criminalité, ???).

B. Associations. Quels problèmes associez-vous avec ces endroits? Essayez de penser à plusieurs possibilités pour chacun.

1. l'hôpital
2. le lycée
3. la prison
4. la rue
5. le travail
6. les grandes villes

C. **Le budget.** Vous êtes chargé(e) de préparer le budget de la nation pour l'année prochaine. Divisez 100% du budget parmi les six catégories suivantes. Quel pourcentage du budget donnez-vous pour...?

- aider les pauvres
- protéger l'environnement
- développer l'économie
- faire de la recherche médicale
- éduquer la population
- la défense nationale

Comment s'y prendre?

Recognizing the future and the conditional

Learning to recognize verbs that indicate future and conditional actions will make reading French easier. A verb whose stem resembles the infinitive and whose endings look like the present tense forms of **avoir** is probably in the future tense. Translate verbs in the future by *will...* How would you translate the last four sentences below?

Je visiterai l'Afrique.	*I will visit Africa.*
Le voyage prendra du temps.	*The trip will take time.*
Tu trouveras les gens courageux.	*You will find the people brave.*
Nous choisirons un itinéraire intéressant.	*???*
Vous aimerez ce continent.	*???*
Les Africains vous plairont.	*???*
Le paysage vous plaira.	*???*

Verbs that have the same stem as the future but the same endings as the **imparfait** are in the conditional. Translate them by *would...* How would you translate the last two sentences?

J'aimerais vivre ici.	*I would like to live here.*
Je vivrais à Dakar.	*I would live in Dakar.*
Nous habiterions près de la ville.	*???*
Tu voudrais venir nous voir?	*???*

Some verbs, like **être**, **pouvoir**, and **faire**, have irregular stems in the future and the conditional (**ser-**, **pourr-**, **fer-**). How would you translate these sentences?

Tu serais heureux ici.	*You would be happy here.*
Tu seras heureux ici.	*???*
On pourrait vivre plus simplement.	*We could live more simply.*
On pourra vivre plus simplement.	*???*

Can you guess the meaning of these sentences?

Il y aura beaucoup de machines.	*???*
Il faudrait trouver des solutions.	*???*
Nous devrions travailler pour la paix (*peace*).	*???*

Savez-vous le faire?

A. C'est possible. D'abord, indiquez si les verbes en caractères gras sont au futur ou au conditionnel et donnez la traduction anglaise. Ensuite, complétez chaque phrase par toutes les réponses qui vous semblent vraies.

1. Dans dix ans...
   - on **vivra** mieux.
   - on **trouvera** des solutions aux problèmes sociaux.
   - le monde **sera** en grand danger.
   - **il y aura** toujours les mêmes problèmes qu'aujourd'hui.
   - **il y aura** plus de paix dans le monde.
2. Si j'étais chef du gouvernement de mon pays...
   - je **pourrais** trouver une solution aux problèmes économiques.
   - ma famille **serait** très heureuse.
   - je **m'occuperais** d'abord des problèmes sociaux.
   - je **choisirais** mon/ma musicien(ne) préféré(e) comme porte-parole (*spokesperson*).
3. Pour améliorer la vie d'aujourd'hui...
   - **il faudrait** limiter la population.
   - on **devrait** développer l'économie.
   - **il faudrait** ne plus gaspiller nos ressources naturelles.
4. Après mes études universitaires...
   - je **pourrai** très bien parler français.
   - je **trouverai** un travail intéressant.
   - on **fera** une grande fête.
   - je **comprendrai** mieux la vie et le monde.

Abidjan, capitale de la Côte-d'Ivoire

B. Une liste. Regardez le texte qui suit (*Une lettre du Zaïre*) et faites une liste de tous les verbes qui sont au futur et de tous ceux (*all those*) qui sont au conditionnel.

Qu'est-ce qui se passe?

Une lettre du Zaïre

Daniel Turquin, Américain d'origine haïtienne et depuis longtemps médecin bénévole pour Humanité internationale, est maintenant en Afrique avec un groupe de musiciens qui font un tour du monde pour encourager la paix mondiale.

En Afrique depuis deux mois, Daniel vient de prendre une décision qui changera le cours de sa vie. Il écrit à sa sœur pour lui apprendre sa décision.

Ma chère Suzanne,

J'ai téléphoné à papa et maman la semaine dernière et ils m'ont dit que tu étais un peu déprimée parce que tu ne te sentais pas satisfaite de ton travail et que tu avais des ennuis avec l'administration de la clinique. Si tu n'es pas contente là où tu es, tu devrais penser à venir me rejoindre en Afrique. Je suis fasciné par les gens et leurs traditions. Dans chaque village que nous visitons, il y a des nouvelles choses à voir. Comme tu sais, je m'intéresse surtout à la musique et à la danse. Nous sommes arrivés au Zaïre la semaine dernière. Je trouve les Zaïrois très chaleureux. J'ai fait quelques vidéos que je t'enverrai.

La vie ici est très simple mais pour la plupart, c'est une vie pleine de joie. Je suis venu ici pour aider, mais à beaucoup d'égards, ce sont les Africains qui m'aident. J'ai trouvé la «joie de vivre» ici. C'est pourquoi j'ai décidé de rester ici en Afrique; je vais rester au moins cinq ans... peut-être même toute ma vie. Que penses-tu de ça, ma chère Suzanne?

Tu m'avais dit que tu pensais venir me rejoindre à la fin de la tournée. Je te demande de réfléchir à la possibilité de rester. Je sais que n'importe qui ne ferait pas ça. Mais je te connais et je sais que tu aimeras l'Afrique autant que moi et qu'une fois arrivée, tu ne voudras plus repartir. Alors, nous serons deux médecins ici au lieu d'un. Comme moi, tu as toujours voulu faire quelque chose qui compte dans le monde.

Et ici, on le pourra! On se joindra aux Africains pour améliorer la vie de ceux qui ont besoin d'aide.

Tu te demandes sans doute comment serait ta vie ici. Je dois t'avouer que je ne sais pas. Je sais seulement que tu serais heureuse. Il est certain que tu vivrais une vie plus simple mais certainement pleine de satisfaction. Moi-même, j'aimerais bien avoir une petite clinique dans un village. Toi, tu préférerais peut-être travailler dans l'hôpital d'une grande ville telle que Kinshasa.

De toute manière, nos connaissances de médecine seront très utiles ici et je suis certain qu'on sera tous les deux très heureux. Je te prie, ma chère Suzanne, de considérer sérieusement ce que je te propose et de m'écrire aussi vite que possible.

Je t'embrasse bien fort,

Daniel

Avez-vous compris?

Dans la lettre. Répondez aux questions suivantes en vous servant de la lettre de Daniel.

1. Qui est Suzanne? Où travaille-t-elle?
2. Qu'est-ce que Daniel a décidé de faire? Pour combien de temps?
3. Pourquoi est-ce qu'il aime l'Afrique? Comment trouve-t-il les Zaïrois? À quoi s'intéresse-t-il surtout?
4. Qu'est-ce qu'il demande à sa sœur de faire? Comment serait sa vie si elle le faisait?
5. Daniel et sa sœur ont toujours voulu faire quelque chose qui compte dans le monde. D'après Daniel, qu'est-ce qu'ils peuvent faire s'ils restent en Afrique?

Une danseuse au Sénégal.

Remarquez que...

L'histoire africaine des deux siècles derniers est une histoire de colonisation et de décolonisation. À la fin du dix-neuvième siècle et au début du vingtième, les quatre coins de l'Afrique étaient sous le contrôle des Européens. Il y a plus de 800 langues indigènes en Afrique, mais de nos jours, la plupart des Africains parlent aussi une langue européenne.

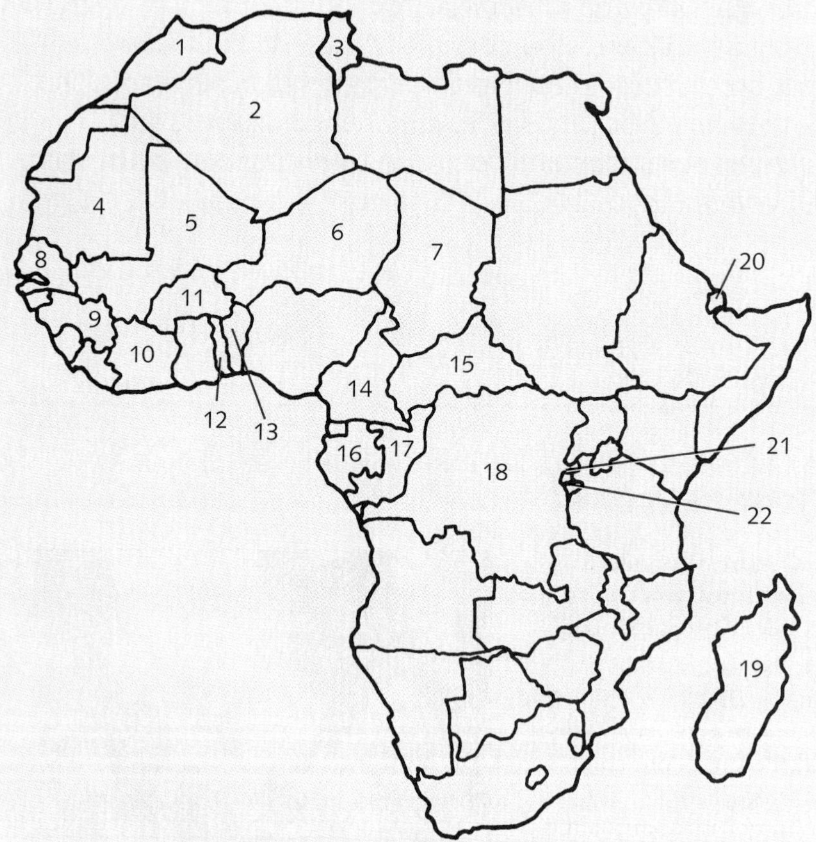

Pays francophones. Voici une liste des pays francophones en Afrique aujourd'hui avec la date d'indépendance de chacun. Regardez la carte et dites quel numéro correspond à chacun de ces pays. Vous pouvez vérifier vos réponses en utilisant la carte du monde francophone au début du livre.

l'Algérie (1962)
le Bénin (1960)
le Burkina-Faso (1960)
le Burundi (1962)
le Cameroun (1960)
le Congo (1960)
la Côte-d'Ivoire (1960)
le Gabon (1960)
la Guinée (1958)
Madagascar (1960)
le Mali (1960)
le Maroc (1956)
la Mauritanie (1960)
le Niger (1960)
la République centrafricaine (1960)
la République de Djibouti (1977)
le Ruanda (1962)
le Sénégal (1960)
le Tchad (1960)
le Togo (1960)
la Tunisie (1956)
le Zaïre (1960)

SUJET DE CONVERSATION 1
Talking about the future

Qu'est-ce qu'on dit?

Êtes-vous plutôt optimiste ou plutôt pessimiste quand vous pensez à **l'avenir**? Comment le voyez-vous?

Sur le plan global...

Est-ce qu'on connaîtra
- la tolérance ou le racisme?
- la compréhension ou **la haine**?
- des progrès médicaux et agricoles ou des maladies et de la famine?
- la liberté ou la tyrannie?
- la sécurité ou le terrorisme?
- **la paix** ou **la guerre**?

Sur le plan individuel...

Est-ce qu'on
- vivra mieux?
- vivra plus longtemps?
- aura plus de temps libre?
- aura une vie plus simple?

Ou est-ce qu'on
- vivra moins bien?
- sera plus malade?
- travaillera plus?
- dépendra plus des ordinateurs et des machines?

Daniel et son nouvel ami Mukala, un des organisateurs du concert, parlent de l'avenir des pays de l'Afrique.

— Les pays **occidentaux** ont toujours **prétendu** avoir **laissé** la démocratie dans leurs **anciennes** colonies mais souvent on ne voyait que des dictatures **puissantes** et de la corruption. C'est pourquoi il y a eu tant de guerres civiles en Afrique et dans le reste du **tiers monde**.

— Mais je vois qu'il y a un mouvement vers la démocratisation dans beaucoup de pays.

— C'est vrai que beaucoup de régimes autocrates ont dû procéder à des élections à cause de l'agitation populaire.

— Mais avec des gouvernements démocratiques, je crois que la situation en Afrique s'améliorera certainement.

— Je reste un peu sceptique. Sans la prospérité, ces nouveaux gouvernements démocratiques seront toujours en danger. La liberté politique et la liberté économique vont ensemble. On ne peut pas avoir l'une sans l'autre. **Tant que** la majorité du peuple vivra dans la pauvreté, il y aura de l'instabilité et il n'y aura pas la paix.

l'avenir *(m) the future* **la *haine** *hatred* **la paix** *peace* **la guerre** *war* **occidental(e)** *western* **prétendre** *to claim* **laisser** *to leave (behind)* **ancien(ne)** *former* **puissant(e)** *powerful* **le tiers monde** *the third world* **tant que** *as long as*

A. **Plus ou moins?** Êtes-vous plutôt optimiste ou plutôt pessimiste face à l'avenir? Exprimez votre opinion en complétant les phrases suivantes avec **plus de**, **moins de** ou **autant de**.

1. Dans vingt ans, il y aura ____ pauvreté dans le monde que maintenant.
2. Il y aura ____ démocratisation.
3. Il y aura ____ dialogues entre les pays du monde.
4. Il y aura ____ régimes autocrates dans le tiers monde.
5. Il y aura ____ crimes dans notre pays.
6. Il y aura ____ maladies dans le monde.
7. Il y aura ____ pollution.
8. Il y aura ____ chômage dans notre pays.
9. Il y aura ____ terrorisme dans notre pays.

B. **On en voit.** Dites si on voit beaucoup les choses suivantes dans votre ville.

EXEMPLE de la pauvreté → **On n'en voit pas.**
ou **On en voit beaucoup.**
ou **On en voit peu.**

1. de la malnutrition
2. du chômage
3. de la drogue
4. de la pollution
5. de la criminalité
6. des sans domicile fixe

C. **Croyances.** Dites si vous croyez aux choses suivantes. Répondez **J'y crois** (*I believe in it*) ou **Je n'y crois pas.**

EXEMPLE les fantômes (*ghosts*) → **J'y crois.**
ou **Je n'y crois pas.**

1. le mariage
2. la vie après la mort
3. la vie extra-terrestre
4. la réincarnation
5. la peine de mort
6. l'astrologie

D. **Est-ce possible?** Utilisez une des expressions données pour exprimer votre avis sur la probabilité des événements suivants d'ici cinquante ans (*fifty years from now*).

1. On vivra dans un monde meilleur.
2. Il y aura une dictature dans notre pays.
3. Les pays du tiers monde seront plus puissants.
4. Tout le monde parlera la même langue.
5. Le SIDA sera guérissable (*curable*).
6. On vivra jusqu'à l'âge de 120 ans.
7. Tout le monde aura une voiture solaire.
8. La vie sera plus simple.

Je crois que oui.
JE SUIS UN PEU SCEPTIQUE.
C'EST BIEN POSSIBLE.
C'est peu probable.
C'est certain.
C'est impossible.

Voilà pourquoi!

Le futur

You have learned to use **aller** + *infinitive* to express planned or anticipated actions. You can also use the future tense forms of the verb to predict or explain what someone *will do*. The future of most verbs is formed by adding the boldfaced endings below to the infinitive of the verb. If an infinitive ends in **-e**, the **e** is dropped.

> **SELF-CHECK**
> 1. What is the future stem for most regular verbs? What if the infinitive ends in **-e**?
> 2. All but two of the future endings look like the forms of the verb **avoir**. Which two are they?

PARLER		FINIR		VENDRE	
je	parler**ai**	je	finir**ai**	je	vendr**ai**
tu	parler**as**	tu	finir**as**	tu	vendr**as**
il/elle/on	parler**a**	il/elle/on	finir**a**	il/elle/on	vendr**a**
nous	parler**ons**	nous	finir**ons**	nous	vendr**ons**
vous	parler**ez**	vous	finir**ez**	vous	vendr**ez**
ils/elles	parler**ont**	ils/elles	finir**ont**	ils/elles	vendr**ont**

Verbs like **acheter** and **payer** have spelling changes in the future stem (**j'achèterai, je paierai**), while those like **préférer** do not (**je préférerai**). Note that the future endings look like the present-tense forms of the verb **avoir**, except for the **nous** and **vous** forms.

The following verbs have irregular stems in the future. Note that they are grouped according to whether their stem ends with **-r**, **-rr**, **-vr**, or **-dr**.

-r	**aller**	**ir-**	→	j'irai, tu iras...
	avoir	**aur-**	→	j'aurai, tu auras...
	être	**ser-**	→	je serai, tu seras...
	faire	**fer-**	→	je ferai, tu feras...
	savoir	**saur-**	→	je saurai, tu sauras...
-rr	**courir**	**courr-**	→	je courrai, tu courras...
	mourir	**mourr-**	→	je mourrai, tu mourras...
	pouvoir	**pourr-**	→	je pourrai, tu pourras...
	voir	**verr-**	→	je verrai, tu verras...
-vr	**devoir**	**devr-**	→	je devrai, tu devras...
	pleuvoir	**pleuvr-**	→	il pleuvra
-dr	**devenir**	**deviendr-**	→	je deviendrai, tu deviendras...
	falloir (il faut)	**faudr-**	→	il faudra
	venir	**viendr-**	→	je viendrai, tu viendras...
	vouloir	**voudr-**	→	je voudrai, tu voudras...

In sentences with **si** (*if*), use the future to say what will happen if certain conditions are true. The verb in the clause with **si** is in the present.

Si nous travaillons ensemble, nous *pourrons* trouver une solution.
Je *viendrai* te voir si tu veux.

Although the future is generally used in French as it is in English, one difference is its use in clauses with **quand, aussitôt que** (*as soon as*), and **tant que** (*as long as*) referring to the future. English uses the present in such clauses.

FRENCH USES FUTURE	ENGLISH USES PRESENT
Quand tu *auras* ton diplôme, qu'est-ce que tu feras?	*When you **have** your degree, what will you do?*
Tant qu'*il y aura* trop de pauvreté, ces démocraties seront en danger.	*As long as **there is** too much poverty, these democracies will be in danger.*

Et ça se prononce comment?

La consonne r et le futur

The future stem of all verbs in French ends in **-r**. To pronounce a French **r**, arch the back of the tongue firmly in the back of the mouth and pronounce a strong English **h** sound. Practice the **r** in these words.

je pourrai **tu trouveras** **il sera** **nous reviendrons** **ils mettront**

When the future stem ends in **-er**, the **e** is often silent if it is preceded by a single consonant.

je sɇrai **tu fɇras** **nous habitɇrons** **ils arrivɇront**

This **e** is generally pronounced like the **e** of **je** when dropping it would bring three pronounced consonants together.

je montrerai **il parlera**

Savez-vous le faire?

A. **Après les études.** D'abord, écoutez chaque question. Remarquez qu'on ne prononce pas chaque **e** barré. Ensuite, demandez à un(e) camarade de classe s'il/si elle fera les choses suivantes après ses études.

Quand tu auras ton diplôme...

EXEMPLE — Est-ce que tu sɇras content(e)?
— **Quand tu auras ton diplôme, est-ce que tu sɇras content(e)?**
— **Je sɇrai très content(e).**

1. Est-ce que tu fɇras un voyage?
2. Est-ce que tu visitɇras l'Europe?
3. Est-ce que tu te mariɇras?
4. Est-ce que tu achètɇras une maison?
5. Où est-ce que tu habitɇras?
6. Est-ce que tu trouvɇras du travail?
7. Est-ce que tu fɇras de la recherche?
8. Est-ce que tu sɇras content(e)?

B. **J'espère que oui!** Dites si vous espérez que les personnes suivantes feront ou ne feront pas les choses indiquées dans les cinq années à venir.

EXEMPLE mon meilleur ami (se marier, être au chômage, acheter une maison)
J'espère que mon meilleur ami se mariera.
J'espère qu'il ne sera pas au chômage.
J'espère qu'il achètera une maison.

1. [*Au prof de français.*] vous (aller en France, avoir des étudiants intelligents, être malade)
2. [*À l'étudiant(e) à côté de vous.*] tu (oublier le français, avoir une vie intéressante, avoir ton diplôme)
3. mon/ma meilleur(e) ami(e) et moi (perdre contact, se téléphoner de temps en temps, habiter ensemble)
4. les pays du tiers monde (développer leur économie, avoir des guerres civiles, établir plus de régimes démocratiques)
5. notre pays (aider plus les pays du tiers monde, dépenser plus d'argent pour la recherche médicale, devenir plus libéral)

C. **Résultats.** Combien de phrases logiques est-ce que vous pouvez faire en cinq minutes en combinant un élément de chaque colonne? Mettez les verbes à la forme convenable.

EXEMPLE **Si on gaspille moins, on protégera l'environnement.**

Si on...	gaspiller moins développer l'économie faire plus de recherche aider les pays pauvres éduquer la population encourager la tolérance travailler ensemble ne pas reconnaître les problèmes sociaux ???	encourager la démocratie mourir trouver un remède contre le SIDA protéger l'environnement avoir plus de crimes avoir moins de chômage développer l'économie trouver des solutions vivre en paix ???

D. **Quand?** Expliquez quand vous ferez les choses suivantes.

EXEMPLE se marier
Je me marierai quand je trouverai l'homme (la femme) parfait(e).
OU **Je ne me marierai jamais.**

1. acheter une maison
2. aller en Europe
3. être content(e)
4. savoir tout faire
5. être surpris(e)
6. avoir des enfants

E. **Résolutions.** La revue *Rock & Folk* a publié ses résolutions pour l'année prochaine. Lisez les résolutions à droite, ensuite écrivez vous-même quatre résolutions.

Résolutions de printemps: Je serai gentil. Je serai positif. Je ne dirai pas de mal de mes chefs. J'aimerai mes collègues. Je dirai bonjour. Je ne tirerai plus au fusil à canon-scié sur les vidéos des Happy Mondays. Je respecterai David Bowie. J'aiderai le rap français. Je voterai. J'irai voir des films français. J'écouterai Peter Gabriel. Je copinerai avec les maisons de disques. Je ne m'abriterai pas derrière mon répondeur-enregistreur. Je visionnerai *toutes* les cassettes vidéos de Boucherie Productions. Je ne me moquerai plus de Prince. Je ne chroniquerai plus les cassettes de la collection Playboy... Oh, et puis non.

un chef *a boss* **tirer** *to shoot* **un fusil à canon-scié** *a sawed-off shotgun* **copiner avec** *to be buddies with* **s'abriter derrière** *to hide behind* **un répondeur-enregistreur** *an answering machine* **visionner** *to view* **se moquer de** *to make fun of*

F. **L'histoire de demain.** Est-ce que vous vous intéressez à la politique? Exprimez votre avis en répondant à chaque question.

1. À votre avis, qui gagnera les prochaines élections nationales dans notre pays?
2. Est-ce que notre pays deviendra plus conservateur ou plus libéral dans les prochaines années?
3. L'année prochaine y aura-t-il plus de chômage ou moins de chômage dans notre pays? À votre avis, dans quelles régions est-ce qu'il y en aura beaucoup? Où est-ce qu'il y en aura le moins?
4. Quels pays du tiers monde deviendront les plus puissants à l'avenir?
5. Dans 50 ans, quel problème sera le plus grave: la maladie, la pollution, le chômage ou la violence?

G. «**Ne me quitte pas.**» Voici les paroles de «Ne me quitte pas», une chanson du célèbre chanteur belge, Jacques Brel. Lisez les paroles et faites une liste des choses que le chanteur fera si la femme qu'il aime ne le quitte pas.

Ne me quitte pas

Ne me quitte pas
Il faut oublier
Tout peut s'oublier
Qui **s'enfuit** déjà
Oublier le temps
Des **malentendus**
Et le temps perdu
À savoir comment
Oublier ces heures
Qui **tuaient** parfois
À coups de pourquoi
Le **cœur** du bonheur
Ne me quitte pas
Ne me quitte pas
Ne me quitte pas
Ne me quitte pas
Moi, je t'offrirai
Des perles de pluie
Venues de pays
Où il ne pleut pas
Je **creuserai** la terre
Jusqu'après ma mort
Pour couvrir ton **corps**
D'**or** et de **lumière**
Je ferai un domaine
Où l'amour sera **roi**
Où l'amour sera loi
Où tu seras **reine**
Ne me quitte pas
Ne me quitte pas
Ne me quitte pas
Ne me quitte pas
Ne me quitte pas
Je t'inventerai
Des mots **insensés**
Que tu comprendras
Je te parlerai
De ces **amants**-là
Qui ont vu deux fois
Leur cœur **s'embraser**
Je te raconterai
L'histoire de ce roi
Mort de n'avoir pas
Pu te rencontrer
Ne me quitte pas
Ne me quitte pas
Ne me quitte pas
Ne me quitte pas
On a vu souvent
Rejaillir le feu
De l'ancien volcan
Qu'on croyait trop vieux
Il est **paraît**-il
Des terres **brûlées**
Donnant plus de **blé**
Qu'un meilleur avril
Et quand vient le soir
Pour qu'un ciel flamboie
Le rouge et le noir
Ne **s'épousent**-ils pas?
Ne me quitte pas
Ne me quitte pas
Ne me quitte pas
Ne me quitte pas
Ne me quitte pas
Je ne vais plus **pleurer**
Je ne vais plus parler
Je **me cacherai** là
À te regarder
Danser et **sourire**
Et à t'écouter
Chanter et puis **rire**
Laisse-moi devenir
L'ombre de ton ombre
L'ombre de ta main
L'ombre de ton chien
Ne me quitte pas
Ne me quitte pas
Ne me quitte pas
Ne me quitte pas

s'enfuir *to flee* **un malentendu** *misunderstanding* **tuer** *to kill* **le cœur** *the heart* **creuser** *to dig* **le corps** *body* **l'or** (*m*) *gold* **la lumière** *light* **le roi** *king* **la reine** *queen* **insensé(e)** *senseless* **des amants** (*m*) *lovers* **s'embraser** *to catch fire* **rejaillir** *to leap up* **paraître** *to appear* **brûlé(e)** *burned* **le blé** *wheat* **s'épouser** *to marry* **pleurer** *to cry* **se cacher** *to hide* **sourire** *to smile* **rire** *to laugh* **laisser** *to let* **l'ombre** (*f*) *shadow*

H. **Un itinéraire.** Vous allez faire le tour du monde et vous voulez visiter quatre pays francophones. Avec un(e) partenaire, préparez votre itinéraire. Dites quels pays vous visiterez, dans quel ordre, combien de temps vous passerez dans chaque endroit et au moins une chose que vous y ferez.

EXEMPLE **D'abord, nous irons au Zaïre. Nous y passerons une semaine. Nous descendrons le Congo en bateau où nous verrons beaucoup d'animaux intéressants. Après, nous irons...**

Voilà pourquoi!

SELF-CHECK

1. Which forms of **voir** and **croire** have a **-y-** instead of an **-i-**?
2. What auxiliary do you use with **voir** and **croire** in the **passé composé**?
3. Which one of these two verbs has an irregular future stem?
4. What are the two uses of **y**? of **en**?

Les verbes **voir** et **croire**

You have already seen the verb **voir** (*to see*) in the infinitive. Here is how you conjugate it. The verb **croire** (*to believe*) is conjugated like **voir**, except in the future.

VOIR (*TO SEE*)	
je **vois**	nous **voyons**
tu **vois**	vous **voyez**
il/elle/on **voit**	ils/elles **voient**

PASSÉ COMPOSÉ: j'**ai vu**
IMPARFAIT: je **voy**ais
FUTUR: je **verr**ai

CROIRE (*TO BELIEVE*)	
je **crois**	nous **croyons**
tu **crois**	vous **croyez**
il/elle/on **croit**	ils/elles **croient**

PASSÉ COMPOSÉ: j'**ai cru**
IMPARFAIT: je **croy**ais
FUTUR: je **croir**ai

Use the preposition **à** to say whether you believe *in* something. One exception is that you use **en** to say *to believe in God* (**croire en Dieu**).

Je ne crois pas *à* la peine de mort. **Mon petit ami ne croit pas *au* mariage.**

Les pronoms **y** et **en** (*reprise*)

You have learned to use **y** to replace a prepositional phrase indicating a place.

Tu viens *au cinéma* avec nous? → **Tu *y* viens avec nous?**
Ils sont encore *dans la cuisine.* → **Ils *y* sont encore.**

You also use **y** to replace a prepositional phrase with **à** followed by a thing, but not by a person or animal. The following verbs take **à** before their objects.

croire à	**Je crois *au végétarisme.***	→ **J'*y* crois.**
s'intéresser à	**Je m'intéresse *à la politique.***	→ **Je m'*y* intéresse.**
participer à	**Ils participent *au concert.***	→ **Ils *y* participent.**
penser à	**Tu penses *au voyage*?**	→ **Tu *y* penses?**
obéir à	**J'obéis toujours *à la loi.***	→ **J'*y* obéis toujours.**
réfléchir à	**Elle réfléchit trop *à ses problèmes.***	→ **Elle *y* réfléchit trop.**
répondre à	**Le professeur a répondu *à ma question.***	→ **Le professeur *y* a répondu.**
réussir à	**Je ne réussis pas *à comprendre.***	→ **Je n'*y* réussis pas.**

In *Chapitre dix*, you learned to use **en** to replace a noun preceded by the partitive, a number, or another quantity expression.

J'ai *des problèmes* aussi dans mon quartier. → **J'*en* ai aussi dans mon quartier.**
Il y a trois *gangs* différents. → **Il y *en* a trois.**
Il y a trop *de violence.* → **Il y *en* a trop.**

Also use **en** to replace a prepositional phrase with **de** followed by something other than a person. The following verbs take **de** before objects.

avoir besoin de	Ils ont besoin *de travail.*	→ Ils *en* ont besoin.
avoir envie de	J'ai envie *de sortir.*	→ J'*en* ai envie.
avoir l'intention de	Il a l'intention *de partir.*	→ Il *en* a l'intention.
s'occuper de	Qui s'occupe *de la maison*?	→ Qui s'*en* occupe?
parler de	Ils parlaient *des élections.*	→ Ils *en* parlaient.
penser de	Que penses-tu *de cette solution*?	→ Qu'*en* penses-tu?
rêver de	Je rêve *de voyager en Afrique.*	→ J'*en* rêve.

Numbers and quantity expressions generally remain after these expressions when the nouns following them are replaced by **en**.

Je m'occupe *de deux grands problèmes.* → Je m'*en* occupe de *deux.*
Il a parlé *de plusieurs solutions.* → Il *en* a parlé de *plusieurs.*

Savez-vous le faire?

A. **Boule de cristal.** Les personnes suivantes voient leur avenir dans une boule de cristal. Complétez chaque phrase pour dire ce qu'elles y voient.

EXEMPLE Mon petit ami y **voit du succès.**

1. Moi, j'y...
2. Mes parents y...
3. Mon/Ma meilleur(e) ami(e) y...
4. Mes camarades de classe et moi, nous y...
5. [*À un(e) autre étudiant(e).*] Est-ce que tu y...?
6. [*Au professeur.*] Est-ce que vous y...?

du succès *des difficultés*
UN TRAVAIL INTÉRESSANT
LE MARIAGE **l'amour**
un voyage beaucoup d'argent
la pauvreté ???
???

B. **Ils y croient.** Nommez une chose à laquelle ces personnes croient ou ne croient pas.

EXEMPLE Mon petit ami **(ne) croit (pas)** à la chance.

1. Moi, je...
2. Mes parents...
3. Mon/Ma meilleur(e) ami(e)...
4. Mes camarades de classe et moi, nous...
5. [*À un(e) autre étudiant(e).*] Est-ce que tu...?
6. [*Au professeur.*] Est-ce que vous...?

à la chance ???
À LA PEINE DE MORT
AUX EXAMENS FACILES
??? au père Noël
à la vie sur d'autres planètes
AU MARIAGE **au divorce**
à la prédestination

C. **Test psychologique.** Vous êtes psychologue et un(e) camarade de classe est votre patient(e). Demandez ce que votre camarade de classe voit dans ces images abstraites.

EXEMPLE — **Qu'est-ce que vous voyez dans cette image?**
— **Je crois que c'est le soleil. / Moi, je vois le soleil.**

EXEMPLE 1. 2.

3. 4. 5.

D. **Questions.** Posez les questions suivantes à un(e) camarade de classe qui doit répondre en remplaçant les mots en caractères gras par **y** ou **en**.

1. Parles-tu souvent **de politique** avec tes amis?
2. Est-ce que la plupart de tes amis croient **à la peine de mort**?
3. À ton avis, pourquoi voit-on de plus en plus **de violence** dans notre société?
4. Penses-tu souvent **à l'avenir**?
5. Est-ce que tu réfléchis trop **à tes problèmes**?
6. Est-ce que tu as quelquefois peur **de l'avenir**?
7. As-tu besoin **de travail**?
8. As-tu envie **de visiter l'Afrique**?

E. **Habitudes.** Complétez les phrases suivantes. Ensuite, demandez à un(e) autre étudiant(e) s'il/si elle fait la même chose en utilisant **y** ou **en**.

EXEMPLE — J'ai besoin d(e)...
— **J'ai besoin d'une nouvelle voiture. Et toi Martine, est-ce que tu en as besoin d'une aussi?**
— **Non, j'en ai déjà une.**

1. Je crois à...
2. Je pense souvent à...
3. J'ai l'intention d(e)...
4. J'ai envie d(e)...
5. Je réfléchis beaucoup à...
6. Je parle souvent d(e)...

F. **Politique.** Vous êtes homme / femme politique et vous êtes interviewé(e) à la télévision française. Préparez la scène avec un(e) partenaire qui va vous poser les questions suivantes. À la fin de l'interview, ajoutez une autre question.

— Pour lutter contre la criminalité, certains croient que l'éducation est la solution, d'autres la prison. Quel est votre avis?

...

— Croyez-vous à la peine de mort?

...

— Croyez-vous que c'est plutôt le chômage ou la drogue qui est à la base de la criminalité dans votre pays?

...

— Si vous gagnez les élections, sera-t-il plus important pour vous de développer l'économie ou de protéger l'environnement?

...

— Que ferez-vous pour lutter contre les maladies?

...

— Comment voyez-vous l'avenir de votre pays?

...

— Et l'avenir du monde?

...

— Quels pays du monde voudriez-vous aider?

...

— ???

Remarquez que...

Avec plus de 500 tribus différentes, le Zaïre est un pays de diversité et de contradictions. Kinshasa, la capitale, est une grande ville moderne mais les deux tiers (*two thirds*) de la population du Zaïre habitent dans des régions rurales où les traditions remontent à plus de mille ans.

Légendes. Laquelle de ces légendes va avec chacune des photos? *Kinshasa, capitale du Zaïre / L'Université de Kinshasa / Les Pygmées, premiers habitants du Zaïre / Nyimi Kok Mabiintsh III, roi des Kubas*

Qu'est-ce qu'on dit?

Daniel et Mukala parlent de la musique. Et vous? Quel genre de musique préférez-vous?

J'aime Je n'aime pas	les musicien(ne)s	qui s'intéressent aux causes politiques. qui jouent du jazz / de la musique populaire / ???. qui dansent aussi. qui chantent dans une autre langue.

J'aime Je n'aime pas	la musique	qu'on entend sur la station de radio ???. qu'on joue dans les discothèques. qu'on faisait pendant les années 50 / 60 / 70 / 80. que mes parents écoutent.

Paul McCartney Willie Nelson Paul Simon Madonna Tina Turner K. D. Lang ???	est un(e) artiste	**dont les chansons** sont bêtes / romantiques / ???. dont les chansons ont un message social. dont j'ai beaucoup de disques compacts. dont j'ai envie de voir un concert. dont je trouve **la voix** jolie / désagréable.

La musique classique Le rock Le blues Le jazz Le rap La musique country	est	plus moins **aussi**	intéressant(e) **que**	le rock. le blues. le jazz. le rap. la musique country. la musique classique.

Luciano Pavarotti Prince Garth Brooks Whitney Houston Paula Abdul Jessye Norman ???	est un(e) meilleur(e) chanteur / chanteuse que n'est pas aussi bon(ne) chanteur / chanteuse que chante mieux que chante moins bien que	???

dont *whose, of whom* **les chansons** (*f*) *songs* **une voix** *a voice* **aussi... que...** *as . . . as . . .*

Daniel et Mukala parlent de la musique au Zaïre.

— **Chaque** fois que j'écoute du jazz zaïrois, j'ai l'impression d'écouter de la musique antillaise.

— Tu as raison. La musique africaine et la musique antillaise se sont beaucoup influencées. Les Antillais d'origine africaine ont mis des éléments africains dans leur musique... et pendant la première **moitié** de ce **siècle**, des **marins** qui venaient de Cuba nous ont **rapporté** de la musique de là-bas comme la rumba, par exemple.

— Comment est-ce que le jazz zaïrois s'est développé?

— Plusieurs groupes ont influencé le jazz zaïrois, dont les plus connus sont le Tout Grand African Jazz et le Tout Puissant OK Jazz. Au début, ils créaient des rythmes qui utilisaient plusieurs guitares et pendant les années cinquante, ils ont **ajouté** des trompettes et des saxophones.

— Il y a une femme que j'ai entendue à la radio et que j'ai beaucoup aimée, mais je ne sais pas son nom exact. C'était quelque chose comme «Belle». Elle ne chantait pas en français. C'était surtout le rythme de ses chansons qui m'a plu.

— C'était peut-être M'Bilia Bel. Généralement, ses chansons ont un message social. Dans une de ses chansons, par exemple, elle parle des problèmes des femmes dans les mariages polygames. Les **paroles** sont très intéressantes.

— Est-ce que tu joues d'un instrument?

— Je joue de la guitare et du likembe. Tu sais ce que c'est, le likembe?

— Non, je connais **le patenge** mais pas le likembe.

— C'est un petit piano qu'on peut **tenir** à la main. Je te le montrerai un jour quand tu viendras chez moi. Et toi, tu joues d'un instrument ou tu chantes?

— Je chante mal. Quand j'étais à l'école secondaire, je jouais de la batterie, mais ça fait longtemps que je n'ai pas joué.

chaque *each, every* **la moitié** *half* **un siècle** *a century* **un marin** *a sailor* **rapporter** *to bring back* **ajouter** *to add* **les paroles** *(f) words* **le patenge** *a type of small drum* **tenir** *to hold*

A. Qui? Vous parlez à un Zaïrois de la musique. Complétez les phrases suivantes avec le nom d'un(e) artiste.

1. ______ est un(e) artiste dont les chansons ont un message social.
2. ______ est un(e) artiste dont les chansons sont romantiques.
3. L'artiste qui gagne le plus d'argent, c'est ______ .
4. L'artiste qui a gagné le plus de Grammys l'année dernière, c'était ______ .
5. ______ est quelqu'un que je voudrais voir en concert.
6. ______ est quelqu'un qui va être populaire pendant longtemps.
7. ______ est quelqu'un qui n'aura pas beaucoup de succès plus tard.
8. L'artiste que mes parents préfèrent, c'est ______ .

B. Préférences. Mukala parle de ses préférences en musique. Écoutez ce qu'il dit une première fois et décidé quel genre de musique il préfère de chaque groupe. Ensuite, écoutez une deuxième fois et dites quelle musique il préfère de toutes et laquelle il n'aime pas du tout.

1. le jazz ou le blues?
2. la musique classique ou l'opéra?
3. la musique pop ou le blues?
4. le blues ou le rap?
5. la musique en général ou le hard rock?

Voilà pourquoi!

SELF-CHECK

1. Which relative pronoun functions as the subject of a verb? Which one functions as the direct object of a verb? Which one replaces prepositional phrases with **de**?
2. What are the possible translations of **dont**?

Les pronoms relatifs qui, que, dont

Sometimes, you need to use a whole phrase to clarify which person or object you are talking about. The phrase that describes a noun is a relative clause. The word that begins the phrase, referring back to the noun described, is a relative pronoun.

— **Quel livre veux-tu?**

— **Le livre**	***qui* est sur la table.**	*The book*	***that** is on the table.*
	***que* j'ai acheté hier.**		***that** I bought yesterday.*
	***dont* tu m'as parlé.**		***about which** you talked to me.*

The use of the relative pronouns **qui, que,** and **dont** depends on how they function in the relative clause. They are all used for both people and things. In the following examples, note how the relative pronouns are used to combine two sentences talking about the same thing. The relative clause is placed immediately after the noun it describes.

- Use **qui** for people or things when they are the subject of the relative clause. Since **qui** is the subject, it is followed by a verb. It can mean *that, which,* or *who.*

M'Bilia Bel est *une artiste zaïroise. Elle* fait du jazz.
M'Bilia Bel est *une artiste zaïroise qui* fait du jazz.

***Le disque* est à moi. *Ce disque* est sur la table.**
***Le disque qui* est sur la table est à moi.**

- Use **que (qu')** for people or things when they are the direct object in the relative clause. It can mean *that, which, whom*, or it may be omitted in English.

  M'Bilia Bel est *une artiste zaïroise.* Je *l'*ai vue en concert.
  M'Bilia Bel est *une artiste zaïroise que* j'ai vue en concert.

  Le disque* est à moi. Il va écouter *ce disque.
  ***Le disque qu'*il va écouter est à moi.**

- Use **dont** for people or things to say *whose* or to replace a prepositional phrase with **de** in verbal expressions like **parler de** and **avoir besoin de**. In the latter case, **dont** can mean *which, of which*, or *about which.*

  M'Bilia Bel est *une artiste zaïroise. Ses* chansons ont un message social.
  M'Bilia Bel est *une artiste zaïroise dont* les chansons ont un message social.

  Le disque* est à moi. Tu parles *de ce disque.
  ***Le disque dont* tu parles est à moi.**

Savez-vous le faire?

A. **Goûts.** Demandez la préférence d'un(e) autre étudiant(e). Utilisez le pronom indiqué.

QUI

EXEMPLE les restaurants (servir de la grande cuisine, ne pas être chers)
— **Est-ce que tu préfères les restaurants qui servent de la grande cuisine ou les restaurants qui ne sont pas chers?**
— **Je préfère les restaurants qui servent de la grande cuisine.**

1. les films (avoir un message social, être amusants)
2. les cours (être faciles, être intéressants)
3. les chanteurs (chanter les vieilles chansons, faire du rap)
4. les voitures (être grosses et confortables, consommer moins)
5. les amis (aimer sortir, préférer rester à la maison)
6. les gens (croire tout savoir, ne pas parler beaucoup)

QUE

EXEMPLE les exercices (toute la classe fait ensemble, nous faisons avec un[e] partenaire)
— **Est-ce que tu préfères les exercices que toute la classe fait ensemble ou les exercices que nous faisons avec un(e) partenaire?**
— **Je préfère les exercices que nous faisons avec un(e) partenaire.**

1. les sports (on fait seul, on fait en groupe)
2. les vêtements (on porte en hiver, on porte en été)
3. les exercices (nous faisons en classe, nous faisons dans le cahier d'exercices)

4. les hommes / les femmes (tu rencontres à la bibliothèque, tu rencontres dans les clubs)
5. la cuisine (on sert dans les fast-foods, on prépare à la maison)
6. les films (on voit sur CBS, on voit sur PBS)

DONT

EXEMPLE les régions (le climat est tropical, le temps change avec les saisons)
— **Est-ce que tu préfères les régions dont le climat est tropical ou les régions dont le temps change avec les saisons?**
— **Je préfère les régions dont le temps change avec les saisons.**

1. les professeurs (les cours sont intéressants mais les examens sont difficiles, les cours sont ennuyeux mais les examens sont faciles)
2. les candidats (la politique protège l'environnement, la politique développe l'économie)
3. les musiciens (les chansons sont romantiques, les chansons ont un message social)
4. un(e) petit(e) ami(e) (la famille est riche mais un peu snob, la famille n'est pas riche mais plutôt sympa)
5. les quartiers (l'architecture est moderne, l'architecture est plus classique)

Dakar, la capitale sénégalaise. Depuis son indépendance en 1960, le Sénégal est l'une des démocraties les plus stables de l'Afrique francophone. Son premier président a été le célèbre poète Léopold Sédar Senghor.

B. Qu'est-ce que c'est? Complétez les descriptions suivantes avec **qui**, **que** ou **dont**. Après, devinez ce qui est décrit.

EXEMPLE VOUS COMPLÉTEZ: C'est un continent qui a 51 pays différents.
dont de nombreux pays sont francophones.
que les Européens ont colonisé au dix-neuvième siècle.

VOUS RÉPONDEZ: **C'est l'Afrique.**

1. C'est un pays ______ est resté neutre pendant la Seconde Guerre mondiale.
______ les langues officielles sont le français, l'allemand, l'italien et le romanche.
______ beaucoup de gens visitent pour faire du ski.
2. C'est un pays ______ le premier président a été le célèbre poète Léopold Senghor.
______ est la destination des participants à la course automobile Paris-Dakar.
______ la France a colonisé en 1882.
3. C'est un pays ______ Sese Seko Mobutu gouverne depuis 30 ans.
______ s'appelait le Congo belge jusqu'en 1971.
______ la capitale s'appelle Kinshasa.
4. C'est une île ______ on voit sur les peintures de Paul Gauguin.
______ le climat est tropical.
______ est dans l'océan Pacifique.
5. C'est un pays ______ se trouve dans le nord de l'Afrique.
______ on voit dans le film *Casablanca.*
______ la langue officielle est l'arabe.
6. C'est une ville ______ a un million d'habitants.
______ les deux tiers des habitants parlent français et un tiers parle anglais.
______ on appelait Ville-Marie en 1642 mais le nom aujourd'hui veut dire **montagne royale**.

C. Goûts. Utilisez un élément de chaque colonne pour expliquer le genre d'homme, de femme ou d'ami(e) que vous aimez ou que vous n'aimez pas.

J'aime... Je n'aime pas...	les hommes les femmes les amis	qui que dont	les idées sont conservatrices / libérales parlent trop / ne parlent pas beaucoup adorent le football américain / le rap / ??? mes parents préfèrent le passé est mystérieux on rencontre dans les clubs / à l'église / ??? ont les yeux bruns / bleus / noirs / ??? sont grand(e)s / passionnant(e)s / ??? ???

D. **C'est à vous!** Écrivez deux ou trois phrases avec un pronom relatif qui décrivent une personne ou une chose. Vos camarades de classe devineront ce que vous décrivez.

EXEMPLE — **C'est un film que tous les enfants adorent, qu'on a fait il y a plus de 50 ans et qui commence et finit au Kansas.**
— **C'est *The Wizard of Oz*, n'est-ce pas?**
— **Oui, c'est ça.**

E. **La musique.** Vous parlez à un(e) ami(e) francophone de la musique qui vous plaît le plus. Préparez une conversation avec un(e) partenaire. Mentionnez les groupes que vous aimez, les chansons que vous préférez et ce qui vous plaît dans leur musique.

Voilà pourquoi!

Le comparatif

To make comparisons, use **plus... que**, **aussi... que**, or **moins... que**. You can compare characteristics of people and things by using these expressions with an adjective.

Tu as une *plus jolie* voix *que* ton frère.
Les paroles de cette chanson sont *aussi intéressantes que* les autres.
Ses concerts maintenant sont *moins amusants qu'*avant.

You can use these expressions with adverbs to compare how much or in what way people do something.

Je vais aux concerts *plus souvent que* mes amis.
Tu chantes *aussi bien que* moi.
Je joue du piano *moins bien qu'*elle.

Use the stressed pronouns (**moi, toi, lui, elle, nous, vous, eux, elles**) after **plus... que**, **aussi... que**, or **moins... que**.

Nous jouons *aussi bien qu'eux.*
Il est *plus grand que moi.*

To say *better*, use **meilleur(e)** as an adjective and **mieux** as an adverb. These words can also mean *best* when they are preceded by the definite article or a possessive adjective.

Son premier disque est bon mais son dernier disque est *meilleur que* le premier.
(**Meilleur** describes what kind.)
Il chante bien mais tu chantes *mieux que* lui.
(**Mieux** describes how.)

SELF-CHECK

1. Which pronouns do you use after **plus... que**, **moins... que**, and **aussi... que**?
2. How would you say *better* in the following two sentences? *She's a better lawyer. She dances better.*

Savez-vous le faire?

A. **Intérêts.** Dites si vous trouvez la première chose plus intéressante, moins intéressante ou aussi intéressante que la seconde.

EXEMPLE le ballet / l'opéra
Pour moi, le ballet est plus (moins, aussi) intéressant que l'opéra.

1. le cinéma / la télévision
2. la littérature / le cinéma
3. le jazz / la musique classique
4. les sports / la littérature
5. la musique / le cinéma
6. les paroles d'une chanson / la mélodie

B. **La vie à l'avenir.** Comparez la vie maintenant et la vie dans 25 ans.

EXEMPLE la vie (compliquée)
Dans 25 ans, la vie sera plus (moins, aussi) compliquée que maintenant.

1. les voitures (rapides, économiques, chères)
2. les gens (conservateurs, libéraux, heureux, pauvres)
3. la vie (difficile, intéressante, simple)
4. notre société (tolérante, violente)
5. l'éducation (importante, facile, chère)

C. **Comment?** Comparez comment on fera les choses suivantes dans 25 ans et comment on les fait maintenant.

EXEMPLE Est-ce qu'on vivra longtemps?
On vivra plus (moins, aussi) longtemps que maintenant.

1. Est-ce qu'on vivra bien?
2. Est-ce qu'on étudiera longtemps?
3. Est-ce qu'on apprendra rapidement?
4. Est-ce qu'on mangera bien?
5. Trouvera-t-on facilement du travail?
6. Changera-t-on souvent de travail?

D. **Quel(le) artiste?** Complétez les questions suivantes avec **meilleur(e)** ou **mieux** et posez-les à un(e) camarade de classe.

1. Tu aimes ______ le rock ou la musique pop?
2. À ton avis, est-ce que Whitney Houston est une ______ artiste que Barbara Streisand?
3. À ton avis, quel est le ______ groupe depuis le commencement du rock?
4. Est-ce que la musique était ______ pendant les années 60 que maintenant?
5. Peux-tu ______ te reposer quand tu écoutes de la musique classique ou du jazz?

E. **Après les études.** Serez-vous content(e) de finir vos études? Est-ce que vous vivrez mieux ou moins bien? Est-ce que votre vie sera plus amusante ou plus ennuyeuse? Écrivez huit phrases qui comparent votre vie maintenant et votre vie comme vous l'imaginez après les études.

Remarquez que...

Léopold Sédar Senghor

Les rythmes de la musique africaine sont connus dans le monde entier et ils ont beaucoup influencé le blues et le jazz en Amérique et en Europe. L'Afrique a produit aussi beaucoup de poètes d'expression française. Les thèmes préférés des poètes de l'Afrique noire sont la dignité de l'être humain, la gloire de la négritude et la lutte contre la souffrance. Parmi les plus célèbres poètes sont Léopold Sédar Senghor, qui a été le premier président du Sénégal, Bernard Dadié, un Ivoirien, et David Diop, un Sénégalais. Ci-dessous vous trouverez un poème de Claude-Emmanuel Abolo Bowole, qui est du Cameroun, et les premiers vers d'un poème de Richard Dogbeh, qui est du Bénin.

Espérance et souffrance. En lisant ces deux poèmes, faites une liste des mots qui expriment l'espoir et une autre liste des mots qui expriment la souffrance.

Préférence...

de Claude-Emmanuel Abolo Bowole

Un Message

À vous qui luttez,
À vous qui rêvez d'un monde meilleur;
À vous qui avez le courage de dire
Ce que vous croyez être **la vérité**...
À vous tous
Qui écrivez...
J'adresse ce message d'espoir
Le monde où nous sommes
Est un monde de haine,
Qui ne le sait?
Le monde où nous sommes
Qu'en ferons-nous toi et moi?
Pouvons-nous en faire
Un monde de paix,
Un monde de fraternité,
Un monde d'amitié,
Un monde de gaieté...

Pitié pour les **affamés**

de Richard Dogbeh

Gens qui **mangez** tous les soirs **à plein ventre**
qui **jetez** aux chiens les **miettes** et les **os**
Ô vous riches dont les réserves **pourrissent**
Ayez pitié des affamés et des mourants
Et **ceux** qui ont **le ventre vide**
Et ceux qui tremblent du lendemain
Et ceux qui le soir aux coins des rues **déambulent** pensifs
à la quête d'un bout de pain
Ô Rois, vous qui êtes nés dans l'opulence
vous qui **jouissez d'**un nom d'une couleur d'une race
Vous qui vivez heureux et il suffit que vous rentriez chez vous
pour que le repas soit prêt
Ayez pitié de ceux qui ruminent leurs pleurs, leurs cris
Ayez pitié de ceux qui **triturent** l'ennui des jours sans pain, sans amour
Ayez pitié de ceux qui **rongent la rouille** des temps
Ayez pitié de ceux qui sentent dans leurs **entrailles** les **convulsions telluriques**
Ayez pitié de ceux qui tremblent sur la terre en pensant à leur ventre
Ayez pitié de ceux qui désirent grandir et qui ne le peuvent pas.

Car la faim c'est tout cela...

la vérité *truth* **affamé(e)** *starving* **manger à plein ventre** *to eat your fill* **jeter** *to throw* **une miette** *crumb* **un os** *bone* **pourrir** *to rot* **ceux** *those* **ventre vide** *empty stomach* **déambuler** *to wander* **à la quête de** *in search of* **jouir de** *to enjoy* **triturer** *to knead* **ronger** *to gnaw* **la rouille** *rust* **les entrailles** (*f*) *guts* **les convulsions** (*f*) **telluriques** *the earth's tremors*

SUJET DE CONVERSATION 3
Discussing options

Qu'est-ce qu'on dit?

À votre avis, que devrait-on faire pour améliorer l'avenir?

Notre gouvernement devrait | s'occuper plus de nos **propres** problèmes sociaux avant d'essayer d'aider le reste du monde.
| aider plus les pays du tiers monde.

On devrait | établir une unité politique qui respecte la diversité sociale.
| essayer de créer une société plus homogène.

Il faudrait se concentrer d'abord sur | la criminalité.
| l'économie et le chômage.
| la faim et le problème des sans domicile fixe.
| l'éducation.
| l'environnement.

Dans notre pays, il faudrait | plus de programmes sociaux.
| moins de programmes sociaux.

Pour lutter contre la drogue, on devrait | avoir plus de prisons.
| avoir plus de police.
| éduquer les jeunes.

Daniel demande à Mukala ce qu'on devrait faire pour améliorer l'avenir de l'Afrique.

— **Il me semble qu'**on pourrait trouver des solutions aux grands problèmes en Afrique si on ne **se battait** pas constamment.
— Eh bien... pour comprendre l'Afrique, il faut reconnaître la diversité d'un pays comme le Zaïre qui se compose de plusieurs tribus importantes.
— J'entends souvent d'autres langues que le français dans la rue.
— Nous parlons français à l'école et c'est la langue officielle, mais il y a 200 autres langues parlées au Zaïre comme le kinkongo, le lingala et le swahili.
— Ça doit être difficile d'avoir une unité politique avec tant de diversité culturelle.
— C'est la même situation dans beaucoup de pays d'Afrique. Quand une société est tellement fragmentée, la démocratie est quelquefois fragile.
— À ton avis, qu'est-ce qu'il faudrait faire pour encourager la démocratie?
— Sur le plan culturel, je pense que nous devrions encourager la diversité en reconnaissant la validité de chaque tradition sociale. Sur le plan économique, je crois qu'on pourrait travailler ensemble si on se concentrait sur les problèmes qui nous touchent tous, comme la faim et **le manque de logement**.

---

propre *own* **il me semble que** *it seems to me that* **se battre** *to fight* **le manque de** *the lack of* **le logement** *housing*

A. **Solutions.** Choisissez la solution qui exprime le mieux votre avis ou proposez-en une autre.

1. Nous devrions encourager (la diversité sociale, l'unité sociale).
2. Pour protéger la démocratie dans le monde, il faudrait (se concentrer d'abord sur les problèmes comme la faim et le manque de logement, se concentrer d'abord sur l'éducation, d'abord développer les économies).
3. Nous devrions (aider plus les pays pauvres, nous occuper de nos propres problèmes sociaux d'abord).
4. Dans notre pays, il faudrait (plus de programmes sociaux, moins de programmes sociaux).
5. Pour lutter contre la drogue, nous devrions (avoir plus de prisons, éduquer les enfants).

B. **Réactions.** Quelle serait votre réaction si les choses suivantes arrivaient? Utilisez: **Je serais heureux (heureuse) / triste / surpris(e) / furieux (furieuse).**

1. S'il y avait une année sans guerre...
2. Si tout le monde était d'accord...
3. S'il n'y avait plus de chômage...
4. Si les cigarettes étaient illégales...
5. S'il était illégal de manger de la viande...
6. Si le service militaire était obligatoire...

Voilà pourquoi!

Le conditionnel

To say that something *would* (*should, could*) *happen* under certain circumstances, or to ask someone if they *would do* something for you, use the conditional. This form of the verb is easy to learn. It has the same stem as the future (page 401) and the same endings as the imperfect.

SELF-CHECK
1. What other verb form has the same stem as the conditional? What other verb form has the same endings?
2. When do you use the conditional?

PARLER		FINIR		VENDRE	
je	parler**ais**	je	finir**ais**	je	vendr**ais**
tu	parler**ais**	tu	finir**ais**	tu	vendr**ais**
il/elle/on	parler**ait**	il/elle/on	finir**ait**	il/elle/on	vendr**ait**
nous	parler**ions**	nous	finir**ions**	nous	vendr**ions**
vous	parler**iez**	vous	finir**iez**	vous	vendr**iez**
ils/elles	parler**aient**	ils/elles	finir**aient**	ils/elles	vendr**aient**

To describe an imagined situation, use a clause with **si** followed by a verb in the imperfect. To say what would happen in the imagined circumstances, use a clause with the verb in the conditional.

Si nous avions l'argent, nous *irions* en Afrique. — *If we had the money, we* ***would go*** *to Africa.*
Si j'étais toi, je *serais* contente. — *If I were you, I* ***would be*** *glad.*
Votre vie *serait* bien différente si vous habitiez dans le tiers monde. — *Your life* ***would be*** *very different if you lived in the third world.*

As you have seen before, the conditional is also used to make or answer polite requests.

Je voudrais un café, s'il vous plaît.	*I would like a coffee, please.*
Est-ce que tu aimerais venir?	*Would you like to come?*
Qui pourrait faire ça?	*Who could do that?*
Qu'est-ce que je devrais faire?	*What should I do?*

Savez-vous le faire?

A. Temps libre. Est-ce que vous feriez les choses suivantes si vous aviez plus de temps?

EXEMPLE travailler plus
Oui, je travaillerais plus parce que j'ai besoin d'argent.
OU **Non, je ne travaillerais pas plus.**

1. dormir plus
2. étudier plus
3. regarder plus la télé
4. sortir danser plus souvent
5. avoir un A dans tous vos cours
6. faire plus d'exercice
7. apprendre à jouer au golf
8. rentrer plus souvent chez vos parents

B. Scrupules. Répondez honnêtement aux questions suivantes.

1. Si vous voyiez la fiancée de votre frère embrasser un autre garçon, est-ce que vous...
   a. le diriez à votre frère?
   b. ne feriez rien?
   c. demanderiez 50 dollars à sa fiancée pour garder le silence?
2. Si vous voyiez une copie de l'examen de fin de semestre / trimestre sur le bureau du prof deux jours avant l'examen, est-ce que vous...
   a. la prendriez?
   b. ne feriez rien?
   c. liriez l'examen tout de suite?
3. Si vous trouviez 100 dollars dans la rue, est-ce que vous...
   a. téléphoneriez à la police?
   b. prendriez l'argent et partiriez?
   c. ne feriez rien?
4. Si vous ne veniez pas en classe le jour d'un examen important parce que vous n'étiez pas préparé(e), est-ce que vous...
   a. expliqueriez la situation au professeur?
   b. diriez au professeur que vous étiez malade?
   c. choisiriez d'avoir un zéro à l'examen?
5. Si vous rencontriez des criminels qui attaquaient votre professeur de français, est-ce que vous...
   a. courriez à une cabine de téléphone pour appeler la police?
   b. resteriez là pour aider votre professeur?
   c. resteriez là pour aider les criminels?

C. Situations. Imaginez ce que vous feriez dans les situations suivantes.

EXEMPLE Si nous n'avions pas cours aujourd'hui...
(aller à la bibliothèque pour étudier, rentrer à la maison, aller au café, ???)
Si nous n'avions pas cours aujourd'hui, j'irais au café.

1. Si le prof me donnait un A dans ce cours... (être content(e), être surpris(e), ???)
2. Si j'étais le prof... (ne pas donner de devoirs, donner des examens difficiles, ???)
3. Si j'avais des vacances cette semaine... (aller à la plage, rester à la maison, faire du ski, ???)
4. Si j'avais beaucoup d'argent... (acheter une voiture, le mettre à la banque, aider les pauvres, ???)
5. Si je pouvais sortir avec une personne célèbre... (dîner avec Mel Gibson, aller danser avec Madonna, passer la journée avec le président des États-Unis, ???)

D. La lampe d'Aladin. Imaginez ce que ces gens feraient s'ils trouvaient la lampe d'Aladin.

1. Mes parents...
2. [*Au professeur.*] Vous...
3. [*À un(e) autre étudiant(e).*] Tu...
4. Nous, la classe de français, nous...
5. Mon/Ma meilleur(e) ami(e)...
6. Moi, je...

faire le tour du monde
DEMANDER BEAUCOUP D'ARGENT
??? DEVENIR ACTEUR / ACTRICE
apprendre à jouer d'un instrument
trouver un remède contre le cancer
demander une copie de l'examen de fin d'année
???
ACHETER UNE ÎLE TROPICALE
aider les pauvres

E. Changements. Si vous pouviez changer ces personnes, comment seraient-elles? Que feraient-elles différemment?

EXEMPLE votre camarade de chambre
Il/Elle se coucherait plus tôt et il/elle ferait plus souvent la lessive.
OU **Je ne changerais rien.**

1. vos professeurs
2. votre meilleur(e) ami(e)
3. vous
4. nous, les Américains / les Canadiens

On fait les courses à Kinshasa.

F. Une journée typique. Imaginez que vous habitez dans un pays du tiers monde. En quoi est-ce que votre journée typique changerait? Avec un(e) partenaire, préparez une description de ce que vous feriez tous les jours.

EXEMPLE **Nous nous lèverions plus tôt...**

G. **Si j'étais...** Lisez ce poème de Claude-Joseph M'Bafou-Zetebeg, un poète du Cameroun. Faites une liste de six choses qu'il ferait s'il était Dieu (*God*).

Si j'étais un Dieu nègre

Si j'étais un Dieu nègre
Je ferais des **rois** nègres
Des rois blancs
Des rois jaunes
Je construirais une grande maison noire
Qui **abriterait** toutes les races du monde
Je ferais une maison noire
Une maison blanche
Une maison jaune
Une maison rouge
Je ferais de l'Afrique ma capitale
Je ferais de Harlem ma résidence privée
Je ferais de l'Europe le pays des Noirs
De l'Asie le pays des Rouges
De l'Amérique le pays des Jaunes
De l'Afrique le pays des Blancs
J'aurais autour de moi
Des **anges** noirs
Des anges blancs
Des anges rouges
Des anges jaunes
Si j'étais un Dieu nègre
Il n'y aurait plus de **déluge**
Il n'y aurait plus ni Sodome ni Gomorrhe
Il y aurait la paix
La paix que mes frères
Prêchent depuis des millénaires
Je ferais un paradis noir
Un paradis blanc
Un paradis rouge
Un paradis jaune
Un paradis de l'Amitié
Où l'homme et la femme
Ne mangeraient plus le fruit défendu
J'enfanterais des nations nouvelles
Des nations d'un pour tous
Et de tous pour un
J'enverrais mes anges
Ambassadeurs sublimes
Mettre un terme aux guerres
Abattre les despotes
Bénir les pauvres
Je ferais du Kilimandjaro
Le vatican de mes frères
Si j'étais un Dieu nègre
Mes yeux **veilleraient sur** le monde
À travers **les cieux**
Fileraient des missiles de la paix
Finirait la haine
Il y aurait la joie
La joie des Noirs
La joie des Blancs
La joie des Rouges
La joie des Jaunes
La joie des peuples Unis
Si j'étais un Dieu nègre
Je marcherais de pays en pays
Invitant les masses à se laver **les cœurs**
Invitant les masses à être bonnes
Invitant les masses à **prier**
Pour ceux qui ne sont plus
Si j'étais un Dieu nègre
Un Dieu blanc
Un Dieu jaune
Un Dieu rouge
Je contribuerais à l'Union des Races.

un roi *a king* **abriter** *to shelter* **un ange** *an angel* **le déluge** *the flood* **prêcher** *to preach* **abattre** *to strike down* **bénir** *to bless* **veiller sur** *to watch over* **les cieux** (*m*) *the heavens* **filer** *to shoot off* **les cœurs** (*m*) *hearts* **prier** *to pray*

Maintenant dites ce que vous feriez si vous étiez: **chef du gouvernement, Dieu, le professeur de français.**

C'est à lire!

Vous allez lire une interview avec la chanteuse de blues Nina Simone publiée dans la revue *Jeune Afrique.* Si vous rencontrez un mot inconnu, essayez d'abord de deviner son sens dans le contexte. En lisant, il vous faudra peut-être chercher certains mots dans un dictionnaire. Avant de lire l'interview, faites l'exercice suivant.

Quel est l'infinitif? Devinez le sens des verbes en caractères gras. Si vous ne pouvez pas déterminer leurs sens, cherchez-les dans un dictionnaire.

1. L'étoile de Nina Simone **a brillé** dans le ciel des cinq continents.
2. Elle **a souffert** du racisme.
3. Un de ses amants la **battait.**
4. Nina **a sillonné** le monde, elle a connu le succès.
5. Maintenant, elle vit à Amsterdam mais elle va **déménager** à Accra, la capitale du Ghāna.
6. Elle a encore beaucoup de projets en tête, mais elle a déjà écrit ses mémoires parce que le public le **réclamait.**
7. Elle **s'est créé** un monde qui est loin d'**avoir livré** tous ses secrets.
8. Le fils d'un de ses fiancés **a été fusillé** publiquement pendant un coup d'état au Libéria.
9. Elle **souhaite** la démocratisation en Afrique.
10. La démocratie **marchera** à condition que tout le monde y participe.

Confidences de la chanteuse américaine

En presque quarante ans de carrière, son destin a croisé celui de personnages extraordinaires et d'amants originaires de tous les horizons. Mais elle est aussi tombée amoureuse de ce continent d'où sont partis ses ancêtres.

L'Afrique de Nina Simone

Une biographie qui vient de paraître en français sous le titre *Ne me quittez pas*, dévoile en 260 pages la vie méconnue d'Eunice Waymon, 59 ans, sixième enfant d'une famille pauvre de la Caroline du Nord, ainsi que les quarante années de scène de son double, une certaine Nina.

Nina Simone est certainement, avec Aretha Franklin, l'une des dernières grandes voix féminines du jazz et du blues. Sa carrière a débuté en 1954, dans un cabaret de Philadelphie. «J'avais, à l'époque, un petit ami hispano, Chico, qui m'avait baptisé Nina, c'est-à-dire fillette en espagnol, raconte l'artiste. Chico m'appelait tout le temps comme ça, et j'aimais beaucoup la sonorité de ce mot. J'aimais bien aussi le prénom Simone depuis que j'avais vu Simone Signoret dans des films français.» Nina Simone. L'étoile était née...

Depuis, elle a brillé dans le ciel des cinq continents. Nina a sillonné le monde, elle a connu le succès, avec des titres comme "I love you," "I put a spell on you" ou encore "Ne me quitte pas" (une reprise de Brel — d'où le titre, qu'elle n'aime pas, de la version française de ses mémoires). Elle a connu la déprime et souffert du racisme. «Ce qui est merveilleux dans une affaire de discrimination, explique-t-elle, c'est qu'on ne peut jamais être certain de son authenticité.»

.....

JEUNE AFRIQUE: Vous vous êtes rendue pour la première fois en Afrique en 1961. Depuis, vous y êtes retournée à plusieurs reprises. Pour vous, l'Afrique a-t-elle changé?

NINA SIMONE: Beaucoup de choses ont changé depuis mon premier passage au Nigeria. Lagos est devenue une mégapole surpeuplée. J'y étais encore il y a quelques semaines...

J.A.: À quelle occasion?

N.S.: Je devais participer à un show en faveur de l'Afrique du Sud à l'International stadium avec Miriam Makeba et d'autres artistes. Le spectacle eut bien lieu, mais sans nous, parce que les organisateurs voulaient que le concert commence à minuit et demi pour s'achever à 6h30 du matin. Miriam et moi avons refusé de nous produire. Ils ont rétorqué que nous pouvions commencer plus tôt, mais pas avant 23h, parce que le protocole prévoyait que nous participions auparavant à d'autres manifestations organisées par le gouvernement nigérien dans le cadre de la journée consacrée à l'Afrique du Sud...

J.A.: Quelle place occupe l'Afrique dans votre cœur?

N.S.: La place numéro un. J'ai été fiancée à un Libérien, C.C. Dennis, le père de l'ancien Premier ministre du Libéria, celui qui a été fusillé publiquement, avec d'autres dignitaires du régime Tolbert, après le coup d'état de 1980. C.C. Dennis est mort de chagrin, deux semaines plus tard. On devait se marier. Je regrette de n'avoir pu le faire, car je vivrais à présent en Afrique. C.C. a été le grand amour de ma vie...

J.A.: Pourquoi avez-vous écrit vos mémoires maintenant? Vous êtes encore en forme...

N.S.: Certes, j'ai encore beaucoup de projets en tête, des concerts, des enregistrements, des voyages à travers le monde, des tas d'histoires à raconter. Mais j'ai écrit mes mémoires parce que le public le réclamait.

.....

J.A.: Avez-vous déjà visité des pays francophones d'Afrique?

N.S.: Bien sûr! La Côte-d'Ivoire, le Maroc. J'adore le Maroc. J'y suis allée, il n'y a pas longtemps, à l'invitation du prince héritier. Je devais donner un concert au profit des hôpitaux qui s'occupent des enfants handicapés. Mais, à la dernière minute, j'ai eu des ennuis. J'avais perdu ma voix.

J.A.: Que pensez-vous du rap?

N.S.: Je déteste. Ce n'est pas de la musique, mais du bruitage.

J.A.: Vous n'aimez pas Public Enemy?

N.S.: C'est du bruit, pas de la musique. Idem pour MC Hammer. Eux, ils appellent ça de la musique. Pour moi, c'est du ramdam...

J.A.: Vous citez parmi vos amis Louis Farrakhan...

N.S.: C'est un grand homme qui cherche à rassembler tous les Noirs sous la même bannière.

J.A.: Certains disent que c'est un extrémiste illuminé...

N.S.: Rien de plus faux! Comme je l'ai écrit dans mon livre, je suis fière d'avoir fait un bout de chemin avec lui...

J.A.: Vous considérez-vous comme une Black, une Negro ou une African-American?

N.S.: Je préfère nettement African-American.

J.A.: Que pensez-vous du combat en cours pour la démocratie en Afrique?

N.S.: Je connais bien Mobutu et — même si celui-ci n'est pas aujourd'hui au pouvoir — Kuanda. Tous deux souhaitent la démocratisation de leur pays. Cela marchera, à condition que la revendication pour la démocratie soit l'expression de la volonté générale.

J.A.: À 59 ans, vous arrive-t-il de penser encore à l'amour?

N.S.: Je ne sais pas. Je voudrais être mariée.

Avez-vous compris?

A. **Questions.** Répondez aux questions suivantes d'après l'interview avec Nina Simone.

1. Quel est le vrai nom de Nina Simone? D'où vient-elle? Pourquoi a-t-elle décidé de s'appeler Nina Simone?
2. Quels genres de musique chante-t-elle? Quel genre n'aime-t-elle pas?
3. Comment est-ce que l'Afrique a changé depuis sa première visite en 1961?
4. Pourquoi est-elle allée au Nigeria quelques semaines avant l'interview? Pourquoi n'a-t-elle finalement pas participé au concert?
5. Quels pays francophones a-t-elle visités en Afrique?
6. Maintenant que Nina Simone a écrit ses mémoires, que va-t-elle faire?

B. **Ne me quittez pas.** La traduction française des mémoires de Nina Simone s'appelle *Ne me quittez pas*, tirée du titre de la chanson de Jacques Brel à la page 405. Relisez les paroles de cette chanson et décidez si c'est un bon titre pour ses mémoires.

Ça y est! C'est à vous!

A. **Organisez-vous.** Vous allez écrire une interview imaginaire avec un(e) musicien(ne) ou un acteur (une actrice) que vous aimez. Choisissez quelqu'un que vous aimez beaucoup et faites une liste de tout ce que vous savez sur cette personne. Ensuite, faites une liste de cinq questions que vous voudriez lui poser sur ses projets pour l'avenir.

B. **Rédaction: Une interview.** Écrivez une interview imaginaire avec un(e) musicien(ne) ou un acteur (une actrice) que vous aimez en utilisant les listes que vous avez préparées dans l'exercice précédent. Posez au moins cinq questions sur son passé et cinq questions sur son avenir. Inventez ses réponses.

C. **Maintenant à vous!** Avec un(e) camarade de classe, présentez l'interview que vous avez préparée dans l'exercice précédent à la classe. Vous jouerez le/la musicien(ne) (l'acteur/l'actrice) et votre partenaire posera les questions. En écoutant l'interview, vos camarades de classe essaieront de penser à d'autres questions à poser.

D. **La musique et la paix.** Vous allez écouter une interview avec un des chefs du groupe Jeunesses musicales, une fédération internationale de musique avec une mission de paix. Écoutez l'interview et répondez aux questions suivantes.

1. Quelle est la mission principale de la fédération Jeunesses musicales?
2. Par quels moyens est-ce qu'ils accomplissent leur mission?
3. Quand est-ce que ce mouvement a commencé? Pourquoi?

Pour vérifier

Après avoir fait les exercices suivants, vérifiez vos réponses dans l'*Appendix C.*

Talking about the future and world problems

A. **Terminaisons.** Lisez rapidement la liste de noms à la page suivante et trouvez l'équivalent français des terminaisons anglaises *-ty*, *-y* et *-ment.* Faites une liste des mots avec chaque terminaison. Est-ce qu'ils sont masculins ou féminins?

B. **Définitions.** Complétez les définitions suivantes avec **qui** ou **que** (**qu'**). Ensuite, décidez quel mot de vocabulaire chaque définition décrit.

1. Les gens ____ n'ont pas de logement..
2. Une activité ____ est illégale.
3. Le temps ____ viendra plus tard.
4. Une chose ____ n'est pas comme le reste.

C. **Gros titres.** Imaginez que vous lisez ces gros titres (*headlines*) au cours des dix prochaines années. Dites ce que vous ressentiriez si ces choses arrivaient.

EXEMPLE **Chercheurs trouvent un remède contre le SIDA**

Je serais content(e) si les chercheurs trouvaient un remède contre le SIDA.

80% de la population au chômage Paix en Afrique
L'ESPAGNOL DEVIENT UNE LANGUE OFFICIELLE AUX ÉTATS-UNIS
L'économie s'améliore **Guerre en Europe**

D. **Espérance.** Dites si vous espérez que les choses indiquées dans les gros titres de l'exercice précédent se réaliseront.

EXEMPLE **J'espère que des chercheurs trouveront un remède contre le SIDA.**

E. **Intérêts.** Dites si vous faites les choses suivantes. Utilisez **y** ou **en** dans votre réponse.

1. Est-ce que vous participez toujours aux élections?
2. Est-ce que vos amis et vous parlez souvent de l'avenir?
3. Est-ce que vous vous intéressez à la situation du tiers monde?

Talking about music

F. **La musique.** Mettez **qui**, **que** ou **dont** dans le blanc et complétez les phrases pour exprimer votre opinion.

1. Le genre de musique _____ j'aime le mieux, c'est... mais... est un genre de musique _____ ne me plaît pas tellement.
2. L'artiste _____ j'ai le plus de disques compacts, c'est...
3. Le dernier concert _____ j'ai vu, c'était... Un concert _____ je voudrais voir, c'est...
4. ... est une chanson _____ j'aime beaucoup le rythme.
5. ... est une chanson _____ a des paroles intéressantes.

Vocabulaire

Talking about the future and world problems

NOMS

l'agitation (*f*)
l'alcoolisme (*m*)
l'avenir (*m*)
le cancer
le chômage
une (ancienne) colonie
la corruption
un crime (violent)
la criminalité
un(e) criminel(le)
le danger
la démocratie
la dépression
une dictature
la diversité culturelle
la drogue
les droits de l'homme (*m*)
l'économie (*f*)
l'éducation (*f*)
l'égalité (*f*)
des élections (*f*)
l'environnement (*m*)
une exception
la faim
la famine
un gang
un gouvernement (autocrate, démocratique)
une guerre (civile)
la *haine
l'inégalité (*f*)
l'instabilité (*f*)
le logement
une loi (sévère)
la maladie
la malnutrition
le manque de
un marin
le meurtre
un(e) meurtrier / meurtrière
la moitié
le mouvement
la paix
les pauvres (*m*)
la pauvreté
la peine de mort
la police
la pollution
la population
la possibilité
la prison
un problème (économique mondial, politique)
un programme (social)
un progrès (agricole, médical)
la prospérité
le racisme
la recherche (médicale)
le régime
les ressources naturelles (*f*)
les sans domicile fixe (*m*)
la sécurité
le SIDA
le siècle
la situation
une société (fragmentée, globale, homogène, violente)
la solution
le tiers monde
la tolérance
une tribu
l'unité (*f*)
la validité
le viol
la violence (domestique)
le vol

ADJECTIFS

africain(e)
ancien(ne)
bénévole
chaque
conservateur(-trice)
fragile
grave
libéral(e)
mondial(e)
occidental(e)
propre
puissant(e)
répandu(e)
sceptique

VERBES

aider
battre
se composer de
se concenter sur
créer
croire (à)
dépenser
développer
éduquer
établir
gaspiller
laisser
lutter (contre)
(se) préoccuper (de)
prétendre
protéger
tourner (vers)

DIVERS

aussitôt que
Il me semble que...
la plupart de
plusieurs
quelques-un(e)s
tant de
tant que

Talking about music

NOMS

une chanson
un concert
un élément
un message
les paroles (*f*)
le rythme
une station de radio
une voix

DIVERS

au début
aussi... que
dont
en tournée
excentrique
ne... rien que

VERBES

ajouter
s' influencer
s' intéresser à une cause
participer à
rapporter
tenir
utiliser

Hemba Helmet Mask
Zaïre
Hamill Gallery of African Art, Boston, Massachusetts
Photo by John Urban

This mask, made by the Suku people of Zaïre, is used in boys' initiation camps and ceremonies. The parallel lines below the eyes symbolize the tears shed during mourning songs that commemorate departed ancestors.

Chapitre 12 Chez le médecin

By the end of this chapter, you should be able to do the following in French:

- Talk about symptoms
- Make recommendations
- Say what people should do
- Express emotions

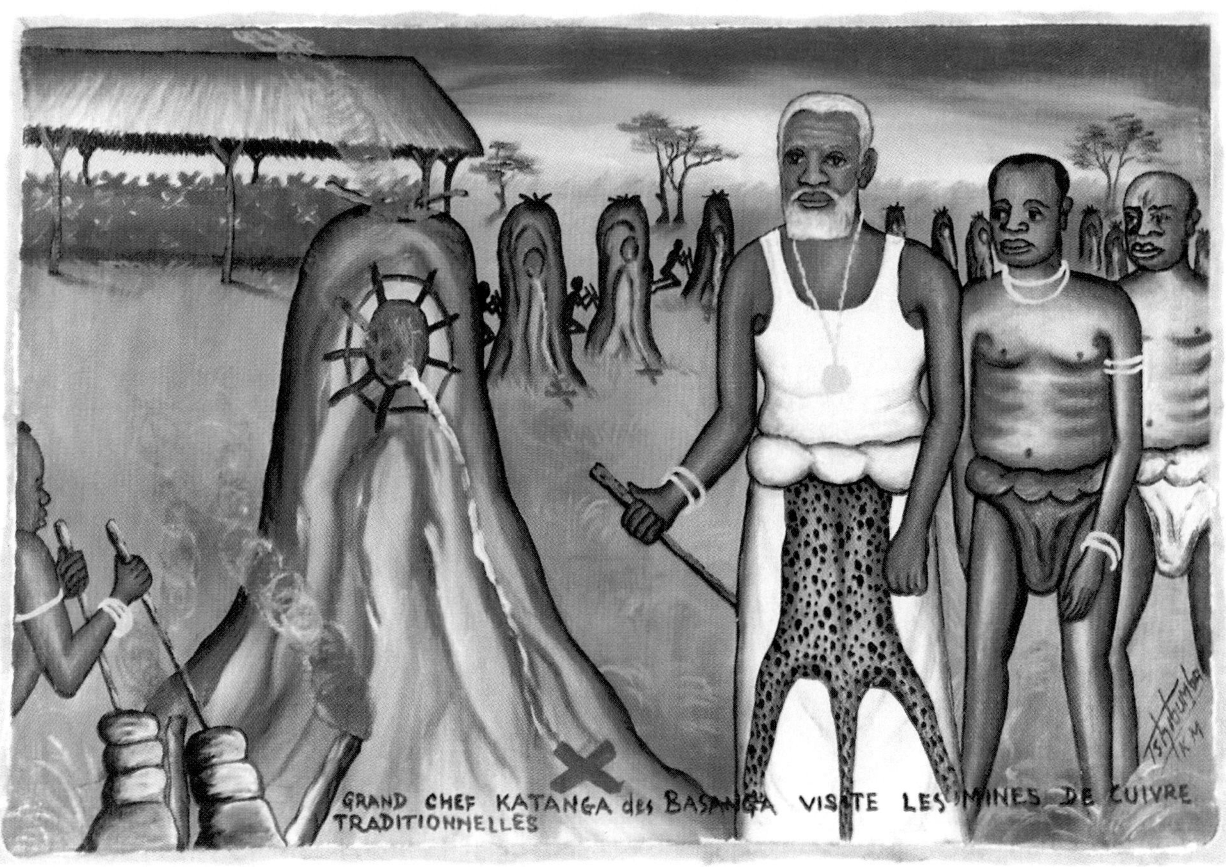

Grand Chef Katanga des Basanga visite les mines de cuivre traditionelles
Tshibumba Kanda-Matulu (circa 1950–)
1977
Collection: Bogumil Jewsiewicki

Kanda-Matulu calls himself a "painter-historian" and aims to tell the history of Zaïre through his art. Each of his paintings portrays a historical event and is accompanied by an explanatory caption in French.

Pour commencer

Daniel a décidé de travailler dans une clinique près de Kinshasa. Il explique à ses assistants comment **soigner les malades** et comment leur parler de leur santé.

D'abord, il faut leur demander où ils **ont mal.**

— Où est-ce que vous avez mal?
— J'ai mal à la tête, à la gorge, au dos, un peu partout.

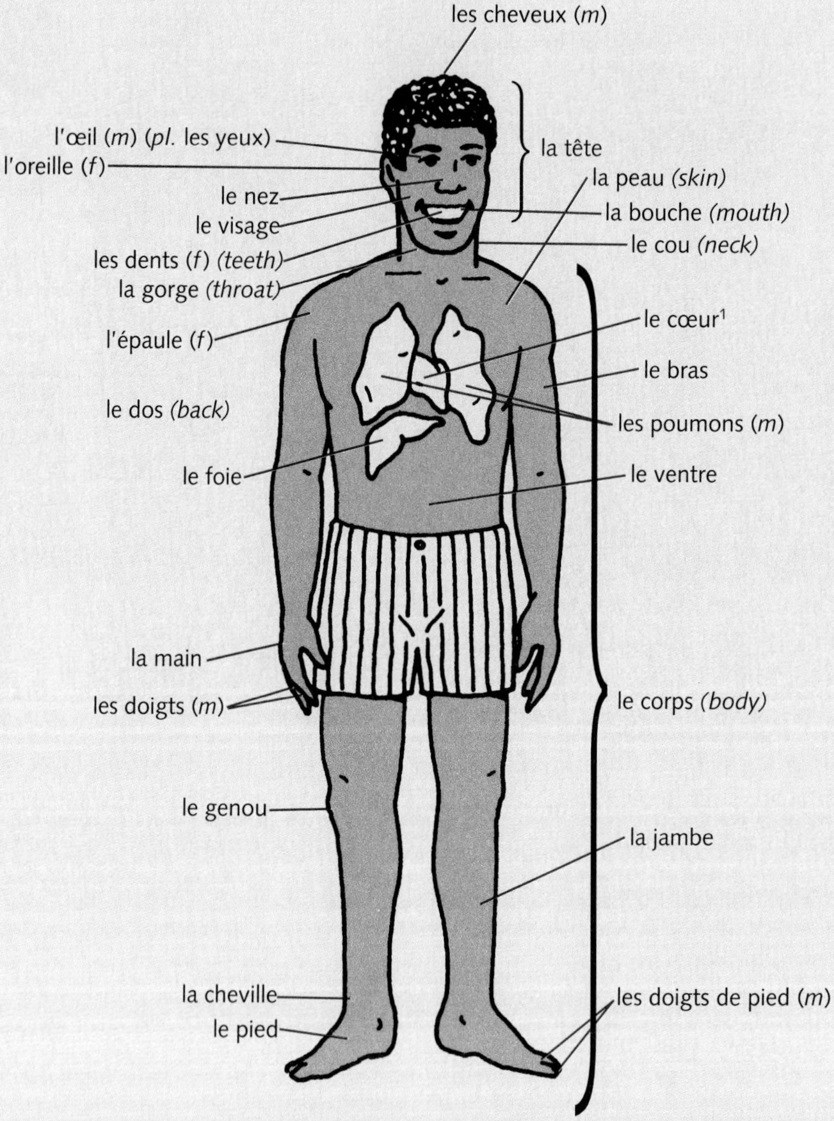

les cheveux (*m*)
l'œil (*m*) (*pl.* les yeux)
l'oreille (*f*)
la tête
le nez
le visage
la peau *(skin)*
la bouche *(mouth)*
les dents (*f*) *(teeth)*
le cou *(neck)*
la gorge *(throat)*
le cœur[1]
l'épaule (*f*)
le bras
le dos *(back)*
les poumons (*m*)
le foie
le ventre
la main
les doigts (*m*)
le corps *(body)*
le genou
la jambe
la cheville
les doigts de pied (*m*)
le pied

SUPPLEMENTAL VOCABULARY

le cerveau *brain*
les cils (*m*) *eyelashes*
le coude *elbow*
les cuisses (*f*) *thighs*
l'estomac (*m*) *stomach*
le front *forehead*
la langue *tongue*
les lèvres (*f*) *lips*
les ongles (*m*) *nails*
le poignet *wrist*
les poils (*m*) *body hair*
la poitrine *chest*
le pouce *thumb*
les reins[2] (*m*) *kidneys*
les sourcils (*m*) *eyebrows*

soigner *to care for* **un(e) malade** *a sick person* **avoir mal (à)** *to hurt*

[1] **Avoir mal au cœur** means *to be nauseated.*
[2] Although **les reins** means *the kidneys,* **avoir mal aux reins** means *to have lower-back pain.*

Il faut aussi les observer pour d'autres symptômes. Un(e) patient(e) peut...

éternuer

avoir le nez qui **coule** ou avoir le nez **bouché**

tousser

avoir de la fièvre

avoir les yeux qui le **démangent**

avoir la main enflée

avoir une indigestion ou vomir

On peut aussi **se blesser**. On peut...

se casser la jambe

se fouler la cheville

se brûler la main

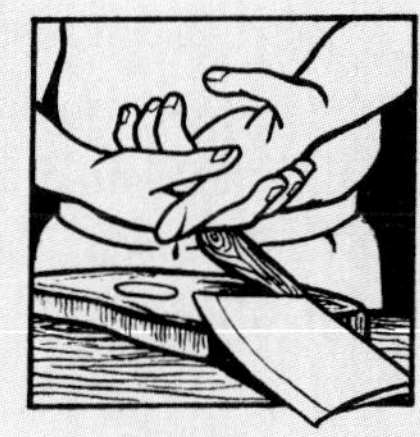
se couper le doigt

couler *to run* **bouché(e)** *stopped up* **démanger** *to itch* **se blesser** *to get hurt, to be wounded* **se fouler** *to sprain*

SUPPLEMENTAL VOCABULARY

SYMPTÔMES
avoir du mal à respirer / à digérer *to have difficulty breathing / digesting*
faire de l'hypertension (*f*) *to have high blood pressure*
avoir la diarrhée
avoir la nausée

MALADIES
l'alcoolisme (*m*)
une angine *tonsillitis*
une attaque (d'apoplexie) *a stroke*
une bronchite
une carie *a cavity*
une crise cardiaque *a heart attack*
le diabète
l'hépatite (*f*)
une maladie des nerfs
la mononucléose
les oreillons (*m*) *mumps*
une pneumonie
la rougeole *measles*
une sinusite
la tuberculose
la varicelle *chicken pox*
un virus

CULTURE NOTE

Normal body temperature in Celsius is 37.

Le/La patient(e) a peut-être...
- des allergies.
- une infection.
- **la grippe.**
- **un rhume.**

Il/Elle doit...
- prendre des médicaments / de l'aspirine.
- prendre des antibiotiques.
- se soigner et se reposer.
- bien manger et boire beaucoup de liquides.

Daniel parle avec Mme Boko, sa première patiente à la clinique.

— Bonjour, madame. **Qu'est-ce qui ne va pas** aujourd'hui?
— Je ne sais pas exactement. Je me sens mal. J'ai souvent très mal au ventre.
— Est-ce que vous **avez des frissons**?
— Non, je **n'**ai **ni** froid **ni** chaud.
— Vous avez perdu l'appétit?
— Quelquefois je n'ai pas faim, mais j'ai très mal au ventre si je ne mange rien. Je ne supporte pas certains **aliments**, surtout **les matières grasses.**
— Qu'est-ce qui vous **rend** malade?
— C'est surtout quand je mange quelque chose de très **gras** ou quand je bois du café que j'ai des **douleurs** et je digère mal. Qu'est-ce qui pourrait causer ça?
— C'est peut-être un ulcère. Je voudrais faire **une analyse de sang** et **une radio** pour vérifier, mais d'abord je vais prendre votre température.

la grippe *the flu* **un rhume** *a cold* **Qu'est-ce qui ne va pas?** *What's wrong?* **avoir des frissons** (*m*) *to have the shivers* **ne... ni... ni** *neither . . . nor* **supporter** *to tolerate* **des aliments** (*m pl*) *food* **les matières grasses** *fat* **rendre** + ***adjectif*** *to make + adjective* **gras(se)** *fatty* **une douleur** *pain* **une analyse de sang** *a blood test* **une radio** *X-ray*

Savez-vous le faire?

A. **Descriptions.** Décrivez le corps des personnes ou des animaux suivants.

EXEMPLE un vampire
Il a les yeux rouges, la peau verte et des grosses dents...

1. une girafe
2. un rat
3. un cyclope
4. un serpent
5. un extra-terrestre
6. la grand-mère du petit chaperon rouge (*Little Red Riding Hood*)

B. **Symptômes logiques.** Quelles parties du corps peuvent logiquement compléter les phrases suivantes? Il y a plusieurs possibilités.

1. J'ai... bouché(e)(s).
2. J'ai... enflé(e)(s).
3. Je me suis cassé...
4. Je me suis foulé...

C. **Maladies.** Décrivez les symptômes qu'on a quand on souffre des maladies suivantes.

EXEMPLE un rhume
On a le nez qui coule, on tousse, on a mal à la gorge et on éternue.

1. une grippe
2. un ulcère
3. des allergies
4. une dépression

D. **Expressions.** Est-ce que vous pouvez deviner quelle traduction à droite correspond à chaque expression à gauche?

être un casse-cou	*to pay an arm and a leg for*
avoir le bras long	*to have influence*
se casser la tête	*to rack one's brains*
être mal dans sa peau	*to know by heart*
payer les yeux de la tête	*to be a nuisance*
connaître par cœur	*to feel ill at ease*
être casse-pieds	*to be a daredevil*

E. **Des allergies.** Imaginez que vous êtes allé(e) chez le médecin parce que vous avez des allergies et qu'il vous pose les questions suivantes. Répondez logiquement.

1. Qu'est-ce qui ne va pas?
2. Est-ce que vous avez de la fièvre?
3. Est-ce que vous avez des frissons?
4. Où est-ce que vous avez mal?
5. Est-ce que vous avez d'autres symptômes?
6. Est-ce que certains aliments vous rendent malade?

F. **Et vous?** Complétez les phrases avec les mots ou les expressions qui vous décrivent le mieux.

1. Le matin, je commence à avoir faim vers (6, 7, 8, 9, 10, 11, ???) heures.
2. Si je ne mange pas le matin, je me sens (bien, mal, fatigué[e], ???).
3. Aujourd'hui, je me sens (bien, mal, fatigué[e], ???).
4. D'habitude, (j'ai chaud, j'ai froid, je n'ai ni froid ni chaud) dans la salle de classe.
5. J'ai (souvent, rarement, parfois) des frissons.
6. (Le café, La viande, La pizza, ???, Rien ne) me fait mal au ventre.

G. **Questions.** Posez les questions suivantes à un(e) camarade de classe.

1. La dernière fois que tu as été malade est-ce que tu avais mal à la tête? à la gorge? Est-ce que tu avais de la fièvre? Est-ce que tu es allé(e) chez le médecin? Qu'est-ce que tu avais? Est-ce que tu as pris des médicaments?
2. Est-ce que tu as des allergies? Pendant quel mois est-ce que tu as des symptômes? Quels symptômes as-tu? Est-ce que tu prends des médicaments? Est-ce que tu vas chez le médecin?

Comment s'y prendre?

Listening for the main idea

When listening to someone speak a foreign language, you must figure out the main idea of what is being said before you can retain any specific information. Once you understand the gist of what the speaker is saying, you can ask for clarification if you wish. Remember that, even in your own language, it is normal to ask someone to repeat something you didn't fully understand. With recorded speech, listen to it more than once. The first time listen for the main idea, then go back and listen again for answers to any questions you might have.

Savez-vous le faire?

A. **Informations médicales.** Vous écoutez une émission sur la médecine à la radio. Écoutez chaque annonce et choisissez ci-dessous le titre qui exprime le mieux l'idée centrale du passage.

ANNONCE 1. ______ ANNONCE 2. ______ ANNONCE 3. ______ ANNONCE 4. ______

a. ***TABAC: SEMAINE DE SEVRAGE***

b. LA LUTTE CONTRE LE SIDA

c. ***50 MILLIONS DE DÉCÈS CHAQUE ANNÉE***

d. *SANTÉ ET ENVIRONNEMENT*

B. **Encore une fois.** Maintenant que vous comprenez l'idée centrale de chaque annonce, écoutez-les une seconde fois pour trouver les détails suivants.

ANNONCE 1. D'où viennent les chercheurs qui font ces recherches? Est-ce qu'ils ont essayé le médicament chez les humains?

ANNONCE 2. Chaque année, combien de décès y a-t-il chez les enfants de moins de cinq ans dans le monde? Quel pourcentage des décès annuels viennent du tiers monde?

ANNONCE 3. Quand est-ce que la journée mondiale de la santé sera célébrée? Quelle organisation parlera des effets de l'environnement sur la santé?

ANNONCE 4. Combien de pharmaciens et médecins se mobiliseront pour la semaine de sevrage tabagique? Pour qui est-ce qu'on organise la semaine de sevrage? Quand est-ce qu'ils espèrent organiser d'autres semaines de sevrage?

Qu'est-ce qui se passe?

Comment soigner un malade

Dans beaucoup de villages zaïrois, il n'y a pas de médecin. Daniel Turquin explique à ses assistants comment soigner les malades quand il n'y a pas de médecin. Écoutez ses explications et faites les exercices suivants.

Avez-vous compris?

A. Comment soigner un malade. Écoutez Daniel expliquer comment soigner un malade. Choisissez l'illustration qui va le mieux avec chacune des quatre conditions qu'il faut observer, d'après Daniel.

CONDITION 1. ______ CONDITION 2. ______ CONDITION 3. ______ CONDITION 4. ______

a.

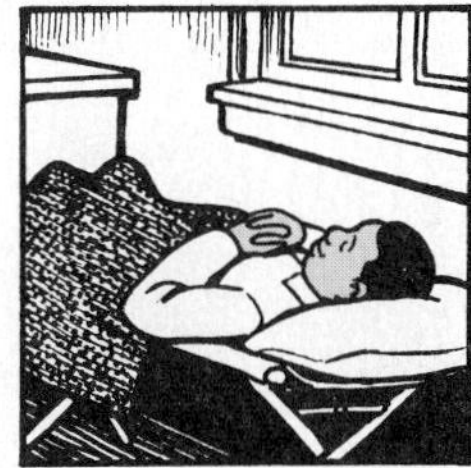

b.

c.

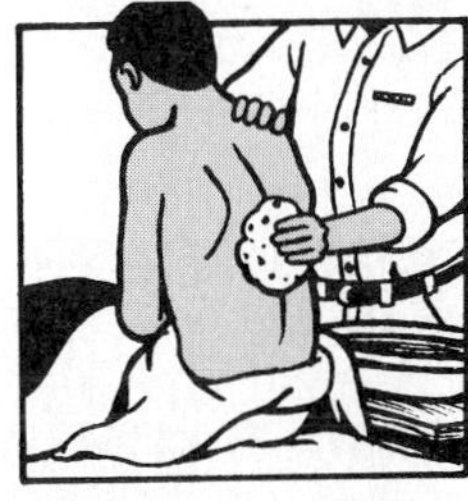

d.

B. Clarification. Écoutez encore la présentation de Daniel et décidez après quelle section (1, 2, 3, 4) il serait logique de poser les questions suivantes pour clarifier ce que vous n'avez pas compris.

a. Pardon monsieur, vous avez dit qu'il faut laver le patient avec de l'eau chaude, de l'eau tiède ou de l'eau froide?
b. Et si le patient souffre d'un ulcère ou de diarrhée, qu'est-ce qu'il peut manger?
c. Faut-il changer les draps *(the sheets)* d'un malade tous les jours?
d. Est-ce que le malade peut boire du vin?

C. Détails. Écoutez encore une fois la présentation de Daniel pour chercher la réponse aux questions suivantes.

1. Comment doit être la chambre d'un malade?
2. Qu'est-ce que le malade peut boire?
3. Faut-il laver le malade tous les jours?
4. Qu'est-ce que le malade peut manger?

Remarquez que...

Le corps humain joue un rôle très important dans l'art indigène de l'Afrique francophone. Qu'est-ce que vous pensez de ces statuettes et de ce masque africains?

Descriptions. Décrivez le corps de ces statuettes et le visage de ce masque.

1.

2.

3.

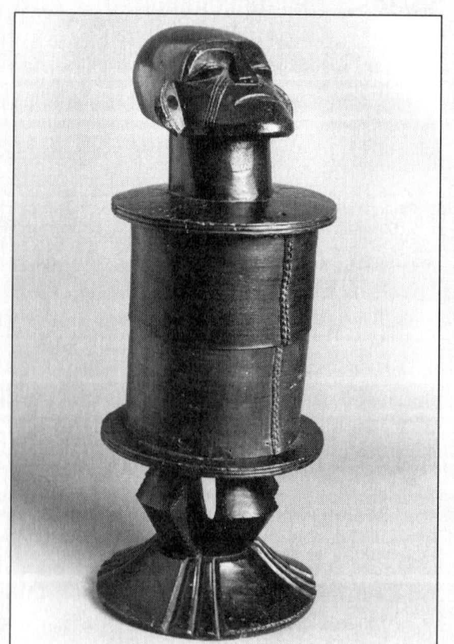

4.

Qu'est-ce qu'on dit?

TEXTBOOK TAPE

Est-ce que vous **êtes tombé(e) malade** récemment? Qu'est-ce que vous aviez? Comment est-ce que vous vous sentiez? Qu'est-ce que vous avez fait?

J'étais très malade.	Je n'avais rien de grave.
J'avais très faim et je mangeais bien.	Je n'avais pas d'appétit et je ne mangeais rien.
J'avais très soif et je buvais beaucoup.	Je ne buvais que très peu. Je n'avais ni faim ni soif.
Je suis allé(e) chez le médecin.	Je ne suis pas allé(e) chez le médecin.
Un(e) ami(e) s'est occupé(e) de moi.	**Personne ne** s'est occupé de moi.
J'ai pris des antibiotiques / de l'aspirine.	Je **n'**ai pris **aucun** médicament.
Cette année, j'ai déjà été malade une / deux / plusieurs fois.	Je n'ai pas été malade cette année.

Daniel donne des conseils à un groupe de femmes **enceintes**.

— Maintenant que vous êtes enceintes, vous devez faire encore plus attention à votre santé.
— Mais qu'est-ce qu'on doit manger de spécial?
— Rien de spécial. Il faut un régime sain et bien équilibré: des produits laitiers, suffisamment de protéines, des céréales, des légumes et des fruits. **Il vaut mieux** ne pas trop grossir. Vous pouvez manger autant de légumes que vous voulez.
— Est-ce qu'il est important de se reposer?
— Normalement on peut continuer sa routine habituelle et il est essentiel de faire de l'exercice. Je vais vous montrer quelques exercices que vous devez faire tous les jours.

tomber malade *to become ill* **personne ne...** *nobody* **ne... aucun(e)** *not any* **enceinte** *pregnant* **il vaut mieux** *it's better*

A. **Et vous?** Complétez les phrases avec les mots ou les expressions qui vous décrivent le mieux.

1. Aujourd'hui, je me sens très bien / assez bien / mal / ???.
2. Maintenant, j'ai faim / j'ai soif / je n'ai ni faim ni soif.
3. J'ai déjà eu / Je n'ai pas eu la grippe cette année.
4. Quand j'ai la grippe, je ne prends rien / je ne prends que de l'aspirine / je prends des antibiotiques / je prends plusieurs sortes de médicaments / je prends ???.
5. Je tombe souvent / Je tombe rarement / Je ne tombe presque jamais malade.
6. Quand je suis malade, je vais presque toujours / je vais souvent / je ne vais presque jamais chez le médecin.
7. Quand je suis malade, ma famille / un(e) ami(e) / personne ne / ??? s'occupe de moi.

B. Conseils. Expliquez ce qu'il faut faire quand on a la grippe en complétant les phrases de la colonne de gauche avec un élément de la colonne de droite.

Il faut...	prendre beaucoup de liquides
Il ne faut pas...	dormir autant que possible
Il vaut mieux...	rester au lit
	sortir avec des amis
	boire beaucoup de bière
	prendre de l'aspirine
	aller chez le médecin
	aller en classe

Voilà pourquoi!

SELF-CHECK

1. What are the antonyms of *quelqu'un*, *quelque chose*, *partout*, and *déjà*?
2. Which negative words are placed between the auxiliary and the past participle in the **passé composé**? Which are placed after the past participle?
3. How do you say *someone special*, *something important*, and *nothing new*?
4. What generally happens to the indefinite and partitive articles after negative expressions? What happens to them after **ne... ni... ni...**?

Les expressions indéfinies et négatives

You already know how to make some negative statements. After a negative question, use **si** instead of **oui** to answer *yes*.

— **Tu *n*'as *pas* mal à la gorge?**
— **Mais *si*, et j'ai mal à la tête aussi.**

Learn these expressions and their antonyms. Do not use **pas** with these negative expressions.

quelqu'un tout le monde	*someone* *everyone*	ne... personne	*no one, nobody*
toujours encore	*still* *still, more, again*	ne... plus	*no longer, no more*
quelque chose tout	*something* *everything*	ne... rien	*nothing*
quelques-un(e)s plusieurs tout / tous / toute(s) beaucoup	*some, a few* *several* *all* *many*	ne... aucun(e)[1]	*none, not any*
toujours souvent quelquefois	*always* *often* *sometimes*	ne... jamais	*never*
et ou	*and* *or*	ne... ni... ni	*neither . . . nor*
partout quelque part	*everywhere* *somewhere*	ne... nulle part	*nowhere*
déjà	*already*	ne... pas encore	*not yet*
beaucoup (de)	*a lot (of)*	ne... que	*only, just*

[1]**Ne... aucun(e)** is only used in the singular. **J'ai trois frères mais je *n*'ai *aucune* sœur.**

The **ne** of negative expressions always precedes the verb. Although the second part of negative expressions follows the verb in most cases, it will precede the verb when it is or refers to the subject of the sentence.

Je *ne* veux *rien*.	*I don't want anything.*
***Rien n'*est plus important.**	*Nothing is more important.*
Je *ne* connais *personne*.	*I don't know anybody.*
***Personne ne* vient.**	*No one is coming.*
Je *n'*aime *ni* la bière *ni* le vin.	*I don't like either beer or wine.*
***Ni* la bière *ni* le Coca *ne* sont bons pour la santé.**	*Neither beer nor cola is good for one's health.*

When the second part of negative expressions follows the verb in the **passé composé**, it goes between the auxiliary and the past participle, except for **personne, nulle part, aucun(e), que** and in most cases **ni... ni**, which are placed after the past participle.

Je *n'*ai *jamais* vu de problème.	BUT	**Je *n'*ai vu *personne*.**
Je *n'*ai *rien* vu.		**Je *ne* suis allé(e) *nulle part*.**
Il *n'*est *plus* venu.		**Il *n'*est venu *que* deux fois.**
		Je *n'*ai bu *ni* vin *ni* bière.

When giving short answers without a verb, drop the **ne** of negative expressions.

— Qu'est-ce que tu prends?	**— Qui s'occupe de toi?**
— *Rien*.	**— *Personne*.**

De precedes adjectives describing **quelque chose, rien, quelqu'un,** and **personne.** Notice the position of **de** and the adjective in the **passé composé** in the second example.

Lui, c'est quelqu'un *d'*intéressant.   **Je n'ai rien fait *de* grave.**

Also remember that the indefinite and partitive articles usually become **de** after negated verbs. After **ne... ni... ni**, these articles are dropped. Note that **ne... que** is not really a negative expression, and **un/une/des/du/de la/de l'** do not become **de** after it. It is a synonym for **seulement** (*only*).

Je *ne* bois *jamais de* café.
Je *n'*ai *pas encore* bu *de* café.
BUT **Je *ne* bois *ni* café *ni* thé.**
Je *ne* prends *que du* café le matin. = **Je prends *seulement du* café le matin.**

Savez-vous le faire?

A. **Non, je ne regrette rien.** La célèbre chanteuse Édith Piaf a chanté une chanson qui, tout en étant remplie (*filled*) d'expressions négatives, a un message très positif. Lisez les paroles de cette chanson et trouvez les expressions négatives. Ensuite, répondez aux questions qui suivent le texte.

Non, je ne regrette rien

Non, rien de rien,
Non, je ne regrette rien
Ni le bien
Qu'on m'a fait,
Ni le mal
Tout **ça m'est** bien **égal**!
Non, rien de rien
Non, je ne regrette rien
C'est payé, **balayé**, oublié
Je me fous du passé!
Avec mes souvenirs
J'ai **allumé le feu**
Mes chagrins, mes plaisirs
Je n'ai plus besoin d'eux
Balayé les amours
Avec leur **trémolo**
Balayé pour toujours
Je repars à zéro.
Non, rien de rien,
Non, je ne regrette rien
Ni le bien
Qu'on m'a fait,
Ni le mal
Tout ça m'est bien égal!
Non, rien de rien,
Non, je ne regrette rien
Car ma vie
Car mes joies
Aujourd'hui
Ça commence avec toi!

Édith Piaf

ça m'est égal *it's all the same to me* **balayer** *to sweep (away)* **je me fous de** (vulgar) *I don't care about* **allumer** *to light* **un feu** *a fire* **un trémolo** *a tremor* **car = parce que**

1. Qu'est-ce que la chanteuse regrette?
2. Elle dit qu'elle n'a plus besoin de plusieurs choses. Quelles sont ces choses?
3. Pourquoi est-ce qu'elle ne pense plus au passé?

B. Chez moi. Complétez les phrases suivantes pour décrire votre famille.

1. Chez moi, tout le monde... mais personne ne...
2. Nous avons plusieurs... mais nous n'avons aucun(e)...
3. Nous avons aussi... et... mais nous n'avons ni... ni...

4. D'habitude, mes parents font quelque chose... mais ils ne font rien...
5. Dans ma chambre, on voit... partout mais on ne voit... nulle part.
6. Quelquefois, ma famille... ensemble mais nous ne... jamais ensemble.

C. **Combien?** Demandez à un(e) camarade de classe combien il/elle a de chaque chose indiquée. Il/Elle doit répondre avec **plusieurs, quelques-un(e)s, ne... que** ou **ne... aucun(e)**.

EXEMPLE chats → **— Combien de chats as-tu?**
— J'en ai plusieurs. / J'en ai quelques-uns. / Je n'en ai qu'un. / Je n'en ai aucun.

1. cours intéressants
2. disques compacts canadiens
3. camarades de chambre
4. amis français
5. petit(e)s ami(e)s
6. examens cette semaine

D. **À l'avenir.** Comment voyez-vous le monde en l'an 2050? Répondez avec l'expression qui exprime le mieux votre opinion.

En l'an 2050...

EXEMPLE Il y aura des guerres. (toujours / ne... plus)
En l'an 2050, il y aura toujours des guerres.
En l'an 2050, il n'y aura plus de guerres.

1. On verra des sans domicile fixe. (souvent / ne... jamais)
2. Il y aura la paix dans le monde. (partout / ne... nulle part)
3. Il y aura de la tyrannie dans le monde. (toujours / ne... plus)
4. Le terrorisme existera. (partout / ne... nulle part)
5. On saura guérir le SIDA. (déjà / ne... pas encore)
6. Il y aura des problèmes sociaux. (beaucoup / ne... aucun)
7. Il y aura les mêmes problèmes sociaux. (toujours / ne... plus)

E. **Ça change?** Votre vie change-t-elle? Répondez aux questions suivantes avec **ne... plus, toujours** ou **encore.**

EXEMPLE Est-ce que vous voulez encore étudier le français l'année prochaine?
Oui, je veux encore étudier le français l'année prochaine.
OU **Non, je ne veux plus étudier le français l'année prochaine.**

1. Est-ce que vous habitez toujours dans la ville où vous êtes né(e)?
2. Est-ce que vous aimez toujours les mêmes sports que vous aimiez quand vous étiez jeune?
3. Rencontrez-vous encore vos amis du lycée de temps en temps?
4. Habitez-vous toujours avec votre famille?
5. Allez-vous encore étudier ici l'année prochaine?
6. Allez-vous toujours habiter au même endroit l'année prochaine?

F. **Pauvre M. Boko.** Ce week-end, M. Boko est resté à la maison. Regardez les illustrations de ce qu'il a fait et répondez aux questions qui suivent.

EXEMPLE Samedi matin, M. Boko se sentait-il déjà mal au petit déjeuner?
Oui, il se sentait déjà mal au petit déjeuner.

samedi après-midi

dimanche matin

1. Est-ce qu'il a mangé des céréales ou des croissants au petit déjeuner?
2. Qu'est-ce qu'il a mangé?
3. Où est-ce qu'il est allé samedi après-midi?
4. Avec qui a-t-il regardé la télé?
5. Est-ce que M. Boko se sentait toujours mal dimanche matin?
6. A-t-il fait quelque chose d'intéressant dimanche matin?
7. Qui a couru avec M. Boko?

G. **Le week-end dernier.** Répondez aux questions suivantes. Si possible, expliquez vos réponses.

EXEMPLE Est-ce que vous avez fait quelque chose de spécial le week-end dernier?
Non, je n'ai rien fait de spécial. J'ai dû travailler.
OU **Oui, j'ai fait quelque chose de spécial. Je suis allé(e) au lac.**

1. Est-ce que vous avez fait quelque chose de spécial le week-end dernier?
2. Est-ce que vous êtes allé(e) quelque part?
3. Est-ce que vous avez passé du temps avec quelqu'un d'intéressant?
4. Avez-vous parlé à quelques-uns de vos amis du lycée?
5. Avez-vous mangé quelque chose d'exotique?
6. Vous avez vu quelque chose d'amusant à la télé?

H. L'inspecteur Maigret. L'inspecteur Maigret pense que vous avez commis un crime. Répondez logiquement à ses accusations.

EXEMPLE Vous avez fait quelque chose de mal.
Mais non, ce n'est pas vrai. Je n'ai rien fait de mal.

1. Vous avez vu la victime plusieurs fois.
2. Vous avez un couteau (*knife*) et un revolver.
3. Vous avez beaucoup de problèmes d'argent.
4. La victime vous a vu(e) quelque part.
5. Vous dites quelque chose d'impossible.
6. Quelqu'un vous a vu(e) avec la victime.
7. Vous connaissiez déjà la victime.
8. Vous allez encore parler avec moi demain matin.

I. **Voilà ce qui s'est passé.** Racontez vos activités d'hier à l'inspecteur, en mettant les verbes entre parenthèses au passé composé ou à l'imparfait.

Monsieur l'inspecteur, vous vous trompez. Je ne suis pas coupable [*guilty*]. Voilà ce que j(e) ______ (faire) hier soir. Il ______ (être) environ cinq heures quand je ______ (rentrer). L'ami qui ______ (m'accompagner) ______ (ne rester) que quelques minutes, juste le temps de prendre un verre et il ______ (partir). Il ______ (faire) mauvais et j' ______ (être) fatigué(e) alors, j(e) ______ (décider) de me reposer un peu avant de dîner. Quand je ______ (se réveiller), j' ______ (avoir) faim et j(e) ______ (commencer) à faire la cuisine. Je ______ (se préparer) un café quand j(e) ______ (remarquer) qu'il n'y ______ (avoir) plus de sucre. Alors, j(e) ______ (décider) d'aller à l'épicerie. J' ______ (acheter) du sucre et je ______ (rentrer) à la maison quand tout à coup j' ______ (entendre) quelqu'un qui ______ (crier [*to shout*]). J(e) ______ (regarder) partout mais il ______ (pleuvoir) très fort et j(e) ______ (ne rien voir). Alors, j(e) ______ (rentrer) chez moi. J(e) ______ (boire) mon café quand j' ______ (entendre) une deuxième fois des cris qui ______ (venir) de la rue. J(e) ______ (regarder) par la fenêtre. La victime ______ (être) devant l'immeuble et elle ______ (pleurer). Quand elle ______ (me voir), elle ______ (crier) de nouveau. Elle ______ (avoir) l'air d'avoir peur de moi. Moi, je ______ (ne pas savoir) ce que j(e) ______ (devoir) faire. Je ______ (descendre) et quand je ______ (sortir) de l'immeuble, j(e) ______ (voir) une voiture de police qui ______ (arriver). Alors, je ______ (rentrer) chez moi et je ______ (se coucher).

Voilà pourquoi!

Les expressions avec **avoir** (*reprise*)

The following **avoir** expressions are useful when describing symptoms and physical or mental conditions.

avoir faim	*to be hungry*	**avoir mal (à)**	*to be sore (in), to hurt (in)*
avoir soif	*to be thirsty*	**avoir peur (de)**	*to be afraid (of)*
avoir sommeil	*to be sleepy*	**avoir des frissons**	*to have the chills*
avoir froid	*to be cold*	**avoir de la fièvre**	*to have a fever*
avoir chaud	*to be hot*	**avoir tort**	*to be wrong*
avoir... ans	*to be . . . (years old)*	**avoir raison**	*to be right*

SELF-CHECK

1. How do you say *to be hungry*, *to be hot*, and *to be sleepy*?
2. When talking about people in general, what form of the verb do you use after expressions such as **il faut** or **c'est important de**?

Les expressions impersonnelles

Use the following expressions to make recommendations about what one should do. When talking in general, rather than to or about a specific person, use the infinitive after them.

Il faut...	*It's necessary to / One has to / You need to . . .*
Il ne faut pas...	*One must not / You shouldn't . . .*
Il vaut mieux...	*It's better to . . .*
C'est important de...	*It's important to . . .*
C'est essentiel de[1]**...**	*It's essential to . . .*

Il faut rester au lit.	*You need to stay in bed.*
Il ne faut pas boire trop d'alcool.	*You shouldn't drink too much alcohol.*
C'est important de bien manger.	*It's important to eat well.*
C'est essentiel de se reposer.	*It's essential to rest.*

Note that **il ne faut pas** means *one shouldn't* and not *it's not necessary,* which is expressed by **ce n'est pas nécessaire.**

Savez-vous le faire?

A. **Qu'est-ce qu'ils ont?** Utilisez une expression avec **avoir** pour décrire ces personnes.

1. 2. 3. 4. 5. 6.

[1]In informal spoken French, people usually use **C'est important / nécessaire / essentiel de...** In formal situations and in written French, people also use **Il est important / nécessaire / essentiel de...**

B. Quelles maladies? Avec quelle(s) maladie(s) est-ce qu'on a les symptômes suivants?

EXEMPLE mal au ventre → **On a mal au ventre quand on a un ulcère.**

1. des frissons
2. de la fièvre
3. mal à la gorge
4. sommeil
5. mal à la tête
6. peur

C. J'aurais... Répondez aux questions suivantes en utilisant une expression avec **avoir.**

Qu'est-ce que vous auriez...

1. si vous n'aviez rien mangé hier ou aujourd'hui?
2. si vous veniez de courir pendant une heure au soleil?
3. si vous étiez né(e) en 1974 et que c'était votre anniversaire aujourd'hui?
4. si vous disiez quelque chose de faux?
5. si vous nagiez en Alaska en hiver?
6. si vous ne dormiez pas pendant deux jours?
7. si vous étiez très malade?

D. Qu'est-ce qu'on doit faire? Qu'est-ce qu'on doit faire dans les situations suivantes?

EXEMPLE Quand on a sommeil? → **Il faut dormir.**

1. Quand on est malade?
2. Quand on a mal à la tête?
3. Quand on a faim?
4. Quand on a chaud?
5. Quand on a soif?
6. Quand on a froid?
7. Quand on a la grippe?
8. Quand on est enceinte?

E. Mauvaises idées. Vous avez un nouvel ami qui a des mauvaises idées sur ce qu'il faut faire pour réussir à l'université. Donnez-lui des conseils en suivant l'exemple.

EXEMPLE On copie les réponses des autres?
Non, il ne faut pas copier les réponses des autres. Il vaut mieux étudier.

1. On arrive en classe en retard?
2. On passe toutes les soirées avec des amis?
3. On attend le dernier moment pour étudier?
4. On dort en classe?
5. On lit le journal en classe?
6. On se dispute avec le professeur?

F. Nouveaux amis. Un Zaïrois vient de commencer ses études à votre université. Donnez-lui des conseils en complétant les phrases suivantes.

EXEMPLE Il vaut mieux...
Il vaut mieux prendre l'autobus pour aller au campus.

1. Il faut...
2. Il ne faut pas...
3. Il vaut mieux...
4. C'est essentiel d(e)...
5. C'est important d(e)...
6. Ce n'est pas important d(e)...

SUJET DE CONVERSATION 2
Saying what people should do

Qu'est-ce qu'on dit?

Vous êtes médecin et votre patient(e) a la grippe. Quels conseils lui donnez-vous?

Il faut que vous... Il ne faut pas que vous...	vous reposiez. preniez beaucoup de liquides. sortiez. mangiez bien. alliez en classe. dormiez beaucoup.

Daniel dit à Mme Boko comment soigner son ulcère.

— C'est bien ce que je pensais: vous avez un ulcère. On peut le **guérir** assez facilement mais il faudra changer votre régime. Vous êtes très stressée?
— Je suppose que oui. Je suis très occupée. Je n'ai pas beaucoup de temps libre.
— Je veux que vous vous reposiez un peu plus et c'est essentiel que vous mangiez mieux.
— Je n'ai pas beaucoup de temps pour les repas.
— C'est important que vous preniez votre temps. Qu'est-ce que vous mangez le matin?
— Je ne prends que du café.
— Il faut que vous mangiez plus le matin. Vous devez manger au moins une tartine... et tant que vous aurez ces douleurs, il vaudrait mieux que vous ne buviez plus de café.
— Faut-il que je prenne des médicaments?
— Oui, je vais vous faire **une ordonnance.**

guérir *to cure* **une ordonnance** *a prescription*

A. **Conseils.** Dites si ce que vous entendez est un bon conseil ou un mauvais conseil pour rester en bonne santé.

EXEMPLE VOUS ENTENDEZ: Il vaut mieux que vous fumiez moins.
VOUS RÉPONDEZ: **C'est un bon conseil.**

B. **Un ulcère.** Votre ami(e) a un ulcère. Complétez les conseils suivants avec **plus** ou **moins.**

1. Si tu es stressé(e), c'est important que tu travailles ______ .
2. C'est essentiel que tu te reposes un peu ______ .
3. Il vaut mieux que tu boives ______ de café.
4. C'est important que tu manges ______ de matières grasses.
5. Il vaut mieux que tu fasses ______ d'exercice si tu es stressé(e).
6. Il faut que tu prennes ______ de temps aux repas.

Voilà pourquoi!

Le subjonctif

Until now, you have used verbs in the indicative mood to say what happens. There is another verb mode called the subjunctive mood. The subjunctive is generally used in the second clause of a sentence when the first clause expresses an attitude or opinion about what should or might be done. Notice that these two clauses will be linked by **que**. Look at the following examples and note how the first clause expresses an attitude about what is being done in the second.

C'est essentiel **que tu prennes tes médicaments.**
Je veux **que vous alliez chez le médecin.**

For most verbs, the subjunctive is formed as follows:

- For **je**, **tu**, **il/elle/on**, and **ils/elles** obtain the root of the subjunctive by dropping the **-ent** ending of the **ils** form of the present indicative and use the present indicative **-er** verb endings: **-e**, **-es**, **-e**, **-ent**.
- For **nous** and **vous**, the subjunctive is identical to the imperfect.

SELF-CHECK

1. What do you use as the subjunctive stem for all verb forms except **nous** and **vous**? What endings do you use?
2. For most verbs, the **nous** and **vous** forms of the subjunctive look just like what other verb form?
3. What seven verbs have irregular subjunctive forms?
4. When do you use the subjunctive?

PRENDRE

Drop the **-ent** of **ils prennent** and use the present indicative **-er** verb endings.			Use the same form as the imperfect.
	que je prenn**e**	que nous pren**ions**	
	que tu prenn**es**	que vous pren**iez**	
	qu'il/elle/on prenn**e**	qu'ils/elles prenn**ent**	

PARLER	FINIR	RENDRE
que je parl**e**	que je finiss**e**	que je rend**e**
que tu parl**es**	que tu finiss**es**	que tu rend**es**
qu'il/elle/on parl**e**	qu'il/elle/on finiss**e**	qu'il/elle/on rend**e**
que nous parl**ions**	que nous finiss**ions**	que nous rend**ions**
que vous parl**iez**	que vous finiss**iez**	que vous rend**iez**
qu'ils/elles parl**ent**	qu'ils/elles finiss**ent**	qu'ils/elles rend**ent**

Most irregular verbs follow the same rule. Note that in the subjunctive, the verbs below on the right have a different stem for the **nous** and **vous** forms.

Il faut...

que je connaisse, que nous connaissions
que je dise, que nous disions
que j'écrive, que nous écrivions
que je parte, que nous partions
que je lise, que nous lisions

que je boive, que nous buvions
que je croie, que nous croyions
que je vienne, que nous venions
que je voie, que nous voyions

The following verbs are irregular in the subjunctive. Note that the verbs in the first row have a different stem for **nous** and **vous** forms, while those in the second row have the same stem for all forms. All except **avoir** and **être** use the regular subjunctive endings.

	ÊTRE **soi- / soy-**	AVOIR **ai- / ay-**	ALLER **aill- / all-**	VOULOIR **veuill- / voul-**
que j(e)	sois	aie	aille	veuille
que tu	sois	aies	ailles	veuilles
qu'il/elle/on	soit	ait	aille	veuille
que nous	soyons	ayons	allions	voulions
que vous	soyez	ayez	alliez	vouliez
qu'ils/elles	soient	aient	aillent	veuillent

	FAIRE **fass-**	SAVOIR **sach-**	POUVOIR **puiss-**
que je	fasse	sache	puisse
que tu	fasses	saches	puisses
qu'il/elle/on	fasse	sache	puisse
que nous	fassions	sachions	puissions
que vous	fassiez	sachiez	puissiez
qu'ils/elles	fassent	sachent	puissent

Learn to use the subjunctive after these expressions that encourage or discourage an action. Notice that verbs in the subjunctive may imply either present or future actions.

Il faut que...	**Il faut** ***que tu ailles*** **chez le médecin.**
Il vaut mieux que...	**Il vaut mieux** ***que vous vous reposiez.***
C'est nécessaire que...	**C'est nécessaire** ***que nous le fassions.***
C'est important que...	**C'est important** ***que tu dormes*** **un peu.**
C'est essentiel que...	**C'est essentiel** ***que je parte.***
C'est dommage que... *It's a shame that . . .*	**C'est dommage** ***que tu sois*** **malade.**
C'est bon / mauvais que...	**C'est bon** ***que tu fasses*** **de l'exercice.**

Note that **il faut que...** and **c'est nécessaire que...** mean the same thing in the affirmative. In the negative, use **ce n'est pas nécessaire que...** to say that something is not necessary, and **il ne faut pas que...** to say that someone *should not* do something.

Ce n'est pas nécessaire ***que tu fasses*** **cela.**	*It's not necessary for you to do that.*
Il ne faut pas ***que tu fasses*** **cela.**	*You shouldn't do that.*

Also use the subjunctive after **vouloir** and **préférer** to say that someone wants or prefers for something to be done.

Ils veulent ***que je vienne.***
Je veux ***que tu le dises*** **à l'infirmière.**
Nous préférons ***que tu le fasses.***

Savez-vous le faire?

A. **Conseils.** Vous êtes conseiller/conseillère. Expliquez à des parents s'il faut ou s'il ne faut pas que les enfants fassent ou sachent les choses suivantes.

EXEMPLE savoir que vous les aimez
Il faut qu'ils sachent que vous les aimez.

1. faire de l'exercice
2. avoir des amis
3. manger toujours du fast-food
4. avoir des responsabilités à la maison
5. savoir nager
6. pouvoir faire tout ce qu'ils veulent
7. vouloir réussir à l'école
8. s'intéresser aux études

B. **La semaine prochaine.** Complétez les phrases suivantes pour dire ce que vous devez faire la semaine prochaine.

1. Il faut que j(e)...
2. Il vaut mieux que j(e)...
3. C'est essentiel que j(e)...
4. C'est important que j(e)...
5. Mes amis veulent que j(e)...

aller à la banque
faire la lessive **???**
venir en cours payer le loyer
me coucher plus tôt ???
MANGER MIEUX

C. **Dans une démocratie.** Dites s'il est important (essentiel, pas nécessaire) que tout le monde fasse les choses suivantes dans une démocratie.

EXEMPLE pouvoir voter → **C'est essentiel que tout le monde puisse voter.**

1. savoir toujours la vérité
2. avoir le droit de vote
3. être éduqué
4. pouvoir voyager librement (*freely*)
5. exprimer son opinion
6. toujours obéir au gouvernement

Alger, la capitale algérienne. L'Algérie a recouvré son indépendance de la France en 1962, après une insurrection de huit ans.

D. **Un candidat.** Vous êtes conseiller/conseillère politique. Dites à votre candidat(e) trois choses qu'il/elle doit faire et trois choses qu'il/elle ne doit pas faire pour être élu(e) (*elected*).

EXEMPLE **Il faut que vous écoutiez les problèmes des autres.**
Il ne faut pas que vous ayez peur d'exprimer votre opinion.

E. **Suggestions.** Dites ce que chacun doit ou ne doit pas faire dans les situations indiquées.

EXEMPLE J'ai mal à la tête. (prendre de l'aspirine, aller à un concert de rock)
Il faut que tu prennes de l'aspirine.
Il ne faut pas que tu ailles à un concert de rock.

1. J'ai la grippe. (dormir beaucoup, prendre des médicaments, aller danser, boire beaucoup d'eau)
2. Mes collègues et moi, nous sommes très stressé(e)s. (être plus calmes, travailler plus, faire plus d'exercice, prendre des vacances)
3. Mon frère fait une dépression. (sortir plus, boire de la bière, penser à ses problèmes, se faire de nouveaux amis)
4. Mes parents grossissent. (faire de l'exercice, regarder la télé toute la journée, manger plus de légumes et moins de sucre)

F. **L'Ange et le Diable.** Vous vous trouvez dans les situations suivantes. Imaginez ce que l'Ange (*Angel*) et le Diable (*Devil*) vous disent de faire. Utilisez **il faut que... / il ne faut pas que...**

EXEMPLE Mes amis m'ont demandé de sortir mais j'ai un examen important demain.
LE DIABLE: **Il faut que tu sortes.**
L'ANGE: **Il faut que tu ailles étudier à la bibliothèque.**

1. Je déteste les pommes mais ma grand-mère m'a fait une tarte aux pommes.
2. J'ai envie d'aller au cinéma avec des amis mais je n'ai pas encore fait mes devoirs pour demain.
3. Mon grand-père est tout seul à l'hôpital mais ma meilleure amie a des billets pour un concert que je veux voir.
4. J'ai cours dans une demi-heure mais j'ai très sommeil.
5. Ma mère m'a demandé de faire la lessive mais il y a un bon film à la télé.
6. J'adore fumer mais le médecin m'a dit d'arrêter.

G. **La loterie.** Votre petit(e) ami(e) vient de gagner à la loterie. Sur une feuille de papier, faites une liste de quatre choses que vous voulez qu'il/elle fasse.

EXEMPLE **Je veux qu'il/elle m'achète une nouvelle voiture...**

H. **Un(e) camarade de chambre.** Sur une feuille de papier, faites une liste de trois choses que vous voulez que votre camarade de chambre fasse et trois choses que vous ne voulez pas qu'il/elle fasse.

EXEMPLE **Je veux qu'il/elle soit amusant(e).**
Je ne veux pas qu'il/elle fume.

I. **Soins spéciaux.** Voici une page du manuel *Là où il n'y a pas de docteur*, publié par Environnement africain. Lisez ce texte. Imaginez ce que Daniel dit aux infirmiers de faire. Complétez ses phrases d'après le texte.

1. Il faut que le malade... liquides.
2. Si le malade montre des signes de déshydratation, il faut qu'il...
3. Si le malade ne peut pas manger d'aliments solides, il faut que vous...
4. La toilette du malade est très importante. Il faut que vous...
5. Si le malade ne peut pas changer de position tout seul, il faut que vous...
6. Si le malade montre des signes de maladies graves, il faut que vous...

Les soins spéciaux chez une personne très malade

1. *LIQUIDES*

Il est très important que le malade prenne suffisamment de liquides. S'il en boit très peu, il faut lui en donner très souvent. S'il a du mal à avaler, il faut lui en donner un tout petit peu toutes les cinq ou dix minutes.

Mesurer la quantité de liquide que le malade prend par jour. Un adulte doit boire deux litres par jour ou plus. Il doit uriner au moins trois à quatre fois par jour. S'il ne boit pas assez, s'il n'urine pas suffisamment ou s'il montre d'autres signes de déshydratation, il faut absolument qu'il boive davantage. Il doit boire des liquides riches en éléments nutritifs, un peu salés. On peut aussi lui donner du sérum buvable. S'il ne peut pas le boire, cherchez un médecin pour qu'il lui administre du sérum physiologique par voie intraveineuse.

2. *LES ALIMENTS*

Si le malade ne peut pas manger des aliments solides, il faut lui donner des soupes, du lait, des jus de fruits et d'autres liquides riches. (Voir chapitre nutrition.)

La bouillie et l'eau de riz sont bonnes, mais il faut les donner avec d'autres aliments un peu plus riches. On peut faire des bouillons à l'œuf, du poulet, du poisson ou de la viande bien hachée. Si le malade mange peu, il faut lui donner à manger souvent.

3. *LA TOILETTE*

La toilette est très importante pour une personne malade. Il faut la laver à l'eau tiède et changer les draps de son lit une fois par jour ou chaque fois qu'ils sont sales.

Pour le malade très affaibli, qui ne peut pas changer de position tout seul, il faut l'aider à changer de position plusieurs fois par jour. C'est ainsi qu'on évite les escarres.

Lorsqu'on change souvent de position un malade, on évite aussi la pneumonie, un danger très grand pour quelqu'un qui est affaibli ou malade et qui passe des journées entières couché. S'il a de la fièvre ou s'il commence à tousser, on doit envisager l'emploi d'un antibiotique et chercher de l'aide médicale.

4. *SURVEILLANCE*

On doit surveiller tout changement dans l'état général du malade qui indique s'il y a une amélioration ou si, au contraire, ça ne va pas bien. Noter soigneusement les données suivantes quatre fois par jour:

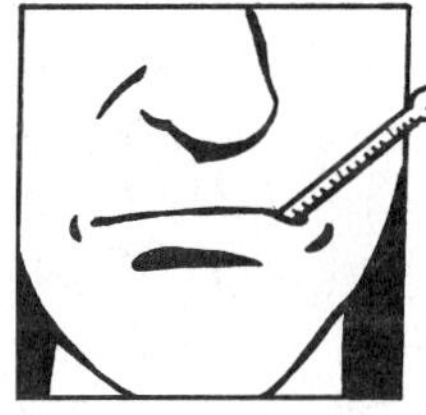

Température: en degrés

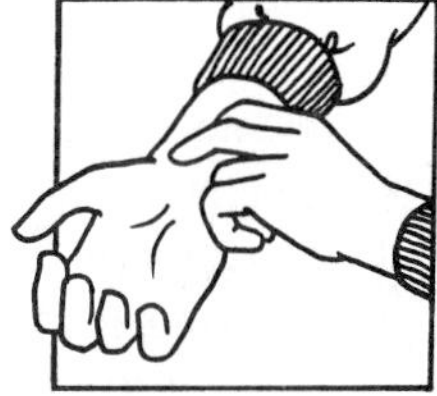

Pouls et respiration: nombre par minute

Lorsqu'on s'occupe d'un malade, il faut être très attentif aux signes de maladies graves ou dangereuses. Si le malade montre l'un de ces signes, *il faut chercher immédiatement l'aide d'un médecin.*

J. **Une consultation.** Avec un(e) partenaire, jouez le rôle d'un(e) patient(e) et votre camarade de classe jouera le rôle du médecin. Préparez une scène où vous décrivez vos symptômes au médecin qui fera son diagnostic et vous conseillera un remède.

Qu'est-ce qu'on dit?

Qu'est-ce qu'on peut dire à un(e) ami(e) malade?

Je regrette que... C'est dommage que...	tu te sentes mal. tu sois malade. tu aies la grippe. tu doives rester au lit. tu ne puisses pas sortir avec nous.

Je suis content(e) que...	tu ailles mieux. tu te sentes mieux. tu n'aies rien de grave. tu puisses sortir avec nous demain.

Avez-vous peur d'aller chez le médecin?

J'ai peur qu(e)...	ce soit quelque chose de grave. on me fasse **une piqûre**. ça me fasse mal. le traitement soit très cher.

Mme Boko parle à son mari de sa consultation chez le médecin.

— Qu'est-ce que le médecin a dit?
— Il a dit que j'avais un ulcère. Mais ce n'est pas grave et ça peut se guérir si je prends ces médicaments.
— Je suis content que ce ne soit pas grave. Qu'est-ce qu'il a dit d'autre?
— Je ne dois plus boire de café... et je dois manger moins de matières grasses aussi.
— C'est dommage. Tu ne vas pas être très agréable sans ton café le matin.
— Le médecin veut aussi que je travaille moins.
— Tu passeras donc plus de temps à la maison?
— Oui, pourquoi?
— J'espère que tu ne t'ennuieras pas. J'ai bien peur que tu sois **de mauvaise humeur**.

une piqûre *shot* **de bonne / mauvaise humeur** *in a good / bad mood*

A. **Émotions.** Choisissez l'expression qui exprimerait le mieux vos sentiments si un(e) ami(e) vous disait les choses suivantes.

Je regrette.		*J'en suis content(e).*
C'est dommage!	**J'espère que oui.**	**Heureusement!**

1. Je ne me sens pas bien.
2. Ma maladie n'est pas grave.
3. Je vais guérir rapidement.
4. Je ne peux pas travailler.
5. Je n'ai pas de fièvre.
6. J'ai perdu l'appétit.

B. **Optimiste ou pessimiste?** Daniel parle avec son ami Mukala de l'avenir. Dites si chaque phrase que vous entendez indique une attitude plutôt optimiste ou pessimiste.

TEXTBOOK TAPE

EXEMPLE VOUS ENTENDEZ: J'ai peur qu'il y ait plus de famine plus tard.
VOUS RÉPONDEZ: **plutôt pessimiste**

Voilà pourquoi!

Le subjonctif pour exprimer la volonté et les émotions

You have already seen that you use the subjunctive after verbs like **vouloir** and **préférer** to say what you want or prefer someone to do.

vouloir que...	**Je veux que tu *prennes* ces médicaments.**
préférer que...	**Ils préfèrent que nous *restions* ici.**
aimer mieux que...	**J'aimerais mieux que tu le *fasses*.**

SELF-CHECK

1. When do you use the infinitive instead of the subjunctive after verbs of emotion? Which expressions require **de** before the infinitive?
2. When negating an infinitive, where do you place **ne** and **pas**? How would you say *I prefer not to go?*

Expressions describing emotions about what is happening or what is going to happen are also followed by a dependent clause with the verb in the subjunctive. Here are the most common expressions of emotion.

être content(e) que...	**Je suis content que tu *ailles* chez le médecin.**
être heureux / heureuse que...	**Elle est heureuse que vous *soyez* son prof.**
être triste que... *to be sad that . . .*	**Nous sommes tristes que tu ne *viennes* pas.**
être désolé(e) que... *to be sorry that . . .*	**Je suis désolé que tu te *sentes* mal.**
regretter que...	**Je regrette que tu *aies* mal à la tête.**
être furieux / furieuse que...	**Ils sont furieux que le médecin ne *fasse* rien.**
avoir peur que...	**Il a peur que nous *soyons* en retard.**
être surpris(e) que...	**Qui est surpris que nous ne le *sachions* pas?**
être étonné(e) que...	**Je suis étonnée que l'hôpital *soit* si cher.**
C'est dommage que...	**C'est dommage que tu *partes* ce soir.**

Note that the verb **espérer** is not followed by the subjunctive.

J'espère qu'il n'*est* pas trop malade. **Nous espérons que les choses *iront* mieux.**

Le subjonctif ou l'infinitif?

If a sentence expresses an attitude that one person has about what someone else is doing, you generally use the subjunctive. When a person is expressing an attitude about his or her own actions, use the infinitive instead. With most of the expressions requiring the subjunctive, the **que** is replaced by **de** before an infinitive. **Vouloir, préférer, aimer mieux,** and **espérer** drop the **que**, and do not add **de** before the infinitive. Compare the following examples.

TALKING ABOUT SOMEONE ELSE	TALKING ABOUT ONESELF
Je veux *que* tu le fasses.	**Je veux le faire.**
I want you to do it.	*I want to do it.*
Nous regrettons *qu'il* ne vienne pas.	**Nous regrettons *de* ne pas venir.**
We're sorry he's not coming.	*We're sorry not to come.*

Expressions such as **il faut, c'est important,** or **c'est dommage** do not have a particular person as the subject. Use the infinitive with them when talking about people in general. With the exception of **il faut** and **il vaut mieux**, these expressions require **de** before an infinitive. Compare:

TALKING ABOUT SOMEONE SPECIFIC	TALKING ABOUT PEOPLE IN GENERAL
Il faut que je mange.	**Il faut manger.**
C'est important que tu comprennes.	**C'est important *de* comprendre.**
C'est dommage qu'il aille à l'hôpital.	**C'est dommage *d'*aller à l'hôpital.**

Savez-vous le faire?

A. À l'hôpital. Vous êtes à l'hôpital. Expliquez vos sentiments dans les situations suivantes.

EXEMPLE L'infirmier est très sympa.
Je suis content(e) qu'il soit sympa.

Je suis content(e) que...
C'est dommage que...
Je regrette que...
C'est bon que...
Je suis surpris(e) que...
Je suis furieux/furieuse que...
Je suis étonné(e) que...
Je suis désolé(e) que...

1. Les repas sont bons.
2. On vous fait une piqûre trois fois par jour.
3. Personne ne vient vous voir.
4. Votre chambre coûte 500 dollars par jour.
5. Il n'y a pas de télévision dans la chambre.
6. Le malade qui partage votre chambre tousse tout le temps.
7. L'autre malade ne dit rien.
8. On peut guérir votre maladie facilement.

B. Réactions. Posez chaque question à un(e) camarade de classe. Après, réagissez à sa réponse.

EXEMPLE — Comment est-ce que tu te sens aujourd'hui?
— Je ne me sens pas très bien.
— Je regrette que tu ne te sentes pas bien.

1. As-tu des allergies?
2. Est-ce que tu es souvent malade?
3. Tu dors bien généralement?
4. Qu'est-ce que tu fais ce week-end?
5. Est-ce que tu veux étudier avec moi?
6. Est-ce que tu comprends le subjonctif?

C. Volonté. Dites si vos parents veulent que vous fassiez les choses suivantes. Ensuite, dites si vous voulez les faire.

EXEMPLE travailler cet été → **Mes parents veulent que je travaille cet été. Moi, je ne veux pas travailler.**

1. aller à l'université cet été
2. se marier
3. avoir beaucoup d'enfants
4. habiter chez eux après vos études
5. leur téléphoner plus souvent
6. leur dire tous vos secrets

D. **Soins médicaux.** Vous ne voulez pas aller chez le médecin. Dites si vous avez peur que le médecin vous fasse les choses suivantes.

1. vous faire une piqûre

2. vous prendre la température

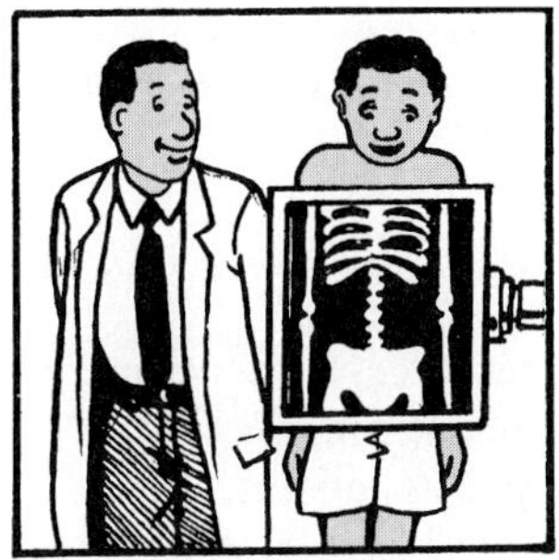

3. vous faire une radio

4. vous faire une analyse de sang

E. **Camarades de chambre.** Faites une liste de cinq choses que votre camarade de chambre fait qui vous plaisent ou qui vous énervent (*annoy*).

EXEMPLE **Je suis content(e) qu'il/elle ne soit pas souvent à la maison. Je suis furieux (furieuse) qu'il/elle ne fasse pas son lit. Je n'aime pas qu'il/elle...**

F. **Idées politiques.** Êtes-vous content(e) du gouvernement ou voudriez-vous des changements? Faites une liste de choses dont vous êtes content(e) et une autre liste de choses qui vous rendent triste ou que vous voudriez que notre gouvernement fasse.

EXEMPLE **Je suis content(e) qu'il y ait la liberté de la presse.**
Je suis triste qu'il y ait tant de sans domicile fixe.
Je veux que...

G. **Émotions.** Complétez les phrases suivantes pour exprimer vos sentiments. D'abord, décidez s'il faut utiliser le subjonctif ou l'infinitif.

1. Je suis content(e) que mes amis...
2. Je suis content(e) de...
3. J'ai peur que mes parents...
4. J'ai peur de...
5. Je suis étonné(e) que...
6. Je suis furieux / furieuse que...
7. Je regrette que...
8. Je regrette de...

H. **Un ami malade.** Avec un(e) partenaire, préparez une scène où l'un(e) de vous dit qu'il/elle ne se sent pas très bien et parle de ses symptômes. L'autre exprime ses regrets et donne des conseils.

I. **Prière des chasseurs nyanga.** Voici une prière (*prayer*) des chasseurs (*hunters*) nyanga au Zaïre. Lisez la prière et faites une liste des choses que les chasseurs veulent et une autre liste des choses dont ils ont peur.

Prière des chasseurs nyanga

Précédez-moi là-bas où je vais chasser.
Aidez-moi,
Que je **tue** beaucoup de **gibier**.

Vous **esprits**,
Donnez-moi votre bénédiction qui dure
Pour que je revienne de la chasse avec du gibier.

Vous mes pères,
Aidez ces chiens.
Qu'ils tuent beaucoup de gibier
Là-bas sur les terres de chasse,
Que je ne doive revenir ici sans gibier.

Vous mes pères,
Aidez-nous.
Là-bas sur les terres de chasse,
Que les chasseurs ne soient blessés
Par les **épines** et les **ronces**.
Que la **sagaie** ne regarde pas le chien
Mais seulement le gibier.

Vous mes pères,
Aidez-nous, vos chasseurs,
Que nous soyons légers
En **pourchassant** le gibier,
En forêt pendant la chasse,
Que nous ne nous blessions pas aux **racines**,
Que les serpents **fuient** loin,
Qu'ils ne réussissent à blesser chiens ou chasseurs.

Vous esprits,
Veillez sur nous
Là-bas en forêt sur les terres de chasse.
Que nous rencontrions du gibier
Qui a les yeux clos en forêt.
Que ce gibier ne blesse ni chiens ni chasseurs!

Des chasseurs zaïrois

tuer *to kill* **le gibier** *wild game* **un esprit** *spirit* **les épines** *(f) thorns* **les ronces** *(f) brambles* **la sagaie** *a type of javelin* **pourchasser** *to pursue, to chase after* **les racines** *(f) roots* **fuir** *to flee* **veiller sur** *to watch over*

C'est à lire!

Vous allez lire la première partie de la pièce de théâtre *Les aventures de Yévi au pays des monstres*, par Sénouvo Agbata Zinsou, né en 1946 à Lomé, au Togo. M. Zinsou est actuellement directeur de la Troupe nationale togolaise, qui fait du théâtre, du ballet et de la musique. Dans ce passage de lecture, vous allez faire la connaissance de Yévi, une araignée (*spider*), d'un conteur (*storyteller*) et d'un géant. En lisant, pensez à deux adjectifs qui décrivent le mieux chacun de ces personnages. Avant de commencer, parcourez (*scan*) la pièce et faites une liste des mots et des expressions qui se répètent plusieurs fois.

Les aventures de Yévi au pays des monstres

Prologue

LE CONTEUR — Donc, vous connaissez Yévi et je n'ai pas besoin de vous le présenter. N'allez surtout pas le confondre avec une vulgaire petite araignée qu'on rencontre dans les coins des murs! Non! C'est un personnage très important.

Entre précipitamment Yévi.

YÉVI — Et alors? Qui a dit que je ne suis pas important? Hein? Qui a dit ça? Je suis dans tous les **contes**, moi.

LE CONTEUR — Bien sûr, calme-toi, Yévi. Calme-toi.

YÉVI — Je veux savoir qui a dit que je ne suis pas important.

LE CONTEUR — Personne, Seigneur Yévi, personne. Calme-toi.

YÉVI — On parle de moi partout. Oui ou non?

LE CONTEUR — Oui, Yévi, oui.

YÉVI — Le conte du soir, à la radio. J'y suis. Oui ou non?

LE CONTEUR — Oui, Yévi, oui.

YÉVI — Les **veillées** dans les villages, les villes...

LE CONTEUR — Oui, Monsieur Yévi. On vous connaît...

YÉVI — Et dans les livres? Les livres de contes. De qui parle-t-on?

LE CONTEUR — C'est de vous, Monsieur Yévi. Rien que de vous.

YÉVI — Et alors? (*Un temps*) Même la télé, la télé est venue me filmer l'autre jour dans un conte, monté par les élèves de l'école... En présence de l'Inspecteur, l'Inspecteur, vous m'entendez!

LE CONTEUR — Justement, Seigneur Yévi, c'est précisément ce conte-là que nous voulons présenter ce soir à nos aimables spectateurs. Alors, Seigneur Yévi, voulez-vous nous rappeler le titre de ce conte...

YÉVI — Bien sûr, il s'agit des «Dernières aventures de Yévi—c'est moi-même—donc... de Yévi au pays des monstres»!

LE CONTEUR — Oui, musique pour la parade des personnages!

Entrent tous les personnages pour la parade.

Tableau I

LE CONTEUR, *à Yévi* — Alors, mon cher ami, ce n'est pas tout de faire **de la fanfaronnade** comme ton numéro de tout à l'heure...

YÉVI — Mon numéro de tout à l'heure... Ça a marché, non? J'ai été applaudi, vivement applaudi, chaleureusement applaudi. Ovationné même.

---

un conte *a story* **les veillées** (*f*) *vigils* **la fanfaronnade** *boasting*

LE CONTEUR — D'accord, mais après tout...

YÉVI — Après tout, quoi? Tu veux dire que j'ai faim?

LE CONTEUR — Ce n'est pas moi qui dis que tu as faim. Mais, c'est que tu as vraiment faim, sérieusement faim.

YÉVI — Mais quoi? La famine, la conjoncture, ce n'est pas moi seul que ça frappe, mais c'est tout le village, tout le monde, y compris toi.

LE CONTEUR — D'accord. Mais sais-tu ce qui fait la différence entre toi et moi? Entre tout le monde et toi?

YÉVI — Ah oui! Certainement, certainement!

LE CONTEUR — Alors, c'est quoi?

YÉVI — C'est que moi, à la différence des autres, je suis un homme important, connu, célèbre, prestigieux!

LE CONTEUR — Non! Mon cher ami, non. La différence, c'est que toi, Yévi, en plus d'être un affamé comme tout le monde, tu es un **con**.

YÉVI — Je suis un con, moi?

LE CONTEUR — Oui, parce que le peu d'énergie que tu as dans les muscles, le peu d'air que tu as dans les poumons, tu les gaspilles dans tes fanfaronnades.

YÉVI — Alors, là, tu m'as insulté. Je ne te pardonnerai pas. Je vais te boxer.

*Il montre **les poings, bombe** le torse et poursuit le conteur qui sort en fuyant. Seul, tout **essoufflé** après avoir poursuivi le conteur.*

Ah! Il m'a... Il m'a... échappé... échappé... Mais je l'aurai... bientôt... Ah! Je suis fatigué... Oh! j'ai mal aux pieds... Aïe! j'ai mal aux genoux... aux reins... Ah! Je comprends: j'ai faim. J'ai encore plus faim qu'avant. Oh! mon ventre! Mon ventre a presque disparu. Vraiment, j'ai faim!

Il crie.

J'ai faim! J'ai faim!

Il voit entrer un géant de cinq mètres de haut.

LE GÉANT — Qui a crié? (*Un temps*) Qui a crié: «J'ai faim»? (*Apercevant Yévi*) C'est toi, espèce de petit insecte, qui as crié?

YÉVI, *tremblant* — Non... Non...

LE GÉANT — Si tu **mens**, je t'**écrase** du coup du **pouce**.

YÉVI — Oui... Oui...

LE GÉANT — Et pourquoi as-tu faim?

YÉVI — Je n'ai rien mangé depuis deux... trois jours...

LE GÉANT — Comment ça, tu n'as pas mangé depuis deux... trois jours? Si tu mens, je t'écrase...

YÉVI — Oh! J'ai mangé, monsieur, j'ai mangé.

LE GÉANT — Quand?

YÉVI — Euh... Tout à l'heure...

LE GÉANT — Comment ça, tu as mangé tout à l'heure et puis tu cries: «J'ai faim»? Si tu mens, je...

YÉVI — J'ai mangé... J'ai mangé...

LE GÉANT, *menaçant* — Comment mangé?

YÉVI — J'ai mangé... j'ai pas mangé. J'ai faim... j'ai pas faim. Bon, c'est comme vous voulez, monsieur.

LE GÉANT, *riant* — Ha - ha - ha! Petit insecte! Tu dis n'importe quoi.

YÉVI — C'est que, monsieur... quand on se trouve en face de vous... vous qui êtes... si fort... Vous qui faites trembler la terre en marchant, vous qui faites tomber les rochers en riant...

LE GÉANT — Assez! Quand on a faim, on ne parle pas.

YÉVI — Oui, monsieur.

LE GÉANT — Quand on a faim, on ne crie pas.

YÉVI — Oui, monsieur.

LE GÉANT — Quand on a faim, on ne court pas.

YÉVI — Oui, monsieur.

LE GÉANT — Quand on a faim, on ne mange pas.

YÉVI — Oui, monsieur.

LE GÉANT, *riant* — Ha - ha - ha! Au revoir, petit insecte.

Il s'en va.

YÉVI — S'il vous plaît, monsieur... s'il vous plaît, grand frère... Oncle... Cousin... Grand-père.

LE GÉANT, *menaçant, se retourne* — Quoi?

YÉVI — Rien, monsieur. Au revoir, monsieur.

LE GÉANT, *riant* — Ha - ha - ha!

YÉVI — Mais... Monsieur... Oncle...

LE GÉANT, *même jeu* — Quoi?

YÉVI — Rien, monsieur... Au revoir, monsieur...

LE GÉANT, *riant* — Ha - ha - ha!

YÉVI — Monsieur, un morceau de... **manioc.**

LE GÉANT, *même jeu* — Quoi?

YÉVI — Rien, monsieur. Au revoir, monsieur.

Le géant s'en va en riant.

---

un con *(vulgar) a jerk* **les poings** *(m) fists* **bomber** *to stick out* **essoufflé(e)** *out of breath* **mentir** *to lie* **écraser** *to crush* **le pouce** *thumb* **riant** *laughing* **le manioc** *manioc (a food-stuff made from a plant root)*

Avez-vous compris?

A. **À votre avis.** Lisez *Les aventures de Yévi au pays des monstres* et répondez aux questions suivantes.

1. Comment est Yévi? Qu'est-ce qu'il demande au géant?
2. Comment est le géant? Donne-t-il quelque chose à manger à Yévi?
3. À votre avis, qui est-ce que les trois personnages (Yévi, le conteur et le géant) représentent?
4. Le conteur dit que Yévi est **con**, un mot vulgaire qui veut dire **imbécile**. Est-ce que vous êtes d'accord? Pourquoi?
5. Avez-vous de la compassion pour Yévi? Pourquoi?
6. À votre avis, est-ce que les trois personnages devraient changer? Si oui, comment faudrait-il qu'ils changent?

B. **Qu'est-ce qu'ils deviendront?** Avec un(e) partenaire, décidez ce qui arrivera à chacun des personnages dans la lecture.

Ça y est! C'est à vous!

A. **Organisez-vous.** Est-ce que vous aimez les feuilletons (*soap operas*)? Vous allez préparer un scénario pour une scène d'un nouveau feuilleton intitulé *Les Docteurs*. Ça peut être une scène dramatique ou une scène comique. Avant de préparer le scénario, répondez à ces questions.

1. **Qui sont-ils?** Faites un portrait physique (grand, petit, gros, un grand nez, les cheveux blonds...) et psychologique (intelligent, bête, sympathique, égoïste...) des personnages.
2. **Que se passe-t-il?** De quel problème parlent-ils? Est-ce que c'est une situation grave? dramatique? comique? idiote?
3. **Que font-ils?** Comment réagissent-ils? Sont-ils de bonne ou de mauvaise humeur? Sont-ils tristes ou heureux? Est-ce qu'ils croient ce que les autres leur disent? Regrettent-ils la situation?
4. **De quoi ont-ils besoin?** Qu'est-ce qu'ils décident de faire? Est-ce que c'est logique? Est-ce que c'est ridicule?

B. **Rédaction: Un scénario.** Comparez vos réponses aux questions de l'exercice précédent à celles de vos camarades de classe. Trouvez des étudiants qui y ont répondu d'une façon similaire et écrivez un scénario pour la scène, que vous jouerez ensuite devant la classe.

C. **Une consultation.** Mukala, l'ami de Daniel, est venu pour une consultation parce qu'il ne se sent pas très bien. Écoutez leur conversation en notant les symptômes, le diagnostic et le remède.

Pour vérifier

Après avoir fait les exercices suivants, vérifiez vos réponses dans l'*Appendix C.*

Talking about health

A. **Bon ou mauvais?** Lisez le passage du livre *Là où il n'y a pas de docteur* à la page suivante. Faites une liste des choses mentionnées qui sont mauvaises pour certaines parties du corps. Après, dites une chose qui est bonne pour la même partie du corps.

EXEMPLE **C'est mauvais pour le foie de boire des boissons alcoolisées. C'est bon pour le foie de manger beaucoup de légumes.**

B. **Négation.** Relisez le passage de *Là où il n'y a pas de docteur* et écrivez une phrase qui explique chacune des choses suivantes.

1. Quelque chose que les femmes enceintes ne doivent jamais faire.
2. Un condiment que les gens qui ont les pieds enflés ne doivent manger qu'en petite quantité.
3. Quelque chose dont la consommation excessive n'est bonne pour personne.

C. **Blessures.** Dites ce que ces gens faisaient quand ils se sont blessés.

1.

2.

3.

Expressing opinions and attitudes

D. **Vacances en Afrique.** Dites à une amie qui va passer les vacances dans les régions tropicales de l'Afrique s'il faut qu'elle fasse les choses suivantes. Commencez les phrases avec **il faut que tu...** ou **il ne faut pas que tu...**

1. avoir un passeport
2. faire attention à ce qu'elle mange
3. aller chez le médecin pour des piqûres
4. prendre l'avion
5. être timide
6. connaître l'histoire de la région

E. **Médecine préventive.** Qu'est-ce qu'il faut faire pour éviter les maladies suivantes? Utilisez des expressions qui encouragent ou découragent.

EXEMPLE le cancer
Pour éviter le cancer, c'est important de manger peu de viande et beaucoup de légumes. C'est mauvais de...

1. une indigestion
2. les maladies de foie
3. un rhume

F. **Un bon médecin.** Un ami qui étudie la médecine veut savoir ce qu'il faut faire pour être un bon médecin. Faites une liste de trois suggestions.

EXEMPLE **Il est essentiel que tu sois patient. Il est bon que...**

De manière générale, les aliments qui sont bons pour nous lorsque nous sommes en bonne santé sont bons pour nous lorsque nous sommes malades. De même, les choses qui nous sont nuisibles lorsque nous sommes en bonne santé nous font encore plus mal lorsque nous sommes malades. Il faut éviter:

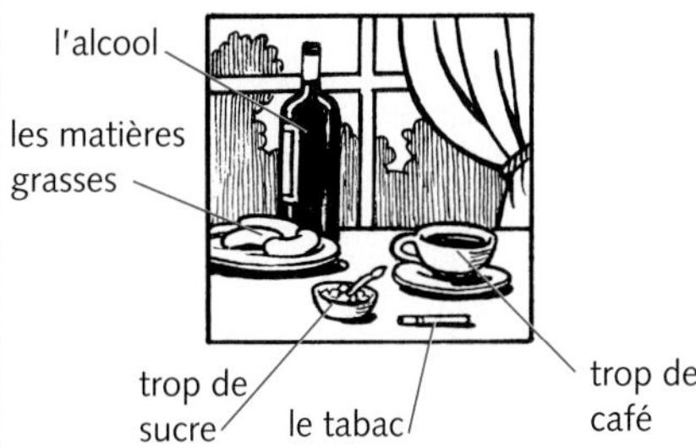

• L'alcool provoque ou aggrave les maladies du foie, de l'estomac et des nerfs. Il cause également des problèmes sociaux.
• Fumer peut causer une toux chronique ou le cancer des poumons et d'autres problèmes. Fumer est particulièrement mauvais pour les gens qui ont des maladies aux poumons comme la tuberculose, l'asthme et la bronchite, et aussi pour les femmes enceintes.
• Une consommation excessive de nourriture grasse ou de café peut provoquer des ulcères d'estomac et d'autres problèmes du système digestif.
• Trop de sucre coupe l'appétit, peut provoquer des problèmes cardiaques et peut être en partie la cause du cancer intestinal.
• Les gens qui ont une tension élevée, certains problèmes de cœur ou les pieds enflés ne doivent utiliser que peu ou pas de sel. Une consommation excessive de sel n'est bonne pour personne.

Vocabulaire

Talking about health

NOMS
des aliments (*m*)
une allergie
une analyse
des antibiotiques (*m*)
un appétit
une aspirine
une clinique
une consultation
la douleur
la fièvre
des frissons (*m*)
la grippe
une indigestion
une infection
un liquide
un(e) malade
les matières grasses (*f*)
des médicaments (*m*)
une ordonnance
un(e) patient(e)
une piqûre
une radio
un rhume
le sang
la santé
un symptôme
un traitement
un ulcère

DIVERS
bouché(e)
de bonne / mauvaise humeur
enceinte
enflé(e)
gras(se)
grave
Qu'est-ce qui ne va pas?

EXPRESSIONS VERBALES
avoir mal à
(se) blesser
(se) brûler
(se) casser
causer
couler
(se) couper
démanger
digérer
donner un conseil
éternuer
se fouler (la cheville...)
(se) guérir
rendre + *adjective*
(se) soigner
supporter
tomber malade
tousser
vomir

Expressing opinions and attitudes

ENCOURAGING AND DISCOURAGING
aimer mieux que...*
c'est bon que...
c'est dommage que...
c'est essentiel que...
c'est important que...
c'est mauvais que...
c'est nécessaire que...
il faut que...*
il vaut mieux que...*
préférer que...*
regretter que...
vouloir que...*

EXPRESSING EMOTIONS
avoir peur que...
être content(e) que...
être désolé(e) que...
être étonné(e) que...
être furieux / furieuse que...
être heureux / heureuse que...
être surpris(e) que...
être triste que...

VOCABULARY NOTE
The expressions listed under ***Expressing opinions and attitudes*** are all followed by the subjunctive. All of these verbal expressions may also be followed by an infinitive. They all replace the **que** by **de** before infinitives except those with an asterisk, which simply drop the **que**.

Pour les parties du corps, voir la page 432.
Pour les expressions affirmatives et négatives, voir les pages 440–441.

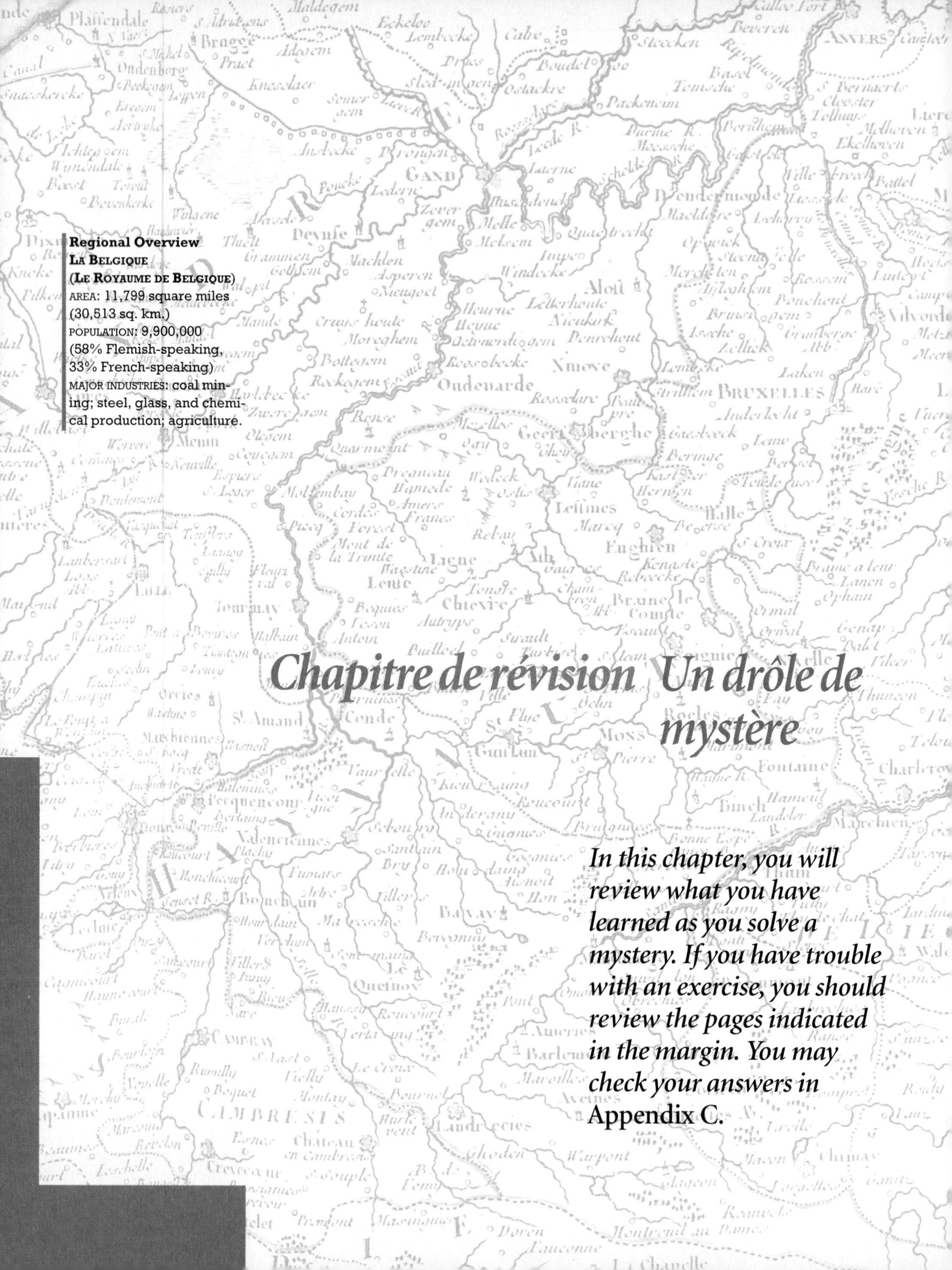

Regional Overview
La Belgique
(Le Royaume de Belgique)
AREA: 11,799 square miles (30,513 sq. km.)
POPULATION: 9,900,000 (58% Flemish-speaking, 33% French-speaking)
MAJOR INDUSTRIES: coal mining; steel, glass, and chemical production; agriculture.

Chapitre de révision *Un drôle de mystère*

In this chapter, you will review what you have learned as you solve a mystery. If you have trouble with an exercise, you should review the pages indicated in the margin. You may check your answers in Appendix C.

Return of the Hunters
Pieter Bruegel (Elder) (1525–1569)
1565
Künsthistorisches Museum, Gemældegalerie, Vienna
Erich Lessing/Art Resource, NY

Bruegel lived and worked in Antwerp, Belgium. This scene, depicting the barrenness of winter, is typical of his paintings, which often portray human activity against the backdrop of a vast landscape.

TEXTBOOK TAPE

Pour commencer

Dans ce chapitre, vous allez résoudre un crime. C'est un meurtre qui a lieu dans un vieux château de la forêt des Ardennes dans le sud de la Belgique. En résolvant le mystère, vous allez aussi réviser ce que vous avez appris dans ce livre. D'abord, faisons la connaissance des personnages du mystère. À votre avis, qui est la victime? Qui est le/la criminel(le)? Quel est le mobile (*motive*)?

Regardez les personnages suivants. Comment sont-ils?

François Fédor, millionaire excentrique

Laurent Lavare, le comptable de François Fédor

Valérie Veutoux, l'ex-femme de François Fédor

Bernard Boncorps, le neveu de François Fédor

Nathalie Lanana, la petite amie de Bernard Boncorps

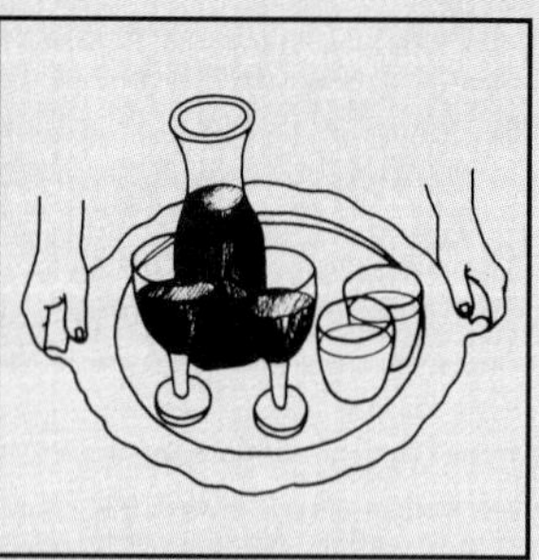

le/la domestique

le détective

Il y a encore un dernier petit détail. Le/La domestique sera joué(e) par votre professeur. Et le détective, qui est-ce? Oui, vous avez deviné juste (comme un bon détective). C'est vous!

Savez-vous le faire?

A. **Descriptions.** Choisissez quatre adjectifs pour décrire chacun des personnages, y compris le/la domestique et le détective.

Pour réviser l'accord des adjectifs, voir les pages 41, 47, 140 et 146.

riche	???	malhonnête	???
BEAU	???	âgé	???
snob	**???**	**bête**	**???**
paresseux **laid**	*blond* SUSPECT	**méchant**	*sympathique*
???	*irresponsable*	???	**(mal)heureux**
désagréable	sexy	froid	**hostile**
grand	**petit**	**intelligent**	???
sportif	MATÉRIALISTE		FRIVOLE
sérieux	intéressant		*puissant*

B. **Explications.** Avec un(e) partenaire, devinez qui va être la victime et qui va commettre le crime. Imaginez une explication. Utilisez un dictionnaire si besoin.

Pour réviser le futur immédiat, voir les pages 157–158.

Un château de la forêt des Ardennes.

Pour réviser les prépositions avec les régions géographiques, voir les pages 246–247.

C. **Où habitent-ils?** Ces personnages habitent dans différents pays européens francophones. Où habitent-ils? (Remarquez qu'on dit **à Monaco** comme si c'était une ville.)

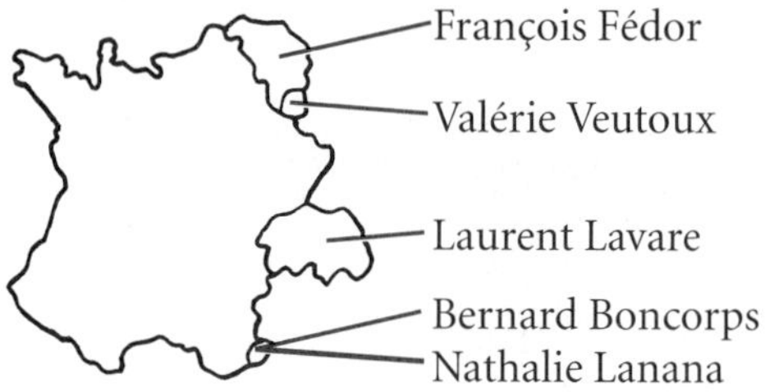

Comment s'y prendre?

Recognizing the pluperfect

The pluperfect tense (**le plus-que-parfait**) indicates that an action preceded another action in the past. When you see the auxiliary verb **avoir** or **être** in the imperfect followed by the past participle, translate it as *had* plus a past participle. Look at these examples and translate the last two.

Quand mon amie m'a invité à déjeuner, j'*avais* déjà *mangé*.
When my friend invited me to lunch, I ***had*** *already* ***eaten****.*

J'ai essayé de te téléphoner mais tu *étais* déjà *parti*.
I tried to call you, but you ***had*** *already* ***left****.*

Quand je suis rentré, toute la famille *était allée* au cinéma, alors j'ai mangé seul.
???

Valérie est arrivée trop tard. Ses amis *étaient* déjà *sortis*.
???

Savez-vous le faire?

A. **D'abord...** Lisez ces phrases et répétez l'action qui a eu lieu (*took place*) en premier.

EXEMPLE Quand le/la domestique s'est couché(e), tous les autres étaient déjà montés dans leur chambre.
Tous les autres étaient montés dans leur chambre.

1. Comme M. Lavare leur avait dit d'arriver vers midi, Valérie et Bernard sont arrivés au château un peu avant.
2. Quand ils se sont levés le lendemain, M. Lavare avait déjà quitté le château.
3. Quand je me suis levé, tout le monde avait déjeuné, alors j'ai mangé tout seul.
4. J'ai dû commencer mon repas avec le plat principal parce que le/la domestique avait déjà servi la soupe quand je me suis mis à table.
5. Je me demandais pourquoi il m'avait dit de venir chez lui et pourquoi il ne m'avait pas indiqué la raison de son invitation.

B. **Qu'est-ce qui s'est passé?** Dans le texte qui suit dans la section ***Qu'est-ce qui se passe?***, trouvez au moins dix exemples du plus-que-parfait.

Qu'est-ce qui se passe?

Un mystère dans les Ardennes

TEXTBOOK TAPE

Certains l'admiraient, d'autres le détestaient. Il avait toujours fait ce qu'il voulait et personne ne disputait ce qu'il faisait. François Fédor habitait dans un vieux château au fond de la forêt des Ardennes. Dans le village, où on ne le voyait jamais, on l'appelait le vieux Midas, parce qu'on disait que tout ce qu'il touchait changeait en or. Personne ne savait exactement d'où venait sa fortune, mais la plupart des gens croyaient qu'il avait fait fortune dans les mines du Zaïre pendant sa jeunesse.

Son aptitude à faire fortune était sans égal. Malheureusement, on pouvait dire la même chose de son aptitude à se faire des ennemis. François Fédor avait toujours négligé les membres de sa famille et il n'avait jamais pris le temps de se faire des amis. Quand je dis qu'il avait négligé les membres de sa famille, je ne veux pas donner l'impression qu'il ne partageait pas sa richesse avec eux; au contraire, ils ne manquaient de rien. Comme dans un trou noir, chaque mois il versait une petite fortune dans les comptes en banque de son neveu Bernard Boncorps et de son ex-femme Valérie Veutoux. Il payait cet argent depuis vingt ans sans garder le moindre contact avec l'un ou l'autre. En fait, il n'avait jamais rencontré son neveu, qui vivait une vie de play-boy à Monaco, grâce à son vieil oncle. Mais il faut ajouter qu'eux n'avaient jamais essayé de venir le voir non plus. Ils acceptaient son argent chaque mois sans questions et ils n'auraient jamais pensé que François Fédor puisse choisir un jour une charité plus méritoire.

C'était donc avec grande surprise que son neveu et son ex-femme avaient reçu un coup de téléphone de Laurent Lavare, le comptable de François Fédor, quelques semaines auparavant. Ils étaient priés de se rendre chez le vieux Midas le dernier jour du mois courant avant midi. Chacun se demandait ce que le vieux Fédor pouvait bien vouloir après tout ce temps. Comme M. Lavare avait refusé de leur donner plus de détails, ils s'étaient laissés emporter par leur imagination. Quand ils étaient arrivés au grand château sombre, Valérie Veutoux, Bernard Boncorps et sa petite amie Nathalie Lanana s'étaient sentis un peu mal à l'aise. Après avoir passé deux journées entières dans le château sans voir leur hôte, le malaise des invités s'était transformé en panique. Mais que pouvaient-ils faire sinon accepter les caprices de leur bienfaiteur et chercher une manière de passer le temps? Quand Bernard n'était pas avec Nathalie, il jouait au billard pendant qu'elle se baignait dans la piscine. Valérie Veutoux restait toute la journée dans sa chambre. Cette attente avait duré presque deux jours quand le/la domestique les avait enfin informés qu'ils verraient M. Fédor au dîner à huit heures, dans la salle à manger.

Accompagné de son comptable, François Fédor les attendait, assis à table, quand ils étaient descendus. Sans dire un mot, le vieil hôte leur avait indiqué d'un geste de la main où chacun devait s'asseoir, à l'autre bout de la table. Le/La domestique avait servi un excellent dîner, mais les invités, qui n'avaient pas l'habitude d'apprécier ce qu'on leur donnait, n'avaient fait aucun compliment. Ils étaient trop curieux de connaître la raison de cette réunion soudaine et inattendue. Si M. Lavare, le comptable, n'avait pas été là, on n'aurait pas dit quatre mots durant tout le dîner.

Le repas fini, François Fédor s'était retiré à la bibliothèque et il avait demandé au/à la domestique de faire entrer son neveu et son ex-femme l'un après l'autre pour boire un cognac avec lui... il avait quelque chose d'important à leur dire. Après une conférence d'une demi-heure avec chacun, le/la domestique les avait raccompagnés à leur chambre et leur avait souhaité une bonne nuit. Devinaient-ils la scène qui les attendait le lendemain matin en sortant de leur chambre? Savaient-ils qu'un détective voudrait leur parler et qu'ils seraient soupçonnés d'un meurtre? Au moins une personne présente cette nuit-là le savait. Mais qui était-ce?

Quand ils s'étaient levés, ils avaient appris que tôt le matin, le/la domestique avait téléphoné à la police pour dire que François Fédor avait été victime d'un meurtre au cours de la nuit. Qui avait commis ce crime? Quel était le mobile du meurtre? Pourquoi est-ce que François Fédor leur avait demandé de venir? Qu'est-ce qu'il leur avait dit seuls dans la bibliothèque? Qu'est-ce que M. Lavare savait? Et le/la domestique? Qu'est-ce qui s'était passé ce soir-là? C'est à vous de résoudre le crime. Qu'est-ce que le célèbre Maigret aurait fait à votre place? Vous allez sans doute vouloir poser beaucoup de questions et prendre des notes.

Avez-vous compris?

A. **Détails.** Lisez le texte «Un mystère dans les Ardennes» et répondez aux questions suivantes.

1. Où est-ce que François Fédor habitait?
2. D'où venait sa fortune?
3. Avait-il beaucoup d'amis?
4. Avec qui partageait-il sa richesse?
5. Qui avait téléphoné à Bernard Boncorps et à Valérie Veutoux pour les inviter au château?
6. Comment avaient-ils réagi à l'invitation?
7. Combien de temps avaient-ils dû attendre avant de voir François Fédor?
8. Qu'est-ce que Bernard Boncorps et Valérie Veutoux avaient appris le lendemain du dîner?
9. À votre avis, qu'est-ce que François Fédor leur avait dit dans la bibliothèque?

B. **Vous êtes le détective.** Pour commencer votre investigation, écoutez la déclaration de chacun des personnages qui a passé la nuit au château. En les écoutant, notez les réponses aux questions qui suivent sur une autre feuille de papier.

BERNARD BONCORPS	VALÉRIE VEUTOUX	LAURENT LAVARE	LE/LA DOMESTIQUE

1. Qu'est-ce que chacun a fait après le dîner?
2. À quelle heure est-ce que chacun s'est couché?
3. Qu'est-ce que chacun a entendu pendant la nuit?

Remarquez que...

Notre mystère se situe dans la forêt des Ardennes, dans le sud de la Belgique. Siège de l'OTAN (Organisation du traité de l'Atlantique Nord), la Belgique a été un champ de bataille pendant les deux guerres mondiales. Au cours de la Première Guerre mondiale, les Allemands ont occupé le pays pendant quatre ans et près d'un million de Belges se sont réfugiés en France, en Grande-Bretagne et aux Pays-Bas. L'histoire s'est répétée pendant la Seconde Guerre mondiale. Occupée à partir de 1940, la Belgique a été libérée par les Alliés en décembre 1944 lors de la célèbre bataille des Ardennes (*Battle of the Bulge*) qui a eu lieu près de la ville de Bastogne. Les villageois de la région racontent que, dans une neige qui leur arrivait jusqu'aux genoux, les troupes américaines ont demandé aux citoyens belges de leur donner leurs draps (*sheets*) de lit pour servir de camouflage. Après la guerre, ces villages ont reçu des boîtes de draps de lit de la part du gouvernement américain. Cette coopération entre l'Amérique et la Belgique au cours de la guerre a continué jusqu'au présent.

Du point de vue linguistique, la Belgique est divisée en deux. Dans le Nord, en Flandre, on parle néerlandais. Le Sud, la Wallonie, est francophone, et Bruxelles, la capitale, est bilingue. L'un des Belges francophones les plus connus est l'écrivain Georges Simenon, créateur du célèbre détective Maigret. Né en 1903 à Liège, une des plus grandes villes de Belgique, Simenon a écrit plus de cent romans policiers.

La Grande Place, Bruxelles, Belgique

Savez-vous le faire?

Pour réviser les prépositions, voir les pages 112 et 294. Pour réviser les meubles, voir la page 111.

A. Il a disparu. Le corps de François Fédor a disparu (*disappeared*). Vous devez bien examiner le lieu du crime. Observez bien tous les indices (*clues*). Voici la chambre de François Fédor avant le dîner et le lendemain du crime. Quelles différences y voyez-vous?

avant le dîner

le lendemain du crime

Pour réviser comment exprimer la possession, voir les pages 114 et 303.

Regardez encore une fois les deux dessins. Demandez au/à la domestique si chaque chose qui se trouve dans la chambre le lendemain du crime et qui n'était pas là la nuit précédente appartenait à François Fédor. Dites à qui pourraient appartenir les choses qui n'étaient pas à lui.

EXEMPLE — **Est-ce que c'était son ordinateur?**
— **Non, cet ordinateur n'était pas à lui. C'est peut-être l'ordinateur de Laurent Lavare.**

B. Absolument pas! Vous interrogez Bernard Boncorps, Valérie Veutoux et Laurent Lavare. Ils répondent tous négativement aux questions suivantes. Que disent-ils? Utilisez une expression négative.

Pour réviser les expressions négatives, voir les pages 440–441.

1. Est-ce que vous avez entendu quelque chose de bizarre pendant la nuit?
2. Avez-vous vu quelqu'un entrer dans la chambre de François Fédor?
3. Est-ce que vous êtes déjà sorti(e) du château ce matin?
4. Est-ce que vous êtes entré(e) dans la chambre de François Fédor pendant la nuit ou ce matin?
5. Vous disputiez-vous quelquefois avec la victime?
6. Avez-vous vu des indices quelque part?
7. Aviez-vous une raison de commettre ce crime?
8. Savez-vous quelque chose d'autre sur ce crime?

C. Dans quelle chambre? Tout le monde a dormi le long du même couloir hier soir. Écoutez le/la domestique pour déterminer qui a dormi dans chaque chambre.

Pour réviser les prépositions, voir les pages 112 et 294.

EXEMPLE — **Valérie Veutoux était au bout du couloir, en face de la salle de bains.**

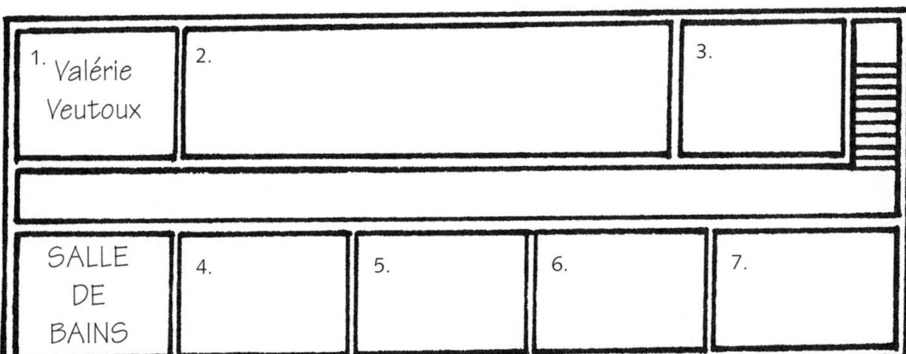

Terwagne, un village dans la forêt des Ardennes.

Pour réviser les pronoms compléments d'object direct et indirect, voir les pages 219 et 255–256.

D. Relations. Utilisez le pronom **le** ou **lui** avec les verbes suivants à l'imparfait pour interroger le/la domestique sur ses relations avec M. Fédor. Écoutez ses réponses.

EXEMPLE connaître depuis longtemps
— **Est-ce que vous le connaissiez depuis longtemps?**
— **Je le connaissais depuis 15 ans.**

1. aimer bien
2. parler de sa famille
3. emprunter quelquefois de l'argent
4. réveiller à la même heure tous les jours
5. servir toujours le petit déjeuner au lit
6. préparer toujours le dîner
7. trouver sévère
8. voir tous les jours

Maintenant demandez au/à la domestique si M. Fédor lui faisait les choses suivantes. Écoutez ses réponses.

EXEMPLE irriter quelquefois
— **Est-ce que M. Fédor vous irritait quelquefois?**
— **Oui, il m'irritait parfois. Ce n'était pas un homme facile.**

1. tout dire
2. payer bien
3. parler de sa vie privée
4. permettre de faire ce que vous vouliez au château

Pour réviser le subjonctif, voir les pages 449–450 et 455–456.

E. Je ne veux pas que... Vous dites aux suspects ce qu'ils doivent et ne doivent pas faire.

EXEMPLE **Je ne veux pas que vous partiez d'ici.**

Il faut que...	partir d'ici
Il ne faut pas que...	dire tout ce que vous savez
Je veux que...	être calmes
Je ne veux pas que...	avoir peur
Il vaut mieux que...	toucher aux affaires de François Fédor
	faire une déposition
	parler à la presse
	m'obéir
	être patients
	???

Pour réviser **savoir** et **connaître**, voir les pages 219 et 222–223.

F. *Savoir* ou *connaître?* Quelles connaissances du crime avez-vous? Dites si vous savez ou si vous connaissez les choses ou les personnes suivantes en utilisant le verbe **savoir** ou **connaître**.

1. la date du crime
2. le/la domestique de François Fédor
3. l'heure approximative du crime
4. le château de François Fédor
5. tous les amis de François Fédor
6. tous les détails de la vie de François Fédor
7. des mobiles possibles
8. l'identité de l'assassin

G. Il faut penser comme le/la criminel(le). Pour attraper le/la criminel(le), il faut savoir penser comme lui/elle. Si vous étiez le/la criminel(le), est-ce que vous feriez les choses suivantes? Utilisez le conditionnel.

Pour réviser le conditionnel, voir les pages 421–422.

Si j'étais le/la criminel(le),...

EXEMPLE faire quelque chose d'inhabituel
Si j'étais le/la criminel(le), je ne ferais rien d'inhabituel.

1. être calme
2. parler beaucoup du crime
3. savoir tous les détails du crime
4. obéir à la police
5. s'intéresser beaucoup à l'investigation
6. dire la vérité
7. avoir envie de partir
8. devenir de plus en plus nerveux / nerveuse
9. accuser quelqu'un d'autre
10. ???

H. Une matinée typique. Voici comment François Fédor passait ses matinées. Décrivez sa journée typique.

Pour réviser les verbes réfléchis, voir la page 323. Pour réviser l'imparfait, voir les pages 340–341.

1.

2.

3.

4.

TOURNEZ S.V.P.

5.

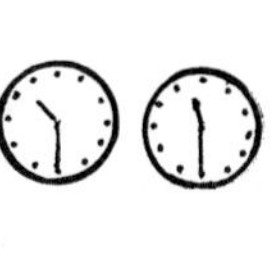

6.

Pour réviser le passé composé et l'imparfait, voir les pages 378–379.

I. Accusations. Dans le château Fédor, chacun des suspects vient vous expliquer pourquoi il/elle soupçonne les autres. Complétez les paragraphes suivants en mettant les verbes entre parenthèses au passé composé ou à l'imparfait.

BERNARD BONCORPS

Je crois que c'est Laurent Lavare, le comptable de mon oncle qui l(e) ______ (tuer *to kill*). J' ______ (entendre) dire récemment qu'il ______ (avoir) des problèmes financiers. Certains disent qu'il ______ (emprunter) des millions de francs à mon oncle sans le lui dire. En fait, un ami suisse qui travaille à la banque de mon oncle m(e) ______ (dire) qu'il y ______ (avoir) très peu d'argent dans son compte. Je pense que mon oncle ______ (apprendre) ce qui ______ (se passer) et je suis certain qu'il ______ (dire) à M. Lavare qu'il ______ (aller) le dénoncer à la police.

VALÉRIE VEUTOUX

Il faut que vous sachiez que Bernard Boncorps ______ (être) furieux contre son oncle. François Fédor ______ (croire) que son neveu ______ (faire) des études de droit à l'Université de Nice. En vérité, Bernard ______ (passer) tout son temps sur les plages et dans les casinos de Monaco. Quand son oncle ______ (comprendre) la situation, il ______ (se fâcher *to get angry*) et il ______ (dire) à son neveu qu'il ______ (vouloir) qu'il vienne finir ses études en Belgique, à l'Université de Liège. Quand sa sœur, la mère de Bernard, ______ (mourir), François lui ______ (promettre) de se charger de l'éducation de son neveu. Bernard ______ (ne pas comprendre) pourquoi son oncle, qu'il n'avait jamais vu, ______ (s'intéresser) après tout ce temps à ce qu'il ______ (faire). Bernard ______ (ne pas vouloir) abandonner sa vie de play-boy sur la Côte d'Azur et il ______ (avoir) peur que sa petite amie, Nathalie Lanana, refuse de venir ici avec lui. Et puis, il faut ajouter aussi que Bernard ______ (avoir) des dettes énormes dans les casinos. Il ______ (ne pas pouvoir) payer ses dettes avec l'argent que son oncle lui ______ (donner) chaque mois. Bernard ______ (ne pas vouloir) attendre la mort naturelle de son oncle pour hériter de sa part de la fortune.

LAURENT LAVARE

Je suis presque certain que Valérie Veutoux ______ (commettre) ce crime. Récemment, elle ______ (faire) la connaissance de Jean Jigaulaux, un jeune homme de 25 ans, et elle ______ (tomber) amoureuse de lui. Ils ______ (sortir) quelques mois ensemble, puis il lui ______ (demander) de l'épouser. La vieille Veutoux ______ (ne pas voir) qu'il ne ______ (vouloir) que son argent et le jeune Jigaulaux ______ (ne pas savoir) qu'elle ne recevrait plus un centime de François Fédor si elle ______ (se remarier). La vaniteuse Valérie Veutoux ______ (sans doute comprendre) qu'elle n'aurait jamais le joli Jigaulaux tant que François Fédor ______ (être) en vie et elle ______ (se débarrasser *to get rid of*) de lui.

J. Éclaircissements. Répondez aux questions suivantes au sujet des suspects indiqués, en vous servant des renseignements que vous avez obtenus dans l'exercice précédent. Utilisez un pronom dans chaque réponse pour remplacer les mots en italique.

Pour réviser les pronoms compléments d'objet direct et indirect, y et en, voir les pages 192–193, 219–220, 255–256, 365 et 406–407.

LAURENT LAVARE

1. Qui a accusé *Laurent Lavare* du crime?
2. D'après son accusateur, est-ce que Laurent Lavare avait *des problèmes financiers*?
3. Est-ce qu'il disait *à François Fédor* qu'il empruntait *de l'argent*?
4. Combien d'argent empruntait-il *à François Fédor*?
5. D'après le banquier, ami de Bernard Boncorps, combien *d'argent* y avait-il dans le compte de son oncle?

BERNARD BONCORPS

1. Est-ce que Bernard Boncorps rendait souvent visite *à son oncle*?
2. Combien de fois est-ce que Bernard avait vu *son oncle*?
3. Qu'est-ce que François Fédor a dit *à sa sœur* juste avant sa mort?
4. Est-ce que Bernard voulait venir *à Liège* pour finir ses études?
5. Combien de temps passait-il *sur les plages et dans les casinos*?
6. Est-ce qu'il avait *des dettes*?
7. Est-ce que Bernard avait assez *d'argent* pour payer *ses dettes*?

VALÉRIE VEUTOUX

1. Qui pense que Valérie Veutoux a tué *François Fédor*?
2. Après combien de temps est-ce que Jean Jigaulaux a demandé *à Valérie Veutoux* de l'épouser?
3. Pourquoi est-ce que le jeune Jigaulaux aimait *la vieille Veutoux*?

K. Comparaisons. Exprimez votre opinion sur les suspects en complétant les phrases suivantes avec un mot comparatif.

Pour réviser le comparatif, voir les pages 54, 373 et 417.

plus	*moins*	**aussi**	**autant**

1. Laurent Lavare a l'air _____ malhonnête que Bernard Boncorps.
2. Valérie Veutoux est _____ méchante que Bernard Boncorps.
3. Valérie Veutoux a _____ de problèmes que Bernard Boncorps.
4. Bernard Boncorps a besoin d(e) _____ d'argent que Laurent Lavare.
5. Laurent Lavare avait _____ de raisons de tuer François Fédor que Valérie Veutoux.
6. Valérie Veutoux avait _____ de mobiles que Bernard Boncorps.
7. Bernard Boncorps avait _____ de mobiles que Laurent Lavare.
8. Laurent Lavare a l'air _____ suspect que Valérie Veutoux.
9. Valérie Veutoux a l'air _____ suspect que Bernard Boncorps.
10. Bernard Boncorps est _____ suspect que Valérie Veutoux.

Pour réviser l'imparfait, voir les pages 340–341.

Pour réviser l'heure, voir la page 21.

L. **Qu'est-ce que vous faisiez?** Écoutez une fois de plus les déclarations de Valérie Veutoux, de Laurent Lavare et de Bernard Boncorps dans l'exercice ***B. Vous êtes le détective*** à la page 470 et notez qui faisait chaque chose à l'heure indiquée.

EXEMPLE déjà être au lit
À dix heures et demie Valérie Veutoux était déjà au lit.

1. avoir mal à la tête
   travailler sur ordinateur
   être au village
2. prendre un verre au café
   lire
   parler au téléphone
3. jouer aux cartes
   dormir

Pour réviser l'usage de **c'est** et **il/elle est**, voir les pages 139–140.

M. **Qui est-ce?** Que savons-nous des suspects? Complétez les phrases suivantes avec **il est** ou **c'est**. Ensuite, dites si vous pensez que chaque phrase décrit plutôt Laurent Lavare ou Bernard Boncorps.

EXEMPLE C'est quelqu'un qui travaille beaucoup. → **C'est Laurent Lavare.**

1. ______ le neveu de François Fédor.
2. ______ comptable.
3. ______ le comptable de François Fédor.
4. ______ suisse.
5. ______ jeune.
6. ______ un play-boy.
7. ______ malhonnête.
8. ______ sportif.
9. ______ une personne bête.
10. ______ peut-être l'assassin.

Pour réviser les pronoms relatifs, voir les pages 413–415.

N. **Les gens du village.** Vous demandez aux gens du village ce qu'ils savaient au sujet de François Fédor. Faites des phrases en utilisant un élément de chaque colonne.

François Fédor était un homme...	qui qu(e)... dont	ne parlait pas beaucoup. le passé était mystérieux. on ne voyait pas souvent. la personnalité était un peu bizarre. tout le monde avait un peu peur. n'avait pas beaucoup d'amis. je ne connaissais pas bien. faisait toujours ce qu'il voulait.

O. Qu'est-ce qu'on a servi? Demandez au/à la domestique s'il/si elle a servi les choses suivantes au dîner le soir du meurtre.

Pour réviser les produits alimentaires, voir les pages 69, 354–356 et 363. Pour réviser l'article partitif, voir les pages 226–227.

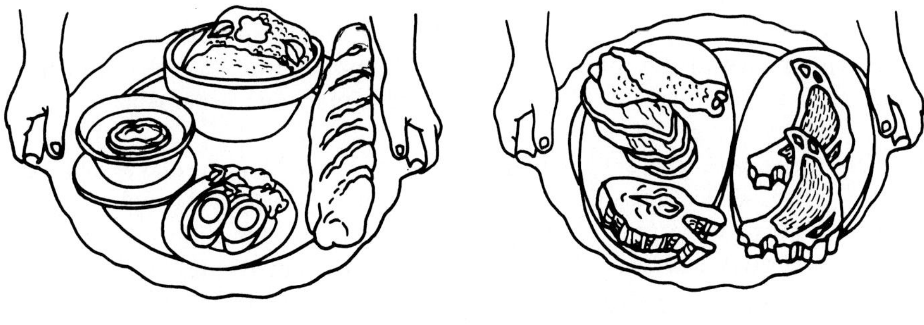

P. Le dîner. Complétez le paragraphe suivant avec l'article défini (**le, la, l', les**), l'article indéfini (**un, une, des**), le partitif (**du, de la, de l'**) ou **de**.

Pour réviser les articles, voir les pages 36–39, 52, 71, 107–108 et 226–227.

______ soir où M. Fédor est mort, j'ai mis la table à sept heures. M. Fédor et Laurent Lavare sont descendus vers sept heures et demie et ils ont pris ______ vin blanc avant de dîner. Durant le repas, M. Fédor n'avait pas très faim; il a mangé ______ soupe et un peu ______ pain mais il n'a pas pris ______ poulet, ______ légumes ou ______ tarte aux pommes. Normalement, il mangeait beaucoup. Il aimait beaucoup ______ viande et ______ pommes de terre mais il ne prenait pas beaucoup ______ choses sucrées. Je pense qu'il n'avait pas ______ appétit parce que ses problèmes le préoccupaient. Il n'a pas bu ______ vin rouge avec son repas, seulement ______ eau minérale et il a pris ______ café quand j'ai servi ______ dessert. Après ______ dîner, M. Fédor s'est retiré à ______ bibliothèque où il a bu un verre ______ cognac. Il est resté assis dans ______ fauteuil près de ______ porte pendant ______ heure, puis il est monté se coucher.

Pour réviser les symptômes et les maladies, voir les pages 432–434.
Pour réviser le passé composé et l'imparfait, voir les pages 378–379.

Q. **Symptômes.** Demandez au/à la domestique si François Fédor a fait les choses suivantes ou s'il avait ces symptômes après le dîner.

1. avoir des frissons
2. vomir
3. prendre des médicaments
4. avoir mal à la tête
5. se sentir fatigué
6. avoir très sommeil
7. monter tout de suite se coucher
8. s'endormir facilement

R. **Valérie se marie.** Vous avez demandé à des collègues d'observer les activités de chacun des suspects. Celui qui suit Valérie Veutoux a rapporté ces photos prises le lendemain du crime. Vous lui demandez de vous raconter la journée de Valérie Veutoux mais ses notes sont en désordre. D'abord, remettez ses notes dans l'ordre; ensuite, racontez la journée de Valérie Veutoux en mettant les verbes au passé composé ou à l'imparfait.

EXEMPLE **Valérie Veutoux est sortie de sa chambre à 8h20 du matin. Elle est descendue...**

- Jean Jigaulaux arrive ici quelques heures après. Il retrouve Valérie Veutoux dans la forêt à midi et ils s'embrassent passionnément.
- Comme Jean est fatigué, il prend une chambre à l'hôtel du village où il passe l'après-midi.
- Valérie Veutoux sort de sa chambre à 8h20 du matin. Elle descend au rez-de-chaussée et elle téléphone à Jean Jigaulaux à Luxembourg. Ensuite, elle téléphone à une agence de voyages à Bruxelles.
- Ils quittent le restaurant à 20h50. À ce moment-là, un chien m'attaque dans les rosiers derrière lesquels je m'étais caché et je les perds de vue.
- À cinq heures, ils montent dans la voiture de Jean Jigaulaux et vont dans le village voisin où ils se marient en secret à 18h20.
- Après la cérémonie, ils dînent au restaurant du village. À part le garçon, ils sont seuls dans le restaurant.
- Pendant le dîner, je les observe de l'extérieur. Jean ne parle pas beaucoup mais Valérie Veutoux lui explique quelque chose.

S. **Réactions.** Valérie Veutoux est furieuse. Imaginez sa réaction quand vous lui dites les choses suivantes.

Pour réviser le subjonctif, voir les pages 449–450 et 455–456.

???	**C'est bon que...**
C'est nécessaire que...	**C'est impossible que...**
C'est important que...	**C'est ridicule que...**
C'EST ESSENTIEL QUE...	
Ça me rend furieuse que...	*Je suis heureuse que...*

EXEMPLE Vous ne pouvez pas partir pour quelques jours.
C'est ridicule que je ne puisse pas partir si je veux.

1. Oui madame, vous êtes suspecte.
2. Nous ne savons pas où se trouve le corps de la victime.
3. Laurent Lavare dit que vous aviez des raisons de tuer François Fédor.
4. Nous savons que vous avez retrouvé M. Jigaulaux dans la forêt.
5. Nous avons des photos de Jean Jigaulaux avec vous.
6. Je veux lui parler demain.
7. Il pourra partir après l'interrogatoire.
8. Vous devez tout nous expliquer.

T. **Deux billets pour Tahiti.** Après une investigation, vous apprenez que François Fédor enregistrait (*recorded*) toutes les conversations téléphoniques chez lui. Vous découvrez que Valérie Veutoux a téléphoné à une agence de voyages à Bruxelles le lendemain du crime. Écoutez la conversation entre Valérie Veutoux et l'agent de voyages, et sur une autre feuille de papier, complétez les détails qui manquent sur l'itinéraire de Valérie ci-dessous.

TEXTBOOK TAPE

Pour réviser comment acheter un billet d'avion, voir la page 258.

ITINÉRAIRE

À l'intention de: (*Nom*) et de (*Nom*)

ALLER — Air France–Vol (*Numéro*)

(*Date*)

Départ de Bruxelles (*Heure*) — Boeing 747

Première classe/Vol direct
Non-fumeur

(*Date*)

Arrivée à Tahiti (*Heure*)

Un repas et une collation seront servis en vol.

Prix du billet: (*Prix*)

Total des deux billets: (*Prix*)

Prévoyez d'arriver à l'aéroport deux heures avant l'heure de départ et n'oubliez pas de reconfirmer votre retour 72 heures avant le départ.

BON VOYAGE!

Pour réviser le futur, voir les pages 401–402.
Pour réviser l'impératif, voir la page 296.

U. Une conversation téléphonique. Voici une transcription de la conversation téléphonique entre Valérie Veutoux et son amant, Jean Jigaulaux le lendemain du crime. La première partie a été effacée (*erased*) accidentellement. Complétez ce qui reste en mettant les verbes entre parenthèses au présent, au futur ou à l'impératif.

— ... Après cela, François ne ______ (faire) plus obstacle à notre bonheur. Nous ______ (pouvoir) nous marier quand tu ______ (vouloir).
— Je ______ (venir) aujourd'hui et nous ______ (se marier) ce soir. Si je ______ (partir) tout de suite, j' ______ (arriver) un peu avant midi.
— À deux kilomètres d'ici, il y a une vieille école abandonnée. ______ (tourner) à gauche juste après cette école et ______ (entrer) dans la forêt. Là, personne ne nous ______ (voir). Je t' ______ (attendre) à cet endroit à midi.
— On ______ (être) heureux ensemble.
— Après demain, nous ______ (partir) pour Tahiti et nous ______ (commencer) notre nouvelle vie ensemble.

Pour réviser comment dire la date, voir la page 217.
Pour réviser les chiffres, voir les pages 11, 73 et 122.

V. Le compte en banque. Quand vous comparez les relevés de compte (*bank statements*) de François Fédor, vous remarquez que quelqu'un avait retiré presque tout son argent ces derniers mois. Combien d'argent est-ce qu'il y avait aux dates suivantes de l'année dernière et de cette année?

EXEMPLE 30/9 201 789 067 francs
Le 30 septembre de l'année dernière, il y avait 201 789 067 (deux cent un million sept cent quatre-vingt-neuf mille, soixante-sept) francs dans son compte.

1. 15/10 160 136 978 francs
2. 10/11 125 194 456 francs
3. 24/12 80 714 387 francs
4. 1/1 15 000 090 francs
5. 15/2 904 506 francs
6. 4/3 113 871 francs

Pour réviser comment poser une question, voir les pages 49 et 87.

W. Une cassette vidéo révélatrice. Vous venez de découvrir qu'une caméra de sécurité cachée dans le couloir filmait chaque personne qui entrait dans la chambre de François Fédor. Entre 20h et 8h du matin la caméra n'a enregistré qu'une seule personne qui est entrée dans la chambre de la victime. La caméra s'est arrêtée à 8h30 le lendemain matin. Préparez cinq questions que vous voudriez poser à Valérie Veutoux.

pourquoi ???
À QUELLE HEURE
COMBIEN DE TEMPS
comment **???** que
quand QUI
quel *où*

X. La dernière volonté de François. Vous avez interrogé Valérie Veutoux et elle a répondu que François Fédor n'était pas vexé qu'elle ait un amant, mais au contraire, qu'il l'avait encouragée à se marier avec lui. Selon elle, est-ce que François Fédor lui a dit qu'il voulait qu'elle fasse les choses suivantes, ou qu'il voulait les faire lui-même?

Pour réviser l'usage de l'infinitif ou du subjonctif, voir les pages 455–456.

EXEMPLES se marier avec Jean Jigaulaux
Il voulait que je me marie avec Jean Jigaulaux.
nous offrir un cadeau de mariage
Il voulait nous offrir un cadeau de mariage.

1. tout savoir sur Jean Jigaulaux
2. dire à Jean Jigaulaux de venir ici
3. se marier tout de suite
4. nous offrir un voyage de noces (*wedding trip*)
5. téléphoner pour réserver le billet pour Tahiti le lendemain
6. partir en lune de miel (*honeymoon*) cette semaine
7. être heureuse
8. venir dans sa chambre après le dîner prendre un chèque pour payer le voyage

Y. Que faisait le/la domestique? Reformulez les questions suivantes avec l'inversion et posez-les au/à la domestique.

Pour réviser l'inversion, voir la page 291.

1. À quelle heure est-ce que vous vous êtes levé(e) le lendemain du crime?
2. Qu'est-ce que vous avez fait après vous être levé(e)?
3. Est-ce que les autres dormaient encore dans le château?
4. Quand est-ce que vous avez découvert que François Fédor était mort?
5. Est-ce que vous étiez surpris(e) de ce que vous avez trouvé?
6. Pourquoi est-ce que vous n'avez pas crié?
7. Est-ce que vous avez réveillé quelqu'un pour vous aider?
8. Vous avez téléphoné à la police à 8h12. À quelle heure est-ce que vous êtes entré(e) dans la chambre?
9. Combien de portes est-ce qu'il y a pour entrer dans la chambre de la victime?
10. Pourquoi est-ce que vous ne dites pas la vérité?
11. Ne faites pas l'innocent(e)! Comment est-ce que vous saviez que François Fédor était mort sans entrer dans sa chambre?
12. Pourquoi est-ce qu'on ne vous voit pas sur la vidéo de sécurité?
13. Pourquoi est-ce que la vidéo s'arrête à 8h30?
14. Alors, est-ce que vous voulez dire que François Fédor n'est pas mort?

Pour réviser le passé composé et l'imparfait, voir les pages 378–379.

Z. Une confession. Le/La domestique confesse que François Fédor n'est pas mort. En lisant sa confession, mettez les verbes entre parenthèses au passé composé ou à l'imparfait.

Je ______ (ne pas vouloir) le faire mais c'______ (être) la seule manière! C'______ (être) la seule manière de sauver le château. M. Fédor m'______ (expliquer) que M. Lavare ______ (venir) de l'informer qu'il avait tout perdu. Il avait tout investi dans une compagnie qui avait fait faillite (*had gone bankrupt*). Il ______ (falloir) vendre le château pour payer les créditeurs. «Mais, non», je lui ______ (dire). Il ______ (savoir) que j'______ (adorer) ce château et que je ferais tout pour ne pas le perdre. Je ______ (naître) pas loin d'ici. Quand j' ______ (être) jeune j(e) ______ (rêver) d'habiter ici un jour et j'______ (inventer) des histoires fantastiques qui ______ (avoir) lieu ici. Mais toutes ces histoires-là ______ (finir) toujours bien. Puis, M. Fédor ______ (suggérer) qu'il y ______ (avoir) peut-être une manière de garder le château et que, si on y ______ (réussir), il me le donnerait. Le château serait à moi pour toujours. C'est alors qu'il m(e)______ (révéler) son plan. Il achèterait une police d'assurance vie de 100 000 000 de francs et j'en serais le/la bénéficiaire. M. Fédor ______ (ne jamais le dire), mais j'______ (avoir) l'impression que c' ______ (être) M. Lavare qui avait inventé ce plan. Je sais que M. Lavare avait dit à M. Fédor que Valérie Veutoux avait pris ce M. Jigaulaux comme amant. Cela ______ (rendre) M. Fédor furieux. Chaque fois que M. Fédor ______ (parler) de son ex-femme avec M. Lavare, l'un ______ (devenir) tout rouge et l'autre tout pâle. La vérité, c'est que c' ______ (être) elle qui avait quitté M. Fédor il y a 15 ans et pas le contraire, comme tout le monde le croit. Il ______ (ne jamais lui pardonner) et il ______ (toujours vouloir) contrôler sa vie. Il ______ (ne pas être) obligé de lui donner cet argent depuis le divorce, mais M. Lavare l'avait persuadé de continuer à lui en donner beaucoup. Il ______ (dire) à M. Fédor que si Valérie Veutoux ______ (dépendre) de lui financièrement, il pourrait contrôler sa vie. M. Fédor m(e) ______ (dire) que M. Lavare inviterait Bernard Boncorps et Valérie Veutoux à la maison. M. Fédor expliquerait à son neveu qu'il ______ (ne plus pouvoir) lui donner d'argent. Mais il dirait à Valérie qu'il ______ (vouloir) qu'elle soit heureuse et qu'il ______ (avoir) l'intention de lui offrir un voyage à Tahiti comme lune de miel (*honeymoon*) si elle ______ (se marier) tout de suite. D'après le plan, tout le monde penserait que Valérie Veutoux avait tué M. Fédor et qu'elle était partie pour Tahiti. On la verrait sur la vidéo entrer dans sa chambre la nuit du meurtre et on croirait qu'elle l'avait tué pour pouvoir se marier avec son jeune amant. Mais en réalité, on tuerait Valérie Veutoux et on laisserait son corps au fond de la forêt. M. Fédor s'habillerait comme elle et il partirait pour Tahiti à sa place. À l'aéroport de Bruxelles, on verrait Mme Veutoux partir pour Tahiti et personne ne saurait que c' ______ (être) elle, la vraie victime. On accuserait Valérie Veutoux de s'être échappée après le meurtre de M. Fédor et on ne la reverrait plus. M. Fédor me laisserait le château et après quelques mois, je mettrais les 100 000 000 de francs d'assurance dans un compte secret pour M. Fédor.

*À ce moment-là, pendant la confession, un policier ______ (entrer) et il ______ (annoncer) que des chasseurs (*hunters*) ______ (venir) de trouver le corps d'une femme morte dans la forêt et ils ______ (donner) la description de Valérie Veutoux.*

Épilogue

TEXTBOOK TAPE

Vous croyez probablement comprendre le mystère du meurtre de François Fédor. Vous pensez que le/la domestique va être puni(e) et que le vieux Midas est parti pour vivre sur une île tropicale. Mais êtes-vous certain(e) d'avoir trouvé les vrais criminels? Ah! Les voilà en croisière quelque part dans l'océan Pacifique. Écoutons un peu leur conversation.

— Quel coup! Tu es un vrai génie, mon chéri. Qui aurait pensé que nous pourrions réussir! Tout le monde pense que je suis morte et que François est l'assassin. Après toutes ces années, nous allons enfin pouvoir vivre ensemble sans nous préoccuper de ce vieux tyran. Je me souviens de la première fois que je t'ai vu quand tu as commencé à travailler pour lui! Quel coup de foudre! Et le pauvre François! Il n'avait aucune idée que je l'ai quitté parce que nous étions amants.

— Je trouve toujours incroyable qu'il ait investi toute sa fortune dans cette compagnie qui n'existait pas. Il avait tellement confiance en moi! Ha ha ha!

— Mais pourquoi pas? Le vrai vieux Midas, c'était toi. Tu avais multiplié dix fois sa fortune. Sans toi, cet imbécile aurait perdu tout son argent longtemps avant! Mais maintenant, toute cette fortune est à nous! S'il avait su que tous ces créditeurs que tu payais n'étaient personne d'autre que moi, son ex-femme! Ha ha ha! Qu'est-ce que tu as fait de son corps?

— Il était vraiment surpris quand, au lieu de l'amener à l'aéroport de Bruxelles, nous sommes allés au fond des Ardennes! Quand je lui ai expliqué que toi et moi, nous étions amants depuis le début, j'ai cru pendant un moment qu'il n'y aurait pas besoin de le tuer. Le pauvre, il a failli avoir une attaque! Et il était très comique, habillé comme toi. Il aurait été une jolie femme, tu sais!

— Quel dommage que nous n'ayons pas de photos! J'aurais aimé voir ça! Ha ha ha! Mais qu'est-ce qu'on dira si on trouve son corps?

— On pensera sans doute que c'est le/la domestique qui l'a tué pour ces 100 000 000 de francs d'assurance!

— Mais il y a un dernier détail que je ne comprends pas. Comment est-ce que tu as persuadé ton jeune associé de jouer le rôle de Jean Jigaulaux? Il a si bien joué! Pendant un moment, j'ai vraiment eu l'impression que j'allais me marier avec lui.

— Ce jeune homme était tellement ambitieux qu'il aurait fait n'importe quoi pour avoir ma clientèle. Je lui ai promis de lui laisser tous mes clients mais il ne savait pas que je n'en avais qu'un, et que c'était François Fédor.

— Ça, c'est trop! Tu es cruel... vicieux! C'est pour ça que je t'aime! Ha ha ha!

Naturellement Valérie Veutoux et Laurent Lavare ont dû changer de noms. Si on vous les présente aujourd'hui, vous ferez la connaissance d'Anabelle Atout et de son mari Richard!

Remarquez que...

L'Europe francophone

En Europe, le français est une langue officielle dans quatre pays, une principauté et une grande île méditerranéenne qui est un département français. En vous aidant des photos et des descriptions, essayez de déterminer quels sont ces endroits.

1. Jusqu'à son indépendance en 1830, elle a été gouvernée par Rome, la Bourgogne, la France, l'Autriche, l'Espagne et les Pays-Bas (*the Netherlands*). Pendant les deux guerres mondiales, elle a été occupée par les Allemands. De nos jours, c'est une monarchie fondée sur une démocratie parlementaire. 58 pour cent de la population (les Flamands) parlent néerlandais et 33 pour cent (les Wallons) parlent français. Cette division culturelle et linguistique a longtemps été une source de conflit. Pour dissiper cet antagonisme, un effort de décentralisation a été fait, donnant plus de pouvoir aux trois régions qui forment ce pays: la Wallonie, la Flandre et Bruxelles.

2. L'unique langue officielle de ce pays est le français. Il s'y trouve quand même plusieurs groupes ethniques ou culturels qui, voulant garder leur propre identité, parlent aussi une autre langue telle que le breton, l'occitan ou le basque. Depuis le moyen âge, ce pays a été une monarchie, un empire et une république. En 1958, Charles de Gaulle a fondé la Cinquième République dont la constitution régit encore aujourd'hui le pays.

Additional Regional Information

LA BELGIQUE
See page 464.

LA FRANCE
See page 28.

LA SUISSE

AREA: 15,941 sq. mi. (41,298 sq. km.).
POPULATION: 6,800,000
CAPITAL: Bern
MAJOR INDUSTRIES: metallurgy, clock and watch making, textile production, tourism, agriculture, banking.
OTHER INFORMATION: The majority of the population (in the northern, central, and eastern parts) speaks German, approximately 19% speak French. They are mostly in the West. About 10% (mostly in the South) speak Italian. **Romanche** is spoken only in a few rural areas. Women have had the vote in national elections only since 1971. Most women still have no voice in local politics.

LE LUXEMBOURG

AREA: 998 sq. mi. (2,586 sq. km.)
POPULATION: 388,000
CAPITAL: Luxembourg City
MAJOR INDUSTRIES: agriculture, hydroelectricity, steel, and tire production.
(*Continued on the next page.*)

3. Ce petit pays (plus petit que l'état de Rhode Island) est un grand-duché. C'est une monarchie constitutionnelle à la tête de laquelle se trouvent le grand-duc, qui détient le pouvoir exécutif, et le chef du gouvernement, qui choisit les ministres. Le français est la langue officielle, mais l'allemand est courant dans l'enseignement et dans la presse. Le luxembourgeois est pourtant la langue dominante.

(*Continued from the previous page.*)
MONACO
AREA: 16 sq. mi.
POPULATION: 29,800
MAJOR INDUSTRIES: tourism, gambling, manufacture of precision instruments and chemicals.

4. C'est une république fédérale composée de 23 cantons (*districts*) liés par la constitution fédérale de 1848. Une grande partie du pouvoir politique reste pourtant toujours au niveau du canton. Siège européen des Nations Unies, ce pays continue à garder la neutralité dans les conflits internationaux depuis 1515. Ce pays a trois langues officielles: l'allemand, le français et l'italien. Dans quelques régions rurales on parle une quatrième langue, le romanche.

5. Cette région, dont la langue officielle est le français, est une principauté depuis plus de 300 ans. Bien qu'elle soit devenue un protectorat de la France en 1861, le prince a gardé le pouvoir absolu jusqu'à l'établissement de la constitution de 1911. Aujourd'hui une monarchie constitutionnelle, cette principauté est célèbre dans le monde entier pour le tourisme, le luxe et le jeu (*gambling*).

6. Faisant partie de la France, cette île méditerranéenne où est né Napoléon est divisée en deux départements.

L'Europe: Un monde en formation

Dès son origine, l'histoire de l'Europe a été l'histoire de conflits, d'invasions, de conquêtes et de guerres entre les pays qui la composent. Pratiquement détruite au niveau politique et économique par les deux guerres mondiales, l'Europe est en train aujourd'hui de se tourner vers l'idée de l'unification.

À cause d'un climat économique en perpétuel changement et des différences culturelles et politiques entre les pays, les obstacles se révèlent nombreux et les progrès lents.

Voici les étapes historiques vers l'unification:

1949: Formation du conseil de l'Europe. Cet organisme dont le pouvoir est très limité ne peut que faire des recommandations que les états membres sont libres d'approuver ou de rejeter. Il se prononce dans le domaine de l'éducation, de la protection de l'environnement et des droits de l'homme.

1951: Traité de Paris. Formation de la CECA (Communauté européenne du charbon et de l'acier). Adoptée par la France, l'Allemagne, l'Italie et les pays du Bénélux (la Belgique, le Luxembourg et les Pays-Bas), la CECA crée une zone de libre échange et un esprit de coopération au cœur de l'Europe.

1957: Le traité de Rome. Le traité de Rome donne naissance à la CEE (Communauté économique européenne). Les principes en sont la libre circulation des biens, des services et des gens parmi les pays membres.

1972: L'Europe des Six (la CEE) devient l'Europe des Neuf avec l'adhésion du Danemark, de l'Irlande et du Royaume-Uni.

1979: Le système monétaire européen et l'unité monétaire européenne (l'ÉCU) sont adoptés mais les accords ne sont pas ratifiés par tous les pays.

1981: La Grèce entre dans la Communauté européenne.

1986: Avec l'entrée du Portugal et de l'Espagne, la CEE devient l'Europe des Douze.

1991: La CEE propose les accords de Maastricht.

1993: L'union douanière est réalisée. Les 12 pays membres ratifient les accords de Maastricht, mais avec certaines modifications.

Le développement de l'Europe est à l'image de son développement historique et culturel. Politiquement, certains pays souhaitent aller plus loin alors que d'autres restent très attachés à l'idée de souveraineté nationale. Par contre, en ce qui concerne les réseaux de communication ou de transport ainsi que les relations commerciales, culturelles et sportives, les progrès sont rapides. Deux événements importants concernant les relations entre la France et le Royaume-Uni reflètent ce rapprochement. D'abord, le tunnel sous la Manche devient réalité grâce à la mise en place d'une liaison ferroviaire (*connection by rail*) en 1994. Sur le plan sportif, le Tour de France, la fameuse course cycliste dont le circuit comprenait déjà plusieurs pays européens, passera désormais (*from now on*) aussi par l'Angleterre.

APPENDIX A
The French Sound System and the International Phonetic Alphabet

Vowels

[a] m**a**dame	[i] qu**i**	[œ] s**œu**r
[e] th**é**	[o] **eau**	[u] v**ou**s
[**ɛ**] **ê**tre	[ɔ] p**o**rte	[y] s**u**r
[ə] qu**e**	[ø] p**eu**	

Semivowels

[j] b**i**en	[ɥ] p**u**is	[w] **ou**i

Nasal Vowels

[ɑ̃] qu**an**d	[ɛ̃] v**in**	[ɔ̃] n**on**

Consonants

[b] **b**leu	[l] **l**ire	[s] **s**ur
[d] **d**ormir	[m] **m**arron	[ʃ] **ch**at
[f] **f**aire	[n] **n**ouveau	[t] **t**riste
[g] **g**ris	[**ɲ**] ensei**gn**er	[v] **v**ers
[**ʒ**] **j**aune	[p] **p**arler	[z] ro**s**e
[k] **qu**and	[R] **r**ester	

Here are sample answers to the self-check questions found throughout the book.

Chapitre préliminaire

p. 3

1. Bonjour, monsieur (**madame, mademoiselle**). / **Bonsoir, monsieur** (**madame, mademoiselle**). **2. mademoiselle** / **madame** / **monsieur** **3. Comment vous appelez-vous?** / **Je m'appelle...** / **Comment allez-vous?** **4.** when a woman is speaking / no

p. 7

1. Salut! / **Comment t'appelles-tu?** / (**Comment**) **Ça va?** **2. Et toi?** **3. Au revoir.** / **À tout à l'heure.**

p. 19

1. je and **j'** **2. ne** (**n'**)**... pas** **3.** Those describing females usually have an additional **-e** at the end (**américain**/**américain*e***).

p. 21

1. with **et quart, et demie**, and **moins le quart** **2.** by using either **du matin** *(in the morning)* or **du soir** *(in the evening)* / by using either **du matin** or **de l'après-midi** *(in the afternoon)*

Chapitre 1

pp. 38–39

1. le, la, l', and **les** / **les** before all plural nouns, **l'** before all singular nouns beginning with a vowel sound (including silent **h**), **le** before masculine singular nouns beginning with a consonant sound, and **la** before feminine singular nouns beginning with a consonant **2.** to say what you like, dislike, or prefer **3.** only in **liaison**

pp. 40–41

1. ils sont and **elles sont** / Use **ils sont** to talk about a group of all males or a mixed group of males and females, and to talk about a group of masculine objects or a mixed group of masculine and feminine objects. Use **elles sont** to talk about a group of all females or a group of all feminine objects. / **ils sont** **2.** Put **ne** (**n'**)**... pas** around the conjugated verb. / before a vowel sound **3.** the masculine singular form / **-s** (unless it ends in **s** or **x**) / **-e** (unless it ends in **-e**) / **-es** / **4. beau** and **vieux** / **beau, belle, beaux, belles** and **vieux, vieille, vieux, vieilles** **5.** In the masculine form, the final consonant is silent, but with the final **-e** of the feminine form, the consonant is no longer final and is pronounced.

p. 46

1. tu / **vous** / **vous** **2.** adjectives ending in **-ien, -if, -eux,** or **-el**/**-ien** → **-ienne** (**canadien** → **canadienne**), **-if** → **-ive** (**sportif** → **sportive**), **-eux** → **-euse** (**paresseux** → **paresseuse**), **-el** → **-elle** (**intellectuel** → **intellectuelle**)

p. 49

1. Put **est-ce que (qu')** at the beginning of a statement, use vocal inflection (raise the pitch of your voice at the end), or put **n'est-ce pas** at the end of a statement. / In all three cases, the pitch of your voice rises at the end. **2. Ne** rhymes with **le** and **n'est** and **n'es** rhyme with **les.**

p. 52

to specify something by saying *the*, to express likes, dislikes, and preferences, to talk about courses, to talk about a general category or an abstract noun

p. 54

plus... que (qu') and **moins... que (qu')**

Chapitre 2

p. 71

un and **une** / Use **un** with masculine nouns and **une** with feminine nouns. / **des**

p. 73

before **un** or **une** / no

p. 78

1. the infinitive (*to* . . .) **2. -er, -ir,** and **-re** **3.** the second

p. 81

1. remove the **-er** / **je** → **-e, tu** → **-es, il/elle** → **-e, nous** → **-ons, vous** → **-ez, ils/elles** → **-ent** **2.** before a vowel sound **3.** all of them except the endings of the **nous** and **vous** forms **4.** after the verb

p. 87

1. Form a question with **est-ce que (qu')** and place the appropriate question word before **est-ce que (qu').** / when **qui** is the subject of the verb or when **où** is followed by **être** **2.** after a **g** / before the **-ons** ending of the **nous** form

Chapitre 3

p. 107

1. *to have* / The forms **tu es / tu as** and **ils ont / ils sont** may seem similar. **2.** no / because it cannot be omitted as it sometimes is in English **3. un hôpital** → **des hôpitaux, une eau minérale** → **des eaux minérales** **4. de (d')**

p. 109

ne (n')... pas / beaucoup

p. 112

1. *there is* or *there are* **2. il n'y a pas de (d')...**

p. 114

1. **la maison de Jean** and **le chien de Marie** 2. **de + le → du, de + les → des** 3. **sa maison** and **sa maison** / **son chien** and **son chien** / no

p. 117

1. A different form is used, depending on whether the noun possessed is plural, masculine singular, feminine singular starting with a consonant, or feminine singular starting with a vowel sound. 2. **notre**, **votre**, and **leur**

p. 122

1. **être** 2. **cent** and **mille**

Chapitre 4

p. 139

1. **Qu'est-ce que c'est?** / **Qui est-ce?** 2. **Il est médecin.** and **C'est un médecin.** / You generally do not use **un/une/des** with occupations. You use them only if you say **C'est.../Ce sont....** 3. **-en → -enne (moyen → moyenne), -if → -ive (sportif → sportive), -eux → -euse (paresseux → paresseuse), -el → -elle (intellectuel → intellectuelle), -er → -ère (cher → chère), -eur → -euse (danseur → danseuse)**

p. 143

1. **Quel âge avez-vous (as-tu)?** / **J'ai __ ans.** 2. **Tu as l'air malade.**

p. 146

1. **nouveau (nouvelle, nouveaux, nouvelles)** 2. **bon (bonne)** and **gros (grosse)** / those ending in **-en (moyen → moyenne)** and those ending in **-el (intellectuel → intellectuelle)** 3. **long (longue)** and **blanc (blanche)** 4. **beaux, nouveaux, vieux,** and **roux**

p. 148

1. **De quelle couleur est/sont...?** / after the noun 2. **grand, beau, bon,** and **mauvais** 3. before a masculine singular noun starting with a vowel sound 4. No, it is followed by the appropriate form of the definite article (**le, la, l', les**).

p. 154

1. when you are referring to people in general / the same form you use for **il/elle** 2. **je vais, tu vas, il/elle/on va, nous allons, vous allez, ils/elles vont** 3. **à + le → au** and **à + les → aux** / **à la** and **à l'**

p. 157

1. Use **aller** followed by an infinitive. / Place **ne (n')... pas** around the conjugated form of **aller.** 2. to say *each, every*

p. 159

before masculine singular nouns starting with a vowel sound

Chapitre 5

p. 177

1. Use the **nous** form of the verb, without the subject pronoun **nous**, or ask a question, using **on**. **2.** It does not end in **-ez** (**faites**). **3.** Place **ne** (**n'**)... **rien** around the conjugated verb.

p. 181

no

p. 184

1. Use the **passé composé.** / two **2.** For **-er** verbs, replace the **-er** ending of the infinitive with **-é** (**parler → parlé**). For **-ir** verbs, replace the **-ir ending** of the infinitive with **-i** (**dormir → dormi**). / **avoir → eu, boire → bu, lire → lu, pleuvoir → plu, voir → vu, être → été, faire → fait, prendre → pris** **3.** Place **ne** (**n'**)... **pas** around the auxiliary.

p. 189

1. Most of them are verbs of motion. **2.** Make it agree with the subject in gender and number.

p. 192

1. It often means *there.* **2.** directly before the verb / directly before the auxiliary / directly before the infinitive

Chapitre 6

p. 211

1. *must, to have to,* and *to owe* / *can* or *to be able* / *to want* **2.** **devoir** = **oi**, **pouvoir** = **eu**, **vouloir** = **eu** **3.** The final consonant of the singular form is silent. The final consonant of the root of the verb in the plural is pronounced.

p. 217

1. **le premier** / Use the regular cardinal numbers (**deux, trois, etc.**). **2.** Use the past participle of **naître** (**né[e][s]**) or **mourir** (**mort[e][s]**) in the **passé composé**, with **être** as the auxiliary. (For example, **il est né..., elles sont mortes...**)

p. 219

1. The final consonant of the singular form is silent. The final consonant of the root of the verb in the plural is pronounced. **2.** *him/it* (masculine) = **le** (**l'**), *her/it* (feminine) = **la** (**l'**), *them* = **les** / directly before the verb / **Ne** precedes the object pronoun and **pas** follows the verb. **3.** before the infinitive / before the auxiliary

p. 222

1. **connaître** / **savoir** **2.** Use **savoir** followed by an infinitive.

p. 226

1. with **des** and the partitive forms (**du, de la, de l'**) 2. Use **des** before all plural nouns, **de l'** before all singular nouns starting with a vowel sound, **du** before masculine singular nouns beginning with a consonant sound, and **de la** before feminine singular nouns beginning with a consonant sound. / when the verb is negated and after expressions of quantity like **beaucoup** 3. the definite article (**le, la, l', les**)

Chapitre 7

p. 246

1. when it is the subject or object of the verb 2. **à** (**Paris**) / **en** (**France**) / **au** (**Canada**) / **en** (**Iraq**) 3. **de** (**d'**) (**Paris**) / **de** (**d'**) (**Autriche**) / **du** (**Mexique**) / **de** (**d'**) (**Iraq**)

p. 250

1. **venir** / **devenir** 2. The final consonant of the singular form is silent. The final consonant of the root of the verb in the plural is pronounced. 3. **être** / **venu(e)(s)**, **revenu(e)(s)**, and **devenu(e)(s)**

p. 253

1. It does not end in -ez (**dites**). 2. **dire** (**dit**) and **écrire** (**écrit**) / **lu**

p. 255

1. verbs of giving and receiving and of communication 2. **à** or **pour** 3. **lui** and **leur**

p. 260

1. **descendre** (**descendu[e][s]**) 2. **me** (**m'**), **te** (**t'**), **nous,** and **vous** / directly before the infinitive / directly before the conjugated verb 3. An unaccented -**e**- is usually dropped, when not pronouncing it would not bring three consonant sounds together. / It is pronounced when dropping it would bring three consonant sounds together.

p. 263

1. **aller, arriver, entrer, monter, partir, rentrer, rester, retourner, sortir, naître, mourir** 2. directly before the auxiliary verb / direct 3. usually **à** or **pour**

Chapitre 8

p. 281

1. yes 2. **être** / **avoir** 3. **partir de** (**d'**)**...**, **pour...**, and **sortir de** (**d'**)**...**, **à...** 4. The final consonant of the singular form is silent. The final consonant of the root of the verb in the plural is pronounced.

p. 285

1. one / two / In **nous prenons** and **vous prenez**, the **e** is pronounced like the **e** in **le**. In **je prends, tu prends,** and **il/elle/on prend,** the e is nasal. In **ils/elles prennent**, it sounds like the **è** in **mère.** 2. **j'ai compris** and **j'ai appris**

p. 291

1. before **il, elle**, or **on,** only when the verb ends in a vowel **2.** after question words when the verb is **être**

p. 294

1. de + le → du, de + les → des 2. dans une rue

p. 296

1. the imperative of the **tu** form of **aller** and **-er** verbs only **2.** directly after the verb, attached to it by a hyphen / It changes to **moi. 3.** directly before the verb **4. être** and **avoir**

p. 302

mettre → mis, permettre → permis, promettre → promis

p. 303

1. after prepositions, when there is no verb, in compound subjects, for emphasis, after **c'est**, after **être à**, with **même(s) 2. lui** and **eux**

Chapitre 9

p. 323

1. Use reflexive verbs when the subject of the verb performs the action for, on, or to himself, herself, or themselves. Use non-reflexives when the action of the verb is performed for, on, or to someone or something else. **2.** Place **ne** before the reflexive pronoun and **pas** after the verb. **3.** in the **je, tu, il/elle/on,** and **ils/elles** forms / the **nous** and **vous** forms

p. 328

1. yes **2.** to the end of the verb / It changes to **toi. 3.** directly before the verb

p. 334

1. when people are doing something to or for each other **2.** no **3.** most verbs indicating actions done to other people / **se regarder, s'écouter,** and **se connaître**

p. 336

1. être 2. directly before the auxiliary verb / Place **ne** before the reflexive pronoun and **pas** after the auxiliary verb. **3.** when the reflexive pronoun is the direct object of the verb

p. 340

1. the **nous** form without the **-ons** ending **2.** to tell what things used to be like (how things used to be, what someone used to do, or what happened over and over in the past) **3.** all of them except those for **nous** and **vous 4.** the letter **-i-**

Chapitre 10

p. 364

1. **de (d')** 2. **en**

p. 370

1. **nous** (**choisissons**), **vous** (**choisissez**), **ils/elles** (**choisissent**) 2. **choisiss- + ais, ais, ait, ions, iez, aient** 3. like a z / like an s

p. 373

1. **nous buvons** and **vous buvez** 2. **plus de fruits que de viande, autant de fruits que de légumes,** and **moins de café que d'eau**

p. 378

1. the **passé composé** / the **imparfait** 2. **passé composé:** to say what happened (a completed event with a beginning and end), to say what changed (a change in condition or state at a precise moment), and to say what happened next (the sequence of events in a narration) / **imparfait:** to say how things used to be (repeated or habitual actions), to describe what someone or something was like (physical or mental states), and to say what was going on (description or setting)

p. 383

1. Add **-ment** to the masculine form if it ends in a vowel; otherwise, add it to the feminine form. 2. at the beginning or end of the sentence or clause / after the verb they modify and after the auxiliary in the **passé composé**

Chapitre 11

p. 401

1. the infinitive / the final **-e** is dropped before adding the endings 2. **nous** (**-ons**) and **vous** (**-ez**)

p. 406

1. **nous** (**voyons, croyons**) and **vous** (**voyez, croyez**) 2. **avoir** 3. **voir** (**verr-**) 4. Use **y** to replace a prepositional phrase indicating a place or to replace a prepositional phrase with **à** followed by a thing. Use **en** to replace a prepositional phrase with **de** followed by a thing or to replace a noun preceded by the partitive, indefinite article, a number, or an expression of quantity.

p. 413

1. **qui / que (qu') / dont** 2. whose, of whom, which, of which, about which

p. 417

1. **moi, toi, lui, elle, nous, vous, eux, elles** 2. **C'est une meilleure avocate. Elle danse mieux.**

p. 421

1. the future / the **imparfait** **2.** to say what would happen under certain circumstances and to make polite requests

Chapitre 12

p. 440

1. ne (n')... personne, ne (n')... rien, ne (n')... nulle part, ne (n')... pas encore **2.** all of them except **personne, nulle part, ni... ni..., aucun(e),** and the **que** of **ne (n')... que** / **personne, nulle part, aucun(e), ni... ni...,** and the **que** of **ne (n')... que** **3. quelqu'un de spécial, quelque chose d'important, rien de nouveau** **4.** They change to **de (d')**. / They are dropped.

p. 445

1. avoir faim, avoir chaud, avoir sommeil **2.** the infinitive

p. 449

1. the present tense form for **ils/elles** without the **-ent** ending / **je** → -e, **tu** → -es, **il/elle/on** → =e, **ils/elles** → =ent **2.** the **imparfait** **3. être, avoir, aller, vouloir, faire, savoir, pouvoir** **4.** generally in a second clause where the first clause expresses an attitude or opinion

p. 455

1. when the subject is talking about his/her own actions / **être content(e), être heureux (heureuse), être triste, être désolé(e), être furieux (furieuse), être surpris(e), être étonné(e), regretter, avoir peur, c'est dommage** **2.** both parts go before the infinitive / **Je préfère ne pas y aller.**

Here are sample answers to the exercises in the **Pour vérifier** section of each chapter of the book. Please note that your answers may vary slightly from those given here and still be correct. In the case of open-ended items, marked *, a sample answer is provided.

Chapitre préliminaire

Pour vérifier PAGE 26

A. Bonjour!

1. Je m'appelle (*your name*).
2. Ça va bien.
3. À demain.
4. À tout à l'heure.

***B. Autoportraits.**

1. Je m'appelle Mme Smith. Je suis de Richmond. J'habite avec ma famille. Je travaille pour l'université.
2. Je m'appelle Sara. Je suis d'Austin. J'habite avec une amie. Je ne travaille pas, j'étudie.
3. Je m'appelle Bill. Je suis de Hope, Arkansas. J'habite à Washington avec ma famille. Je travaille beaucoup.
4. Je m'appelle Elizabeth. Je suis de Londres. J'habite avec ma famille. Je travaille pour le gouvernement.

C. Réponses.

1. Oui, je comprends. / Non, je ne comprends pas.
2. C'est (*day of the week*).
3. Il est (*time of day*).
4. Ça veut dire *close*.
5. Ça veut dire *month*.

*6. Je suis en classe de huit heures à midi.

D. Chiffres.

1. vingt-sept
2. douze

*3. vingt-cinq

4. un
5. cinq

E. En classe.

1. Asseyez-vous!
2. Donnez-moi votre feuille de papier!
3. Ouvrez votre livre! / Lisez!

Chapitre 1

Pour vérifier PAGE 60

A. Qui est-ce?

1. C'est un garçon.
2. C'est une fille.
3. Ce sont des jeunes.

***B. Descriptions.**

1. Il est actif.
2. Elle est paresseuse.
3. Ils sont sympathiques.

***C. Comparaisons.**

1. Il est plus sportif.
2. Elle est plus paresseuse.

***D. Questions.**

1. — Est-ce que tu es marié(e)?
   — Oui, je suis marié(e). / Non je ne suis pas marié(e).
   — Tu es d'ici, n'est-ce pas?
   — Oui, je suis d'ici. / Non je suis de Dallas.
   — Est-ce que tu es sportif (sportive)?
   — Oui, je suis sportif (sportive). / Non, je ne suis pas sportif (sportive).
2. — Est-ce que le professeur est difficile?
   — Oui, il/elle est difficile. / Non, il/elle n'est pas difficile.
   — Est-ce que le professeur est français?
   — Oui, il/elle est français(e).
3. — Est-ce que les étudiants sont intelligents/sympathiques/agréables?
   — Oui, ils sont / Non, ils ne sont pas intelligents/sympathiques/agréables.

***E. J'étudie...**

J'étudie à l'Université du Texas à Austin. J'étudie les sciences. J'aime beaucoup la biologie mais je n'aime pas la physique. Je ne comprends pas la chimie mais je comprends le français. La chimie est plus difficile que la biologie.

***F. L'Université de Nice.**

L'Université de Nice est plus/moins moderne que l'Université X (*the name of your university*). L'Université X est plus vieille mais plus grande et plus belle que l'Université de Nice.

***G. L'université.**

1. J'aime beaucoup la bibliothèque. Elle est grande et jolie. **2.** Je n'aime pas les salles de classe. Elles sont petites et laides. **3.** J'aime le campus. Il est agréable et joli. **4.** J'aime les cours. Ils sont intéressants. Ils ne sont pas très difficiles.

Chapitre 2

Pour vérifier PAGE 94

***A. Au café.**

— Monsieur, s'il vous plaît.
— Bonjour, monsieur/mademoiselle. Vous désirez?
— Pour moi, un thé au citron.
— Très bien, monsieur/mademoiselle.

***B. L'addition, s'il vous plaît.**

— S'il vous plaît, monsieur. C'est combien?
— Ça fait 16 francs.
— Voilà 20 francs.
— Et voici votre monnaie.

***C. J'aime...**

1. À la maison, j'aime bricoler.
   j'aime lire.
   j'aime écouter la radio.
2. J'aime aller danser avec des amis.
   J'aime prendre un verre au café.
   J'aime aller voir un film au cinéma.
3. Je n'aime pas dormir tard.
   Je n'aime pas manger dans un fast-food.
   Je n'aime pas regarder la télévision.

***D. Invitations.**

1. — Est-ce que tu voudrais jouer au basket-ball demain après-midi?
   — D'accord! À quelle heure?
   — Vers deux heures?
2. — Est-ce que tu voudrais prendre un verre ce soir?
   — D'accord! À quelle heure?
   — Vers sept heures?
3. — Est-ce que tu voudrais faire du jogging demain matin?
   — D'accord! À quelle heure?
   — Vers six heures?
4. — Est-ce que tu voudrais voir un film au cinéma samedi soir?
   — D'accord! À quelle heure?
   — Vers huit heures?

***E. Questions.**

1. — Qu'est-ce que tu étudies beaucoup?
   — Le français.
2. — Comment est-ce que tu joues au tennis?
   — Assez bien.
3. — Avec qui est-ce que tu aimes sortir le week-end?
   — Avec des amis.
4. — Où est-ce que tu dînes souvent?
   — Au restaurant Green Pastures.

*F. On...

1. Il / Elle aime sortir le samedi soir.
2. J'invite rarement des amis à la maison.
3. Ils / elles aiment danser le week-end.
4. Nous jouons quelquefois à des jeux vidéo.

Chapitre 3

Pour vérifier PAGE 128

A. Mon appartement.

ligne

1 J'habite / Je partage
2 loyer
3 embêtant; fume
4 salon
5 loyer

***B. Quel...?**

1. Quelle est l'adresse?
2. Quel est le numéro de téléphone?
3. Quel est le code postal?

C. Le loyer.

1. trois cent cinq dollars.
2. six cent quarante dollars.
3. deux cent cinquante dollars.

D. Une chambre d'hôtel.

ligne

1 avons; des; avons; de; a
2 de; de; as
3 avons; une; un
4 ont; des; n'ai; de
5 avez; des

E. La Maison Blanche.

1. Il y a / Nous avons beaucoup de chambres.
2. Oui, elles sont grandes.
3. Oui, il est joli et vieux.

***F. Chez Claude et Thomas.**

1. Leur appartement est au deuxième étage.
2. Il y a un ascenseur et un escalier.
3. Ils ont un téléviseur.
4. Il y a une table et un fauteuil.
5. L'appartement est agréable.

Chapitre 4

Pour vérifier PAGE 164

A. Conversations.

— êtes
— sommes; fils; fille
— s'appellent
— s'appellent

B. Professions.

1. médecin ou infirmière
2. acteurs
3. serveuse
4. musiciens

C. Quel adjectif?

1. fatigué(e)
2. vieille; gris
3. de taille moyenne

***D. Personnages.**

1. Il est gros. Il a les cheveux gris et une barbe grise.
2. Elle est belle. Il est grand et laid.
3. Il est petit (court, gros, bleu).

E. Jamais content.

1. Ce; mauvais
2. Cette; ennuyeuse
3. Cet; bête
4. Ces; mauvais

F. Devinette.

1. plus tard
2. demain après-midi
3. mercredi
4. le mois prochain
5. ce week-end

***G. Projets.**

1. Plus tard, je vais faire du shopping.
2. Demain après-midi, je vais écouter des disques.
3. Mercredi, je vais retrouver des amis.
4. Le mois prochain, je vais aller à la plage.
5. Ce week-end, je vais acheter des livres.

Chapitre 5

Pour vérifier PAGE 198

*A. **Quel temps fait-il?**

1. Il fait très froid et il neige.
2. Il fait très chaud et il fait du soleil.
3. Il fait frais et il pleut.
4. Il fait souvent beau et il fait du vent.

*B. **Et cette semaine?**

1. Demain en Alaska, il va faire froid et il va neiger.
2. Demain en Arizona, il va faire chaud.
3. Demain à Londres, il va faire frais et il va pleuvoir.
4. Demain en Californie, il va pleuvoir.

1. Hier en Alaska, il a fait froid et il a neigé.
2. Hier en Arizona, il a plu.
3. Hier à Londres, il a fait frais.
4. Hier en Californie, il a fait du vent.

C. **Moi, j'ai...**

1. Éric a sommeil.
2. Nous avons faim.
3. J'ai l'intention de voyager. / J'ai envie de voyager.

D. **Suggestions.**

1. On fait du ski? / Faisons du ski.
2. On fait du shopping? / Faisons du shopping.
3. On va au restaurant? / Allons au restaurant.
4. On fait une promenade? / Faisons une promenade.

*E. **Activités**

1. Moi, je fais souvent la cuisine.
2. Mes amis et moi, nous faisons souvent du bateau.
3. Mon ami Bill fait souvent du camping.
4. Mon amie Leili fait souvent de l'exercice.
5. Les jeunes Américains font souvent du sport.

*F. **La dernière fois.**

1. Je suis rentré(e) après minuit vendredi dernier.
2. Je suis parti(e) en week-end en été.
3. J'ai passé toute la journée à la maison hier.
4. Je suis allé(e) à la plage il y a six mois.
5. J'ai été malade le mois dernier.
6. J'ai eu un examen la semaine dernière.

Chapitre 6

Pour vérifier PAGE 232

A. Invitations.

1. — veux
   — peux; dois
2. — connaissez
   — avons fait
   — avez envie
   — veut

B. Casse-tête.

1. le 1er juillet
2. le 1er juin
3. le 1er août
4. le 1er janvier
5. le 21 juillet

***C. À la boum.**

— J'aime les fruits, les canapés et le vin. Tu veux des fruits? des canapés? du vin?

***D. Ça te dit?**

— Allô? Qui est à l'appareil?
— C'est Jeanne.
— Bonjour, Jeanne. Comment ça va?
— Ça va. Écoute, tu es libre ce soir?
— Oui. Qu'est-ce que tu as envie de faire?
— J'ai envie de louer une cassette vidéo. Je vais louer *Astérix le Gaulois.*
— Qu'est-ce que c'est?
— C'est un dessin animé. C'est très amusant.
— Je veux bien. À ce soir!

Chapitre 7

Pour vérifier PAGE 268

***A. Associations.**

un aéroport
des bagages
un billet
un départ
un passeport
un vol

une île tropicale
aller à la plage
faire de la planche à voile
faire de la plongée sous-marine
faire du ski nautique
goûter la cuisine locale

B. **Une famille internationale.**

1. viens — Je viens de Bruxelles, en Belgique.
2. vient — Il vient d' Honolulu, Hawaï / d'Oklahoma City, Oklahoma.
3. viennent — Ils viennent de Mexico, au Mexique.

*C. **Les dernières vacances.**

1. Je n'ai pas nagé. J'ai fait du ski.
2. Je n'ai pas visité une île tropicale mais j'ai visité Paris.
3. J'ai fait du shopping et j'ai fait de la planche à voile.
4. J'ai visité des musées et je suis allé(e) au théâtre.
5. J'ai fait de l'exercice et j'ai goûté la cuisine locale.
6. Je n'ai pas couru le long des plages mais j'ai passé l'après-midi assis(e) sur la plage.
7. J'ai fait un pique-nique à la campagne et à la plage.
8. Je suis allé(e) voir des amis. Je ne suis pas resté(e) à la maison.

D. **Qui?**

1. écrivent; lit; rend
2. lisons; écrit; dit
3. lisez; disent; écrit

E. **Conversations.**

1. — nous
   — vous
2. — m'
   — t'
3. — lui
   — m' lui

Chapitre 8

Pour vérifier PAGE 310

A. **À la réception.**

1. avec un grand lit; salle de bains
2. seule
3. compris; supplément; servi
4. clé; étage
5. régler; départ; chèques de voyage; cartes de crédit; espèces
6. séjour

— Bonjour, monsieur.
— Bonjour, madame / mademoiselle / monsieur.
— Vous avez une chambre pour deux personnes?
— Est-ce que vous préférez une chambre à deux lits ou avec un grand lit? Et avec ou sans salle de bains?
— Nous préférons une chambre avec salle de bains et avec un grand lit.
— C'est pour une seule nuit?
— Non, c'est pour deux nuits.
— Très bien. Nous avons une chambre avec salle de bains à 400 francs.

— Est-ce que le petit déjeuner est compris?
— Non, madame. Il y a un supplément de 35 francs par personne. Le petit déjeuner est servi entre sept heures et dix heures dans la salle à manger.
— Eh bien, on prend la chambre à 400 francs.
— Vous avez la chambre **48.** Voici votre clé. Votre chambre est au quatrième étage.
— Vous préférez que je vous paie maintenant?
— Non, vous pouvez régler la note à votre départ. Vous pouvez payer par chèques de voyage, par carte de crédit ou en espèces. Bon séjour!

B. Une journée comme les autres.

1. Moi, je sors quelquefois le vendredi soir mais je prends rarement un taxi. Vendredi dernier, je ne suis pas sorti(e) et je n'ai pas pris de taxi.
2. Mes amis sortent souvent le dimanche soir et ils dorment souvent en classe le lendemain. Ils sont sortis dimanche dernier mais ils n'ont pas dormi en classe le lendemain.
3. Mon meilleur ami part souvent en week-end et il va toujours à la plage. Samedi dernier il est parti en week-end et il est allé à la plage.
4. Chez moi, nous ne servons jamais le dîner après huit heures. Nous sortons quelquefois au restaurant. Samedi dernier, nous n'avons pas servi le dîner après huit heures parce que nous sommes sortis au restaurant.

***C. Directions.**

Sortez de la sous-préfecture et tournez à droite dans la rue Duplessis/ Allez tout droit jusqu' à la rue de Nozière et tournez à droite. Continuez jusqu' à la rue Lamartine. La gendarmerie est au coin de la rue.

***D. Que portent-ils?**

1. Alain porte une chemise, une cravate, un pantalon et un blouson.
2. Catherine porte une robe et un chapeau.
3. L'hôtelier porte une chemise et une cravate.
4. La dame porte un short et un T-shirt. L'homme porte un maillot de bain.

E. Un vol.

1. Une hôtesse met une jupe et un chemisier.
2. Un homme d'affaires met un costume, une chemise et une cravate.
3. Moi, je mets un costume/un tailleur.
4. Les étudiants mettent un jean, un T-shirt et un anorak.

Chapitre 9

Pour vérifier PAGE 390

***A. Les enfants sages.**

1. Les enfants sages se brossent les dents tous les jours.
2. Ils ne se couchent pas tard.
3. Ils se lèvent tôt.
4. Ils ne s'ennuient pas en classe.
5. Ils s'intéressent à tout.

B. Un examen important.

1. Couche-toi tôt.
2. Calme-toi!
3. Ne t'endors pas pendant l'examen.
4. Ne te dépêche pas pendant l'examen.

***C. Demain.**

1. Je vais me lever tard.
2. Je vais me laver les cheveux.
3. Je vais me promener avec mes amis.
4. Je vais me rendre chez ma grand-mère.
5. Je vais me souvenir de faire le ménage.
6. Je vais me reposer un peu.

D. Hier. (N'oubliez pas que c'est Rose qui parle.)

1. André s'est levé vers quatre heures et il s'est reposé pendant l'après-midi.
2. André et Mamie se sont retrouvés en ville et ils se sont embrassés.
3. Moi, je me suis couchée et je me suis endormie tout de suite.

E. Un bon rapport.

1. Nous nous embrassons souvent.
2. Nous ne nous disputons pas.
3. Nous nous téléphonons.

F. En classe.

1. Nous ne nous sommes pas disputé(e)s.
2. Nous ne nous sommes pas embrassé(e)s.
3. Nous nous sommes amusé(e)s.
4. Nous nous sommes parlé (en français, naturellement).
5. Nous nous sommes vu(e)s.
6. Nous ne nous sommes pas ennuyé(e)s.

***G. À cette époque-là.**

1. un chien; il n'y avait pas de chien.
2. la musique classique; je préférais les Beatles.
3. danser; je ne savais pas.
4. à Denver; elle habitait à Chicago.
5. aller au cinéma; nous aimions regarder la télé.
6. au tennis; je jouais du piano.

Chapitre 10

Pour vérifier PAGE 388

***A. Questions?**

1. En France, on mange des tartines, des croissants, du beurre et de la confiture. Aux États-Unis et au Canada, on mange des œufs au bacon ou des céréales et du pain grillé.

2. Dans une pâtisserie, on vend des pâtisseries (des tartes, des gâteaux). Dans une charcuterie, on vend du jambon, des saucisses et des plats préparés. Dans une épicerie, on vend des fruits, des légumes et du fromage.
3. On peut y commander des hamburgers, des frites et de la salade.

B. **Ingrédients.**

1. Elle a besoin de 250 grammes d'oignons, de 60 grammes de beurre et d'un litre de bouillon pour faire de la soupe à l'oignon.
2. Elle a besoin de 700 grammes de bœuf, d'une bouteille de vin rouge, de 50 grammes de beurre, et de 100 grammes d'oignons pour faire du bœuf bourguignon.

*C. **À la boucherie.**

— Bonjour, madame.
— Bonjour, madame / monsieur / mademoiselle, vous désirez?
— Je voudrais du bifteck, s'il vous plaît.
— Combien, madame / monsieur / mademoiselle?
— 500 grammes, s'il vous plaît.
— Et avec ça?
— C'est tout, merci. C'est combien?
— 50 francs.
— Voici, madame. Au revoir.

À la boulangerie.
— Bonjour, monsieur.
— Bonjour, madame / monsieur / mademoiselle, vous désirez?
— Je voudrais un pain complet et une baguette, s'il vous plaît.
— Et avec ça?
— C'est tout, merci. C'est combien?
— Dix francs pour le pain complet et 7 francs pour la baguette. Ça fait 17 francs.
— Voici 20 francs.
— Et voici votre monnaie. Merci, madame / monsieur / mademoiselle.
— Merci. Au revoir, monsieur.

D. **C'est-à-dire...**

1. grossit
2. as maigri
3. vieillissons
4. réfléchis
5. grandissent
6. rougissez

E. **La jeunesse.** (N'oubliez pas que c'est André qui parle.)
étais; habitaient; nous voyions; la trouvais; étais; je n'étais; je n'avais pas; j'ai décidé; l'aimais; Je suis allé; je suis arrivé; je l'ai vue; s'embrassaient; je savais (j'ai su); ce n'était pas; aimait

Chapitre 11

Pour vérifier PAGE 428

A. Terminaisons.

-ty=-té (féminin)
criminalité
égalité
inégalité
instabilité
pauvreté
possibilité
prospérité
sécurité
société
validité

-y=-ie (féminin)
colonie
démocratie
économie

-ment=-ment (masculin)
environnement
gouvernement
mouvement

B. Définitions.

1. qui; les sans domicile fixe
2. qui; un crime
3. qui; l'avenir
4. qui; une exception

***C. Gros titres.**

1. Je ne serais pas content(e) si 80% de la population était au chômage.
2. Je serais très heureux (heureuse) s'il y avait la paix en Afrique.
3. Je serais surpris(e) si l'espagnol devenait une langue officielle aux États-Unis.
4. Je serais content(e) si l'économie s'améliorait.
5. Je serais triste s'il y avait la guerre en Europe.

***D. Espérance.**

1. J'espère que 80% de la population ne sera pas au chômage.
2. J'espère qu'il y aura la paix en Afrique.
3. J'espère que l'espagnol deviendra une langue officielle aux États-Unis.
4. J'espère que l'économie s'améliorera.
5. J'espère qu'il n'y aura pas la guerre en Europe.

E. Intérêts.

1. J'y participe toujours / je n'y participe pas toujours.
2. Nous en parlons souvent / nous n'en parlons pas souvent.
3. Je m'y intéresse / je ne m'y intéresse pas.

***F. La musique.**

1. que; la musique classique; le rock; qui
2. dont; Sting.
3. que; Paul McCartney; que; Johnny Hallyday
4. *Fool on the Hill*; dont
5. *Ne me quitte pas*; qui

Chapitre 12

Pour vérifier PAGE 462

*A. **Bon ou mauvais?**

1. C'est mauvais pour les poumons de fumer. C'est bon pour les poumons de faire de l'exercice.
2. C'est mauvais pour l'estomac de manger trop de matières grasses. C'est bon pour l'estomac de manger des légumes.
3. C'est mauvais pour le cœur de manger trop de sucre. C'est bon pour le cœur de faire de l'exercice.
4. C'est mauvais pour la tension d'utiliser trop de sel. C'est bon pour la tension de manger des fruits.

*B. **Négation.**

1. Elles ne doivent jamais fumer.
2. Ils ne doivent pas utiliser beaucoup de sel.
3. On ne doit pas boire trop d'alcool.

C. **Blessures.**

1. Il coupait de la viande.
2. Il faisait du ski.
3. Elle mangeait de la soupe.

D. **Vacances en Afrique.**

1. Il faut que tu aies un passeport.
2. Il faut que tu fasses attention à ce que tu manges.
3. Il faut que tu ailles chez le médecin pour des piqûres.
4. Il faut que tu prennes l'avion.
5. Il ne faut pas que tu sois timide.
6. Il faut que tu connaisses l'histoire de la région.

*E. **Médecine préventive.**

1. Pour éviter une indigestion, c'est important de manger peu de matières grasses et beaucoup de fruits et de légumes.
2. Pour éviter les maladies de foie, c'est important de boire peu d'alcool.
3. Pour éviter un rhume, c'est important de manger des oranges. C'est mauvais d'avoir froid.

*F. **Un bon médecin.**

1. Il est essentiel que tu saches donner des piqûres.
2. Il est bon que tu études beaucoup.
3. Il ne faut pas que tu fumes et il faut que tu fasses de l'exercice.

Here are sample answers to the exercises found in the ***Chapitre de révision.*** Please note that your answers may vary slightly from those given here and still be correct. In the case of open-ended items, marked *, a sample answer is provided.

Chapitre de révision

Pour commencer

Savez-vous le faire? PAGES 467–468

***A. Descriptions.**

1. François Fédor	vieux, intelligent, sérieux, riche
2. Laurent Lavare	petit, malhonnête, laid, désagréable
3. Valérie Veutoux	riche, snob, petite, blonde
4. Bernard Boncorps	beau, grand, sportif, irresponsable
5. Nathalie Lanana	blonde, petite, frivole, paresseuse
6. Le/La domestique	suspect(e), intelligent(e), sérieux(-euse) intéressant(e)
7. Le détective	intelligent, sérieux, froid, âgé

***B. Explications.**

François Fédor va être la victime et Valérie Veutoux et Bernard Boncorps vont commettre le crime parce qu'ils veulent son argent.

C. Où habitent-ils?

1. François Fédor habite en Belgique.
2. Valérie Veutoux habite au Luxembourg.
3. Laurent Lavare habite en Suisse.
4. Bernard Boncorps et Nathalie Lanana habitent à Monaco.

Comment s'y prendre

Savez-vous le faire? PAGE 468

A. D'abord...

1. M. Lavare leur avait dit d'arriver vers midi.
2. M. Lavare avait quitté le château.
3. Tout le monde avait déjeuné.
4. Le/La domestique avait servi la soupe.
5. Il m'avait dit de venir chez lui.

B. Qu'est-ce qui s'est passé?

ligne(s)	
1	avait toujours fait
6	avait fait fortune
9–10	avait toujours négligé
10	n'avait jamais pris
11	avait negligé

6–17	n'avait jamais rencontré
18	n'avaient jamais essayé
21	avaient reçu
25	avait refusé
26	ils s'étaient laissés
27	étaient arrivés
28	s'étaient sentis
30	s'était transformé
39–40	avait duré
41–42	les avait enfin informés
45	étaient descendus

B. (*continued*)

45	leur avait indiqué
47	avait servi
48	n'avaient fait
50	n'avait pas été
52	s'était retiré
52	avait demandé
55–56	les avait raccompagnés
56	leur avait souhaité
60	s'étaient levés
60	avaient appris
61	avait téléphoné
61	avait été
62	avait commis
63	leur avait demandé
64	leur avait dit
65	s'était passé

Qu'est-ce qui se passe?

Avez-vous compris? PAGE 470

A. Détails.

1. Il habitait dans un château au fond de la forêt des Ardennes.
2. Personne ne savait d'où venait sa fortune mais on croyait qu'il avait fait fortune dans les mines du Zaïre.
3. Non, il n'en avait pas beaucoup.
4. Il la partageait avec son neveu, Bernard Boncorps et son ex-femme, Valérie Veutoux.
5. Laurent Lavare leur avait téléphoné.
6. Ils étaient surpris.
7. Ils ont dû attendre presque deux jours.
8. Ils avaient appris que François Fédor était mort.

*9. À mon avis, il leur avait dit qu'il n'allait plus leur donner d'argent.

*B. **Vous êtes le détective.**

Bernard Boncorps

1. Il est allé au village avec Nathalie et ils ont pris un verre. Ensuite ils sont rentrés et ils ont joué aux cartes.
2. Il s'est couché vers 2h.
3. Il n'a rien entendu.

Valérie Veutoux

1. Elle s'est couchée tout de suite après le dîner pour lire.
2. Voir #1.
3. Elle n'a rien entendu.

Laurent Lavare

1. Il a travaillé sur ordinateur pendant deux heures. Ensuite il a téléphoné chez lui et puis il a pris un bain.
2. Il s'est couché vers minuit et demi.
3. Il n'a rien entendu sauf deux chats qui se battaient.

Le/La domestique

1. Il/Elle a passé une heure dans la cuisine.
2. Il/Elle s'est couché(e) vers dix heures.
3. Il/Elle a cru entendre quelqu'un dans le couloir trois ou quatre fois pendant la nuit.

Savez-vous le faire? PAGE 472–484

*A. **Il a disparu.**

Le lendemain du crime...

1. Il y avait un pantalon et une cravate sur le lit.
2. Il y avait des chaussures près du lit.
3. La lampe était par terre.
4. Il y avait deux verres sur la petite table.
5. Il y avait une chaussure près de la porte.
6. Il y avait un ordinateur sur le bureau.
7. Le tableau de François Fédor avait disparu.

À qui est-ce?

1. — Est-ce que c'était son pantalon?
   — Oui, ce pantalon était à lui.
2. — Est-ce que c'était sa cravate?
   — Oui, cette cravate était à lui.
3. — Est-ce que c'étaient ses chaussures près du lit?
   — Oui, ces chaussures étaient à lui.
4. — Est-ce que la chaussure près de la porte était à lui?
   — Non, cette chaussure n'était pas à lui.
   — C'était peut-être la chaussure de Valérie Veutoux.

B. Absolument pas!

1. Non, je n'ai rien entendu de bizarre.
2. Non, je n'ai vu personne y entrer.
3. Non, je ne suis pas encore sorti(e) ce matin.
4. Non, je n'y suis entré(e) ni pendant la nuit ni ce matin.
5. Non, je ne me disputais jamais avec lui.
6. Non, je n'en ai vu nulle part.
7. Non, je n'avais aucune raison pour le commettre.
8. Non, je ne sais rien d'autre sur ce crime.

***C. Dans quelle chambre?**

1. Valérie Veutoux était au bout du couloir, en face de la salle de bains.
2. François Fédor était dans la plus grande chambre, à côté de la chambre de Valérie Veutoux.
3. Bernard Boncorps était dans la chambre entre la chambre de François Fédor et l'escalier.
4. Laurent Lavare était dans la chambre à côté de la salle de bains.
5. Le/La domestique était dans la chambre en face de la chambre de François Fédor.
6. Il n'y avait personne dans la chambre à droite de la chambre du/de la domestique.
7. Nathalie Lanana était dans la chambre en face de la chambre de Bernard Boncorps.

D. Relations.

1. Est-ce que vous l'aimiez bien?
2. Est-ce que vous lui parliez de sa famille?
3. Est-ce que vous lui empruntiez quelquefois de l'argent?
4. Est-ce que vous le réveilliez à la même heure tous les jours?
5. Est-ce que vous lui serviez toujours le petit déjeuner au lit?
6. Est-ce que vous lui prépariez toujours le dîner?
7. Est-ce que vous le trouviez sévère?
8. Est-ce que vous le voyiez tous les jours?

1. Est-ce que M. Fédor vous disait tout?
2. Est-ce qu'il vous payait bien?
3. Est-ce qu'il vous parlait de sa vie privée?
4. Est-ce qu'il vous permettait de faire ce que vous vouliez au château?

***E. Je ne veux pas que...**

1. Il faut que vous me disiez tout ce que vous savez.
2. Je veux que vous soyez calmes.
3. Il ne faut pas que vous ayez peur.
4. Il vaut mieux que vous ne touchiez pas aux affaires de M. Fédor.
5. Il faut que vous fassiez une déposition.
6. Je ne veux pas que vous parliez à la presse.
7. Il vaut mieux que vous m'obéissiez.
8. Il faut que vous soyez patients.

F. *Savoir* ou *connaître*?

1. Je ne sais pas la date du crime.
2. Je connais le/la domestique de François Fédor.
3. Je sais l'heure approximative du crime.
4. Je connais le château de François Fédor.
5. Je ne connais pas tous les amis de François Fédor.
6. Je ne sais (connais) pas tous les détails de la vie passée de François Fédor.
7. Je sais des mobiles possibles.
8. Je ne sais pas l'identité de l'assassin.

G. Il faut penser comme le/la criminel(le).

Si j'étais le/la criminel(le)...

1. je serais calme.
2. je ne parlerais pas beaucoup du crime.
3. je saurais tous les détails du crime.
4. j'obéirais à la police.
5. je m'intéresserais beaucoup à l'investigation.
6. je ne dirais pas la vérité.
7. j'aurais envie de partir.
8. je deviendrais de plus en plus nerveux/nerveuse.
9. j'accuserais quelqu'un d'autre.

H. Une matinée typique.

1. Il se réveillait à huit heures.
2. Il se levait à huit heures et quart.
3. Il prenait son café dans sa chambre à huit heures et demie.
4. Il se brossait les dents à neuf heures moins le quart.
5. Il s'habillait à neuf heures.
6. Il se promenait de dix heures et demie à onze heures et demie.

I. Accusations.

Bernard Boncorps

l'a tué; J'ai entendu dire; il avait; a emprunté (empruntait); m'a dit qu'il y avait; a appris; se passait; a dit; il allait

Valérie Veutoux

était; croyait; faisait; passait; a compris; s'est fâché; a dit; voulait; est morte; lui a promis; ne comprenait pas; s'intéressait; faisait; ne voulait pas (n'a pas voulu); avait (a eu); avait; ne pouvait pas; lui donnait; ne voulait pas

Laurent Lavare

a commis; a fait; est tombée; sont sortis; lui a demandé; ne voyait pas; voulait; ne savait pas; se remariait; a sans doute compris; était; s'est débarrassée

J. Eclaircissements.

Laurent Lavare

1. C'est Bernard Boncorps qui l'a accusé du crime.
2. Oui, il en avait.
3. Non, il ne lui disait pas qu'il en empruntait.

4. Il lui empruntait des millions de francs.
5. Il y en avait très peu.

Bernard Boncorps

1. Non, il ne lui rendait jamais visite.
2. Il ne l'avait jamais vu.
3. Il lui a dit qu'il se chargerait de l'éducation de son neveu.
4. Non, il ne voulait pas y venir.
5. Il y passait tout son temps.
6. Oui, il en avait.
7. Non, il n'en avait pas assez pour les payer.

Valérie Veutoux

1. C'est Laurent Lavare qui pense qu'elle l'a tué.
2. Il lui a demandé de l'épouser après quelques mois.
3. Il l'aimait pour son argent.

***K. Comparaisons.**

1. aussi/plus/moins
2. aussi/plus/moins
3. autant/moins/moins
4. autant/plus/moins
5. autant/plus/moins
6. autant/plus/moins
7. autant/plus/moins
8. aussi/plus/moins
9. aussi/plus/moins
10. aussi/plus/moins

L. Qu'est-ce que vous faisiez?

1. À onze heures, Laurent Lavare travaillait sur ordinateur.
   Valérie Veutoux avait mal à la tête.
   Bernard Boncorps était au village.
2. À minuit moins le quart,
   Laurent Lavare parlait au téléphone.
   Valérie Veutoux lisait.
   Bernard Boncorps prenait un verre au café.
3. À une heure et quart,
   Laurent Lavare et Valérie Veutoux dormaient.
   Bernard Boncorps jouait aux cartes.

M. Qui est-ce?

1. C'est; Bernard Boncorps.
2. Il est; Laurent Lavare.
3. C'est; Laurent Lavare.
4. Il est; Laurent Lavare.
5. Il est; Bernard Boncorps.
6. C'est; Bernard Boncorps.
7. Il est; Bernard Boncorps ou Laurent Lavare.
8. Il est; Bernard Boncorps.

9. C'est; Bernard Boncorps.
10. C'est; Bernard Boncorps ou Laurent Lavare.

N. Les gens du village.

1. François Fédor était un homme qui ne parlait pas beaucoup.
2. François Fédor était un homme dont le passé était mystérieux.
3. François Fédor était un homme qu'on ne voyait pas souvent.
4. François Fédor était un homme dont la personnalité était un peu bizarre.
5. François Fédor était un homme dont tout le monde avait un peu peur.
6. François Fédor était un homme qui n'avait pas beaucoup d'amis.
7. François Fédor était un homme que je ne connaissais pas bien.
8. François Fédor était un homme qui faisait toujours ce qu'il voulait.

O. Qu'est-ce qu'on a servi?

À noter: Les réponses du/de la domestique à vos questions sont indiquées entre parenthèses.

1. Avez-vous servi du pain? (Oui.)
2. Avez-vous servi de la soupe à l'oignon? (Oui.)
3. Avez-vous servi du pâté? (Non.)
4. Avez-vous servi des œufs durs? (Non.)
5. Avez-vous servi du poulet? (**Oui.**)
6. Avez-vous servi des côtes de porc? (Non.)
7. Avez-vous servi du poisson/du saumon? (Non.)
8. Avez-vous servi des carrottes? (Non.)
9. Avez-vous servi des pommes de terre? (Oui.)
10 Avez-vous servi des haricots verts? (Oui.)
11. Avez-vous servi des petits pois? (Non.)
12. Avez-vous servi du riz? (Non.)
13. Avez-vous servi de la tarte aux pommes? (Oui.)
14. Avez-vous servi de la glace? (Non.)
15. Avez-vous servi du gâteau au chocolat? (Non.)
16. Avez-vous servi du fromage? (Non.)
17. Avez-vous servi du vin rouge? (Oui.)
18. Avez-vous servi de l'eau minérale? (Oui.)
19. Avez-vous servi du café? (Oui.)

P. Le dîner.

ligne

1 Le
2 du
3 de la
4 de; de; de; de
5 la; les
6 de; d'
7 de
8 de l'; du; le
9 le; la; de
10 le/un; la; une

Q. Symptômes.

À noter: les réponses du/de la domestique à vos questions sont indiquées entre parenthèses.

1. Est-ce que François Fédor avait des frissons? (Non.)
2. Est-ce que François Fédor a vomi? (Non.)
3. Est-ce que François Fédor a pris des médicaments? (Oui.)
4. Est-ce que François Fédor avait mal à la tête? (Non.)
5. Est-ce que François Fédor se sentait fatigué? (Non.)
6. Est-ce que François Fédor avait très sommeil? (Non.)
7. Est-ce que François Fédor est monté tout de suite se coucher? (Non. Il est resté une heure dans la bibliothèque.)
8. Est-ce que François Fédor s'est endormi facilement? (Je ne sais pas, mais d'habitude il ne dormait pas bien.)

R. Valérie se marie.

1. Valérie est sortie de sa chambre à huit heures vingt du matin. Elle est descendue au rez-de-chaussée et elle a téléphoné à Jean Jigaulaux à Luxembourg. Ensuite, elle a téléphoné à une agence de voyages à Bruxelles.
2. Jean Jigaulaux est arrivé ici quelques heures après. Il a retrouvé Valérie Veutoux dans la forêt à midi et ils se sont embrassés passionnément.
3. Comme Jean était fatigué, il a pris une chambre à l'hôtel du village où il a passé l'après-midi.
4. À cinq heures, ils sont montés dans la voiture de Jean Jigaulaux et sont allés dans le village voisin où il se sont mariés en secret à 18h20.
5. Après la cérémonie, ils ont dîné au restaurant du village. À part le garçon, ils étaient seuls.
6. Pendant le dîner, je les ai observés de l'extérieur. Jean ne parlait pas beaucoup mais Valérie Veutoux lui expliquait quelque chose.
7. Ils ont quitté le restaurant à 20h50. À ce moment-là, un chien m'a attaqué(e) dans les rosiers derrière lesquels je me cachais et je les ai perdus de vue.

***S. Réactions.**

1. C'est ridicule que je sois suspecte.
2. C'est nécessaire que vous sachiez où se trouve le corps de la victime.
3. Ça me rend furieuse que M. Lavare dise que j'ai des raisons de tuer François Fédor.
4. C'est important que vous sachiez que j'ai retrouvé M. Jigaulaux dans la forêt.
5. C'est impossible que vous ayez des photos de Jean Jigaulaux avec moi.
6. C'est bon que vous vouliez lui parler demain.
7. Je suis heureuse qu'il puisse partir après l'interrogatoire.
8. C'est impossible que je doive tout vous expliquer.

T. Deux billets pour Tahiti.

1. Valérie Veutoux / Jean Jigaulaux
2. (numéro du vol) 612
3. (date du départ) le 4 mai
4. (heure du départ) 15h
5. (date d'arrivée) le 5 mai
6. (heure d'arrivée) 6h

7. (prix du billet) 5 896
8. (total des deux billets) 11 792

U. **Une conversation téléphonique.**

ligne

1 fera
2 pourrons; voudras
3 viendrai; nous marierons; pars
4 j'arriverai
5 Tourne
6 entre
7 verra; Je t'attendrai
8 sera
9 partirons; commencerons

V. **Le compte en banque.**

1. Le quinze octobre de l'année dernière, il y avait cent soixante millions cent trente-six mille neuf cent soixante-dix-huit francs dans son compte.
2. Le dix novembre de l'année dernière, il y avait cent vingt-cinq millions cent quatre-vingt-quatorze mille quatre cent cinquante-six francs dans son compte.
3. Le vingt-quatre décembre de l'année dernière, il y avait quatre-vingts millions sept cent quatorze mille trois cent quatre-vingt-sept francs dans son compte.
4. Le premier janvier de cette année, il y avait quinze millions quatre-vingt-dix francs dans son compte.
5. Le quinze février de cette année, il y avait neuf cent quatre mille cinq cent six francs dans son compte.
6. Le quatre avril de cette année, il y avait cent treize mille huit cent soixante et onze francs dans son compte.

*W. **Une cassette vidéo révélatrice.**

1. Pourquoi êtes-vous entrée dans la chambre de François Fédor?
2. À quelle heure y êtes-vous entrée?
3. Combien de temps y êtes-vous restée?
4. Où êtes-vous allée après?
5. Avec qui avez-vous parlé?

X. **La dernière volonté de François.**

1. Il voulait tout savoir sur Jean Jigaulaux.
2. Il voulait que je dise à Jean Jigaulaux de venir ici.
3. Il voulait que je me marie tout de suite.
4. Il voulait nous offrir un voyage de noces.
5. Il voulait que je téléphone pour réserver le billet pour Tahiti le lendemain.
6. Il voulait que je parte en lune de miel cette semaine.
7. Il voulait que je sois heureuse.
8. Il voulait que je vienne dans sa chambre après le dîner prendre un chèque pour payer le voyage.

Y. Que faisait le/la domestique?

1. À quelle heure vous êtes-vous levé(e) le lendemain du crime?
2. Qu'avez-vous fait après vous être levé(e)?
3. Les autres dormaient-ils encore dans le château?
4. Quand avez-vous découvert que François Fédor était mort?
5. Étiez-vous surpris(e) de ce que vous avez trouvé?
6. Pourquoi n'avez-vous pas crié?
7. Avez-vous réveillé quelqu'un pour vous aider?
8. Vous avez téléphoné à la police à 8h12. À quelle heure êtes-vous entré(e) dans la chambre?
9. Combien de portes y a-t-il pour entrer dans la chambre de la victime?
10. Pourquoi ne dites-vous pas la vérité?
11. Ne faites pas l'innocent(e)! Comment saviez-vous que François Fédor était mort sans entrer dans sa chambre?
12. Pourquoi ne vous voit-on pas sur la vidéo de sécurité?
13. Pourquoi la vidéo s'arrête-t-elle à 8h30?
14. Alors, voulez-vous dire que François Fédor n'est pas mort?

Z. Une confession.

ligne	
1	ne voulais pas; était; était
2	a expliqué
3	venait
4	fallait
5	ai dit
6	savait; adorais
7	suis né(e); étais; rêvais
8	inventais
9	avaient; finissaient
10	a suggéré; avait
11	réussissait
12	a révélé
14	ne l'a jamais dit; j'avais
15	était
17	a rendu (rendait); parlait
18	devenait
19	était
20	ne lui a jamais pardonné
21	a toujours voulu (voulait toujours); n'était pas
23	disait (a dit)
24	dépendait
25	a dit
26	ne pouvait plus
27	voulait
28	avait
29	se mariait
36	était
40	est entré; a annoncé
41	venaient
42	ont donné

Tableau des verbes

The superscript number before each verb is correlated with the **Vocabulaire français-anglais**, where the same superscript number follows verbs that are conjugated the same way. Numbers in parentheses after entries in the verb charts indicate in which chapter the present indicative of the verb is presented.

Verbes auxiliaires

VERBE INFINITIF	INDICATIF PRÉSENT	INDICATIF PASSÉ COMPOSÉ	INDICATIF IMPARFAIT	INDICATIF FUTUR	CONDITIONNEL PRÉSENT	SUBJONCTIF PRÉSENT	IMPÉRATIF
[1]avoir	ai	ai eu	avais	aurai	aurais	aie	
to have (3)	as	as eu	avais	auras	aurais	aies	aie
	a	a eu	avait	aura	aurait	ait	
	avons	avons eu	avions	aurons	aurions	ayons	ayons
	avez	avez eu	aviez	aurez	auriez	ayez	ayez
	ont	ont eu	avaient	auront	auraient	aient	
[2]être	suis	ai été	étais	serai	serais	sois	
to be (1)	es	as été	étais	seras	serais	sois	sois
	est	a été	était	sera	serait	soit	
	sommes	avons été	étions	serons	serions	soyons	soyons
	êtes	avez été	étiez	serez	seriez	soyez	soyez
	sont	ont été	étaient	seront	seraient	soient	

Verbes réguliers

VERBE INFINITIF	INDICATIF PRÉSENT	INDICATIF PASSÉ COMPOSÉ	INDICATIF IMPARFAIT	INDICATIF FUTUR	CONDITIONNEL PRÉSENT	SUBJONCTIF PRÉSENT	IMPÉRATIF
[3]**-er** verbs							
parler	parle	ai parlé	parlais	parlerai	parlerais	parle	
to talk,	parles	as parlé	parlais	parleras	parlerais	parles	parle
to speak (2)	parle	a parlé	parlait	parlera	parlerait	parle	
	parlons	avons parlé	parlions	parlerons	parlerions	parlions	parlons
	parlez	avez parlé	parliez	parlerez	parleriez	parliez	parlez
	parlent	ont parlé	parlaient	parleront	parleraient	parlent	
[4]**-ir** verbs							
dormir	dors	ai dormi	dormais	dormirai	dormirais	dorme	
to sleep (8)	dors	as dormi	dormais	dormiras	dormirais	dormes	dors
	dort	a dormi	dormait	dormira	dormirait	dorme	
	dormons	avons dormi	dormions	dormirons	dormirions	dormions	dormons
	dormez	avez dormi	dormiez	dormirez	dormiriez	dormiez	dormez
	dorment	ont dormi	dormaient	dormiront	dormiraient	dorment	

Verbes réguliers (suite)

VERBE	INDICATIF				CONDITIONNEL	SUBJONCTIF	IMPÉRATIF
INFINITIF	PRÉSENT	PASSÉ COMPOSÉ	IMPARFAIT	FUTUR	PRÉSENT	PRÉSENT	
[5]**-ir** verbs							
finir	finis	ai fini	finissais	finirai	finirais	finisse	
to finish (10)	finis	as fini	finissais	finiras	finirais	finisses	finis
	finit	a fini	finissait	finira	finirait	finisse	
	finissons	avons fini	finissions	finirons	finirions	finissions	finissons
	finissez	avez fini	finissiez	finirez	finiriez	finissiez	finissez
	finissent	ont fini	finissaient	finiront	finiraient	finissent	
[6]**-re** verbs							
vendre	vends	ai vendu	vendais	vendrai	vendrais	vende	
to sell (7)	vends	as vendu	vendais	vendras	vendrais	vendes	vends
	vend	a vendu	vendait	vendra	vendrait	vende	
	vendons	avons vendu	vendions	vendrons	vendrions	vendions	vendons
	vendez	avez vendu	vendiez	vendrez	vendriez	vendiez	vendez
	vendent	ont vendu	vendaient	vendront	vendraient	vendent	

Verbes réfléchis

VERBE	INDICATIF				CONDITIONNEL	SUBJONCTIF	IMPÉRATIF
INFINITIF	PRÉSENT	PASSÉ COMPOSÉ	IMPARFAIT	FUTUR		PRÉSENT	
se laver	me lave	me suis lavé(e)	me lavais	me laverai	me laverais	me lave	
to wash	te laves	t'es lavé(e)	te lavais	te laveras	te laverais	te laves	lave-toi
oneself (9)	se lave	s'est lavé(e)	se lavait	se lavera	se laverait	se lave	
	nous lavons	nous sommes lavé(e)s	nous lavions	nous laverons	nous laverions	nous lavions	lavons-nous
	vous lavez	vous êtes lavé(e)(s)	vous laviez	vous laverez	vous laveriez	vous laviez	lavez-vous
	se lavent	se sont lavé(e)s	se lavaient	se laveront	se laveraient	se lavent	

Verbes à changements orthographiques

VERBE	INDICATIF				CONDITIONNEL	SUBJONCTIF	IMPÉRATIF
INFINITIF	PRÉSENT	PASSÉ COMPOSÉ	IMPARFAIT	FUTUR		PRÉSENT	
[7]préférer	préfère	ai préféré	préférais	préférerai	préférerais	préfère	
to prefer (9)	préfères	as préféré	préférais	préféreras	préférerais	préfères	préfère
	préfère	a préféré	préférait	préférera	préférerait	préfère	
	préférons	avons préféré	préférions	préférerons	préférerions	préférions	préférons
	préférez	avez préféré	préfériez	préférerez	préféreriez	préfériez	préférez
	préfèrent	ont préféré	préféraient	préféreront	préféreraient	préfèrent	
[8]acheter	achète	ai acheté	achetais	achèterai	achèterais	achète	
to buy (9)	achètes	as acheté	achetais	achèteras	achèterais	achètes	achète
	achète	a acheté	achetait	achètera	achèterait	achète	
	achetons	avons acheté	achetions	achèterons	achèterions	achetions	achetons
	achetez	avez acheté	achetiez	achèterez	achèteriez	achetiez	achetez
	achètent	ont acheté	achetaient	achèteront	achèteraient	achètent	

Verbes à changements orthographiques (suite)

VERBE INFINITIF	INDICATIF PRÉSENT	PASSÉ COMPOSÉ	IMPARFAIT	FUTUR	CONDITIONNEL PRÉSENT	SUBJONCTIF PRÉSENT	IMPÉRATIF
[9]appeler	appelle	ai appelé	appelais	appellerai	appellerais	appelle	
to call (9)	appelles	as appelé	appelais	appelleras	appellerais	appelles	appelle
	appelle	a appelé	appelait	appellera	appellerait	appelle	
	appelons	avons appelé	appelions	appellerons	appellerions	appelions	appelons
	appelez	avez appelé	appeliez	appellerez	appelleriez	appeliez	appelez
	appellent	ont appelé	appelaient	appelleront	appelleraient	appellent	
[10]essayer	essaie	ai essayé	essayais	essaierai	essaierais	essaie	
to try (9)	essaies	as essayé	essayais	essaieras	essaierais	essaies	essaie
	essaie	a essayé	essayait	essaiera	essaierait	essaie	
	essayons	avons essayé	essayions	essaierons	essaierions	essayions	essayons
	essayez	avez essayé	essayiez	essaierez	essaieriez	essayiez	essayez
	essaient	ont essayé	essayaient	essaieront	essaieraient	essaient	
[11]manger	mange	ai mangé	mangeais	mangerai	mangerais	mange	
to eat (2)	manges	as mangé	mangeais	mangeras	mangerais	manges	mange
	mange	a mangé	mangeait	mangera	mangerait	mange	
	mangeons	avons mangé	mangions	mangerons	mangerions	mangions	mangeons
	mangez	avez mangé	mangiez	mangerez	mangeriez	mangiez	mangez
	mangent	ont mangé	mangeaient	mangeront	mangeraient	mangent	
[12]commencer	commence	ai commencé	commençais	commencerai	commencerais	commence	
to begin (2)	commences	as commencé	commençais	commenceras	commencerais	commences	commence
	commence	a commencé	commençait	commencera	commencerait	commence	
	commençons	avons commencé	commencions	commencerons	commencerions	commencions	commençons
	commencez	avez commencé	commenciez	commencerez	commenceriez	commenciez	commencez
	commencent	ont commencé	commençaient	commenceront	commenceraient	commencent	

Verbes irréguliers

VERBE INFINITIF	INDICATIF PRÉSENT	PASSÉ COMPOSÉ	IMPARFAIT	FUTUR	CONDITIONNEL	SUBJONCTIF PRÉSENT	IMPÉRATIF
[13]aller	vais	suis allé(e)	allais	irai	irais	aille	
to go (4)	vas	es allé(e)	allais	iras	irais	ailles	va
	va	est allé(e)	allait	ira	irait	aille	
	allons	sommes allé(e)s	allions	irons	irions	allions	allons
	allez	êtes allé(e)(s)	alliez	irez	iriez	alliez	allez
	vont	sont allé(e)s	allaient	iront	iraient	aillent	
[14]s'asseoir	m'assieds	me suis assis(e)	m'asseyais	m'assiérai	m'assiérais	m'asseye	
to sit	t'assieds	t'es assis(e)	t'asseyais	t'assiéras	t'assiérais	t'asseyes	assieds-toi
(down)	s'assied	s'est assis(e)	s'asseyait	s'assiéra	s'assiérait	s'asseye	
	nous asseyons	nous sommes assis(es)	nous asseyions	nous assiérons	nous assiérions	nous asseyions	asseyons-nous
	vous asseyez	vous êtes assis(es)	vous asseyiez	vous assiérez	vous assiériez	vous asseyiez	asseyez-vous
	s'asseyent	se sont assis(es)	s'asseyaient	s'assiéront	s'assiéraient	s'asseyent	

Verbes irréguliers (suite)

VERBE INFINITIF	INDICATIF PRÉSENT	PASSÉ COMPOSÉ	IMPARFAIT	FUTUR	CONDITIONNEL	SUBJONCTIF PRÉSENT	IMPÉRATIF
15 battre	bats	ai battu	battais	battrai	battrais	batte	
to beat	bats	as battu	battais	battras	battrais	battes	bats
	bat	a battu	battait	battra	battrait	batte	
	battons	avons battu	battions	battrons	battrions	battions	battons
	battez	avez battu	battiez	battrez	battriez	battiez	battez
	battent	ont battu	battaient	battront	battraient	battent	
16 boire	bois	ai bu	buvais	boirai	boirais	boive	
to drink (10)	bois	as bu	buvais	boiras	boirais	boives	bois
	boit	a bu	buvait	boira	boirait	boive	
	buvons	avons bu	buvions	boirons	boirions	buvions	buvons
	buvez	avez bu	buviez	boirez	boiriez	buviez	buvez
	boivent	ont bu	buvaient	boiront	boiraient	boivent	
17 conduire	conduis	ai conduit	conduisais	conduirai	conduirais	conduise	
to drive	conduis	as conduit	conduisais	conduiras	conduirais	conduises	conduis
	conduit	a conduit	conduisait	conduira	conduirait	conduise	
	conduisons	avons conduit	conduisions	conduirons	conduirions	conduisions	conduisons
	conduisez	avez conduit	conduisiez	conduirez	conduiriez	conduisiez	conduisez
	conduisent	ont conduit	conduisaient	conduiront	conduiraient	conduisent	
18 connaître	connais	ai connu	connaissais	connaîtrai	connaîtrais	connaisse	
to be	connais	as connu	connaissais	connaîtras	connaîtrais	connaisses	connais
acquainted with,	connaît	a connu	connaissait	connaîtra	connaîtrait	connaisse	
to know (6)	connaissons	avons connu	connaissions	connaîtrons	connaîtrions	connaissions	connaissons
	connaissez	avez connu	connaissiez	connaîtrez	connaîtriez	connaissiez	connaissez
	connaissent	ont connu	connaissaient	connaîtront	connaîtraient	connaissent	
19 courir	cours	ai couru	courais	courrai	courrais	coure	
to run (8)	cours	as couru	courais	courras	courrais	coures	cours
	court	a couru	courait	courra	courrait	coure	
	courons	avons couru	courions	courrons	courrions	courions	courons
	courez	avez couru	couriez	courrez	courriez	couriez	courez
	courent	ont couru	couraient	courront	courraient	courent	
20 croire	crois	ai cru	croyais	croirai	croirais	croie	
to believe (11)	crois	as cru	croyais	croiras	croirais	croies	crois
	croit	a cru	croyait	croira	croirait	croie	
	croyons	avons cru	croyions	croirons	croirions	croyions	croyons
	croyez	avez cru	croyiez	croirez	croiriez	croyiez	croyez
	croient	ont cru	croyaient	croiront	croiraient	croient	
21 devoir	dois	ai dû	devais	devrai	devrais	doive	
must,	dois	as dû	devais	devras	devrais	doives	
to have to,	doit	a dû	devait	devra	devrait	doive	
to owe (6)	devons	avons dû	devions	devrons	devrions	devions	
	devez	avez dû	deviez	devrez	devriez	deviez	
	doivent	ont dû	devaient	devront	devraient	doivent	

Verbes irréguliers (suite)

VERBE INFINITIF	INDICATIF PRÉSENT	PASSÉ COMPOSÉ	IMPARFAIT	FUTUR	CONDITIONNEL	SUBJONCTIF PRÉSENT	IMPÉRATIF
22dire	dis	ai dit	disais	dirai	dirais	dise	
to say,	dis	as dit	disais	diras	dirais	dises	dis
to tell (7)	dit	a dit	disait	dira	dirait	dise	
	disons	avons dit	disions	dirons	dirions	disions	disons
	dites	avez dit	disiez	direz	diriez	disiez	dites
	disent	ont dit	disaient	diront	diraient	disent	
23écrire	écris	ai écrit	écrivais	écrirai	écrirais	écrive	
to write (7)	écris	as écrit	écrivais	écriras	écrirais	écrives	écris
	écrit	a écrit	écrivait	écrira	écrirait	écrive	
	écrivons	avons écrit	écrivions	écrirons	écririons	écrivions	écrivons
	écrivez	avez écrit	écriviez	écrirez	écririez	écriviez	écrivez
	écrivent	ont écrit	écrivaient	écriront	écriraient	écrivent	
24envoyer	envoie	ai envoyé	envoyais	enverrai	enverrais	envoie	
to send	envoies	as envoyé	envoyais	enverras	enverrais	envoies	envoie
	envoie	a envoyé	envoyait	enverra	enverrait	envoie	
	envoyons	avons envoyé	envoyions	enverrons	enverrions	envoyions	envoyons
	envoyez	avez envoyé	envoyiez	enverrez	enverriez	envoyiez	envoyez
	envoient	ont envoyé	envoyaient	enverront	enverraient	envoient	
25faire	fais	ai fait	faisais	ferai	ferais	fasse	
to do,	fais	as fait	faisais	feras	ferais	fasses	fais
to make (5)	fait	a fait	faisait	fera	ferait	fasse	
	faisons	avons fait	faisions	ferons	ferions	fassions	faisons
	faites	avez fait	faisiez	ferez	feriez	fassiez	faites
	font	ont fait	faisaient	feront	feraient	fassent	
26falloir *to be necessary* (7)	faut	a fallu	fallait	faudra	faudrait	faille	
27lire	lis	ai lu	lisais	lirai	lirais	lise	
to read (7)	lis	as lu	lisais	liras	lirais	lises	lis
	lit	a lu	lisait	lira	lirait	lise	
	lisons	avons lu	lisions	lirons	lirions	lisions	lisons
	lisez	avez lu	lisiez	lirez	liriez	lisiez	lisez
	lisent	ont lu	lisaient	liront	liraient	lisent	
28mettre	mets	ai mis	mettais	mettrai	mettrais	mette	
to put,	mets	as mis	mettais	mettras	mettrais	mettes	mets
to place,	met	a mis	mettait	mettra	mettrait	mette	
to set (8)	mettons	avons mis	mettions	mettrons	mettrions	mettions	mettons
	mettez	avez mis	mettiez	mettrez	mettriez	mettiez	mettez
	mettent	ont mis	mettaient	mettront	mettraient	mettent	
29ouvrir	ouvre	ai ouvert	ouvrais	ouvrirai	ouvrirais	ouvre	
to open	ouvres	as ouvert	ouvrais	ouvriras	ouvrirais	ouvres	ouvre
	ouvre	a ouvert	ouvrait	ouvrira	ouvrirait	ouvre	
	ouvrons	avons ouvert	ouvrions	ouvrirons	ouvririons	ouvrions	ouvrons
	ouvrez	avez ouvert	ouvriez	ouvrirez	ouvririez	ouvriez	ouvrez
	ouvrent	ont ouvert	ouvraient	ouvriront	ouvriraient	ouvrent	

Verbes irréguliers (suite)

VERBE INFINITIF	INDICATIF PRÉSENT	PASSÉ COMPOSÉ	IMPARFAIT	FUTUR	CONDITIONNEL	SUBJONCTIF PRÉSENT	IMPÉRATIF
30pleuvoir	pleut	a plu	pleuvait	pleuvra	pleuvrait	pleuve	
to rain (5)							
31pouvoir	peux	ai pu	pouvais	pourrai	pourrais	puisse	
to be able,	peux	as pu	pouvais	pourras	pourrais	puisses	
can (6)	peut	a pu	pouvait	pourra	pourrait	puisse	
	pouvons	avons pu	pouvions	pourrons	pourrions	puissions	
	pouvez	avez pu	pouviez	pourrez	pourriez	puissiez	
	peuvent	ont pu	pouvaient	pourront	pourraient	puissent	
32prendre	prends	ai pris	prenais	prendrai	prendrais	prenne	
to take (8)	prends	as pris	prenais	prendras	prendrais	prennes	prends
	prend	a pris	prenait	prendra	prendrait	prenne	
	prenons	avons pris	prenions	prendrons	prendrions	prenions	prenons
	prenez	avez pris	preniez	prendrez	prendriez	preniez	prenez
	prennent	ont pris	prenaient	prendront	prendraient	prennent	
33recevoir	reçois	ai reçu	recevais	recevrai	recevrais	reçoive	
to receive	reçois	as reçu	recevais	recevras	recevrais	reçoives	reçois
	reçoit	a reçu	recevait	recevra	recevrait	reçoive	
	recevons	avons reçu	recevions	recevrons	recevrions	recevions	recevons
	recevez	avez reçu	receviez	recevrez	recevriez	receviez	recevez
	reçoivent	ont reçu	recevaient	recevront	recevraient	reçoivent	
34rire	ris	ai ri	riais	rirai	rirais	rie	
to laugh	ris	as ri	riais	riras	rirais	ries	ris
	rit	a ri	riait	rira	rirait	rie	
	rions	avons ri	riions	rirons	ririons	riions	rions
	riez	avez ri	riiez	rirez	ririez	riiez	riez
	rient	ont ri	riaient	riront	riraient	rient	
35savoir	sais	ai su	savais	saurai	saurais	sache	
to know (6)	sais	as su	savais	sauras	saurais	saches	sache
	sait	a su	savait	saura	saurait	sache	
	savons	avons su	savions	saurons	saurions	sachions	sachons
	savez	avez su	saviez	saurez	sauriez	sachiez	sachez
	savent	ont su	savaient	sauront	sauraient	sachent	
36suivre	suis	ai suivi	suivais	suivrai	suivrais	suive	
to follow	suis	as suivi	suivais	suivras	suivrais	suives	suis
	suit	a suivi	suivait	suivra	suivrait	suive	
	suivons	avons suivi	suivions	suivrons	suivrions	suivions	suivons
	suivez	avez suivi	suiviez	suivrez	suivriez	suiviez	suivez
	suivent	ont suivi	suivaient	suivront	suivraient	suivent	
37venir	viens	suis venu(e)	venais	viendrai	viendrais	vienne	
to come (7)	viens	es venu(e)	venais	viendras	viendrais	viennes	viens
	vient	est venu(e)	venait	viendra	viendrait	vienne	
	venons	sommes venu(e)s	venions	viendrons	viendrions	venions	venons
	venez	êtes venu(e)(s)	veniez	viendrez	viendriez	veniez	venez
	viennent	sont venu(e)s	venaient	viendront	viendraient	viennent	

Verbes irréguliers (suite)

VERBE INFINITIF	INDICATIF PRÉSENT	PASSÉ COMPOSÉ	IMPARFAIT	FUTUR	CONDITIONNEL	SUBJONCTIF PRÉSENT	IMPÉRATIF
38vivre	vis	ai vécu	vivais	vivrai	vivrais	vive	
to live	vis	as vécu	vivais	vivras	vivrais	vives	vis
	vit	a vécu	vivait	vivra	vivrait	vive	
	vivons	avons vécu	vivions	vivrons	vivrions	vivions	vivons
	vivez	avez vécu	viviez	vivrez	vivriez	viviez	vivez
	vivent	ont vécu	vivaient	vivront	vivraient	vivent	
39voir	vois	ai vu	voyais	verrai	verrais	voie	
to see (11)	vois	as vu	voyais	verras	verrais	voies	vois
	voit	a vu	voyait	verra	verrait	voie	
	voyons	avons vu	voyions	verrons	verrions	voyions	voyons
	voyez	avez vu	voyiez	verrez	verriez	voyiez	voyez
	voient	ont vu	voyaient	verront	verraient	voient	
40vouloir	veux	ai voulu	voulais	voudrai	voudrais	veuille	
to want,	veux	as voulu	voulais	voudras	voudrais	veuilles	veuille
to wish (6)	veut	a voulu	voulait	voudra	voudrait	veuille	
	voulons	avons voulu	voulions	voudrons	voudrions	voulions	veuillons
	voulez	avez voulu	vouliez	voudrez	voudriez	vouliez	veuillez
	veulent	ont voulu	voulaient	voudront	voudraient	veuillent	

VOCABULAIRE
français-anglais

This list contains both active vocabulary and words appearing in readings and realia in *Qu'est-ce qu'on dit?*. The definitions of active vocabulary words are followed by the number of the chapter where they are first presented. A (P) refers to the *Chapitre préliminaire*. Since verbs are sometimes introduced in the infinitive before the conjugation of the present indicative is presented, refer to the verb charts in *Appendix D* or the *Index* to find out the chapter where conjugations are introduced. Superscript numbers following verbs refer to the verb charts in *Appendix D*, indicating the position in the charts of that verb or a verb with a similar conjugation. A superscript [ê] indicates that the verb is conjugated with **être** in the **passé composé**. You may presume that verbs without [ê] are conjugated with **avoir** in the **passé composé**. An (*m*), (*f*), or (*pl*) following a noun indicates that it is masculine, feminine, or plural. *Inv* means that a word is invariable. An asterisk before a word beginning with an **h** indicates that the **h** is aspirate.

A

à to, at, in (P); **À bientôt.** See you soon. (P); **à cause de** due to, because of (7); **à côté (de)** next to (8); **À demain.** See you tomorrow. (P); **à la campagne** in the country (3); **à la maison** at home (P); **à l'avance** in advance (8); **à l'étranger** abroad (7); **à l'heure** on time (7); **à l'intérieur** inside (10); **À quelle heure?** At what time? (P); **À tout à l'heure.** See you in a little while. (P); **au café** at the café (2); **au centre-ville** downtown (3); **au chômage** unemployed (4); **au coin (de)** on the corner (of) (8); **au premier étage** on the second floor (3); **Au revoir.** Good-bye. (P); **à votre avis** in your opinion (9); **café au lait** coffee with milk (2); **j'habite à** (+ *city*) I live in (+ *city*) (P)
abonnement (*m*) subscription
abonner: s'abonner[3ê] **à** to subscribe to
abord: d'abord first (4)
abricot (*m*) apricot
abriter[3] to shelter
abstenir: s'abstenir[37ê] **(de)** to abstain (from)
accent: sans accent without an accent (P)
accepter[3] to accept (8)
accident (*m*) accident (5)
accompagner[3] to accompany
accord: D'accord! Okay! Agreed! (2)
accorder: s'accorder[3ê] to grant each other
accueil (*m*) welcome, reception
accueillant(e) welcoming
achat (*m*) purchase
acheter[8] to buy (4)
achever: s'achever[8ê] to end
acteur (*m*) actor (4)
actif(-ive) active (1)
activité (*f*) activity (4)
actrice (*f*) actress (4)
adapter: s'adapter[3ê] to adapt (10)
addition (*f*) check, bill (2)
admirer[3] to admire (7)
adorer[3] to love, to adore (4)
adresse (*f*) address (3)
adresser: s'adresser à[3ê] to go and see
aérien(ne) aerial
aéroport (*m*) airport (7)
affaibli(e) weakened
affaires (*fpl*) things (3), business (4); **femme d'affaires** businesswoman (4); **homme d'affaires** businessman (4)
affichage (*m*) display
affiche (*f*) poster (3)
africain(e) African (11)
Afrique (*f*) Africa (7)
âge: Quel âge a...? How old is . . .? (4)
âgé(e) old (4)
agence de voyages (*f*) travel agency (7)
agent de voyages (*m*) travel agent (7)
aggraver[3] to worsen
agir[5] to act, to take action (10)
agitation (*f*) agitation (11)
agneau (*m*) lamb
agréable pleasant (1)
agricole agricultural (11)
aider[3] to help (11)
aigle (*m*) eagle
ail (*m*) garlic
aile (*f*) wing
ailleurs elsewhere
aimer[3] to like (2); **J'aime...** I like . . . (1); **aimer mieux** to like better (2); **J'aimerais...** I would like . . . (7); **s'aimer**[3ê] to love each other (9); **Tu aimes...?** Do you like . . . ? (1)
ainsi thus
air (*m*) look, appearance; **avoir l'air** (+ *adjective*) to look / to seem (+ *adjective*) (4); **de plein air** outdoor (4)
aise: mal à l'aise ill at ease
ajouter[3] to add (11)
alcool (*m*) alcohol (10)
alcoolisé(e) alcoholic (6)
alcoolisme (*m*) alcoholism (11)
Algérie (*f*) Algeria (7)
algérien(ne) Algerian (6)
aliment (*m*) food (12)
Allemagne (*f*) Germany (7)
allemand (*m*) German (1)
allemand(e) German
aller[13ê] to go (2); **aller**[13ê] **très bien à quelqu'un** to look very good on someone (8); **Allez au tableau.** Go to the board. (P); **Comment vas-tu/allez-vous?** How are you? (P); **Comment ça va?** How is it going?, How are you? (P); **Ça va.** It's going okay. (P); **On va...?** Shall we go . . . ? (2); **Qu'est-ce qui ne va pas?** What's wrong? (12); **s'en aller**[13ê] to go away
aller simple (*m*) one-way ticket (7); **billet aller-retour** (*m*) round-trip ticket (7)
allergie (*f*) allergy (12)
allô hello (*on the telephone*) (6)
allumer[3] to light
allumette (*f*) match
alors so, then (1)
amande (*f*) almond
amant(e) (*m/f*) lover
amélioration (*f*) improvement
améliorer[3] to improve (5)
aménagé(e) fitted out
amener[8] to take
américain(e) American (P)
Amérique du Nord (*f*) North America (7)
Amérique du Sud (*f*) South America (7)
ami(e) (*m/f*) friend (P), **petit ami** (*m*) boyfriend (4); **petite amie** (*f*) girlfriend (4)
amitié (*f*) friendship
amour (*m*) love (6)
amoureux (-euse) in love
amovible detachable
amphithéâtre (*m*) lecture hall (1)
amusant(e) funny; **c'est amusant** it's fun (1)
amuser: s'amuser [3ê] to have fun (9)
an (*m*) year; **avoir**[1]**... ans** to be . . . years old (4); **jour de l'an** (*m*) New Year's Day
analyse (*f*) analysis, test (12)
ananas (*m*) pineapple
ancêtre (*mf*) ancestor
anchois (*m*) anchovy
ancien(ne) former (11), old
andouillette (*f*) sausage of chitterlings
anglais (*m*) English (P)
anglais(e) English
angoissé(e) anguished
animal (*m*) (*pl* **animaux**) animal (3)
animé(e) animated (8); **dessin animé** (*m*) cartoon (6)
année (*f*) year (4); **des années soixante** from the sixties (4)
anniversaire (*m*) birthday (6)
annonce (*f*) advertisement (9)
annuaire (*m*) telephone book
anorak (*m*) ski jacket, anorak (8)
antibiotique (*m*) antibiotic (12)
antillais(e) West Indian
Antilles (*fpl*) West Indies (7)
août (*m*) August (6)
apéritif (*m*) pre-dinner drink (10)
appareil (*m*) apparatus, appliance; **appareil-photo** camera; **Qui est à l'appareil?** Who's calling? (6)
apparenté(e) related
appartement (*m*) apartment (3)
appartenance (*f*) belonging
appartenir[37] to belong

appeler[9] to call; **Comment s'appelle...** What is . . . 's name? (4); **Comment t'appelles-tu?** What is your name? (*informal*) (P); **Comment vous appelez-vous?** What is your name? (*formal*) (P); **Je m'appelle...** My name is . . . (P); **s'appeler**[9ê] to be named, to be called (9)
appétit (*m*) appetite (12)
apporter[3] to bring (6)
apprendre[32] to learn (8)
approcher: s'approcher[3ê] **(de)** to approach
après after, afterwards (2); **d'après** according to
après-demain day after tomorrow (8)
après-midi (*m*) afternoon (P); **Il est une heure de l'après-midi.** It's one o'clock in the afternoon. (P); **l'après-midi** in the afternoon, afternoons (2)
arbre (*m*) tree
arc: tir à l'arc (*m*) archery
argent (*m*) money (7), silver
Argentine (*f*) Argentina (7)
armée (*f*) army
arrêt (*m*) stop; **arrêt d'autobus** (*m*) bus stop (3)
arrêter: s'arrêter [3ê] **(de)** to stop
arrière (*m*) rear, back
arrivée (*f*) arrival (7)
arriver[3ê] to arrive (5), to happen (9)
arrondissement (*m*) district
arroser[3] to sprinkle
article (*m*) article (7)
ascenseur (*m*) elevator (3)
Asie (*f*) Asia (7)
aspirine (*f*) aspirin (12)
asseoir: Asseyez-vous. Sit down. (P); **s'asseoir**[14ê] to sit (down) (10)
assez fairly, rather (P); **assez (de)** enough (10)
assiette (*f*) plate
assis(e) seated (7)
assister[3] **à** to attend
associer[3] to associate
assurance (*f*) insurance
astutieux(-euse) astute
atelier (*m*) workshop
atout (*m*) trump, winning card
atteler[9] to harness
attenant(e) adjoining
attendre[6] to wait (for) (7)
attente (*f*) waiting
attention: faire[25] **attention (à)** to pay attention (to) (10)
attirant(e) attractive
attirer[3] to attract
attrait (*m*) attraction
attraper[3] to catch
auberge: auberge de jeunesse (*f*) youth hostel (8)
aucun(e): ne... aucune(e) no, none, not one (9)
au-dessus above
aujourd'hui today (P)
auparavant beforehand
aussi too, also (P); **aussi... que** as . . . as (11)
aussitôt que as soon as (11)
Australie (*f*) Australia (7)
autant (de)... (que) as much . . . (as), as many . . . (as) (10)
autobus (*m*) bus (3); **arrêt d'autobus** (*m*) bus stop (3)
autocar (*m*) bus (5); **en autocar** by bus (5)
autocrate (*m*) autocrat (11)
automne (*m*) autumn, fall (5); **en automne** in autumn (5)
autoportrait (*m*) self-portrait
autour de around
autre other (4); **quelquefois... d'autres fois** sometimes . . . other times (2)
autrefois in the past (9)
avaler[3] to swallow
avance (*f*) advance (11); **en avance** early (6)
avant before, beforehand (2); **avant de** (+ *infinitive*) before (+ *-ing form of the verb*) (8)
avec with (P); **Avec plaisir!** Gladly!, With pleasure! (6)
avenir (*m*) future (11)
aventure: film d'aventures (*m*) adventure movie (6)
avenue (*f*) avenue (8)
averse (*f*) shower
avion (*m*) airplane (5); **en avion** by airplane (5)
avis (*m*) opinion (9)
avocat(e) (*m/f*) lawyer (4)
avoir[1] to have (3); **avoir... ans** to be . . . years old (4) **avoir besoin de** to need (5); **avoir chaud** to be hot (5); **avoir envie de** to feel like, to desire (5); **avoir faim** to be hungry (5); **avoir froid** to be cold (5); **avoir l'air** (+ *adjective*) to look/to seem (+ *adjective*) (4); **avoir lieu** to take place (9); **avoir l'intention de** to plan on, to intend to (5); **avoir mal (à)** to hurt, to ache (12); **avoir peur (de)** to be afraid (of), to fear (5); **avoir raison** to be right (5); **avoir soif** to be thirsty (5); **avoir sommeil** to be sleepy (5); **avoir tort** to be wrong (5); **il y a** there is, there are (3); **Quel âge a...?** How old is . . . ? (4)
avouer[3] to admit
avril (*m*) April (6)

B

bagages (*mpl*) baggage (7)
baguette (*f*) loaf of French bread (10)
baie (*f*) bay
baigner: se baigner[3ê] to bathe, to go swimming
bain (*m*) bath (9); **maillot de bain** (*m*) swimsuit (8); **salle de bains** (*f*) bathroom 3
baiser[3] to kiss
baiser (*m*) kiss
bal (*m*) dance
baliser[3] to mark with signs
balnéaire swimming
banane (*f*) banana (10)
banlieue (*f*) suburbs (3); **en banlieue** in the suburbs (3)
bannière (*f*) banner
banque (*f*) bank (7)
banquette (*f*) bench, seat
bar (*m*) bar (4)
barbe (*f*) beard (4)
bas (*m*) bottom
baser: en se basant sur based on
basket-ball (*m*) basketball (2)
bataille (*f*) battle
bateau (*m*) boat (5); **faire du bateau** to go boating (5)
bâtiment (*m*) building (1)
batterie (*f*) drums (9)
battre[15] to beat (11); **se battre**[15ê] to fight (11)
bavette (*f*) undercut
beau (bel, belle, *pl.* **beaux, belles)** beautiful, handsome (1); **beaux-arts** (*mpl*) fine arts (1); **belle-sœur** (*f*) sister-in-law; **Il fait beau.** The weather's nice. (5)
beaucoup a lot (P); **beaucoup de** a lot of (3)
beige beige (4)
beignet (*m*) fritter
Belgique (*f*) Belgium (7)
bénévole voluntary
besoin (*m*) need; **avoir besoin de** to need (5)
bête (*f*) animal, beast
bête dumb (1)
beurre (*m*) butter (10)
beurré(e) buttered
biais (*m*) means, device
bibliothèque (*f*) library (P)
bidet (*m*) bidet (8)
bien well (P), very; **Bien sûr!** Of course! (2); **Je voudrais bien.** Sure, I'd like to. (2); **bien-être** (*m*) well-being
bientôt soon (P); **À bientôt.** See you soon. (P)
bienvenu(e) welcome
bière (*f*) beer (2)
bifteck (*m*) steak (10)
bikini (*m*) bikini (8)
billet (aller-retour) (*m*) (round-trip) ticket (7)
biologie (*f*) biology (1)
biscotte (*f*) melba toast (10)
bistrot (*m*) restaurant, pub
blanc(he) white (4); **vin blanc** (*m*) white wine (2)
blanquette (*f*) sauce prepared with wine
blesser[3] to wound (12); **se blesser**[3ê] to wound oneself (12)
bleu(e) blue (4)
blond(e) blond (4)
blouson (*m*) windbreaker jacket (8)
blues (*m*) blues (*music*) (6)
bœuf (*m*) beef, ox
boire[16] to drink (5)
boisson (*f*) drink (6)
boîte (*f*) can; **en boîte** canned (10)
bol (*m*) bowl
bombardement (*m*) bombing
bon(ne) good (4); **Bonne idée!** Good idea! (2); **Bon séjour!** Have a nice stay! (8)
bonheur (*m*) happiness
bonjour hello, good day (P)
bonsoir good evening (P)
bord (*m*) edge; **à bord** on board; **bord de mer** (*m*) seaside; **au bord de** along the edge of
bordeaux wine-colored
bordure: en bordure de along the edge of

bouche (*f*) mouth (12)
bouché(e) stopped up (12); **cidre bouché** (*m*) bottled cider
boucherie (*f*) butcher's shop (10)
boue (*f*) mud
bouger[11] to move
bouillabaisse (*f*) fish soup
bouillie (*f*) mush, porridge
bouillir to boil
boulangerie (*f*) bakery (10)
boule (*f*) ball
boulevard (*m*) boulevard (8)
boum (*f*) party, bash (6); **faire une boum** to give a party (6)
bout (*m*) end, bit; **au bout (de)** at the end (of) (8)
bouteille (*f*) bottle (10)
bouton (*m*) button, pimple
branché(e) swinging
bras (*m*) arm (12)
Brésil (*m*) Brazil (7)
bricolage (*m*) handiwork
bricoler[3] to tinker around (2)
briller[3] to shine
briser[3] to break
brochette (*f*) skewer
brosser: se brosser[3è] to brush (9)
broyeur (*m*) grinder
bruit (*m*) noise (7)
bruitage (*m*) sound effects
brûler[3] to burn (12); **se brûler**[3è] to burn oneself (12)
brun(e) brown, brunette, dark-haired (4)
Bruxelles Brussels (7)
bureau (*m*) desk (3); office (8); **bureau de poste** (*m*) post office (8); **bureau de tabac** (*m*) tobacco shop (8)
buvable drinkable

C

ça that (P); **Ça fait... francs.** That's . . . francs. (2); **Ça me plaît!** I like it! (6); **Ça s'écrit comment?** How is that written? (P); **Ça te dit?** How does that sound to you?, Does that sound like fun? (6); **Ça va.** It's going okay. (P); **C'est ça!** That's right!; **comme ci comme ça** so-so (2); **Comment ça va?** How is it going?, How are you? (P); **Qu'est-ce que ça veut dire?** What does that mean? (P)
cabine d'essayage (*f*) fitting room (8)
cabinet: cabinet de toilette (*m*) toilet (3)
cadre (*m*) executive, framework, setting
café (*m*) coffee, café (2); **café au lait** coffee with milk (2)
cahier (*m*) notebook (P)
californien(ne) Californian (1)
câlin(e) cuddly
calme calm (1)
calmer: se calmer[3è] to calm down (9)
camarade (*mf*) pal; **camarade de chambre** (*mf*) roommate (3); **camarade de classe** classmate
campagne (*f*) country (3), campaign
camping (*m*) camping (5)
campus (*m*) campus (1)
Canada (*m*) Canada (7)
canadien(ne) Canadian (P)
canapé (*m*) open-faced sandwich (6), sofa
canard (*m*) duck (10)
cancer (*m*) cancer (11)
canne à sucre (*f*) sugar cane
capote (*f*) top, hood
car because
caractère (*m*) character; **en caractères gras** boldfaced
carafe (*f*) decanter (10)
caraïbe Caribbean
carotte (*f*) carrot (10)
carrière (*f*) career
carte (*f*) card (7), menu, map; **carte de crédit** (*f*) credit card (7); **carte d'identité** (*f*) identity card (7); **carte postale** (*f*) postcard (7)
cas: dans tous les cas in any case
case (*f*) box
casse-cou (*inv*) (*mf*) daredevil
casse-pieds (*inv*) (*mf*) nuisance
casser[3] to break (12); **se casser**[3è] **le bras** to break one's arm (12)
cassette (*f*) cassette (P); **cassette vidéo** (*f*) video cassette (3)
cassoulet (*m*) Southern French bean casserole
cathédrale (*f*) cathedral (8)
cause (*f*) cause (11); **à cause de** due to, because of (7)
causer[3] to cause (12)
ce (cet, cette) this, that (4); **ce que** what, that which; **ce qui** what, that which, **ces** these, those (4); **ce soir** tonight (2); **c'est** it's, that's (P); **ce sont** they are, those are (4); **ce week-end** this weekend (2)
célèbre famous (6)
célébrer[7] to celebrate
célibataire single, unmarried (1)
celui (celle) the one
cendre (*f*) ash
cendrier (*m*) ashtray
cent (*m*) one hundred (2)
centaine (*f*) one hundred
centime (*m*) centime (*one hundredth of a franc*) (2)
central(e) (*mpl* **centraux**) central
centre (*m*) center; **centre commercial** (*m*) shopping center, mall (4)
centre-ville (*m*) downtown (3)
cercle (*m*) circle
céréales (*fpl*) cereal (10)
cerise (*f*) cherry (6)
certain(e) certain; **certains** some, certain people (10)
certes true, indeed; of course
cervelle (*f*) brain
ceux (celles) those
chacun(e) each one
chaîne (*f*) chain, **chaîne stéréo** stereo (3)
chaise (*f*) chair (3)
chalet de ski (*m*) ski lodge (8)
chaleur (*f*) warmth (7)
chaleureux(-euse) warm-hearted
chambre (*f*) bedroom (3); **camarade de chambre** (*mf*) roommate (3)
champ (*m*) field
champêtre country, rustic
champignon (*m*) mushroom
chance (*f*) luck (5)
changement (*m*) change
changer[11] to change, **changer**[11] **de l'argent** to exchange money (7)
chanson (*f*) song (11)
chanter[3] to sing (2)
chanteur(-euse) (*m/f*) singer (4)
chapeau (*m*) hat (8)
chaque each, every (9)
charcuterie (*f*) delicatessen (10)
charger: se charger[11è] **de** to take charge of
charmant(e) charming
charte (*f*) charter
chasse (*f*) hunt, hunting
chasser[3] to hunt
chat (*m*) cat (3)
châtain (*inv*) chestnut brown (hair) (4)
château (*m*) castle (10)
chaud(e) hot; **avoir**[1] **chaud** to be hot (5); **chocolat chaud** (*m*) hot chocolate (2); **Il fait chaud.** It's hot. (5)
chauffé(e) heated
chaussette (*f*) sock (7)
chaussure (*f*) shoe (8)
chef head, boss
chef-d'œuvre (*m*) masterpiece
chemin (*m*) roadway; **indiquer le chemin** to show the way (8)
chemise (*f*) shirt (8); **chemise de nuit** (*f*) nightshirt (8)
chemisier (*m*) blouse (8)
chêne (*m*) oak
chèque (*m*) check; **chèque de voyage** (*m*) traveler's check (7)
cher(-ère) expensive (3)
chercher[3] to look for (3); **aller**[13è] **chercher** / **venir**[37è] **chercher quelqu'un** to go get / come get someone (7)
chercheur(-euse) (*m/f*) researcher
chéri(e) (*m/f*) honey, darling
chevet: livre de chevet (*m*) bedside book
cheveux (*mpl*) hair (4)
cheville (*f*) ankle (12)
chèvre (*m*) goat
chez at . . . 's house/place, to . . . 's house/place (2)
chien (*m*) dog (3)
chiffre (*m*) number
chimie (*f*) chemistry (1)
Chine (*f*) China (7)
chips (*fpl*) chips (6)
chirurgie (*f*) surgery
choc (*m*) shock, impact
chocolat (*m*) chocolate (2); **gâteau au chocolat** (*m*) chocolate cake (6)
choisir[5] **(de faire)** to choose (to do) (10)
choix (*m*) choice (10)
chômage (*m*) unemployment (11); **être au chômage** to be unemployed (4)
choqué(e) shocked
chose (*f*) thing (3); **quelque chose** something (2)

chou (*m*) cabbage
chouette neat (7)
chou-fleur (*m*) cauliflower
chute (*f*) fall
ci: ce livre-ci this book; **ci-dessous** below; **ci-dessus** above; **comme ci comme ça** so-so (2)
ciboule (*f*) chive
ciel (*m*) sky
cinéma (*m*) cinema, movie theater (2)
cinq five (P)
cinquante fifty (2)
circulation (*f*) traffic (8)
cirque (*m*) circus
citoyen(ne) (*m/f*) citizen
citoyenneté (*f*) citizenship
citron: thé au citron (*m*) tea with lemon (2)
civet (*m*) stew
civil(e) civil (11)
clairement clearly
classe class(room) (1); **en classe** in class (P); **en classe touriste** in second class, in coach (7)
classique: musique classique (*f*) classical music (6)
clavier (*m*) keyboard (9)
clé (*f*) key (8)
climatisé(e) air-conditioned
clinique (*f*) clinic (12)
clos(e) closed
club (*m*) nightclub (5)
cobaye (*m*) guinea-pig
Coca (*m*) cola
coco (*m*) coconut
cocotte (*f*) casserole
code: code postal (*m*) zip code (3)
cœur (*m*) heart (12)
coffre (*m*) trunk; **coffre-fort** (*m*) safe
coiffure (*f*) hairstyle
coin (*m*) corner; **au coin (de)** on the corner (of) (8)
col (*m*) pass
colère: en colère angry
collant (*m*) pantyhose, tights (8)
collection (*f*) collection (6)
Colombie (*f*) Columbia (7)
colonie (*f*) colony (11)
colonne (*f*) column
combattre[15] to fight, to combat (12)
combien how much, how many (P); **combien de** how many, how much (3); **Vous êtes combien?** How many are there (of you)? (4)
comédie (*f*) comedy (6); **comédie musicale** (*f*) musical (6)
commander[3] to order (10)
comme like, since (1), as (10); **comme ci comme ça** so-so (2)
commencer[12] to begin (2)
comment how (2); **Ça s'écrit comment?** How do you write that? (P); **Comment?** What? (P); **Comment vas-tu/allez-vous?** How are you? (P); **Comment ça va?** How is it going?, How are you? (P); **Comment dit-on... en français?** How do you say . . . in French? (P); **Comment est (sont)...** What is (are) . . . like? (1); **Comment s'appelle...?** What is . . . 's name? (4)
commerçant(e) (*m/f*) shopkeeper, merchant (10)
commerce (*m*) business
commercial : centre commercial (*m*) shopping center, mall (4)
commettre[28] to commit
commode (*f*) dresser (3)
commode convenient (3)
commodité (*f*) convenience
compact: disque compact (*m*) compact disc (3); **lecteur de disques compacts** (*m*) compact disc player (3)
compagnie (*f*) company
complet: pain complet (*m*) wholegrain bread (10)
compliqué(e) complicated (1)
composer[3]**: se composer**[3ê] **de** to be made up of (11)
compote (*f*) stewed fruit
compotier (*m*) fruit bowl
compréhension (*f*) understanding (11)
comprenant(e) including
comprendre[32] to understand (8), to include (9); **Est-ce que vous comprenez?** Do you understand? (P); **Je comprends.** I understand. (P)
compris(e) included (8)
comptabilité (*f*) accounting (1)
comptable (*mf*) accountant
compte en banque (*m*) bank account
compter[3] to count (on), to plan (7); **Comptez de zéro à trente.** Count from zero to thirty. (P)
concentrer[3]: **se concentrer**[3ê] **sur** to concentrate on (11)
concert (*m*) concert (4)
concevoir[33] to conceive
concombre (*m*) cucumber
concours (*m*) competition
concurrent(e) (*m/f*) competitor
confiance (*f*) confidence
confidence (*f*) secret
confit de canard (*m*) conserve of duck
confiture (*f*) jam (10)
conflit (*m*) conflict
confondre[6] to confuse
confortable comfortable (3)
conjoncture (*f*) situation
connaissance (*f*) acquaintance (6), knowledge
connaître[18] to know, to be familiar with (6)
connu(e) known (7)
conquérant(e) (*m/f*) conqueror
conquête (*f*) conquest
conseiller(-ère) (*m/f*) counselor, advisor
conseil (*m*) a piece of advice (9)
conservateur(-trice) conservative (11)
conserver[3] to keep
consommation (*f*) consumption, drink
consonne (*f*) consonant
constamment constantly (10)
constituer[3] to constitute, to make up
construire[17] to construct, to build
consultation (*f*) consultation, medical visit (12)
conte (*m*) story
contemporain(e) contemporary
contenir[37] to contain
content(e) happy, glad (4)
continuer[3] to continue (8)
contraire (*m*) contrary
contre against (11); **par contre** on the contrary (9)
contrebas: en contrebas de below
convenable appropriate, suitable
convenir[37] to be suitable
copain (*m*) (male) friend, pal (6)
copieux(-euse) plentiful, copious (10)
copine (*f*) (female) friend, pal (6)
coquillage (*m*) shellfish
coquilles St-Jacques (*fpl*) scallops (10)
corps (*m*) body (12)
corruption (*f*) corruption (11)
costard (*m*) suit (*familiar*)
costume (*m*) suit (8)
cote (*f*) rating
côte (*f*) coast; **côte de porc** (*f*) pork chop (10)
côté: à côté (de) next to (8); **de l'autre côté (de)** on the other side (of) (8); **voisin(e) d'à côté** (*m/f*) next door neighbor (6)
coton: en coton cotton (8)
cou (*m*) neck (12)
coucher: se coucher[3ê] to go to bed (9)
coulée (*f*) flow
couler[3] to run (*liquids*) (12)
couleur color; **De quelle couleur est (sont)...?** What color is (are) . . . ? (4)
coulis (*m*) purée
couloir (*m*) hall (8)
coup (*m*) stroke, blow; **coup de foudre** (*m*) love at first sight (9); **coup de téléphone** (*m*) telephone call
coupe (*f*) dessert dish, cutting
couper[3] to cut (12); **se couper**[3ê] to cut oneself (12)
couple (*m*) couple (9)
courant(e) present, current, common
courir[19] to run (7)
cours (*m*) class, course (P); **au cours de** in the course of; **suivre**[36] **un cours** to take a course (5)
course (*f*) errand (5); **faire**[25] **des courses** to run errands (5); **faire**[25] **les courses** to go grocery shopping (10)
court(e) short (4); **court métrage** (*m*) short film
cousin(e) (*m/f*) cousin (4)
coutume (*f*) custom
couvrir[29] to cover
crayon (*m*) pencil (P)
cravate (*f*) necktie (8)
crédit: carte de crédit (*f*) credit card (7)
créer[3] to create (11)
crème (*f*) cream
crevette (*f*) shrimp (10)
crier[3] to shout
crime (*m*) crime (11)
criminalité (*f*) crime (11)
criminel(le) (*m/f*) criminal (11)
crise cardiaque (*f*) heart attack
croc (*m*) fang
croire (à) to believe (in) (9); **je crois** I think (4)

croiser[3] to cross
croisière (*f*) cruise (8)
croissant (*m*) croissant (10)
croque-madame (*m*) toasted ham-and-cheese sandwich with egg on top
croque-monsieur (*m*) toasted ham-and-cheese sandwich
cru(e) raw
crudités (*fpl*) raw vegetables
cuiller (*f*) spoon
cuillerée (*f*) spoonful (10)
cuirassé (*m*) battleship
cuire to cook
cuisine (*f*) kitchen (3); cooking (5)
cuisinière (*f*) stove (3)
cuisson (*f*) cooking
culturel(le) cultural (4)
cuve (*f*) vat
cyclisme (*m*) cycling

D

dame (*f*) lady (1)
danger (*m*) danger (11)
dans in (2); **dans la rue...** on . . . street (8)
danser[3] to dance (2)
danseur(-euse) (*m/f*) dancer (4)
date (*f*) date (6); **Quelle date sommes-nous?** What is the date? (6); **Quelle est la date aujourd'hui?** What is the date today? (6)
daurade (*f*) sea bream
davantage more
de from (P), of (2), about; **d'abord** first (4); **D'accord!** Okay! Agreed! (2); **d'après** according to; **de bonne / mauvaise humeur** in a good / bad mood (12); **de la, de l'** some; **de l'autre côté (de)** on the other side (of) (8); **de luxe** deluxe (7); **De quelle couleur est (sont)...?** What color is (are) . . . ? (4); **de taille moyenne** medium-sized (4); **d'habitude** usually (2)
débarquer[3] to disembark
début (*m*) beginning; **au début** at first (11)
débuter[3] to start
décembre (*m*) December (6)
décennie (*f*) decade
décidément decidedly, for sure
décider[3] to decide (7); **se décider**[3ê] to make up one's mind
découper[3] to cut out
découverte (*f*) discovery
découvrir[29] to discover
décrire[3] to describe (7)
défaire[25]: **défaire ses valises** to unpack (8)
défendu(e) forbidden
défi (*m*) challenge
défini(e) definite
degré (*m*) degree (12)
dégustation (*f*) sampling
dehors outside (9)
déjà already (7)
déjeuner (*m*) lunch (7); **petit déjeuner** (*m*) breakfast (7)
déjeuner[3] to have lunch (2)
délai (*m*) delay (7)
délicieux(-euse) delicious (6)
délivrance (*f*) issue
demain tomorrow (P)
demander[3] to ask (7); **se demander**[3ê] to wonder
démanger[11] to itch (12)
demi (*m*) draft beer
demi(e) half (10); **Il est deux heures et demie.** It's half past two. (P)
démocratie (*f*) democracy (11)
démocratique democratic (11)
dent (*f*) tooth (9)
dentaire dental
départ (*m*) departure (7)
dépêcher: se dépêcher[3ê] to hurry (9)
dépendre[6] **(de)** to depend (on) (5)
dépenser[3] to spend (11)
déplier[3] to unfold
dépression (*f*) depression (11)
déprime (*f*) depression
déprimé(e) depressed
depuis since, for, from (9)
dernier(-ère) last (5)
derrière behind (3)
des some (3)
dés (*mpl*) dice
dès right after; **dès que** as soon as
désagréable unpleasant (1)
descendre[6ê] to go down, to stay (*at a hotel*), to get off (5)
désirer[3] to desire; **Vous désirez?** May I help you? (2)
désolé(e) sorry (12)
dessert (*m*) dessert (6)
desservir[4] to serve
dessin (*m*) drawing (1); **dessin animé** (*m*) cartoon (6)
dessiner[3] to draw
destin (*m*) destiny, fate
détenir[37] to hold, to possess
détente (*f*) relaxation
détenteur(-trice) (*m/f*) holder
détester[3] to hate; **se détester**[3ê] to hate each other (9)
dette (*f*) debt
deux two (P); **deux-tiers** two-thirds
deuxième second (3)
devant in front of (3)
développer[3] to develop (11); **se développer**[3ê] to develop (11)
devenir[37ê] to become (7)
deviner[3] to guess (9)
dévoiler[3] to unveil
devoir[21] to have to, should, ought to, to owe (6)
devoirs (*mpl*) homework (P)
diable (*m*) devil
diamant (*m*) diamond
dictature (*f*) dictatorship (11)
dictée (*f*) dictation
dieu (*m*) God
différemment differently (10)
différent(e) different (1)
difficile difficult (P)
difficulté (*f*) difficulty (9)
digérer[7] to digest (12)
dimanche Sunday (P)
dîner (*m*) dinner (7)
dîner[3] to have dinner, to dine (2)
diplômé(e) (*m/f*) graduate
dire[22] to say, to tell (7); **Ça te dit?** Does that sound like fun to you? (6); **Comment dit-on... en français?** How do you say . . . in French? (P); **Qu'est-ce que ça veut dire?** What does that mean? (P)
direct(e) direct (7)
discuter[3] to discuss
disparaître[18] to disappear; **disparu(e)** having disappeared, dead
disponible available
disposer[3] **de** to have available
disputer: se disputer[3ê] **(avec)** to argue (with) (9)
disque (*m*) record; **disque compact** (*m*) compact disc (3); **lecteur de disques compacts** (*m*) compact disc player (3)
distingué(e) distinguished
distraction (*f*) fun activity
divan (*m*) divan, couch (3)
diversité (*f*) diversity (11)
diviser[3] to divide; **se diviser**[3ê] **(en)** to divide (into)
divorcé(e) divorced (4)
divorcer[12] to divorce (9)
dix ten (P); **dix-huit** eighteen (P); **dix-neuf** nineteen (P); **dix-sept** seventeen (P)
doigt (*m*) finger (12); **doigt de pied** (*m*) toe (12)
domaine (*m*) estate
domestique (*mf*) servant
domestique domestic (11); **tâche domestique** (*f*) household chore (9)
domicile: les sans domicile fixe (*mpl*) homeless people (11)
dommage: c'est dommage it's a shame, what a pity (5)
donc therefore, so, thus, then (5)
données (*fpl*) data
donner[3] to give (2); **donner**[3] **à manger à** to feed (7); **Donnez-moi votre feuille de papier.** Give me your sheet of paper. (P)
dont of which, whose (11)
dormir[4] to sleep (2)
dos (*m*) back (12)
dossier (*m*) seat back
doté(e) (de) endowed (with)
douane (*f*) customs (7)
douche (*f*) shower (8)
douleur (*f*) pain, ache (12)
douloureux(-euse) painful
doute (*m*) doubt
doux (douce) sweet, soft, gentle
douzaine (*f*) dozen (10)
douze twelve (P)
drame (*m*) drama (6)
dresser[3] to set up
drogue (*f*) drug(s) (11)
droit (*m*) right (*legal*) (11); law (*field of study*); **tout droit** straight (8)
droite (*f*) right (*direction*) (8): **à droite (de)** to the right (of) (8)
du (de la, de l', des) some (6)
duc (*m*) duke

dunette (*f*) poop deck
dur(e) hard; **œuf dur** (*m*) hard-boiled egg (10)
durant during
durée (*f*) duration
durer[3] to last

E

eau (*f*) water (2)
écailler[3] to open (*shellfish*)
échange (*m*) exchange
échanger[11] to exchange
échapper[3] to escape; **s'échapper**[3ê] to escape
échelle (*f*) ladder
éclairage (*m*) lighting
éclaircie (*f*) sunny spell
éclairé(e) lighted
école (*f*) school (8)
écolo(giste) (*mf*) environmentalist
économie (*f*) economy (11); **faire des économies** to save money (7)
économique economic (11); **sciences économiques** (*fpl*) economics
écossé(e) shelled
écoute: être à l'écoute de to be listening to
écouter[3] to listen (to) (2); **Écoutez les cassettes.** Listen to the cassettes. (P)
écran (*m*) screen
écraser[3] to crush
écrire[23] to write (7); **Ça s'écrit comment?** How do you write that? (P); **Écrivez la réponse au numéro 1 de l'exercice E.** Write the answer to number 1 of exercise E. (P)
écrivain (*m*) writer
édifice (*m*) building
éducation (*f*) education (11)
éduquer[3] to educate (11)
effectuer[3] to carry out, to make
efforcer: s'efforcer[12] **(de)** to endeavor
égal(e) (*mpl* **égaux**) equal; **Ça m'est égal.** It's all the same to me.
égalité (*f*) equality (11)
égard (*m*) respect
église (*f*) church (4)
Égypte (*f*) Egypt (7)
élections (*fpl*) election(s) (11)
élément (*m*) element (11)
élevé(e) high, elevated (8)
elle she (1), her (8); **elles** they (1), them (8)
embêtant(e) annoying (3)
embrasser[3] to kiss; **s'embrasser**[3ê] to kiss, to embrace (9)
émeraude (*f*) emerald
émincé(e) thinly sliced
emmener[8] to take
emploi (*m*) employment
emporter[3] to carry away
emprunter[3] to borrow (7)
en in (P); **de temps en temps** from time to time (4); **en avance** early (6); **en coton** cotton (8); **en face (de)** across from, facing (8); **en retard** late (7); **en soie** silk (8); **en solde** on sale (8); **en vacances** on vacation (7); **être en train de...** to be busy . . . (4); **payer en espèces** to pay cash (8)
en some, about it / them, of it / them (10); **Je t'en prie.** You're welcome. (6); **Je vous en prie.** You're welcome. (2); **Qu'en penses-tu?** What do you think (about it)? (4); **s'en aller** to go away
encastrable able to be built in
enceinte (acoustique) (*f*) speaker
enceinte pregnant (12)
enchaîné(e) chained up
Enchanté(e). Delighted to meet you. (P)
encore still, again (10); **ne... pas encore** not yet (7)
endormir: s'endormir[4ê] to fall asleep (9)
endroit (*m*) place (8)
énerver[3] to irritate
enfant (*mf*) child (1)
enfer (*m*) hell
enfin finally (9)
enflé(e) swollen (12)
engager[11] to hire
englober[3] to encompass
ennemi(e) (*m/f*) enemy
ennui (*m*) trouble
ennuyer: s'ennuyer[10ê] **(de)** to get bored (with), to be bored (of) (9)
ennuyeux(-euse) boring (1)
énorme enormous
enseignement (*m*) teaching
enseigner[3] to teach (9)
ensemble together (2)
ensuite next, then (4)
entendre[6] to hear (7); **s'entendre**[6ê] to get along (9)
entier(-ère) entire, whole
entouré(e) (de) surrounded (by) (11)
entre between (3), among
entrée (*f*) first course (10), entry ticket, entrance
entrer[3ê] **(dans)** to enter, to go in (5)
envahir[5] to invade
envers towards (9)
envie: avoir[1] **envie de** to feel like, to desire (5)
environ around, about (10)
environnement (*m*) environment (11)
environs (*mpl*) surrounding area
envisager[11] to contemplate
envoûtant(e) bewitching
envoyer[24] to send
épais(se) thick
épaule (*f*) shoulder (12)
épicé(e) spicy
épicerie (*f*) grocer's shop (10)
épineux(-euse) thorny, prickly
éplucher[3] to peel
époque (*f*) time period (9); **à cette époque-là** at that time, in those days (9)
épouser[3] to marry
épouvante: film d'épouvante (*m*) horror movie (6)
époux (épouse) (*m/f*) spouse
épuisé(e) exhausted (8)
équestre: centre équestre (*m*) riding school
équilibré(e) balanced
équilibriste (*mf*) tightrope walker
équipe (*f*) team
équipé(e) fitted out
équipée (*f*) venture
équitation (*f*) horse-riding
ériger[11] to build, to erect
escalade (*f*) (rock)climbing
escale (*f*) stopover (7)
escalier (*m*) stairs, staircase (3)
escargot (*m*) snail
escarre (*f*) bedsore
espace (*m*) space
espadon (*m*) swordfish
Espagne (*f*) Spain (7)
espagnol (*m*) Spanish (P)
espagnol(e) Spanish
espèce (*f*) sort; **payer**[10] **en espèces** to pay cash (8)
espérer[7] to hope (9)
espoir (*m*) hope
esprit (*m*) mind, spirit
essayage (*m*) fitting; **cabine d'essayage** (*f*) fitting room (8)
essayer[10] to try on (8); **essayer**[11] **(de faire)** to try (to do) (9)
essentiel(le) essential (12)
est (*m*) east
est-ce que (*question marker*); **Est-ce que vous comprenez?** Do you understand? (P)
estival(e) summer, **station estivale** (*f*) summer resort (8)
et and (P)
établir[5] to establish (11)
établissement (*m*) establishment
étage (*m*) floor (3); **au premier étage** on the second floor (3); **à l'étage** on the same floor
étagère (*f*) shelf, bookcase (3)
étalon (*m*) stallion
étape (*f*) stopping place
état (*m*) state; **États-Unis** (*mpl*) United States (7)
été (*m*) summer (5); **en été** in summer (5)
éternuer[3] to sneeze (12)
étoile (*f*) star
étonner[3] to surprise, to amaze (10)
étranger(ère) foreign (7); **à l'étranger** abroad (7)
être[2] to be (1); **c'est** it's, that's (P); **être à** to belong to (8); **être en train de...** to be busy . . . (4) **je suis** I am (P); **Comment est (sont)...** What is (are) . . . like? (1); **le français est...** French is . . . (P); **Nous sommes le...** Today is . . . . (6); **Nous sommes six.** There are six of us. (4); **Quelle date sommes-nous?** What is the date? (6); **vous êtes** you are (P)
être humain (*m*) human being
étroit(e) tight (8)
études (*fpl*) studies (1)
étudiant(e) (*m/f*) student (P)
étudier[3] to study (1); **Étudiez les mots de vocabulaire.** Study the vocabulary words. (P)
Europe (*f*) Europe (7)
européen(ne) European (4)
eux them (8)
évader: s'évader[3ê] to escape
évasion (*f*) escape

événement (*m*) event
évidemment of course, obviously (10)
éviter[3] to avoid (10)
examen (*m*) test, exam (1)
excentrique eccentric (11)
exception (*f*) exception (11)
exclu(e) excluded
exercice (*m*) exercise (P)
exotique exotic (7)
expliquer[3] to explain
exploser[3] to explode
exposition (*f*) exposition (4); **matériel d'exposition** (*m*) display items
express (*m*) expresso (2)
exprimer[3] to express
extra great, terrific
extrait (*m*) excerpt
extroverti(e) outgoing, extrovert (1)

F

face: en face (de) across from, facing (8); **face à** across from
facile easy (P)
facilement easily (9)
façon (*f*) way
faculté (fac) (*f*) faculty, campus
faillir: j'ai failli tomber I almost fell
faim (*f*) hunger (11); **avoir**[1] **faim** to be hungry (5)
faire[25] to do (2), to make (5) **Ça fait... francs.** That's . . .francs. (2); **Ça ne se fait pas.** That is not done! (10); **faire attention (à)** to pay attention (to) (10); **faire de la planche à voile** to go windsurfing (7); **faire de la plongée sous-marine** to go scuba diving (7); **faire de l'exercice** to exercise (5); **faire des haltères** to lift weights (10); **faire du bateau** to go boating (5); **faire du camping** to go camping (5); **faire du jardinage** to garden (5); **faire du jogging** to go jogging (2); **faire du shopping** to go shopping (4); **faire du ski (nautique)** to go (water-)skiing (5); **faire du sport** to play sports (5); **faire la connaissance de** to meet, to make the acquaintance of (6); **faire la cuisine** to cook (5); **faire les courses** to go grocery shopping (10); **faire le tour du monde** to take a trip around the world (8); **faire mal** to hurt (12); **faire ses valises** to pack one's bags (7); **faire une boum** to give a party (6); **faire une croisière** to go on a cruise (8); **faire une promenade** to go for a walk (5); **faire un pique-nique** to have a picnic (7); **faire un tour** to go for a ride / walk / run (5); **faire un voyage** to take a trip (5); **Faites les devoirs dans le cahier.** Do the homework in the notebook. (P); **Il fait beau (chaud / du soleil / du vent / frais / froid / mauvais).** It's nice (hot / sunny / windy / cool / cold / bad). (5); **Je fais du 42.** I wear a 42. (8); **Quel temps fait-il?** What's the weather like? (5); **tout à fait** completely (9)
faisan (*m*) pheasant
falloir[26]**: il faut...** it is necessary . . . , one must . . . , one should . . . (7), **il ne faut pas** one shouldn't . . . (7)
fameux(-euse) famous (6)
familial(e) (*mpl* **familiaux**) family
familier(-ère) familiar, informal
familièrement colloquially
famille (*f*) family (P)
famine (*f*) famine, starvation (11)
fanfaronnade (*f*) boasting
fantastique fantastic; **film fantastique** (*m*) fantasy movie
farci(e) stuffed
farine (*f*) flour
fast-food (*m*) fastfood (restaurant) (2)
fatigué(e) tired (4)
faute (*f*) lack
fauteuil (*m*) armchair (3)
faux (fausse) false
favoriser[3] to favor, to further
femme (*f*) woman (1), wife (4); **femme d'affaires** (*f*) businesswoman (4)
fenêtre (*f*) window (3)
fenouil (*m*) fennel
fer (*m*) iron
férié(e): jour férié (*m*) holiday
ferme (*f*) farm
fermer[3] to close (2); **Fermez votre livre.** Close your book. (P)
fête (*f*) holiday, celebration; **fête du travail** (*f*) Labor Day (6); **Fête nationale** (*f*) national holiday (6)
fêter[3] to celebrate (6)
feu (*m*) fire
feuille de papier (*f*) sheet of paper (P)
feuilleté(e) flaky (*pastry*)
février (*m*) February (6)
ficelle (*f*) string
fiche (*f*) form
fier(-ère) proud
fièvre (*f*) fever (12)
figure (*f*) face (9)
fille (*f*) girl (1); daughter (4)
fillette (*f*) little girl
film (*m*) movie (2)
fils (*m*) son (4)
fin (*f*) end (8)
financier(-ère) financial
finir[5] **(de faire)** to finish (doing) (10)
finition (*f*) finishing
fixe fixed (10); **sans domicile fixe** (*mpl*) homeless people (11)
flamboyer[10] to flame up
fleur (*f*) flower (4)
fleuri(e) flowery
fleuve (*m*) river
flotter[3] to float
foie (*m*) liver (12)
fois (*f*) time, occasion (2); **à la fois** at the same time
folk (*m*) folk music (6)
fonction (*f*) function; **en fonction de** according to; **voiture de fonction** (*f*) company car
fonctionner[3] to function, to work
fond (*m*) bottom
fondre[6] to melt
football (*m*) soccer (2)
forcément necessarily, inevitably
forêt (*f*) forest
forfait (*m*) set price
forme (*f*) shape
formidable fantastic
formulaire (*m*) form
formule (*f*) formula, system
fort(e) strong (10)
fou (folle) crazy
foudre: coup de foudre (*m*) love at first sight (9)
fouler: se fouler[3é] **la cheville** to sprain one's ankle (12)
four (*m*) oven
fourrure (*f*) fur
foyer des étudiants (*m*) student center (1)
fragile fragile (11)
fragmenté(e) fragmented (11)
fraîcheur (*f*) freshness, coolness
frais (fraîche) fresh (10); **Il fait frais.** It's cool. (5)
fraise (*f*) strawberry (6)
framboise (*f*) raspberry
franc (*m*) franc (2)
français(e) French (1)
France (*f*) France (7)
franchir[5] to cross
francophone French-speaking (7)
frapper[3] to strike
frénésie (*f*) frenzy
fréquemment frequently (9)
fréquenter[3] to frequent, to hang out at
frère (*m*) brother (4)
frire to fry
frisé(e) curly
frisée (*f*) curly endive
frisson (*m*) shiver, chill (12)
frites (*fpl*) French fries (2)
frivole frivolous (1)
froid(e) cold; **avoir**[1] **froid** to be cold (5); **Il fait froid.** It's cold. (5)
fromage (*m*) cheese (6); **sandwich au fromage** (*m*) cheese sandwich (2)
frontière (*f*) border
fruit (*m*) fruit (6); **fruits de mer** (*mpl*) seafood (10); **jus de fruits** (*m*) fruit juice (2)
fuir to flee, to run away
fumée (*f*) smoke
fumer[3] to smoke (3)
fumerolle (*f*) wisp of smoke
fumeur: section (non-)fumeur (*f*) (non-)smoking section (7)
furieux(-euse) furious (12)
fusiller[3] to shoot

G

gagner[3] to win (2), to reach
gai(e) gay, lively
gang (*m*) gang (11)
garage (*m*) garage (4)
garantir[5] to guarantee
garçon (*m*) boy (1), waiter (2)
garder[3] to keep

garni(e) served with vegetables
garniture (*f*) garnish
gaspiller[3] to waste (11)
gâteau (*m*) cake (6)
gauche (*f*) left (8); **à gauche (de)** to the left (of) (8)
gaulois(e) from Gaul (*ancient name for the region of modern France*)
géant (*m*) giant
gêné(e) embarrassed (10)
général: en général generally (2)
génie (*m*) genius
genou (*m*) knee (12)
genre (*m*) kind, type (6)
gens (*mpl*) people (1)
gestion (*f*) management
gibier (*m*) wild game
glace (*f*) ice cream (6); ice
glacier (*m*) ice cream shop
global(e) (*m*) (*pl* **globaux**) global (11)
gloire (*f*) glory
goéland (*m*) seagull
gommage (*m*) rubbing out
gorge (*f*) throat (12)
gosse (*mf*) kid
gouffre (*m*) abyss
goulu(e) gluttonous
gousse (*f*) clove
goût (*m*) taste
goûter[3] to taste (7)
goutte (*f*) drop
gouvernement (*m*) government (11)
grâce à thanks to
gramme (*m*) gram (10)
grand(e) big, large (1)
Grande-Bretagne (*f*) Great Britain (7)
grandeur nature (*f*) life-sized
grandir[5] to grow up, to get big (10)
grand-mère (*f*) grandmother (4)
grand-père (*m*) grandfather (4)
grands-parents (*mpl*) grandparents (4)
gras(se) (*f*) fatty (12); **en caractères gras** boldfaced; **matière grasse** (*f*) fat (12)
grasset(te) chubby
gratuit(e) free
gratuitement without charge
grave serious, grave (11)
gravir[5] to climb
Grèce (*f*) Greece
grillé(e) grilled, **pain grillé(e)** toast (10)
grimpe (*f*) climb (*familiar*)
grimper[3] to climb
grippe (*f*) influenza (flu) (12)
gris(e) gray (4)
gronder[3] to rumble, to grumble; to scold
grondin (*m*) gurnard
gros(se) big (4)
grossir[5] to get fat, to gain weight (10)
gruyère (*m*) gruyère cheese
gouvernement (*m*) government (11)
guadeloupéen(ne) Guadelupian (7)
guépard (*m*) cheetah
guérir[5] to cure, to heal (12); **se guérir**[5é] to get well (12)
guerre (*f*) war (9)
guide (*m*) guide, guidebook (7)
guitare (*f*) guitar (9)

H

habiller: s'habiller[3é] to get dressed (9)
habitation (*f*) residence
habiter[3] to live (2); **j'habite à** (+ *city*) I live in (+ *city*) (P)
habitude (*f*) habit; **d'habitude** usually (2)
habituel(le) customary, usual
***haché(e)** chopped (up)
***haine** (*f*) hatred (11)
haltères: faire[25] **des haltères** to lift weights (10)
***hamburger** (*m*) hamburger (10)
***hard rock** (*m*) hard rock (6)
***haricots verts** (*mpl*) green beans (10)
***hasard: par hasard** by chance (9)
***haut: dans les hauts** high above; **(tout) en haut** at the (very) top
***haut(e)** high
***hauteur** (*f*) height
hébergement (*m*) accommodation
hériter[3] to inherit
héritier(-ère): prince héritier (*m*) crown prince
hésiter[3] to hesitate
heure (*f*) hour; **à l'heure** on time (7); **À tout à l'heure.** See you in a little while. (P); **Il est... heure(s).** It's . . . o'clock.; **tout à l'heure** in a little while (P), a little while ago; **Quelle heure est-il?** What time is it? (P)
heureusement luckily
heureux(-euse) happy (9)
hier yesterday (5)
hilarant(e) hilarious
histoire (*f*) history (1); story (7)
historique historical (7)
hiver (*m*) winter (5); **en hiver** in winter (5)
***homard** (*m*) lobster (10)
homme (*m*) man (1); **homme d'affaires** (*m*) businessman(4)
homogène homogeneous (11)
honnête honest
honneur: être[2] **à l'honneur** to have the place of honor
hôpital (*m*) hospital (8)
horrible horrible (6)
***hors-** outside of (9); **dimensions *hors-tout** (*fpl*) overall dimensions; ***hors-d'œuvre** (*m*) appetizer (10)
hôte (*m*) host
hôtel (*m*) hotel (5)
hôtelier(-ère) (*m/f*) hotel-keeper
huile (*f*) oil (10)
huit eight (P)
huître (*f*) oyster (10)
humain(e): sciences humaines (*f*) humanities
humeur (*f*) mood (12); **de bonne / mauvaise humeur** in a good / bad mood (12)

I

ici here (P); **par ici** this way (10)
idéaliste idealistic (1)
idée (*f*) idea (2)
idem ditto
identité: carte d'identité (*f*) identity card (7)
il he, it (1); **il faut...** it is necessary . . . , one must . . . , one should . . . (7); **il ne faut pas** one shouldn't . . . (7); **ils** they (1); **il y a** there is, there are (3) ago (5); **s'il vous plaît** please (P); **Qu'est-ce qu'il y a?** What's the matter? (10)
île (*f*) island (7)
immeuble (*m*) apartment building (3)
immobilier(-ère) real estate
impatient(e) impatient (1)
imperméable (*m*) raincoat (8)
important(e) important (12)
importer: n'importe où (just) anywhere (3); **n'importe quel(le)** (just) any; **n'importe qui** (just) anyone; **n'importe quoi** (just) anything
impressionnant(e) impressive
inattendu(e) unexpected
incliné(e) leaning
inclus(e) included
indicatif régional (*m*) area code
indigène native
indigestion (*f*) indigestion (12)
indiquer[3] to show, to indicate (8)
inégalité (*f*) inequality (11)
infection (*f*) infection (12)
infirmier(-ère) (*m/f*) nurse (4)
influencer: s'influencer[12é] to influence each other (11)
informatique (*f*) computer science (1)
infusion (*f*) herbal tea
innover[3] to innovate
inquiétant(e) disturbing
insister[3] to insiste (7)
insonorisé(e) soundproofed
instabilité (*f*) instability (11)
intellectuel(le) intellectual (1)
intelligent(e) intelligent (1)
intention: avoir[1] **l'intention de** to plan on, to intend to (5)
interdit(e) forbidden
intéressant(e) interesting (P)
intéresser: s'intéresser[3é] **à** to be interested in (9)
intérieur: à l'intérieur inside (10)
interprète (*mf*) interpreter
interrompre[6] to interrupt
introverti(e) introverted (1)
invité(e) (*m/f*) guest
inviter[3] **(à)** to invite (to) (2)
irréel(le) unreal
irriter[3] to irritate
Israël (*m*) Israel (7)
Italie (*f*) Italy (7)
italien(ne) Italian (4)
itinéraire (*m*) itinerary (7)

J

jaillir[5] to shoot out
jamais: ne... jamais never (2)
jambe (*f*) leg (12)
jambon (*m*) ham (6)

janvier (*m*) January (6)
Japon (*m*) Japan (7)
japonais(e) Japanese (4)
jardin (*m*) garden (4)
jardinage (*m*) gardening (5)
jardiner[3] to garden
jaune yellow (4)
jazz (*m*) jazz (3)
je I (P); **Je vous en prie.** You're welcome. (2)
jean (*m*) jeans (8)
jet (*m*) stream
jeu (*m*) game (2); **jeu de société** (*m*) board game; **jeu vidéo** (*m*) video game (2)
jeudi Thursday (P)
jeune young (1); **jeunes** (*mpl/fpl*) young people
jeunesse (*f*) youth (9); **auberge de jeunesse** (*f*) youth hostel (8)
jogging (*m*) jogging outfit (8); **faire**[25] **du jogging** to go jogging (2)
joie (*f*) joy
joindre: se joindre à to join
joli(e) pretty (1)
jouer[3] **à** to play (*a sport or game*) (2); **jouer**[3] **de** to play (*music*) (9)
jour (*m*) day (5); **tous les jours** every day (2)
journal (*m*) newspaper, journal (7)
journée (*f*) day, daytime (2); **toute la journée** the whole day (2)
juillet (*m*) July (6)
juin (*m*) June (6)
jumeau (jumelle) (*m/f*) twin; **sœur jumelle** (*f*) twin sister (1)
jupe (*f*) skirt (8)
jus (*m*) juice (2); **jus de fruits** (*m*) fruit juice (2)
jusqu'à until, up to (6)
juste fair; **juste là** right there (8)

K

kilo kilo (*2.2 pounds*) (10)

L

la the (1), her, it (6)
là there (3); **là-bas** over there
laboratoire: laboratoire de langues (*m*) language laboratory (1)
lac (*m*) lake (4)
laid(e) ugly (1)
laisser[3] to leave (11), to let; **laissez-passer** (*m*) pass
lait (*m*) milk (10); **café au lait** coffee with milk (2)
laitier(-ère) milk, dairy (10)
laitue (*f*) lettuce (10)
langouste (*f*) spiny lobster
langoustines (*fpl*) scampi
langue (*f*) language (1); tongue
largeur (*f*) width
lavabo (*m*) washbasin, sink (8)
lave (*f*) lava
laver[3] to wash (9); **se laver**[3ê] to wash (up) (9)
le the (1), him (6); **Je suis en cours le lundi.** I'm in class on Mondays. (P); **le matin** in the morning, mornings, **le week-end** on the weekend (2)
lecteur: lecteur de disques compacts (*m*) compact disc player (3)
lecture (*f*) reading
léger(-ère) light (10)
léguer[3] to leave, to bequeath
légume (*m*) vegetable (10)
lendemain (*m*) the next day (8)
lentement slowly (10)
lequel (laquelle, lesquels, lesquelles) which one(s)
les the (1); them (6);
lessive (*f*) laundry (5)
lettre (*f*) letter (7); **lettres** (*fpl*) study of literature
leur their (3); (to, for) them (7)
lever: Levez-vous. Get up. (P); **se lever**[8ê] to get up (9)
libéral(e) (*mpl* **libéraux**) liberal (11)
liberté (*f*) freedom (12)
librairie (*f*) bookstore (4)
libre free (2)
lier[3] to connect
lieu (*m*) place; **avoir**[1] **lieu** to take place (9)
ligne (*f*) figure (10); line
limande (*f*) dab
liquide (*m*) liquid (12)
lire[27] to read (2); **Lisez la page 21.** Read page 21. (P)
lissé: au lissé until smooth
lit (*m*) bed (3)
literie (*f*) bedding
litre (*m*) liter (*approximately one quart*) (10)
littérature (*f*) literature (1)
livraison (*f*) delivery
livre (*m*) book (P)
livre (*f*) pound, half-kilo (10)
local(e) (*mpl* **locaux**) local (7)
location (*f*) rental
logement (*m*) housing, lodging (11)
loi (*f*) law (11)
loin (de) far (from) (3)
loisir (*m*) leisure activity
Londres London (7)
long: le long de along (7)
long(ue) long (4)
longtemps a long time (5)
lors de at the time of
lorsque when
louer[3] to rent (4)
loup (*m*) wolf
loyer (*m*) rent (3)
lui (to, for) him (7)
lundi Monday (P)
lune (*f*) moon
lunettes (*fpl*) glasses (4)
lutter[3] **(contre)** to struggle (against), to fight (11)
luxe (*m*) luxury; **de luxe** deluxe (7)
lycée (*m*) secondary school (8)

M

macérer[7] to soak
madame (Mme) madam (Mrs.) (P)
mademoiselle (Mlle) miss (P)
magasin (*m*) store, shop (4)
magie (*f*) magic
magnétoscope (*m*) video cassette recorder (3)
magnifique magnificent, fantastic (7)
majoré(e) with a surcharge
mai (*m*) May (6)
maigrir[5] to slim down, to lose weight (10)
maillot de bain (*m*) swimsuit (8)
main (*f*) hand (9)
maintenant now (P)
maintien (*m*) maintenance
mairie (*f*) town hall
mais but (P)
maison (*f*) house (3); **à la maison** at home (P)
maître (*m*) master
maîtrise (*f*) master's degree
mal (*m*) bad, evil; **avoir**[1] **mal (à)** to ache (12); **faire**[25] **mal** to hurt (12)
mal badly (2); **mal à l'aise** ill at ease
malade (*mf*) sick person
malade ill, sick (4)
maladie (*f*) illness (11)
malheureusement unfortunately (5)
malheureux(-euse) unhappy (9)
malhonnête dishonest
malnutrition (*f*) malnutrition (11)
mamie (*f*) granny
mandat (*m*) money order
manège (*m*) merry-go-round
manger[11] to eat (2); **donner**[3] **à manger à** to feed (7); **salle à manger** (*f*) dining room (3)
manière (*f*) manner, way
manifestation sportive (*f*) sports event
manque (*m*) lack (11)
manquer[3] to miss, to lack
manteau (*m*) (full-length) coat (8)
manuscrit (*m*) manuscript
maquillage (*m*) make-up
maquiller: se maquiller[3ê] to put on make-up
marchand(e) (*m/f*) merchant, shopkeeper
marché (*m*) market (8)
marcher[3] to work, to walk, to march
mardi Tuesday (P)
maréchal (*m*) marshall
mari (*m*) husband (4)
mariage (*m*) marriage
marié(e) married (1)
marier : se marier[3ê] **(avec)** to get married (to) (9)
marinier(-ère): moules marinières (*f*) mussels cooked with onions
marketing (*m*) marketing (1)
marque (*f*) brand
marquer[3] to mark, to indicate
marron (*inv*) chestnut brown (4)
mars (*m*) March (6)
masque (*m*) mask
matériel d'exposition (*m*) display items
mathématiques (*fpl*) mathematics (1)
matière grasse (*f*) fat (12)

matin (*m*) morning (P); **À huit heures du matin.** At eight o'clock in the morning. (P)
matinée (*f*) morning hours
mauvais(e) bad (4); **Il fait mauvais.** The weather's bad. (5)
me (to, for) me (7), myself (9); **Ça me plaît!** I like it! (6)
méchant(e) mean (1)
méconnu(e) unrecognized
médaille (*f*) medal
médecin (*m*) doctor, physician (4)
médical(e) (*mpl* **médicaux**) medical (11)
médicaments (*mpl*) medicine (12)
médiocre mediocre (10)
méfiance (*f*) mistrust
meilleur(e) better, best (3)
même same (1); **moi-même** myself; **quand même** all the same
menacer[12] to threaten
ménage (*m*) housework (5), household (9)
ménager(-ère) household
mener[8] to lead
menthe (*f*) mint
mentir[4] to lie
menu (*m*) menu (10)
mer (*f*) sea (7); **bord de mer** (*m*) seaside
merci thank you (P)
mercredi Wednesday (P)
mère (*f*) mother (4)
méritoire deserving
merveilleux(-euse) marvellous
message (*m*) message (11)
métier (*m*) occupation
métrage: court métrage (*m*) short film
métro (*m*) subway (8)
mettre[28] to put (on), to place (8); **Mets...!** Put . . . ! (3); **mettre**[28] **la table** to set the table; **mise en bouteille** bottled; **mise en relief** highlighted, accentuated; **se mettre**[28ê] **d'accord** to come to an agreement
meuble (*m*) piece of furniture
meublé(e) furnished
meurtre (*m*) murder (11)
meurtrier (*m*) murderer (11)
meurtrière (*f*) murderess (11)
Mexico Mexico City (7)
Mexique (*m*) Mexico (7)
mi- mid-, half-
midi (*m*) noon (P)
mie: pain de mie (*m*) soft sandwich bread
mieux better (2); **il vaut mieux** it's better, you had better (12); **J'aime mieux** I prefer (2)
mille one thousand (3)
millénaire (*m*) one thousand years
million: un million (de) (*m*) one million (3)
mince thin
minéral(e) (*mpl* **minéraux**): **eau minérale** (*f*) mineral water (2)
minitel (*m*) French electronic mail and information system
minuit (*m*) midnight (P)
minute (*f*) minute; **il y a quelques minutes** a few minutes ago (5)
miroir (*m*) mirror
mise en tension (*f*) on/off switch
mobile (*m*) motive
mode (*f*) fashion
moderne modern (1)
moi me (1); **chez moi** at my house (3); **Donnez-moi votre feuille de papier.** Give me your sheet of paper. (P)
moindre: le moindre the least
moins (de)... que less . . . than (1); fewer . . . than (10); **Il est trois heures moins le quart.** It's a quarter to three. (P); **le moins** the least (8)
mois (*m*) month (3); **par mois** per month (3)
moitié (*f*) half (11)
moment: à ce moment-là at that time (10); **au dernier moment** at the last minute (7); **Un moment!** One moment! (6)
mon (ma, mes) my (3); **ma famille** my family (P)
monde (*m*) world (8); **faire**[25] **le tour du monde** to take a trip around the world (8); **tout le monde** everybody, everyone (4)
mondial(e) (*mpl* **mondiaux**) world(-wide) (11)
monnaie (*f*) change (2); money
monsieur (M.) mister (Mr.), sir (P); **monsieur** (*m*) man
montagne (*f*) mountain (7)
monter[3ê] to go up (3); to get on (5)
montrer[3] to show (7)
morceau (*m*) piece (10)
mort (*f*) death; **peine de mort** (*f*) death penalty, capital punishment (11)
mort(e) dead (4)
Moscou Moscow (4)
mot (*m*) word (P)
moules marinières (*fpl*) mussels cooked with onions
moulin (*m*) mill
mourant(e) dying
mourir to die (6); **Il/Elle est mort(e)** He/She died. He/She is dead. (6)
moustache (*f*) mustache (4)
moutarde (*f*) mustard
mouvement (*m*) movement (11)
moyen (*m*) means (8); **moyen de transport** (*m*) means of transportation (8)
moyen(ne) medium (4); **de taille moyenne** medium-sized (4); **Moyen-Orient** (*m*) Middle East
moyenne (*f*) average
muet(te) silent
mur (*m*) wall (3)
musée (*m*) museum (4)
musicien(ne) (*m/f*) musician (4)
musique (*f*) music (1)

N

nager[11] to swim (4)
naissance (*f*) birth (9)
naître to be born (6); **Il/Elle est né(e).** He/She was born. (6)
nationalité (*f*) nationality (3)
naturaliste (*mf*) nudist
nature (*f*) nature; **grandeur nature** (*f*) life-sized; **omelette nature** (*f*) plain omelet
naturel(le) natural (11)
nautique: ski nautique water-skiing (5)
navette (*f*) shuttle
navire (*m*) ship
ne: je ne comprends pas I don't understand (P); **ne... aucun(e)** none, not one (9); **ne... jamais** never (2); **ne... ni... ni...** neither . . . nor (12); **ne... nulle part** nowhere (12); **ne... pas (du tout)** not (at all) (1); **ne... pas encore** not yet (7); **ne... personne** nobody, no one (12); **ne... plus** no more, no longer (10); **ne... que** only (7); **ne... rien** nothing (5); **ne... rien que** nothing but (11); **n'est-ce pas?** right? (1); **n'importe où** (just) anywhere (3)
nécessaire necessary (12)
néerlandais(e) Dutch
négliger[11] to neglect
négociant(e) (*m/f*) merchant
neige (*f*) snow
neiger[11] to snow (5)
nerf (*m*) nerve; **nerfs à vif** nerves on edge
nettement clearly
neuf nine (P)
neuf (neuve) brand new
neveu (*m*) nephew (4)
nez (*m*) nose (12)
ni: ne... ni... ni... neither . . . nor (12)
nièce (*f*) niece (4)
niveau (*m*) level
Noël (*m*) Christmas (6)
noir(e) black (4)
nom (*m*) name (3)
nombreux(-euse) numerous
nommer[3] to name
non no (P), not; **non plus** neither (3)
nord (*m*) north; **Amérique du Nord** (*f*) North America (7)
note (*f*) grade, note; **régler**[7] **la note** to pay the bill (8)
noter[3] to note, to notice
notre (*pl* **nos**) our (3)
nourriture (*f*) food, nourishment (11)
nous we (1); (to, for) us (7); **avec nous** with us (2); **Nous sommes le...** Today is . . . (6); **Nous sommes six.** There are six of us. (4)
nouveau (nouvel, nouvelle) new (4)
novembre (*m*) November (6)
noyau (*m*) pit
nu(e) naked
nuageux(-euse) cloudy
nuisible harmful
nuit (*f*) night (5)
nul(le) zero, really bad (9); **ne... nulle part** nowhere (12)
numéro (*m*) number (P)
numéroté(e) numbered

obéir[5] **(à)** to obey (10)
obligeance (*f*) kindness
obtenir[37] to get, to obtain (7)
occasion: d'occasion second-hand
occupé(e) busy (6)

occuper[3] to occupy; **s'occuper**[3ê] **de** to take care of (9)
octobre (*m*) October (6)
odeur (*f*) smell, odor
œil (*pl* **yeux**) (4) (*m*) eye (12)
œuf (*m*) egg (10)
œuvre (*f*) work
office de tourisme (*m*) tourist office (7)
offrir[29] to offer (10)
oignon (*m*) onion (10)
oiseau (*m*) bird
omelette (*f*) omelet (10)
on one, they, we, people (4); **Comment dit-on... en français?** How do you say . . . in French? (P); **On...?** Shall we . . . ? (2)
oncle (*m*) uncle (4)
onze eleven (P)
optimiste optimistic (1)
or (*m*) gold
orange (*inv*) orange (6)
ordinateur (*m*) computer (2)
ordonnance (*f*) prescription (12)
ordre (*m*) order
oreille (*f*) ear (12)
organiser[3] to organize; **s'organiser**[3ê] to get organized
originaire de coming from
os (*m*) bone
ou or (P)
où where (2); **n'importe où** (just) anywhere (3)
oublier[3] to forget (7)
ouest (*m*) west
oui yes (P)
outre-mer overseas
ouverture (*f*) opening
ouvrir[29] to open; **Ouvrez votre livre à la page 23.** Open your book to page 23. (P).

P

page (*f*) page (P)
paiement (*m*) payment
pain (*m*) bread (6); **pain au chocolat** (*m*) croissant with chocolate filling (10); **pain grillé** toast (10)
paix (*f*) peace (11)
palourde (*f*) clam
pantalon (*m*) pants (8)
papier: feuille de papier (*f*) sheet of paper (P)
Pâques (*fpl*) Easter (6)
par per (3); by (8); **par contre** on the other hand (9); **par *hasard** by chance (9); **par ici** this way (10); **par terre** on the ground (7)
paradis (*m*) paradise, heaven
paraître[18] to appear
parapente (*f*) paragliding
parapluie (*m*) umbrella (8)
parc (*m*) park (4)
parce que because (P)
parents (*mpl*) parents (4)
paresseux(-euse) lazy (1)
parfait(e) perfect (2)
parfois sometimes (10)
parking (*m*) parking lot (8)
parler[3] **(de)** to talk (about), to speak (about), (2); **je parle** I speak (P); **se parler**[3ê] to talk to each other (9)
parmi among
parole (*f*) word, lyric (11)
parsemer[8] to sprinkle
part: ne... nulle part nowhere (12); **quelque part** somewhere (12)
partager[11] to share (3)
partenaire (*mf*) partner
participer[3] **(à)** to participate (in) (11)
partie part (*f*); **en partie** partially
partir[4ê] **(de... pour)** to leave (from . . . for), to go away (5); **à partir de** starting from
partout everywhere (3)
pas not (P); **je ne comprends pas** I don't understand (P); **ne... pas (du tout)** not (at all) (1); **ne... pas encore** not yet (7)
passé(e) past (5)
passeport (*m*) passport (7)
passer[3] to spend, to pass (2); **passer**[3ê] **chez** to pass by the house of (6); **passer**[3] **un film** to show a movie (6); **se passer**[3ê] to happen (9)
passe-temps (*m*) pastime
passion (*f*) passion (4)
pâte (*f*) paste
pâté (*m*) meat spread (6)
patient(e) (*m/f*) patient (12)
patient(e) patient (1)
patin à roulettes (*m*) roller skate
pâtisserie (*f*) pastry shop (10), pastry (10)
patrimoine (*m*) patrimony
patron(ne) (*m/f*) owner, boss (10)
pauvre poor (11)
pauvreté (*f*) poverty (11)
pavé (*m*) thick slice
payant(e) not free
payer[10] to pay (7)
pays (*m*) country (3)
paysage (*m*) countryside (7)
peau (*f*) skin (12)
pêche (*f*) peach (10), fishing
pêcheur (*m*) fisherman
peine de mort (*f*) death penalty (11)
pendant during, for (5); **pendant que** while (9)
penser[3] to think (2); **je pense que** I think that (P)
pension (*f*) room and board
perdre[6] to lose, to waste (*time*) (7)
père (*m*) father (4)
permettre[28] **(de)** to permit, to allow (8)
Pérou (*m*) Peru (7)
persil (*m*) parsley
personnage (*m*) character
personne (*f*) person (8); **ne... personne** nobody, no one (12)
pessimiste pessimistic (1)
petit(e) small, little (1); **petit ami** (*m*) boyfriend (4); **petite amie** (*f*) girlfriend (4); **petite annonce** (*f*) classified ad (9); **petit déjeuner** (*m*) breakfast (7); **petit-enfant** (*m*) grandchild; **petits pois** (*mpl*) peas (10)
peu little (1); **à peu près** approximately
peur: avoir[1] **peur (de)** to be afraid (of), to fear (5)
peut-être perhaps, maybe (2)
pharmacie (*f*) pharmacy (8)
pharmacien(ne) (*m/f*) pharmacist (4)
philosophe (*mf*) philosopher
philosophie (*f*) philosophy (1)
photo (*f*) photo (4)
phrase (*f*) sentence (P)
physique (*f*) physics (1)
physique physical
piano (*m*) piano (9)
pièce (*f*) room (3)
pied (*m*) foot (12); **aller**[13ê] **à pied** to walk, to go on foot (8); **doigt de pied** toe (12)
pincée (*f*) pinch
pique-nique (*m*) picnic (7)
piqûre (*f*) shot (12)
piscine (*f*) swimming pool (4)
pitié (*f*) pity
placard (*m*) closet (3)
place (*f*) square, place (8); **Retournez à votre place.** Return to your place(s). (P)
plage (*f*) beach (4)
plaire to please (7); **Ça me plaît!** I like it! (6); **s'il vous plaît** please (P)
plaisance (*f*) pleasure
plaisant(e) pleasant
plaisir (*m*) pleasure (6)
plan (*m*) map (7), level; **plan d'eau** (*m*) stretch of water
planche à voile (*f*) windsurfing (7)
plante (*f*) plant (3)
plaquer[3] to jilt, to dump
plaque tournante (*f*) turntable, hub
plat (*m*) dish (10)
plat(e) flat; **œuf au plat** (*m*) fried egg
plateau (*m*) tray
platine (*f*) turntable
plein(e) full; **de plein air** outdoor (4); **plein de** full of, a lot of (6)
pleur (*m*) tear, sobbing
pleurer[3] to cry
pleuvoir[30] to rain (5)
plongée sous-marine (*f*) scuba diving (7)
plonger[11] to dive, to plunge
pluie (*f*) rain
plupart: la plupart de (*f*) the majority of (9)
plus: ne... plus (de) no more, no longer (10); **non plus** neither (3); **plus... que** more . . . than (1); **plus de... (que)** more . . . (than) (10); **plus tard** later (4)
plusieurs several (11)
plutôt rather (1); **plutôt que** rather than
poêle (*f*) frying pan
poêlée (de) (*f*) frying pan full (of)
poème (*m*) poem (7)
poésie (*f*) poetry
poids (*m*) weight (10)
poignée (*f*) handful, handle
poire (*f*) pear (10)
poireau (*m*) leek
pois: petits pois (*mpl*) peas (10)
poisson (*m*) fish (10)
poissonnerie (*f*) fish shop (10)
poivre (*m*) pepper (10)
poivron (*m*) (bell) pepper

poli(e) polite
police (*f*) police (11)
policier(-ère) detective; police (6)
politique (*f*) policy
politique political (11); **homme politique** (*m*) politician
pollution (*f*) pollution (11)
pomme (*f*) apple (6); **pomme de terre** (*f*) potato (10)
pop: musique pop (*f*) pop music (6)
population (*f*) population (11)
portant(e) sur dealing with
porte (*f*) door (3)
porter[3] to wear (4)
poser[3] to place; **poser une question** to ask a question (7)
possibilité (*f*) possibility (11)
postal(e): carte postale (*f*) postcard (7); **code postal** (*m*) zip code (3)
poste: bureau de poste (*m*) post office (8)
poubelle (*f*) trash can
poudre (*f*) powder
poulet (*m*) chicken (10)
pouls (*m*) pulse
poumon (*m*) lung (12)
pour for (P), in order to (1); **pour que** so that
pourquoi why (2)
poursuivre[36] to pursue
pourtant however (9)
poussière (*f*) dust
pouvoir (*m*) power
pouvoir[31] to be able, can (6)
pratique (*f*) practice
pratiquer[3] to practice
préavis (*m*) notice
précédent(e) preceding
préféré(e) favorite (3)
préférer[7] to prefer (2)
premier(-ère) first (3)
prendre[32] to take (3); **prendre un verre** to have a drink (2); **Prenez un stylo.** Take out a pen (P)
prénom (*m*) first name (3)
préoccuper[3] to worry (11); **se préoccuper**[3ê] **(de)** to worry (about) (11)
préparatifs (*mpl*) preparations (7)
préparer[3] to prepare (2); **préparer**[3] **les cours** to study for classes (2)
près (de) near (3); **à peu près** approximately
présentation (*f*) introduction
présenter[3] to introduce (4); **Je vous/te présente...** I would like to introduce . . . to you. (4)
préservatif (*m*) condom (9)
presque almost, nearly (2)
pressé(e) hurried (9)
prétendre[6] to claim (11)
prêt(e) ready
prêter[3] to loan, to lend (7)
preuve (*f*) proof
prévision du temps (*f*) weather forecast
prévoir[39] to plan, to schedule
prier[3] to beg, to request; **Je vous en prie.** You're welcome. (2)
primaire: école primaire (*f*) elementary school
principal(e) (*mpl* **principaux**) main (10)
principauté (*f*) principality
printemps (*m*) spring; **au printemps** in spring (5)
prise (*f*) plug, grip
prison (*f*) prison (11)
privé(e) private (8)
prix (*m*) price (7)
probablement probably
problème (*m*) problem (9)
procéder[7] **à des élections** to hold elections
prochain(e) next (4); **le prochain cours** the next class (P)
proche near
produire[17] to produce; **se produire**[17ê] to appear
produit (*m*) product (10); **produit en boîte** (*m*) canned good (10)
professeur (*m*) professor (P)
profession (*f*) profession (4)
profiter[3] **de** to take advantage of (7)
profondeur (*f*) depth
programme (*m*) program (11)
projet (*m*) plan (4)
projeté(e) projected
promenade (*f*) walk (5)
promener: se promener[8ê] to go walking (9)
promettre[28] **(de)** to promise (8)
promouvoir to promote
pronom (*m*) pronoun
proposer: se proposer[3ê] **de** to intend
propre own (8)
propriétaire (*m*) owner, proprietor
propriété (*f*) property
prospérité (*f*) prosperity (11)
protéger[7] to protect (11)
protéine (*f*) protein (10)
proximité: à proximité de in the vicinity of
psychologie (*f*) psychology (1)
publicité (*f*) advertising, advertisement
publier[3] to publish
puis then (4)
puissant(e) powerful (11)
pull (*m*) pullover sweater (8)
punir[5] to punish
purée (*f*) mashed potatoes
pyjama (*m*) pyjamas (8)

Q

quai (*m*) quay, wharf
quand when (2); **quand même** all the same
quarante forty (2)
quart (*m*) quarter; **Il est deux heures et quart.** It's a quarter past two. (P)
quartier (*m*) neighborhood (3)
quatorze fourteen (P)
quatre four (P)
quatre-vingts eighty (2)
quatre-vingt-dix ninety (2)
que that (P), than (2); **ce que** what, that which; **ne... que** only (7); **ne... rien que** nothing but (11); **Qu'est-ce que ça veut dire?** What does that mean? (P)
quel(le) which, what (3); **À quelle heure?** At what time? (P); **n'importe quel(le)** (just) any; **Quel âge a...?** How old is . . . ? (4); **Quel temps fait-il?** What's the weather like? (5)
quelconque any
quelque some; **quelque chose** something (2); **quelque part** somewhere (12); **quelques** a few (5); **quelqu'un** someone, somebody (5)
quelquefois sometimes (2)
quelques-un(e)s (*m/f*) a few (11)
question (*f*) question (P)
qui who (2); **ce qui** what, that, which
quinze fifteen (P)
quitter[3] to leave (5); **Ne quitte/quittez pas!** Don't hang up! (6); **se quitter**[3ê] to leave each other (9)
quoi what; **n'importe quoi** (just) anything
quotidien(ne) daily (9)

R

rabattre[15] to fold back
racisme (*m*) racism (11)
raconter[3] to tell, to recount (7)
rade (*f*) harbor
radio (*f*) radio (2), X-ray (12)
rafale (*f*) blast, gust
raie (*f*) skate (fish) (10)
raisin (*m*) grape(s) (6)
raison (*f*) reason; **avoir**[1] **raison** to be right (5)
ramdam (*m*) racket
randonnée (*f*) hike
rapport (*m*) relationship
rapporter[3] to bring back (11)
rarement rarely (2)
rasoir (*m*) razor
rassembler[3] to bring together
rassis(e) stale
rassurant(e) reassuring
rater[3] to miss
ravigote (*f*) dressing
ravitailler: se ravitailler[3ê] to stock up
réagir[5] **(à)** to react (to) (10)
réalisation (*f*) carrying out
réaliste realistic (1)
récemment recently (5)
réception (*f*) front desk (8)
recette (*f*) recipe
recevoir[33] to receive
recherche (*f*) research (11)
réclamer[3] to ask for, to claim
recommander[3] to recommend (8)
reconnaître[18] to recognize (6); **se reconnaître**[18ê] to recognize each other (9)
reconstruire[17] to reconstruct
rédaction (*f*) composition (7)
réduire[17] to reduce
refermer[3] to close back up
réfléchi(e) reflexive
réfléchir[5] **(à)** to think (about), to reflect (on) (10)
réfrigérateur (*m*) refrigerator (3)
réfugier: se réfugier[3ê] to take refuge
regard (*m*) look
regarder[3] to look at, to watch (2); **se regarder**[3ê] to look at each other (9)

régime (*m*) diet (10); regime (11); **être**[2] **au régime** to be on a diet (10)
régir[5] to govern
règle (*f*) rule
règlement (*m*) payment
régler[7] to adjust; **régler**[7] **la note** to pay the bill (8)
regretter[3] to regret (6)
rein (*m*) kidney; **reins** (*mpl*) lower back
rejoindre to join (7)
relais (*m*) inn
relier[3] to connect
remarquer[3] to notice
remède (*m*) remedy, cure
remercier[3] **(de)** to thank (for) (10)
remettre[28] **en cause** to bring into question
remise (*f*) reduction, discount; **remise en forme** (*f*) getting back into shape
rencontre (*f*) meeting
rencontrer[3] to meet, to run into (7); **se rencontrer**[3ê] to run into each other (9)
rendez-vous (*m*) date, appointment (6)
rendormir: se rendormir[4ê] to fall back asleep
rendre[6] to return, to give back (7); **rendre**[6] (+ *adjective*) to make (+ *adjective*) (12); **rendre**[6] **visite à** to visit (*someone*) (7); **se rendre**[6ê] **(à / chez)** to go (to) (9)
rénové(e) renovated
renseignements (*mpl*) information (7)
rentrée (*f*) return
rentrer[3ê] to return, to come / go home (4)
répandu(e) widespread (12)
repartir[4ê] to start again
repas (*m*) meal (8)
répéter[7] to repeat; **Répétez, s'il vous plaît.** Repeat, please (P)
répondre[6] **(à)** to answer (7); **Répondez à la question.** Answer the question. (P)
réponse (*f*) answer (P)
repos: en repos dormant
reposant(e) restful (7)
reposé(e) rested (5)
reposer[3] to set down; **se reposer**[3ê] to rest (9)
reprise (*f*) resumption, remake, occasion
réservation (*f*) reservation (7)
réserve: sous réserve de subject to
réserver[3] to reserve (7)
résidence: résidence universitaire (*f*) dormitory, residence hall (1)
résoudre to solve
ressembler[3] **à** to look like, to resemble (4)
ressentir[4] to feel
ressources (*fpl*) resources (11)
restaurant (*m*) restaurant (2); **dîner**[3] **au restaurant** to dine out (2); **restaurant universitaire** (*m*) university dining hall (1)
rester[3ê] to stay (2)
résultat (*m*) result
retard: en retard late (7)
retirer[3] to take out, to withdraw
retour (*m*) return; **billet aller-retour** round-trip ticket (7)
retourner[3ê] to return (5); **Retournez à votre place.** Return to your place(s). (P)
rétrécir[5] to shrink
retrouver[3] to meet (4); **se retrouver**[3ê] to meet (each other) (9)
réussir[5] **(à)** to succeed (in) (10)
rêve (*m*) dream (7)
réveil (*m*) awakening, alarm clock
réveiller[3] to wake up (9); **se réveiller**[3ê] to wake up (9)
révélateur(-trice) revealing
revendication (*f*) demand
revendre[6] to resell, to sell back (7)
revenir[37ê] to come back (7)
rêver[3] **(de)** to dream (about) (7)
rêveur(-euse) dreamy
réviser[3] to review
revoir[39] to see again; **Au revoir.** Good-bye (P)
revue (*f*) magazine (7)
rez-de-chaussée (*m*) ground floor (3)
rhum (*m*) rum
rhume (*m*) cold (12)
ride (*f*) wrinkle
rideau (*m*) curtain
ridicule ridiculous
rien: ne... rien nothing (5); **ne... rien que** nothing but (11)
rillettes (*fpl*) potted pork or goose
rire[34] to laugh
riz (*m*) rice (10)
robe (*f*) dress (8)
rocher (*m*) rock, boulder
rocheux(-euse) rocky
rock (*m*) rock (music) (6)
rognon (*m*) kidney
roi (*m*) king
roman (*m*) novel (7)
rosbif (*m*) roast beef (10)
rose pink (4)
rosier (*m*) rosebush
rôti(e) roasted
rouage (*m*) cogwheel
roue (*f*) wheel
rouge red (4); **vin rouge** (*m*) red wine (2)
rougir[5] to turn red, to blush (10)
roulette: patin à roulette (*m*) roller skate
roux (rousse) red (*hair*) (4)
rue (*f*) street (3)
ruminer[3] to ponder
rupture (*f*) breaking up
Russie (*f*) Russia (7)
rythme (*m*) rhythm (11)

S

sable (*m*) sand
sac (*m*) purse (8)
sage good, well-behaved (9)
sain(e) healthy (10)
Saint-Valentin (*f*) Valentine's Day (6)
saison (*f*) season
salade salad (10)
sale dirty
salé(e) salted
salle (*f*) room; **salle à manger** (*f*) dining room (3); **salle de bains** (*f*) bathroom (3); **salle de classe** (*f*) classroom (1)
salon (*m*) living room (3)
saluer[3] to greet (9)
Salut! Hi!, Bye! (P)
samedi Saturday (P)
sandwich (*m*) sandwich (2)
sang (*m*) blood (12)
sanglier (*m*) wild boar
sans without (P); **les sans domicile fixe** (*mpl*) homeless people (11)
santé (*f*) health (12)
sauce (*f*) sauce (10)
saucière (*f*) sauceboat
saucisse (*f*) sausage link (10)
saucisson (*m*) sausage (6)
sauf except (2)
saumon (*m*) salmon (10)
saupoudrer[3] to sprinkle
sauvage wild
sauver[3] to save
sauvetage (*m*) rescue, saving
savoir[35] to know (how) (6); **Je ne sais pas.** I don't know. (P)
saxophone (*m*) saxophone (9)
scène (*f*) stage
sceptique sceptical (11)
sciences (*fpl*) science; **film de science-fiction** (*m*) science fiction movie (6); **sciences économiques** (*fpl*) economics; **sciences humaines** (*fpl*) humanities; **sciences politiques** (*fpl*) political science (1); **sciences sociales** (*fpl*) social sciences (1)
se herself, himself, itself, oneself, themselves (9); **Où se trouve...?** Where is . . . located? (3)
séance (*f*) showing (6)
sec (sèche) dry
secrétaire (*mf*) secretary (4)
section: section (non-)fumeur (*f*) (non-)smoking section (7)
sécurité (*f*) security, safety (11)
séduisant(e) seductive
sein (*m*) breast
seize sixteen (P)
séjour (*m*) stay (8)
séjourner[3] to stay
sel (*m*) salt (10)
selon according to
semaine (*f*) week (5); **en semaine** weekdays
sembler[3] to seem; **Il me semble que...** It seems to me that . . . (11)
semer[8] to sow
Sénégal (*m*) Senegal (7)
sens (*m*) meaning
sentier (*m*) path
sentir: se sentir[4ê] to feel (9)
sept seven (P)
septembre (*m*) September (6)
série: en série standard-equipped
sérieux(-euse) serious (1)
serpenter[3] to wind
serveur (*m*) waiter (4)
serveuse (*f*) waitress (4)
servir[4] to serve (6); **servi(e)** served (8); **se servir**[4ê] **de** to use
seul(e) alone (P), single (8), lonely (9), only
sévère strict (11)
sevrage (*m*) weaning, severance
sexuel(le) sexual (9)
shopping: faire[25] **du shopping** to go shopping (4)
short (*m*) shorts (8)

si if (2), yes (6); **s'il te/vous plaît** please (P)
SIDA (*m*) AIDS (9)
siècle (*m*) century (11)
siège (*m*) seat
sigle (*m*) set of initials
signaler[3] to draw attention to
sillonner[3] to cross
simple: billet aller simple one-way ticket (7)
sinon if not
site (*m*) site (7)
situation (*f*) situation (11)
situer: se situer[3ê] to be situated
six six (P)
ski (nautique) (*m*) (water-)skiing (5)
social(e) (*mpl* **sociaux**) social (11)
société (*f*) society (11); **jeu de société** (*m*) board game
sœur (*f*) sister (1); **belle-sœur** (*f*) sister-in-law
soi oneself
soie: en soie silk (8)
soif: avoir[1] **soif:** to be thirsty (5)
soigner[3] to take care of (12); **se soigner**[3ê] to take care of oneself (12)
soigneusement carefully
soin (*m*) care
soir (*m*) evening (P); **ce soir** tonight (2)
soirée (*f*) evening (5)
soixante sixty (2)
soixante-dix seventy (2)
soja (*m*) soya
sol (*m*) ground
solde: en solde on sale (8)
soleil: Il fait du soleil. It's sunny. (5)
solitaire lonely
solution (*f*) solution (11)
somme (*f*) sum
sommeil (*m*) sleep; **avoir**[1] **sommeil** to be sleepy (5)
sommet (*m*) summit
son (sa, ses) her, his, its (3)
sondage (*m*) poll (9)
sonner[3] to ring
sonorité (*f*) sound
sorcière (*f*) witch
sorte (*f*) kind, sort (6)
sortie (*f*) exit, outing, evening out
sortir[4ê] **(de)** to go out (2); to leave (5)
soudain suddenly (10)
soudain(e) sudden
souffle (*m*) breath
souffrance (*f*) suffering
souffrir[29] **(de)** to suffer (from)
soufre (*m*) sulphur
souhait (*m*) wish
souhaiter[3] to wish
soumettre: se soumettre[28ê] **à** to submit to
soupçonner[3] to suspect
soupe (*f*) soup (10); **soupe à l'oignon** (*f*) onion soup (10)
souper[3] to have supper
souple flexible
sous under (3); **sous réserve de** subject to
sous-sol (*m*) basement (3)
sous-marin(e) underwater; **plongée sous-marine** (*f*) scuba diving (7)
sous-vêtements (*mpl*) underwear (8)
soutenu(e) supported
souvenir (*m*) memory
souvenir: se souvenir[37ê] **(de)** to remember (9)
souvent often (2)
spécialité (*f*) specialty (8)
spectacle (*m*) show
spéléo(-logie) (*f*) cave exploring
sport (*m*) sport (1)
sportif(-ive) athletic (1)
stade (*m*) stadium (8)
stage (*m*) training
standard (*m*) switchboard
station: station de radio (*f*) radio station (11); **station estivale** (*f*) summer resort (8); **station-service** (*f*) service station (8)
stéréo: chaîne stéréo (*f*) stereo (3)
stress (*m*) stress (10)
stylo (*m*) pen (P)
succursale (*f*) branch office / store (5)
sucer[12] to suck
sucre (*m*) sugar (10)
sucré(e) sweet, sugary
sud (*m*) south; **Amérique du Sud** (*f*) South America (7)
suffire: il suffit de... it's enough to . . .
suffisamment sufficiently (10)
suffisant(e) sufficient
suggérer[7] to suggest (6)
Suisse (*f*) Switzerland (7)
suite: toute de suite right away (8)
suivant(e) following
suivre[36] to follow; **suivre**[36] **un cours** to take a course (5)
sujet (*m*) subject
super great (6)
supermarché (*m*) supermarket (8)
supplément (*m*) extra charge (8)
sur on (3); **sept jours sur sept** seven days out of seven
sûr(e) sure; **Bien sûr!** Of course! (2)
sûrement surely
surgelé(e) frozen (10)
surpeuplé(e) overpopulated
surprenant(e) surprising
surpris(e) surprised (12)
surtout especially, above all (4)
surveiller[3] to keep watch over
sympathique (sympa) nice (1)
symptôme (*m*) symptom (12)

T

tabac (*m*) tobacco; **bureau de tabac** (*m*) tobacco shop (8)
table (*f*) table (3)
tableau (*m*) board (P); painting, picture (3)
tâche: tâche domestique (*f*) household chore (9)
taille (*f*) size (8); **de taille moyenne** medium-sized (4)
tailleur (*m*) lady's suit (8)
talent (*m*) talent (9)
talon (*m*) heel
tant (de) so much, so many (11); **tant que** as long as (11)
tante (*f*) aunt (4)
tard late (2); **plus tard** later (4)
tarte (*f*) pie (6)
tartelette aux fraises (*f*) strawberry tart (10)
tartine (*f*) bread and butter sandwich (with jam) (10)
tas (*m*) pile; **un tas de** a bunch of
taxi (*m*) taxi (8)
te (to, for) you (7), yourself (9); **Ça te dit?** Does that sound like fun to you? (6); **Je t'en prie.** You're welcome. (6); **Je te présente...** I would like to introduce . . . to you. (4); **Je t'invite à...** I invite you to . . . (6); **s'il te plaît** please (6)
tel(le) que such as
télécopie (*f*) fax
téléphone (*m*) telephone (2) **parler au téléphone** to talk on the telephone (2)
téléphoner[3] **(à)** to telephone (7); **se téléphoner**[3ê] to telephone each other (9)
téléviseur (*m*) television set (3)
télévision (télé) (*f*) television (2)
tellement so much, so (6)
température (*f*) temperature (12)
temps (*m*) time (2), weather (5); **de temps en temps** from time to time (4)
tenir[37] to hold (11)
tennis (*m*) tennis (2)
tentation (*f*) temptation
terme: mettre[28] **terme à** to put an end to
terminaison (*f*) ending
terrain: sur le terrain on site
terrasse (*f*) terrace (10)
terre (*f*) earth; **par terre** on the ground (7); **pomme de terre** (*f*) potato (10)
terrorisme (*m*) terrorism (11)
tête (*f*) head (12)
thé (*m*) tea (2)
théâtre (*m*) theater (4)
thon (*m*) tuna (10)
tiers: deux-tiers two-thirds; **tiers monde** (*m*) third world (11)
timide shy, timid (1)
titulaire (*m/f*) holder
toi you (P); **chez toi** at your house (3) **Et toi?** And you? (P)
toilette: cabinet de toilette (*m*) toilet (3)
tolérance (*f*) tolerance (11)
tomate (*f*) tomato (10)
tomber[3ê] to fall, **tomber**[3ê] **amoureux(-euse)** to fall in love; **tomber**[3ê] **malade** to get sick (12)
ton (ta, tes) your (3)
tort: avoir[1] **tort** to be wrong (5)
tôt early (5)
toujours always (2), still (7)
tour (*m*) drive, ride, walk, run (5); **faire**[25] **le tour du monde** to take a trip around the world (8)
tourisme: office de tourisme (*m*) tourist office (7)
touriste (*m/f*) tourist (7); **en classe touriste** in coach (7)
touristique tourist (7)
tournée (*f*) tour
tourner[3] to turn (8); **se tourner**[3ê] **(vers)** to turn (towards) (11)
tourte (*f*) pie

Toussaint (*f*) All Saints' Day (6)
tousser[3] to cough (12)
tout (toute, tous, toutes) everything (3), all, whole (4); **ne... pas du tout** not at all (1); **tous les jours** every day (2); **tout à coup** all of a sudden (10); **tout à fait** completely (9); **tout à l'heure** in a little while (P), a while ago; **tout de suite** right away (8); **tout droit** straight (8) **toute la journée** the whole day (2); **toutes sortes de...** all kinds of . . . (6); **tout le monde** everybody, everyone (4); **tout près (de)** right by, very near (3)
train (*m*) train (5); **en train** by train (5) **être**[2] **en train de...** to be busy . . . (4)
traitement (*m*) treatment (12)
tranche (*f*) slice (10)
tranquille tranquil, calm (6)
transmettre[28] to pass on
transport: moyen de transport (*m*) means of transportation (8)
travail (*m*) work (5); **fête du travail** Labor Day (6)
travailler[3] to work (2); **je travaille** I work (P)
traverser[3] to cross (8)
treize thirteen (P)
tremper[3] to soak
trentaine (*f*) about thirty
trente thirty (P)
très very (P)
tribu (*f*) tribe (11)
triste sad (4)
trois three (P)
troisième third (3)
trompette (*f*) trumpet (9)
trop too, too much (3); **trop de** too much, too many (10)
tropical(e) tropical (*mpl* **tropicaux**) tropical (7)
trou (*m*) hole
trouver[3] to find (5) **Où se trouve(nt)...** Where is (are) . . . located? (3)
tu you (1)
tuer[3] to kill
typique typical
tyrannie (*f*) tyranny (11)

U

ulcère (*m*) ulcer (12)
un(e) one (P), a (1); **un(e) ami(e)** a friend (P)
unité (*f*) unity (11)
universitaire university (1); **résidence universitaire** (*f*) dormitory, residence hall (1); **restaurant universitaire** (*m*) university dining hall (1)
université (*f*) university (P)
us: us (*mpl*) **et coutumes** (*fpl*) habits and customs
usine (*f*) factory
utile useful
utiliser[3] to use, to utilize (11)

V

vacances (*fpl*) vacation; **en vacances** on vacation (7)
valeur (*f*) value
validité (*f*) validity (11)
valise (*f*) suitcase (3); **(dé)faire**[25] **ses valises** to (un)pack one's bags (7)
vallée (*f*) valley
valoir: il vaut mieux (que)... it's better, you had better (12)
varié(e) varied
veau (*m*) veal
veillée (*f*) evening together
vélo (*m*) bicycle (3)
vendeur(-euse) (*m/f*) salesperson
vendre[6] to sell (7)
vendredi Friday (P)
venir[37ê] to come (2); **venir de** (+ *infinitive*) to have just (+ *past participle*) (10)
vent: Il fait du vent. It's windy. (5)
vente (*f*) sale
ventre (*m*) stomach, belly (12)
verdoyant(e) green
verglaçant(e) icy
vérifier[3] to check
vérité (*f*) truth
verre (*m*) glass (2)
vers (*m*) verse
vers towards (2)
vert(e) green (4)
vêtements (*mpl*) clothes (3)
veuve (*f*) widow (9)
vexer[3] to vex, to upset
viande (*f*) meat (6)
vidéo: cassette vidéo (*f*) video cassette (3); **jeu vidéo** (*m*) video game (2)
vider[3] to empty
vie (*f*) life (9)
vieillir[5] to age, to get old (10)
Viêt-nam (*m*) Vietnam (7)
vieux (vieil, vieille) old (1)
vif(-ive) lively, bright
vigueur: en vigueur in effect
village (*m*) village, town
villageois(e) (*m/f*) villager
ville city (3); **en ville** in town (3)
vin (*m*) wine (2)
vinaigre (*m*) vinegar (10)
vingt twenty (P)
viol (*m*) rape (11)
violence (*f*) violence (11)
violent(e) violent (11)
violet(te) violet (4)
visage (*m*) face (12)
visiter[3] to visit (a place) (5)
vitamines (*fpl*) vitamins (10)
vite quickly, fast (10)
vivant(e) alive
vivier (*m*) fish reservoir
vivre[38] to live
vocabulaire: mot de vocabulaire (*m*) vocabulary word (P)
voici here is, here are (2)
voie (*f*) way; **par voie intraveineuse** intravenously
voilà there is, there are (2)
voile (*f*) sailing; **planche à voile** (*f*) windsurfing (7)
voilier (*m*) sailboat
voir[39] to see (1)
voisin(e) (*m/f*) neighbor (6)
voiture (*f*) car (3)
voix (*f*) voice (11)
vol (*m*) flight (7), theft (11)
volaille (*f*) poultry
volcan (*m*) volcano (7)
volonté (*f*) will
volontiers gladly, willingly
vomir[5] to vomit (12)
votre (*pl* **vos**) your (3); **Ouvrez votre livre.** Open your book. (P)
vouloir to want (6); **Je voudrais...** I would like . . . (2); **Qu'est-ce que ça veut dire?** What does that mean? (P)
vous (to, for) you (P); **s'il vous plaît** please (P)
voyage (*m*) trip (5); **agence de voyages** (*f*) travel agency (7); **agent de voyages** (*m*) travel agent (7); **chèque de voyage** (*m*) traveler's check (7)
voyager[11] to travel (2)
voyelle (*f*) vowel
vrai(e) true
vraiment truly (10)
vue (*f*) view (3)

W.-C. (*mpl*) water closet, toilet (3)
week-end (*m*) weekend (P); **le week-end** on the weekend (2); **partir**[4ê] **en week-end** to go away for the week-end (5)

y there (5); **il y a** there is, there are (3)
yaourt (*m*) yoghurt (10)
yeux (*mpl*) eyes (4)

Z

Zaïre (*m*) Zaire (7)
zéro zero (P)

The *Vocabulaire anglais-français* includes all words presented in *Qu'est-ce qu'on dit?* for active use. An asterisk before a word beginning with **h** indicates that the **h** is aspirate. Masculine nouns are followed by (*m*), feminine nouns by (*f*), and plural nouns by (*pl*). If you wish to know in which chapter a word or expression was taught, look up the French equivalent in the *Vocabulaire français-anglais*, where the chapter number is indicated in parentheses after the entry. The conjugation of a verb may also be found by looking up the French equivalent in the *Vocabulaire français-anglais*, where the verbs are followed by a superscript indicating where the conjugation is found in the verb charts in *Appendix D*.

A

a un(e)
able: be able pouvoir
about environ; **What do you think about it?** Qu'en penses-tu?, Qu'en pensez-vous?
above all surtout
abroad à l'étranger
accent: without an accent sans accent
accept accepter
accident accident (*m*)
accounting comptabilité (*f*)
ache douleur (*f*)
ache avoir mal (à)
acquaintance: make the acquaintance of faire la connaissance de
across from en face (de)
act agir
active actif(-ive)
activity activité (*f*)
actor acteur (*m*)
actress actrice (*f*)
adapt s'adapter
add ajouter
address adresse (*f*)
admire admirer
adore adorer
advance avance (*f*); **in advance** à l'avance
advantage: take advantage of profiter de
adventure: adventure movie film d'aventures (*m*)
advertisement: classified advertisement petite annonce (*f*)
advice conseils (*mpl*) ; **give a piece of advice** donner un conseil
aerobics: do aerobics faire de l'aérobic
afraid: be afraid (of) avoir peur (de)
Africa Afrique (*f*)
African africain(e)
after après; **day after tomorrow** après-demain
afternoon après-midi (*m*); **It's one o'clock in the afternoon.** Il est une heure de l'après-midi.; **in the afternoon** l'après-midi
again encore
against contre
age vieillir
agency: travel agency agence de voyages (*f*)
agent: travel agent agent de voyages (*m*)
agitation agitation (*f*)
ago il y a
Agreed! D'accord!
agricultural agricole
AIDS SIDA (*m*)
airplane avion (*m*)
airport aéroport (*m*)
alcohol alcool (*m*)
alcoholic alcoolisé(e)
alcoholism alcoolisme (*m*)
Algeria Algérie (*f*)
Algerian algérien(ne)
all tout (toute, tous, toutes); **above all** surtout; **all of a sudden** tout à coup; **All Saints' Day** Toussaint (*f*); **all sorts of** toutes sortes de; **not at all** ne... pas du tout
allergy allergie (*f*)
allow permettre (de)
almost presque
alone seul(e)
along le long de; **get along** s'entendre
already déjà
also aussi
always toujours
amaze étonner; **amazed** étonné(e)
America: North America Amérique du Nord (*f*); **South America** Amérique du Sud (*f*)
American américain(e)
an un(e)
analysis analyse (*f*)
and et
animal animal (*m*) (*pl* animaux)
animated animé(e)
ankle cheville (*f*)
annoying embêtant(e)
answer réponse (*f*)
answer répondre (à)
antibiotic antibiotique (*m*)
anywhere n'importe où
apartment appartement (*m*); **apartment building** immeuble (*m*)
appetite appétit (*m*)
appetizer *hors-d'œuvre (*m*)
apple pomme (*f*)
appointment rendez-vous (*m*)
April avril (*m*)
Argentina Argentine (*f*)
argue (with) se disputer (avec)
arm bras (*m*)
armchair fauteuil (*m*)
around vers, environ; **take a trip around the world** faire le tour du monde
arrival arrivée (*f*)
arrive arriver
article article (*m*)
as comme; **as . . . as** aussi... que; **as long as** tant que; **as many . . . (as)** autant de... (que); **as much . . . (as)** autant (de)... (que); **as soon as** aussitôt que
Asia Asie (*f*)
ask demander; **ask a question** poser une question
asleep: fall asleep s'endormir
aspirin aspirine (*f*)
at à; **at home** à la maison; **at . . . 's house/place** chez...
athletic sportif(-ive)
attention: pay attention (to) faire attention (à)
August août (*m*)
aunt tante (*f*)
Australia Australie (*f*)
autocrat autocrate (*m*)
autumn automne (*m*)
avenue avenue (*f*)
avoid éviter
away: right away tout de suite

B

back dos (*m*)
back: bring back rapporter; **come back** revenir; **sell back** revendre
bacon bacon (*m*)
bad mauvais(e); **really bad** nul(le)
badly mal
baggage bagages (*mpl*)
bakery boulangerie (*f*)
banana banane (*f*)
bank banque (*f*)
bar bar (*m*)
basement sous-sol (*m*)
basketball basket-ball (*m*)
bath bain (*m*)
bathroom salle de bains (*f*)
be être; **be able** pouvoir; **be afraid (of)** avoir peur (de); **be busy doing something** être en train de faire quelque chose; **be cold** avoir froid; **be familiar with** connaître; **be hot** avoir chaud; **be hungry** avoir faim; **be interested in** s'intéresser à; **be right** avoir raison; **be sleepy** avoir sommeil; **be thirsty** avoir soif; **be wrong** avoir tort; **be . . . years old** avoir... ans; **here is/are** voilà; **How are you?** Comment allez-vous?; **How is it going?** Comment ça va?; **isn't it?** n'est-ce pas?; **It's hot.** Il fait chaud.; **That's . . . francs.** Ça fait... francs.; **There are six of us.** Nous sommes six.; **there is/are** il y a, voilà; **The weather's nice (bad / cold / cool / hot / sunny / windy).** Il fait beau (mauvais / froid / frais / chaud / du soleil / du vent).; **You're welcome.** Je t'en prie., Je vous en prie.

beach plage (*f*)
beans: green beans *haricots verts (*mpl*)
beard barbe (*f*)
beat battre
beautiful beau (bel, belle, *pl* beaux, belles)
because parce que; **because of** à cause de
become devenir
bed lit (*m*); **go to bed** se coucher
bedroom chambre (*f*)
beef: roast beef rosbif (*m*)
beer bière (*f*); **draft beer** demi (*m*)
before avant; **before (doing)** avant de (faire)
begin commencer
behind derrière
beige beige
Belgium Belgique (*f*)
believe (in) croire (à)
belly ventre (*m*)
belong to être à
best le/la meilleur(e)
better meilleur(e) (*adjectif*), mieux (*adverbe*); **it's better, you had better** il vaut mieux
between entre
bicycle vélo (*m*)
big grand(e), gros(se); **get big** grandir
bikini bikini (*m*)
bill addition (*f*); **pay the bill** (*at a hotel*) régler la note
biology biologie (*f*)
birth naissance (*f*)
birthday anniversaire (*m*)
black noir(e)
blond blond(e)
blood sang (*m*)
blouse chemisier (*m*)
blue bleu(e)
blues (*music*) blues (*m*)
blush rougir
board tableau (*m*)
boat bateau (*m*)
boating: go boating faire du bateau
body corps (*m*)
book livre (*m*)
bookcase étagère (*f*)
bookstore librairie (*f*)
bored: be bored, get bored s'ennuyer (de)
boring ennuyeux(-euse)
born: be born naître; **He/She was born.** Il/Elle est né(e).
borrow emprunter
boss patron(ne) (*m/f*)
bottle bouteille (*f*)
boulevard boulevard (*m*)
boy garçon (*m*)
boyfriend petit ami (*m*)
branch office succursale (*f*)
Brazil Brésil (*m*)
bread pain (*m*); **bread-and-butter sandwich** tartine (*f*); **loaf of French bread** baguette (*f*)
break casser; **break one's arm** se casser le bras
breakfast petit déjeuner (*m*)
bring apporter; **bring back** rapporter
brother frère (*m*)
brown marron, brun(e), (*hair*) châtain
brunette brun(e)
brush (one's teeth) (se) brosser (les dents)
Brussels Bruxelles
building bâtiment (*m*); **apartment building** immeuble (*m*)
burn brûler; **burn oneself** se brûler
bus autobus (*m*), autocar (*m*); **bus stop** arrêt d'autobus (*m*)
business affaires (*fpl*); **business course** cours de commerce (*m*)
businessman homme d'affaires (*m*)
businesswoman femme d'affaires (*f*)
busy occupé(e); **be busy doing something** être en train de faire quelque chose
but mais; **nothing but** ne... rien que
butcher's shop boucherie (*f*)
butter beurre (*m*); **bread-and-butter sandwich** tartine (*f*)
buy acheter
by par; **by bus** en autobus, en autocar; **by chance** par *hasard; **right by** tout près (de)
Bye! Salut!

C

café café (*m*)
cake gâteau (*m*)
Californian californien(ne)
call appeler, téléphoner; **Who's calling?** Qui est à l'appareil?
calm calme
calm down se calmer
camping camping (*m*); **go camping** faire du camping
campus campus (*m*)
can (be able) pouvoir
Canada Canada (*m*)
Canadian canadien(ne)
cancer cancer (*m*)
canned good produit en boîte (*m*)
capital punishment peine de mort (*f*)
car voiture (*f*)
card carte (*f*); **credit card** carte de crédit (*f*); **identity card** carte d'identité (*f*)
care: take care of s'occuper de; (*health*) (se) soigner
carrot carotte (*f*)
cartoon dessin animé (*m*)
cash: pay cash payer en espèces
cassette cassette (*f*); **video cassette** cassette vidéo (*f*); **video cassette player** magnétoscope (*m*)
castle château (*m*)
cat chat (*m*)
cathedral cathédrale (*f*)
cause cause (*f*)
cause causer
celebrate fêter
celebration fête (*f*)
center: shopping center centre commercial (*m*); **student center** foyer des étudiants (*m*)
central central(e) (*mpl* centraux)
century siècle (*m*)
cereal céréales (*fpl*)
certain certain(e)
chair chaise (*f*)
chalet: ski chalet chalet de ski (*m*)
chance: by chance par *hasard
change monnaie (*f*); **Here's your change.** Voici votre monnaie.
change changer
charge: extra charge supplément (*m*)
check chèque (*m*), addition (*f*); **traveler's check** chèque de voyage (*m*)
cheese fromage (*m*); **cheese sandwich** sandwich au fromage (*m*)
chemistry chimie (*m*)
cherry cerise (*f*)
chicken poulet (*m*)
child enfant (*mf*)
chill frisson (*m*)
China Chine (*f*)
chips chips (*fpl*)
chocolate chocolat (*m*); **chocolate cake** gâteau au chocolat (*m*)
choice choix (*m*)
choose (to do) choisir (de faire)
chop: pork chop côte de porc (*f*)
chore: household chore tâche domestique (*f*)
Christmas Noël (*m*)
church église (*f*)
cinema cinéma (*m*)
city ville (*f*)
composition rédaction (*f*)
computer ordinateur (*m*); **computer science** informatique (*f*)
concentrate on se concentrer sur
concert concert (*m*)
conservative conservateur(-trice)
constantly constamment
consultation consultation (*f*)
continue continuer
contrary: on the contrary par contre
convenient commode
cook faire la cuisine; (faire) cuire
cooking cuisine (*f*)
cool: The weather's cool. Il fait frais.
copious copieux(-euse)
corner coin (*m*); **on the corner (of)** au coin (de)
corruption corruption (*f*)
cotton coton (*m*)
couch divan (*m*)
cough tousser
count (on) compter (sur)
country pays (*m*), campagne (*f*); **country music** musique country (*f*)
couple couple (*m*)
course cours (*m*); **first course** (of a meal) entrée (*f*); **Of course!** Bien sûr!, Évidemment!; **take a course** suivre un cours
cousin cousin(e) (*m/f*)
create créer
credit card carte de crédit (*f*)
crime crime (*m*), criminalité (*f*)
criminel criminel(le) (*m/f*)
cross traverser
cruise croisière (*f*); **go on a cruise** faire une croisière
cultural culturel(le)

cure guérir
customs douane (*f*)
cut (oneself) (se) couper

D

daily quotidien(ne)
dairy laitier(-ère)
dance danser
dancer danseur(-euse) (*m/f*)
danger danger (*m*)
dark-haired brun(e)
date date (*f*); rendez-vous (*m*); **What is the date?** Quelle date sommes-nous?, Quelle est la date?
daughter fille (*f*)
day jour (*m*), journée (*f*); **All Saints' Day** Toussaint (*f*); **day after tomorrow** après-demain; **good day** bonjour; **every day** tous les jours; **Labor Day** fête du travail (*f*); **New Year's Day** jour de l'an (*m*); **the next day** le lendemain (*m*); **the whole day** toute la journée; **Valentine's Day** Saint-Valentin (*f*); **What day is today?** Quel jour est-ce aujourd'hui?
daytime journée (*f*)
dead mort(e)
death penalty peine de mort (*f*)
decanter carafe (*f*)
December décembre (*m*)
decide décider
degree degré (*m*)
delay délai (*m*)
delicatessen charcuterie (*f*)
delicious délicieux(-euse)
delighted: Delighted to meet you. Enchanté(e).
deluxe de luxe
democracy démocratie (*f*)
democratic démocratique
departure départ (*m*)
depend (on) dépendre (de)
depression dépression (*f*)
describe décrire
desire avoir envie de
desk bureau (*m*); **front desk** réception (*f*)
dessert dessert (*m*)
detective policier(-ère)
develop (se) développer
dictatorship dictature (*f*)
die mourir; **He/She died.** Il/Elle est mort(e).
diet régime (*m*); **be on a diet** être au régime
different différent(e)
differently différemment
difficult difficile
difficulty difficulté (*f*)
digest digérer
dine (out) dîner (au restaurant)
dining: dining room salle à manger (*f*); **dining hall** restaurant universitaire (*m*)
dinner dîner (*m*)
dinner: have dinner dîner
direct direct(e)
disc: compact disc disque compact (*m*); **compact disc player** lecteur de disques compacts (*m*)
dish plat (*m*)
divan divan (*m*)
diversity diversité (*f*)
diving: scuba diving plongée sous-marine (*f*)
divorce divorcer
divorced divorcé(e)
do faire; **That is not done!** Ça ne se fait pas.
doctor médecin (*m*)
dog chien (*m*)
domestic domestique
door porte (*f*)
dormitory résidence universitaire (*f*)
down: go down descendre
downtown centre-ville (*m*)
dozen douzaine (*f*)
draft beer demi (*m*)
drama drame (*m*); **drama course** cours de théâtre (*m*)
drawing dessin (*m*)
dream rêve (*m*)
dream (about) rêver (de)
dress robe (*f*)
dressed: get dressed s'habiller
dresser commode (*f*)
drink boisson (*f*); **have a drink** prendre un verre
drink boire
drive: go for a drive faire un tour en voiture
drug(s) drogue (*f*)
drums batterie (*f*)
duck canard (*m*)
due to à cause de
dumb bête
during pendant

E

each chaque
ear oreille (*f*)
early tôt, en avance
easily facilement
Easter Pâques (*fpl*)
easy facile
eat manger
economic économique
economy économie (*f*)
educate éduquer
education éducation (*f*)
egg œuf (*m*); **hard-boiled egg** œuf dur (*m*)
Egypt Égypte (*f*)
eight *huit
eighteen dix-huit
eighty quatre-vingts
election(s) élections (*fpl*)
element élément (*m*)
elevated élevé(e)
elevator ascenseur (*m*)
eleven onze
embarrassed gêné(e)
embrace s'embrasser
end fin (*f*); **at the end (of)** au bout (de)
English anglais (*m*)
English anglais**(e)**
enough assez (de)
enter entrer (dans)
environment environnement (*m*)
equality égalité (*f*)
errand course (*f*); **run errands** faire des courses
especially surtout
essential essentiel
establish établir
Europe Europe (*f*)
European européen(ne)
evening soir (*m*), soirée (*f*); **At ten o'clock in the evening.** À dix heures du soir.; **good evening** bonsoir; **in the evening, evenings** le soir
every day tous les jours
everybody tout le monde
everyone tout le monde
everything tout
everywhere partout
exam examen (*m*)
excentric excentrique
except sauf
exception exception (*f*)
exchange money changer de l'argent
exercise exercice (*m*)
exercise faire de l'exercice
exhausted épuisé(e)
exotic exotique
expensive cher (chère)
exposition exposition (*f*)
expresso express (*m*)
extra charge supplément (*m*)
extrovert extroverti(e)
eye œil (*m*) (*pl* yeux)

F

face figure (*f*), visage (*m*)
facing en face (de)
fairly (much) assez
fall automne (*m*)
fall tomber; **fall asleep** s'endormir
familiar: be familiar with connaître
family famille (*f*)
famine famine (*f*)
famous célèbre, fameux(-euse)
fanstastic magnifique
far (from) loin (de)
fast vite
fastfood fast-food (*m*); **fast-food restaurant** fast-food (*m*)
fat matière grasse (*f*)
fat gros(se); **get fat** grossir
father père (*m*)
fatty gras(se)
favorite préféré(e)
fear avoir peur (de)
February février (*m*)
feed donner à manger à
feel se sentir; **feel like doing** avoir envie de faire
fever fièvre (*f*)
few: a few quelques, quelques-un(e)s
fewer . . . than moins ... que
fifteen quinze
fifty cinquante
fight se battre; **fight (against)** lutter (contre), combattre

figure ligne (*f*)
finally enfin
fine arts beaux-arts (*mpl*)
finger doigt (*m*)
finish (doing) finir (de faire)
first premier(-ère), d'abord; **at first** au début; **first floor** rez-de-chaussée (*m*); **first course (of a meal)** entrée (*f*); **first name** prénom (*m*); **in first class** en première classe; **love at first sight** coup de foudre (*m*)
fish poisson (*m*); **fish shop** poissonnerie (*f*)
fitting room cabine d'essayage (*f*)
five cinq
flight vol (*m*)
floor étage (*m*); **ground floor** rez-de-chaussée (*m*); **on the second floor** au premier étage
flower fleur (*f*)
flu grippe (*f*)
folk music folk (*m*)
food aliment (*m*), nourriture (*f*)
foot pied (*m*)
for pour, pendant, depuis; **for the last three days** depuis les trois derniers jours
foreign étranger(-ère)
forget oublier
former ancien(ne)
forty quarante
four quatre
fourteen quatorze
fragile fragile
fragmented fragmenté(e)
franc franc (*m*)
France France (*f*)
free libre
freedom liberté (*f*)
French français (*m*); **French class** cours de français (*m*)
French français(e); **French fries** frites (*f*)
French-speaking francophone
frequently fréquemment
fresh frais (fraîche)
Friday vendredi (*m*)
friend ami(e) (*m/f*), copain (*m*), copine (*f*)
fries: French fries frites (*fpl*)
frivolous frivole
from de
front: front desk réception (*f*); **in front of** devant
frozen surgelé(e)
fruit fruit (*m*); **fruit juice** jus de fruits (*m*)
full plein(e)
fun amusant(e); **Does that sound like fun?** Ça te dit?; **have fun (doing)** s'amuser (à faire)
furious furieux(-euse)
future avenir (*m*)

G

gain weight grossir
game: video game jeu vidéo (*m*)
gang gang (*m*)
garden jardin (*m*)
garden faire du jardinage
gardening jardinage (*m*)
general: in general en général
generally généralement
German allemand (*m*)
German allemand(e)
Germany Allemagne (*f*)
get obtenir; **get along** s'entendre; **get big** grandir; **get dressed** s'habiller; **get fat** grossir; **get married (to)** se marier (avec); **get off** descendre (de); **get old** vieillir; **get on** monter (dans); **get sick** tomber malade; **get up** se lever; **get well** se guérir; **go/come get someone** aller/venir chercher quelqu'un
girl fille (*f*)
girlfriend petite amie (*f*)
give donner; **give a party** faire une boum; **give back** rendre
glad content(e)
Gladly! Avec plaisir!
glass verre (*m*); **a glass of** un verre de
glasses lunettes (*fpl*)
global global(e) (*mpl* globaux)
go aller, se rendre (à/chez); **go away** partir; **go boating** faire du bateau; **go camping** faire du camping; **go down** descendre; **go for a ride/drive** faire un tour; **go for a walk** faire une promenade; **go grocery shopping** faire les courses; **go in** entrer (dans); **go home** rentrer; **go jogging** faire du jogging; **go on a cruise** faire une croisière; **go on foot** aller à pied; **go out** sortir (de); **go scuba diving** faire de la plongée sous-marine; **go shopping** faire du shopping; **go (water-)skiing** faire du ski (nautique); **go to bed** se coucher; **go up** monter; **go walking** se promener; **go windsurfing** faire de la planche à voile; **How's it going?** Comment ça va?; **It's going okay.** Ça va.
good: canned good produit en boîte (*m*)
good bon(ne), sage; **good day** bonjour; **good evening** bonsoir
Good-bye. Au revoir.
government gouvernement (*m*)
gram gramme (*m*)
grandfather grand-père (*m*)
grandmother grand-mère (*f*)
grandparents grands-parents (*mpl*)
grape(s) raisin (*m*)
gray gris(e)
great super
Great Britain Grande-Bretagne (*f*)
green vert(e); **green beans** *haricots verts (*mpl*)
greet saluer
grocer's shop épicerie (*f*)
grocery: go grocery shopping faire les courses
ground: ground floor rez-de-chaussée (*m*); **on the ground** par terre
grow up grandir
Guadelupian guadeloupéen(ne)
guess deviner
guide guide (*m*)
guidebook guide (*m*)
guitar guitare (*f*)

H

hair cheveux (*mpl*)
half moitié (*f*)
half demi(e); **It's half past two.** Il est deux heures et demie.
hall couloir (*m*); **lecture hall** amphithéâtre (*m*); **dining hall** restaurant universitaire (*m*); **residence hall** résidence universitaire (*f*)
ham jambon (*m*); **ham sandwich** sandwich au jambon (*m*)
hamburger *hamburger (*m*)
hand main (*f*); **on the other hand** par contre
handsome beau (bel, belle)
hang up: Don't hang up! Ne quitte/quittez pas!
happen se passer, arriver
happy content(e); heureux(-euse)
hard rock *hard rock (*m*)
hard-boiled egg œuf dur (*m*)
hat chapeau (*m*)
hate (each other) (se) détester
hatred *haine (*f*)
have avoir; **have a drink** prendre un verre; **have a picnic** faire un pique-nique; **have dinner** dîner; **have fun (doing)** s'amuser (à faire); **have just (done)** venir de (faire); **have lunch** déjeuner
he il
head tête (*f*)
heal guérir
health santé (*f*)
healthy sain(e)
hear entendre
heart cœur (*m*)
hearty copieux(-euse)
hello bonjour; **hello** (*on the telephone*) allô
help aider
her la; **to her** lui; **with her** avec elle
her son (sa, ses)
here ici; **here is/are** voici
Hi! Salut!
high élevé(e)
him le; **to him** lui; **with him** avec lui
his son (sa, ses)
historical historique
history histoire (*f*)
hold tenir
holiday fête (*f*); **national holiday** fête nationale (*f*)
home: at home à la maison; **come/go home** rentrer
homeless les sans domicile fixe (*mpl*)
homework devoirs (*mpl*)
homogeneous homogène
hope espérer
horrible horrible
horror movie film d'épouvante (*m*)
hospital hôpital (*m*)
hostel: youth hostel auberge de jeunesse (*f*)
hot chaud(e); **be hot** avoir chaud; **hot chocolate** chocolat chaud; **The weather's hot.** Il fait chaud.
hotel hôtel (*m*)

hour heure (*f*)
house maison (*f*); **at my house** chez moi; **pass by the house of** passer chez
household ménage (*m*); **household chore** tâche domestique (*f*)
housework ménage (*m*)
housing logement (*m*)
how comment; **how many** combien (de); **how much** combien (de); **How old is... ?** Quel âge a... ?; **How's the weather?** Quel temps fait-il?
however pourtant
hundred: one hundred cent
hunger faim (*f*)
hungry: be hungry avoir faim
hurry se dépêcher (de); **hurried** pressé(e)
hurt avoir mal (à); **hurt (someone)** faire mal (à quelqu'un)
husband mari (*m*)

I

I je
ice cream glace (*f*)
idea idée (*f*)
idealistic idéaliste
identity card carte d'identité (*f*)
if si
ill malade
illness maladie (*f*)
impatient impatient(e)
important important(e)
improve améliorer
in dans, en; **I live in** (+ *city*) j'habite à (+ *city*); **in advance** à l'avance; **in front of** devant; **in order to** pour; **in the country** à la campagne; **in the morning** le matin; **in your opinion** à votre avis
included compris(e)
Indies: West Indies Antilles (*fpl*)
indigestion indigestion (*f*)
inequality inégalité (*f*)
infection infection (*f*)
influence each other s'influencer
influenza grippe (*f*)
information renseignements (*mpl*)
inside à l'intérieur
insiste insister
instability instabilité (*f*)
intellectual intellectuel(le)
intelligent intelligent(e)
intend avoir l'intention de
interested: be interested in s'intéresser à
interesting intéressant(e)
introduce présenter; **I would like to introduce . . . to you.** Je vous/te présente...
introverted introverti(e)
invite inviter (à)
island île (*f*)
Israel Israël (*m*)
it il, elle, ce, le, la
Italian italien(ne)
Italy Italie (*f*)
itch démanger
itinerary itinéraire (*m*)
its son (sa, ses)

J

jacket: windbreaker jacket blouson (*m*); **ski jacket** anorak (*m*)
jam confiture (*f*)
January janvier (*m*)
Japan Japon (*m*)
Japanese japonais(e)
jazz jazz (*m*)
jeans jean (*m*)
jogging jogging (*m*); **go jogging** faire du jogging; **jogging outfit** (tenue de) jogging (*m*)
join rejoindre
journal journal (*m*)
juice jus (*m*)
July juillet (*m*)
June juin (*m*)
just: have just (done) venir de (faire)

K

key clé (*f*)
keyboard clavier (*m*)
kilo kilo (*m*)
kind genre (*m*); **all kinds of . . .** toutes sortes de...
kiss baiser (*m*)
kiss s'embrasser
kitchen cuisine (*f*)
knee genou (*m*)
know savoir, connaître; **known** connu(e)

L

Labor Day fête du travail (*f*)
laboratory: language laboratory laboratoire de langues (*m*)
lack of manque de (*m*)
lady dame (*f*); **lady's suit** tailleur (*m*)
lake lac (*m*)
language langue (*f*); **language laboratory** laboratoire de langues (*m*)
large grand(e)
last dernier(-ère)
late tard, en retard; **later** plus tard
laundry lessive (*f*)
law loi (*f*)
lawyer avocat(e) (*m/f*)
lazy paresseux(-euse)
learn apprendre
leave laisser, partir (de... pour), quitter, sortir (de); **leave each other** se quitter
lecture hall amphithéâtre (*m*)
left gauche (*f*); **to the left (of)** à gauche (de)
leg jambe (*f*)
lemon citron (*m*); **tea with lemon** thé au citron (*m*)
lend prêter
less . . . than moins (de)... que
letter lettre (*f*)
lettuce laitue (*f*)
liberal libéral(e)
library bibliothèque (*f*)
life vie (*f*)
lift weights faire des haltères
light (*weight*) léger(-ère)
like aimer; **I like it!** Ça me plaît!; **I would like . . .** Je voudrais...
like comme; **What is (are) . . . like?** Comment est (sont)...
liquid liquide (*m*)
listen (to) écouter
liter litre (*m*)
literature littérature (*f*)
little peu (de); **a little** un peu (de)
little petit(e)
live habiter
liver foie (*m*)
living room salon (*m*)
loan prêt (*m*)
loan prêter
lobster *homard (*m*)
local local(e) (*mpl* locaux)
located: Where is . . . located? Où se trouve...?
lodge: ski lodge chalet de ski (*m*)
lodging logement (*m*)
London Londres
lonely seul(e)
long long(ue); **a long time** longtemps; **as long as** tant que; **no longer** ne... plus; **look (at) (each other)** (se) regarder; **look** (+ *adjective*) avoir l'air (+ *adjectif*); **look for** chercher; **look like** ressembler à; **look very good on someone** aller très bien à quelqu'un
lose perdre; **lose weight** maigrir
lot: a lot (of) beaucoup (de), plein de
love amour (*m*); **love story** film d'amour (*m*); **love at first sight** coup de foudre (*m*)
love (each other) (s')aimer, adorer
luck chance (*f*)
lunch déjeuner (*m*); **have lunch** déjeuner
lung poumon (*m*)
lyrics paroles (*fpl*)

M

madam (Mrs.) madame (Mme)
magazine revue (*f*)
magnificent magnifique
main principal(e) (*mpl* principaux)
majority: the majority of la plupart de
make faire; **make** (+ *adjective*) rendre (+ *adjectif*); **made up of** composé(e) de
mall centre commercial (*m*)
malnutrition malnutrition (*f*)
man homme (*m*); monsieur (*m*)
many beaucoup (de); **how many** combien (de); **so many** tant (de); **too many** trop (de)
map plan (*m*)
March mars (*m*)
market marché (*m*)
marketing marketing (*m*)
marriage mariage (*m*)
married marié(e); **get married (to)** se marier (avec)
mathematics mathématiques (*fpl*)

matter: What's the matter? Qu'est-ce qu'il y a?
May mai (*m*)
maybe peut-être
me me, moi
meal repas (*m*)
mean: What does that mean? Qu'est-ce que ça veut dire?
mean méchant(e)
means of transportation moyen de transport (*m*)
meat viande (*f*); **meat spread** pâté (*m*)
medical médical(e) (*mpl* médicaux); **medical visit** consultation (*f*)
medicine médicaments (*mpl*)
mediocre médiocre
medium moyen(ne); **medium-sized** de taille moyenne
meet faire la connaissance de, rencontrer, retrouver; **meet each other** se rencontrer, se retrouver
melba toast biscotte (*f*)
menu menu (*m*)
merchant commerçant(e) (*m/f*)
message message (*m*)
Mexico Mexique (*m*); **Mexico City** Mexico
midnight minuit (*m*)
milk lait (*m*)
milk (*product*) laitier(-ère)
million: one million un million (de)
mineral water eau minérale (*f*)
minute minute (*f*); **at the last minute** au dernier moment
miss mademoiselle (Mlle)
mister (Mr.) monsieur (M.)
modern moderne
moment moment (*m*)
Monday lundi (*m*)
money argent (*m*); **save money** faire des économies
month mois (*m*)
mood; in a good/bad mood de bonne/mauvaise humeur
more: no more ne... plus (de); **more . . . than** plus (de)... (que)
morning matin (*m*); **at eight o'clock in the morning** à huit heures du matin; **in the morning, mornings** le matin; **morning hours** matinée (*f*)
Moscow Moscou
mother mère (*f*)
mountain montagne (*f*)
mouth bouche (*f*)
movement mouvement (*m*)
movie film (*m*); **go to the movies** aller au cinéma; **movie theater** cinéma (*m*); **show a movie** passer un film
much beaucoup (de); **as much . . . (as)** autant de... (que); **how much** combien (de); **so much** tant (de), tellement (de); **too much** trop (de)
murder meurtre (*m*)
murderer (murderess) meurtrier(-ère) (*m/f*)
museum musée (*m*)
music musique (*f*)
musical comédie musicale (*f*)
musician musicien(ne) (*m/f*)
must devoir; **one/you must . . .** il faut...
mustache moustache (*f*)
my mon (ma, mes); **at my house** chez moi

N

name nom (*m*); **My name is . . .** Je m'appelle...; **What is . . . 's name?** Comment s'appelle...?; **What is your name?** Comment t'appelles-tu? (*familiar*); Comment vous appelez-vous? (*formal*)
named: be named s'appeler
nationality nationalité (*f*)
natural naturel(le)
near près (de)
nearly presque
neat: That's neat! C'est chouette!
necessary nécessaire; **it is necessary . . .** il faut..., il est nécessaire (de)...
neck cou (*m*)
necktie cravate (*f*)
need avoir besoin de
neighborhood quartier (*m*)
neither non plus; **neither . . . nor** ne... ni... ni...
nephew neveu (*m*)
never ne... jamais
new nouveau (nouvel, nouvelle); **New Year's Day** jour de l'an (*m*)
newspaper journal (*m*)
next ensuite; prochain(e); **next door neighbor** voisin(e) d'à côté (*m/f*); **next to** à côté (de); **the next day** le lendemain (*m*)
nice sympathique (sympa); **The weather's nice.** Il fait beau.
niece nièce (*f*)
night nuit (*f*)
nightclub club (*m*)
nightshirt chemise de nuit (*f*)
nine neuf
nineteen dix-neuf
ninety quatre-vingt-dix
no non; **no longer** ne... plus; **no more** ne... plus (de); **no one** ne... personne
nobody ne... personne
noise bruit (*m*)
none ne... aucun(e)
non-smoking section section non-fumeur (*f*)
noon midi (*m*)
nor: neither . . . nor ne... ni... ni
North America Amérique du Nord (*f*)
nose nez (*m*)
not ne... pas; **not at all** ne... pas du tout; **not one** ne... aucun(e); **not yet** ne... pas encore
notebook cahier (*m*)
nothing ne... rien; **nothing but** ne... rien que
nourishment nourriture (*f*)
novel roman (*m*)
November novembre (*m*)
now maintenant
nowhere ne... nulle part
nul(le) zéro
number numéro (*m*); **telephone number** numéro de téléphone (*m*)
nurse infirmier(-ère) (*m/f*)

O

obey obéir (à)
obtain obtenir
obviously évidemment
o'clock: It's . . . o'clock. Il est... heure(s).
October octobre (*m*)
of de; **Of course!** Bien sûr!; Évidemment!
off: get off descendre (de)
office bureau (*m*); **post office** bureau de poste (*m*); **tourist office** office de tourisme (*m*)
offer offrir
often souvent
oil huile (*f*)
okay d'accord; **It's going okay.** Ça va.
old vieux (vieil, vieille), âgé(e); **be . . . years old** avoir... ans; **get old** vieillir; **How old is . . . ?** Quel âge a...?
omelet omelette (*f*)
on sur; **I'm in class on Mondays.** Je suis en cours le lundi.; **on . . . street** dans la rue...; **on the corner (of)** au coin (de); **on the ground** par terre; **on the weekend** le week-end; **on time** à l'heure; **on vacation** en vacances
one on; **no one** ne... personne; **not one** ne... aucun(e)
one un(e)
one-way ticket aller simple (*m*)
onion oignon (*m*)
only seulement, ne... que
open ouvrir
opinion avis (*m*); **in your opinion** à votre avis
optimistic optimiste
or ou
orange orange (*f*)
orange orange
order commander
other autre; **on the other hand** par contre; **on the other side (of)** de l'autre côté (de)
ought to devoir
our notre (*pl* nos)
out: dine out dîner au restaurant; **go out** sortir (de)
outdoor de plein air
outgoing extroverti(e)
outside dehors, en plein air; **outside of** *hors
over there là-bas
owe devoir
own propre
owner patron(ne) (*m/f*)
oyster huître (*f*)

P

pack one's bags faire ses valises
page page (*f*)
pain douleur (*f*)
painting tableau (*m*)
pal copain (*m*), copine (*f*)
pants pantalon (*m*)
panty hose collants (*mpl*)

paper papier (*m*); **sheet of paper** feuille de papier (*f*)
parents parents (*mpl*)
park parc (*m*)
parking lot parking (*m*)
participate (in) participer (à)
party boum (*f*); **give a party** faire une boum
pass passer; **pass by the house of** passer chez
passion passion (*f*)
passport passeport (*m*)
past: in the past autrefois
past passé(e)
pastry pâtisserie (*f*); **pastry shop** pâtisserie (*f*)
patient patient(e) (*m/f*)
patient patient(e)
pay payer; **pay attention (to)** faire attention (à); **pay the bill** régler la note
peace paix (*f*)
peaceful tranquille
peach pêche (*f*)
pear poire (*f*)
peas petits pois (*mpl*)
pen stylo (*m*)
penalty: death penalty peine de mort (*f*)
pencil crayon (*m*)
people gens (*mpl*), on; **poor people** les pauvres (*mpl*); **some people** certains; **young people** jeunes (*mpl*)
pepper poivre (*m*)
per par
perfect parfait(e)
perhaps peut-être
period: time period époque (*f*)
permit permettre (de)
person personne (*f*)
Peru Pérou (*m*)
pessimistic pessimiste
pharmacist pharmacien(ne) (*m/f*)
pharmacy pharmacie (*f*)
philosophy philosophie (*f*)
photo photo (*f*)
physician médecin (*m*)
physics physique (*f*)
piano piano (*m*)
picnic pique-nique (*m*)
picture tableau (*m*)
pie tarte (*f*)
piece morceau (*m*)
pink rose
pity: what a pity c'est dommage
place endroit (*m*); **at . . . 's place** chez; **take place** avoir lieu
place mettre
plan projet (*m*)
plan on avoir l'intention de, compter sur
plant plante (*f*)
play (a sport) jouer (à un sport), faire (du sport); **play (an instrument)** jouer (d'un instrument)
player: compact disc player lecteur de disques compacts (*m*)
pleasant agréable
please plaire
please s'il te plaît (*familiar*), s'il vous plaît (*formal*)
poem poème (*m*)
police police (*f*)
political politique; **political science** sciences politiques (*fpl*)
poll sondage (*m*)
pollution pollution (*f*)
pool: swimming pool piscine (*f*)
poor pauvre
pop music musique pop (*f*)
population population (*f*)
pork chop côte de porc (*f*)
possibility possibilité (*f*)
post office bureau de poste (*m*)
postcard carte postale (*f*)
poster affiche (*f*)
potato pomme de terre (*f*)
pound livre (*f*)
poverty pauvreté (*f*)
powerful puissant(e)
pre-dinner drink apéritif (*m*)
prefer préférer, aimer mieux
pregnant enceinte
preparations préparatifs (*mpl*)
prepare préparer
prescription ordonnance (*f*)
pretty joli(e)
price prix (*m*)
prison prison (*f*)
private privé(e)
problem problème (*m*)
product produit (*m*)
profession profession (*f*)
professor professeur
program programme (*m*)
promise promettre (de)
prosperity prospérité (*f*)
protect protéger
protein protéine (*f*)
psychology psychologie (*f*)
pullover sweater pull (*m*)
punishment: capital punishment peine de mort (*f*)
purse sac (*m*)
put (on) mettre
pyjamas pyjama (*m*)

Q

quarter quart (*m*); **It's a quarter past two.** Il est deux heures et quart.
question question (*f*); **ask a question** poser une question
quickly vite

R

racism racisme (*m*)
radio radio (*f*); **radio station** station de radio (*f*)
rain pleuvoir
raincoat imperméable (*m*)
rape viol (*m*)
rarely rarement
rather assez, plutôt
react (to) réagir (à)
read lire
realistic réaliste
recently récemment
recognize (each other) (se) reconnaître
recommend recommander
recorder: video cassette recorder magnétoscope (*m*)
recount raconter
red rouge, (*hair*) roux (rousse); **turn red** rougir
reflect (on) réfléchir (à)
refrigerator réfrigérateur (*m*)
regret regretter
remember se souvenir (de)
rent loyer (*m*)
rent louer
repeat répéter
research recherche (*f*)
resell revendre
resemble ressembler à
reservation réservation (*f*)
reserve réserver
residence hall résidence universitaire (*f*)
resort: summer resort station estivale (*f*)
resources ressources (*fpl*)
rest se reposer; **rested** reposé(e)
restaurant restaurant (*m*)
restful reposant(e)
return rentrer, retourner, (*something*) rendre
rhythm rythme (*m*)
rice riz (*m*)
ride: go for a ride faire un tour en voiture (à vélo)
right (*legal*) droit (*m*), (*direction*) droite (*f*); **to the right (of)** à droite (de)
right: right away tout de suite; **right by** tout près (de); **right there** juste là; **right?** n'est-ce pas?; **be right** avoir raison
roast beef rosbif (*m*)
rock rock (*m*); **hard rock** *hard rock (*m*)
room pièce (*f*), salle (*f*); **dining room** salle à manger (*f*); **fitting room** cabine d'essayage (*f*); **living room** salon (*m*)
roommate camarade de chambre (*mf*)
round-trip ticket billet aller-retour (*m*)
run courir, (*liquids*) couler; **run errands** faire des courses; **run into** rencontrer
Russia Russie (*f*)

S

sad triste
safety sécurité (*f*)
saint: All Saints' Day Toussaint (*f*)
salad salade (*f*)
sale: on sale en solde
salmon saumon (*m*)
salt sel (*m*)
same même
sandwich sandwich (*m*); **bread-and-butter sandwich** tartine (*f*); **open-faced sandwich** canapé (*m*)
Saturday samedi (*m*)
sauce sauce (*f*)
sausage saucisson (*m*); **sausage link** saucisse (*f*)
save money faire des économies

saxophone saxophone (*m*)
say dire; **How do you say . . . in French?** Comment dit-on... en français?
sceptical sceptique
school école (*f*); **secondary school** lycée (*m*)
science sciences (*fpl*); **computer science** informatique (*f*); **political science** sciences politiques (*fpl*); **science fiction** science-fiction (*f*); **social sciences** sciences sociales (*fpl*)
scuba diving plongée sous-marine (*f*)
sea mer (*f*)
seafood fruits de mer (*mpl*)
seated assis(e)
second deuxième; **in second class** en classe touriste
secretary secrétaire (*mf*)
section: (non-)smoking section section (non-)fumeur (*f*)
security sécurité (*f*)
see voir; **See you in a little while.** À tout à l'heure.; **See you soon.** À bientôt.; **See you tomorrow.** À demain.
seem (+ *adjective*) avoir l'air (+ *adjectif*); **It seems to me that . . .** Il me semble que...
sell vendre; **sell back** revendre
Senegal Sénégal (*m*)
sentence phrase (*f*)
September septembre (*m*)
serious sérieux(-euse), grave
serve servir; **served** servi(e)
service station station-service (*f*)
set: television set téléviseur (*m*)
seven sept
seventeen dix-sept
seventy soixante-dix
several plusieurs
sexual sexuel(le)
shall: Shall we . . . ? On... ?; **What shall we do?** Qu'est-ce qu'on fait?
shame: it's a shame c'est dommage
share partager
she elle
sheet of paper feuille de papier (*f*)
shelf étagère (*f*)
shirt chemise (*f*)
shivers frissons (*mpl*)
shoe chaussure (*f*)
shop magasin (*m*); **butcher's shop** boucherie (*f*); **fish shop** poissonnerie (*f*); **pastry shop** pâtisserie (*f*); **tobacco shop** bureau de tabac (*m*)
shopkeeper commerçant(e) (*m/f*)
shopping center centre commercial (*m*); **go grocery shopping** faire les courses; **go shopping** faire du shopping
short court(e)
shorts short (*m*)
shot piqûre (*f*)
should devoir; **one/you shouldn't . . .** il ne faut pas
shoulder épaule (*f*)
show montrer, indiquer; **show a movie** passer un film
shower douche (*f*)
showing séance (*f*)
shrimp crevette (*f*)
shy timide
sick malade; **get sick** tomber malade; **sick person** malade (*mf*)
side côté (*m*); **on the other side (of)** de l'autre côté (de)
sight: love at first sight coup de foudre (*m*)
silk soie (*f*); **made of silk** en soie
since depuis
sing chanter
singer chanteur(-euse) (*m/f*)
single célibataire, seul(e)
sink lavabo
sir monsieur (M.)
sister sœur (*f*)
sit (down) s'asseoir; **Please sit down.** Asseyez-vous, s'il vous plaît.
site site (*m*)
situation situation (*f*)
six six
sixteen seize
sixty soixante; **from the sixties** des années soixante
size taille (*f*); **medium-sized** de taille moyenne
skate (*fish*) raie (*f*)
ski ski (*m*); **ski lodge** chalet de ski (*m*); **ski jacket** anorak (*m*)
ski faire du ski; **water-ski** faire du ski nautique
skiing ski (*m*); **water-skiing** ski nautique (*m*)
skin peau (*f*)
skirt jupe (*f*)
sleep dormir
sleepy: be sleepy avoir sommeil
slice tranche (*f*)
slim down maigrir
slowly lentement
small petit(e)
smoke fumer
smoking section section fumeur (*f*)
sneeze éternuer
snow neiger
so tellement, alors, donc; **so much, so many** tant (de); tellement (de); **so-so** comme ci comme ça
soccer football (*m*)
social social(e) (*mpl* sociaux); **social sciences** sciences sociales (*fpl*)
society société (*f*)
sock chaussette (*f*)
solution solution (*f*)
some du, de la, de l', des; **some people** certains
somebody quelqu'un
someone quelqu'un
something quelque chose
sometimes quelquefois, parfois
somewhere quelque part
son fils (*m*)
song chanson (*f*)
soon bientôt; **as soon as** aussitôt que
sorry désolé(e)
sorts: all sorts of toutes sortes de
sound: Does that sound like fun? Ça te dit?
soup soupe (*f*); **onion soup** soupe à l'oignon (*f*)
South America Amérique du Sud (*f*)
Spain Espagne (*f*)
Spanish espagnol (*m*)
Spanish espagnol(e)
speak (about) parler (de)
specialty spécialité (*f*)
spend (*money*) dépenser, (*time*) passer
spoonful cuillerée (*f*)
sport sport (*m*); **play sports** faire du sport
sprain (one's ankle) se fouler (la cheville)
spread: meat spread pâté (*m*)
spring printemps (*m*); **in spring** au printemps
square place (*f*)
stadium stade (*m*)
staircase escalier (*m*)
stairs escalier (*m*)
starvation famine (*f*)
station: radio station station de radio (*f*); **service station** station-service (*f*)
stay séjour (*m*); **Have a nice stay!** Bon séjour!
stay rester, (*at a hotel*) descendre (dans); **Stay on the line!** Ne quitte/quittez pas!
steak bifteck (*m*)
stereo chaîne stéréo (*f*)
still encore, toujours
stomach ventre (*m*)
stop: bus stop arrêt d'autobus (*m*)
stopover escale (*f*)
stopped up bouché(e)
store magasin (*m*)
story histoire (*f*)
stove cuisinière (*f*)
straight tout droit
strawberry fraise (*f*)
street rue (*f*)
stress stress (*m*)
strict sévère
strong fort(e)
struggle (against) lutter (contre)
student étudiant(e); **student center** foyer des étudiants (*m*)
studies études (*fpl*)
study étudier, préparer les cours
suburbs banlieue (*f*); **in the suburbs** en banlieue
subway métro (*m*)
succeed (in) réussir (à)
sudden: all of a sudden tout à coup
suddenly soudain
suffer souffrir
sufficiently suffisamment
sugar sucre (*m*)
suggest suggérer
suit costume (*m*); **lady's suit** tailleur (*m*)
suitcase valise (*f*)
summer été (*m*); **in summer** en été; **summer resort** station estivale (*f*)
Sunday dimanche (*m*)
sunny: It's sunny. Il fait du soleil.
supermarket supermarché (*m*)
surprise étonner; **surprised** étonné(e), surpris(e)
surrounded (by) entouré(e) (de)
sweater: pullover sweater pull (*m*)
swim nager
swimming pool piscine (*f*)
swimsuit maillot de bain (*m*)
Switzerland Suisse (*f*)

swollen enflé(e)
symptom symptôme (*m*)

T

T-shirt T-shirt (*m*)
table table (*f*)
take prendre; **take a course** suivre un cours; **take advantage of** profiter de; **take a trip around the world** faire le tour du monde; **take care of** s'occuper de, (*health*) (se) soigner; **take place** avoir lieu
talent talent (*m*)
talk (about) parler (de); **talk on the phone** parler au téléphone
tart tartelette (*f*)
taste goûter
taxi taxi (*m*)
tea (with lemon) thé (au citron) (*m*)
teach enseigner
technical technique
telephone téléphone (*m*); **talk on the telephone** parler au téléphone; **telephone number** numéro de téléphone (*m*)
telephone (each other) (se) téléphoner
television télévision (télé) (*f*); **television set** téléviseur (*m*)
tell dire, raconter
temperature température (*f*)
ten dix
tennis tennis (*m*)
terrace terrasse (*f*)
terrorism terrorisme (*m*)
test analyse (*f*), examen (*m*), contrôle (*m*)
than: less . . . than moins de... que; **more . . . than** plus de... que
thank (for) remercier (de); **thank you** merci
that ça
that ce (cet, cette)
that que; **I think that . . .** je pense que...
the le (la, les)
theater théâtre (*m*)
theft vol (*m*)
their leur(s)
them les; **to them** leur; **with them** avec eux, avec elles
then alors, donc, ensuite, puis
there là, y; **How many are there of you?** Vous êtes combien?; **over there** là-bas; **right there** juste là; **there is, there are** il y a, voilà
therefore donc
these ces
they ils, elles, ce, on
thing(s) chose(s) (*f*), affaires (*fpl*)
think (about) réfléchir (à), penser (à); **What do you think (about it)?** Qu'en penses-tu?, Qu'en pensez-vous?
third troisième; **third world** tiers monde (*m*)
thirsty: be thirsty avoir soif
thirteen treize
thirty trente
this ce (cet, cette); **this way** par ici
those ces
three trois
throat gorge (*f*)
Thursday jeudi (*m*)
thus donc
ticket billet (*m*); **one-way ticket** aller simple (*m*); **round-trip ticket** billet aller-retour (*m*)
tight étroit(e)
time (*clock*) heure (*f*), (*occasion*) fois (*f*), temps (*m*); **a long time** longtemps; **at that time** à ce moment-là; **At what time?** À quelle heure?; **on time** à l'heure; **from time to time** de temps en temps; **time period** époque (*f*); **What time is it?** Quelle heure est-il?
timid timide
tinker around bricoler
tired fatigué(e)
thousand: one thousand mille
to à; **to . . . 's house/place** chez
toast pain grillé (*m*); **melba toast** biscotte (*f*)
tobacco tabac (*m*); **tobacco shop** bureau de tabac (*m*)
today aujourd'hui; **Today is . . .** Nous sommes le..., Aujourd'hui, c'est le...
toe doigt de pied (*m*)
together ensemble
toilet cabinet de toilette (*m*); W.-C. (*mpl*)
tolerance tolérance (*f*)
tomato tomate (*f*)
tomorrow demain; **day after tomorrow** après-demain
tonight ce soir
too aussi, trop; **too many** trop (de); **too much** trop (de)
tooth dent (*f*)
tourist touriste (*mf*) ; **tourist office** office de tourisme (*m*)
tourist touristique
towards vers
town: in town en ville
traffic circulation (*f*)
train train (*m*); **by train** en train
tranquil tranquille
transportation: means of transportation moyen de transport (*m*)
travel: travel agency agence de voyages (*f*); **travel agent** agent de voyages (*m*)
travel voyager
traveler's check chèque de voyage (*m*)
treatment traitement (*m*)
tribe tribu (*f*)
trip voyage (*m*); **take a trip** faire un voyage; **take a trip around the world** faire le tour du monde
tropical tropical(e) (*mpl* tropicaux)
truly vraiment
trumpet trompette (*f*)
try (on) essayer
Tuesday mardi (*m*)
tuna thon (*m*)
turn (towards) (se) tourner (vers); **turn red** rougir
twelve douze
twenty vingt
twin brother frère jumeau (*f*)
twin sister sœur jumelle (*f*)
two deux
type genre (*m*)
tyranny tyrannie (*f*)

ugly laid(e)
ulcer ulcère (*m*)
umbrella parapluie (*m*)
uncle oncle (*m*)
under sous
understand comprendre
understanding compréhension (*f*)
underwear sous-vêtements (*mpl*)
unemployed au chômage
unemployment chômage (*m*)
unfortunately malheureusement
unhappy malheureux(-euse)
United States États-Unis (*mpl*)
unity unité (*f*)
university université (*f*)
university universitaire
unmarried célibataire
unpack défaire ses valises
unpleasant désagréable
until jusqu'à; **It's a quarter until three.** Il est trois heures moins le quart.
up: get up se lever; **go up** monter; **up to** jusqu'à
us nous
use utiliser
usually d'habitude
utilize utiliser

vacation vacances (*fpl*); **on vacation** en vacances
Valentine's Day Saint-Valentin (*f*)
validity validité (*f*)
vegetable légume (*m*); **vegetable soup** soupe aux légumes (*f*)
very très
video: video cassette cassette vidéo (*f*); **video cassette recorder** magnétoscope (*m*); **video game** jeu vidéo (*m*)
Vietnam Viêt-nam (*m*)
view vue (*f*)
vinegar vinaigre (*m*)
violence violence (*f*)
violent violent(e)
violet violet(te)
visit: medical visit consultation (*f*)
visit (*place*) visiter, (*someone*) rendre visite à
vitamins vitamines (*fpl*)
vocabulary vocabulaire (*m*)
voice voix (*f*)
volcano volcan (*m*)
vomit vomir

wait attendre
waiter garçon (*m*), serveur (*m*)
waitress serveuse (*f*)

wake up (se) réveiller
walk promenade (*f*); **go for a walk** faire une promenade, se promener
walk aller à pied
wall mur (*m*)
want vouloir
war guerre (*f*)
warmth chaleur (*f*)
wash (se) laver; **wash clothes** faire la lessive
washbasin lavabo (*m*)
waste gaspiller, (*time*) perdre du temps
watch regarder
water eau (*f*); **water closet** W.-C. (*mpl*)
waterskiing ski nautique (*m*)
way: show the way indiquer le chemin; **this way** par ici
we nous, on; **Shall we . . . ?** On...?; **What shall we do?** Qu'est-ce qu'on fait?
wear porter; **I wear a 42.** Je fais du 42.
weather temps (*m*); **The weather's nice (bad/cold/cool/hot/sunny/windy).** Il fait beau (mauvais/froid/frais/chaud/du soleil/du vent).
Wednesday mercredi (*m*)
week semaine (*f*)
weekend week-end (*m*); **on the weekend** le week-end; **go away for the weekend** partir en/pour le week-end
weight poids (*m*); **gain weight** grossir; **lift weights** faire des haltères; **lose weight** maigrir, perdre du poids
welcome bienvenue
welcome: You're welcome. Je t'en prie, Je vous en prie.
well bien; **well-behaved** sage; **get well** se guérir
west: West Indies Antilles (*fpl*)
what qu'est-ce que, que, comment, quel(le); **What day is today?** Quel jour est-ce aujourd'hui?; **What is (are) . . . like?** Comment est (sont)...?; **What is . . . 's name?** Comment s'appelle...?; **What's the weather like?** Quel temps fait-il?
when quand
where où
which quel(le); que, qui; **about/of which** dont
while: See you in a little while. À tout à l'heure.
white blanc(he)
who qui
whole tout (toute); **the whole day** toute la journée
wholegrain bread pain complet (*m*)
whose dont
why pourquoi
widespread répandu(e)
widow veuve (*f*)
wife femme (*f*)
win gagner
wind vent (*m*)
windbreaker jacket blouson (*m*)
window fenêtre (*f*)
windsurfing: go windsurfing faire de la planche à voile
windy: It's windy. Il fait du vent.
wine vin (*m*)
winter hiver (*m*); **in winter** en hiver
with avec; **coffee with milk** café au lait
without sans
woman femme (*f*)
word(s) mot(s) (*m*); (*lyrics*) paroles (*fpl*)
work travail (*m*)
work travailler
world monde (*m*); **take a trip around the world** faire le tour du monde
world-(wide) mondial(e) (*mpl* mondiaux)
worry (about) (se) préoccuper (de)
would: I would like to . . . je voudrais...
wound (oneself) (se) blesser
write écrire; **How do you write that?** Ça s'écrit comment?
wrong: be wrong avoir tort; **What's wrong?** Qu'est-ce qui ne va pas?

X-ray radio (*f*)

year an (*m*), année (*f*); **be . . . years old** avoir... ans; **New Year's Day** jour de l'an (*m*)
yellow jaune
yes oui, si
yesterday hier
yet: not yet ne... pas encore
yoghurt yaourt (*m*)
you tu, vous, te; **with you** avec toi, avec vous; **You're welcome.** Je t'en prie., Je vous en prie.
young jeune
your ton (ta, tes); votre (vos)
youth jeunesse (*f*); **youth hostel** auberge de jeunesse (*f*)

Z

Zaire Zaïre (*m*)
zero zéro (*m*), nul(le)
zip code code postal (*m*)

A

B

C

D

E

F

G

H

I

J

L

N

P

Q

R

S

T

U

V

Text Credits

5 & 10, Editions Albert René; **14,** Document France Télécom - *Les pages jaunes* - édition 1991; **24,** *Paris Vision* brochure from France Tourisme 1992; **36,** cartoon: *Le Figaro magazine* no. 13960, 15 juillet 1989; **56,** grade report: *Direct from France*, National Textbook Company 1991; **58,** I.M.E.F. ; **70,** Vin d'Alsace; **70,** Geriko, **70,** Kanterbräu; **74,** Document France Télécom - *Les pages jaunes* - édition 1991; **75,** Aux trois obus; **80,** "Quels sont tes loisirs préférés?", Vidéo-Presse, Vol. XX, no. 9, mai 1991; **83,** L'Idéal; **86,** Le Trapèze; **90,** "Les bonnes tables", *Nice-matin*, 3 août 1992; **91,** Aux trois obus; **104,** Source: Brochure touristique *Destination Québec, Vacances d'été* (édition 1993). La reproduction de cette carte a été autorisée par le ministère du Tourisme du Québec; **119,** Université Laval; **120,** Document France Télécom - *Les pages jaunes* - édition 1991; **121,** *Annuaire téléphonique Montréal* 1992-1993, Bell Québec Communications; **123,** Source: Brochure touristique *Destination Québec, Vacances d'été* (édition 1993). La reproduction de ce tableau a été autorisée par le ministère du Tourisme du Québec; **124,** 3 Suisses; **125,** subscription form and cover: *Brune*, No. 5, 1992; **126,** excerpt from "Mon pays" by Gilles Vigneault from the brochure *Réalités du Québec*, a document of the Ministère des Relations internationales; **128,** *Le Journal de Montréal*, Vol XXVII, no. 171, 2 décembre 1990; **145,** 3 Suisses; **151,** "Face à ses concurrents" *Parcours*, B.C. Editions; **151,** Parc Safari; **155,** Galérie Le Chariot; **157,** Cinéma Imax; **157,** Université McGill; **155 & 157,** Parc Olympique; **157,** Maisons de la culture; **161,** "Quelle place occupent tes grands-parents dans ta vie?" de F. Gagnon, Vidéo-Presse, Vol. XX, no. 9, mai 1991; **174,** *L'Officiel des spectacles* no. 2379, 1992; **180,** weather map: IGN Paris 1991; **182,** temperature chart: Copyright Le Figaro 1993; **194,** "Les weekends des Français", *Figaro Magazine*, copyright Figaro magazine/SOFRES, no. 13960, 1989; **204,** "Tous les films de la semaine", *Pariscope*, no. 1262, p. 86; **205,** "Vos programmes", *Le Figaro TV Magazine* August 1987; **206,** Celine Carterie; **224,** calendar: Editions Quo Vadis; **230,** "Grandeur et décadence du cinéma" *Jeune et jolie*, no. 48, 1991; **232,** Editions Albert René; **238,** Le Conseil Général pour une politique du patrimoine; **238,** La Nova restaurant; **238,** Promenade en mer avec Erick; **239,** Ballades avec Jacques; **239,** Alizéa fitness center; **239,** Parc Zoologique; **240,** excerpt of "Le volcanisme", from the brochure *Guadeloupe: Antilles françaises: La Basse-Terre* , Office Départemental du Tourisme de la Guadeloupe; **240,** map of la Soufrière from *Bonjour la Guadeloupe* by Jean Michel Renault, Editions du Pelican; **254,** *Geo Magazine* , text copyright Geo Magazine, Ulysses photo by Kevin Fleming, Ulysse et Circé, Louvre AGR, photo R.M.N.; **254,** *L'Entreprise*, no. 82, juillet-août 1992; **254,** *Rock & Folk*, no. 287, juillet 1991; **264,** Avis; **265,** Air France Jet Tours of Martinique; **275,** Ecotel; **276,** Le Relais du Moulin; **276,** La Marina; **277 & 293,** excerpts from the Michelin Guide, *France Hôtels et Restaurants*, édition 1993, Pneu Michelin, Services de Tourisme; **278,** Document France Télécom - *Les pages jaunes* - édition 1991; **287,** Air Gabon; **298,** map of Pointe-à-Pitre from *Bonjour la Guadeloupe* by Jean Michel Renault, Editions du Pelican; **307,** "A qui" de *Haïti blues Echopoèmes* par J.F. Ménard, Editions L'Harmattan; **309,** *Selected Hotels of France*, French Government Tourist Office; **330 & 344,** *Camping en Bretagne*, 1991; **345,** Excerpts from "Tous les matins je me lève" vu dans *Vogue Hommes* no. 152, septembre 1992; **349,** *Rouen Poche*, no. 92, du 15 au 21 juillet 1987; **357, 358, & 359,** Le Restaurant Maraichers; **366,** recipes from *Je sais cuisiner*, by Ginette Mathiot, Albin Michel; **387,** *Savoir préparer les salades: Idées recettes*, E.P.P. La bonne cuisine à la portée de tous, 1983; **404,** "Résolutions de printemps" text and cover, *Rock & Folk*, no. 296, avril 1992; **405,** "Ne me quittes pas" by Jacques Brel; **412,** Cover of M'Bilia Bel CD, Shanachie Records Corp. 1991; **419,** "Préférence" par Claude-Emmanuel Abolo Bowole vu dans le livre *Poèmes de demain*, Editions

Some notes about the types used in this book:

Minion was used for most of the text, including the words you are reading right now. Robert Slimbach based this 1990 design on the work of Claude Garamond and Aldus Manutius, whose "old style" metal typefaces of the late Renaissance were renowned for their openness and clarity. *Minion* was the name given to a particular size of type in the early days of typefounding (very close to the size you are now reading).

Ondine was created by Adrian Frutiger, one of the greatest type designers of the 20th century. *Ondine* is the word used by the French to describe the female water spirits in Germanic and Scandinavian mythology (it is derived from the word *onde*, one of whose English meanings is *wave*).

Mistral was designed by Roger Excoffon, a noted French advertising art director. He modeled the type's letterforms on his own handwriting, but also succeeded in capturing the verve of the brush-written alphabets used by generations of Francophone signpainters. *Mistral* is the Provençal name for a violent, cold, dry wind that sweeps down the Rhône valley to the coast along the Mediterranean Sea.

We felt that it would be particularly appropriate to set this book in typefaces that originated in the Francophone world, and hope that you agree with our choices!

Nouvelles du Sud, 1980; **419,** "Pitié pour les Affamés" par Richard Dogbeh, vu dans *Poésie du Bénin,* Editions Nouvelles du Sud; **424,** "Si j'étais un dieu nègre" par A. Martin Honoré Zeufack vu dans le livre *Poèmes de demain* , Editions Nouvelles du Sud, 1980; **425,** "L'Afrique de Nina Simone", *Jeune Afrique*, no. 1626, du 5 au 11 mars 1992; **442,** lyrics for "Non, je ne regrette rien" by C. Dumont and M. Vaucaire; **453,** *Là où il n'y a pas de docteur,* par David Wener, ENDA; **458,** Fragment de "Prières des chasseurs nyanga" traduit par D. Biebuyck in *Textes sacrés d'Afrique Noire.* Editions Gallimard; **459,** "La tortue qui chante" de *Les aventures de Yévi au pays des monstres,* Hatier 1987.

Maps

Reproduction of rare maps on the chapter openers courtesy of the Smith Collection, University of Southern Maine Libraries. Pages **xxviii,** "Carte réduite du globe terrestre", **234**, "Isle de la Guadeloupe, les Saintes et Marie Galante", **312**, "Costes de France depuis Brest jusqu'à Dunkerque et celles d'Angleterre qui leur sont opposées", **28**, "Carte des costes de Provence depuis l'embouchure du Rhône jusqu'au Var" reprinted from Bellin, Jacques Nicolas. *Le petit atlas maritime... en cinq volumes.* Paris: Jacques Nicolas Bellin, 1764. Page **96**, "Carte de la Nouvelle France... pour l'establissement de la Compagne" by Chatelain, Henry Abraham. Amsterdam: 1719. Page **390**, "Afrique", reprinted from Buy de Mornas, Claud. *Atlas méthodique et élémentaire de géographie et d'histoire.* Paris: 1761. Pages **464**, "La Flandre le Haynaut à Paris" and **160**, "L'isle de France" reprinted from Le Rouge, George Louis. *Atlas nouveau portatif, Tome 1er, 2e.* Paris: George Louis Le rouge, Le Fils Prault, and Le Veuve Robinot, 1756-1759.

Additional Art Credits

Page **438,** *(Top left)* Snuff Mortar, by Luluwa. Wood. © The University of Iowa Museum of Art, The Stanley Collection. *(Top right)* Mask from Lega, Zaire. Wood, fiber, white paint. Photo by Ann Hutchison. © Virginia Museum of Fine Arts. *(Bottom left)* Bell. Wood. © American Museum of Natural History. *(Bottom right)* Lidded container. Wood, bark. © Ken Heinen/National Museum of African Art, Eliot Elisafon Archives, Smithsonian Institution.

Photo Credits

Page **iii,** Carol Palmer; **iv-v,** S. Tansey/Odyssey Productions; **2,** G.S. Zimbel/Monkmeyer Press *(top)*; Matt Jacob/The Image Works *(bottom)*; **6,** R. Lucas/The Image Works *(left)*; Peter Menzel/Stock Boston *(right);* **9,** Andrew Brilliant *(left);* Carol Palmer *(right);* **17,** Beryl Goldberg; **25,** Beryl Goldberg *(top);* David Simpson/Stock Boston *(bottom);* **32,** R. Lucas/The Image Works; **35,** Beryl Goldberg; **42,** Fredrik D. Bodin *(left);* Andrew Brilliant *(right);* **43,** Beryl Goldberg; **54,** Beryl Goldberg; **55** Palmer/Brilliant *(top);* Spencer Grant/Stock Boston *(bottom left);* Topham/The Image Works *(bottom right);* **57,** Beryl Goldberg *(top and bottom);* **68,** Beryl Goldberg *(top);* Palmer/Brilliant *(bottom);* **69,** Mike Mazzaschi/Stock Boston; **84,** Beryl Goldberg; **89,** Beryl Goldberg; **90,** Hugh Rogers/Monkmeyer Press; **92,** Carol Palmer *(top);* Frank White/Gamma-Liaison *(bottom);* **98,** Robert Fried/Stock Boston; **110,** Mark Antman/The Image Works; **123,** George Hunter/Odyssey Productions; **127,** Beryl Goldberg; **136,** Mark Antman/The Image Works *(top);* Lee Snider/The Image Works *(bottom);* **144,** SUPERSTOCK; **149,** Charles Nes/Liaison International;

170, John Elk/Stock Boston *(top left);* Eric Bouvet/Gamma-Liaison *(top right);* Robert Fried *(bottom);* **183,** Beryl Goldberg; **188,** Faria Castro/Gamma-Liaison; **197,** Beryl Goldberg *(top);* Mark Antman/The Image Works *(bottom left);* Philippe Gontier/The Image Works *(middle right);* Palmer & Brilliant *(bottom right);* **208,** Stuart Cohen/Comstock; **210,** Mark Antman/The Image Works *(top);* Ray Stott/The Image Works *(bottom)* ; **214,** R. Lucas/The Image Works; **220,** Eric Carle/Stock Boston; **221,** Jean-Claude LeJeune/Stock Boston *(top left);* Peter Menzel/Stock Boston *(top right);* Beryl Goldberg *(bottom);* **230,** The Bettmann Archive; **237,** S. Vidler/SUPERSTOCK; **279,** Michael Doneff; **295,** K. Scholz/SUPERSTOCK; **299,** French West Indies Tourist Board *(top);* Joe Petrocik *(bottom);* **306,** Wide World Photo *(top);* G. de Steinheil/SUPERSTOCK *(bottom);* **307,** Christopher Harris/SUPERSTOCK; **314,** Henri Cartier-Bresson/Magnum; **320** S. Vidler/SUPERSTOCK; **327,** S. Vidler/SUPERSTOCK; **332,** Ulrike Welsch; **345,** Ulrike Welsch; **361,** Stuart Cohen/Comstock; **362,** Beryl Goldberg; **368,** Stuart Cohen/Comstock; **374,** Hugh Rogers/Monkmeyer; **377,** R. Manley/SUPERSTOCK; **379,** Stuart Cohen/Comstock; **385,** Stuart Cohen *(top);* Ulrike Welsch *(bottom);* **386,** Gamma Presse Images; **387,** Philippe Gontier/The Image Works; **395,** Georg Gerster/Comstock; **397,** Betty Press/Monkmeyer Press; **409,** SUPERSTOCK; **410,** Daniel Laine *(top);* R. Manley/SUPERSTOCK *(bottom left);* R. Manley/SUPERSTOCK *(bottom right);* **415,** H. Kanus/SUPERSTOCK; **419,** AP/Wide World Photo; **423,** Anthony Suau/Gamma-Liaison; **426,** Rene Perez/Wide World Photo; **442,** Wide World Photo; **451,** Stephen Ferry/Gamma-Liaison; **458,** Wendy Stone/Gamma-Liaison; **467,** Martin Rogers/Stock Boston; **471,** S. Vidler/SUPERSTOCK; **473,** David Simpson/Stock Boston; **486,** Lee Snider/The Image Works *(top);* Kurgan-Lisnet/Liaison International *(bottom);* **487,** Guy Marché/FPG International *(top);* **488,** Eberhard Otto/FPG International *(top);* Ted Funk/FPG International *(bottom).*